'it is hard to imagine that this biograp[hy]

Si[...]

'. . . a remarkable and outstanding achievement . . . informed by the kind of insight into personal relations that is the mark not of an academic but of a considerable novelist'.

H. M. Daleski, Hebrew University of Jerusalem

'[This is] a work of impeccable scholarship, and comes provided with an impressive apparatus of notes, appendices, chronological tables, family trees, an exemplary index, and complete lists of Lawrence's prose and verse writings in the relevant period, making it an invaluable resource for serious students of Lawrence; but it is also written in a lucid, unpretentious style which lay readers will find accessible and enjoyable.'

David Lodge, *The New York Review of Books*

'This is a superb biography. Apart from the compelling narrative there are judicious excursions into the mix of rurality and the mining industry that formed the background to Lawrence's life. There are portraits of the family members and . . . insights into Lawrence's admiring bluestockings and into the less well-known early works that led up to *Sons and Lovers* . . . Cambridge have already given us . . . a decent edition of Lawrence's fiction; now they are embarked on what should be the definitive life.'

Anthony Curtis, *The Financial Times*

'[Worthen] has researched deeply, reading everything even remotely relevant, and is able to be authoritative where others have conjectured. [This] is a warm as well as a serious book, for he clearly loves his subject, and makes us share his feeling. The theme of the development of the miner's son and sickly scholarship boy with warring parents is a wonderful one, and he grasps all its possibilities in the 500 pages of his narrative.'

Claire Tomalin, *The Independent on Sunday*

'One of this biography's great merits is that Worthen understands the dangers of creating a life from a work of fiction. He uses Lawrence's fiction intelligently. He never forgets that even the most apparently autobiographical novels rearrange real events in order to make an artistic point. They cannot be trusted, as too many biographers trust them, to do the biographer's work for him. The other great merit, apart from the wonderfully detailed and engrossing reconstruction of a period and a society, is its attitude to Lawrence himself. Worthen is unfailingly sympathetic, as a biographer should be, yet he never falls into the trap of supposing his hero to be perfect . . . This definitive book will be a hard act . . . to follow.'

Allan Massie, *Weekend Telegraph*

'Worthen's depiction of Eastwood is on something of a scholarly par with Lawrence's evocation of it in *Sons and Lovers*.'

Janet Byrne, *The New York Times Book Review*

'Literary scholars who thought they knew Lawrence and his circle well will be suprised by the subtlety, aptness, and psychological nuance of Worthen's presentation and interpretation. It is as if for the first time we see Lawrence whole . . . this persuasive biography is compulsive reading from cover to cover. A major event in modern literary studies.'

Keith Cushman, *Library Journal*

'Worthen sets the record straight in a thousand little ways, and there emerges a complex genius, ruthless, sensitive and fully alive.'

Publishers' Weekly

'. . . extremely thorough and careful . . .'

Jeffrey Meyers

The Cambridge Biography

D. H. LAWRENCE

1885–1930

◆

DAVID ELLIS

MARK KINKEAD-WEEKES

JOHN WORTHEN

The author of *The early years, 1885–1912*, John Worthen, was born in London during the Second World War and educated at Downing College, Cambridge and the University of Kent. He is the author of several books on D. H. Lawrence, most recently *D. H. Lawrence: A Literary Life*, and has edited a number of Lawrence's works for Cambridge University Press. Having taught in America, Scotland and England, he now lives in South Wales, where he is Professor of English at the University College of Swansea.

Steven Herrmann

D. H. LAWRENCE

THE EARLY YEARS

1885–1912

◆

JOHN WORTHEN

CAMBRIDGE
UNIVERSITY PRESS

Published by the Press Syndicate of the University of Cambridge
The Pitt Building, Trumpington Street, Cambridge CB2 1RP
40 West 20th Street, New York, NY 10011–4211, USA
10 Stamford Road, Oakleigh, Victoria 3166,
Australia

© Cambridge University Press 1992. Acknowledgement
is made to William Heinemann Ltd in the UK and the
Viking Press in the USA for the authorisation granted
to Cambridge University Press through the Frieda
Lawrence Estate for quotation from the works of
D. H. Lawrence.

First published 1991
First paperback edition 1992

Printed in Great Britain at the University Press,
Cambridge

British Library cataloguing in publication data

Worthen, John
D. H. Lawrence: the early years, 1885–1912. – (The
Cambridge biography).
1. Fiction in English. Lawrence, D. H. (David Herbert),
1885–1930
I. Title
823.912

Library of Congress cataloging in publication data

Worthen, John
D. H. Lawrence: the early years, 1885–1912/John Worthen.
p.   cm. – (The Cambridge biography)
Includes index.
ISBN 0-521-25419-1 (hardback). 0-521-43772-5 (paperback)
1. Lawrence, D. H. (David Herbert).
1885–1930 – Biography – Youth.
2. Authors, English – 20th century – Biography – Youth. I. Title.
II. Series.
PR6023.A93Z957 1991
823'.912–dc20   90–23423
[B]   CIP

ISBN 0 521 25419 1 hardback
ISBN 0 521 43772 5 paperback

To M and F

It is perhaps absurd for any man to write his own autobiography. The one person I find it impossible to 'know', is myself. I have dozens of little pictures of what purports to be myself, and which is me? None of them. The little animal is now a bigger animal. But what sort of animal it is, I do not know, and do not vastly care.

The little animal was a pasty-faced boy born to have bronchitis and a weak chest, but otherwise lively enough. A little animal that

D. H. Lawrence: 'Mushrooms' (University of Cincinnati)

What separates us from the characters about whom we write is not knowledge, either objective or subjective, but their experience of time in the story we are telling. This separation allows us, the storytellers, the power of knowing the whole. Yet, equally, this separation renders us powerless: we cannot control our characters, after the narration has begun. We are obliged to follow them, and this following is through and across the time, which they are living and which we oversee.

The time, and therefore the story, belongs to them. Yet the meaning of the story, what makes it worthy of being told, is what we can see and what inspires us because we are beyond its time.

John Berger: 'Once Through a Lens' (1984)

Oh, I could go on and on for pages about Christie's young life, inventing and observing, remembering and borrowing. But why?   All is chaos and unexplainable.   These things happened. He is as he is, you are as you are.   Act on that: all is chaos.   The end is coming, truly.
          It is just so much wasted effort to attempt to understand anything.
                    Lots of people never had a chance, are ground down, and other clichés. Far from kicking against the pricks, they love their condition and vote conservative.

B. S. Johnson: *Christie Malry's Own Double-Entry* (1973)

CONTENTS

CONTENTS

◆

AUTHORS' PREFACE

The need for a new Biography of a writer about whose life – to put it mildly – much has been written, arises from the mass of new information in the Cambridge collected *Letters* and *Works*, which makes all existing biographies out of date. This can be said without insult or injury to previous biographers, whose work we gratefully acknowledge. But it would be strange indeed if over two thousand unpublished letters and postcards, the editing and annotation of the thousands previously known, and the researches of an international team into how and when each of the writings came into existence, did not substantially alter and correct the existing picture of Lawrence's life. We are deeply indebted to all the Cambridge editors who have allowed us access to their work, published and unpublished.

No amount of new material, however, can make any biographical overview the final word, and we express this conviction in the form of one work by three authors: not only a new 'Life' but also, we believe, a new kind of biography. Each author has taken responsibility for a different period of Lawrence's life, the first volume ending with the completion of *Sons and Lovers*, the second with Lawrence's departure from Europe in 1922. From the beginning, we have collaborated very closely, and subjected one another's work to intensive scrutiny and comment. We have acted as research assistants to one another, have challenged the half-conscious tendency of every biographer to turn a blind eye to inconvenient items of evidence and have argued out fundamental positions. Nevertheless, though the whole will be joint work – in that sense – from first to last, each author is finally responsible for the Lawrence who emerges from his particular period. Three Lawrences, striking the reader as both the same and different, will (we believe) answer all the more to ordinary experience of other people.

There might seem, however, to be danger here of dissonant or even contradictory answers to the question of who Lawrence was and what he was really like. Can three people, however closely they work together, be sufficiently in harmony to capture Lawrence's identity? It seems to us that the assumptions which prompt such questions are dubious. Our culture does often appear bound by the idea of a personal core or centre, an 'essential self', out of which character grows in a process of development. Yet in Lawrence's own writings, though there is plenty of support for the notion of an essential self, there is also a characteristic and no less powerful emphasis on fluidity and change. It was Lawrence who denounced 'the old stable ego of the character' in the kinds of novel he no longer wanted to write, and whose preferred way of imagining his progress through life was in terms of rebirth, again and again, into new states of being. To have three people write his life is an explicit (even dramatic) acknowledgement that, however important the continuities, the Lawrence of the last years (for example) is so different from the 19-year-old who visited the Haggs Farm, that it sometimes seems only by accident that they share the same name. There is a hardly less striking and significant difference between the writer who sent off *Sons and Lovers* to its publisher in November 1912, and the author of *Women in Love* expelled from Cornwall, by order of the military authorities, less than five years later.

There are of course important continuities in Lawrence's life, because certain elements in his nature remained constant: he himself felt, at the age of 43, that 'I am somewhere still the same Bert who rushed with such joy to the Haggs.' We are confident that we agree enough about these not to produce a contradictory effect upon readers of all three volumes. Our biography overall, and our individual volumes themselves, will not however show Lawrence's life evolving with steady emotional logic from initial premises. Of all the dangers biographers have to fear, the so-called 'genetic fallacy' – explanation in terms of origins – should be less in evidence here. We have learned to distrust hindsight, because reading the later man back into the earlier always implies determinism. We believe that our one work by three writers, each allowing his particular material rather than any over-view to dictate his form, will produce the necessary tension between a continuous and a continuously changing Lawrence, in a way that no synoptic view could achieve. In biographies which succeed in rising above the conscientious enumeration of one thing after another, a pattern of interpretation is established early, and later events are then selected and arranged with a predictability which plays false to the actualities and unexpectedness of life – especially life as our subject himself saw it.

Avoiding this predictability, through three points of view, has seemed to us very important – and we hope our procedure has an additional advantage. Because our biography is based on more documentary evidence than any previous one, and because (unlike some biographers) we have always acknowledged Lawrence to be a writer, each volume has to be detailed, and long – and for the reader to find the same manner in three lengthy books might be more than flesh and blood could bear. Variety of approach will at least mean variety of style: three different voices to tell Lawrence's story – but at the same time give the lie, by their very difference, to the idea that any single view, however detailed and comprehensive, could ever be 'definitive'; any pattern of interpretation *the* pattern.

David Ellis – Mark Kinkead-Weekes – John Worthen
Canterbury – Ramsgate – Swansea
March 1990

ILLUSTRATIONS

xvii

MAPS

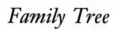

Family Tree

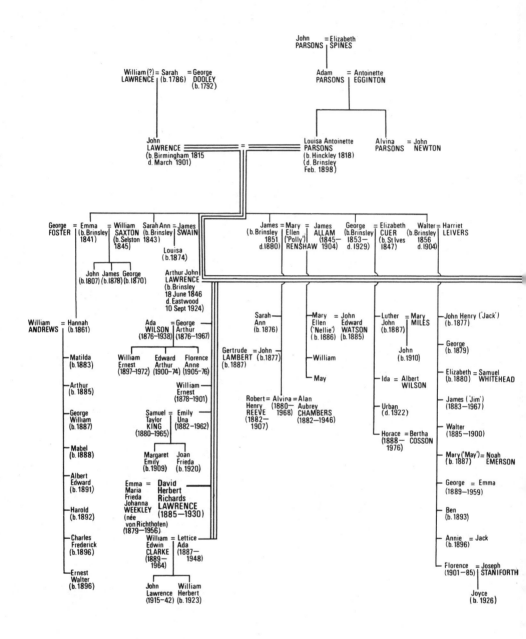

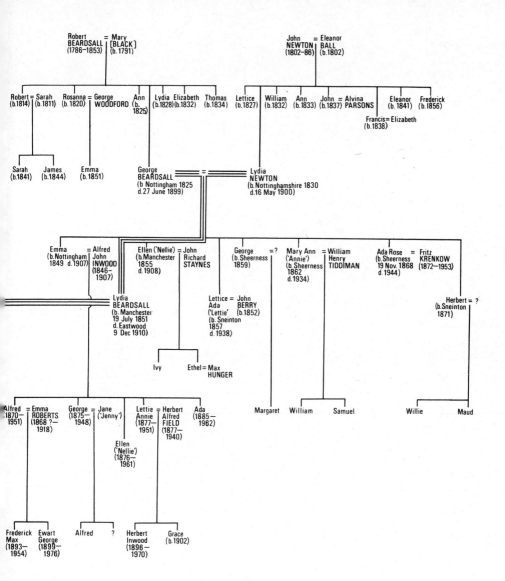

Robert BEARDSALL (1786–1853) = Mary [BLACK] (b. 1791)

John NEWTON (1802–86) = Eleanor BALL (b. 1802)

Robert (b. 1814) = Sarah (b. 1811) | Rosanna (b. 1820) = George WOODFORD | Ann (b. 1825) | Lydia (b. 1828) | Elizabeth (b. 1832) | Thomas (b. 1834)

Lettice (b. 1827) | William (b. 1832) | Ann (b. 1833) | John (b. 1837) = Alvina PARSONS | Eleanor (b. 1841) | Frederick (b. 1856)

Francis = Elizabeth (b. 1838)

Sarah (b. 1841) | James (b. 1844) | Emma (b. 1851)

George BEARDSALL (b Nottingham 1825 d. 27 June 1899) = Lydia NEWTON (b. Nottinghamshire 1830 d. 16 May 1900)

Emma (b. Nottingham 1849 d. 1907) = Alfred John INWOOD (1846–1907)

Ellen ('Nellie') (b. Manchester 1855 d. 1908) = John Richard STAYNES

George (b. Sheerness 1859) = ?

Mary Ann ('Annie') (b. Sheerness 1862 d. 1934) = William Henry TIDDIMAN

Ada Rose (b. Sheerness 19 Nov. 1868 d. 1944) = Fritz KRENKOW (1872–1953)

Lydia BEARDSALL (b. Manchester 19 July 1851 d. Eastwood 9 Dec 1910)

Lettice Ada ('Lettie') (b. Sneinton 1857 d. 1938) = John BERRY (b. 1852)

Herbert (b. Sneinton 1871) = ?

Ivy | Ethel = Max HUNGER

Alfred (1870–1951) = Emma ROBERTS (1868 ?–1918)

George (1875–1948) = Jane ('Jenny')

Lettie Annie (1877–1951) = Herbert Alfred FIELD (1877–1940)

Ada (1885–1962)

Margaret | William | Samuel

Willie | Maud

Ellen ('Nellie') (1876–1961)

Frederick Max (1893–1954) | Ewart George (1899–1976)

Alfred | ?

Herbert Inwood (1896–1970) | Grace (b. 1902)

CHRONOLOGY

(The chronology of Lawrence's writing will be found in
Appendices I and II.)

DHL=D. H. Lawrence   Frieda=Frieda Weekley, née von Richthofen

? December 1815	John Lawrence born, Deritend, Birmingham
1825	George Beardsall born, Nottingham
27 February 1838	John Lawrence marries Louisa Antoinette Parsons, Old Radford, Nottingham
18 June 1846	Arthur John Lawrence born, Brinsley
26 December 1847	George Beardsall marries Lydia Newton, Sneinton, Nottingham
19 July 1851	Lydia Beardsall born, Ancoats, Manchester
27 December 1875	Arthur John Lawrence marries Lydia Beardsall, Sneinton, Nottingham
26 September 1876	George Arthur Lawrence born, Brinsley
22 July 1878	William Ernest Lawrence born, New Cross
11 August 1879	Frieda born, Metz
24 February 1880	James Lawrence killed, Brinsley pit
21 March 1882	Emily Una Lawrence born, New Cross
1883	Lawrence family moves to 8a, Victoria Street, Eastwood
11 September 1885	DHL born, Eastwood
29 January 1887	Jessie Chambers born, Carlton
16 June 1887	Lettice Ada Lawrence born, Eastwood
late 1887	Lawrence family moves to 57, The Breach, Eastwood
20 May–20 October 1889	DHL attends Infant section, Beauvale Board School

1891	Lawrence family moves to 3, Walker Street, Eastwood
1892–8	DHL attends Boys' section, Beauvale Board School
1898	Chambers family moves to Haggs Farm, Underwood, Notts.
14 September 1898–July 1901	DHL attends Nottingham High School
20 March 1900	Arrest of DHL's uncle Walter Lawrence for manslaughter
13 July 1900	Trial and release of Walter Lawrence
July 1901	DHL leaves Nottingham High School
? late September–December 1901	Clerk with J. H. Haywood Ltd, Nottingham
11 October 1901	Death of DHL's brother Ernest Lawrence
late December 1901	DHL ill with pneumonia
c. April 1902	Month at Skegness convalescing
October 1902–July 1905	Pupil-teacher at British School, Eastwood
31 October 1903	Peterborough, Skegness
21 November 1903	Arthur Lawrence fractures leg, Brinsley pit
March 1904	DHL begins part-time attendance at Pupil-teacher Centre, Ilkeston
4 April 1904	Death of Walter Lawrence
5 November 1904	Emily Lawrence marries Sam King, Eastwood
December 1904	DHL sits King's Scholarship Examination
19 December 1904	Arthur Lawrence injured, Brinsley pit
early 1905	Lawrence family moves to 97, Lynn Croft, Eastwood
June 1905	DHL at Great Yarmouth, Hunstanton, etc.
late June 1905	Sits University of London Matriculation Examination
August 1905–September 1906	Uncertificated assistant teacher at British School, Eastwood
Easter 1906	Break with Jessie Chambers
August 1906	Lawrence family holiday at Mablethorpe, Lincolnshire

October 1906–June 1908	DHL student at University College, Nottingham
10–24 August 1907	Lawrence family holiday at Robin Hood's Bay, Yorkshire
30 September 1907	Emily King's first child born dead
7 December 1907	'A Prelude' in *Nottinghamshire Guardian*
19 March 1908	'Art and the Individual' read to Eastwood Debating Society
June–July 1908	Sits Nottingham University College examinations
8–22 August 1908	Lawrence family holiday at Flamborough, Yorkshire
16–24 September 1908	DHL at 50, Dulverton Rd, Leicester, with Ada and Fritz Krenkow
25 September 1908	Unsuccessful interview for teaching post in Stockport
26 September–3 October 1908	London: interviewed in Croydon
11 October–23 December 1908	Croydon: certificated assistant teacher at Davidson Road School
24 October 1908	Hampton Court
7 November 1908	Epsom, Dorking, Reigate
14 November 1908	Barnet
5 December 1908	London
23 December 1908–10 January 1909	Eastwood for Christmas holidays
10 January–8 April 1909	Croydon
9 February 1909	Emily King's daughter Margaret born
8–18 April 1909	DHL at Eastwood for Easter holidays
18 April–28 May 1909	Croydon
8–9 May 1909	Brighton, Rottingdean
22 May 1909	Caterham
28 May–6 June 1909	Eastwood for Whitsuntide holiday (attends Mabel Cooper's wedding on 2 June)
6 June–29 July 1909	Croydon
29–31 July 1909	Harrow-on-the-Hill
31 July–14 August 1909	Lawrence family holiday at Shanklin, Isle of Wight
14–29 August 1909	DHL at Eastwood for Summer holidays
29 August–23 December 1909	Croydon
c. 11 September 1909	London to meet Ford Madox Hueffer

November 1909	Sequence of poems, 'A Still Afternoon', in *English Review*
14 November 1909	London and Hampstead (further visits on 16 and 20 November)
27–8 November 1909	Jessie Chambers visits DHL in London
11–12 December 1909	DHL in London
23 December 1909–9 January 1910	Eastwood for Christmas holidays
9 January–24 March 1910	Croydon
21 January 1910	London
February 1910	'Goose Fair' in *English Review*
8–11 February 1910	Ill and absent from school
9 March 1910	Hampstead
?19 March 1910	London with Alice Dax
25 March–3 April 1910	Eastwood for Easter holidays
3 April–13 May 1910	Croydon
13–22 May 1910	Eastwood for Whitsuntide holidays
22 May–28 July 1910	Croydon
23 July 1910	London
28 July–6 August 1910	Eastwood and Nottingham for Summer holidays
1 August 1910	Breaks 'betrothal of six years standing' to Jessie Chambers
6–12 August 1910	Holiday with George Neville in Blackpool, Fleetwood and Barrow-in-Furness
c. 10 August 1910	Lydia Lawrence falls ill in Leicester
12–22 August 1910	DHL in Eastwood, with visits to Leicester
22–8 August 1910	Leicester
28 August–4 September 1910	Croydon
4 September 1910	Leicester
4 September–6 October 1910	Croydon
?late September 1910	Lydia Lawrence brought back to Eastwood
October 1910	'Three Poems' in *English Review*
6–9 October 1910	DHL in Eastwood: visits Nottingham's Goose Fair: sees Louie Burrows
9–21 October 1910	Croydon
21–3 October 1910	Eastwood
23 October–4 November 1910	Croydon

4–7 November 1910	Eastwood
7–23 November 1910	Croydon
23 November–13 December 1910	Eastwood
2 December 1910	Copy of *The White Peacock* for Lydia Lawrence arrives
3 December 1910	Leicester: becomes engaged to Louie Burrows
9 December 1910	Lydia Lawrence dies
11 December 1910	DHL meets Jessie Chambers, gives her poems
12 December 1910	Lydia Lawrence buried
13–24 December 1910	DHL in Croydon
24–31 December 1910	Christmas holidays in Brighton with Ada Lawrence and Frances Cooper
31 December 1910–8 January 1911	Quorn (home of Louie Burrows)
8 January–14 April 1911	Croydon
19 January 1911	*The White Peacock* published in New York (20 January in London)
9 March 1911	Lawrence family moves to Queen's Square, Eastwood
14–23 April 1911	DHL in Eastwood and probably Quorn for Easter holidays
17 April 1911	Matlock with Louie Burrows
23 April–4 June 1911	Croydon
13 May 1911	With Louie Burrows in London (including Buckingham Palace and Westminster Abbey)
June 1911	'Odour of Chrysanthemums' in *English Review*
4–11 June 1911	Quorn, Eastwood and Leicester for Whitsuntide holidays
11–17 June 1911	Croydon
17–25 June 1911	Quorn and Eastwood (holiday for George V's Coronation)
25 June–27 July 1911	Croydon
12 July 1911	Dover
19 July 1911	London
27 July 1911	Quorn
28 July 1911	Eastwood

29 July–12 August 1911	Summer holidays in North Wales with Louie Burrows and Ada Lawrence: later joined by George Neville
12–19 August 1911	Eastwood, Eakring
19–?21 August 1911	Shirebrook, with Harry and Alice Dax
22–7 August 1911	Eastwood, Lincoln, Quorn
27 August–27 October 1911	Croydon
September 1911	'A Fragment of Stained Glass' in *English Review*
13–15 October 1911	Visits Edward Garnett at 'The Cearne', near Edenbridge, Kent
27–9 October 1911	Quorn and Eastwood
29 October 1911–4 January 1912	Croydon
November 1911	Review of *Contemporary German Poetry* in *English Review*
4 November 1911	Two poems in *Nation*
18–19 November 1911	'The Cearne': falls ill
19 November–22 December 1911	Ill with pneumonia and absent from school
24 December 1911–4 January 1912	Louie Burrows in Croydon
January 1912	Reviews of *The Minnesingers* and *The Oxford Book of German Verse* in *English Review*
4–6 January 1912	DHL with Louie Burrows at Redhill
6 January–3 February 1912	DHL at Bournemouth for convalescence
3–9 February 1912	'The Cearne'
4 February 1912	Breaks engagement with Louie Burrows
9 February–3 March 1912	Eastwood, with visits to Nottingham
13 February 1912	Meets Louie Burrows in Nottingham; sequel 'which startled *me*'
14 February 1912	Meets Alice Dax in Nottingham
?3 March 1912	Visits Professor Ernest Weekley, meets Frieda: sees Chambers family at Arno Vale in afternoon: to Shirebrook
3–8 March 1912	Shirebrook, with Alice and Harry Dax
8–25 March 1912	Eastwood, with visits to Nottingham
17 March 1912	Nottingham: ?sees Frieda
between 18 and 23 March 1912	Sees *Man and Superman* with Frieda in Nottingham

25–31 March 1912	Bradnop, Staffs., with George Neville
31 March–23 April 1912	Eastwood, with visits to Nottingham
9 April 1912	Nottingham, meets Agnes Mason: ?sees Frieda
23–5 April 1912	Leicester, with Ada and Fritz Krenkow
25–8 April 1912	London, Kew Gardens with Irene and Margaret Brinton and 'The Cearne' with Frieda
28–9 April 1912	Leicester
29 April–3 May 1912	Eastwood
3 May 1912	London; meets Frieda, travels (via Dover and Ostend) to Metz
4–7 May 1912	With Frieda in Metz
7 May 1912	Trouble with military policeman in Metz
8 May 1912	DHL goes to Trier
8–11 May 1912	Trier
11 May 1912	To Waldbröl (via Koblenz, Niederlahnstein, Troisdorf, Hennef)
11 May 1912	First three of eight 'Schoolmaster' poems in *Saturday Westminster Gazette*, 11 May–1 June
11–24 May 1912	Waldbröl
15 May 1912	To Nümbrecht with Hannah Krenkow: hail-storm
19 May 1912	To Bonn and Drachenfels
23 May 1912	*The Trespasser*
24 May 1912	To Munich, meets Frieda
25 May 1912	DHL and Frieda to Beuerberg: stay till 1 June
June 1912	'Snapdragon' in *English Review*
1 June–5 August 1912	DHL and Frieda in Icking
3 August 1912	'French Sons of Germany' in *Saturday Westminster Gazette*
5 August 1912	DHL and Frieda leave Icking: to Wolfratshausen on foot, Bichl by train, Bad Tölz on foot
6 August 1912	To Röhrlmoos hay-hut on foot
7 August 1912	To Café Hubertus on foot and (later) Achensee farmhouse by omnibus
8 August 1912	To Jenbach on foot, then to Kufstein by train

9 August 1912	To Jenbach by train, then to Mayrhofen
9–26 August 1912	DHL and Frieda in Mayrhofen; joined by David Garnett *c.* 18 August, later by Harold Hobson
10 August 1912	'Hail in the Rhine-Land' in *Saturday Westminster Gazette*
26 August 1912	To hay-hut beyond Ginzling on foot
27 August 1912	To Dominicus-Hütte on foot
28 August 1912	Over the Pfitscherjoch pass on foot to Gasthof Elefant
29 August 1912	To Sterzing on foot: Garnett and Hobson to Munich
29 August–1 September 1912	DHL and Frieda in Sterzing
1 September 1912	To Jaufen Haus on foot
2 September 1912	Back to Sterzing on foot: then to Bozen by train
3 September 1912	To Trento by train
4 September 1912	To Riva, Lago di Garda, by train
4–18 September 1912	Riva
18 September 1912–2 April 1913	Villa Igea in Villa
2 November 1912	All Souls' Day
December 1912	'Snap-Dragon' in *Georgian Poetry 1911–1912*
February 1913	*Love Poems and Others*
22 March 1913	'Christs in the Tirol' in *Saturday Westminster Gazette*
March 1913	'The Soiled Rose' in *Forum*; review of *Georgian Poetry: 1911–1912* in *Rhythm*
2–10 April 1913	San Gaudenzio, Lago di Garda
29 May 1913	*Sons and Lovers*

D. H. LAWRENCE

1885–1912

PART ONE

◆

Eastwood
and
Nottingham

◆

CHAPTER ONE

1815–1883

ANTECEDENTS

I. The Legacy of Eastwood

Our first image of D. H. Lawrence comes from October 1885, a month after his birth in the small Midlands mining town of Eastwood. Willie Hopkin – local shopkeeper and intellectual – recalled seeing Lawrence's mother Lydia 'coming out of Victoria Street wheeling the baby in a three-wheeled pram; two wheels being wood and the rims iron. You could hear them coming a long way off. Mrs Lawrence was neatly dressed in black, with a little black bonnet that was always a feature of her attire'.[1] Respectable, always in black, 'tiny and pleasant and restrained', keeping herself to herself except when out with a noisy pram: that was the Lydia Lawrence whom Eastwood knew. Hopkin asked how the new baby was, Lawrence being 'a snuffly-nosed little beggar, seldom without a cold'. Mrs Lawrence

uncovered his face and I marvelled at the frail little specimen of humanity. I saw that Mrs. Lawrence seemed very concerned, and she said that she sometimes wondered if she would be able to raise him. It was at my tongue's end to remark to Mrs. Lawrence that he did not resemble his father, either in appearance or frame, but when I saw her worried face, I pulled myself up and said nothing.[2]

A photograph from a little later of the baby in his pram survives (see Illustration 4): though he may have had an ear infection at 10 months,[3] he hardly looks frail, though (as in other early photographs) his mouth is open: a sign of that 'snuffly-nose'. But the baby clothes are remarkable: probably supplied by Lydia Lawrence's better-off sisters, the white hat, lace collar and lace-frilled pelisse (probably velvet) would have contrasted sharply with the black of his mother's clothes and the grime of the mining town. Lawrence's division between his parents had already begun: the sickly baby, dressed up so splendidly, was also the son of Arthur John Lawrence, a miner who worked underground for more than fifty years, and who was immensely tough. No wonder Hopkin was surprised.

For it was the healthy who survived best in Eastwood. There were regular epidemics: measles, diphtheria, diarrhoea, scarlet fever and whooping cough; in the late nineteenth century, respiratory diseases (tuberculosis and bronchitis) accounted for 17% of deaths in the area. The writer who died of pleurisy and tuberculosis in 1930, at the age of 44, remarked just before he died that 'I have had bronchitis since I was a fortnight old.'[4] But many families suffered worse than the Lawrences. The Cooper family with their five daughters would be next-door neighbours in Lynn Croft in the 1900s, and Tom Cooper the Lawrences' landlord. The mother, Thirza Cooper, died of 'Pulmonary tuberculosis & cardiac failure' in July 1904 at the age of 55: and all five daughters suffered from tuberculosis. Ethel died of 'Phthisis/Pulmonalis/Exhaustion' early in 1905, when she was 17; Mabel Hannah Cooper Marson died of 'Pulmonary Tuberculosis' at the age of 34, in February 1916; Francis ('Frankie') died of 'Pulmonary Tuberculosis and Exhaustion', also at 34, in December 1918; Florence Cooper Wilson died of 'Laryngeal Tuberculosis' in July 1924, at 43; and Gertrude ('Gertie') – also suffering from tuberculosis, and living with Lawrence's sister Ada in nearby Ripley from 1919 – had a lung removed in 1926, when she was 41.[5] Gertrude was the only one of the sisters to live beyond her mid-forties: she died at the age of 57. What is significant, of course, is that Lawrence's infection did not develop into tuberculosis for many years; he was simply a boy – and an adult – with a 'weak chest', subject to colds and coughs and 'flu'.

But he carried away with him, as a legacy of his Eastwood childhood, his weak chest – and the tubercle itself: the family doctor apparently told his mother in 1901 that her son was tubercular. And although he physically left Eastwood, and spiritually and intellectually moved away from its attitudes, attachments and beliefs – shortly before he died his sister Ada remarked that 'He hates it. It makes him ill whenever he sees it'[6] – yet he also remained extraordinarily close to it. He belonged to it even when it seemed inevitable that he should stop belonging; he carried the experience of Eastwood with him like the lungs which were the relics of his childhood there.

II Lawrences

The house at 8a, Victoria Street, Eastwood, where Lawrence was born (see Illustration 10), still has a shop-window; Lydia Lawrence had a small draper's shop there for a few years. Its possibility as a shop was probably among the reasons why, late in 1883, the Lawrence family (then of New Cross, Sutton-in-Ashfield, 5 miles away) took the house.

But only one of the reasons. At the bottom of Victoria Street ran Princes Street, where Arthur's youngest brother Walter and his family lived at no. 9; less than a mile away, in Brinsley, lived Arthur's brother George and his family, as well as the family of Mary Ellen (known as Polly) Lawrence, the widow of his third brother James. Both George and Walter had been working at Brinsley when James Lawrence had been killed there in 1880; and it had been in Brinsley that Arthur himself had worked as a miner, first as a child, and then again in the mid 1870s. Arthur Lawrence's two married sisters and his parents also lived in Brinsley; the latter had occupied Quarry Cottage – the house where all their children had been born – since the late 1840s. So when the New Cross Lawrences came to Eastwood, they returned to the centre of Arthur Lawrence's family. D. H. Lawrence was to be born into a family in which, on his father's side, none lived farther from each other than a mile and half, and some nearer than 60 yards. This gives the first clue to one of the crucial differences between Lydia and her husband, during their years in Eastwood: the contrast between her isolation, resulting from her separation from her own family, and his involvement in and closeness to the community surrounding the old family centre.

The man who was most probably D. H. Lawrence's great-grandfather, William Lawrence, was however not from Brinsley.* He had worked in the metal industry in and around the growing town of Birmingham at the turn of the eighteenth century; and late in 1815, his wife Sarah had given birth to their son John in Deritend, a suburb of Birmingham: John had been christened on Christmas Day 1815, and was reputedly 'brought up as a tiny baby in some military hospital – or home'.[7] The Lawrences had a story that they had French ancestors; that John's father had been a refugee from the French Revolution who 'fought against Napoleon in Waterloo' (iii. 282) and who married an English barmaid, or – in another version – that John had been found as a child wandering on the battlefield of Waterloo. It was also said – and this is the only real possibility – that John's father had been killed at Waterloo. That might explain the baby's military upbringing; the father had certainly died before 1837, when his wife Sarah married again. But all these stories were probably invented, with John's birth in the magic year '1815' helping them along. The newspapers of the 1880s continued to record the deaths of soldiers who had fought at the battle, as the romance of Waterloo throve in the popular imagination; at least one cottage in East-

---

* Paul Lawrence, Framesmith, appears as 'Father' when John Lawrence (born in Birmingham) got married in 1838, and therefore appears to be the family great-grandfather, rather than William. But Sarah Lawrence, John's mother, had married a tailor (George Dooley) the previous year, and since Paul was a witness to the marriage, unless there was a divorce in the family (which is extremely unlikely) John's actual father must have been dead by 1837. Nor can Paul Lawrence's name be found in the surviving Birmingham parish records between 1809 and 1829; while we know that John Lawrence was born in Birmingham (Census 1841, 1851, 1861, etc.). It is more likely that Paul Lawrence was a male relation – perhaps an uncle – and that he stood in for the deceased 'Father'. The only 'John Lawrence' whose christening appears in the (incomplete) Birmingham records around 1815–17, however, is also the only boy with a mother called Sarah; and his father is William Lawrence.

wood had been built for a Waterloo veteran, in Three Tunns Road; the father of William Whitehead, Lawrence's headmaster at Beauvale School, had been a Waterloo hero; a sword reputedly from Waterloo had hung in Quarry Cottage.[8] But if the Lawrences' origins had originally been with a French Laurens family, such origins are now lost in obscurity:* all that can be said is that they had Birmingham origins early in the nineteenth century. It is possible that there was French blood on the other side of the family: in 1838, John Lawrence married Louisa Antoinette Parsons; and though she came from a traditionally nonconformist family living in Hinckley in Leicestershire, she was the daughter of Antoinette Egginton. The name certainly suggests French sympathies, if not actual connections.

By 1837 Sarah Lawrence had remarried; she and her husband George Dooley moved to Brinsley. They were probably responsible for Brinsley becoming the Lawrence family centre. Her son John had grown up apprenticed to a tailor, quite possibly his future stepfather George Dooley; he also settled in Brinsley after his marriage the following year, and worked there as a tailor: he may once have been a military tailor (iii. 282). But his reputation was as a rower, wrestler, boxer and dancer: 'He was famous in South Notts as the best dancer and the best boxer' (iii. 282). Tall and powerful, according to family legend he once met Ben Caunt in an informal fight and beat him; Caunt became 'Champion of England' in 1840 after winning a 101 round fight. John Lawrence in the 1890s was remembered by his granddaughter Ada as 'a big, shambling, generous-hearted man whose waistcoat front was always powdered with snuff'; his grandson D. H. Lawrence saw him as 'a tall, silent, strange man' (iii. 282). He was reputed to weigh twenty stone, but was nevertheless a dandy; his grandson never forgot the snuffbox he carried.[9] By the 1890s, he had grown 'very deaf and didn't talk much', but his grandchildren remembered him as always kind and never forgetting to ask ' "Would you like some apples, my duckies?" At our nods he would shuffle into the garden and fill our pockets with Keswicks from the old tree'. Another story of his gentleness (and his wife's fierceness) is linked to the same tree; D. H. Lawrence's elder brother George remembered how

I was once up an apple tree and along comes grandfather, spots me up the tree, you know, reaches his long arms, caught me round the middle, set me down on the [hesitation] ... and bent down and he said 'Are your pockets full, ducky?' And I

---

* When DHL chose the family surname 'Morel' in his autobiographical novel *Sons and Lovers*, he was again suggesting the French connection: uncommon in England (although there was a firm of Nottingham photographers called Morel), the name was and is common in France. 'Morel' is also the dark nightshade, the bitter (morello) cherry and an edible, dusky fungus: a sense of darkness is conveyed by them all.

nodded, I couldn't speak; he taps me on the behind, you know, and said 'Then run, Granny's comin'.' He wouldn't lay a finger on a child. Granny would.

'Granny' – Louisa Lawrence – was also notorious for her 'sharp, querulous' tongue.[10]

John Lawrence worked much of his life as a company tailor for the Eastwood firm of Barber Walker & Co., which ran Brinsley pit: 'In those days the company supplied the men with thick flannel vests, or singlets, and the moleskin trousers lined at the top with flannel, in which the colliers worked'.[11] After the company stopped providing clothing, John Lawrence stayed in Brinsley as a tailor and shared the shop with his wife, who sold haberdashery. He still made and sold miners' clothing; his grandson remembered 'the great rolls of coarse flannel and pit-cloth which stood in the corner of my grandfather's shop when I was a small boy, and the big, strange old sewing-machine, like nothing else on earth, which sewed the massive pit-trousers'. Every week, Louisa Lawrence 'travelled in the carrier's cart to the Nottingham warehouses where she bought her small stock'; when Lydia Lawrence started her shop in Eastwood, she was thus following her mother-in-law's trade, though by the 1890s Louisa Lawrence's once flourishing business in Brinsley 'had declined sadly', which probably contributed to her short temperedness: 'Many of the boxes on the shelves were empty and there were only a few red handkerchiefs, shoulder shawls, aprons and cotton odds and ends in the others'.[12]

The four male children of John and Louisa Lawrence all worked as colliers, and may well have started at Brinsley colliery, only 200 yards away – though with the region dotted with collieries, large and small, there can be no certainty about which first took them on. They all eventually had jobs at Brinsley. The Lawrences' elder daughter Emma married a miner, George Foster, and after his death she married another miner, William Saxton, four years younger than herself. Her sister Sarah was the only member of the family not to be linked with the mining industry; she married James Swain, the sexton at Brinsley church (where the young Arthur Lawrence had sung in the choir), and reportedly felt superior. Her nieces and nephews were not fond of visiting her, though they enjoyed going to see aunt Emma, widowed for the second time by the 1890s, and whose generosity 'was as boundless as her "superior" sister's was confined'. 'At her home we were sure of a wholehearted reception, and as we hurried through her garden, among the madonna lilies, red-hot pokers and golden rod we could hear her voice, telling whoever happened to be within hearing distance, that her darlings were arriving, and expecting her listeners to be astonished about it'.[13] That suggests the warmth of Brinsley, and of the Lawrence relations there.

In the Brinsley of the 1850s and 1860s, the Lawrences and their web of close connections with the colliery were not unusual; the 1861 Census shows house after house of colliers, mine officials and railway workers. The Midland Railway Company had been set up in 1832, and its railways were opening from the 1840s; the movement of large quantities of coal, hitherto dependent upon canal transport, had become possible. The mines of Barber Walker & Co., like those of its competitors, developed simultaneously with the network of railway lines; there had been coal mined at Brinsley since at least the late seventeenth century, but in 1843 the main shaft had been purchased by Barber Walker, and over the next twelve years it was deepened and extended. Lawrence would describe at the start of *Sons and Lovers* how the six Barber Walker Eastwood pits were 'like black studs on the countryside, linked by a loop of fine chain, the railway'.[14] That was the colliery (or 'mineral') railway: one loop going east, to Moorgreen, High Park and Watnall pits, the other coming down to Brinsley from Underwood; together they joined the railway line at Langley Mill; coal wagons from Eastwood could be seen all over the country. When Lawrence came to use material about his own family, in *Sons and Lovers*, he did not start with an account of incompatible personalities, or even of family history: he began with the history of mining in the region, for that was the significant history of most of the families there, including the Brinsley Lawrences.*

Arthur Lawrence, born in 1846, the eldest son of John and Louisa Lawrence, remembered starting work at the pit at the age of 7.[15] This would not have been unusual; the 1861 Census records his 11-year–old brother James as 'Coal Miner', and although children were not supposed to work underground before they were 10, the same Census reveals some 8-year-olds similarly employed. Thomas Renshaw, for example, whose sister Polly married James Lawrence, was 8 years old and 'Coal Miner' in the 1861 Census, along with his 10- and 11-year-old brothers; they probably worked sorting coal. By the age of 7, Arthur had had some infant schooling from Miss Eyte of Brinsley; the Sunday schools run by all the local chapels and churches, which he continued to attend, included writing and reading classes. A local schoolmaster had commented in 1842 that 'the collier children are more tired on the whole than others, but equally anxious to learn'; the

---

* I make frequent reference to the persons and action of *Sons and Lovers*. It should be emphasised that the novel is used only sparingly for illustrations of events in the Lawrence household: it has not been drawn upon except when other evidence confirms its versions of life. Many things in the novel are not true of real life; many things from real life do not appear in the novel; and a novel – even an autobiographical one – is not an appropriate source for the events of real life. See below, 'The Use of Sources'.

vicar of Eastwood did 'not think they are more backward in their education than others'.[16] Arthur Lawrence only ever went to Infant school and Sunday school; even as a 7-year-old he would have worked a twelve hour day, five days a week; and although short-time working and lay-offs when demand for coal was slack would have meant that he was not always employed, he would not have fitted into normal school hours. Unlike his mother, who never learned to write, he could sign his name and – with some difficulty – read; as an adult he was able to deal with the (limited) paper work entailed by his job as a butty. His son remembered how 'when I was a little boy, my father used to buy a scrubby yearly almanack with the sun and moon and stars on the cover ... crammed in corners it had little anecdotes and humorisms, with a moral tag'.[17] Arthur Lawrence's everyday reading probably went no further than the almanac and the newspaper.

His first job, after going underground at the age of 10, would have been opening and shutting the wind- and fire-proof doors for the passage of ponies and coal tubs. He would probably have progressed to working with the ponies; then, as a 'dayman', he would have joined a team of three or four men working under the direction of two or three 'butties'. The butties were responsible for the working of a specified section, a 'stall', of the coal face; the managers paid them each week (by weight) for the coal the stall produced, which was weighed at the pit-head in tubs marked with their stall number. The daymen – on a fixed daily wage – loaded the coal into the tubs, despatched them to the bottom of the shaft and got rid of waste material; they worked behind the 'holers', also on daily wages, who actually cut the coal by digging out the bottom of the seam to create a hole into which the overhanging coal could be broken. The butties themselves worked as supervisors and holers. After the weekly wages of the daymen and holers had been paid, and expenses for blasting powder and candles had been met, the butties would divide up the remaining money. They thus received the profits after the wages of the others had been paid. If the daymen had been slack, or inefficient or – more likely – one of them had had an accident which slowed down or stopped the filling and movement of coal tubs, then the butties' profits suffered. When he was about 17 or 18, Arthur would perhaps have started as a holer – the most profitable job in the pit below the level of butty or manager, but also the most dangerous.

Arthur Lawrence did well. Like his father, he was always physically very strong, and he worked underground from 1856 until at least 1912. He became a thoroughly experienced and highly regarded workman: 'a perfect gentleman to work with', according to a man who worked with him 'to the day of his retirement'. He earned the relatively good wages possible for a successful coal miner in the developing industry, especially during the great

days of the 1870s. According to a family friend, he was 'a first-rate workman
... invariably called upon when there was a particularly difficult job to be
done in the pit'.[18] By the time he was 20, in 1867, he had moved to New
Annesley to work at the newly opened pit. By 1875 he had progressed to the
position of butty: 'Mining Contractor' – the official term – is his profession
on his marriage certificate. It was very common for butties to take family as
their daymen: brothers, uncles, strong young sons. All would profit if the
butty were an efficient organiser, a safe worker, and could rely upon his
team – and if the daymen's wages went into the same family as the butty's
profits. Arthur Lawrence's brother Walter, in the 1880s, worked with him
as a holer for a time; but Arthur Lawrence must often have wished for other
– and more reliable – family members to join him.[19]

His three brothers, who had remained in Brinsley – the 1871 Census
shows them still living at home, when they were 20, 18 and 16 – were
getting married; James in 1874, George and Walter in 1877. Arthur, with
his skills, experience and good wages, would then have been as his son
D. H. Lawrence re-imagined him in *Sons and Lovers*: 'well-set-up, erect and
very smart. He had wavy, black hair that shone again, and a vigorous black
beard that had never been shaved. His cheeks were ruddy, and his red, moist
mouth was noticeable because he laughed so often and so heartily.' In a
surviving photograph his good clothes are conspicuous, but he looks warily
at the camera: he is a handsome, well-dressed man in his late twenties who
prides himself on his appearance (see Illustration 3). A skilled workman, and
also an accomplished dancer – he actually taught dancing, though it is not
known where or for how long – he does not look altogether sure of himself.
Family tradition, assisted by the story told in *Sons and Lovers*, says that he
met and fell in love with the 23-year-old Lydia Beardsall at a family Christmas party in Nottingham.[20] As her uncle John Newton was married to
Arthur's aunt Alvina, they probably met at their relatives' house at 34
Whitbread Street, New Basford, Nottingham. The year was 1874.

III Beardsalls

Lydia's background and family were quite different. Born in 1851 in
Ancoats, Manchester, she belonged on her father's side to a Nottingham
family which had once been comparatively 'well-to-do' (iii. 282), but was
now 'a family chiefly noted for its decay'. The Beardsalls were full of stories
of having 'once held large lands along the Trent' and having been 'richest
among the town's wealthy tanners, in the old years'.[21] But they had been
'ruined in a smash in the lace industry' (iii. 282). Lydia's mother's family,
the Newtons, included the 'Artist, composer of music' John Newton, and –

a generation back – the famous hymn writer John Newton, friend of Cow-per. But in the Nottingham lace industry where the family had once been owners and partners, most of the male Newtons and Beardsalls were now workmen: they appeared in the 1881 Census variously as 'pattern hand', 'lace designer', 'lace maker', 'lace mender' and 'engine fitter'.

Originally a 'framesmith apprentice', Lydia's father, George Beardsall, had become an engine mechanic. He had married Lydia Newton in Decem-ber 1847, and their first child Emma was born in 1849. At some point, George Beardsall began to specialise as an engine fitter: 'a working engineer whose duties consist in the fitting together of machine or engine parts': what would today be called an engine assembler. In Ancoats, where their second and favourite daughter Lydia ('Liddie') was born,[22] he probably worked on the engines of one of the numerous cotton mills. In 1853, when the family moved to Longsight, 2 miles south of Manchester, George Beardsall was presumably working as a fitter for the London and North-western Railway Company: if so, he was obviously not a specialist fitter for lace machines. In 1855, after the birth of the third child, Ellen ('Nellie'), they went back to Sneinton in Nottingham; and here their fourth child, Lettice ('Lettie'), was born. In 1858 George Beardsall was taken on as a fitter at the Sheerness Dockyards on the Isle of Sheppey, Kent; their first son, George, was born in Sheerness in 1859. His brother-in-law Francis Newton's two eldest children were born in Sheerness in 1865 and 1867, showing that some of his family had also moved there.[23] George Beardsall's frequent moves, however, though they demonstrate a skilled workman who could turn his hand to anything, suggest a degree of restlessness – and perhaps the hurt pride at not being appreciated which his family remembered.

In Sheerness, the family lived in Marine Town. The details about them uncovered by Roy Spencer are highly significant; they tended to live in places rather beyond their means; they had pretensions which their actual income of around £90 a year could barely support. (Arthur Lawrence, a bachelor, would have been earning around £100 a year in the early 1870s.)

How it may be asked could a hired dockyard fitter with a wife and five children earning 5s 8d a day afford to live in the smartest and newest of Sheerness's five towns? The answer is that he could not. But with an instinct for choosing the right place, he had taken the family to the very edge of Marine Town, to an unpaved cul-de-sac of tiny, two-up-two-down cottages . . . The house was no more than nine feet wide . . .[24]

Here the Beardsall family of two adults and five children somehow managed to house a lodger as well; they must have been desperate for his rent. To add to their financial difficulties and to the overcrowding, two more children (Mary Ann – 'Annie' – and Ada) were born in Sheerness, in 1862 and 1868.

And then catastrophe struck. On 16 February 1870, George Beardsall was severely hurt in an accident at work when he fell 9 feet to the ground. He suffered 'almost complete lameness', and showed symptoms of angina pectoris; he was rendered 'permanently unfit', and was granted 'a £20 compassionate gratuity in consideration of injury'.[25] He never worked again. It was a disaster for the family, even though he was subsequently granted a special compassionate allowance of £18-5-0 a year. For one thing, he had to repay his original gratuity; between 1871 and 1874 his income was only £12-5-0 a year. For another, only one of the daughters was married (Emma, in 1869) while their elder son was only 10 and could not support them. They did the only possible thing; they moved back to Sneinton, to be in the midst of their relations and get what help they could. And the three remaining elder daughters started work.

Lydia Beardsall would have liked to be a teacher. She had worked briefly and unsuccessfully as a pupil-teacher in Sheerness, when she was 13; she apparently tried to start a school there, and seems to have taught a little later (unqualified, apart from her time as a pupil-teacher) in a Dame's school. In 1910, Lawrence recreated her in that last job, in a fictional sketch of her early life he called 'Matilda'; while Mrs Morel in *Sons and Lovers* recalls 'the funny old mistress, whose assistant she had become ... in the private school'. Lydia Beardsall may also have worked as a governess.[26] But family needs in 1870 took priority. By April 1871, according to the Census, Lydia, Nellie and Lettie (19, 16 and 14 respectively) were all lace drawers in the Nottingham lace industry; pulling out the long cotton draw-threads (or lacers) which separate machine-made lace made in strips, keeping the web firm and making it convenient to handle on a wide machine. It was a 'sweated' trade for home workers which – with three daughters working at it – would have filled the house with cotton thread and lace, just as the Radfords' house described in *Sons and Lovers* is 'smothered':

The mother ... was drawing thread from a vast web of lace. A clump of fluff and ravelled cotton was at her right hand, a heap of three-quarter-inch lace lay on her left, whilst in front of her was the mountain of the lace web, piling the hearthrug. Threads of curly cotton, pulled out from between the lengths of lace, strewed over the fender and the fireplace. Paul dared not go forward, for fear of treading on piles of white stuff ...

The room was all lace—and it was so dark and warm, that the white, snowy stuff seemed the more distinct.[27]

The Beardsall house in John Street, Sneinton, must have looked like that permanently. To add to their problems, an eighth child had been born to the family in March 1871, but Lydia loved Herbert 'dearly when he was a little blond boy',[28] and was partly responsible for his upbringing until she left home to get married, four years later.

IV Lydia and Arthur

Meeting Arthur Lawrence at Christmas 1874 would have seemed to Lydia to open her way forward from a life which, after childhood freedom in Sheerness, was now shut in by sweated labour and poverty – poverty felt the more intensely because it had struck a family acutely sensitive to its standing. Mrs Morel, in *Sons and Lovers*, married to a collier and living in a colliery village, regrets her years of freedom as a child, and wonders if she is 'the same person . . . as had run so lightly on the breakwater at Sheerness, ten years before'.[29] Lydia Beardsall may well have started to feel that in Sneinton during the years while George Beardsall was repaying his gratuity and the daughters were lace drawing. In the 1870s, however, miners' wages were particularly high: the 27-year-old Arthur Lawrence was weekly bringing in more than George Beardsall's pension did in two months.

So although Lydia's daughter Ada described her mother as having a 'rather quiet, reserved and ladylike' nature – she was nicknamed 'The Mouse' as a child – and though she had been 'brought up in a strict and Puritanical atmosphere', she could not have helped being impressed by the young man's income and by the prospect of being rescued from poverty. Arthur Lawrence, too, may have presented himself as rather more than an ordinary collier. Family tradition says that he did not tell Lydia that he worked underground (the main social division between colliery workers being whether they got black at work or not); and she, who had 'never visited a mining village',[30] would not have seen through the official title of 'Mining Contractor': though it is worth adding that in *Sons and Lovers*, Lawrence shows Gertrude Coppard discovering on first meeting Walter Morel that he is a miner, and admiring how he 'risked his life daily, and with gaiety'. However, Lawrence's contemporary and friend, George Neville, stated that he heard (many years later) how Lydia had been 'under the impression that Arthur Lawrence had some kind of a staff job at the collieries, was an official of sorts, permanently employed and at a fixed salary'.[31] Such a job – with a secure income – would have been rather more acceptable to Lydia and her family; and while it is impossible to be certain about what Arthur Lawrence told Lydia, or what she may have wanted to hear, it is important that she came to believe that she had been deceived.

Arthur Lawrence would perhaps most have impressed Lydia by what

15

their daughter Ada described as 'his overflowing humour and good spirits'. This tends to be overlooked in written accounts of him; but it survives in recollections of his mending the household's boots and shoes. He was

never more happy than when seated tailorwise on the rug, with the hobbing iron, hammering away and singing at the top of his voice. If the pans and kettles leaked he could always mend them, and when the eight-day clock was out of order we loved to watch him take it to pieces, carefully putting the screws and spare parts in saucers, and boiling the works in a big saucepan to clean them thoroughly.[32]

Lawrence recreated such times in *Sons and Lovers*: Walter Morel 'always sang when he mended boots, because of the jolly sound of hammering'. There was little enough of Arthur Lawrence's cheerfulness, his practicality, his liveliness, his 'musical voice, his gallant manner' in the house in Sneinton.[33] Lawrence's fiction 'Matilda' recreates George Beardsall as stern and sardonic, his wife muted, the children uneasily caught between their parents. Arthur Lawrence's energy, openness and humour were immensely attractive: Lydia, lace drawing and almost certainly disappointed with her life, found him irresistible. Perhaps, like Gertrude Coppard in *Sons and Lovers*, she would have married him even if she had known he was simply a collier without that precious 'fixed salary': though she would not then have been able to hold it against him that he had deceived her.

The year-long wait before Lydia and Arthur married suggests that they were being sensible: that he was economising and saving and that they were buying furniture (out of his wages) for their house. They were going to live at Brinsley, where Arthur had gone back to work. On 27 December 1875, the day after Lydia's parents' wedding anniversary, they married at St Stephen's Parish Church in Sneinton – just ten minutes' walk from the Beardsall house in John Street – with Lydia 'looking, in the words of her sister, "like an angel" in her dove-coloured silk dress and bonnet'.[34] They may have lodged with his parents in Quarry Cottage; it is rather more likely that they rented a small house of their own nearby, quite probably a house owned by Arthur's parents. Family tradition – this time perpetuated by Lawrence in *Sons and Lovers* – suggested that Arthur Lawrence deceived Lydia by allowing her to think that the house and its furniture belonged to him, when both actually belonged to his mother.[35] When Lydia found out, it seemed a repetition of his deceitfulness about his job, and again he was not forgiven.

Their differences were part of what had attracted them to each other; the extrovert carelessness, the warmth and immediacy in Arthur: the principledness, the educated and ladylike reserve in Lydia. 'She was never effusive or demonstrative in any way', reported her daughter Ada.[36] Those very differences would grow to be a source of dispute. Lydia's family, though poverty-stricken, always attempted to maintain what gentility they could; although George Beardsall had appeared as a 'fitter' on his older children's birth certificates, at his daughters' marriages (including those he did not himself attend) he appeared as 'Engineer'. His six daughters were clearly prepared to give him the status he wanted, though 'Formerly an Engine Fitter' appeared on his death certificate. Although he had actually never earned as much as Arthur Lawrence even when working full-time, he went on clinging to his right to the respect owed the middle classes (to which he had never belonged). Just as the household he ruled was, he hoped, superior, its inmates refined, moral and religious, so his daughters were 'ladies' – even if they worked at drawing lace. It is striking that all of them, except Lydia, succeeded in marrying (by Beardsall standards) respectably; and that three of the five married to considerable social and financial advantage. Emma had married Alfred John Inwood, in the skilled trade of compositor – the so-called 'aristocrat of labour': in 1877, Nellie married John Richard Staynes, 'Warehouseman' on his marriage certificate but later 'Lace Manufacturer': he ended up owning houses in Nottingham (i. 184 n. 1), and his wife ran a superior boarding house at Skegness in the early 1900s (Lydia's children went there for holidays). Annie, in 1887, married William Henry Tiddiman, in the relatively well-paid skilled trade of gilder: Lettie, in 1888, married John Berry, the widowed manager of a brick works; and Ada, in 1896 – at 28, but pretending to be 24 – married the merchant Fritz Krenkow,[37] who did not have to work for his living and whose father was described as 'Gentleman' on his son's marriage certificate; Ada and Fritz Krenkow had a house with two maids and a library (i. 77, 81). The marriages of Nellie, Lettie and Ada were particularly advantageous; it was almost certainly Nellie who helped Lydia Lawrence with money and children's clothes in the early 1880s. Lydia's marriage was, by Beardsall standards, socially degrading, while financially it was by far the most risky. But it followed directly on the consequences of the 1870 catastrophe; and although her marriage had probably seemed exhilarating at the time, Lydia spent a good deal of her life ensuring that her children did not forget how it had degraded her.

Lydia Beardsall was both angered by and attracted to her father. A family friend once heard her remark: 'My father was exacting. He made us wait on him hand and foot, and I used to say, "I'll never have a husband like you," then I'd have to fly. But it taught me not to dance attention on a man and to let a boy learn to help himself.'[38] She impressed her children with her admiration for him, while also making sure that her mother's fate of being ignored or treated as a servant would never be her own. Even though (as she

17

came to see it) Arthur Lawrence had tricked her, no man would ever lord it over *her*. In some ways, Lydia was clearly very like her father: George Beardsall, recreated as George Coppard in *Sons and Lovers*, was naturally ironic and harsh in his judgement of others, and the portrait of Mrs Morel's father preferring 'theology in reading' and drawing 'near in sympathy only to one man, the Apostle Paul'[39] is (according to family tradition) horribly true of George Beardsall. *Christian influences in maternal line.*

The Beardsall family was strictly Wesleyan Methodist, and Lydia's daughter Ada remembered her as 'deeply religious', too; until her son Ernest's death in 1901 she regularly sang and played hymns on the piano. Interestingly enough, however, Lawrence very largely misses out Mrs Morel's religion in *Sons and Lovers*, which makes her superior moral code particularly personal. But Lydia Lawrence's religion was typical of one strand in the nonconformist tradition: her daughter Emily remembered her replying to a man trying to engage her in a religious discussion: 'I am a Christian woman, and I live up to it, and don't want to be drawn into a discussion'. Her faith was simple, uncomplicated and – secular rather than spiritual – the sterner for that reason. Her children remembered their mother's secular strengths; she was, according to Ada, 'a stickler for truth, having great contempt for anything petty, vain or frivolous'.[40] Feeling herself deceived, she was remorseless about deceit in others, making it the more ironical that the history of her own family which she passed on was so denatured by myth as to make it essentially romance. But the divergence between the history and the romance indicates how desperately her experience fuelled her need to sustain the myth, and to encourage her children to adopt it: we actually know far less about the later lives of the Beardsall parents than about earlier days, because they vanish into the family romance which Lydia encouraged. She also became sterner as she got older, and forgot her original reaction to her husband's charm and good humour, the extrovert recklessness, the warmth and tall-story telling of 1874. A few years later, she saw such things as frivolity and lies. Lydia Lawrence – again, like her father – seems to have spent much of her life ignoring her partner, and a lot of the rest of it blaming him, while never admitting that she had married him because he had been able to rescue her from her home, and because she had been charmed by him.[41]

The parallel between father and daughter is a topic Lawrence recreated in 'Matilda' and *Sons and Lovers*. In 'Matilda', Matilda 'had her mother's small, svelte figure, and brown, fine, curling hair, but her sagacious brow, her eyes, with their imperious stare, or with their blue concentrated interest, and her close-knit lips were from her father'. In *Sons and Lovers*, Gertrude's 'proud and unyielding' temper comes from her father's side of the family; she is 'a puritan, like her father', with his 'clear, defiant blue eyes'.[42] George Beardsall struck everyone as 'imperious' to the point of tyranny, particularly towards his womenfolk; in 'Matilda' Robert Wootton is 'a man of overweening pride' and, like Wootton, George Beardsall was handsome, sardonic, capable of 'biting sarcasm'. Above all, he was embittered by his failure to do better for himself, especially after his crippling accident; in 'Matilda' Wootton feels that 'his life will pass in insignificance'[43] – a fear Lydia Beardsall certainly shared. But even before his accident, George Beardsall's pride had been easily wounded. Relatively little is known about him, so two anecdotes preserved in 'Matilda' are particularly revealing. One – before his conversion to Methodism – describes his falling in love with a beautiful girl whom he later discovered 'was not as good as she might be': 'He had turned his indignation upon her, and she had laughed. Maddened, he had fetched her a knock upon the lips. She sprang like a devil and beat him wildly on the face. He left her, and she flaunted before him with strange men. People talked about him, which he could not endure . . .'[44] The other story tells how, only six months after Robert Wootton's marriage, his wife – though expecting their first child – decided to economise by doing the housework herself.

When she told him, he answered with a coldness that pained her:
"Well, you please yourself. I suppose other women do their own work."
She never understood to her dying day that he felt this still another humiliation, that his wife should have to drudge for him.[45]

The story goes on to describe how she began by washing his overalls – workingman's overalls ' "swarfed" with machine oil' – and rubbed the skin off her fingers while doing so. She then showed her hands to her husband, tearfully expecting his sympathy and commendation. He refused: her sacrifice hurt his pride too deeply. 'What do you want? . . . What do you think I married you for? Did you think you were going to be a lady? A working man's wife expects to work. They'll get hard enough.'[46] Both stories reveal the touchy and dreadfully vulnerable pride which George Beardsall passed down both to his daughter Lydia and to his grandson. If Lydia Lawrence felt embittered by her marriage and by Arthur Lawrence when she found out the facts about his job, his income and his house, if she felt herself deceived and her pride assaulted – then she too found it very difficult to forgive him, or to forgive herself. She seems to have abandoned her hopes of being 'a lady', and to have set herself to slave for her children – not her husband – in a succession of alien places which she would never accept as her home: and so far as possible she turned the children away from their father. It was a punishment that ought to have made her husband suffer too;

if it did not, that would have made her even angrier. She communicated to all her children the bitterness with which she accepted her fate.

The contrast was enormous, too, between the moral, puritan, 'superior' but poverty-stricken Beardsalls of Sneinton, and the comfortably-off Lawrences of Brinsley – the famous boxer and provincial tailor who owned houses, his shrewd but shrewish wife, the energetic, successful, but uneducated and non-intellectual collier sons. Both families would, by income and occupation, properly be reckoned working-class, with the Lawrences the nineteenth-century success story; the Beardsalls were declining, despite their efforts to stay genteel. But when Lydia Beardsall married Arthur Lawrence, she moved away from her family's traditions of good times and rich relations, into a much more ordinary family, and into a succession of dirty, insanitary, reputedly immoral and squalidly sprawling colliery villages. The Beardsalls were now living in a Nottingham slum: but they had continued to feel superior to their neighbours. The Lawrences unashamedly lived where they could earn, among people like themselves.

Lydia found herself, too, married to a man who for their first eight years together had to travel to where work was most financially rewarding. He may well have been laid off at Brinsley pit in 1877 (many miners were); at any rate the family moved on to New Cross. While Lydia's sisters' marriages took them to Leicester, to Arlsey in Bedfordshire, to Harrow-on-the-Hill on the outskirts of London, Lydia's own marriage led from Brinsley to New Cross, briefly to South Normanton, back to New Cross and finally to Eastwood: ugly, rough, fast-growing and quickly deteriorating colliery villages near Nottingham: all, like Eastwood, places 'where 98 per cent. of the population depend on coal mining for their existence'.[47]

Lydia Lawrence, however, went on being her father's daughter. She went on looking the 'ladylike girl' of her youth, and her interests were not those of her neighbours. Her daughter Ada wrote how 'Some people were ill-natured enough to say that she "put it on" when she spoke, for her English was good and her accent so different' – it may well have been Kentish; but, all the same, 'How ladylike we thought she looked when dressed for chapel in her black costume, and black silk blouse, little black bonnet decorated with black and white ospreys (she never wore a hat), and an elegant black and white feather boa round her neck'. Against this respectably dressed and consciously different figure – 'small and slight' with 'tiny hands and feet, and a sure carriage' – it has been traditional to set that of a very rough diamond indeed in Arthur Lawrence; 'with black wavy hair, dark brown beard and moustache ... dark flashing eyes and a ruddy complexion':[48] a collier, certainly unintellectual and frequently in the public house. It would be sensible not to insist on the roughness – a collier could not afford to be soft, though Arthur Lawrence was often charming and could be gentle: nor on the fact that his education had equipped him no further than to write what he needed to as a butty, and to read a newspaper with some difficulty. Nor is it right to lay particular stress upon his drinking. Nearly all colliers drank, and Arthur Lawrence apparently drank no more than the rest; mining is a hot, dry and dusty job, and drinking very little during eight hours or so underground (miners could only drink what they took with them: cold tea was usual) meant that they ended up extremely thirsty. If they could afford it, the pub on the way home or in the evening – with their workmates – was part of the routine. The crucial point was whether they missed work because of their drinking. Arthur's brother Walter did, and his family suffered. Arthur Lawrence did not: even the much despised Walter Morel in *Sons and Lovers* 'practically never had to miss work owing to his drinking'. It would be better to stress that Arthur Lawrence belonged to the place where he was born and lived, and found his amusement there; and that he resented attempts to make him different from the men he worked alongside, went to the pubs with and drank with. In this can be seen the source of the sympathy his son found with the mining community he wrote about, in particular after the death of Lydia Lawrence.[49]

Arthur Lawrence's feelings were always in absolute contrast to those of his wife. When Lydia came to live in Eastwood, her grandfather John Newton, together with other Newton relations, was living in Kimberley, 2 miles away on the Nottingham road; but the rest of her family either still lived in and around Nottingham, 12 miles away, or – as they married – dispersed around the country. And Lydia's real interests always lay beyond the Eastwood community. She was interested in religion, like her father: in intellectual discussion, in books. Her daughter Ada remembered the local minister visiting her to discuss 'religion and philosophy'[50] – something remarkable for a miner's wife (and doubtless remarked by her neighbours). She was not only a great reader; she was 'an esteemed friend and co-worker' of the Eastwood branch of the Women's Co-operative Guild, playing 'an active part in the local branch work, being treasurer for many years'.[51] In *Sons and Lovers* Mrs Morel is also a member of the Guild: 'The women were supposed to discuss the benefits to be derived from co-operation, and other social questions.' Virginia Woolf recognised how the Guild gave women

in the first place the rarest of all possessions – a room where they could sit down and think remote from boiling saucepans and crying children; and then that room became not merely a sitting-room and a meeting place, but a workshop where, laying their heads together, they could remodel their houses, could remodel their lives, could beat out this reform and that . . .[52]

The organisation had developed enormously from its beginnings in 1883;

by the 1890s many branches were becoming much more than a forum for general discussion. They were acquiring a bad reputation among the men of the industrial communities for 'making women think too much of themselves': as Lawrence knew, 'The guild was called by some hostile husbands, who found their wives getting too independent, the "clat-fart" shop: that is, the gossip shop'. ('Clat' is gossip and 'fart' shows what the colliers thought of it.) But Guild branches – which kept in touch with each other through a column in the *Co-operative News* – came into their own at times like the 1893 miners' lock-out, when 'The determined stand made by the miners' wives to enable their husbands to resist the proposed reduction was greatly aided by the support of Co-operative Societies and the Women's Guild'.[53] Guild branches also developed into self-help institutions, with members 'earnestly endeavouring first to educate themselves, and then to educate others': Lydia Lawrence would have found confirmed, for example, the idea that 'education was to be the workers' best weapon'. Some groups (particularly in the big cities of the Midlands and the South of England) were radical and actively political; suffragism and even birth-control ('moral hygiene') would have been on their agenda. We know very little about the Eastwood branch, but we can be fairly sure that it was not militant; it was regarded by intellectual radicals like Willie Hopkin as conservative. But in all branches women were encouraged to train themselves (and others) to go about things 'in a business-like way' and to listen to and to read books on the history of industrialism and the co-operative movement. Lydia Lawrence, for example, entered a competition on Robert Owen's philosophy of co-operation which the national organisation ran in 1897; she had to answer 22 questions, to read a 136-page book, and if possible four other recommended texts. The Guild helped her feel that she was part of a group of working-class women striving in the country at large, not simply buried in Eastwood: it created a kind of community for her. The weekly Guild meetings offered support to women living their lives in the kitchens which were the traditional arena for the display of male authority. Above all, the Guild brought together women determined to ensure 'that their children should have chances denied to themselves'.[54] What was life to Arthur Lawrence – the community of men, the nearby relations, the gossip of the immediate locality, its amusements, its work, the friends in public houses in the evenings – was alien to Lydia Lawrence. She actively resented them and her husband's attachment to them. His visits to the pub – the focus of so much anger and bitterness in the Lawrence marriage – were not just to drink. In the words of an Eastwood miner a generation later, 'Got to be a man, to go in the pubs: or you were out of it'. In the pub, Arthur Lawrence was with men whom he understood, and who understood him; 'their interests were his interests', and in the pub he was 'more sure of himself' than he could be in his own home.[55] For Lydia Lawrence, such visits were a waste of money, self-indulgent and dangerous: the husband who drank and ruined his family was a threat of which she – knowing from her own experience what happened when a family's wage-earner suddenly stopped earning – was very conscious. And she was not going to compromise her standards: her daughter Ada remembered how 'she was a staunch teetotaller, and would have no strong drink in the house'. She never compromised, any more than her father would have done. She brought up her children strictly, and instilled in them the puritan stoicism with which she confronted her own fate. Lawrence remembered 'Mother's constant motto to me "Blessed is he that expecteth little, for he shall not be disappointed" ' (i. 248).[56]

Eastwood remained a place which she always disliked. In 1910, her feelings about it still rankled: in comparison with her sister Lettie's home in Harrow-on-the-Hill, Eastwood – she wrote – 'looks rather a dirty mean place'.[57] The occasions when Arthur Lawrence left the Midlands can be counted on the fingers of one hand:* there was no reason for him to go further afield. Lydia Lawrence's relations, however, were scattered over the country; her children went to see her sister Nellie, in Skegness; she herself paid visits to her sisters Lettie and Ada; she must also have visited her sister Emma, who lived in North London. She was never sufficiently well-off to travel freely, but – particularly when her own children were grown up – she visited her sisters at least once a year, and perhaps more often. That would have confirmed the opinion of her neighbours in Eastwood that she thought herself too good for the place; her family and her interests lay outside it. She had relatively few friends in Eastwood, where she lived for twenty-six years, though she was widely respected: but there are ways in which respect precludes friendship. To be more exact, she never accepted that Eastwood *was* her community; she could, literally, look beyond it, to another world of human affairs; intellectual, literary, social, moral. And she brought up her children to live their lives beyond it.

Yet her travels were always more extensive morally and intellectually than they could be geographically. Her education, and her time as a teacher – be it ever so brief – had equipped her to read and write fluently: her son D. H. Lawrence recalled how 'She wrote a fine Italian hand, and a clever and amusing letter when she felt like it';[58] something borne out by her surviving correspondence. He frequently mentioned her reading; he gave a corre-

---

* To London in 1901, when his son Ernest died; to Mablethorpe in 1906, for the first of the family holidays which the Lawrence family took – in some improvement of their financial situation – over the next few years; to Robin Hood's Bay, Flamborough and Shanklin for holidays 1907–9.

spondent in August 1910 a vivid picture of her 'reading a translation of Flaubert's *Sentimental Education*' and wearing 'a severe look of disapproval' (i. 174). Very few women in Eastwood would have read Flaubert. She may have been keeping up with her intellectual son: in his play *A Collier's Friday Night*, Lawrence showed Mrs Lambert (a recreation of Lydia Lawrence) reading her student son Ernest's copy of the *New Age*, a radical weekly started in 1907, lively and iconoclastic, including contributions by Shaw, Wells, Bennett and Chesterton. But most of Lydia Lawrence's reading was not on that level; 'as she grew older she read novels again, and got terribly impatient with *Diana of the Crossways* and terribly thrilled by *East Lynne*'.[59] The Mechanics' Institute Library in Eastwood was stacked with such novels: Mrs Morel in *Sons and Lovers* gives Lily Western 'a little thing of Annie Swans [sic]' to read – there were eight Annie Swan novels in the library by 1895. Mrs Lawrence also read *Wuthering Heights* and liked Barrie and Scott. Lawrence's visits as an adolescent to the library on Thursday evenings, recreated in *Sons and Lovers*, show how necessary books were to the household; books for the mother and her children which the young Lawrence borrowed: 'every week piles of books . . . to be enjoyed when we were all in bed'. Ada, too, remembered how her mother 'loved to read';[60] reading was her great escape from the community in which she lived.

V   Differences

When D. H. Lawrence came to draw upon the lives of his grandparents and the young life of his parents in his writing, he did so from an interestingly one-sided point of view. He wrote comparatively little about his grandparents on his father's side; and very little indeed about the troops of uncles, aunts and young cousins in Eastwood, Ilkeston and Brinsley by whom the Eastwood Lawrences were surrounded (there were actually eighteen cousins living within a couple of miles). The family story about having French ancestors appears in *Sons and Lovers*,[61] and brief portraits of his father's parents appear in 'Daughters of the Vicar' – while his paternal grandmother plays a small role in 'Odour of Chrysanthemums' and *The Widowing of Mrs. Holroyd*; but, apart from those, he recreated only the story of the death of his uncle James (in Brinsley pit in 1880) in 'Odour of Chrysanthemums' and *The Widowing of Mrs. Holroyd*; and he used the story of his uncle Walter's manslaughter of his son in an early version of *Sons and Lovers*. Both the stories he drew from this side of the family – about his uncle James and his cousin Walter – were about accident and violent death, of the kind which got into the mining community newspapers. The stories were not about the links of family that mattered so much for the Lawrences, and only incidentally about the community in which they flourished. In none of the fiction, however, is there any significant alteration of social or economic facts.

Lawrence treated his mother's family very differently. In Croydon in 1910, he began a novel – 'Matilda' – to be based on his mother's early life. He only completed forty-eight pages of it; but the surviving fragment shows recreations of Lydia's parents and Lydia as a child, and includes numerous stories from Beardsall family history. Having abandoned that, Lawrence reused much of the material in *Sons and Lovers*, with the addition of an account of the later life of Gertrude Coppard which in many respects parallels that of Lydia Beardsall. He made no equivalent use of his father's background or family; Mr Morel's family is practically non-existent, apart from a brief conversation Mrs Morel has with her mother-in-law. There are no uncles, aunts or cousins: Paul grows up effectively isolated from any such contacts. Although Lawrence had once planned to use his maternal aunt Ada Krenkow at length in *Sons and Lovers*, he never did; there is, however, the full-length portrait of his mother as Gertrude Morel in the novel; there is the mother in *The White Peacock* (who is actually given the name 'Beardsall'), and a good deal of Lydia Lawrence in both Mrs Bates, in 'Odour of Chrysanthemums', and her counterpart Mrs. Holroyd, in *The Widowing of Mrs. Holroyd*.

Not only did he use the material from his mother's family much more freely than from his father's; he also significantly altered it. It is impossible to say whether he did this as a conscious revision of the facts, or because the Beardsall history he had learned from his mother was so entwined with myth. The latter is more likely; he gave recreations of his maternal grandparents the genuine middle classness to which their originals had only aspired. In 'Matilda' he recreated George Beardsall as Robert Wootton, 'a man of capacity' who – though starting as only a turner – grows to be 'foreman in an engineering shop ... where were made difficult machines newly patented':[62] he earns £4 a week, which is £200 a year, more than twice what George Beardsall had earned. In *Sons and Lovers*, George Beardsall appears as George Coppard, 'an engineer', then 'foreman of the engineers in the dockyard at Sheerness' – a very striking upgrading from George Beardsall's trade of 'fitter'. There is no equivalent to George Beardsall's accident, and the family's subsequent crippling poverty; instead, the Coppard family leave Sheerness when Gertrude is 'twenty, owing to her health ... Her father had retired home to Nottingham.'[63] A real-life return in poverty and desperation is recreated as a move for 'her health': as if lace drawing in a Nottingham slum would have been better for Lydia Beardsall than the fresh air of Sheerness.

Such changes make the marriage of Gertrude Coppard to Walter Morel an even more strikingly unlikely partnership than that of Lydia and Arthur Lawrence. Gertrude is truly middle-class; her husband more crudely working-class. The novel – and Lawrence – perhaps need the starkness of the contrast; in 1913, the subtleties of distinction between lower-middle-class, skilled working-class and ordinary working-class life would have escaped most middle-class readers, even though society was more acutely class-conscious than today. But there also seems little doubt that Lawrence really believed that his mother's family was middle-class; that was the Beardsall myth. It would have been natural enough for Lydia Lawrence in the early years of her marriage to romanticise her life at her parents' home, and to make those parents the images of middle-class respectability which in real-life they certainly had not been. She can actually be seen in the process of doing that in George Neville's recollection (which can only have originated with her) of her father as 'a tradesman carrying on business in the Peashill Rise district of the city' and her family 'in quite good circumstances'. Another neighbour remembered how, around the year 1904, she talked of 'how her father, finding himself possessed of six daughters, came from Kent to Nottingham where they could earn a living in the lace trade'.[64] The idea of the generous and far-sighted father safeguarding his daughters' future by returning to Nottingham 'where they could earn a living' is a splendid reversal of the truth: poverty-stricken himself, George Beardsall had taken his daughters to Nottingham to scrape together the family's income by sweated labour.

The myth of the Beardsall family, however, became enshrined in both family and literary history; it became an established fact in the early 1930s that the writer D. H. Lawrence had had a working-class father and a middle-class mother.[65] In actuality, both families were working-class: one child had been educated to the age of 13, the other to the age of 7. But the most powerful class distinctions always operate in borderline areas; and what divided the Beardsalls from the the Lawrences was ideology, myth and expectation: that made for a deep and lasting division. It was as parents, in particular, that Lydia and Arthur Lawrence showed their affiliations. In their resentment of each other, each tended to project upon their children an exclusive version of how they themselves saw the world. Arthur Lawrence, like Walter Morel, naturally saw his sons as potential partners at work, his future mates at Brinsley. The pit was full of such family groups.[66] What, says Walter Morel, is the point of making his son William 'a stool-harsed Jack' in the Co-op office?

"All he'll do is to wear his britches behind out an' earn nowt . . . Put 'im i' th' pit we me, an' 'e'll earn an easy ten shillin a wik from th' start. But six shillin' wearin' his truck-end out on a stool, 's better than ten shillin' i' th' pit wi' me, I know."

"He is *not* going in the pit," said Mrs Morel, "and there's an end of it."[67]

Walter Morel's voice must have been raised frequently in the Lawrence household. Their eldest son, George, did indeed work at a colliery – though perhaps not as a collier – for a short time. The second son, Ernest, although tall, active, physically very strong and from Arthur Lawrence's point of view an ideal fellow worker, never did: like William in *Sons and Lovers*, he started work at 14 in that 'Co-op office'. Mrs Morel's voice was also heard, and it dominated. Arthur Lawrence even had ambitions for his third son: but, as a contemporary remembered, 'There was never a hope, despite his father's hints. His frail physique and his mother's cultivated hatred of the industry . . . precluded all that'.[68]

But that brief argument in the novel sums up the crucial difference between Arthur and Lydia Lawrence. The father saw his children as like himself, and wanted them to belong to the place where they were born, and become his working partners in it: to belong to the community, like their Brinsley grandparents, their aunts, their uncles, their cousins. Lydia Lawrence saw another life for them, as potential adults who could leave Eastwood and ideally recover what she, and her family, had lost in economic and social independence. It was an argument which, in different shapes and forms, dominated the Lawrences' marriage and the lives of their children.

And it was in these respects that, in the generation of Lydia and Arthur, the differences of outlook within two families became sharpened and divisive. The differences came to a complex kind of flowering and expression in the life and work of D. H. Lawrence. He contained the differences within himself, as the product of his upbringing; and he was continually articulate about them, in his ceaseless attempts to come to terms with them.

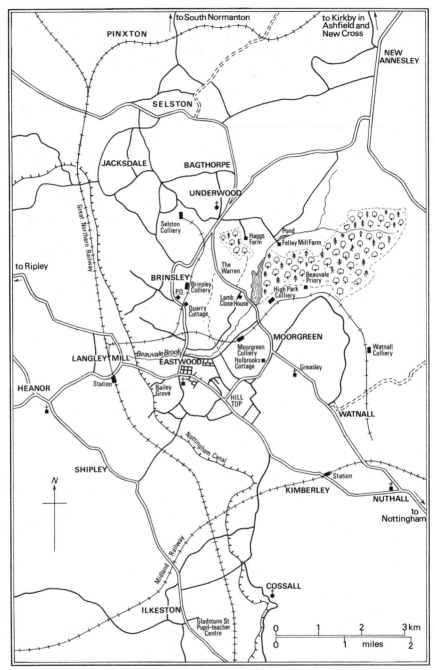

Eastwood and its Surroundings

CHAPTER TWO

♦

1883–1892

HOME AT EASTWOOD

I Houses and Money

The Lawrence family must be seen not only as individuals like Arthur, or Lydia; they are also figures in an industrial landscape. The Eastwood to which the Lawrence family came in 1883 was an expanding village – and already more of a small town than a village. Wright's 1883 local Directory described it as

a parish, and large and improving village on the Alfreton road, Erewash river, Nottingham and Cromford canals, and borders of Derbyshire. It is a mile from Langley Mill station, on the Erewash Valley branch of the Midland railway, half-a-mile from the Eastwood station, on the Great Northern Co.'s line from Nottingham to Pinxton, 8½ miles N.W. from Nottingham, 10½ from Derby, and 135 from London.[1]

But the whole village was transforming itself: 'improving', as the language of the time had it: growing wealthier, attracting inhabitants. As Wright's Directory pointed out, Eastwood lay at the centre of a network of canals and railways built to transport the coal that lay beneath the valleys which surrounded it. Between 1803 and 1848, the coal shipped out of the region by canal increased from 254,268 tons to 427,670 tons per year; but by 1869, sales by railway alone totalled 1,709,061 tons, while sales by canal had fallen back to 192,902 tons. There had been a 442% growth in coal sales between 1849 and 1869, following the coming of the railway, and the growth of that 'fine chain' between the 'black studs' of the mines.[2]

The population of Eastwood had been under 2,000 in 1861, but it had climbed to 3,500 by 1881, to 4,500 by 1886; by 1893, it had grown to more than 5,000. New chapels had been built for the expanding population (the Congregational chapel in 1868: the Wesleyan in 1876); whole new streets and squares of houses had been erected, new shops opened, the old green spaces built over, the old smallholdings sold for building land. The population filling Eastwood was the élite of the industrial working class, which came there to make its livelihood out of the hard, dangerous but also comparatively well-rewarded trade of coal-mining; there were ten pits within easy walking distance of the town. The wages of colliers in the

Eastwood district more than doubled between the 1850s and 1914, while in the same period the wages of Nottinghamshire agricultural workers rose by less than 50%; as a result, 'At the end of the nineteenth century, farmworkers in Nottinghamshire's Leen Valley were making around £1 a week whereas local face-workers were able to earn nearly 8s. a shift'.[3] Skilled workers in other crafts too, whose earnings had been higher than those of miners in the 1850s, were considerably less well off by the turn of the century. It had been that rise in the earning power of the collier which had ensured that Arthur Lawrence and his brothers had become colliers, in the first place: and it now brought Arthur and his family, along with thousands of others, to live in Eastwood. By 1910, when D. H. Lawrence was 25, there were over 4,400 men working in the Eastwood collieries: more than the entire population of Eastwood when he was born.

The Lawrences had come back to the Eastwood region partly because it was so near the Lawrence family home at Brinsley; partly because they almost certainly wanted to get out of New Cross, where diphtheria had broken out in 1882 and 1883; and partly because of the opportunities for doing well which Eastwood itself offered. Arthur could get work in the pit at Brinsley, just a mile away; Lydia could make something of the small shop for which 8a, Victoria Street was suitable. In 1875–6, they had actually lived in Brinsley, near – if not with – Arthur's parents; this time, a mile away in Eastwood, they would not be so close to Lydia's in-laws. And Arthur's brother Walter and family were literally round the corner. Arthur and Lydia's own family was growing: their first child, George, had been born in Brinsley in 1876; Ernest and Emily had been born in New Cross in 1878 and 1882 respectively.

But Brinsley was still the family centre. Arthur could have walked over and back while they were living in New Cross; he probably came back to Brinsley for his brother James's funeral at the end of February 1880, and five months later Arthur, Lydia and their two children all returned to Brinsley for a special family occasion. Neither George nor Ernest had yet been christened – perhaps the family had been too often on the move (in July 1880 they were actually living, briefly, in South Normanton); but on 4 July James's daughter Alvina, born to his widow Polly a month after his death, was to be christened. George and Ernest were brought back to be christened the same day; the whole family of brothers, sisters, husbands, wives and parents must have met in Brinsley for the occasion.

Arthur and Lydia had then gone back with their children to South Normanton, and for another brief period to New Cross; but they may well already have planned to return to the Brinsley region. The diphtheria in New Cross was perhaps only their direct provocation for making the decision. The growing family needed a settled and healthier home, as well as more space, and Arthur probably wanted to be nearer his parents (his father was nearly 70); while Polly Lawrence, bringing up three children on her own in Brinsley, needed all the family support she could get. And there was, for Lydia, the prospect of the shop in Eastwood: it may have been her price for coming back so close to the centre of her husband's family. Kelly's Directory for 1888 announces it (and its appearance in the directory shows that it was a settled establishment): 'Lawrence Arthur, Haberdash. Victoria Street': Wright's for 1891 was still listing 'Lawrence Arthur, Smallwear and lace dealer'. But the shop was Lydia's; Arthur had signed on for work as a butty at Brinsley Colliery on 26 November 1883. Lydia Lawrence 'sold lace caps and aprons and linen, etc., in the front room'.[4]

It was not only the trade of the expanding village which a shop like Lydia Lawrence's might hope to catch. Eastwood's shopkeepers were a class apart: late in life, D. H. Lawrence described his mother's attitude to them and the attraction of that shop-window in Victoria Street. Henry Saxton, local councillor and elder statesman of the Congregational chapel, owned the grocers' shop on the corner of Victoria Street and Scargill Street, just three yards down the hill from the Lawrences.

Henry Saxton was a burly bullying fellow with fair curly hair, and though he never pronounced an "h" in the right place, he had a great opinion of Henry . . .

My mother seemed, however, to have a respect for him. She, after all, was only a collier's wife . . . she looked up to Henry Saxton with tender respect. And, since I was foreordained to accept all her values, I had to look up to Henry Saxton too.

He was, of course, terribly respectable. He was Sunday School Superintendent, he was a deacon at the Congregational Chapel . . . She thought him an infinitely more wonderful man than my father. Why, in heaven's name? Because he was a chapel man, and far more than that, because he was successful . . . she was worshipping success, because she hadn't got it.[5]

Henry Saxton was successful in the way Eastwood rated success. If Lydia Lawrence felt that her marriage was a failure and that the task of raising children was a continual and wearisome drudge, always against the odds, even the Henry Saxton who lived on the corner could be admirable. And with her Lawrence mother-in-law already in business (but not, a mile away, in competition), the prospect of being a shopkeeper and sharing in just a little of that respectability – and (ideally) that success – must have been attractive.

The shop, however, did not last long: probably no longer than the family's residence at 8a, Victoria Street, in spite of the continued entries in the local directories. It did not have the advantages of a shop up on the Nottingham Road; and according to Willie Hopkin (himself a shopkeeper),

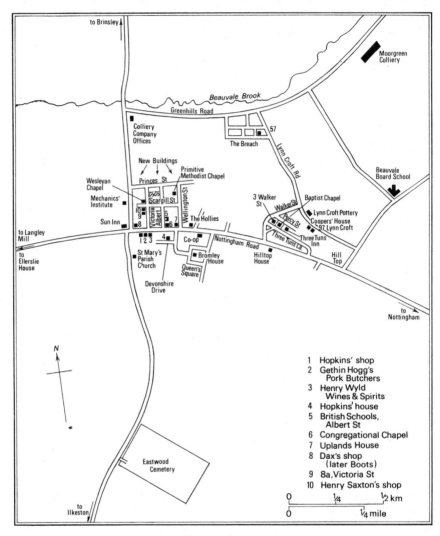

to Brinsley

Moorgreen Colliery

Beauvale Brook

Greenhills Road

Colliery Company Offices

57

The Breach

Lynn Croft Rd

Beauvale Board School

New Buildings

Primitive Methodist Chapel

Wesleyan Chapel

Princes St

Mechanics' Institute

Scargill St

Wellington St

3 Walker St

Walker St

Baptist Chapel

Lynn Croft Pottery

Coopers' House

97 Lynn Croft

Percy St

Sun Inn

The Hollies

to Langley Mill

Co-op

Nottingham Road

Three Tuns La.

Three Tuns Inn

to Ellerslie House

St Mary's Parish Church

Bromley House

Hilltop House

Hill Top

Queen's Square

to Nottingham

Devonshire Drive

N

1   Hopkins' shop
2   Gethin Hogg's
    Pork Butchers
3   Henry Wyld
    Wines & Spirits
4   Hopkins' house
5   British Schools,
    Albert St
6   Congregational Chapel
7   Uplands House
8   Dax's shop
    (later Boots)
9   8a, Victoria St
10 Henry Saxton's shop

Eastwood Cemetery

0   ¼   ½ km

0   ¼ mile

to Ilkeston

Eastwood *c.* 1907

it 'was not a very great success. They found that people in Eastwood, as elsewhere, got into debt and did not pay.'[6] And, by 1887, Lydia had two more children and less time to spare: David Herbert had been born on 11 September 1885 and Lettice Ada in June 1887; and Bert (as his family called him) was particularly prone to illness. The shop was abandoned.

The Lawrence family's progress through the houses of Eastwood, however, charts their advance. Though they had come with three young children, the Victoria Street house would have felt even smaller when two more had been born. Like the majority of the houses in the 'New Buildings' – 'two quadrangles of dwellings with a street all round, rising like barracks on the hill-slope'[7] – it had two rooms downstairs, kitchen and front parlour: the stairs led off directly from the parlour, and beneath them was a pantry. Upstairs were two bedrooms. And although the New Buildings had been built by Barber Walker & Co. only in the 1870s, they were not an attractive place to live. A good deal of Eastwood's housing had been built by the colliery companies; Walter Lawrence and family, round the corner in Princes Street, were also living in a Barber Walker & Co. house in the New Buildings.[8] But more streets had been erected in the New Buildings than originally planned; the houses had no gardens, only access on to a great wind-swept square space between the blocks, studded with wooden line posts, between which washing was always drying and children playing. Lawrence remembered how the New Buildings 'were unpopular. It was "common" to live in the Square.' And since Arthur was a Barber Walker & Co. butty, he could not only live in one of the Company houses, but had priority in moving into a better house. The blocks known as the 'Breach', down in the valley near Beauvale Brook, offered a good deal more space and cleanliness than the New Buildings, although they had been built at almost the same time. 'It was a little less common to live in the Breach',[9] Lawrence recalled; the houses had not only the usual two bedrooms upstairs, but spacious attics as well; and they had been built almost on the edge of the country. Best of all, they had their own gardens. Late in 1887 the Lawrence family – all seven of them – moved into no. 57, an end house in the Breach (see Illustration 11), which cost them 5/6 a week in rent. That was 6d a week more than most of the houses: but the end house had a side porch, with a door not opening directly into the front room (or parlour), a strip of side garden – and, with only one adjoining neighbour, just a little more privacy and quiet. The garden was important: Ada never forgot the 'white currant bushes by the house and the old-fashioned white rose trees in the little front garden';[10] the smuts and dust from Moorgreen colliery generally blew the other way, the whole area was cleaner than the New Buildings had been and the slope in front of the house was a perfect place for children to play.

The family stayed in the Breach until 1891. But the Breach houses – 'substantial, and decent: tall, solid, respectable blocks'[11] – were still 'common' by the highest Eastwood standards and turned out to have their own disadvantages. Although the front of the Lawrences' house faced south, looking over the 'common gardens' and up the slope, no collier's family lived in the parlour. It was kept for Sunday afternoons and special occasions; the kitchen at the back was the living-room, and its windows looked into the yard. Beyond the kitchen was a small scullery: and outside the back door was the narrow strip of garden leading to the lane that stank in summer from the 'ashpits' – lavatories using ashes to cover their contents – which stood at the end of every garden, and which were emptied at night by the night-soil men. Somebody else who grew up in such surroundings remembered how 'when it was hot in the summer the stench from the ash pits would make me sick and I didn't want to go out'. It was this feature which made the Breach unpleasant: Ada recalled how 'My mother never liked being there, partly because the houses were in a hollow, principally because the backs looked out on to drab patches of garden with ashpits at the bottom.'[12]

In 1891, the Lawrences made a break from colliery company houses and took the chance of renting a new house in a superb position. They moved up the hill into one of six brand-new terrace houses popularly known (from the prosperity of their occupants) as 'piano row', and built in Walker Street between 1890 and 1891 by the Mellor family, who ran the Lynn Croft pottery at the end of the road. According to a deleted paragraph in the *Sons and Lovers* manuscript about the very similar move of the Morel family up to 'Scargill Street', 'of the six four were unfinished' when they moved in. The Walker Street houses had bay windows and a marvellous view out over 'the great open space of the cockleshell valley'[13] towards Crich Stand; they had no back lane of ashpits, no drab gardens, no other houses backing on to them; behind the brief back garden of no. 3 was only the high wall around the Baptist chapel. The houses in Walker Street felt more like semi-detached houses than houses in a row: 'There was one entry or passage to each two houses, with a common back yard and garden path to each two houses also . . . The house consisted of scullery, living-room and parlour on the ground floor, with three bedrooms, the staircase running up with "winders" from the living-room.' And there was gas laid on for the first time in a Lawrence house.[14] Without the great attics, there was a little less space than they had had in the Breach; and in spite of having a 'little front garden' where grew 'pink Jerusalem cowslips' and a 'mezereon tree that smelled so sweet' (v. 645), they missed the long garden. But otherwise the house was better in every way.

When the family moved up the hill, Lawrence was 6 years old; he was starting to experience the way in which his family were themselves part of the improvement in the 'large and improving village' of which Wright's 1883 Directory spoke. His brother George had gone out to work that year, which suggests why the family may have been better off. May Chambers, the daughter of neighbours along the road from the Breach, had a memory of a conversation with some of the Lawrence children around 1892, shortly after they had moved to Walker Street: 'There was an empty house in the Breach where they had lived formerly—"But we don't live there now," explained his sister [Emily, then 9 or 10] as we crossed the plank that bridged the brook. "We wouldn't live in the Breach for anything. We live up at Brickyard Closes in those houses with bay windows."'[15] Such distinctions were crucial in late nineteenth-century Eastwood. Another neighbour's child, Mabel Thurlby, described the move as 'a great lift for the family, for we who lived on Lynn Croft [at the end of Walker Street] never, as a rule, mixed with the children of the Breach'. She remembered how 'The first thing Mrs Lawrence did was to buy new lace curtains for the bay-windowed "parlour,"' though at this stage the Lawrences' curtains were suspended only by tape: the 'bamboo pole' deemed respectable in Lynn Croft was still too expensive for them. Walker Street, too, was only partly built up, so that the Lawrence children – like the Morel children in *Sons and Lovers* – felt themselves 'quite select'.[16] May Chambers first saw the inside of the Walker Street house around 1897:

I was warmly welcomed and taken in to be shown with pride the parlour, the carpet, the suite, the vases and ornaments, the family group in a handsome frame on the wall facing the bay window. We peeped through the curtains at the wide view over the valley crowning its far side. They turned again to the family group, telling me when and where taken, and I stood admiring everything when the elder sister [Emily] asked:

'Have you got a suite?'[17]

By local standards, that was the significant question; and by 1897 the Lawrence's parlour had one, a set of matching mahogany chairs.* It was still not a question that a visitor should be asked. '"Mind your own business," snapped the mother. "If you ask me no questions, you get no lies, do you,

---

* One chair was damaged a few years later:

He and his younger sister [Ada] had been romping about and broken the back or leg of a chair belonging to the front room suite.

'Mother was so mad she called in Father, and they both carried on ridiculously. It might be a crime we'd committed instead of a measly chair damaged. Oh, yes, it's spoiled the suite if it can't be repaired neatly. But even so, what's a measly chair to make such a fuss about? . . . They keep on saying how much they paid for that suite,' Bert continued, 'and what each chair cost, making out that we've destroyed so much money's worth . . .'[18]

child?"'[19] However sharp Lydia Lawrence was on Emily's rudeness, it was a natural question for one of the Lawrence children to ask, acutely conscious as they were of such things as tape, bamboo poles and their newly-discovered distance from the Breach. Ada, the other daughter, remembered how proud they were of the Walker Street house and furniture:

of our front room or parlour with its well-made mahogany and horse-hair suite of furniture – the little mahogany chiffonier and the oval Spanish mahogany table, which my mother insisted on covering with a fawn and green tapestry table-cloth to match the Brussels carpet. Here again were oleographs, heavily framed in gilt, and the family portrait in the place of honour over the mantelpiece.[20]

The oleographs – reproductions printed in oil-colours, in imitation of oil-paintings – were relatively expensive compared with the more common steel-engravings. Ada remembered feeling how 'there was something about our house which made it different from those of our neighbours . . . mother would have nothing cheap or tawdry, preferring bareness.'[21] George Neville, the son of a miner neighbour in Lynn Croft, confirms that impression of the Walker Street house: 'Upstairs all was neatness and snowy whiteness . . . The hallmark in the whole place was orderliness, neatness and cleanliness.' Eventually the lace curtains in the parlour – Lawrence remembered how 'my mother was rather proud of them' – acquired their bamboo curtain pole, as well as a large pelargonium in a pot beside them: and the parlour was complete at last.[22]

But however much Eastwood's miners' families stood out in their community as 'improving', it would be wrong to suggest that they were well off. As a contemporary of Lawrence's put it, there was an 'endless struggle for bread' which, nevertheless, 'did not imply dire poverty'. Emily Lawrence always recalled her mother's habitual answer to the children's request 'Can we have toast for our tea, mother?' – 'If you have toast you can't have butter, you'll have to have dripping or lard'; while if there was bacon for tea, Arthur Lawrence would have the bacon 'and we had the dip' (the dripping).[23] Even in winter, with full-time working, money had to be saved for anything except the basic necessities, and against the hard times during strikes or part-time working which were bound to come. In summer, things were much worse. A contemporary of Lawrence remembered:

In winter time, from September to April, the pits worked 5½ shifts per week; in summer time, from April to September, the pits worked an average of 2–3 shifts a week . . . when the pits were working short time, Lawrence's father would do casual work for Josiah Hodgkinson [owner of land between Walker Street and Lynn Croft], such as cleaning out dykes, trimming hedges and repairing fences. At harvest time he would help with the haymaking and gathering in the hay.[24]

Even with the additional casual labour, Lydia Lawrence would fairly often have received only 25/- – the amount Mrs Morel regularly gets in *Sons and Lovers*. And although Arthur Lawrence would have earned between 35/- and 50/- a week in winter, and occasionally even more (up to 100/- at exceptional times), like all miners he would have kept back between 5/- and 15/- for himself, and still more when very well off. An account of an Eastwood miner in a pub who 'tosses up half a sovereign saying "that goes before I go, tonight"' was 'true: I was there' according to a contemporary of Arthur Lawrence; the young miner Joe in Lawrence's play *The Daughter-in-Law* regards 5/- out of a total strike-pay of 10/- as 'non a whackin' sight o' pocket money for a man's week'.[25] In *Sons and Lovers*, if Walter Morel earns 'forty shillings, he kept ten; from thirty five, he kept five; from thirty two, he kept four; from twenty eight, he kept three; from twenty four, he kept two; from twenty, he kept one and six; from eighteen, he kept a shilling; from sixteen, he kept sixpence'. Lydia Lawrence would only very rarely have received 40/- a week; her regular expectation was nearer 30/-. Mrs Lambert, in *A Collier's Friday Night*, regards 28/- as a particularly bad week's wages for winter; Mrs Bates, in 'Odour of Chrysanthemums', is outraged when her husband keeps 10/- out of a winter wage of 33/-. Neville records one occasion during short-time working when Arthur Lawrence brought back only 17/3: Lydia Lawrence explained that 'He's been every day, but they were all quarters or halves'.[26] Her regular anger with her husband was not because he earned small sums (they were not his fault), but because he continued to keep a comparatively large proportion for himself. Neville says that Arthur Lawrence kept 3/- of the 17/3 'for a bit of tobacco and a glass of beer': in 1922, in what was probably an exaggeration, Lawrence recalled his mother complaining: 'I said to our master, I said to him, Now look here, Arthur, if you think you're going to give me thirty shillings, and keep twelve for yourself— — — —'[27] Arthur Lawrence never seems to have kept that much; but he would have spent money on betting, on skittles and football matches and on clothes; and perhaps on items like the fancy walking-stick and the canary Mr Morel buys in *Sons and Lovers*. It is also possible that he sometimes helped his sister Emma (twice widowed) and his sister-in-law Polly (also widowed), while his brother Walter's family would have had problems after Walter's death in 1904.[28]

The statement in *Sons and Lovers*, however, that Walter Morel earns less as he grows older because the colliery officials he offends revenge themselves by ensuring that he 'came gradually to have worse and worse stalls' – the same was suggested of Arthur Lawrence by his daughter Ada – cannot have been true, in spite of Arthur Lawrence's notorious hostility to his 'petty bosses in the pit'.[29] The seam in Brinsley colliery was extremely variable, and no official could have arranged for a particular butty always to get 'worse and worse stalls': particularly as he shared his stall with at least one and perhaps two other butties. The reason sounds like an excuse given to an angry wife by a man earning less money than she expected, or a charge made by an angry wife wishing to put her husband in the wrong.

Out of the 30/- a week which Lydia Lawrence would get from her husband in reasonably good times, between 5/6 and 6/6 went on rent, between 5/6 and 7/- on the various insurance schemes to which the family subscribed (the sick club for medical treatment, the club for money if Arthur Lawrence were injured): there were also gas and water bills to pay. Another 6/- or 7/- went on the groceries from the Friday-night market and the local Co-op: Lawrence remembered his family's Co-op number (1553 A.L.) 'better than the date of my birth'. For the Lawrence household, as for many others, the Co-op was an institution of primary importance: not only for its good-quality goods at reasonable prices, but because the purchase of a share in it meant that a full dividend was paid quarterly. The quarterly Co-op dividend was one of such a family's few opportunities of acquiring a small lump sum; it would often have been earmarked for clothing. (In *Sons and Lovers*, when she needs to buy her son's first season-ticket, Mrs Morel is miserable about having to break into her Co-op share: if she does, she will not in future get a full dividend.)[30] That accounted for almost two-thirds of Lydia Lawrence's money. Nevertheless, some had to be saved: and clothing and any extras had to come out of the rest. The young Lawrence did not hate the lack of money itself, but what he felt was the 'dreadful indignity' of the endless carefulness to which they were subjected. That sounds exactly like his maternal grandfather. A luxury like a visit to the local travelling theatre was rare: 'we used to long for the twopence it cost to go in', Lawrence remembered. As late as 1926 he was still describing in vivid terms the constraints of his early life: 'To be sick meant the doctor; that meant any extra shilling went for the doctor's fee and medicine . . . Boots and clothes had to be saved up for slowly, week by week. Every little thing we needed extra, meant saving and scraping for . . .' A doctor's home visit could cost 2/6; he was only called in as a last resort.[31]

In this small town, however, the Lawrence children stood out as rather advantaged. This was entirely because of their mother's genius for economising, for keeping going during hard times and for making their money go a long way – for example, by 'preferring bareness'. And, above all, she was adept at making sure that it was the children who profited from her economies. The young D. H. Lawrence, Mabel Thurlby recalled, 'was the only child with paints' for painting the clay marbles they baked on Saturday afternoons in the cooling kilns of the Lynn Croft pottery; 'his mother

bought them, sixpence they were'. The same child was struck by the contrast between Lydia Lawrence at market, buying a jam dish and complaining 'I shall have to go short, I've paid fourpence for this', and her not
grumbling about paints which cost twopence more, 'because they were for
him, you see'.[32] The young Lawrence probably received sixpence each week
for collecting his father's earnings from the colliery company offices on
Greenhills Lane: Paul Morel gets sixpence, which is his 'only income'.
Another neighbour's child who collected the wages, however, got only 'a
penny for my trouble', while yet another child 'got only a halfpenny'. One
of Lawrence's cousins, not unfortunately a reliable witness, also remarked
how Bert Lawrence 'was one of the first boys in Eastwood to have a nice
brand new bicycle; he was the envy of all the other people in the village'. In
August 1899, the family's financial standing is shown by their acquisition of
a second-hand 'Pianette' from William Needham, of Nottingham: it cost
£6-0-0 and the bill was paid by 1 November.* Again, it was for the children:
Ada (then 12) played it, and remembered how 'Some of our happiest hours
were spent at our old piano with its faded green silk front. It had to be
touched gently to bring out the tinkling notes.'[33]

The other way the children benefited was in their education. Sending
Lawrence to Nottingham High School in 1898 and then to Nottingham
University College in 1906 'involved great sacrifices on the rest of the
family', as George Neville knew.[34] But Lydia Lawrence saw to it that they
made the sacrifice, just as she had always sacrificed herself.

However, all this economising exacted its price, in Lydia Lawrence's
unrelenting and wearying work – the cleaning, the washing, the shopping,
the baking, the cooking, the mending, the making of clothes – and her strict

---

* A new one would have cost around nineteen guineas. Alice Hall remembered that Lydia
Lawrence's sister Ada 'one time . . . sent a piano for the Lawrences', but it cannot have been
this one. In February 1896 Lydia Lawrence bought 10 £1 shares in a local brick works, which
suggest a sudden windfall rather than careful saving: her sister Ada was getting married in
December 1896 to the relatively prosperous Fritz Krenkow, which may have had something
to do with it; and the brick works had a future relation (Max Hunger, who married her niece
Ethel) connected with it. In February 1896 she was probably saving to buy her son George
out of the army (that took £18 in November 1896), and was keeping the money safe by
investing it. Her son Ernest had however started work in 1892, and by 1896 his income must
have been making some difference to the family: he would have brought in at least 18/- a
week. Emily's dressmaking would also have been bringing in between 5/- and 8/- a week.
These things would have helped offset the effects of the miners' lock-out of the winter
1893–4. But – the lock-out apart – the Lawrences' prosperity had probably been increasing
anyway in the early 1890s, as food prices fell: 'The Co-operative Wholesale Society
estimated that the average family grocery, which would have cost 7s. 6½d. in 1882, cost only
5s. 11d in 1888 and as little as 4s. 10½d in 1895. But the cost of living began to increase again
from the mid 1890s . . . rising to 6s. 4¼d. in 1914'. The purchasing power of the pound also
fell, from 20s. in 1896 to only 16s. 3d. in 1912.[35]

attitude towards wastefulness. She baked their bread and 'always said that one of their home-made loaves was as good as two of the baker's': but both *A Collier's Friday Night* and *Sons and Lovers* record the waves of moral disapproval generated by the mother when her children are careless enough to let the loaves burn.[36] The young Lawrence suffered the same reaction when he damaged the chair in the 'suite'. And the ruthless scraping and saving also helped further to alienate Arthur Lawrence – the only regular breadwinner of the household – from the rest of his family. Neville recalled an incident connected with Lawrence's acquisition of a new suit, sometime around 1906 – a time when Arthur Lawrence would not have been earning what he had in the 1870s or 1880s, and when prices were higher too. Lawrence was going to College; he

had been a little ashamed at the necessity of making his clothes last so long, as it was absolutely necessary that he should do; they were threadbare and darned to the last extremity, though always neat and tidy, before they could possibly be discarded. I was, indeed, glad for his sake, to hear that it had been found possible for him to have a new suit.

Neville goes on to describe how Arthur Lawrence, confronted by that suit, first asked 'And wheer did that cum from?', and then – the crucial question – 'Is it peed for?' Mrs Lawrence replied, 'Yes it is *peed* for' and, Neville continued,

I remember the expression, and the infinite scorn of her tones as she mocked his dialectical 'peed' for 'paid'; one of the very few times I ever heard her use any of the local dialect. But its very use, the accent, and the scorn were very regrettable, for they lashed old Lawrence to fury – the only time I remember seeing him in anything approaching an actual rage.
    'Yer can mock me, an' be off-hand wi' me, an' turn yer nose up, but if it is peed for it's my money as peed for it; an' it's a damned shame. 'Ere I ain't got a copper even ter get mesen a drink, an' 'e can 'ave owt 'e wants. What's 'e want wi' new suits? An' if 'e does why can't he goo out an' earn 'em? Not get you ter rob me for 'em.'[37]

The language cannot be an accurate record, but the tone is utterly convincing. By 1906, after thirty years of privileged children in the house – privileged, Arthur Lawrence felt, at his expense – the man so often ignored by his family was showing his resentment. The other side of Lydia Lawrence's saving and the family's 'improvement' over the years, with their books and paints and bicycle and piano, was a husband who felt himself ignored, his feelings set aside and his years of earnings taken advantage of; within three years, for some reason (almost certainly age, compounded by an injury at work) he had stopped working as a butty. From then on he was employed by other butties as a dayman, often only working part-time.[38]

But, in this family, the mahogany and horsehair suite, the paints, the bicycle, the piano, the new suit and above all the education of the youngest children, had a special meaning. The Lawrences were part of an economically advancing working class but – because of Lydia Lawrence's insistence and slaving work – they were also aiming, against the odds, at particular and special improvement. Ada Lawrence remembered her mother as a woman 'who fought all her life to give her children opportunities of becoming something more than miners and factory hands. Had it not been for her my brother would have gone down the pit with father.'[39] Arthur Lawrence's reasons for hoping his sons would join him at Brinsley were described above: he knew very well that if his sons had started work as miners, the family's income would have been suddenly and dramatically bettered. But Lydia Lawrence's different perspective, supported by her Women's Guild, was that of a woman who did not feel herself a natural part of her community. It was not just a question of income; the material advantages her children shared, like their continuing education, were steps towards the life for which she was trying to prepare them. George, Ernest, Bert and Ada not only got good jobs; they also left the working class.

After the tragic death of her son Ernest in 1901, however, Lydia Lawrence 'never appeared to be quite comfortable in the Walker Street home'; Lynn Croft, at the end of the road (a contemporary remembered), 'attracted Mrs Lawrence to make yet another advance from Walker Street'. They moved into 97, Lynn Croft early in 1905, during Arthur Lawrence's last years as a butty. The street was 'not so pleasant' as Walker Street, but the house – owned by the miners' check-weighman Tom Cooper, next door – was 'slightly larger', genuinely semi-detached and cost 6/6 a week in rent.[40] It was 'a comfortable house, comfortably furnished,' with 'a little entrance hall, with the stairs and the doors to the other rooms opening out from it. There was a cooking range in the scullery as well as in the living-room, a china closet in addition to the pantry, a cupboard under the side window where the school books were kept . . .' No longer did the stairs descend into the living room, and the extra cooking range could be used by a servant; by 1910, a girl called Minnie was helping Lydia Lawrence. The Lawrences thus almost caught up with the Neville family, who had moved into Lynn Croft (into a house they owned) as early as 1893, as well as with the Thurlbys and their bamboo curtain pole. The Lawrences lost their magnificent view out to Crich Stand: but here, at last, they had a 'lovely garden' – the only real lack in Walker Street – and Ada recalled how 'Mother was happy here amongst the flowers.'[41] The garden itself backed on to a field; from the big window of the living-room, Lawrence wrote in 1910, when I turn my head, I see over the large daisies and the lilies the many chimneys of the town – a town village – shining red, and behind them the assertive church tower, and then at the back, some four or five miles off, another misty village with a square church-tower blocked on the sky on the top of the hill. (i. 174)

Eastwood could offer nothing more refined in its working-class housing. The only better houses were the double houses along Devonshire Drive, where the Hopkins lived, and the big free-standing houses along Nottingham Road: Uplands House, Ellerslie House, The Hollies; the houses of the local shopkeepers and bourgeoisie, where lived bank and colliery managers, doctors, engineers and the professional classes.[42]

II James, George, Walter

There is another way of understanding the particular tensions and problems of the Lawrences of Eastwood: by seeing them in the context of the families of Arthur Lawrence's three younger brothers.

James, born in 1851, was also working as a collier by the age of 11: but, unlike his brother Arthur, he never learned to write (he witnessed the birth registration of his son John in December 1877 with a cross). He was still living in the parental home at the age of 21, in 1871, but probably moved to Eastwood soon afterwards: perhaps when he got married in November 1874 to the 20-year-old Polly Renshaw, daughter of a Brinsley farm labourer. At the age of 25, on 2 January 1877, he went back to work at Brinsley pit as a holer; at the same age, Arthur was a butty, which makes it probable that he had done better for himself than James had. Arthur was also five years older before he got married. In 1876 James and Polly Lawrence had a daughter Sarah, and their second child, John, in 1877, a year when all three younger sons of John Lawrence celebrated the arrival of their first sons. Unlike Arthur, whose first son had been named George after his maternal grandfather in 1876, all three younger brothers included the name John.[43] By now James and Polly Lawrence were living in a house only 200 yards from the parental home at Quarry Cottage, and feet away from the colliery railway line that ran up to Brinsley pit; they were just beside the entrance to the colliery itself.

On 24 February 1880, when Polly Lawrence was eight months pregnant, James Lawrence was caught in a fall of roof underground while he was 'holing'. 'He was found by three other colliers named Thos. Wardle, George Clifford, and Samuel Cosford, but death had taken place.' He had been trapped and suffocated. At least one of his brothers – Walter – was working underground in the same pit at the time, and his brother George probably was too. The body was brought out and buried on 26 February in

Brinsley churchyard; Polly Lawrence gave birth to her third child, Alvina, on 27 March 1880.[44] Her other children were then 4 and 2.

Such are the facts; but the story of his death was told and retold in the Lawrence family. D. H. Lawrence heard it from his grandmother Louisa Lawrence around 1892, when he was 7 years old: 'I heard my Grandmother say ... "Like a blessed smiling babe he looked – he did that"' (i. 199). Lawrence drew upon the story – and upon that particular memory of how the body looked – in both his story 'Odour of Chrysanthemums' and his play *The Widowing of Mrs. Holroyd*.

Arthur Lawrence was hurt several times underground: badly in November 1903, when he was left with a limp for the rest of his life by the 'compound fracture of the right leg'; again in 1904, when he 'was struck on the back by a fall of bind, and, falling on a quantity of debris, was badly crushed internally'. He was hurt again in July 1909 (i. 132). But mining accidents in British collieries during the period were appallingly frequent: 'Between 1868 and 1919 a miner was killed every six hours, seriously injured every two hours, and injured badly enough to need a week off work every two or three minutes'.[45] Yet nothing in the family history of Lydia and Arthur comes near the awful tragedy of the Brinsley family. Polly Lawrence – whose own mother, Sarah, had died at the age of 37 – married again, in 1884; her new husband James Allam's own first partner had died the previous year. But Polly Lawrence herself died at the age of only 41 in 1895: her children were than 19, 17 and 15. The small boy Paul Morel in *Sons and Lovers*, who prays 'very often ... "Lord, let my father die" ... "Let him be killed at pit"',[46] knows very well how easily such an accident might happen; but the security of Lawrence's own background is striking compared with his uncle James's family. Although she was often ill, Lydia Lawrence lived to the age of 59; Arthur Lawrence, in spite of his injuries at work, to 78.

Lawrence's uncle George was born in Brinsley in 1853: he started his working life as a miner (and was still one in 1871), styling himself 'Mining Engineer'; but at some stage he started working in the post-office shop in Brinsley. He also 'belonged to the Methodists at Brinsley', and was well known as 'quite a different type from his brother Arthur'. He eventually became sub-post-master, and his level of education is demonstrated by his clear and confident handwriting; he took over his parents' house – Quarry Cottage – after they died, renaming it 'Garden Vale'. (Lawrence, late in life, told a friend how his uncle had spoiled it (v. 593).)[47] But Lawrence also described how one of his uncles – probably George – was the originator of 'Lawrence's Salve': 'an ointment prized by the miners ... His uncle would heat the plaster before the fire until it was piping hot, and then slap it on to the aching back of the victim. "And then how the miners yelled!"' He certainly profited by such enterprise; by the mid-1890s he had advanced to being one of the managers of the Albert Street Schools in Eastwood: and by 1896 he was serving on Brinsley Parish Council, where he continued for many years.[48]

He and his wife Elizabeth, married in March 1877, had three sons (Luther John, Urban and Horace) and one daughter (Ida). The two elder sons, like their father, started work in the pit, but both eventually worked elsewhere: Luther became a chemist, and Urban was the manager of a retail store when he died, rather young. The daughter married Albert Wilson, who worked at a colliery, but not as a miner. Horace, the youngest son, was the only man in his immediate family never to work in the colliery.

George's family demonstrates, therefore, exactly the same pattern of upward movement characteristic of the Lawrences of Eastwood, where there were also three sons, one very briefly working at the colliery before being apprenticed to a picture framer, one excelling in business, one becoming a schoolteacher: the latter two never working at the pit. Although two of George's three sons started as miners, all the sons eventually moved into less dangerous and better paid jobs than their father. Arthur Lawrence was, however, never the respected local councillor and pillar of his community which his younger brother became; he is reported to have ridiculed George as a 'pious humbug'. Nor was Lydia Lawrence like George's wife Elizabeth: the latter notorious for her meanness in the quantity of sweets bought for a penny at the post-office shop ('she never gave us enough'), and for being (as her nephew described her) 'the champion butter spreader. She can make a pound of butter go farther than any woman I know. I watched to see how she does it, and she spreads it on, then scrapes it off, and there's a smear on the bread, but most of the butter is back in the butter dish.' And Elizabeth Lawrence reportedly had no interest in books, or in any of the things that illuminated Lydia Lawrence's life. There was little contact between the two families.[49]

Most of what we know about Lawrence's uncle Walter and his family comes from events which took place in 1900. Before then, Walter had signed on at Brinsley pit when he was 18, in 1874, as a dayman: in 1877 he was working at South Normanton; by 1878 he was back at Brinsley, where he was a holer. In 1885, after a stint at Selston colliery, he was again back at Brinsley, working as a holer in the team where his brother Arthur was butty. But he did not stay with his brother: by 1888 he was working for another former member of Arthur Lawrence's team.[50] His frequent changes of work and workplace suggest someone rather feckless, rootless and perhaps ill-tempered; that was certainly the reputation he had in the Lawrence family.

He had married Harriet Leivers, daughter of an Eastwood coal-miner, in April 1877. They had nine surviving children, the eldest born only twenty-five days after the wedding; another child died in infancy.[51] John ('Jack'), Walter Jnr and Ben became miners like their father (Walter was at work by the time he was 15): their daughters Elizabeth, Mary ('May'), Annie and Florence all married miners. Jim became a bricker and tiler, while George was a professional footballer. By 1900, the family was living and working in Ilkeston, just over the Derbyshire border.

On 18 March 1900 Walter Lawrence killed his son Walter by throwing a carving steel at him; the steel penetrated his ear, and went into his brain. The boy died a few days later. There were lengthy reports in the local papers, which give us a unique insight into Walter Lawrence's family, and into the kind of quarrels that happened in a miner's kitchen. The row between father and son was about position and priority, about earning and money; about who earned what, and what rights this entailed. Walter Lawrence was well known as a man who – because he drank too much – was sometimes unable to work (or earn) as much as he should. He was notorious in the Lawrence family for being exactly the kind of workman his brothers Arthur and George were not – one unsure of a regular weekly pay-packet. In contrast, George Neville testified that Arthur Lawrence 'never neglected his work' and that 'From the point of view of his earnings his first thought was always for his home'.[52] But by 1900 Walter Lawrence was not able to work regularly 'through being unwell' (as his wife put it, in court), or through not wanting to (as his son Walter sneered); and the consequent economic problems of the family joined with the tensions in the family caused by a 15-year-old son who was starting to earn good money.

The quarrel naturally took place in the confined space of the miner's kitchen, where the whole large family lived; where those who sat and ate and read the newspaper were occupying the places wanted by others, who also wanted to sit and eat; where quarrels naturally simmered, with the quarrelling parties hardly ever losing sight of each other. In Walter Lawrence's words, taken down by the police, 'his son came in whilst they were at tea, and wanted one of them to shift for him. The prisoner asked him to wait a minute, and he could have his place. The lad said he should not.' The hierarchy of the room creates oppositions; quarrels about who sits where are also quarrels about role and earning power and status. When D. H. Lawrence recreated the quarrels leading up to the killing (whose details he had probably forgotten) for the version he used in the 1911 draft of his novel 'Paul Morel', he concentrated at first on the position of the table in the room: Walter Morel – significantly – wants it where he can sit with his elbows on it, in his own chair, directly by the fireplace, while the son wants the table for reading. The fatal quarrel is provoked by his son's disgust with Morel's eating habits.[53]

Walter's wife Harriet was the court at Ilkeston's first witness:

On Sunday, the 18th inst., about four o'clock in the afternoon, she and her husband were getting their tea, the latter having an egg and she eating toasted pyclet [tea-cake or crumpet]. Deceased came in and sat on a stand between the sofa and the fireplace, and asked for his tea. She replied 'All right, my boy, wait a minute,' to which deceased replied 'Mother, are there any more eggs?' She told him 'No,' upon which deceased turned to his father and said, 'Those who do the least work have the most eggs.' Witness said 'Hold your noise, and don't let us have any bother about it.' Her husband had not been able to work regularly through being unwell, and the deceased had thought his father ought to have gone to work oftener than he did. The lad repeated his statement about the eggs, and the father then said 'If you don't give over I shall throw something at you.' Deceased continued his aggravating language, and while her back was turned for a moment she heard the lad call out, 'Oh, mother, dad's killed me!' She did not see anything thrown, but the lad rolled off the stand on to the sofa. Blood was streaming out of his left ear . . .

Walter Lawrence also gave his version of what happened, in spite of the Coroner cautioning him:

On Sunday afternoon they sat at tea when deceased came in and said 'I want my tea.' His mother told him to sit down a minute and he could have it. Deceased replied 'I shant; I want it now.' Witness then told him to wait a minute and he could have his place. The lad again replied 'I shant.' His mother asked him if he would have a pyclet, and he refused, saying 'I go to work the same as other folks, and I shall have some eggs.' His mother said there are none. Deceased used a lot of impudent talk to both of them, and would not hold his noise, although prisoner told him many a time to do so. Then his mother began to 'chastise' him – he meant she told the lad to hold his noise, but the lad went on, and the prisoner then exclaimed, 'If you don't, I'll throw "summat" at you.' At that time witness had an egg in his left hand eating it, and the newspaper was on the corner of the table and he was reading it while he was getting his tea. The steel [i.e. the carving steel] lay between his own and his wife's saucers, and as the lad kept on with his impudence prisoner drew the steel out and 'merely threw it at him,' not intending to hit him, but simply to get him to hold his noise. Deceased sat on a stand near the fire, and was leaning on the sofa at the moment, and that caused the steel to catch him. If he had kept still the steel would not have touched him. Witness saw deceased put his hand up to his ear twice, and the second time there was a spot of blood in the middle. Then his mother jumped up and took him to the doctor. Deceased had just put the pyclet on the table, which he had been toasting, and his mother was about to butter it for him. The idea of hurting him never entered witness's head.[54]

The mother's role in the reports of the 'Domestic Tragedy at Ilkeston' (as the *Ilkeston Advertiser* and *Nottinghamshire Guardian* both called it) is fascinating. Harriet Lawrence was naturally the one who tried to interpose between the warring menfolk; she attempted to 'chastise' her son, in the dialect sense of 'restrain', though in fact she was an extremely strong woman with a reputation for laying about her (see Illustration 19). She was also about to butter her son's pyclet for him at the moment of the tragedy, which (characteristically for a woman waiting upon her menfolk) she did not see, because 'her back was turned for a moment'. In the circumstances, however, it might have been judicious of her not to have seen what happened. She said that the carving steel 'was usually kept in the knife box' and that 'She did not know it was on the table', although (according to Walter Lawrence) it lay between his saucer and hers. It seems at least possible that the steel was where it usually was, and where she obviously expected it to be – in the knife drawer. Walter Lawrence may well have taken the steel out of the drawer (his phrase 'drew the steel out' certainly suggests so) to throw at his son. But Harriet Lawrence remained a loyal wife and did not see what he actually did. Walter Lawrence was committed to trial at the Assizes in Derby.*

The affair demonstrates some of the enormous differences between Arthur's household in Eastwood, and that of his brother in Ilkeston. Arthur had two sons almost of the same age, Ernest and Bert; the former was earning a good salary as a clerk in London, the latter was, in March 1900, a scholarship boy at Nottingham High School. Walter's two eldest sons were both miners like their father. The father Lawrence wrote about in *A Collier's Friday Night* accuses his student son of staying out of work because he does

---

* At the Assizes, on 13 July, in front of Mr Justice Wright, Walter Lawrence was defended ('at the request of his Lordship') by Mr Dominic Daly; evidence was given by the 10-year-old second son, George, that

> on the day in question his brother (the deceased) came home and commenced grumbling about what had been obtained for his tea. His father told him that he should hit him if he did not hold his noise. The boy went on grumbling, however, and his father then threw a steel at him. – By Mr Daly: The prisoner was reading the newspaper at the time and was not at all angry . . . Prisoner did say that had the boy remained still the steel would not have struck him. Lawrence, so far as the witness knew, was a respectable man and had not been in any trouble before. – For the defence Mr Daly contended that the case was more one of accident than anything and not one in which a man could be convicted of the serious crime of manslaughter.

Walter Lawrence was found guilty of manslaughter, but – as he had been in prison for fourteen weeks awaiting trial – was told by Mr Justice Wright: 'Prisoner may go now. (Applause.)' We can hear his family joining in that applause. But he lived for only another three years: he died on 3 April 1904 of 'Progressive Bulbar Paralysis', a disease in which 'the muscles of facial expression, of mastication, of articulation, and of swallowing suffer progressive loss of power. The cause of the nerve degeneration is not known, although in some cases it is a syphilitic infection.'[55] The disease probably accounts for the peculiarly distressing expression of Walter's face in a surviving picture of him: see Illustration 18.

47

not want to 'dirty his fingers'; his wife accuses the father, in turn, of wanting to 'drag all the lads into the pit, and you only begrudge them because I wouldn't let them'.[56] Lydia Lawrence settled that argument her own way in Eastwood; Harriet and Walter Lawrence (she a coal-miner's daughter who had never learned to write – she marked her husband's death certificate with a cross) settled it the other way in Ilkeston, where the money brought in by their sons helped make up for the deficiencies in their father's income.

George Neville, again, is our source for the response Arthur Lawrence would make when angered with his son Bert's still being a student at the age of 21, in 1906: 'I speak raight out an' say tha'rt not worth thee salt. Too damn lazy to work like anybody else's kids an' get owt for theesen'.[57] Walter Lawrence's son's complaint, in 1900, that 'Those who do the least work have the most eggs' could be nicely applied – though with the roles reversed – to the Lambert family in *A Collier's Friday Night*, where it is the (non-employed) children for whom their mother gets the tinned apricots and the grapes for their tea, to the anger of the (employed) father. When the latter starts to eat the grapes, and is warned by his wife not to eat all of them – 'There's somebody else!' – he retorts:

'Somebody else'! Yes, there *is* 'somebody else'! *(he pushes the plate away and the grapes roll on the table)*: I know they was not bought for me! I know it! I know it!! *(his voice is rising)* 'Somebody else'!! Yes, there *is* somebody else. I'm not daft: I'm not a fool! *(The mother turns away her head with a gesture of contempt. The father continues with maddening tipsy ironic snarl.)* I'm not a fool! I can see it, I can see it!! I'm not daft! There's nothing for me. Nothing's got for me. Noo—! You can get things for them—you can, but you begrudge me every bit I put in my mouth.[58]

The privilege and priority of the man's role (in its particular manifestation as that of father and breadwinner) are both asserted and under attack, in the fictional Lamberts and the real-life Lawrences of Eastwood. This should remind us of another of the contradictions of the period; that the man who earned the family's bread by his work down pit and who was, by the standards of the working class, earning good money, was also raising children who – as with the Lawrences of Eastwood, and with uncle George's family in Brinsley – would leave the working class behind. Their opinion of the father's and man's role would inevitably change; and, as they went away from home to take up jobs elsewhere, the bulk of their earning would no longer come back to their families.

The quarrel at Ilkeston, then, dreadful as it must have been, was in one way a time-honoured one between the rising and the older male generations in a working-class environment of rigid priorities and status; one in which quarrels and violence were never very far away. The quarrels in the

Lawrence family of Eastwood, as people like Neville reported them, were very different. In the first place, they were verbal rather than physical. There is no record of them becoming violent; Arthur Lawrence never seems to have been violent to his children, either, and the worst that Lawrence showed Walter Morel doing to his wife in *Sons and Lovers* was throwing a small drawer at her which just catches her on the temple. In many Eastwood families, as the local paper shows, husbands behaved far more violently to their wives. Arthur Lawrence, however, locked Lydia out of the Victoria Street house on one occasion, and she spent the night in an outhouse; Lawrence reported that his father 'was very bad before I was born' (i. 190), and *Sons and Lovers* shows Walter Morel locking a pregnant Gertrude Morel out. The local paper records such happenings in Eastwood.[59]

But the quarrels of the Eastwood Lawrences generally demonstrated a significant reversal of female and male roles. To that degree, the Lawrence family of Eastwood was unusual, even within the Lawrence family as a whole; and to a large extent that must have been because of Lydia Lawrence and the struggle which cost her (in one way) her marriage.

It was with a new perception not only of the man's role within the family that Lawrence himself grew up, but with a new expectation of what as a man he might achieve in the world at large. As a boy, he sometimes wore an apron, scrubbed the floor and blackleaded the grate; he did the same kind of household tasks – cooking, preparing food, tidying and cleaning – for the Chambers family at the Haggs Farm, when he was a teenager (but was then very careful not to let the boys in that family – two of them miners – catch him at it). He experimented as a child with cooking, making toffee and potato cakes: he also gathered 'the girls together to go blackberrying', though we know by his own account that picking blackberries was a job for 'children ... women ... half grown youths'.[60] He was even able, to the amazement of the shopkeeper, to discuss the 'difference of two qualities' of grocery: 'Do you know another lad as 'ud stand and talk like a woman about groceries?' This was a community in which it could be said that 'You're braver than most men if you dare go in a shop'. He even helped his Croydon landlady with the dusting in 1911 (i. 248). Arthur Lawrence was an extremely handy man (witness his mending of boots and shoes, his soldering, his making of household utensils): but he shopped, cooked and cleaned only on very rare occasions. (In *Sons and Lovers*, Mrs Morel declares that Morel's fellow butty, Barker, is 'ten times the man you are' because – while his wife is pregnant – he goes 'buying in the week's groceries and meat on the Friday nights': Walter Morel, however, sweeps the house when Gertrude Morel is pregnant.)[61] All his life, D. H. Lawrence went on doing his own shopping and cooking and cleaning; but people misunderstood if they thought it was because he came from the working class. Just the opposite: it was a sign of his emancipation from the traditional male roles of the working class. His mother, well aware of how her father had tyrannised over his womenfolk in such things, was ensuring that her own son at least would not grow up thinking of women as servants.

The numerous reports of Lawrence's being considered effeminate, as a child and adolescent, have therefore some grounding in his resolutely non-male behaviour. More than once he was taxed with his preference for girls, 'but disdained it', remarking to May Chambers:

'I like girls, and I'm going about with them whatever they say. Why shouldn't I?'
  'Why not boys?' I asked.
  'Girls are ever so much nicer. Besides, I don't like boys' games, they're so rough. It's beyond me why they make such a fuss about it.'[62]

Girls grew up quicker, were more interesting in their talk, did not despise him as an outsider and would let him compete with them on equal terms (or even lead them). There seems to have been an interesting division in the young Lawrence between his preference for girls as companions, and his later feelings of attraction towards men such as Alan Chambers and George Neville, in his teens: both of them athletic and not particularly intellectual. Lawrence, as formed by his physique and by his childhood in the company of women, was cut off from the man's usual athletic and non-intellectual world and – of course – continually subjected to his mother's version of Arthur Lawrence as morally degenerate and physically repulsive. He went quite a long way in the direction of preferring girls and women as companions and intellectual equals, so that there was always some woman to whom he was very close; in 1913 he wrote that 'It is hopeless for me to try to do anything without I have a woman at the back of me' (i. 503). But he also grew up looking with physical and aesthetic envy at non-intellectual boys and men: feeling for them what (much later) he would admit was love. The subject will come up again in a consideration of Lawrence's adolescence and sexual maturing. Here it is simply important to stress how his childhood and upbringing naturally took him on a counter course to the prevailing sexual codes, mores and manners of the mining working class.

Again, late in life, and mockingly, Lawrence recalled his mother's hopes that her 'clever' son 'might one day be a professor or a clergyman or perhaps even a little Mr Gladstone. That would have been rising in the world—on the ladder. Flights of genius were nonsense—you had to be clever & rise in the world, step by step'.[63] There was reason for Lawrence to mock that in 1928; by then, he had taken his choices and made his own way, and it was a very different way from any for which his mother might have hoped. But, back in the 1890s and 1900s, he had benefited enormously from the shift in perspective which his mother had inculcated. Louie Burrows recalled, probably of the period around 1910 (when Lawrence was 25), that 'His admiration for his aunt who had social aspirations [i. e. Aunt Ada Krenkow] was a heartfelt one – tho' he made as if to round on her for snobbery. He was at this time wickedly ambitious socially – tho' it was the last thing he would admit or condone in another.'[64] That nicely suggests the contradiction and ambiguity in his attitude. But his ambition as he grew up was no longer confined to being a man earning a good wage in the local industry, or being a dominant and successful father-figure and head of family (the two role models which his father consciously or unconsciously offered him). Lawrence was brought up to believe he could make a mark on the world, not just in Eastwood or as the father of a family: his brother Ernest actually excelled in 'getting on' in the world. His mother might not have thought Lawrence's actual career much of a 'rise in the world', and she was deeply suspicious of his ambition to be a writer: but at least she had a perspective on a world in which her children could rise.

III Sisters and Brothers

Lawrence was born on 11 September 1885 and christened in the parish church on 29 November.[65] Lydia Lawrence did not want another child – 'My mother never wanted me to be born', Lawrence remarked in 1919 (iii. 333); bringing up three small children in the Victoria Street house, and trying to run a shop too, were presumably quite enough for her. But Lawrence was not her last child: Ada was born in June 1887, when he was 21 months old. His elder sister, Emily, was 3½ years older than he, and always helped to mother the younger children; Lawrence remembered running away from her down the road to Moorgreen Colliery, as a child of 4 or 5, and 'hour after hour' watching the horses and the trucks at the level-crossing. Emily, however – like her counterpart Annie Morel in 'Paul Morel' – was 'stocked with invaluable "Ugly Duckling" and "Little Folks" stories', and could keep him enthralled: she was 'a splendid companion, so enthusiastic, such a one for yarning'. Ada recalled of Emily how 'Bert and I loved her to read aloud to us when mother was out. She knitted well, and during each winter made woollen gloves and stockings, working furiously while she thrilled us with adventure stories, such as "Coral Island", "Swiss Family Robinson" or tales from "Little Folks".'[66] She would also 'recite sentimental poetry at great length', and Lawrence remembered how 'I used to pull her hair till she cried, but she went on and on, the tears streaming

51

down her face.' Like Paul Morel, he enormously enjoyed her gusto; as a child 'she was so unhesitating, so sure and uncritical, so unlike himself'.[67]

It was a household of girls and women in which the young Lawrence was brought up, especially as he was 'always delicate' and at home a great deal more than most boys; home was the woman's realm.[68] Ada became his constant companion in his youth and grew up very close to him. 'You and I', Lawrence addressed her in 1911: 'there are some things which we shall share, we alone, all our lives ... You are my one, *real* relative in the world: only you' (i. 231). When Lawrence gave the youthful Paul Morel no younger sister as a companion, in *Sons and Lovers*, he was considerably revising his own experience as a child, and making Paul far more independent in himself and considerably more dependent upon his mother than he himself had been. When the young Paul Morel goes out, it is with his younger brother Arthur; they are 'the lads'.[69] When Lawrence went out to play, it would have been with Ada.

The young Lawrence would have seen considerably less of his elder brothers and still less of his father. When he was on night-shifts, Arthur Lawrence came home just as his children were having breakfast, at 7.30 in the morning; he 'used to arrive home, black and tired, just as we were downstairs in our nightdresses. Then night met morning face to face, and the contact was not always happy.'[70] Arthur Lawrence slept during the day, had his main meal when he got up and went out at around 8.30 at night. When on day-shifts, he got up summer and winter at 4.45 a.m.; he made his own breakfast, prepared his own 'snap tin' containing his midday food and was out of the house by 5.30. Unless the pit was on part-time or short-time working, his children would not see him until 4.30 in the afternoon, when he would come home and have his main meal of the day. He loved his garden, and in summer he worked on his allotment in the evenings: he must have supplied vegetables for the household. If he could afford it – as he normally could, between Friday and Monday – he would go out to join his friends in the pub for the rest of the evening; the children would usually be in bed before he was home. If he stayed in, he might do some household jobs; best of all were the times when, like Walter Morel, he mended the boots and shoes, or told stories of life down pit; the children enjoyed these even more than their mother's 'stories from Andersen'. But, like Walter Morel, he would then go to bed very early, often before the children. 'There was nothing remained for him to stay up for, when he had finished tinkering, and had skimmed the head lines of the newspaper'.[71] Two family friends reported, however, that Arthur Lawrence 'was never allowed to stay downstairs': 'they always told him to get to bed, Arthur': 'the Little Woman ... would then instruct him to hold his tongue or go to bed'. Alice Hall remembered an occasion when he 'wanted to tell us about somebody roast-ing a hedgehog on the way to Felley, over the common he'd gone, but they wouldn't let him finish. They just told him to get to bed and they all ignored him, and it made one feel very uncomfortable, in his own house'. George Neville remembered the same about Arthur Lawrence's attempts to give his point of view, or to air someone else's grievance: Lydia would instruct him 'Hold your tongue, Sir, or be off to bed.'[72] Only at weekends, on holidays and during short-time working or strikes was their father much of a presence in the Lawrence children's lives.

Of Lawrence's two elder brothers, George was always reckoned the handsome one of the family; not tall (he was only 5ft. 4½in.) but powerfully built and good looking, with 'regular features and dark brown wavy hair'.[73] He was, however, a rather distant elder brother for the younger members of the family; he was much older than they (9 years older than Bert) and went to work at the age of 14 in High Park Colliery, before being apprenticed to George Carlin, picture framer. His earnings would have helped a little with the family income, but his boyish promises to his mother were quickly broken: a family friend recalled Lydia Lawrence speaking with 'comical emphasis' about them '. . . he was never going to leave me. "I shall always stop with you, mother, and take care of you," he used to say. And at seventeen he was arming a girl round.' Worse was to follow. In August 1895 – 19 years old, presumably bored and looking for adventure (his younger brother recalled his 'raffling round') – he walked over to Ilkeston with a friend and signed on for seven years in the army with the King's Own Scottish Borderers. In fact, he was in the army only a year and 97 days; his mother somehow managed to pay £18 in 1896 to purchase his release.[74] One of her sisters may have helped. But it would have been a dreadful blow to her careful saving and budgeting; and the moral was doubtless drawn for the benefit of the younger children.

George then got a job locally as a turner; but with his buxom girl friend Ada Wilson three months pregnant, he married her in May 1897. They probably lived with his parents for a short while, but not for long: his wife was 'a girl that they didn't really like. They thought she wasn't quite suitable for him'.[75] The couple moved a mile away to Hill Top, Eastwood, where their son William Ernest was born in November 1897. George and his family subsequently went to live in Nottingham, where he worked for the engineering firm of Berry's; here his maternal uncle George Beardsall (who had done well for himself) was a partner, and able to keep an eye on him. The fact that George's son, the 4-year-old William Ernest, came back to Eastwood to live with his grandparents in the early 1900s may suggest that George's family was finding it difficult to survive in Nottingham: though they may just have been taking the chance of getting a young child off their hands while Ada was pregnant.[76] George changed jobs frequently, and at this stage of his life drank a good deal; he was in many ways reckless and like his father, whom he always admired tremendously. George Neville remembered George Lawrence at this period as 'bluff, hail-fellow-well-met and more like his father than any of the others': Lydia Lawrence may have been glad to bring up her grandson herself for a while. Later in the 1900s, however, having been a trial and trouble to his parents, George was the first of the family to settle down; in time he became extremely respectable, teetotal and pious. As a lay preacher in Nottingham he 'used to spend the whole Saturday afternoon, if he wasn't working, getting his sermon ready for the Sunday'.[77] Imprudence and recklessness were thus followed by extreme respectability; which suggests yet another of the oppositions haunting the Lawrence children's lives as they grew up. If, of all the children, George had been most like his father when young, he became more and more like a parody of his mother as he got older: pious, strict and sternly condemnatory of folly and immorality. He deeply disapproved of his younger brother going away with a married woman in 1912: 'I didn't like that at all. Aye . . . And I don't think I saw him again for quite a number of years'.[78]

The second brother, William Ernest, two years younger than George, was in every way closer to his younger brother and sisters: 'Tall, well built, with thick brown hair with reddish tints and twinkling blue eyes . . . Always full of fun and humour, he was the life and soul of the house, and no party seemed complete unless he was there to play the fool': he was also 'rather a dandy'. He made a marvellous success of his career: having done extremely well at school – in December 1890 he was placed top of a list of pupils awarded prizes by the trustees for 'general good conduct. regularity in attendance and proficiency' – he had to leave school at 14 like George, in order to start earning;[79] he began work in the Co-op at Langley Mill, a mile west of Eastwood. From there, at the age of 18, he went to work in the offices of the Shipley Colliery Company; then spent a year as correspondent, shorthand writer and typist with a cycle firm in Coventry. By the time he was 19 he was tutoring local boys in shorthand and typing, both in private lessons at home and in the evening classes at the British school, before – like his counterpart William in *Sons and Lovers* – he got a job in an office in London, probably (like William) at 'a hundred and twenty a year'. Here he 'learned French and Latin and worked at law, and the young women adored him'. There were always women around Ernest: *Sons and Lovers* suggests through the character of William how dashing and attractive and fickle in his tastes Ernest was. He was also the tallest of the family: six

foot, 'like grandfather who was over six feet'; and <u>he was also like his</u>
<u>grandfather John Lawrence in being a tremendous athlete: swimmer, run-</u>
<u>ner, cyclist and 'champion footballer'</u>.[80] The Lawrence family still preserves
the glass inkstand, shaped like an anvil, which at the age of 12 he won for
running: he won prizes for swimming too. *Sons and Lovers* describes how the
fictional William wins cycle races, jumps higher hedges and throws stones
further than any other boy in the neighbourhood. When he grew older,
Ernest – like his father – came to love dancing, and attended 'A fancy dress
ball, in connection with Mr. J. S. Clay's dancing classes' in February 1896:
like his counterpart in *Sons and Lovers*, he went as a 'Scotchman'.[81] <u>Ernest</u>
<u>was, naturally, the great hero of his younger sisters and brother</u>; Ada tells a
lovely story of a funeral she and Bert were having for two accidentally
suffocated rabbits: 'Ernest suddenly appeared wearing a black silk hat and
long black streamers, and carrying one of father's huge white handkerchiefs
into which he bellowed so loud and long that the neighbours hurried out to
see what was to do. In spite of our real grief at our loss, we collapsed in
laughter at the ridiculous faces he was pulling.'[82] He gave them all their
nicknames: Ada remembered how 'My sister Emily, because of the colour of
her hair, was "Injun Top-knot"; Bert, whose hair was light brown in those
days was "Billy White-nob": and I "Corkscrews", because of my curls.'
Emily was also known as 'Pamela' or 'Pem' while Bert was 'Billy Godly':
Ernest himself was 'Red-nob'.

He was a great reader, and also wrote poems. After he went to London in
1897, when Ada was 10 and Bert 12, 'his homecomings were the greatest
events of our lives'.[83] One letter he sent to Bert from London in October
1897 survives, addressed to 'My dear William Whytteoun' (i.e. 'White-
'un'): it is full of love and playfulness. His brother is 'you great big monster',
'you big bellied rascal', 'you monstrous piggleum': and Ernest wishes, at the
end of his letter, that he too could be enjoying Goose Fair at home.

Well my laddie I hope that you have a jolly good time, and enjoy yourself as much as
ever I used to, and I did use to.
    So now my dear old tremendous one I must dry up with best wishes for any of
your Friends, and tell Ada I will write to her next time but I have not time this turn.
    Goodbye for a time.
                        Your affectionate Brother,
                        W. E. Lawrence
                        pp *Red Nob*[84]

When Emily and Bert failed to write to him, a couple of years later, they got
a letter from the 'Killemwenucachem Club', certifying that 'if "His
Monstrous" alias "White Nob" alias "Big Sogger" alias "Tremendous

Belly" and "Her serene Highness Pem" alias "Injun Top knot" alias "Scrubbs" do not reply to my last epistle, I the President of the above Club will send down vengeance swift and sure'. His family kept his poems, his letters, his postcards, his sketches; his death in 1901 was a fearful blow.[85]

Until Ernest's death, too, 'Mother always took part in our games and joined in our songs. He had been the life and soul of them. After he died she would stay in the kitchen in her rocking chair, pretending to read.' For the young Lawrence, his mother had been at the centre of his world; he remembered wondering, as a child, 'why God was a man, and not a woman. In heaven, God was the fount of right and wrong, and on earth, woman. Women know best. Men didn't care. God knows best of all. — That was my childish arrangement of the moral scheme.' Like Paul Morel as a small child, 'he trotted after his mother like her shadow'.[86] There are countless stories of his love for her, her love and support for him, and of their preternatural closeness. Another sentence in *Sons and Lovers* perhaps sums up the particular nature of Lawrence's feelings for his mother: 'He was so conscious of what other people felt, particularly his mother.' Ada, too, was aware of how – compared with other children – they had been brought up to be 'conscious of more. The anxieties of our mother were shared by us. She never concealed the fact that she had not enough money to clothe and feed us as adequately as she wished.' As a result, though loved and reassured by her – Ada remembered how 'we felt in her a wealth of love and a security past all understanding'[87] – all the children took on a special burden of sympathy.

And yet there was in Lawrence, all his life, a kind of hypersensitivity to others, to their feelings of pain in particular, which many people remarked: and the boy learned it from his experience of his expressive yet reserved and undemonstrative mother. She made him conscious not only of her problems with money, but of how she reacted to her husband and to her marriage: when he was still young, she told him the story of her married life in a way he never forgot (and himself had to retell, to exorcise it). In response, he learned to be preternaturally attuned to feelings: adept at learning the significance of a phrase from his mother, a gesture, a sniff (very characteristic of her), a fleeting grimace, as Lydia Lawrence shared her frustration or anger. Paul Morel looks at his mother's face while she is ironing, and sees it 'brave and rich with life, but as if she had been done out of her rights'. It is a complex emotion; but it seems to be characteristic of what Lydia Lawrence, too, subtly communicated to her son when he was very young. In *Sons and Lovers*, when Mrs Morel cannot bear herself, 'the feeling was transmitted to the other children⌜.⌝ ⟨, but particularly to Paul.⟩ She never suffered alone any more: the children suffered with her.' Like Paul Morel, Lawrence sometimes 'seemed old for his years' as a result:[88] he ended up at 23 feeling that 'In some things I'm grey old' (i. 81).

IV   Father and Mother

Lawrence's sympathy with his mother also necessitated a powerful reaction against his father: May Chambers recalled him confessing 'I have to hate him for Mother's sake'. Lydia Lawrence seems not only to have excluded her husband from the everyday life of the home, but as far as possible to have forced the children into making a moral choice against him. The children's polarisation between their loyalties to father and to mother led to what Ada called the 'misery in our childhood'.[89] They were by no means always unhappy children; but the conflicts of possessiveness were an everyday reality. A friend recorded Lawrence's memory from the 1920s of how his mother

would gather the children in a row and they would sit quaking, waiting for their father to return while she would picture his shortcomings blacker and blacker to their childish horror. At last the father would come in softly, taking off his shoes, hoping to escape unnoticed to bed, but that was never allowed him. She would burst out upon him, reviling him for a drunken sot, a good-for-nothing father. She would turn to the whimpering children and ask them if they were not disgusted with such a father. He would look at the row of frightened children, and say 'Never mind, my duckies, you needna be afraid of me. I'll do ye na harm.'[90]

We can see both Lawrence parents claiming 'their' children in that anec-dote; but Lydia Lawrence won hands down. Ada recalled how 'we all idolised her', and George remembered her as 'a wonderful woman'; her daughter Emily's children still bear witness to the strength of that current of feeling.[91]

Yet none of the other children had so violent a reaction against their father as Lawrence did. A surviving letter from Ernest to his father is extremely cheerful and friendly, and George's later recollections show how very fond he was 'of my old dad. He was a man. And admitted that he liked his beer, I'm perfectly well aware, but otherwise our old dad was a fine fellow, and he, Bert, made me very vexed with some of the slighting remarks he made in his book about my old dad'. Emily retained fond memories of her father: 'He knew the names of the birds and animals and that. He was very good at that': while as a little girl, Ada – to whom her father 'listened indulgently' – was his favourite.[92] Her account of him is full of understand-ing. Lawrence was exceptional in his deep hatred of his father: he was the only one of the children to take over his mother's attitude completely. His feelings were clear; almost everyone who knew him, even slightly, observed them. When – probably in the middle 1890s – Arthur Lawrence was hurt down pit and had to go to hospital, a neighbour's child remembered how 'We children were watching near the cab, and as the driver mounted the box, Bertie turned and said: "Now we are going to be very happy while Father is away."' May Chambers recalled a meal in the Lawrence household around 1902 (when Lawrence was 17) to which she was invited:

> Bert and I sat on the sofa; and when his father took his place, I felt Bert draw himself together, humping himself up and bending his head over his plate. When the father talked to me, the son twitched my dress or nudged me. He hardly answered when his father spoke to him . . . There was such a hateful feeling coming from Bert that I was almost frightened.[93]

A few days later, May – puzzled by Lawrence's attitude to his father – 'tried to find a word to fit Bert's attitude and discovered it was *vengeful*': he 'seemed to send out jagged waves of hate and loathing that made me shudder'. George Neville recorded Lawrence saying, after a row with his father around 1906, 'He *is* a beast, a beast to mother, a beast to all of us': Jessie Chambers remembered how 'Lawrence broke into a storm of abuse against his father' while on holiday in 1907, and Paul Morel prays 'each night, for twenty years' that his father will either stop drinking or die in an accident.[94] From 1910, we have Lawrence's own testimony: 'I was born hating my father: as early as ever I can remember, I shivered with horror when he touched me' (i. 190). The same year, he declared that he had 'never had but one parent' (i. 181); and, finally, in 1911 he told the local minister how 'disgusting, irritating, and selfish as a maggot' (i. 220) his father was, remarking to Ada at the same time that 'It is astonishing how hard and bitter I feel towards him' (i. 230).

Arthur Lawrence was boastful and (George Neville believed this was the main problem) 'mean in soul': he willingly gave up neither money nor his comforts,[95] while Lawrence never forgot how ready his father was to believe the worst of his children 'and reluctant of the best' (i. 351). But hatred is something different. The hatred, as the 1910 remark suggests, started early, and was from the start combined with a violent physical repulsion. It was never just a conscious or intellectual response to what he felt had been his father's unfair and vicious treatment of his mother, though that was often his later understanding (and explanation) of it. The shiver of horror sounds more like a victim recalling an assault than a son remembering his father's touch: yet several people spoke of Arthur Lawrence as *not* violent to his children – as, indeed, particularly tender and gentle towards them. One neighbour remembered him 'as he staggered up the entry with three of them clinging round his neck like a bunch of cherries'; while even Walter

Morel in *Sons and Lovers* is 'very affectionate, indulgent' to his eldest son. The worst recorded of Arthur Lawrence is threatened anger:

The nearest he ever did was once when Ada riled him, and he got hold of her hair – she had long curly hair – curls down her back – and he said 'for two pins I'll swing you round the room with your hair.' But he didn't. He threatened very often when Bert was very rude to him as a little boy – he threatened to 'skelp him' as he called it – but I never saw him touch him once. Never. He threatened to, but he never did.

The worst the children ever got – probably from their mother rather than their father – was 'a quick smack. Nothing else.'[96]

Lawrence's revulsion can be understood as that of a boy who feels threatened and repulsed by his father, and whose answer is to retreat into a child's version of his mother's feelings; he grew up with a 'distaste for being caressed (except on occasions)' (i. 51), with a strong sense of untouchableness which was his 'sort of pride' (i. 165). He was an unusually sensitive child, and – like his mother – acutely aware of things he found distasteful. When his younger sister smacked her tongue against her palate when eating, for example, he would 'yell in anger . . . "Mother, she's clapping!"' Ada tells us that, again like Lydia Lawrence, her brother 'loathed the smell of pit dirt'; he rejected, very powerfully (if unconsciously) his father's actual physical presence, together with his warmth, tenderness and touch: his inhibition in Arthur Lawrence's presence could actually exert a paralysing effect on him.[97] His father had similar problems with him: George Neville, who sat at Lawrence's bedside in the evening during his pneumonia in the winter of 1901–2, remembered how Arthur Lawrence

would come into the bedroom in stockinged feet, and with his slippers in his hand would stand behind the screen awaiting my signal. If I signalled 'asleep', he would come softly to the foot of the bed and just look and look at the poor wasted figure, while the tears would trickle unheeded down his face and hurry off his beard. If he heard the ravings of his delirious son, he would just stand quietly behind the screen, cry quietly for a time, and then move softly away to his bed. Often I did not hear him go.

Neville also remembered how Arthur Lawrence 'would pick up a jar or something his son had been decorating, hold it, and gaze at it when he thought no one was observing him'.[98] These anecdotes not only reveal Arthur Lawrence's tenderness towards his son: they suggest how his feelings normally showed themselves. He might be gentle, or compassionate, or violent, or sulky, or rude, or tremendously cheerful or thoroughly boisterous: but he always let you know what he was feeling.

This, however, seems to have become one of the things which Lydia Lawrence could not stand about her husband. Whether Arthur Lawrence was cheerful or sad or angry, his very physical presence came to irritate her.[99] But whereas that made her even cooler and more impassive than usual, her emotionally dependent son's reaction tended to take physical form. When possessed by irritation, he became the boy who 'drew himself together, humping himself up' in the presence of his father: on at least one occasion he actually squared up to his father, to fight him.[100] His hatred became a violent passion of rejection and loathing: his rejection of his father was a counterpart to what sounds very like sexual revulsion in his mother. Once again we have to be very cautious of treating *Sons and Lovers* as a recreation of real life; Paul insists that his mother once 'had a passion' for his father:

"That's what one *must have*, I think," he continued; "the real, real flame of feeling through another person, once, only once, if it only lasts three months. See, my mother looks as if she'd *had* everything that was necessary for her living and developing. There's not a tiny bit of a feeling of sterility about her."

"No," said Miriam.

"And with my father, at first, I'm sure she had the real, real thing . . ."[101]

Miriam's cautious agreement inevitably sounds sceptical; Lydia Lawrence's reaction to her husband probably had far more in common with the revulsions of Mrs Morel than with the sexual theories of Paul.

It took Lawrence years to get over his feeling of hatred for his father; but the process probably started later in the year after his mother died. Arthur Lawrence was no longer working as a butty at Brinsley but was doing odd shifts for other butties on a part-time basis. Lawrence responded to the news from his sister Ada: 'I'm glad father's got a lighter job. Give him my love. Does he want for anything' (i. 316). It is practically the first sign of fellow-feeling towards his father in twenty-six years: his loyalty to Lydia Lawrence had helped inhibit it before.

V Language

'Home' means more than the four walls of the Lawrence houses in Eastwood. A good friend of Lawrence's from 1901, Jessie Chambers – May's sister, and from 1898 living outside Eastwood itself, on a farm 2 miles away – wrote about Lawrence and his community that

Lawrence belonged absolutely to the stock from which he sprang; bone of their bone. There was no distance between him and the people amongst whom he lived; when he talked to them he spoke out of the same heritage of thought and feeling; he was like them, only greater, in a sense he contained them in himself. He had a marvellous understanding of collier folk, men and women; he knew just how they felt about things and what their reactions were . . . He was quite at home with them, and they with him, whereas I always felt, and was, an outsider, a 'foreigner' as they would say. But Lawrence was not a 'foreigner', he was one of them in an extremely close and subtle relationship.[102]

She went on to say that the fact that Lawrence ended up leaving 'his common people' was 'accidental and not intentional':

I am quite sure that he did not intend or wish in the least to make a complete break. It was never deliberate, he somehow blundered into it . . . after the break with his Nottingham life he made more than one attempt, half-hearted perhaps, but then he received no encouragement, to re-establish some kind of relationship. But there were too many irreconcilable elements in the situation . . .[103]

There always remained, of course, 'some kind of relationship' between Lawrence and the Eastwood region; friends to whom he felt attached still remained there. In a rather different way, Eastwood retained connections with members of his own family, in particular his sisters Emily and Ada; his father lived there, and subsequently at Ripley (just a few miles away) until his death in 1924.

But Jessie Chambers's sentimentalising portrayal of Lawrence's belonging to 'the stock from which he sprang' ignores the fact that his relationship with Eastwood had been, from the start, coloured by his relationship with his mother, and by the aspiration to another life which her efforts for her children continually created. To her, Eastwood was only the last in a succession of grimy and depressing places to which she felt she had been condemned, unknowing, when she got married. Her own distance from the place may be gauged by the fact that 'She spoke King's English, without an accent, and never in her life could even imitate a sentence of the dialect which my father spoke, and which we children spoke out of doors.'[104] If George Neville's anecdote about the new suit can be trusted, then she could actually imitate her husband's dialect perfectly well – if she chose. But she did not choose; it was not her language. Arthur Lawrence was all his life a dialect speaker: the dialect audible in memorable phrases like 'the doom of St Paul's' (i. 534), which his son never forgot. Only when confronted by his son (with whom he sometimes dropped his vernacular speech) or with his son's educated friends was he known to talk '*in the most perfect King's English, with an affected voice and accent*, entirely forsaking the local dialect he usually employed. But before he had proceeded far in this strain, he was generally interrupted by a shriek of laughter, led by D. H., well seconded by the Little Woman [Lydia Lawrence] . . .'[105] Arthur Lawrence, like his son, was a gifted mimic: it is one of the necessities of life for people living between cultural and linguistic divisions to be able to impersonate those who sound superior.

Whereas Neville makes Arthur Lawrence's 'superior' accent sound ineffectual, it is probable that the performance was actually directed at the refinement of people like Neville – the latter being noted for his 'excellent English and refined accent' (i. 67). Ernest Lambert's father in *A Collier's Friday Night* also adopts 'an exaggerated imitation of his son's English' when annoyed with his superior wife and son; while Walter Morel in *Sons and Lovers* – another 'good mimic' – parodies the 'fat, squeaky voice, with its attempt at good English'[106] of the underground manager, as the latter attempts to put him in his place. Lawrence himself, for the benefit of his teachers, adopted an 'exquisite accent' (i. 64) in place of his Midlands accent while at college. It was a strategy that, in varying forms, he adopted all his life, as the class outsider is forced to do in England.

He also made a special point, up to 1912, of using the French he had learned at High school, and which had distinguished him from the other Eastwood boys. He encouraged Jessie Chambers to keep a diary in French, which he corrected; French peppers his surviving early letters, and he used it on special occasions, such as embarrassedly thanking his headmaster for a congratulatory present in 1904 (i. 25); he read Maupassant, Stendhal, Baudelaire, Verlaine in French, sometimes out loud (i. 68): he tried writing poetry in French. He seems to have spoken French whenever possible: with his headmaster's wife in Croydon, for example; with a Brazilian pianist and her husband he met in 1911 (i. 308); he was called on by a school colleague to help entertain a Frenchman and his sister (i. 318–19), and on at least one occasion a friend heard him 'airing his French' with a barmaid. In 1909, fed up with teaching, he wanted to 'go to France as soon as I can' (i. 140) – something he explained in 1910 as his 'old desire' (i. 215). And in *The White Peacock*, 'The Witch à la Mode' and 'The Old Adam' he gave three of his autobiographical fictional heroes French connections. He tended to make France, and French – like the vermouth and absinthe he drank in cafés[107] – symbolic of the decadent poet's life, of witty cultivation and an amoral pose; but still more it was a reminder of how far he aimed to travel from the limitations (and language) of Eastwood, and of how cultivated (in a non-Eastwood sense) he was.

His mimicry of all kinds of dialect and accent, however, was brilliant. Alice Hall recalled how, like his father, he was particularly adept at parodying the superior and the refined: 'it was our delight to get him to impersonate anyone we knew. The local clergymen were the ones we liked best, or the different folks that attended the Christian Endeavour meeting including his sisters and some of their friends'.[108] Late in life, he celebrated two of his family's languages in his poem 'Red-Herring'. But while 'My father was a working man/and a collier was he', and 'My mother was a superior soul/a superior soul was she', the children belonged to both and to neither:

> We children were the in-betweens
> little non-descripts were we,
> indoors we called each other *you*,
> outside, it was *tha* and *thee*.[109]

And yet even that is not an absolute truth. It all depended upon whom the children were outside with, when they spoke. It is striking that the young Paul Morel hardly ever speaks in dialect, inside or outside his home; and with the Chambers family, for example, with whom they were 'outside' a good deal, the Lawrence children did not speak dialect. May Chambers recalled, as an exception, how 'We sometimes talked in the dialect. Bert was very good and gave us samples new to us. "Hoad the faece, woman!" his father had said to his mother.'[110] But Lawrence's own command of the dialect was masterly; it was not only outdoors, as a child, that he spoke it. Willie Hopkin remembered his 'intimate knowledge' of it:

Sometimes when at my house he and I would speak it for a time, much to the bewilderment of any visitor from elsewhere. These words – 'How are you getting on? I hear you have been ill. I do hope it was nothing serious.' Spoken in the dialect would be – 'How are ter gerring on surrey? I hear as thou's bin badly. I dow hope its nowt serious.'[111]

Lawrence's dialect speech was not only mimicry. It was one of his actual voices; it was an Eastwood voice (he always kept his Midlands accent) – but it was not his mother's voice. It was both his own, and not his own; part of himself, for which he retained a deep nostalgia, but also a voice which he came to feel he had betrayed. His very choice and mixture of voices was a sign of the 'queer jumble of the old England and the new' where he came into consciousness.[112]

For, above all, Lawrence's dialect voice was one he could choose to use: could use to give 'samples' to the Chambers family, or to add local colour to a letter to a cultivated friend (i. 58), or to bewilder visitors with – or to write in. It was by no means simply the voice of one who was 'bone of their bone'. As a writer he consciously and carefully used the dialect voice. When a correspondent wrote to him in 1915 to suggest how his transcription of the dialect in the *Prussian Officer* collection of stories could be improved – 'dosta', for example, to replace Lawrence's 'does ter' – Lawrence revealed how deliberately constructed his written dialect was:

The difficulty is, that one reads with the eye, as well as with the ear. Consequently 'dosta' is read as one word, and the mind mechanically halts, saying 'What strange word is this?' And to pull up the mind like that is fatal. Have you ever tried reading dialect – those Yorkshire stories one used to see, or even William Barnes' poetry? It is difficult, even painful ... Unless the effect of sound is conveyed simultaneously with eye-picture, there is discrepancy and awkwardness ... I would gladly use 'dosta' if I thought it would be instinctively understood, would not cost an effort.[113]

That carefully constructed written dialect drew on a knowledge of, an intimacy with, the language of his father's world and his father's friends; it is a perfect example of his extraordinary intimacy with the place in which he grew up, and yet of his simultaneous and controlling detachment from it.

VI Chapel

Yet another of *Sons and Lovers*'s divergences from the realities of the Lawrence family's life in Eastwood is that it hardly mentions the part played by religion or chapel in the Morel family. Mrs Morel is visited by a Congregational minister, and William and his London girlfriend Gipsy go to chapel; but Paul is 21 before it is mentioned that 'the same people had sat in the same places ever since he was a boy'. The novel concentrates upon the life of the Morel children at home; but also suggests that religion has not been particularly important in Paul's life. And no sooner does the novel describe him going to chapel than it also describes him 'beginning to question the orthodox creed'.[114]

But chapel had been a formative experience in Lawrence's childhood. The Lawrences were traditionally Church of England; Arthur Lawrence had sung in Brinsley church choir as a young man, and his children were all christened in the Church of England (Bert Lawrence in Eastwood parish church). Yet Arthur Lawrence was not a church-goer: and only rarely went to chapel. Religion had been far more important in Lydia Lawrence's family.

Lydia, however, must have broken away from her family's Wesleyanism, for she attended the Congregational chapel during her years in Eastwood. We do not know what turned her away from her family's denomination; it may well have been the effect of the chapels and ministers she knew before she got to Eastwood: it may have been the particular nature of the Congregational chapel in Eastwood which attracted her.[115]

Lawrence described, late in life, his relief that he had been brought up a nonconformist: and his pleasure that, within nonconformity, Congregationalism had been the religion of his childhood. The Wesleyan Methodists in Eastwood, whose chapel was in the New Buildings, though of course 'Low-church', were – with their Anglican antecedents – traditionally Tory rather than Liberal. On the other hand, Lawrence described the Eastwood

Primitive Methodists as 'always having "revivals" and being "saved," and I always had a horror of being saved'.[116] What he meant was that the Primitive Methodists – who had split from the Wesleyan Methodists in 1810 precisely over that fondness for 'revivals' – tended to be socially radical and decidedly working-class: the emerging Labour party drew heavily from them. In Eastwood they were 'the uneducated people', with their pleasure in the denunciation of kings and rulers in the book of Revelation, and their Tuesday night services 'in the great barn-like Pentecost chapel' just along the road from the Victoria Street house. In the Church of England, however, Lawrence noted, 'one would hardly have escaped those snobbish hierarchies of class, which spoil so much for a child';[117] the established Church in Eastwood was inevitably linked with the owning classes, with the Tory party and with the local gentry.

But the Congregationalists in Eastwood, as elsewhere, tended to represent reforming liberalism (with both a small and large 'l'); and though drawing their membership from the working class, they constituted something of an aristocracy of miners and their families. Their Gothic-revival chapel itself, in Nottingham Road, was popularly known as 'Butty's Lump'. 'The promoters of the scheme for building the new chapel were influential at the colliery'; it was rumoured that 'the surest means of securing a good "stall" in the pit was to make a handsome donation to the building fund'.[118] 'Perhaps', added Jessie Chambers ironically, 'that explains why our chapel had its air of elegance'. But Eastwood's Congregational chapel was more than elegant: it had status, with its spire, its fine stone cladding and its architect's design. It was not just the rough work of a local builder. The 'barn-like' Primitive Methodist chapel in the Squares, by contrast, was designed by a local builder, F. W. Stubbs; and though only built 1896–7, had to be partly rebuilt in the 1920s because it was near to collapse.

As well as a degree of superiority within the working class, compared with the other nonconformist churches in Eastwood, there had also traditionally been a strong intellectual tradition in Congregationalism – from which the young Lawrence continued to profit. That, too, may have attracted Lydia Lawrence to Congregationalism.[119] But she was not – according to Alice Hall – active in the chapel; the doctrine of self-improvement she found at the Women's Co-operative Guild at its Monday night meetings was rather more important to her. Nevertheless, chapel attendance was as natural to her as her respectability, and she had great respect for the Rev. Robert Reid, Minister from 1897. Her children all went to chapel regularly; their attendance was yet another of the ways in which they were encouraged to grow up sharing her values and ideals.[120]

But chapel attendance for the children not only meant services on

Sundays. There was Sunday school in the morning in the Albert Street schoolroom next to the chapel. The Sunday school teachers were from all walks of life, from the minister himself (the Rev. J. Loosemoore when Lawrence was young, the Rev. Robert Reid from the time he was 12), prominent shopkeepers like Henry Saxton and George Henry Cullen, local men like Mr Rimmington 'with his round white beard and his ferocity' – who always 'shulled' his peas on Saturday night to keep the sabbath holy – down to the local blacksmith, who was Lawrence's own teacher and who seems to have been brought in to deal with collier children who proved too much for the other teachers.[121] In *The Lost Girl*, Lawrence recreated his memories of the blacksmith:

His influence was more than effectual. It consisted in gripping any recalcitrant boy just above the knee, and jesting with him in a jocular manner, in the dialect. The blacksmith's hand was all a blacksmith's hand need be, and his dialect was as broad as could be wished. Between the grip and the homely idiom no boy could endure without squealing.[122]

Morning Sunday school would be followed by a service in the chapel itself; and there would be another Sunday school class in the afternoon: 'boys on one side, girls on the other, in small groups, each class with its teacher'.[123] Once a month, in place of the afternoon class there would be recitals of pieces (poems and texts) learned for the occasion, and both May and Jessie Chambers remembered the 11-year-old Lawrence forgetting his poem and provoking his sister Emily to hysterical giggles. With 'a tortured face'. he turned to the Sunday school superintendent and got permission to consult the text, which he then recited correctly, and 'got down from the platform with a white face': May Chambers did not 'remember seeing him on the platform ever again.' However ill Lawrence was as a child, at times he managed a regular attendance at Sunday school; in February 1894, at the age of $8\frac{1}{2}$, he got the prize of a book for it.[124]

The Congregational child grew up belonging to an institution which dominated not only Sunday but life during the rest of the week. In the words of Jessie Chambers, 'The chapel at Eastwood became the centre of our social life.'[125] The chapel provided magic lantern shows and penny readings for the smaller children; lectures and talks on subjects such as temperance were presented to them at a very early age. Under the auspices of the various chapels, the Band of Hope (a non-denominational Christian temperance association) appealed to children to renounce alcohol: Lydia Lawrence ensured that her children all signed up. The process of religious education continued at school, with services and religious instruction: and the schools would at times work together with the chapels in sponsoring

Band of Hope talks and demonstrations. We know from Ernest Lawrence what a 'big thing' the latter had been to him in his early teens, and that was probably true of his brothers and sisters as well.[126]

The main effect of these years of attendance and instruction, as Lawrence described them in 1928, was a kind of unconscious submersion in the language and imagery of the Bible and of the hymns which he sang. When he was a child, naturally enough, dogma and doctrine did not go very deep; but as an adult he continued to experience the 'sense of wonder':

I am eternally grateful for the wonder with which it filled my childhood.

> Sun of my soul, thou Saviour dear,
> It is not night if Thou be near—

That was the last hymn at the board-school. It did not mean to me any Christian dogma or any salvation. Just the words, "Sun of my soul, thou Saviour dear," penetrated me with wonder and the mystery of twilight. At another time the last hymn was:

> Fair waved the golden corn
> In Canaan's pleasant land—

And again I loved "Canaan's pleasant land." The wonder of "Canaan," which could never be localized.[127]

He never forgot the hymns: one even got into *The Plumed Serpent* in 1926, and he sang them all his life. One friend recalled his performance of the Ira Sankey hymn 'Oh to be Nothing, Nothing', while another discovered how Lawrence knew 'all the Moody and Sankey revival songs, the Salvation Army tunes, every word of all the verses. One followed another in growing dramatic effect, until the climax was reached in *Throw out the life-line*. He stood up and threw out an imaginary lasso to the drowning souls, hauling them in strenuously.'[128]

And yet the influence and power of chapel went far beyond a memory stocked with hymns and a sense of wonder. When he came to write his play *David* in 1925 he could still reproduce the language and cadences of the Authorised Version at will: his consciousness was truly soaked in the Bible. Attitudes associated with chapel also played a considerable part in the Lawrence children's upbringing; and the habits of mind inculcated by Congregationalism went very deep indeed. Lawrence was brought up to believe that his father was not only a bad father and a bad husband, but a wicked man. He drank and was not 'a chapel man': he was therefore an outsider in an otherwise decent family. Chapel and its enclosing standards provided yet another of the ways in which Lydia Lawrence was able to keep her children alienated from their father. Religious teaching also ruled the consciousness of the growing child:

From earliest years right into manhood, like any other nonconformist child I had the Bible poured every day into my helpless consciousness . . . but also it was day in, day out, year in, year out expounded, dogmatically, and always morally expounded, whether it was in day-school or Sunday School, at home or in Band of Hope or Christian Endeavour.[129]

The Congregationalists may have had an intellectual tradition, but it hardly affected the children who went to Sunday school, the Band of Hope and the religious association Christian Endeavour. Bible-based teaching insisted on conscious and constant choice of the Christian faith, on the Bible's supremacy in all matters of faith, above all on the Christian child being eternally morally vigilant: and Lawrence would later affirm how, as a result, all the processes of his emotion and thought had been affected.[130]

His growing up to be a man and a writer who insisted that his attitudes were primarily religious shows his successful resistance to his early training as much as its lasting influence. His achievement was neither to become trapped within the codes and restrictions of the faith preached to him as a child, nor simply to abandon religion, along with any conception of man as a religious being, when he broke with chapel Christianity around the age of 22. He came to believe in the absolute primacy, in human life, of processes of feeling and consciousness which were physical and non-rational: he became convinced that the most important perceptions need have little to do with ideas or thought. And although such conclusions were (in one sense) absolutely alien to the formal and moral teachings of the Congregational chapel, they were all the same developments, in a very twentieth-century mind and sensibility, of his early religious experience. The chapel had always stressed revelation and insight rather than authority, the individual rather than the group, and the absolute rightness of the individual's revelation of truth. Power and glory were more significant than thoughtful responsibility, and more could be expected from violent, revelatory change than from progressive alteration. The chapel religion which really soaked into the young Lawrence, and altered the colour of his mind, had little to do with the moral disciplines which were also preached; he was affected incalculably by the emotional patterns of the religion in which he grew up.

68

VII Parents Recreated

Lawrence often drew upon the mining community in his fiction between 1909 and 1912, but his accounts are rather selective. In the first place, it is families and family life upon which he almost exclusively concentrates: not upon the work of the men, nor (apart from in the sketch 'Strike-Pay') upon their amusements, nor upon the education of children outside the home nor upon religious life outside the family circle. In the second place, within the families upon which he chooses to concentrate, the children tend to be either very small, as in 'The Miner at Home', 'Odour of Chrysanthemums', *The Widowing of Mrs. Holroyd* and the first part of 'Paul Morel' – in all of which the father is frequently absent, and the mother bearing up against heavy odds; or they are adolescent, as in the second half of 'Paul Morel' and in *A Collier's Friday Night*. This time, the children are seen rebelling against the father and supporting the mother. These works show, in effect, a resolution of the younger children's situation.* What is particularly interesting, of course, is the absence of other situations: for example, of families which are not divided: or of a miner's children being like, and sympathetic to, their father; or of wives who are not discontented outsiders; or, in the adolescent families, of children who follow their father's career.

When Lawrence wrote about parents in his early fiction too, he frequently (and naturally) divided them into the oppositions he had observed in his own immediate family. In addition to the Morel parents in *Sons and Lovers*, he recreated aspects of the lives of his uncle James and aunt Polly in 'Odour of Chrysanthemums' and in *The Widowing of Mrs. Holroyd*. In both cases, however, the reality is significantly altered. Aunt Polly was a local labourer's daughter, while Elizabeth Bates and Mrs Holroyd, like Mrs Morel, are educated women who not only do not belong to the locality but are literally strangers to it. And all three fictional creations exercise a restraining and restrictive influence upon their children. There is also a marriage foreshadowed in 'Daughters of the Vicar' between the clergyman's daughter Louisa – brought up apart from the life of the community – and the man born into it, and living in the middle of it, Alfred Durant; and at the end of the first version of the story, which Lawrence wrote in 1911, the offspring of such parents are also foreshadowed:

* There are no children in 'Two Marriages', the early version of 'Daughters of the Vicar': Alfred is grown-up, and he and Louisa only look forward to having children at the very end of the story. Nor are there children in 'Strike-Pay' or 'A Sick Collier'. In 'The Christening', the father is old, the mother dead, the daughters in their twenties and the adolescent miner son rebelling against his father; in 'Her Turn', the children are again grown-up but play no part in the tale.

Her children would be born into a real home, whose very stuff would have in it some of their father's spirit—and their mother's—and of their forefathers' and fore-mothers'. It would be nearly like a living thing, of their own blood. It was indeed a home. She dreamed of the boy, like Alfred, who would have the home when she left it. He would be like Alfred, but she would educate him.

She had several children, and was not disappointed.[131]

That ending smacks of fantasy; it is a slightly despairing attempt to bring together incompatible things, though the date – 1911 – is also perhaps significant; it was the year when, freed from the daily influence of his mother, Lawrence was trying to write a new kind of fiction about a miner's family. Yet the very fact that the son of Alfred and Louisa will be educated – and, even more strikingly, that 'she would educate him', not even that 'she would have him educated' – still suggests the kind of difference, and sometimes alienation, in their children which the educated mothers are responsible for creating.

In 'Odour of Chrysanthemums', as Lawrence first revised it in 1910, it is clear how Elizabeth Bates attempts to create in her children something of her own sense of difference, of apartness from the place and its way of life. Her speech is stressed by Lawrence as an inevitable sign of that difference. Mrs Bates does not speak dialect, as her son John naturally does; she is articulate, and he almost non-verbal, and her particular stress on his language is an attempt to *educate* him; to make him aware of himself as she is aware of him, and of herself. It is a struggle; John has already acquired the speech habits of his father and of the locality. He asks her 'Can I 'ave summat t'eat?' and that is not only a request for his tea; it is his way of standing up against her, and of unconsciously stressing his loyalty to place and to father. And that is something she wants to nip in the bud: '"Summat t'eat" – who says that! You can have "something to eat" when you have your tea.' The boy is also carving a piece of wood, and she cautions him:

'Don't make a litter,' she said.

'They on'y go on th' steerfoot mat,' he replied.

'Very well,' said his mother, repeating his words to correct their vulgar pronunci-ation, 'see they do only go on the stairfoot mat, and then shake it when you've done.'

She turned away. Her son was very much like herself, yet something in him always pained her, and roused her opposition.[132]

What rouses her opposition is that her son has already acquired his father's manners and dialect; and that reminds her of her own isolation in such a community. Accordingly, she wants to educate him into another (less 'vulgar') pronunciation, and into non-masculine habits like shaking out the stairfoot mat when he has made it dirty. A little earlier, he has put his arms on a table laid with a cloth; she immediately shouts '"Take your arms off the table!"'[133] Her husband's arms on the table, when he comes in from pit, will dirty her table-cloth, and that much she has to accept; but the boy need not be so like his father as to rest *his* arms on the cloth.

We can compare the situation of the father's return home in *A Collier's Friday Night*, when he 'lays his grimed arms wearily along the table', and his wife remarks 'Here, that's a clean cloth'. The stage direction notes 'she does not speak unkindly': it is something she is prepared for: 'The mother takes a newspaper and spreads it over the cloth for him.'[134] But Mrs Bates, in the story, is less pragmatic: she is sharply critical of this local masculine habit. She wishes, in fact, to detach her son from the community and its habits, as she herself is detached and dissociated; she wants to reclaim a child 'very much like herself'. The opening of the story has shown the crude ugliness of the environment around her cottage, near the pit-head; but when her son tears off 'the ragged pink locks of the pale chrysanthemums' and drops the petals 'in handfuls along the path', she responds 'Don't do that—it *does* look nasty . . .'[135] How can a woman who feels so acutely the ugliness of fallen flower petals continue to live in such a place? Her solution is to live her life in a spirit of opposition to it, and to everything it stands for; and (so far as she can) to make her children like herself: different, opposed, alien.

It is upon such a struggle that Lawrence's presentation of mining family parents and their young children focuses. He recognised it as his mother's struggle, in particular; but things often taken to be personal traits of Lydia Lawrence – a desire to see her children educated and getting on in the world rather than staying in Eastwood or following their father down the pit – were actually the goals of thousands of working-class women of the period, and precisely those articulated and fostered by the Women's Co-operative Guild.

But a woman's attempt to repossess her children would, of course, in its turn, have aroused the opposition and sometimes the active hostility of the male members of the community. That is made extraordinarily vivid in *Sons and Lovers*, when Mr Morel cuts his son William's hair. The novel shows how Mrs Morel 'was proud of him, he was so pretty. She was not well off now, but her sisters kept the boy in clothes. Then, with his little white hat curled with an ostrich feather, and his white coat, he was a joy to her, the twining wisps of hair clustering round his head.'[136] There is not much joy in Mrs Morel's life, but she finds it in her son; and the obvious comparison is with that photograph of the young D. H. Lawrence in his pram, with his white hat and his lace collar. Mrs Morel however, lying in bed half asleep one Sunday morning, hears the chatter of father and son:

When she came downstairs, a great fire glowed in the grate, the room was hot, the breakfast was roughly laid. And seated in his armchair, against the chimney piece, sat Morel, rather timid: and standing between his legs, the child,—cropped like a sheep, with such an odd round poll—looking wondering at her: and on a newspaper spread out upon the hearth rug, a myriad of crescent-shaped curls, like the petals of a marigold scattered in the reddening firelight.

Mrs Morel stood still. It was her first baby. She went very white, and was unable to speak.[137]

Her immediate reaction is extremely violent: 'I could kill you, I could!' She also goes towards Morel with her hands raised, as if about to hit him. She then strokes and fondles the child, faltering 'Oh—my boy'; and finally snatches him up, burying her face in his shoulder and crying, although Lawrence tells us that she is 'one of those women who cannot cry: whom it hurts as it hurts a man'.[138]

Why has Morel cut the child's hair? He gives his own reason: 'Yer non want ter make a wench on 'im'. The child is unmasculine, his hair is too long for a boy; in Bestwood, a boy must *be* a boy. But he is specifically, too, Mrs Morel's 'pretty'; in his white clothes, with an ostrich feather in his hat, he is an alien in a colliery village: he is, after all, dressed in clothes provided by Mrs Morel's better-off sisters. She is making him a proof of another life, outside; and he becomes, too, a compensation for her own unhappiness and alienation. Morel's act of cutting his hair is not only a statement about what a man's son should be like, and about what *his* son should be like; it is an act of repossession, as the 'odd round poll' suggests the working man with hair cut short because of his job. Mr Morel has attempted to stop the child being Mrs Morel's; and standing between his father's knees, with his hair cut short, William has become his father's son.[139]

Mrs Morel's violence and her desire to recapture the child are her possessive reaction to Morel's possessiveness; her tears are those of a woman who has had her child taken from her, and who cannot be certain that she will recover him, to live for her in the future. The episode creates in miniature the conflict over the children which much of the early part of the novel will be about, and which Lawrence had himself learned at home in Eastwood; the needs of parents to father and mother 'their' children and to foster 'their' futures.

VIII Conflict and Choice

Growing up in the kind of household in which he did, the conflict of possessiveness was an everyday reality for Lawrence. Even something as ordinary as the children's pets brought it out. Ada remembered how her brother 'loved all animals'; some time before he was 12, a schoolfriend, Arthur ('Pussy') Templeman, gave him two tame white rats which 'loved to run all over us, among my long hair and under Bert's waistcoat – down his sleeves and into his pockets to sleep'.[140] But at different times the children also had rabbits, a gold fish, a puppy they called Rex, a wild rabbit they called Adolf and 'other little wild animals . . . which had sulked and refused to live, and brought storms of tears and trouble in our house of lunatics'. In 1919 Lawrence could still write with extraordinary power about the children's love for Rex: in particular their 'mute despair' when their uncle (whose dog he was) arrived to take Rex away: 'After which, black tears, and a little wound which is still alive in our hearts.'[141] As so often happens, their pets focused the children's emotional distresses and emphasised the family's divisions. They brought out the children's desire for love, and their fear of losing it. Ada remembered how, when Rex first arrived in their house, 'We begged to be allowed to take him to bed for the first night. Mother wouldn't hear of it . . .' But her brother Bert could not bear the puppy's anguished howling: 'he crept downstairs and quietly brought the wretched little fellow to bed, where he cuddled close to him and slept soundly until morning, when we hurried down and put him back on the sofa before mother was up'. In the 1911 version of his novel 'Paul Morel', Lawrence created an autobiographical alter ego whose pets 'were more anxiety to him, as his mother said, than a family of children was to most men'.[142] The family pets also emphasised the nagging but caring worries of Lydia Lawrence while bringing out Arthur Lawrence's humour, affection and carelessness. Mrs Lawrence, unemotional and undemonstrative, with her well-run and well-kept house – and as the one who bore the brunt of her children's inevitable distress over the deaths of pets – 'did not care for close contact with animals. She was too fastidious.'[143] But their father, though laughing at his children's softness and sentimentality, was also their ally. He brought them their wild animals, took Rex out on Sunday mornings – 'My mother would not walk a yard with him' – and ended up tramping 'many miles' looking for the puppy when it got lost. Lydia Lawrence not only 'detested animals about the house' (Lawrence remembered her disgust when Rex left dead rats on the hearthrug) but 'could not bear the mix-up of human with animal life'.[144] Her tone towards the destructive Rex – 'I'll teach you, my Jockey! Do you think I'm going to spend my life darning after your destructive little teeth! I'll show you if I will.' – contrasts beautifully with Lawrence's memory of his father's talking to the puppy in 'a funny, high, sing-song falsetto which he seemed to produce at the top of his head': ''s a pretty little dog! 's a pretty little doggy! – ay! – yes! – he is, yes! – Wag thy strunt, then! Wag thy strunt, Raxie! – Ha-ha! – Nay, tha munna –' In 1919, when he wrote that account, Lawrence could present his father's language of the affections sympathetically; but we can guess how it originally must have grated on him, just as it grated on his mother. He was not a child who talked like that. We might compare Connie Chatterley's reaction to Parkin's caressive dialect in the second version of *Lady Chatterley's Lover*: 'something in her spirit, and in her will, stiffened with resistance, from the intimacy': his dialect makes her feel 'so curiously *caught*, netted'.[145]

In their quarrels, his parents both claimed 'their' children. It was precisely this kind of parental conflict (a conflict of cultures, hopes and aims) which Lawrence knew in his bones, and expressed so forcefully in his life's writing. But in his early writing Lawrence is continually both resolving and then reopening the problem. It is like a wound; he cannot leave it alone; he continually presents and re-presents characters who insist upon and who exude coolness, separateness and isolation – while he confronts them with characters radiating warmth, physical immediacy and easy intimacy with their locality. And these are never simply his own parents: they are versions of himself, too, and reflections of the community he knew so intimately as a child and adult. He not only grew up as an observant and detached aspirant to middle-class life; he grew up to be the kind of social being who was permanently nostalgic for fellowship, warmth and community. Back in the Midlands in 1915, he described 'These men, whom I love so much – and the life has such a power over me' (ii. 489).[146] And yet he had left them behind, irrevocably. The role of 'writer' was perhaps the adult's way of continuing to enact both the possibilities which had been so powerfully engendered and cultivated in him; but the child had been driven simply to choose between his parents.

CHAPTER THREE

◆

1892–1901

LAUNCHING INTO LIFE

I Beauvale Board School

D. H. Lawrence started school on 20 May 1889, at the age of 3 years and 8 months; rather early to go to the Infants' section of Beauvale Board School, a mile's walk from the family home in the Breach (the journey would be made four times a day, since the pupils went home for the lunch break).[1] Ernest was, however, also going to Beauvale school, and doubtless took his younger brother with him.

The experiment was not, however, a success. Lawrence was withdrawn on 20 October 1889 and did not return to school until September 1892, when he was 7, and started attending the Boys' section at Beauvale. Ada started at the Infants that year, and her brother took her by the hand to school.[2] In 1928, Lawrence wrote briefly about his first day at school – though we do not know which of his two school starts he was referring to: 'I shall never forget the anguish with which I wept the first day. I was captured. I was roped in. The other boys felt the same. They hated school because they felt captives there. They hated the masters because they felt them as jailers.'[3] But his anguish as a child may not really have been a result of being 'captured', as he put it in 1928, so much as a reaction to a raw new experience. His first prolonged absence from school, and what we know of his propensity for extreme reaction to first contact with anything new,* strongly suggest the latter. The 1928 memoir is primarily concerned with establishing its author's working-class origins, and with making him just one of the 'other boys': and to that extent is unreliable.†

There are, of course, other possible explanations for the three-year gap. The young Lawrence had health problems; 'always had a runny nose, now I

---

* See a 1909 letter written after his return to Croydon from Eastwood:
    I think it is my liver which is upset by nervous excitement. I get much better of this absurdity, but still it comes, and I expect it. Very rarely have I been able to enjoy the first weeks of anything, even a holiday, because I am always a bit sick as the result of my change. So I've had a little bout now . . . Lots of folk are like it – to a more or less degree. I always remember poor Charlotte Brontë, who was much worse than I. That's enough of my homesickness. (i. 106)
† See Appendix IV.

never remember him without a runny nose, never'. He may have had pneumonia: a remark he made in 1913 suggested a serious childhood illness (ii. 72). Illness certainly kept him at home some of the time. He would not, for example, get into the list of pupils 'who had made the most attendances' at Beauvale in February 1897.[4] But we can also link the age of this first unfortunate experiment in schooling with the age at which Paul Morel, in *Sons and Lovers*, is found by his mother crying for no apparent reason: 'three or four'. The young Lawrence cried in just the same way: he himself recalled 'going into a corner to cry, as I used to do as a child' (ii. 393), and his sister Ada remembered how 'Sometimes, for no apparent reason, he would burst into tears and irritate mother, who would say "Bless the child – whatever is he crying for now?" Bert invariably sobbed, "I don't know," and continued to cry.'[5] In 1913, his wife Frieda – worried about his fits of depression, but reassured by Ada that 'he always had those humps' – remarked 'I think I'll put him on a little stool in the garden like his mother, "now cry there, misery" ' (i. 532, 531). In *Sons and Lovers*, Mrs Morel does exactly that with Paul; his crying makes her 'feel beside herself', and having tried to 'reason him out of it, or to amuse him, without effect', she carries him into the back yard, puts him in his chair and says:

"Now cry there, Misery!"
And then a butterfly on the rhubarb leaves perhaps caught his eye, or at last he cried himself to sleep. These fits were not often, but they caused a shadow in Mrs Morel's heart, and her treatment of Paul was different from that of the other children.

Such crying seems to be of the kind which D. W. Winnicott has called 'sad crying':

something which means that your infant has ... started to take responsibility for environment. Instead of just reacting to circumstances he has come to feel responsible for the circumstances. The trouble is that he starts off feeling *totally* responsible for what happens to him and for the external factors in his life. Only gradually does he sort out what he *is* responsible for from all that he *feels* responsible for.[6]

We have no way of knowing what it was Lawrence might have been feeling responsible for: though an informed guess would pinpoint his mother's gloominess and anger, and the tensions of the family group. But what happened to him at school would certainly not have helped. There were four staff members (one teacher and three pupil-teachers), and 220 children on the books; classes of over 50 were common. The frail Lawrence would have been lost in a crowd of children; and if they noticed him, then they despised him 'because he couldn't take part in their games'.[7] The depressions he suffered were also the reverse side of the anger he felt for the other children, for his mother who had sent him and with himself. If he stayed away from school, however, he could remain where he thought he wanted to be – at home. His prolonged absence from school meant that, even more than most working-class children, he grew up in the company of women. While other boys were at school together, Lawrence was at home for an extra three years with his mother, his younger sister Ada and the women neighbours: hearing women's talk and bearing responsibility.

When finally he went back to the Boys' section of Beauvale Board School, he was desperately unhappy. Mabel Thurlby remembered him

standing at the stile which was quite near my home, crying . . . I said 'what are you crying for?' 'I don't want to go to school.' I said, 'come on.' I dragged him along: I pushed him into the boy's part, you know, where they had to go in the Board School; and at lunchtime, when we came out, he was waiting for me. So I said, 'what are you waiting for?' He said, 'to go home . . .' I don't think there was a more unhappy child went into that Board school than Lawrence.[8]

When Paul Morel goes to school in the 1911 'Paul Morel', too, 'the trouble of his life began': he hates it because of his 'horror of being thrust into public'. And, not surprisingly, at school Lawrence 'displayed no remarkable ability'. A description of how he looked at school when he was 8 is given by his friend George Neville: 'He was a thin, pale, weakly lad always scrupulously clean, neat and tidy, with no energy for our oft-times over-robust games, and no apparent inclination to attempt to join us. A book and a quiet corner were always his delight and he would much more often be found with girl companions than with boys.'[9] 'Paul Morel' also describes how the 8-year-old Paul dares not even run across 'the Squares' for fear of attracting attention: 'The "Squares" urchins, some of whom knew him by name, jeered him, because, they said, he was "proud".' On another occasion, Paul is set on by a gang of boys: he does not fight back, but simply radiates hatred.[10]

This quiet, studious, rather frail and thoroughly self-conscious boy had yet another obstacle in front of him at Beauvale. Ada remembered how he always appeared 'under the shadow of Ernest, who was set up by the headmaster [William Whitehead] as a model for the other children. He told Bert that he would never be fit to tie his brother's boot-laces . . .' Memories of Ernest, seven years older, dogged him for years: 'the head master had the unpleasant habit of drawing unfavourable comparisons between him and his brother'. Another teacher commented later that Lawrence struck him 'as being rather effeminate, compared with his brother. He was fortunate in being a member of a very clever class'. It was just the sort of comparison a nervous, bullied and unhappy child could do without: it 'depressed and discouraged' him.[11]

The difference, however, could hardly have been more extreme. Ernest had combined athletic prowess with excellent academic and (it turned out) commercial ability. Lawrence, however, 'never played with boys, never joined in their games, and at playtime always shunned other boys'; never ran, or raced, or jumped or threw; was never a local celebrity and shining example like Ernest. Lawrence,

in his elementary school days . . . did not get on with other boys. They despised him because he couldn't take part in their games. I well remember the day when I was passing the [Beauvale] school as the scholars were leaving for dinner. He was walking between two girls, and a number of Breach Boys walked behind him monotonously chanting 'Dicky Dicky Denches plays with the Wenches.' That charge branded any boy as effeminate – the local term is 'Mardarse.' Bert's chin was in the air as though he cared no jot but his eyes were full of anger and mortification . . .

I said to his tormentors 'Why don't you leave him alone,' to which one replied, 'Well, he's allus wi' wenches and he never plees wi' us.'[12]

The two girls Lawrence walked between were probably Mabel Thurlby and Gertrude Cooper: the former remembered how they helped protect him against his tormentors. Eastwood was not a good place to be a boy known as 'Mardarse', or 'Mardy Lawrence', or simply 'Mardy' (the word means 'soft'): to be in appearance a quiet, pale rather studious boy whose 'weakness and unpopularity with boys . . . drove him into the arms of girls'.[13] But even the girls did not necessarily find him easy to get on with. One of them, at the age of 90, recalled him: 'Shy boy he was. Very shy. Well set up, mind. Nice looking. But, ooh, he kept himself to himself. You couldn't really get to know him . . . he never used to play with the rest of us, not from what I can remember'. May Chambers's first memory of Lawrence, from around 1893, is not of a boy playing with girls but of a boy, surrounded by children younger than himself, watching the girls at play.[14] Mortified at school, and cut off from his beloved home, it is not surprising that he was miserable. School, too, confirmed how much he was his mother's son, not his father's.

His marked sensitivity, upon which all of his contemporaries commented, must have been scarred continually at Beauvale by boys and girls alike, as well as by the notorious toughness of the teachers: a contemporary of Lawrence's in the Boys' section, J. C. P. Taylor, recalled 'the softening up process at the hands of Nocker [Bradley] during transit through Standard IV'. One of the very few accounts we have of Lawrence's being physically aggressive, also from Taylor, suggests his distance (literally at arm's length) from his contemporaries: 'As a youngster he could become suddenly contumacious and refractory. In our day we grew to anticipate and forestall that vicious stab in the left breast with two stiff fingers, which could be very painful. It was usually accompanied by that fiendish whinny by which he expressed his glee'.[15] But, in response to his feeling of difference, and to the attacks made on him at school, at quite an early age 'he began hittin' back wi' his tongue an' he could get at us wheer it hurt'. His brother George also recalled that 'very sharp tongue': 'yes, it was as our old dad used to say: "to take the skin off your back" – and he could . . . he was sharp as a needle was our young Bert, you know. He was. He was'. His mother employed the same weapon. George Neville recalled 'that sharp little tongue of hers': and Lawrence remembered his father shouting at her 'I'll make you tremble at the sound of my footstep!': at which his mother, although furious, 'only gave one of her peculiar amused little laughs and replied: Which boots will you wear?'[16] It is significant that Lawrence's verbal skills both dealt with his tormentors and distinguished him from them. Language itself was a divide, a separator, for the boy who already felt himself to be an outsider.

It must be said, however, that his sister Ada – who knew him at home – gives a very different account of him as a boy growing up. As a brother he was intensely lively and creative:

much of our early life was very happy, and many days are fixed in my memory, days of such care-free joy with Bert that I know I can never experience again. It seemed inevitable that Bert should spend his life creating things. He was never content to copy others, and perhaps found more pleasure in inventing games that in playing them . . . he had a genius for inventing games, especially indoors.[17]

Others who experienced that creativity found it harder to cope with. Mabel Thurlby remembered how 'One day he looked across the field and said, " 'Everywhere is blue and gold.' Now you say a line." Of course I could not.' When she found, however, that he 'talked to the flowers', she told him, 'You *are* potty.' Two schoolfriends found him disturbing, even 'uncanny', in recollection: 'Do you remember when he used to take us on the meadows, and in the field, and put us through our paces performing his little plays? Bert would say to us, "You are a bird, you are a rabbit, you are a flower, you are a horse, you are a cow . . ." ' We find him, around the age of 19, insisting to a group of friends on an outing 'Now it's your turn, you've got to compose a little poem'. The creativity, however, was something most of his contemporaries never saw; if they saw it, they didn't like it, or found it 'uncanny'.[18]

II Scholarship Boy

Willie Hopkin remarked that, when Lawrence left Beauvale school in July 1898, at the age of 12, 'he was not distinguished for anything, unless it was his tidy habits and his love of study, and a marked difference from the rest'.

That was not quite true; he had begun to distinguish himself during the year before he left. In October 1897 he had passed a drawing examination 'with credit': and in July 1898 he was one of six boys in Standard VII to receive a certificate for 'excellence in Reporting a lecture on "Alcohol and the Human Body"' given in May – his first recorded (but no longer extant) piece of prose writing. A contemporary remembered him being 'outstanding at English, and his essays were frequently read to the class by the teacher'. Above all, he distinguished himself in sitting an exam on 23 July 1898 and winning one of the scholarships which the Nottinghamshire County Council had recently begun to offer, to the High School in Nottingham.[19] His brother Ernest, now in his twentieth year, was particularly keen that his younger brother 'should have, if possible, a better educational start in life than he himself was able to get', and helped him; while Whitehead, the Headmaster at Beauvale – always proud of Ernest's achievements (he copied Ernest's letter of thanks for a reference into the school log-book in July 1896, four years after Ernest had left) – learned to see talent in the younger brother too, and 'specially coached Lawrence for the examination'.[20]

Lawrence was obviously worth coaching. The boy who had given him the white rats, 'Pussy' Templeman, who was entered for the scholarship the same year, remembered the extra work being done 'generally in the same room' as the normal lessons, and being mainly in Geography, History and Grammar: 'This occurred on most days, for half of the day . . . Mr Whitehead was very stern; and at times severe, especially if we allowed our attention to be momentarily diverted while receiving instruction'. Templeman also remembered how 'neither my parents nor myself had any idea of what this was all about. My opinion was that the exam. result might reflect credit on the teachers – or otherwise'. But 'Mrs. Lawrence had a more correct idea. She seemed to me to be a well educated lady – she was certainly well educated in comparison to my own parents'.[21] Lydia Lawrence and Ernest knew what Bert might gain from a scholarship; not only release from Beauvale, but an advance to an excellent and predominantly middle-class school.

But winning a scholarship was not enough; whether the family could afford to let him take it up also mattered. George, Ernest and Emily had all gone out to work at 14. May Chambers remembered meeting Lydia Lawrence shortly after the news of her son's scholarship success had come through, and presents a striking picture of how she took the news.

I thought Mrs. Lawrence must have a headache. Her elbow was on the coping stone on the low wall, her head resting on her hand. In her black dress and soiled apron she impressed me as one in deep misery.

Bert came a few steps to meet me, and said in a tense voice:

'I've won that scholarship.'

My eyes and mouth opened in speechless admiration, and his face suddenly shone with joy, then clouded with anxiety.

'She's wondering if she'll let me go. I hope she does. I want to go.'

The problem, Mrs Lawrence explained, was simply the money:

But Bert broke in, 'There is some money found [i.e. provided], Mother.'

'Aye, my lad, there's a little found, but there's a lot wants finding. Why, look at his clothes and boots and dinners and train fare and books.'

'There's enough for books and train fare and a little more, I think, and I can wear my Sunday suit and boots,' he arranged eagerly.

'And they won't wear out? And what will you wear for Sunday? Tell me that. Oh, I don't know!'

And she turned up the entry with her weary step and her shoulders a little more bowed.

'Skimp, skimp, I'm tired of skimping.'[22]

Lydia Lawrence had lived through years of difficulty, when none of her children was earning; and then through years of disappointment. George, though respectably apprenticed, had run away into the army and had had to be bought out; he had then immediately got married, and had a baby – so brought no money into the Eastwood home. The family had not been able to afford to keep Ernest on at school in 1892, although his abilities had clearly fitted him for it. When he finally got his excellent job in London, however, in 1897, he very rarely sent money back home. Only Emily – bringing in perhaps 10/- a week by 1898, perhaps from a dressmaking job – was any help.[23]

After all this, there was now to be yet another drain on the family's resources, stretching forward for at least another three years. The careers of Arthur Templeman and Clem Taylor can, in contrast, give us an idea of what happened to intelligent boys in Eastwood who were perhaps fortunate enough not to win scholarships. Templeman was 'kept at school until I was 13 years of age when I got a job as an errand boy in Boots' Chemists branch shop with a weekly wage of 2/6d. After 6 months I went to work at the Colliery at 1/4d. per day'. He eventually became a Colliery Training officer. But even the colliery job which he took when he was 13 or 14 would have meant a yearly income of some £25, without travel or extra expenses. Taylor, too, got a job in a shop when he left school, at 'four and sixpence a week', but that too was only 'an abortive attempt to escape the pit'. The shop closed; and by the age of 14 he was working at High Park Colliery as a pony driver, at a similar wage to Templeman.[24] The scholarship which Lawrence won paid only £14 a year, of which the school took £9-0-0 in fees (the balance being sent to the scholar after his term reports had been examined). There were clothes and books and (worst of all) a season-ticket to buy. In the chapter 'Paul Launches into Life' in *Sons and Lovers*, Lawrence provides an acute description of a low-waged family buying a season-ticket. It has to be bought, as in the end it will save money: but where is the lump sum for buying it to come from?

> In the morning he filled in the form for his season ticket, and took it to the station. When he got back, his mother was just beginning to wash the floor. He sat crouched up on the sofa.
> "He says it'll be here by Saturday," he said.
> "And how much will it be?"
> "About one pound eleven," he said.
> She went on washing the floor in silence.
> "Is it a lot?" he asked.
> "It's no more than I thought," she answered.
> ... At last she said:
> "That William promised me, when he went to London, as he'd give me a pound a month. He has given me ten shillings—twice ..."[25]

Paul, 'crouched up on the sofa', making himself small, is doing the right thing while a floor is being washed. But he is also showing how guilty he feels. Although he doesn't know exactly how bad 'one pound eleven' is, he has a fair idea. His mother's silent floor washing tells him that; it also demands his sympathy. It is a demonstration of her own stoicism in the face of such challenges; it is because of her capacity to go on slaving, she is saying, that she can afford to buy him a season-ticket when she has to.

So although Paul might find the 'launching into life' exciting, he also learns how hard it is on *her*. She does not want to repress her sense of the unfairness of it all, even though it is what she wants. She makes her attack, however, upon her other son, the one who is earning. What is the point of all her work, her saving and skimping, if such a son and such thanklessness are the result? And thus it is that Paul is obliged to take on the responsibility of his own success.

III Nottingham High School

In the Lawrence family, Lydia's 'determination and self-sacrifice' carried the day; it was decided that 'somehow means should be found for Bert to attend the High School'.[26] Just after his thirteenth birthday, Lawrence began to travel each day from Eastwood to Nottingham. School started at 9.00, and went on till 4.15 (except on Wednesday and Saturday half holidays). It was an exhausting life: 2½ miles walk to the station at Kimberley meant 'starting from home shortly after seven o'clock in the morning, and returning just before seven at night, with always a pile of lessons to do later ... Even in those days, Lawrence had that little, troublesome, hacking cough that used to bring his left hand so sharply to his mouth ...' Later, Lawrence told his friend Jessie Chambers

it would probably have been better for him if he had never won the scholarship. It was a great strain, he said, when one was only eleven [13], to have the long walk to the station and a daily train to catch. There was always the anxiety lest one should miss it, and again he was obliged to be away from home for the midday meal.[27]

A contemporary at Nottingham remembered him as 'a slim boy, pale of face, with fair hair which was accentuated by his always wearing a black suit of clothes'. The dark suit was doubtless at first his 'good' Sunday suit, though later he had an 'Eton suit' with its traditional cut-away jacket: the paleness was strain as well as ill health. Lawrence was 'not only a poor boy, but he was a train boy. The school was half an hour's walk from the Railway station, and walking it was taken for granted ... his means would not allow even a ride on the new electric trams'. He missed both lunch at home, and the main meal eaten by his father (if on day-shifts) at around 4.30 in the afternoon. He sometimes went to his married brother George's house in Nottingham for his midday meal; but that meant half an hour's walk each way.[28] It is not surprising that he stayed pale.

In some ways, too, particularly after the closeness and familiarity (and violence and contempt) of the Beauvale school, the life of the scholarship boy at Nottingham High School was strangely quiet, unfamiliar and isolating. The effect can be imagined of this upon a boy who though 'pleasant and quick' also tended to be quiet and reserved. One of his two closest friends at the school, Ernest Woodford, confessed in 1957 that

I knew (and *know*) very little about him; nevertheless I was one of his closest associates. That requires some thinking over ... He attracted no attention. He was a normal scholarship boy – by which I mean he was much withdrawn into himself, no doubt through the sensitiveness which comes to a boy who is denied the things other boys have ...[29]

Woodford was the son of a schoolmaster from Granby in Nottinghamshire; Lawrence's other closest friend, Tommy Marsden, was the son of an extremely well-known and prosperous Nottingham grocer, who owned a chain of shops in the area. Woodford found his friendship with Lawrence, too, 'almost confined to lesson time and play time'. The scholarship boy could not afford games ('the parents of such were not affluent enough to provide sports outfits'), or take part in other out-of-school activities. There was always the train to catch, 'and the homework time lessening'.[30]

83

Relatively few other children from working-class families in Eastwood pursued the same course. Templeman failed the exam, and Taylor never even took it; George Neville, one year behind Lawrence at Beauvale school, was successful in the 1899 exam. During the eighteen years between 1882 and 1899, however, only three miners' sons ever attended Nottingham High School – Lawrence was the second and Neville the third – although the sons of colliery clerks, cashiers and managers were numerous. The other boys who travelled from Eastwood every day were the sons of Eastwood's shopkeepers and its professional class. On the same train as Lawrence and Neville in 1899, for example, would have been Tom Gillott and his two brothers (sons of a civil engineer living at Uplands House in the Nottingham Road), Willie and Cyril Wyld (sons of the Wine and Spirit Merchant), Laurence Wyld (son of the Head Clerk at Barber Walker & Co.) and Duncan Meakin (son of the horse-dealer and farming family of Hill Top House, Nottingham Road). The last of these, at least – and he was probably not alone – 'appeared to consider himself as socially somewhat superior to us', Neville remembered, and it was 'something unusual for him to travel in our compartment'. But, like them, Lawrence wore the 'Eton coat and collar' of the High School Boy,[31] something else that would have marked him out in the streets of Eastwood on his way to and from the station. He was mixing with the middle classes without actually rising into them.

His social advance, however, coincided with that of his brother Ernest in London, who found himself mixing with a higher social class altogether. When he came back to Eastwood for holidays, he too stood out in the streets. May Chambers's father remarked 'I never see such a young fool in my life as that lad of Lawrence's, Ernest, do they call him. There I met him walking down the street in a top hat, frock coat, and yellow kid gloves'. Ernest, though, knew exactly what he was doing. Using fashionable London slang, he wrote to his brother Bert about a planned visit.

I will astonish the natives. Fancy my walking up the length of our church at Christmas with my overcoat thrown lightly over my arm, a Frock Coat waddling about my knees, and Silk Hat held out from me at an angle of 45½ degrees, as though I wanted to take the collection, and Oh! I forgot! the gloves and umbrella. You know when a fellow has a Sleever he has perforce to carry an umbrella, for you see the rain in these parts has such a dreadfully nasty way of coming down without first consulting its victims, and to be in a shower with a Silker, almost spoils it.[32]

Ada and Lawrence 'asked for nothing better than to walk down Eastwood Main street with him' when Ernest was wearing his frock coat and silk hat. Lydia Lawrence liked it too: 'The feathers in mother's bonnet seemed to nod triumphantly.'[33]

In 1928, Lawrence gave his own account of his High School career: 'at age of twelve won a scholarship for Nottingham High School, considered best day school in England – purely bourgeois school – quite happy there, but the scholarship boys were a class apart – D. H. made a couple of bourgeois friendships, but they were odd fish – he instinctively recoiled away from the bourgeoisie, regular sort –'.[34] The account has, of course, the bias of all Lawrence's late autobiographical writing. What is important, however, is his dual stress: on the class orientation of the school, and on his being 'a class apart'. At Beauvale school, he had been in a group happy to despise education in all its forms; Lawrence remembered the 'endless refrain' of his school-mates, ' "When I go down pit you'll see what —— sums I'll do"', and a contemporary recalled the 'three R's' which really mattered to the boys at Beauvale: 'ripping, repairing and road-laying'.[35] The young Lawrence had been isolated because he was *not* one of his peer group. Now, at Nottingham High School, he suffered a quieter version of the same experience; only this time it was the middle-class children with whom he did not fit. Ernest Woodford remembered an incident

when a master (Trafford) had gone through a Geometrical rider on the blackboard, and a small nasal voice at the back of the class said – "now you just do that again". Everyone expected the roof to fall in –, but Trafford, like the gentleman he was, went through the rider once more without comment. The comments were freely provided by the class after the lesson.[36]

The nervousness of a snuffly-nosed outsider who cannot catch the tone in which to address a master is obvious; as is the way in which a 'gentleman' can deal with an awkward scholarship boy, and the manner in which Lawrence's class, of potential gentlemen, resolve the matter afterwards. Frieda Lawrence passed on the story of how bitter it was to Lawrence 'when a friend at the high school who took him home to tea, refused to continue the friendship as soon as he heard Lawrence was a miner's son'.[37] She probably heard the story from Lawrence around 1912–13, and registered a 'bitter' memory which, by 1928, had been suppressed.

However, one of the 'odd fish' he met at school apparently formed a more significant friendship with him than Ernest Woodford did. Thomas Haynes Marsden signed his name – adding 'alias "dreamer"' – into Emily Lawrence's birthday book, an indication that he visited the Walker Street house.[38] And in 1918, planning to move back up to the Midlands, and hearing that a house in Bolehill (near Wirksworth in Derbyshire) was to let, Lawrence told Willie Hopkin that 'It is a very pleasant little house, and I should love to have it . . . I used to stay there when Miss Marsden was alive' (iii. 222). Elizabeth Marsden, who had died in 1913, was Tommy Marsden's aunt, and had been a schoolteacher at Bulwell; the fact that Lawrence 'used to stay' in Bolehill suggests that his connection with the Marsden family went further than with his other High School acquaintances. He probably accompanied Tommy Marsden when the latter was visiting his aunt, though it is also possible – if less likely – that he got to know Elizabeth Marsden in some other connection or at some later date.[39] We know nothing else about the friendship; but it at least suggests that Lawrence's later account of his recoil away from the bourgeoisie, as a child and adolescent, was not entirely true.

IV 'Shocking Affair at Ilkeston'

He made an extremely good start in the High School's Shell Form (intermediate between the IIIrd and IVth Forms) in his first term, Christmas 1898; he came second, with the general comment 'Very satisfactory': not surprisingly, his family kept his school report.

Form Work	No. of boys			
English Subjects	17		2	Good
French	17		1.	Very good
German	17		2	Good
Scripture	17		11.	Fair
Writing	47		4.	Very good
Drawing	33		12.	Quite satisfactory
Science	78		4.	Moderate
Mathematics	43	Arith.	1.	He works very intelligently
		Alg.	3.	
Diligence –			Very good	
Conduct –			Very good	
Times late			_____	
Times detained			_____	
Excuses brought			_____	
Times absent			_____	

[40]

The small classes in four of his subjects are striking; he had experienced nothing like it at Beauvale. The report is on a model pupil.

When he moved higher in the school, into the Lower Modern IVth, he was 5th; but in the Upper Modern IVth, at Easter 1900, he won the form prize. Passing into the Modern Vth for the summer term, however, in July 1900 he was only 16th out of 21 boys; he did best that term in Mathematics (winning a prize), but was only 13th in English and German and 19th in

French. He spent his last year in the Modern VIth, ending up as 15th out of 19, and only 7th even in Mathematics. He left school in July 1901.[41]

Everyone agrees that Nottingham High School under its distinguished headmaster Dr James Gow was an excellent school, and Lawrence was obviously a talented boy. It is therefore particularly interesting that, after his success in the Shell and IVth forms, he did so badly in the Vth and VIth forms. That may tell us something about the kind of education the school offered: it was shaped increasingly, in the higher classes, to University preparation. In the Modern VIth, during Lawrence's last year, when he was only 15, he was in the same class as boys of 18 and 19 who were going on to University.

And yet that is perhaps not a sufficient explanation for the sudden plunge in his performance after Easter 1900. Only eleven boys were older than he in the Modern VIth, and seven were younger (four of whom were above him in the final marks). But Lawrence would also have known, all through the school, that he would be leaving in the summer before his sixteenth birthday, and that he would be going on neither to higher education nor to a career as a professional man. Only the quite exceptional working-class boy, who won prizes and awards and scholarships every year (which Lawrence had not), could look forward to such a future. And he knew that, unlike many of the other boys, what he did at school (and how well he did), would probably make not the slightest difference to his subsequent career. The most he could realistically hope for was to be a clerk or a teacher; and those he could be without a High School education. We know that he would have preferred to become a teacher; but, as George Neville recalled, 'neither of us could follow our own inclination and become pupil teachers, because we had not sufficient "backing influence" to gain us admission'.[42] Until the Education Act of 1902, such influence lay in the hands of the school governors. Lawrence knew that he would be leaving school in the summer of 1901 to become a clerk in a factory: what did school matter, in that last year?

But matters may not be quite so simple as that suggests. For one thing, Lawrence started to do badly not during his last year, but in the summer of 1900. Teachers know how a sudden or dramatic falling off in a pupil's performance is very likely due to factors which have nothing to do with academic work; and Lawrence's examination performance in the winter of 1904 shows that he could, in wholly academic terms, perform quite out-standingly – something he signally failed to do in his last four terms at school. We need to consider whether anything in his home circumstances changed, between the end of the spring term 1900 and the summer of 1901.

By far the biggest event in his home life would have been the effect upon the household in Walker Street, Eastwood, of his uncle Walter's arrest in Ilkeston, two miles away, on Tuesday 20 March 1900 for maliciously wounding his son Walter. The boy died on Thursday 22 March and Walter Lawrence was charged with manslaughter. The Coroner's jury on the 24th returned a verdict of 'manslaughter, brought about by great provocation';[43] the following week, on 29 March, the Petty Sessions committed Walter Lawrence to trial at the next Assizes.

It is impossible to know the effect of all this upon the Lawrence family of Eastwood. The local newspapers were full of the story: the Eastwood newspaper went out of its way to connect the affair with Eastwood – 'A sad case occurred at Ilkeston last week, the facts of which will be keenly interesting to Eastwood and Brinsley people as the parties hail from these localities'. Even the Nottingham newspapers reported the event, with a short report in the *Nottinghamshire Guardian* on 24 March ('Tragic Occurrence at Ilkeston') and a lengthy account on 31 March ('Shocking Affair at Ilkeston') both identical with the reports in the Eastwood paper.[44] In Walker Street, there was doubtless a mixture of shock, shame and family solidarity – modified, on Lydia's side, by an even stronger sense of difference.

Arthur's family would have felt publicly shown up as brutal and violent; Lydia's reaction is not hard to imagine, as she worked to construct the particular myth of the difference between her own family and her husband's: and also to ensure that the children of her own marriage would be unlike their father in manners, outlook and profession. Largely because of Lydia Lawrence's tough-mindedness and forcefulness, the role of the husband in the Lawrence family of Eastwood was utterly different from that of Walter Lawrence in Ilkeston. The children in Eastwood, as Lydia Lawrence had brought them up, would never have abused their father – even if that father had been capable of manslaughter: nor would they have reason to complain that he was not working, or that food in the household was not being fairly distributed. And – very much to the point – at the age of nearly 15, Bert was not (like the 15-year-old Walter in Ilkeston) a miner, with the pugnacious outlook of a collier boy challenging a father who drinks. Because of Lydia's insistence, he was a scholarship boy at Nottingham High School.

Yet Lawrence's sudden falling away in performance at Nottingham High School suggests not only that the Walker Street household was even more than usually divided and unhappy, but that Lawrence himself was powerfully affected. The death of Lydia Lawrence's widowed mother in May would further have sharpened Lydia's sense of the tyranny of husbands and fathers.[45] She would have been reminded of how she herself had set out to be different; and how her children must be, too. At school Lawrence was subject, already, to a sense of being temporarily raised into a middle-class world. This awareness would have been terribly heightened by his mother's determined polarisation of the Walker Street family, as well as by the public demonstration that the Lawrences were working-class, that brutal violence was their normal answer to problems and that they quarrelled absurdly but savagely over eggs and pyclets. The story broke in the newspapers right at the end of the school spring term in March 1900. But his contemporaries would not have been slow in connecting him with it, and Lawrence would have gone back after Easter in the full blaze of its notoriety. If anything was calculated to make the reserved boy still more reserved, the self-conscious boy still more self-conscious, it would have been the sense of exposure and humiliation to which, as a boy, he was always liable. The eyes of others would now have been upon him with a vengeance. It is tempting to wonder whether the anecdote Frieda Lawrence remembered – the schoolfriend's family rejecting Lawrence because he was a miner's son – should be modified to make their objection the fact that he was a murderer's nephew.

At the age of 15 and 10 months, however, after his relatively unsuccessful last year at school – and having been a drain on the family resources for the past three years – it was imperative that Lawrence leave school and get a job. Within three months he was a clerk in a Nottingham factory.

V   Education Recreated

For an intensely autobiographical writer, Lawrence wrote remarkably little either about his own time at school, or indeed about any children at school, until he created *The Rainbow* in 1914–15. In none of his early short stories or plays is the subject even touched on; but, even more surprisingly, it enters the various versions of *Sons and Lovers* only tangentially. Paul Morel's elder brother William leaves school at 13, and – apart from his success at sports – we learn almost nothing about his time there, though his career at the Co-op and subsequently in London is given in some detail. But, quite remarkably, in the published novel there is no account of Paul at school either, in spite of a whole chapter describing his growing up. His education is handled only incidentally. In a passage primarily about William's successes we hear that 'Annie was now studying to be a teacher. Paul, also very clever, was getting on well, having lessons in French and German from his Godfather, the clergyman who was still a friend to Mrs Morel'. That rather gives the impression that Paul has not gone to school at all; and it is true that the young Lawrence did (in addition to his normal schooling) receive French lessons from the governess to a local family, Miss Fanny

Wright, probably before going to Nottingham High School in 1898.[46] However, Paul does indeed go to 'board school', as is shown when he is collecting his father's wages from the Company Offices and Mr Winterbottom (the cashier) sneers at his failure to add up the stoppages correctly: ' "Don't they teach you to count at the Board School?" he asked. "Nowt but algibbra an' French," said a collier.' Paul tells his mother afterwards: 'An' they say "Nowt but algibbra an' French." They *don't* teach me French at the board school.' But apart from occasional remarks about the children coming home from school, and the fact that school closes early on a Friday, there are very few references to Paul at school. In his job interview, Mr Jordan asks him what school he went to, and Paul answers 'The board school.' And while Paul is 'looking for work' when he is 14, we are suddenly told how 'He suffered very much from the first contact with anything. When he was seven, the starting school had been a nightmare and a torture to him. But afterwards he liked it'.[47] It is odd that such an experience of 'nightmare' and 'torture' should have been omitted; as well as the way in which 'afterwards he liked it'. In the 1911 'Paul Morel' there are a couple more details, particularly about Paul's hatred of appearing in public, but nothing extensive. Knowing as we do about Paul's 'convulsions of self consciousness' when exposed to other people, for example at the Colliery offices or at school, we are entitled as novel readers to wonder why his school years are largely omitted from the account of his young life;[48] particularly as we know that Lawrence at Beauvale school had made a strikingly odd impression. He had been the object of some people's contempt and of some people's sympathy, but either way the experience had been important to him. His experience at Nottingham High School had been similarly mixed.

The reason seems to be that Lawrence created in Paul Morel, from the start, a character often very unlike himself indeed. Apart from his relationship with his mother, Paul is a more ordinary child than Lawrence himself had been. His younger brother Arthur, however, was conceived as an oversensitive, highly intelligent child, who (remarkably for one of his background) goes on to High School and then to College. Lawrence has therefore no use for his own academic ability in Paul, or for him to have much inclination towards books. And it is striking how, when Paul starts to go through the same kinds of experiences as the young Lawrence, the experiences are significantly modified. So, for example, Paul – like Lawrence – plays with girls, unusually for the place and the period. But the novel provides a good reason for it:

The children of Scargill Street felt quite select. At the end where the Morels lived, there were not many young things. So the few were more united. Boys and girls played together, the girls ⟨uniting⟩ ⌜joining⌝ in the fights and the rough games, the boys taking part in the dancing games and rings and make belief of the girls. ⟨When Paul grew up, and met some tall woman in the street dragging her brats along, he would think:

"There's Alice Chambers! How many times have I ridden on her back, and she on mine, at charging."⟩[49]

There is probably an element of autobiographical truth in this; the six houses at the end of Walker Street (in what was known as 'Mellors' corner', after the builder) were certainly rather isolated. Yet the stress by Lawrence's contemporaries lies so much upon his physical weakness and his difference from the other boys – and so much, too, upon the fact that girls were his companions at school, and when he was not playing – that the novel's version appears to be a conscious alteration. Paul is *not* weak, although he is often ill; he plays games like anyone else, and fights like the other children, who 'would fight, hate with a fury of hatred, and flee home in terror'.[50]

It seems certain, then, that Lawrence's normalisation of his own young life into that of Paul is extended to his school career as well. Paul does not do markedly better than the other children at school; he does not go to High School; he does not stand out as an oddity, either in himself or in his attitude towards work; in fact, he does not stand out at all, as we are rarely allowed to see anything of his school life. It is Arthur who is conceived as the oddity, and the academic star.

The novel's logic thus dictates that the formation of Paul's character by his attitude towards father and mother is what really matters. The novel is focused upon Paul at home; his relationship with his parents, not with school, is made the important experience of his youth. The sharpness of Lawrence's realisation of class attitudes, of differences between himself and others in their background, as he experienced them *outside* the home – and would certainly have felt them at school – is replaced by Paul's awareness of the difference between his father and mother as he sees them *within* the home.

But Paul's realisation of class distinction, and of his own isolation in his community, is very acutely felt at moments. He experiences it poignantly when he collects the wages from the Colliery offices; he feels small, inadequate, but above all *different*, and he cannot cope with the experience. Mabel Thurlby explains that that was true of the young Lawrence in the identical situation:

The most unhappy day of Bertie Lawrence's week was Friday when, with a calico bag clutched in his hand, he had to go to the offices on Nether Green to draw his father's wages . . . I always got a beating when I reached home, because my pinafore was so dirty from pushing Bertie between the miners to reach the counter when his father's name was called.[51]

He would not assert himself: he did not behave like a miner's son. His 'convulsions of self consciousness', as he felt himself observed, were probably identical with those of Paul Morel.

In that way, however, the novel – with its 'normal' hero – dealt with the problem which, in their different ways, both his schools had been for Lawrence. School was simply omitted. It was only much later, in *The Rainbow*, that Lawrence's fiction first began to explore the experience of the child who does not fit in with school. He was then working with a character in many ways his antithesis: Tom Brangwen. Tom is sent to the Grammar School in Derby as 'an unwilling failure from the first'; print repels him, and he 'hated books as if they were his enemies'; he finds writing intolerable 'and would have been torn to pieces rather than attempt to write another word'. And so the Grammar School 'got used to him, setting him down as a hopeless duffer at learning'.[52] This is all quite different from Lawrence's own experience.

Yet Lawrence does convey, brilliantly, the kind of humiliation which Tom experiences at school; and he also stresses the fact that Tom's perceptions are 'delicate, very delicate', which makes his humiliation the more intense as he struggles to learn. In one interesting touch, the only thing Tom can do well is mathematics, for which he has 'an instinct': 'but if this failed him, he was helpless as an idiot. So that he felt that the ground was never sure under his feet, he was nowhere.'[53] Lawrence's own instinct for mathematics was striking even in his first bad term at High School, in the Modern Vth during the summer of 1900, when he was 14 and his sudden academic weakness in English and foreign languages became noticeable. Tom's sense 'of failure all the while, of incapacity' may well have become Lawrence's too, in his last year at the High School; the feeling of being in the wrong place, and of being easily and frequently humiliated. Just after telling us that Paul, having left school, is 14 and looking for work, Lawrence describes how 'when there was any clog in his soul's quick running, his face went stupid and ugly. He was the sort of boy that becomes a clown and a lout as soon as he is not understood, or feels himself held cheap . . .'[54] Paul's feeling of being a clown, of being misunderstood and seen as a fool, offers a strange parallel to what Tom Brangwen experiences; and it is striking that it should come into *Sons and Lovers* at exactly the point where some kind of summary of Paul's life at school might have been expected. It is one of the few clues to what Lawrence may have gone through at Nottingham High School.

Tom Brangwen's experience at school, however, also shows the *distance* between the child who does not fit in and the world of school. Tom's granddaughter Ursula Brangwen, in *The Rainbow*'s third generation, feels something rather different. When she is young, 'the common school and the companionship of the village children, niggardly and begrudging' oppress her; she goes with relief to the Grammar School in Nottingham, having 'a passionate craving to escape from the belittling circumstances of life, the little jealousies, the little differences, the little meannesses'. Her education is presented largely in terms of her own sense of superiority (particularly class superiority); her 'hill of learning' enables her, literally, to look down 'on the smoke and confusion and the manufacturing, engrossed activity of the town': 'Up here, in the Grammar School, she fancied the air was finer, beyond the factory smoke.' What, for the miners of Paul Morel's Bestwood, are proofs of the pretentious folly of schools – algebra and French – are exactly the subjects which make Ursula feel liberated. It is the learning itself she values; teachers and schoolmistresses are the objects of her contempt.[55] Only in the chapter 'Shame' does Lawrence do anything to capture the dynamics of school, of study, of relationships; and then partly from the teacher's point of view.

In general, instead, he presents Ursula's education as a process of separation from the village in which she grows up. The people who knew her as a child, who 'had held "Urtler Brangwen" one of themselves, and had given her her place in the native village, as in a family' cannot understand that she should grow up 'different'.

" 'Ello Urs'ler, 'ow are yer goin' on?" they said when they met her. And it demanded of her in the old voice the old response. And something in her must respond and belong to people who knew her. But something else denied bitterly. What was true of her ten years ago was not true now ... They said she was proud and conceited, that she was too big for her shoes nowadays. They said, she needn't pretend, because they knew what she was. They had known her since she was born. They quoted this and that about her. And she was ashamed because she really did feel different from the people she had lived amongst. It hurt her that she could not be at her ease with them any more.[56]

Paul Morel is never exposed to such a feeling – in spite of the fact that his divided background might easily have provoked it. But in *The Rainbow* Lawrence finally explored the experience of the child whose education and experience effectively detach it from its community. There are countless ways in which Ursula's experience cannot be compared with Lawrence's own, and in which Ursula's life is fictional and not autobiographical; and yet, as an exploratory writer, Lawrence seems here to be covering a good deal of the ground which he had denied himself in *Sons and Lovers*. And the conclusion he comes to about the village child whose education carries it beyond the village is that, for good or ill, it cannot return; the differences, once established, cannot be abolished. Ursula feels 'the old voice' demanded of her when she meets her old acquaintances, just as Lawrence retained his dialect voice as a permanent legacy of Eastwood: but his reaction to Eastwood, from quite early in his life, was more than the common reaction of the twentieth-century scholarship boy, moving out of his class: it was to feel different from the people he had lived amongst.[57]

VI   Haywoods: and Death in the Family

Lawrence left school in July 1901. Ernest, after leaving school, had added to his qualifications by studying shorthand and typing at night-school. The best his younger brother could have expected, even after a High School career, would have been a desk job in some manufacturer's office; even with the languages he had learned at school, he was rather less qualified than Ernest had been at his age. But he had to get a job. In *Sons and Lovers*, Mrs Morel tells her son he must hunt in the advertisement columns of the newspapers:

He looked at her. It seemed to him a bitter humiliation and an anguish to go through. But he said nothing. When he got up in the morning, his whole being was knotted up over this one thought:

   "I've got to go and look for advertisements for a job."

   It stood in front of the morning, that thought, killing all joy and even life, for him. His heart felt like a tight knot.[58]

Life sometimes seems nothing but a succession of such humiliations for Paul – which is odd, since much of the time he is such a normal boy. But in his reaction there is probably a good deal of the tortured self-exposure which Lawrence's own hunt for a job entailed. As Paul goes up the street, he feels that everyone knows he is going to the Co-op reading-room to scan the advertisements: something even more embarrassing, probably, for the boy who had recently been at High School and who had always felt an outsider.

   The actual advertisement Lawrence found cannot now be traced; it would have been like this example in the *Nottingham Daily Guardian*: 'Youth (intelligent) Wanted, for Manufacturer's Office, aged about 15. – Address, own handwriting, P22 "Guardian" Office.'[59] The advert Lawrence answered had been placed by the Nottingham firm of surgical garments manufacturers, J. H. Haywood, of 9 Castle Gate, Nottingham and Wood Street, London. Lawrence had ready a letter of application which his brother Ernest had helped him draft (i. 21), which stated (not quite

94

accurately) that he had won prizes in French and German at school. In fact he had been top in French in his first term, and had won the term prize in the Upper Modern IVth. The letter was designed to be valid from Lawrence's sixteenth birthday, on 11 September 1901, but was probably used earlier; it got him an interview. Paul's interview in *Sons and Lovers* stresses once again how easily he is reduced to a 'feeling of ignominy and of rage', as the manager gets him to translate a letter in French and then criticises his translation. But – like Paul – Lawrence was successful at his interview, and around the end of September, with a salary of probably 8/- a week, he started work at Haywoods as a junior clerk.[60]

He was, particularly with strangers, always very quiet as a boy and youth – 'gentle and reserved' was how Jessie Chambers thought of him in the summer of 1901 – and he made little impression on anyone at Haywoods during his time there. Like Paul Morel at Jordans, he 'talked to them very little'. In 1950, an employee named A. E. Gill claimed to remember him 'quite well' – 'but did not associate with him out of business hours, as he had to travel by train home . . . he was a very quiet and reserved young man. Tall and dark-haired, very little to say in conversation, both in work time and outside.'[61] Lawrence was neither dark nor especially tall, but certainly silent. Paul Morel arrives at work just after 8.00 a.m.; Lawrence, dressed in his school suit, would have had to catch the same 7.00 a.m. train he had taken to school – Ernest Woodford remembered him going to Haywoods 'still in his black suit, carrying a basket with his midday food'. When Paul arrives he copies the letters which contain the orders, is given checking and invoicing to do, makes up parcels and takes the orders down to the work girls who do the making of the elastic web garments. When the made-up items come back, he packs, addresses and weighs them, and takes them down to the postal clerk. He has an hour's break between 1.00 p.m. and 2.00 p.m., in which he eats the food he has brought from home and then wanders round Nottingham. Work slackens off during the afternoon. At 5.00 p.m. there is a tea-break; after tea, he works until 8.00 p.m., with 'the big evening post to get off'; then leaves for home on the 8.20 p.m. train. He gets home at 9.20 p.m.[62]

Lawrence's day must have contained many of those elements, and perhaps all of them; and like Paul, 'all the time he was there, his health suffered from the darkness, and lack of air, and the long hours'. His sister Ada, in 1929, still remembered how 'He didn't like it, but he wanted to help mother.' Haywoods was only a small concern, inhabiting 'an old building without modern lighting and ventilation'; the Chambers family heard from Lawrence about the fuss made of his health by 'two old ladies – overlookers of the concern':

'Oh, those old women! They smell so funny. They think I'm not strong and fuss around me, and I get the full blast of that stuffy, musty smell and the scent of the pomade they use on their hair! I'm sure I nearly faint. But they mean to be kindness itself, and so I shall have to put up with it.'

And he sent us into gusts of laughter, mimicking their tones in forcing him to accept and use cough lozenges they had bought for him.[63]

But the most important event of his first weeks at Haywoods had nothing to do with his work. Ernest was still working as a clerk in London, at the solicitors John Holman and Sons; he was also enaged to be married, to the 23-year-old Louisa Lily Western ('Gipsy') Dennis, a cheerful and – according to Ernest – chatty stenographer who worked in London. A surviving photograph of her was taken by Ernest himself, who had added photography to his accomplishments (see Illustrations 5 and 6); he also wrote her at least one poem.[64] Ernest and Gipsy went to Eastwood together at least twice – the second visit being on 27 July 1901: but Ernest went home to Eastwood by himself for the Goose Fair holiday, Thursday 3 to Sunday 6 October. He was clearly tired and run down; his letters home for months had been saying 'I really do seem to get busier every week' and 'I have been so very busy', though back in March he had told Emily how 'Both Gipsy and I are keeping in splendid health.' But in October he apparently showed his mother the small patch of inflammation on his throat which marked the beginning of erysipelas: an infectious disease, often called 'St Anthony's Fire', which shows itself in a severe inflammation of the face or throat and leads to acute blood-poisoning.[65] Ernest's feeling of tiredness, and his general run-down condition, were characteristic of the early stages of erysipelas.

He went to the Congregational chapel with the family in Eastwood on Sunday evening, before staying with his brother George in Nottingham on the Sunday night and catching the first train back to London on Monday morning. He went to work as usual that day, but was too ill to get up on the Tuesday; he developed pneumonia as a result of the erysipelas, which is frequently accompanied by a temperature of 104–105°. Either on Wednesday 9th or Thursday 10th a telegram arrived in Eastwood warning of his illness, and Lydia Lawrence (perhaps accompanied, but more likely followed, by her husband) went to London. She found her way to Ernest's lodgings in Catford; Ernest, with his head and face shockingly inflamed and swollen, was delirious from his extremely high temperature and did not recognise her.[66] Two doctors had declared his condition hopeless, and on Friday 11 October he died. His mother (who was present) registered his death; and his parents brought him back to Eastwood on the Saturday night. May Chambers happened to be at Langley Mill station when that train arrived: 'in the stream of passengers I saw only one figure, short, black, bowed, but tearless, stunned with grief but wearily attending the work of the moment. Her husband followed heavily behind as she went to attend to the coffin's transfer. Her face looked shrunken under the small bonnet; grief and pain seemed concentrated in the pitiful eyes.'[67] The funeral took place in Eastwood cemetery on Monday 14th: four days later there was an obituary in the local paper which was elegiac in its praise of Ernest's hard work and his business acumen.

His knowledge for a young man was considerable, London's gaiety could not wrest from him his love for work and his keen desire to get on, and after business hours his evenings were spent in the study of French and German languages, a knowledge of which he acquired sufficient to converse and write letters. To undertake so much was too much, but his large mind, his keen desire for hard work, his ambition to make himself thoroughly fitting to fill a high post, to get on and be useful in the world was so great.[68]

It is of Lydia Lawrence that we naturally think most; she had invested so much hope in her sons, had been so proud of Ernest's success: particularly in comparison with George's escapades. Ernest had always been the high-flyer, the marvellous success of the family, with his dazzling smile and the 'touch of the audacious which added to his attraction',[69] his sense of fun, his winning ways, his stylish clothes, his tremendous energy and capacity for hard work and his London salary. He was perhaps the only real success Lydia Lawrence could claim from all her married life. She had probably needed him more than he needed her; she had not approved of his engagement. His extraordinary place in her affections can be gauged by her remark that 'she looked forward more to meeting her son Ernest in heaven than Jesus Christ Himself': a heart-rending confession for a woman as strict in religion as herself. A muted protest against his death even appeared on the printed funeral card announcing his entry into 'the Land of Light October 11, 1901': 'Even so Father, For so it seemeth good in Thy Sight.'[70]

May Chambers remembered how 'Daily at school we talked of the tragedy of Mrs. Lawrence's life'. A letter Lydia wrote to her sister Ada a week after Ernest's death gives some indication of her state.

18 October 1901

My dear Ada,

I should have answered your dear letter yesterday but several friends came in and I was cleaning upstairs. Though I was upstairs most of the day I did very little and Ah my heart was so heavy, it did seem – all so dark, so dreary.

I had a lot of letters yesterday, ones from Emma, Nellie, Miss Coulson, Miss Loosemoore and another from Mr Walton saying that their staff had made arrangements to follow him and bring a wreath.

He was surprised to hear from Louie that he was buried on Monday.

Louie's cross was a large beautiful one but sadly crushed and faded. The inscription on it was

'The last token of Gipsy's love to my beloved, whom I hope to
meet some day in heaven my dearest one.'

On Wednesday one came from Mr and Miss Coulson. Emily and Ada have gone every day and the flowers were keeping very fresh and beautiful but I expect the heavy rain of yesterday afternoon has dashed them.

Yes dear Ada that was a beautiful thought, taken from Satan's clutches to his Father's keeping through his Saviour's prayers.

I was so sorry dear Ada that you left your purse, I did not see it till yesterday so I have sent the money for feel you may want it, and will bring or send the purse. There were 2/-[1], 1/-[1], 6d[1] and 6d in coppers, nothing else of any value.

Mrs Kirk came to see me on Wednesday, she was very kind indeed everybody is.

Yourself and Fritz not the least by far, I was so thankful to have you and missed you so much.

Mr Ineson came soon after you left and stayed some time, he offered a beautiful prayer.

I know dear Ada I am in all your thoughts and prayers God bless you both.

Bert sent me a very kind little note on Tuesday, assuring me of his deepest sympathy and saying that the loss of so bright and promising a son was enough to break his mother's heart.

It nearly has but for the sake of the others I hide as much as I can.

Goodbye dear Ada

Love much love to Truly your loving

Liddie[71]

Her resolution to do the cleaning (itself a kind of therapy; but like Mrs Morel cleaning during the discussion of the season-ticket, also a demonstration of how she was standing up against suffering); her quotation from Gipsy Dennis's wreath, combined with the acute observation that, of all the wreaths, Gipsy's is the one 'crushed and faded' (she also refuses to call her 'Gipsy'[72]); the tough-minded and unsentimental observation that although the flowers have lasted well, the rain yesterday will have 'dashed them'; her compliment for the 'beautiful thought', with its references to 'Satan's clutches' – probably those of money, drink and women; her concern for Ada's money and purse and her careful enumeration of the coins; her hiding 'for the sake of the others' – her other children, presumably – 'as much as I can'; the error in 'Love much love to Truly . . .' (instead of 'Love much love from Truly . . .') – the whole letter is a tribute to her capacity to mask and suppress feeling, and to reveal her feelings in spite of her tight-lipped resolution. What matters to her is the sympathy of her Eastwood circle, and – even more – of her family; she writes to one sister, refers to her brother-in-law Fritz, to her sisters Nellie and Emma, to her youngest brother Bert and to her daughters Emily and Ada. Arthur Lawrence, however, is not mentioned: the letter could be that of a widow.

In the absence of any knowledge of Arthur Lawrence's feelings, it is appropriate to cite the reaction of Mr Morel in *Sons and Lovers* after the death of his son William; it may even be authentically Arthur Lawrence's. When Mr Morel is brought the news at work, he leans 'up against a truck side, his hand over his eyes. He was not crying.' His son Paul looks around the industrial landscape: he watches a weighing machine: he is embarrassed, and looks at anything and everything except his father 'leaning against the truck as if he were tired'. We hear little else except that Mr Morel subsequently refuses to walk round by 'Shipstone' – Shipley – where his son used to work, and that he always avoids the cemetery where he is buried. However, long after the death, when his son Paul is starting to do well, his father suddenly comments (as if he has been acutely conscious of it for years): ' "Yes, an' that other lad 'ud 'a done as much, if they hadna ha' killed 'im," he said, quietly.'[73] The 'they' is important: it means London, it means those who believe in business and in 'getting on': it means those outside his community.

Through all this, D. H. Lawrence worked away in his surgical garments factory. *Sons and Lovers* describes Paul's helpless attempts to interest his mother in his activities, after the death of his brother William: 'Night after night he forced himself to tell her things, although she did not listen.' Lydia Lawrence's letter shows what she would suppress; but she would not have been able to simulate liveliness, or interest in her younger son. Then, according to May Chambers, 'there was a heavy, grey fog for several days, and he went down with pneumonia'.[74] The warehouse work, his long hours in all weathers, his own frailty and – we may hazard – his mother's failure to attend to him, all came together in an illness which nearly killed him.

There was perhaps another cause too. George Neville tells us all we know about it. Lawrence, he wrote, found it very hard to cope with the work-girls at Haywoods: 'He used to tell me of the things they had said to him. They were perfect beasts; they were little devils, he said. They were filthier than anybody he had ever conceived; and they *would* persist in thrusting their filth upon him.'[75] They were not the first; at Beauvale School 'Pussy' Templeman and another boy 'had striven to acquaint Lawrence with the more advanced vulgar expressions, only to discover his horror', and Neville also reports Lawrence's violent reaction to smutty stories told on the train to Nottingham during his High School days. He was a natural target for such treatment: it was the one kind of language he could not control, and he was unable to hide his violent reaction. Even his sister Ada knew that 'Bert would never tolerate vulgarity and dirty stories.'[76] Neville further commented that the work-girls 'appear to have taken a sheer delight in searing his youthful innocence'; he provides a very convincing account of Lawrence's idealisation of women and his usual politeness and charm:

There was always the same scrupulous uncovering of the head, accompanied by his queer little jerky half-bow, a bright smile and a clear and well accented 'Hello, Mrs So-and-so! And how are *you* today?' But no stopping to gossip . . . along he went, leaving a gladdened heart behind him.

'Aye! He *is* a nice lad, isn't he?' I have heard it scores and scores of times . . .[77]

It was, however, that very 'niceness' – the politeness, innocence and 'superiority' of the reserved ex-High School Boy – which provoked the work-girls at Haywoods. One of them later recalled him: 'the Lawrence she described . . . was rather shy, not too popular because people thought him "stand-offish", a boy who never made the slightest advances to girls but always stood on the outskirts of groups of girls chatting about their boyfriends on Monday mornings, listening to them with a kind of fascinated horror'.[78] He was not one of them; they inevitably thought him stuck-up, and their natural response was to try and take him down a peg.

But not only did they enjoy making his ears burn; on one occasion, according to Neville, they cornered him in his lunch hour and attempted to remove his trousers.

I am certain that they would be utterly astonished when Lawrence got fairly started. Though only slim, he was tall and wiry, with very long arms and fingers, and in a rage he could be a very demon. I gathered that he had set about those girls with teeth, hoof and claw . . . and finally driven them off, afraid of the fury they had aroused.[79]

Neville said that the incident came 'a little time before his attack of pneumonia, and in my own mind I have always felt that the incident was directly responsible for the attack'.[80] It would certainly have added to his feelings of isolation and victimisation, his hatred of the factory and his desperation to leave.

The way Lawrence handled his memory of the work-girls at Haywoods when he came to write 'Paul Morel' and *Sons and Lovers*, however, tells quite a different story. There is absolutely no trace of coarseness in them, in speech or action – indeed, they are almost uncannily sensitive to Paul; there is no possibility of them committing the kind of assault on Paul which they had made first on Lawrence's sensitivity, and then on his person. The novel's cleaning up of experience for a middle-class audience, together with its recreation of Lawrence as Paul, purely working-class Paul, accounts for this; but in fact Paul has no 'superiority' which might be found offensive. In the factory, as in the village, if you did not like Lawrence you could easily dismiss him as a mother's-boy, stuck-up, over-educated and odd; as a permanent outsider and weakling. But Lawrence, in 1912–13, made Paul Morel the unselfconscious being he was himself then in the process of becoming, and which he desperately wanted to be. Paul was part of his own self-therapy, and thus of the 'shed[ding] of sicknesses' which he later described the novel as having accomplished (ii. 90).*

Pneumonia in 1901 could be a killer. It had contributed to Ernest's death; its pattern was well known, as it built to a crisis of inflammation, temperature and the filling of the lungs. 'As the crisis approached, there seemed a breathlessness among people. "Eh, that Bertie Lawrence'll ne'er o'er break it," would say a woman to me on my way to school; or "It'll be t'biggest wonder in t'world if he isna laid wi' t'other lad," would say a collier on my way home.' At the time of 'the crisis', it was reported how 'The doctor says there is a spot about the size of a crown on his lungs that is clear. If that can be kept clear, he may live – that's what I heard today.'[81]

And live he did. His illness marked the division in his life between childhood and adolescence. He fell ill as a loved and frail but not extraordinary child; he recovered to be the pivot of his mother's hopes, needs and affection. His voice broke during his illness, though it always remained high-pitched and sometimes squeaky; and he also got too big for his clothes, in an adolescent spurt of growth which made his mother complain: 'He'll need a new suit before he can be dressed, and new boots, I'll wager.'[82] The suit he had worn to school and to Haywoods had to be discarded. He grew to be five foot nine inches tall, but was always slender, and often struck people as taller than he really was.

His 1901 illness was a kind of parallel to whatever it had been in 1889 – crying fits, probably illness, stress and tension – which had taken him away from school for almost three years. His pneumonia in 1901, which left his health permanently delicate, saved him from the fourteen-hour absence from home, five-and-a-half days a week, which the factory meant; it marked the division between the 'prisoner of industrialism' which Paul Morel feels he is (and remains), and the very different, and very differently occupied, young man D. H. Lawrence would be.[83]

---

* In 1919, however, DHL recreated something a little akin to the assault at Haywoods. In the story 'Tickets Please', because of his sexual philandering a young male tram inspector is offensive to the women tram conductors, who gang up on him and attack him. Their motive is sexual revenge; but they attack him 'to see him taken down a peg or two'.[84] The story owes perhaps just that single element to the 1901 incident.

And, once again, it kept him at home. Between December 1901 and the autumn of 1902 – except for a period at the Staynes boarding-house in Skegness in the spring[85] – Lawrence became for Lydia Lawrence the son who could replace Ernest in her love and hopes. She needed him for that.

◆

CHAPTER FOUR

WIDENING CIRCLES

I The Chambers Family

To a boy growing up in Eastwood, the big industrial cities – Derby, Nottingham – with schools, industries, colleges, opportunities – lay only a few miles to the east and south: they contained the future to which he was probably destined (or condemned). Lawrence had been to Nottingham to school, and again to work. But stretching out beyond Eastwood in the other direction lay great tracts of farming land and unspoiled country, particularly to the north. The industry of the region was surrounded by the countryside; going along the hedgerows on his way to Brinsley pit, Arthur Lawrence gathered mushrooms and herbs and saw rabbits in the fields. And about two miles north of Eastwood, and only a mile to the north-east of Brinsley, lay the Haggs Farm: the home of the Chambers family.

The Chambers family, like the Lawrences, were original residents of the area; Edmund Chambers had been born and brought up in Eastwood. His father, Jonathan, though styling himself 'Gentleman', was a pawnbroker known locally as 'Pawny' who later became the owner of an off-licence in The Breach. He and his wife 'had been staunch chapel people all their lives, and their pew in the Congregational chapel was in the same aisle as the Lawrences', only across the gangway'. Edmund was first employed as an assistant in Burton's grocery shop in Nottingham; but in 1881 he married Ann Oats, the daughter of a Nottingham joiner, and in the early 1890s returned to Eastwood with his growing family to a smallholding on Greenhills Road, only a hundred yards or so from The Breach, where the Lawrence family had lived since 1887.[1] From here he ran a milk round. In 1891, the Lawrence family moved up the hill to the bay-windowed house in Walker Street: but, in the words of Mrs Chambers's daughter Jessie, Mrs Lawrence and Mrs Chambers 'struck up a sudden friendship one Sunday evening after chapel. They found themselves together in the porch, glanced at one another, smiled, and walked out side by side . . . A mysterious affinity drew them together, and they had a heart to heart talk.'[2] But the affinity was not so mysterious as Jessie suggests; Mrs Chambers's youngest son David described how his mother and Mrs Lawrence were both strangers to the colliery community and they found in the Chapel a degree of culture that was otherwise entirely lacking in their lives; this was the only place in which they felt really at home in an otherwise alien world. It is difficult for us to realise today what the Chapel way of life meant to the more sensitive and refined members of a colliery village. It imposed upon them, of course, a rigid puritan morality, but this represented no sacrifice on their part as it was the only rule of life they knew and was part of the air they breathed. In addition, meeting at the Chapel enabled the two mothers to exchange confidences and share their troubles, and they had much to talk about: they both hated the mining community to which their husbands had brought them. My mother was rather frightened of it: she had never before seen men coming home black from head to foot with coaldust, and dreaded to hear their rough loud voices and strange dialect, and their heavy boots dragging along the pavement.[3]

It must have been a relief to Ann Chambers when, in 1898, her family became tenants of the Haggs Farm (see Illustration 20) – though she now added the job of helping with the farm to cooking and cleaning for a large family. Edmund Chambers continued his milk round, but his eldest son Alan (born 1882) was old enough to help him with the farm work and May (born 1883) to help her mother; so the younger members of the family (Jessie and Mollie born in 1887 and 1896, Hubert, Bernard and David in 1888, 1890 and 1898) grew up in a very different environment.

The Lawrences and the Chambers family – at least the two mothers – kept in contact through the Congregational chapel on Sundays, though Ann Chambers could get there only when Edmund could drive her to Eastwood. But the two women do not seem to have been particularly close; not until the summer of 1901, two or three years after the Chambers's move, did Lydia Lawrence and her son Bert take up the invitation to see the farm, and walk the field paths out to the Haggs on a school half-holiday.

Lawrence was in his last term at Nottingham High School, and the Chambers brothers and sisters (apart from May, who knew him already) felt shy of him; he was 'still something of a stranger from another world'; though his behaviour shows how relaxed he felt with them, from the start, this 'vivacious young man in his Eton clothes and with his impetuous manners'. The world he came from, May Chambers felt, was where 'bay windows and front room furniture and new clothes were so very important': she expected him to think their old house and severely plain furnishings 'very countrified'.[4] But the Haggs Farm became, to the young Lawrence, a place – and a family – which drew him away from Eastwood on every possible opportunity, for the next seven years or so, until the autumn of 1908.

Whatever I forget, I shall never forget the Haggs – I loved it so. I loved to come to you all, it really was a new life began in me there. The water-pippin by the door – those maiden-blush roses that Flower [the horse] would lean over and eat – and Trip [the bull-terrier] floundering round – And stewed figs for tea in winter, and in August green stewed apples. Do you still have them? Tell your mother I never forget, no matter where life carries us ... Oh I'd love to be nineteen again, and coming up through the Warren and catching the first glimpse of the buildings. Then I'd sit on the sofa under the window, and we'd crowd round the little table to tea, in that tiny little kitchen I was so at home in.[5]

The 'new life' which 'began in me there' included, from the first, the marvellous, empty and magical wood, through which he walked to the Haggs, and which surrounded it on the west and stretched away to the south and the east. May Chambers described how, on the young Lawrence's very first visit, she took him to see the gamekeeper's hut in the wood, and then out to see the view from the wood 'as if we were looking from a big window':[6] a view he later described frequently in his fiction. But he drew so much upon the place, and upon the wood, that particular identifications are almost irrelevant. The landscape of his first novel, *The White Peacock*, is steeped in the countryside around the Haggs; the same woods and fields were the setting for his first poems, and then appeared in his stories 'A Prelude' and 'A Modern Lover' (and its later counterpart 'The Shades of Spring'); and again in 'A Fragment of Stained Glass', 'Second-Best' and 'Love Among the Haystacks'. Great stretches of *Sons and Lovers* drew upon that particular landscape; and it recurred in the fragments of the 'Burns Novel' written just before the end of 1912. It went on appearing long after Lawrence had left the Haggs, Eastwood and England; the wood in *Lady Chatterley's Lover*, which Lawrence finished early in 1928, is in almost every way a recreation of the wood, with the same keeper's hut and the identical view from the 'window' he had seen that day in 1901.

Going to the Haggs, too, he discovered something of nature's wildness to supplement what he knew from the neat gardens and allotments of East-wood. For a town boy, oppressed by living 'among bricks and mortar', he was growing up extraordinarily knowledgeable about plants, wild flowers and nature in general. His interest doubtless started with his parents; his mother loved her scraps of garden, and we know he helped his father with the family allotment. His father, however, was 'very good on wild life, and he knew ... he knew the names of the birds and animals and that. He was very good at that.' Like his son, he was an expert on wild flowers, fungi and herbs; he gathered the latter for the bitter herb-tea he made, just as his son did. More than any of the other children, Bert Lawrence acquired Arthur Lawrence's particular expertise; the unspoken appreciation, the quickness of recognition. Characteristically, he supplemented it with book-learning:

he acquired a copy of W. T. Gordon's *Our Country's Flowers: And How to Know Them* in July 1900.[7] He grew to seem almost uncanny in his empathy with wild things; often shy with people until he knew them well, he found he could move joyously and unselfconsciously in the natural world.

And yet his first visits to the Haggs and its wood, in the summer of 1901, might have been his last – the relationship between the families being so tenuous – had it not been for his own desperate illness that winter. Following this, he had months in which to recuperate, and one of the first outings he made was to the Haggs. Edmund Chambers 'suggested that, in a few days, when he got stronger, he could ride up in the milkcart and join his lads in the hayfield': and 'Since Bert was recuperating, he spent much time at our farm, the walk back and forth thought to be beneficial.' He wrote lengthy letters to the Chambers family while convalescing in Skegness in April 1902, and when he returned to Eastwood began to spend time at the Haggs regularly. His visits continued even after he started as a pupil-teacher at Eastwood's British school in the autumn of 1902: 'at least once a week, sometimes oftener and always at holiday times, and especially at Christmas'.[8]

And the family, too, quite unlike his own, grew to expect him; grew to love him as he loved them. The image of the boy who 'rushed with such joy to the Haggs' inevitably suggests one who was escaping from Eastwood and from his family home. Jessie Chambers described what she remembered of the particular atmosphere of the Lawrence household in the early 1900s: an atmosphere both exciting and disturbing.

There seemed to be a tightness in the air, as if something unusual might happen at any minute. It was somehow exciting, yet it made me feel a little sick . . . It was not due specifically to anything that was said or done, though happenings there had sharp edges and a dramatic quality that made them stand out in one's memory. It was a constant quality, something one felt immediately on entering the house. I liked to go, just to feel, as it were, or to listen to the curious, powerful vibration, so different from our house, or any house I have ever known.[9]

The tremendous tension of oppositions, the strict moral tone and the years of anger combined to make that 'vibration'. The Haggs was certainly not a peaceful or quarrel-free household: the carefree and arrogantly male Edmund Chambers, the self-sacrificing Ann Chambers demanding emotional sympathy from her children, the superior eldest son Alan, the tensions between the younger brothers and sisters – in short, the very strong-willed attitudes of everyone in the Chambers family never made for peacefulness. But at the Haggs there was always liveliness, there was a freedom from inhibition and above all there was a tremendous capacity for sheer pleasure as well as for quarrels. There were not the same standards of conduct, speech and attitude to be maintained which could make life so tense in Walker Street. Will Holbrook, who married May Chambers in 1906, remembered that Lawrence 'loved to come where he could do and say just what he pleased, even to using strong language to win his point'.[10] Angers and differences were expressed in the Chambers family, not bottled up and brooded over to issue just occasionally as catastrophic and unforgivable rows; and Lawrence was struck by what he later confusedly wrote down as the 'wholesome happiness on of a farm' (i. 103).

Lawrence found that he fitted wonderfully into this in some ways substitute family at the Haggs; 'fitted . . . as though he had been born into it': 'became almost one of the family'.[11] Alan, three years older, and May (the first to leave home) were a little aloof from him to start with. Jessie, Hubert and Bernard were his natural companions, and he was effectively an elder brother to the younger children. David Chambers, 3 when Lawrence first came to the Haggs, wrote how

His vitality seemed to illumine the house and stimulate the entire household. He had what might be called an electric presence, raising the potential of everyone around him. As for me, I adored him. I looked for his coming at weekends and I could not imagine a Christmas without him. I think everyone loved him at this time; he combined with his vivacity a sweetness of disposition that was quite irresistible.[12]

It might seem easy to overestimate the importance of the Haggs for Lawrence; after all, he was there for only a few hours every week, compared with the days he spent at home. And yet, as an adolescent growing up in a tense and demanding home environment, even those few hours were important. It is never too late to have a happy childhood, and Lawrence discovered his at the Haggs. 'In later years he said that in those days [the period up to 1906] he was only happy when he was either at The Haggs or on the way there.' The Chambers family were warm and cheerful companions who loved and admired him, and in whose company he flourished: no longer was he any kind of outsider. 'It was a splendid time for all of us, and Bert was always the centre to whom we all looked as leader, a position he thoroughly enjoyed'; they could talk, they could sing; they read aloud, took part in charades, danced and played all the usual party games.[13] The boy who had invented those games for his younger sister now found a whole family to play with him. The other side of the quiet and often withdrawn boy we associate with Eastwood was a figure of dynamic and demanding energy; lively, stimulating, responsive, and – once in a context he found sympathetic – thoroughly assured. (His assurance was one of the things which probably developed at the Haggs.) As a result, Jessie Chambers remembered how 'In our home his name was a synonym for joy – radiant joy in simply being alive. He communicated that joy to all of us, and made us even happy with one another while he was there, – no small achievement in a family like ours!'[14]

The Chambers parents loved him as much as their children did – Ann Chambers 'like one of her own'; he found them knowledgeable, sympathetic and undemanding. As a result, he could be with them the gay and spirited son he found it so hard to be at home (though clearly his brother Ernest and sister Ada had seen that side of him). 'Ah, you Haggites see the best of me!' he once remarked. He could also be helpful in the Chambers family – eight or nine would commonly sit down to meals, plus Lawrence – in ways that Lydia Lawrence's household management (and the presence of his two unmarried sisters) would not have allowed him to be at home. At the Haggs, he 'set about household tasks, such as cooking, and even washing, and would help to prepare the family meal and lay the table. With Bert in charge, the meal was a family party.'[15] We don't hear again of his being so irresistibly happy, relaxed and stimulating until he went away with Frieda in 1912, when friends reported similar stories of his vivacity, his capacity for games and mimicry and fun, and the sheer sense of adventure which he brought to ordinary life. And his life-long nostalgia for 'a few folk' with whom to live the good life, somewhere in the country, goes directly back to these years at the Haggs. As Jessie put it, 'is that Golden Age of which D.H.L. dreamed in some remote past any further back than his own boyhood & youth?'[16]

The 'new life', of course, was not without its complications. 'He told us rather shamefacedly that his mother said he might as well pack his things and come and live with us': Jessie Chambers remembered that being said as early as 1902.[17] He had survived the winter 1901–2, and his mother had claimed him with particular love; but now she found him escaping to the Haggs and must have feared she was losing him again. Nor can it have been easy for any of the Eastwood family to welcome back the boy who so hugely enjoyed his visits to the Haggs: it inevitably seemed a criticism of *them* . . . The seeds of his family's later annoyance with Jessie Chambers were sown long before his visits to the Haggs became primarily for her sake. Both his sisters, as well as his mother, shared in the resentment. May Chambers remembered the kind of gossip there was:

My parents were blamed for encouraging him to spend so much time at our house.' We as a family were stealing him from his mother. My sister [Jessie] was claiming his time which should be spent in the open air. She was taking far too much for granted. He came just for his health and not because of any liking for any particular one of us.

I tried to get my parents to forbid him our house . . . I thought he should stay away if his family hated him to come, and he scolded:

'They don't hate it, really. It's just the way they carry on. If it wasn't this, it would be something else. But I shall come,' he said with quiet obstinacy, 'and nothing will stop me unless your father and mother say I can't come.'

Lawrence also complained 'how he had to tell his family everything he did while at our house' – something which added to May's resentment.[18] But he kept going to the Haggs; before 1906, it was always more a place than a particular person which took him there, and even more a family than a place. But he knew that 'if it wasn't this, it would be something else': Lydia Lawrence would have resented any such power as the Haggs and the Chambers family had begun to exert over him.

The farm kitchen also gave him a quite new feeling for, and knowledge of, rural working-class life. The Chambers family were always fairly poor – 'Miriam was even poorer than he',* he remarked later:[19] though as tenant farmers, doing most of the farm work themselves, they would not have been subject to the low earnings of farm workers in the late nineteenth-century period, relative to those of industrial workers. But the farm could neither give all of them employment nor support the family as a whole: by 1907, two of the Chambers sons were working as coal-miners. The Chambers family, with the three eldest sons employed either on the farm or in the pit, and the two eldest daughters both schoolteachers, offers another microcosm of a working-class family in the midst of a period of change. It helps us see how the Lawrence family, with none of its sons working in the local industry, was less than typical of both the region and of the period.

But at the Haggs Lawrence experienced working-class family life of a different kind from any he would have known in Eastwood itself; a life not marked by a hoped-for advance to status in the cramped confines of the small town, nor containing an angry breadwinner hostile to the distance from him which his family had cultivated. The Chambers were fairly badly-off people who were nevertheless remarkably aware of books and literature: their love of such things spread cheerfully and effortlessly over the divides that gaped in the Lawrence family. Jessie Chambers remembered, for example, how when she was four years old Edmund Chambers read out loud *Tess of the D'Urbervilles* to her mother when it was serialised in the *Nottinghamshire Guardian* (the only provincial paper to print it) between July and December 1891; she recalled how her mother 'was flushed and excited, and kept making little exclamations of surprise and dismay'. But Edmund and Ann Chambers also 'adored Barrie, *The Little Minister* and *A Window in Thrums*', and their family grew up to read voraciously.[20] Into such a family Lawrence fitted marvellously. Even May Chambers, self-confessedly 'only

---

* Here, as elsewhere, 'Miriam' and 'Muriel' normally refer to recreations of Jessie Chambers.

on the outer fringe' of Lawrence's circle, recalled how in company with him,

> we delighted in even merely knowing the great names of literature. We read something of all, though I, an outcast, did not join the circle around the parlour fire where passages were read aloud and sometimes plays in their entirety.
>
> Bert was always eager to talk about books and poetry, and brought special ones we 'simply must read.' Maupassant, and Ibsen, Tolstoy, Anatole France, besides our English writers, were familiar names with us . . .[21]

The stimulus of such reading out loud and discussion, in a non-academic environment and by people whose feet were very firmly on the ground, was yet another of the pleasures of the Haggs.

For books were yet another source of division in the Lawrence family. The Lawrences had always spent more money on books than other families did. In their Christmas stockings, as children, 'Usually we each had a book or some small toy': a neighbour remembered how, as a child, 'Ada had a book with Arabian Nights stories in it, princesses with veils and painted slippers and rouge on their cheeks and men with baggy trousers . . . we couldn't have afforded books like that'.[22] We know some of the other books given to and owned by the children: Lawrence's sisters gave him *Hero Charlie*, by Mary Hamden, 'on his eleventh Birthday', while Maria Cummin's *The Lamplighter* was given Emily Lawrence by 'her brother and sister' in 1897. With his sisters, he read adventure stories such as '*Coral Island, The Swiss Family Robinson, The Gorilla Hunters*, etc.'; later he enjoyed the works of Marryat and James Fenimore Cooper. The children also read children's magazines: *The Prize, The Chatterbox* and *Child's Own* – none of them cheap, but all of them 'improving' and religious. The money spent on books and magazines angered Arthur Lawrence, who 'felt no desire to read anything but newspapers'; Lawrence recalled how 'My father hated books, hated the sight of anyone reading or writing.' Books and reading symbolised for him the kind of genteel, leisured waste of time characteristic of women and children at home. 'It's only fools as sits wi' their noses stuck i' books, that's what *I* say', remarks Walter Morel, who 'canna see what there is i' books, ter sit borin' your nose in 'em for'.[23]

On the other hand, Lydia Lawrence encouraged and was proud of her children's reading. Emily, in spite of winning prize books and reading out loud to her younger brother and sister, was never a great reader, and nor was George. But Ernest, unlike his younger brother in so many ways, shared his passion for books; he was locally famous for it. His obituary remarked how, at the Mechanics' Institute library 'there was no more familiar figure than his, he was a great reader from a boy, and in his early teens he had become acquainted with most of the present day writers and many of the past'.[24] Ernest bought a set of the twenty-volume anthology *International Library of Famous Literature*, edited by Dr Richard Garnett, sometime between August 1900 (when it was first published) and his death just over a year later; it cost him £8-18-6, a vast sum of money even for a London clerk who was doing well, and suggests what respect he had for books (and how buying them was more important than sending money home to Eastwood). Jessie Chambers recalled that very set:

One of the most treasured possessions of the Lawrence household was a set of large volumes bound in green cloth containing long extracts from famous authors.* The books had belonged to Ernest, and were regarded with a reverence amounting to awe. Lawrence must have made many literary acquaintances through the medium of these volumes. As a mark of rare favour I was once allowed to borrow one of them, but the favour was never repeated.[25]

The same set, together with the prize and presentation books won by the younger brother as a student, appears in the stage directions for the family-kitchen setting of *A Collier's Friday Night*, which describes an evening between 1906 and 1909.

The upper case is full of books, seen through the two flimsy glass doors: a large set of the "Worlds Famous Literature" in dark green at the top – then on the next shelf prize books in calf and gold, and imitation soft-leather poetry books, and a Nuttalls dictionary and Cassell's ⟨English⟩ 'French', German and Latin dictionaries.

Another '*four shelves of books*' – '*ill-assorted school-books, with an edition of Lessing florid in green and gilt, but tarnished*'[26] – are mentioned earlier in the same stage direction. Such a stage direction (like the detail of the mother reading the *New Age*) insists that *this* collier's kitchen is something special. The books behind glass in the case possess an odd kind of sanctity; their bindings, and the kind of books they are, suggest not only literary but scholarly tastes.

At the Haggs Lawrence could not only read and study, but also share his reading and his fascination with language, which naturally included diction-ary and reference-book knowledge. May Chambers remembered it: ' " 'A black ousel!' " he would say. "There is such a thing. It's a blackbird. I

---

* Lawrence doubtless read widely in them. And yet Garnett's collection was a memorial to the masterpieces of the period up to the last quarter of the nineteenth century; it contains only scraps of Ibsen and Hardy; no Wilde, Shaw, William James or Nietzsche; its Darwin is brief and uncompelling, like its T. H. Huxley; its Haeckel only a scrap of travelogue. A strength of the set is its focus on American writing: but the extracts are short, and their main function is to provoke a taste for the books from which they come. The volumes are not designed for serious study.

looked *ousel* up. 'You black ousel,' our mother said to the girls. 'You black ousel.' " And he rolled it over his tongue.' The three occasions on which May Chambers remembered his relish for language all concerned words which Lawrence had heard his mother using. 'Mother does know a lot of old words, and they come out when she's mad': ' "Tears! tears thick as pipe-stails streaming! Tears dropping like peas! And neither kind will do you any good, you saucy madam!" That's what mother said this morning to the girls.' Lawrence's father was well known for his liveliness as a talker,[27] and some of his idioms stayed in his son's memory for years: 'It would wear the heart out of a wheel-barrow trundle, as my father would say', suddenly bubbled up out of a letter Lawrence wrote in 1913 (i. 506). However, if Lawrence acquired from both his parents fluency, unexpectedness and rich-ness of language – and from his mother, in particular, consciousness of language – then the Haggs was the place where he brought it to fruition. From around 1905 Jessie would become the particular audience for his writing; but the Haggs family all shared in his youthful literary, intellectual and linguistic excitements. As late as the summer of 1908, after a week working with the Haggs family on the hay harvest, Lawrence's plans for a week of rest included an evening with friends at the Haggs:

in the low parlour I shall read Verlaine to the girls (in French – the nut-brown eyes of Louie [Burrows] will laugh and scold me; the soft dark eyes of Emily [Jessie Chambers] will look at me, pensive, doubtful – not quite sure what I mean) – and perhaps I'll read Whitman; we shall walk arm in arm through the woods home in the moonlight. (i. 68)

II Pupil-Teacher

The spring and summer of 1902 following his illness had been a turning point for Lawrence. It was one thing to enjoy his convalescence, go to the Haggs and explore the delights of the family there. But the biggest question was: What should he do for a career, now that he was finally well again? The fact that he did not return to Haywoods, or to any other work as a clerk, suggests that his mother had recognised the link between his illness and his job, and that his brains could save him from the rigours of a factory. The obvious career for him was schoolteaching, which – according to George Neville – Lawrence 'longed for'. During the late nineteenth century, elementary schoolteachers were still being recruited almost completely from the 'respectable' working class; and the passage of the 1902 Education Act, the changes that followed in the administration of local education, and in particular the increasing stress upon the training of teachers in undenominational colleges, such as the Day Training Department now established at the University College of Nottingham, combined to make teaching seem an eminently sensible choice. Lydia Lawrence's brief career as a pupil-teacher had got her nowhere; forty years later her son had a far better chance. The decision was taken that, after all, Lawrence should become a teacher; and following what Neville remembered as 'considerable "effort" ', he began duties in October 1902 as a pupil-teacher under George Holderness, headmaster of the Boys' section of the Albert Street Schools, Eastwood.[28] The local Congregational minister, the Rev. Robert Reid, who acted as correspondent between the managers of the school and the local education authority, was probably responsible for getting Lawrence his place. At the end of September, the Boys' section had lost a pupil-teacher, Samuel J. Bunting, when he won a scholarship: but there was the usual influx of pupils from the Infants' department at the start of October. By 10 October, George Holderness was struggling to teach three classes simultaneously: 'It has been impossible to work as it should be done', he recorded in his log-book. He told Reid about his problems, and Reid laid the matter before the school managers. It cannot be a coincidence that Lawrence started work on Monday 24 October; the necessary £12 a year had presumably been found to pay him.[29]

It is to this period that an anecdote told by May Chambers probably belongs. The Lawrence family in the period 1901–3 must have been particularly hard-up, with no money coming in from anyone in the family apart from Arthur – but with, for example, the money for Ernest's headstone and grave surround to pay off: the whole cost of his funeral had come to just under £30, which would have been another dreadful extra burden on the family budget.[30] There would have been doctor's bills to pay, too, from Lawrence's illness in the winter of 1901–2: while Arthur Lawrence's serious accident of November 1903 (he was in hospital for a month and off work longer) would have made things still worse. Lawrence, around the time he started as a pupil-teacher, was wearing boots which had been given him second-hand by friends; and he was thoroughly self-conscious about them. May Chambers recalled how he 'thrust them under my nose to find out if the gift had been talked about'. As a pupil-teacher, furthermore, he would be paid only 'a shilling a week with a yearly increase supposed to cover the cost of books'.[31] Accordingly, he had to go out to work while waiting to start, and probably at other times too during the next few years; he told his friends who were going to evening classes that, with his aptitude for maths shown at the High School, he had had to take an opportunity

to earn a few shillings on market night keeping accounts for the leading pork butcher. He shivered as he told us, dreading the publicity.

'Don't pass by when you go to science class,' he begged. 'Bang on the window or something to let me see you, and I shan't feel so lonely.'[32]

Each of the group of friends, May Chambers remembered, individually drew his attention 'as he sat on a high stool at the desk in the butcher's shop just beyond the window display'; and on their way back they all 'grinned in sympathy with him in his prison. He wore his cap and looked cold, and smiled back anxiously and enviously, and there we faced him and cheered him up, he assured us, by not passing him by forgotten.'[33] The anecdote helps us imagine the loneliness and the sense of being abandoned which he must have experienced in the autumn of 1901 at Haywood's Nottingham factory; even now he was a boy who desperately needed to feel neither 'forgotten' nor exposed to 'publicity' as he worked in Gethin Hogg's Pork Butcher's shop, only a few minutes walk from home.

Pupil-teachers, as the name suggests, both taught and were taught: from 1846 they had traditionally been instructed by the headmasters under whom they served, as they worked towards the examination for the teacher's certificate. Lawrence had to take instruction from George Holderness for an hour before lessons started, which meant an eight-o'clock start. May Chambers, now herself a pupil-teacher in the Girls' department at Albert Street, was very aware of Lawrence's dilemma when he passed from the headmaster's tuition to the far harder confrontation with his own class: 'Bert begged me to look out for him and "give him a smile to cheer," for he was frightened to death. The sort of boy he was not strong enough to play with he was now to try to teach.'[34] George Holderness made a laconic comment in the school log-book on Lawrence's arrival at Albert Street: 'The third Standard has this week been mainly under the care of D. H. Lawrence, a young person 17 years old, who has finished a three years' course at the Nottingham High School, and who has come with a view to becoming a Pupil Teacher.' Holderness, however, was soon impressed by Lawrence's work. Standard III – 9 year olds – remained Lawrence's class, and by 4 May 1903 had 'made very good progress in all subjects'; in June 1903, its work had 'progressed satisfactorily'.[35] That July, Lawrence heard that, together with his fellow pupil-teacher in the Boys' Department, Richard Pogmore, he had passed the first year's examination. In September 1903 he started at Albert Street with the same class, now Standard IV.

But the training of pupil-teaching was undergoing considerable changes. 'Required to teach all day, the pupil-teachers were dependent upon the headteacher for the improvement of their own knowledge and this had to be accomplished outside normal school hours';[36] as early as 1870 it had been recommended that pupil-teachers should receive part-time instruction in special centres set up for them. This meant they would be absent from their schools on a regular basis, and would not just get their instruction from the head teachers for an hour each morning. Head teachers, however, often resisted the loss of staff entailed by the new arrangement: and George Holderness was no exception. He hung on to his pupil-teachers as long as he could: not until March 1904 was Lawrence at last given permission to attend the Ilkeston centre, set up in 1899 and the nearest to Eastwood, just over the Derbyshire border (i. 26).[37] On 7 June 1904, George Holderness had received a message from his director of Education outlining his pupil's timetable; he added his own comments in the log-book. 'D. H. Lawrence is to attend the Ilkeston Pupil teacher centre on Tuesday & Thursday mornings, Wednesday and Friday afternoons & Saturday mornings. Pointed out that these times would considerably interfere with School work unless more help is granted.' In spite of his protests, word came through on 7 July that 'the Pupil Teachers are to attend the Ilkeston Centre beginning on Saturday [9 July], and that if this interfere with the ordinary lessons on the Time Table. collective lessons, such as Singing, should be given during their absence.'[38]

Though his headmaster in Eastwood suffered, Lawrence remembered his days at the Ilkeston centre as particularly enjoyable: 'I wish they could be repeated' (i. 28) he wrote to one of the teachers in the summer of 1905. Thomas Beacroft, a 'dapper little gentleman', only 33 but a headmaster since he was 28, brisk and direct and a very strict disciplinarian, was principal at the centre, which currently operated in a room in the Gladstone Street Schools. Confronted by Lawrence, Beacroft 'quickly perceived his unusual gifts ... they got on extremely well together':[39] Lawrence himself paid tribute to 'the greatest assistance' he had received from Beacroft (i. 26). Thomas Alfred Beacroft had had no University training (he had attended York Training College); his main subjects were Geography, History, Music, Art and Mathematics – and it was as a mathematician that Lawrence continued to shine. He remembered in 1924 how tables of logarithms used to give him 'a certain thrill' (v. 64), while his fellow pupil-teacher Richard ('Dick') Pogmore recalled how good Lawrence was at algebra.

I remember being at Teachers' Centre one Saturday morning when it was held in the Gladstone Street Schools [i.e. before July 1904], and Mr Beacroft, who was always pretty hot tempered, had set us a problem. Not one of us could do it. And he suddenly stormed at us, 'Oh! You – not one of you as good as Lawrence! He did it yesterday in a few minutes.' And he turned the blackboard around and showed us Lawrence's working on the board.[40]

It was at the centre that Lawrence first met Louie Burrows, from Cossall, to whom he was later engaged; there, too, went George Neville and Richard Pogmore from Eastwood, May and Jessie Chambers from Underwood and a man called Gilbert Noon from Cotmanhay. A group was thus formed which shared the journey to Ilkeston, the work and the social life which followed: George Neville and Dick Pogmore (the latter at one stage rather fond of Ada Lawrence) were both regular visitors to the Lynn Croft house, while Louie Burrows and Gilbert Noon both went to college with Lawrence in 1906.[41]

The centre was to assist pupil-teachers to prepare better for the examinations leading up to the certificate. During his second year as a pupil-teacher, 1903–4, Lawrence was studying for the King's Scholarship exam, which would get him a training college or day training college place; he was being paid only £17-0-0 a year, and it was doubtless the period he remembered teaching 'for 2/6 a week' (v. 479). Not until his third year did his salary rise to £24-0-0.[42] H. M. Inspector called at the British School at the start of the year to hear 'the Reading and Recitation of D. H. Lawrence the Scholarship candidate'; on 25 November 1904, Lawrence was granted three weeks' absence from Albert Street: one for the exam itself, and two for a fortnight's preparation at the centre, the local Education Committee having resolved that such pupils 'be allowed to attend ... every day during the fortnight immediately preceding'. Lawrence later described his method of study in a note written for the *Schoolmaster*: his habit was 'to make condensed notes of each subject as I studied it from the text-book; then to learn the notes by heart. I always took the greatest care to let no spelling or grammatical error go unrectified in these notes, and thus acquired the habit of writing quickly and correctly ...'[43] May Chambers remembered how nervous Lawrence was before examinations:

> We didn't think he could ever fail on any subject, but he would look desperate and say: 'What if I fail?' We would say he was too modest, that if we knew half he knew we should go down on our knees and give heart-felt thanks. But he refused to be assured and would look tragic and say, 'Wouldn't it be awful if I did fail!' When the results came out, his name would top the list or come second. But not before he had made himself quite ill with worry and doubt.

The anxiety is revealing: without a job, hardly earning, dependent on his family, he felt he had to succeed.[44]

Succeed he did. On 25 February 1905, Beacroft sent him to the Nottingham Shire Hall to hear his result: '1st Division 1st Class', as George Holderness proudly recorded it in his school log. He sent Lawrence a book as a way of congratulating him (i. 25). 2,603 male candidates had sat the exam that year; only 37 got into the first division of Class 1. Lawrence's friend Gilbert Noon got into the second division of Class 1; the following year, Jessie Chambers and Louie Burrows would also get into Class 1 (divisions three and four respectively), and George Neville would be in Class 2. The local paper called Lawrence's result a 'brilliant success'; his fellow pupils at the Centre planned to chair him through Ilkeston, but he got to hear of the plan and did not go that day. He had to write that letter to the *Schoolmaster*, and to send a photograph and write a note for the *Teacher*. He remarked in the former that 'I must say that no one is more astonished than myself at my own success', though 'I attribute my success in a great measure to a love of literature'. From now on, he remembered, he was 'considered clever'.[45]

Problems continued at Albert Street, however, because of the absence of pupil-teachers at Ilkeston. On 10 April 1905, with Richard Pogmore absent ill, George Holderness noted that 'This afternoon with Lawrence at the P.T. Centre, work was almost impossible. The master endeavoured to take Stands. 3.5.6.7 – over 90 boys'. Six weeks later, Lawrence brought a message from Beacroft that his attendance at Ilkeston was required 'for the whole of the next two weeks'. Holderness again resisted: 'Pointed out that with the present staff this would be impossible, as it would leave over 100 for the Master alone. Arranged for him to attend every morning and for Pogmore to stay away on Tuesday and Thursday.'[46] It must have been a relief for his headmaster when Lawrence ended his days at the Centre in July 1905.

Beacroft had wanted Lawrence so often because he was helping him (and other pupils) prepare for the London Matriculation exam in the summer of 1905. This exam would enable Lawrence to enter the day-training department of Nottingham University College, where he would follow the Normal (i.e. non-degree) course leading to the teacher's certificate: 'to be in the profession without attendance at a training college was a very serious handicap'.[47] It was not actually necessary to go to college to obtain one's certificate; many teachers (Jessie Chambers among them) qualified by taking the external examination. But Lawrence was obviously academically exceptional; and his mother, at least, hoped that he might follow a degree course at Nottingham and not just study for his teacher's certificate.

He passed his matriculation examination in June 1905 – this time, however, only in the second class, after the misery of 'pen-driving in the city heat' (i. 27) in Nottingham: a trip to Norfolk immediately afterwards with Ada and some friends (but without his mother or Jessie Chambers) was probably a reward for his hard work. He could in theory have gone to college in the autumn of 1905, but returned to Albert Street on 1 August 1905 to spend a year as a full-time teacher: he needed £20 'in a lump sum to pay the entrance fee' at Nottingham.[48] It was full-time teaching at last: a grim year, with a class fast growing up. He remembered how 'I had to fight bitterly for my authority' (i. 39). He later referred to it as 'savage teaching', though George Holderness was full of praise for his work: at the March 1906 Quarterly examinations, the headmaster noted how 'The whole of the work in Standard 5, under the charge of D. H. Lawrence was especially well done'. In 1908, writing a reference for Lawrence, Holderness summed up his opinion of his work at Albert Street:

He served his apprenticeship with me, and in every respect gave thorough satisfaction. He is hard-working and painstaking, energetic and bright in his manner, and at the same time kind and considerate for others. I have been in charge of these schools 28 years and during that period have had many teachers, but in my opinion, none of greater promise than Mr. Lawrence.
I can confidently recommend him as an exceptionally efficient teacher.[49]

But what he could save out of his £55 salary was not sufficient to cover all his expenses, and he went back to teaching at Albert Street for an extra eight weeks at the start of the autumn term in 1906, stopping only on 28 September, a few days before the start of the College term.[50] Once again, 'though it was obvious that it would mean a very great struggle to bear the expense', Lydia Lawrence 'decided that the sacrifice must be made', and the family began saving 'every possible penny towards sending Lawrence to college'. When they had been young, Lydia Lawrence had always made as much of her children's clothing as she could; she still continued to mend and patch their clothes. Emily Lawrence remembered an adage of hers: 'There is no disgrace in a patch, but there is in a hole.' Sons and Lovers describes William, working as a clerk, putting on a shirt so patched that it is impossible to tell where or what the original material is. The usual problems arose with expensive items like boots and suits; Mrs Lambert, in A Collier's Friday Night, worries about the expense of a new pair of boots for her student son; Ada Lawrence remembered how her brother's going to college 'meant a good deal of sacrifice by his mother'.[51] It was around this time that Lawrence finally acquired the suit ('peed for') which led to the distressing row about money with his father.

One of the things that eventually helped the family's finances was the fact that Ada herself started work as a full-time (though uncertificated) teacher in June 1907, half-way through Lawrence's course; she had also attended the Ilkeston centre and passed the King's Scholarship exam in 1906, in Class 3. Lawrence's sister Emily, having been 'out in service' in Eastwood, had got married in November 1904 and was no longer living at home:[52] but Lawrence's prolonged period of education and training meant that he would be the last of his family to become financially independent, at the age of 23.

III Jessie Chambers

Perhaps the most significant thing about these years of training, however, was Lawrence's developing relationship with Jessie Chambers. The third child of the Chambers family, Jessie had been born on 29 January 1887. She was strikingly attractive as an adolescent – 'like a lovely Italian picture', with rich brown curls – though she was never physically as graceful as her 'brown curled' head suggested (see Illustration 22). Louie Burrows, who first saw her in 1904, noticed a 'somewhat large nose and spare chin with eyes brown and steadfast – serious and rather undulating in her carriage, gay only as a duty – and then effortfully – thin lips with a very pleasant expression'. Another woman described how she looked in 1910: 'Her short, soft, dark curls flouted the convention of a hat and belied the firm lines of her nose and chin. She was tanned as a gipsy, and wore a claret-red frock of simple cut that suited her colouring.' Jessie remembered first seeing Lawrence around 1896, but was close to him from 1902 until he left England in 1912.[53]

The Lawrence she first saw at Eastwood's Congregational Sunday school was a 'slight, fair boy of about eleven', even then 'the perfect pattern of a scholarship boy'.[54] But she saw little more of him or of his family until Lydia Lawrence and her youngest son paid their first visit to the Haggs Farm, in the spring of 1901. It was Jessie's sister May who showed Lawrence round, however, and Jessie's brothers Bernard and Hubert who gravitated to the young Lawrence as companions, while Lawrence himself eventually made a particular friend of the eldest son Alan.

Like Lawrence, Jessie was a bookish child. Her brother David described how, as a child and as an adolescent, she

had a passion for poetry and went about the house and on the way from school reciting specially the poems of Scott – *Marmion*, *The Lay of the Last Minstrel*; and also Wordsworth. She recited *Lucy Gray* to me with a tragic intensity which I have never forgotten. I could see those footsteps in the snow and their disappearance over the broken ridge and I often wished we could have something more cheerful.[55]

David was not her only brother to respond unhappily to her 'passion for poetry'; her sister May remembered how Hubert and Bernard

took delight in bursting in on her rhapsodical moods and shattering her poetical day-dreams in a wild scrimmage of slaps and bangs. I remember them once waiting for her as she came along reciting *The Lay of the Last Minstrel* or 'Lucy Gray' and springing out on her as she went by. Then they took to their heels, for the chase was on.

For though Jessie was at times intense and rhapsodic, she could also – says David – be 'equal to anybody'. Her brothers learned this to their cost: May recalled how 'In lighter moods, she would wind a scarf round each fist and challenge them both to a fight.'[56] But those 'lighter moods' were rare; she was characteristically either angry with her family because of the drudgery in the farm kitchen to which she felt her menfolk confined her, or grimly aloof from the family apart from her mother. As Louie Burrows put it, Jessie was in general 'gay only as a duty'.

Lawrence's first contacts with the Haggs family, on his Wednesday after-noon half-holidays, came when 'he would step quietly into our kitchen, often bringing some magazine or other to our book-loving household'. Throughout the period of his visits to the Haggs, 'Books . . . flowed through the house, and floods of talk about their authors'. However, of all the family, Jessie was the most deeply stirred by what she read. It was therefore natural that, after his convalescence in the spring of 1902, when he was 16½, the 15-year-old Jessie should have been most drawn to him. Like their mothers, they shared a passion for what lay beyond the immediacies of their different worlds: 'Right from infancy I had been aware of a world that glimmered beyond the surrounding world of fact, and I dreaded lest the circumstances of my life should shut me out, compel me to live, as it were, in the dark, and prevent me from ever becoming a sharer in the feast of the human spirit.'[57]

But Jessie was also the first person Lawrence was drawn to in the kind of sympathy which was so characteristic of him as an adult: he seemed to understand Jessie very well from the start. Just when he met her she was 'in a state of furious discontent and rebellion' against her family; in particular she felt her lack of education to be 'a constant humiliation'.[58] At the age of 15, in April 1902, a monitress at Underwood National School, she was assisting in the Infants' classes – a post of responsibility; yet it was hardly helping *her* forward. The young Lawrence was thus almost magically trans-ported into her life, to be the person who would help release her. He was a little older than she; had read more and was better educated; but he was prepared, even eager, to share what he had learned, especially in the appre-ciative atmosphere which he found at the Haggs. As well as bringing books for the family, Lawrence started to bring them especially for Jessie; and the two of them soon became their families' representatives when books were borrowed from the Mechanics' Institute Library in Eastwood. Jessie's visit to the library 'was . . . the outstanding event of the week'. Lawrence

would take possession of my list and pounce on the book he was looking for; he always seemed to know just where to look for it. We were both excited by this hunting among books . . . Then Lawrence and I would set off for my home literally burdened with books. During the walk we discussed what we had read last, but our discussion was not exactly criticism, indeed it was not criticism at all, but a vivid re-creation of the substance of our reading.[59]

Unlike the dipping and tasting which the Lawrence family's Garnett anthology would have encouraged, this was the beginning of a 'kind of orgy of reading' in which both Lawrence and Jessie engaged, and which began to detach them to some extent from the other members of their families:

> our reading became a kind of personal experience. Scott's novels in particular we talked over in this way, and the scenes and events of his stories were more real to us than our actual surroundings . . . And to say that we *read* the books gives no adequate idea of what really happened. It was the entering into possession of a new world, a widening and enlargement of life.[60]

Lawrence probably recalled Jessie's attitude towards that 'widening and enlargement of life' when he came to write *The Rainbow* in 1914–15. It is exactly what the first generation of 'Brangwen women' – like Jessie, in danger of being trapped on their farm – yearn for; while in the third generation Ursula Brangwen (who like Jessie becomes a teacher) determines to possess the 'new world' for herself.[61]

In their early years, it was mostly novels which excited Lawrence and Jessie, and created their sense of 'enlargement'; Scott, Charles Reade, James Fenimore Cooper, Stevenson. They read these in their first period of 'sheer revelling in books', before the end of 1904. By then they had also begun to read George Eliot, Charlotte Brontë and Thackeray, together with a good deal of poetry, mostly from Palgrave's *Golden Treasury*. 'Lawrence carried the little red volume in his pocket and read to me on every opportunity, usually out in the fields. He must have read almost every poem to me at one time or another'. But they read other poetry too. Lawrence got to know William Blake; Blake's life and work fascinated him, and Jessie gave him *Songs of Innocence* and *Songs of Experience* for Christmas, probably in 1905.[62] Blake's passionate dialectic, his hatred of scientific truth and fact, his insistence upon the supreme value of the individual in the face of the social norm – these became things which stayed with Lawrence. Swinburne, too, became a favourite poet of Lawrence's. He was able to describe his 'love of literature' as having played an important part in his examination success, while Violet Hunt noted how, when she first knew Lawrence in London late in 1909, he was 'more conversant with decadent poetry' than either she or Ford Madox Hueffer, the editor of the *English Review*: 'and that is saying a great deal'. Hueffer himself paid tribute to Lawrence's knowledge of literature: 'I have never known any young man of his age who was so well read in all the dullnesses that spread between Milton and George Eliot . . . he moved amongst the high things of culture with a tranquil assurance . . .'[63]

Lawrence also read Jessie poetry when she came to the Lawrence home in Walker Street and later in Lynn Croft – but, here, the sheer pleasure of reading was constrained; he would sit 'ready to close the book and swiftly put it away if a step should sound outside in the entry'.[64] He did not want to be found reading poetry by his family: in particular by his father or by Emily. Hence the reading 'out in the fields' or in the little parlour at the Haggs.

By the spring of 1906, when Lawrence was 20½ and Jessie 19, they were reading Lamb, Emerson, Thoreau and Carlyle; and what Jessie called Lawrence's 'early flamboyant delight in reading was changing into a seriousness that was at times almost frightening in its intensity'. He later described himself as 'suffering acutely from Carlyliophobia' in 1906 (i. 49); he read *Sartor Resartus*, *The French Revolution*, *Lectures on Heroes*, perhaps *Past and Present*.[65] What had bitten him were almost certainly Carlyle's energetic denunciations of Mammon and self-consciousness, and his assertions of Soul, Aristocracy and Individual. At times, reading Carlyle, one can hear the swingeing certainties of Lawrence's prose. And yet it is remarkably hard to point to passages in Lawrence's writing which precisely demonstrate Carlyle's influence. This is because, as with nearly all his reading, Lawrence took from Carlyle what he needed – and then transformed it into his own way of understanding and feeling. This *possession* of the thoughts of others, this capacity to turn them into what he wanted, was characteristic of Lawrence's intelligence. Reading was no longer a general kind of 'enlargement': it was starting to be a way of illuminating the world, part of the self-education with which Lawrence and Jessie assisted each other. Hueffer once remarked when Lawrence confessed to knowing Carlyle and Ruskin, 'You're the only man I've ever met . . . who really has read all those people.' That was the direct result of his years of reading and discussion with Jessie Chambers: Lawrence once remarked to her 'I've been a better education to you than any academic sort.'[66] What they now experienced was in its own way a period as important as school had been, or college would be.

The period of reading and discovery of books with Jessie had been a particularly important time for her too. Without the experience of High School which Lawrence had had, she had become – at the age of 16, in the late summer of 1903 – a pupil-teacher in the Infants' department at Underwood school, spending three days a week there and two days at the pupil-teacher centre at Ilkeston. It had been an exhausting life: one day in January

1903, before becoming an official pupil-teacher, she had been obliged to go home ill 'through being overworked with a large Standard III', and the same would happen in October 1903: 'left today on account of being over-worked'. As a pupil-teacher going to Ilkeston, she had 'to walk three miles or more to Langley Mill station to catch a train, and back again at night, and then do her homework in the evening'.[67] Her brother David Chambers also had a memory of her at Underwood school around 1906:

I saw her myself . . . call out a great hulking lad nearly as big as herself, and give him two strokes of the cane. His mother – a vast woman – waited for her as she came out and told her what would happen to her if she ever dared to lay her hands on her Sam again. The children shouted after her as she went down the village street. She walked on with her head high as though she saw and heard nothing. She was about nineteen at the time, at the height of her glory.[68]

Like his memories of Louie Burrows, who also became a teacher, Lawrence's memories of what he had heard about Jessie, or of what she herself had told him, were vital when he came to write about Ursula's experience as a teacher in chapter XIII of *The Rainbow*; there he presented some of the struggle of these years, the enormous difficulty of being a woman in 'The Man's World'. More than any other member of her family, apart from her independently minded sister May, Jessie had been determined (as her brother David put it) to 'break away from the drudgery of the farm kitchen and make her escape into the world of books where her imagination could expand'.[69] Her determination was, however, very far from being as vague as her ambition; like thousands of other women in the period who were also looking for a profession, she decided to 'make her escape' by qualifying herself as a teacher and by that means make herself genuinely independent. In December 1905, she sat the King's Scholarship exam, as Lawrence had done in 1904, obtaining (like him) a place in the 1st Class; in August 1906, she transferred to the Mixed section of Underwood school and worked there as an uncertificated teacher, studying in the even-ings, until she took her certificate examinations late in 1908. This was quite unlike Lawrence, who at the equivalent stage of his career would go to Nottingham University College, taking his certificate examinations in the summer of 1908 after some leisure to study and to prepare for them. At Nottingham, Lawrence would also be able to go on reading widely, particu-larly in history and philosophy and literature; and though he always pro-fessed himself disappointed with his course (and with his teachers), his time as a student would give him two valuable extra years to read and write which Jessie Chambers never had.

IV Eastwood Friends

Although we know something about many of the friends and acquaintances Lawrence had, growing up in Eastwood, there are some striking gaps. We know most of all about the group of pupil-teachers who met in Ilkeston: Jessie Chambers, Louie Burrows, Ada Lawrence, Richard Pogmore, George Neville, Gilbert Noon. We know rather less about friends and neighbours in Eastwood who were not in that group. Some people are now only names, like Ethel Harris – whose autograph album Lawrence adorned so carefully around 1903.[70] Others, like the Coopers, are a little more vivid. The families had known each other for some time – Ada Lawrence and Frances (normally 'Frankie') Cooper were in the same form at school (see Illustration 25): Ethel visited the Lawrences in Walker Street. The Coopers were the Lawrences' next door neighbours when they moved to Lynn Croft early in 1905. Four of the five daughters (the eldest, Florence, was already married) were soon in and out of the Lawrence household like members of the family. Ethel Cooper died in 1905; but the recreation as 'Gertie Coomber' of Gertrude Cooper – usually called 'Gertie' or 'Grit' – in Lawrence's play *A Collier's Friday Night* shows the style of the friendship in these years: extremely close, gossipy, non-intellectual. George Neville described the habitual lounging walk of the middle sister, Frances, as she came into the Lawrences' kitchen, 'spick, span and immaculate'; an Eastwood acquaintance added that Frankie Cooper 'was very much in love' with Lawrence: 'very sweet on him but he just simply didn't feel the same towards her, you know'. The families stayed close: Lawrence was at Mabel's wedding on 2 June 1909, and went to see Frankie Cooper just before she died in Lynn Croft in 1918; Gertie Cooper would make her home with Ada and her husband.[71]

More obscure, however, is Mabel Limb, the daughter of a local miner and one of Lawrence's earliest Eastwood acquaintances. What we know about her mostly comes from the letters and cards Lawrence wrote her, and from her appearance in the draft plot for the very first 'Paul Morel'. Most of the characters in the plot appear under their own names: 'Miss Wright', 'Gertie' and 'Aunt Ada' for example. Coinciding with the Morel family's 'Move from Breach' in chapter IV of the plot appears 'Mrs Limb': the Lawrences moved from The Breach to Walker Street in 1891, and the Limb family were only a few doors away, around the corner in Percy Street. The two families probably got to know each other then. Chapter V records 'Return of Father' and 'walk with Mabel': Mabel appears by name in chapters VI and VII; and when 'William' – the Paul Morel figure – makes friends with 'Flossie' (apparently a version of Flossie Cullen with elements of Jessie

Chambers), we find 'Mabel jealous'. Mabel's name appears again in chapter VIII; and in Part II, when William starts 'at Haywoods' (1901 in real life) and is going to 'Miss Wright' for painting (meeting 'Flossie much'), he 'neglects Mabel – she becomes engaged'. Mabel Limb, born in 1886, was only 16 in 1902, so the engagement is probably fictional. But we know that Mabel Limb was a childhood friend of Lawrence's (i. 35 n. 4) – Lawrence recalled to Ada 'How jolly we used to play in their house!' (i. 230) – and her sister Emmeline, usually 'Emmie', appeared under her own name in *Sons and Lovers*. Emmie, a dressmaker, beame a close friend of Ada Lawrence and was a bridesmaid at her wedding in 1913.[72]

Mabel stayed a family friend; she was one of the party during the second week of the Lawrence family holiday to Robin Hood's Bay in 1907, and she would probably have gone to Shanklin with the Lawrences in 1909 if she had not been so ill: Lawrence wrote to her how 'Mother has been wishing you might be with us, for certainly it would do you good' (i. 133). But Mabel had had problems with her health for a long time. An acquaintance knew her as a 'semi-invalid'; she may have been the girl remembered by May Chambers as 'ill with consumption' to whom Lawrence used to go and read after getting home from College.[73] Lawrence wrote to her 'are you still getting fatter' in September 1908 (i. 77), and again a month later: 'I want to see you plump at Christmas' (i. 82). But she died of 'Ovarian disease' – probably cancer – at the age of 23, on 28 December 1909. Fourteen months later, Lawrence wrote to Ada how 'I often dream of Mabel Limb – oh, so often. I am tired of life being so ugly and cruel . . .' (i. 230).

Unlike the Cooper girls, Mabel Limb did not belong to the group which went to Ilkeston, or to chapel and discussed the sermon. She was simply one of the ordinary people who knew Lawrence in Eastwood, and made up his social circle there: who called round at the Lawrences' house, as so many people did. She was one of the people whom Lawrence left behind when he left Eastwood, but did not forget. She may not have been well enough to work: the section 'occupation' on her death certificate simply records 'daughter of William Limb, Coal Miner'. One small detail in Lawrence's surviving correspondence provides us with a clue to their relationship. Lawrence was always careful about expressing emotions in his cards and letters: his surviving postcard to his mother, for example, concludes simply 'DHL' (i. 27). DHL was his usual form of farewell: 'Yours DHL' (i. 24) or 'Yrs DHL' (i. 30). But Mabel Limb was one of only three correspondents before 1910 to get 'Love' (i. 35, 95, 134) and 'love from DHL' (i. 82), the other two being Gertrude and Frances Cooper (i. 36 and 90). Mabel also got kisses in the form of 'x's.[74] There is a considerable contrast between the style of a letter Lawrence wrote in November 1908 to Louie Burrows, a women he was fond of and found sexually attractive – 'My dear Louise . . . Au revoir – soyez encore gai. Yrs DHL' (i. 95) – and that of a card to Mabel Limb he wrote only four days later: 'Dearest Mab . . . With Love DHL xxx' (i. 95). Only Lawrence's old friends got the loving salutations: they were the people whose friendship went back to an innocent and untroubled time – and continued out of loyalty to the old days. The 'Paul Morel' plot suggests that there may, at one time, have been a particular liking between Lawrence and Mabel Limb, something probably predating Lawrence's friendship with Jessie Chambers and the intellectual friendships of his teens. May Chambers records almost all that is known of it: she remembered Lawrence remarking, around 1901,

'. . . Oh, what do you think? Mabel says I'm a monster. Imagine, a monster! Me a monster!' he cried.

'I bet she means it, too,' I said.

'She pretended to, but she doesn't really. She doesn't know what it means. I was making fun of her, and she got mad. Why should she mean it?' he asked aggressively.

'Because perhaps she thinks you don't play fair. You don't stay friends with just me but have a lot of friends because you like each one for something the others haven't got.'

'Well, that's all right, isn't it?' he wanted to know. 'I do like one for this, and one for that, but what's wrong with that?'

'I bet that's why she called you a monster, just the same!' I answered.[75]

Exactly as in the 'Paul Morel' plot, it was Lawrence's moving between old friends and newer ones which upset Mabel. She was the kind of person who had made up his childhood circle in Eastwood: the kind of person he inevitably moved away from, over the years, as – like Ursula in *The Rainbow* – he grew to feel 'different' from the people he had lived amongst. Yet he remained in a kind of sympathy with them, too: Ursula also finds that 'something in her must respond and belong to people who knew her. But something else denied bitterly . . .'[76] Since we know a little about her, Mabel Limb has to stand in for all those whom Lawrence also remembered, and left behind, but whose names we hardly know.

CHAPTER FIVE

1905–1906

WRITING AND PAINTING

I 'A collier's son a poet!'

Although Lawrence was training to be a teacher, something else of crucial importance happened during his first year of full-time employment as an uncertificated teacher at Albert Street in 1905–6. He began, Jessie Chambers recalled, 'to talk definitely of writing'. Not, at this stage, of writing as a career; everything up to this point in his life pointed to his being a teacher – his background, his prolonged education, his training, his spectacular examination success in 1904, his matriculation in 1905 and his family's expectations of him. 'My mother looks to me', he would remark in May 1908 (i. 50), meaning that she expected him to succeed as a professional man and to provide his parents with some financial help. Yet, from 1905 at least, he also had his eye upon another way of life altogether: something quite unlike the career for which he was destined. He had probably been thinking of starting to write for a long time before he actually began. When in the spring of 1905 he asked Jessie Chambers 'Have you ever thought of writing?' her reply came back 'at once', as if it were a question she had been waiting for.

'Oh yes ... I've thought of it all my life. Have you?'
  'Yes, I have,' he said in the same quiet tone. 'Well, let's make a start. I'm sure we could do something if we tried. Lots of the things we say, the things you say, would go ever so well into a book.'[1]

Considering the attention to literature that he and Jessie had been paying since 1902–3, it was not at all surprising that his ambitions should have taken the same direction: like Jessie, he felt as if he had been preparing himself to write 'all my life'. The surprising thing, perhaps, is that it should have taken so long for him to start. That suggests the strength of the various feelings of inhibition which Jessie Chambers also remembered.

And although Lawrence made it clear that his mother did not approve of what he actually wrote between 1905 and 1910, her influence upon his initial idea of writing can hardly be overestimated. The sentences in *Sons and Lovers* about Mrs Morel's Guild activities, including her writing, convey the reaction to books and writing of young children in a working-class family as they grow up during the 1890s: and are probably close to the literal truth about the family in Walker Street: 'Sometimes Mrs. Morel read a paper. It seemed queer to the children to see their mother, who was always busy about the house, sitting writing in her rapid fashion, thinking, referring to books, and writing again. They felt for her on such occasions the deepest respect.' Writing not only commands 'respect' but is from the start something the children associate particularly with their mother. As pointed out above, Lydia Lawrence wrote at least one essay for a competition organised by the Guild, as well as (presumably) papers for local meetings.[2]

She also sometimes wrote for herself and not for the Guild. Lydia Lawrence's family was proud of its famous hymn-writing ancestor John Newton; poetry was in the Beardsall family – or in part of it. And one of Lydia's poems survives, probably written before 1900 (her mother actually died in May 1900).

My Mother's Hands

Such beautiful, beautiful hands,
    They're neither white nor small,
And you I know would scarcely think
    That they were fair at all
I've looked on hands whose [...] & true
    As [...] dreams might be
Yet are these aged, wrinkled hands,
    Most beautiful to me

Such beautiful, beautiful hands
    Though hearts are weary & sad
These patient hands kept toiling on
    That the children might be glad
I almost weep when looking back
    To childhood's distant day;
I think how these hands rested not
    While mine were at their play.

Such beautiful, beautiful hands
    They're growing feeble now,
For time and pain have left their mark,
    On hands and heart and brow.
Alas Alas the nearing time!
    And the sad sad day to me
When 'neath the daisies out of sight
    These hands will folded be.

> And, oh, beyond this shadow lamp
>   Where all is bright & fair
> I know full well these dear old hands
>   · Will palms of victory bear.
> Where crystal streams through endless years
>   Flow over golden strands
> And where the old grow young again
>   I'll clasp my mother's hands.[3]

The concerns of the poem – the sentiments of a child's love for a parent, the pains and responsibilities of parents, the hope of an after-life which will make up for such pains – are precisely those which might have been expected both from Lydia Lawrence and from John Newton's granddaughter. The conventionality of the expression and form is not surprising; the sentimental ballad, whose form Lydia Lawrence adopts, was a powerful and pervasive influence upon nineteenth-century poetry, and here draws on the imagery of the nonconformist hymn. The poem is a good clue to what 'poetry' meant in Lydia Lawrence's life, and how she would have expressed the idea to her children. It is something rather exalted, emotional and religious: although it may originate in everyday feelings and reactions, it is about concepts rather than about everyday life. Two poems by her son Ernest are, too, of just that kind.[4]

May Chambers recorded how Lydia Lawrence's writing of poetry affected her youngest son: the events she described probably date from around 1898, when Lawrence was 13.

One afternoon, Bert was in high glee and hopped about the doorstep, his eyes shining.

'You'd never guess, I shall have to tell you, because you'd never guess in ever so long.' He paused dramatically. 'Mother's writing poetry! She is, you may not believe it, but she is.'

His mother came to the door, an exercise book almost hidden in the folds of her skirt as it hung from her hand.

'Well, child, how's your mother?'

But he burst out, 'I've told her!'

'Aye, clatting! I might have known. It's nothing, child.'

But Bert cried, 'It is, it is. It's poetry.'

'Nonsense. I just amuse myself sometimes with making up verses.'

'She's going to send it to a mag,' he announced.

'He means a magazine, child,' Mrs. Lawrence explained.

'She sent some once before,' Bert volunteered.

'Aye, and that's all that came of it. I expect it got into the wastepaper basket. But come in. We are all by ourselves, for a wonder. Just the two of us.'

Nothing more was said about the poetry, though that afternoon her son sketched glowing pictures of his mother becoming famous and making them rich.[5]

And yet the very idea of 'writing' was linked, from the start, with attitudes alien to Eastwood. Lydia Lawrence apparently wrote her poetry when she was alone in the house with her son, and when the masculine world was safely distanced. Her skirt almost hides the evidence of the exercise book as she comes to the door and can be seen by the world outside; her son naively but significantly associates 'poetry' with a world of wealth and success lying far beyond the life the Lawrences live in Eastwood, but to which 'writing' might be the key.

Lawrence was under no illusions about the oddity of his becoming a writer in Eastwood. To Jessie Chambers he remarked 'one night . . . softly':

'It will be *poetry*.'
I took fire at that.
'Well, isn't that the very greatest thing?'
'Ah, *you* say that,' he replied. 'But what will the others say? That I'm a fool. A collier's son a poet!'
'I can't see that that has anything to do with it,' I answered sincerely. 'What does your father's occupation matter?' Lawrence and his father had little connection with one another in my mind. He shook his head, and we went on . . .[6]

Being a poet while also being a miner's son was not a problem which mattered to Jessie Chambers. She didn't think of Lawrence and his father as inhabiting the same moral or mental landscape; she did not live with the particular tensions of the house in Lynn Croft.

But for Lawrence, home was an immediate obstacle. The family lived in the kitchen: the bedrooms were only for dressing and sleeping. What you did in the kitchen was visible to, and commented on by, the whole family. 'Poetry' – 'pottery' as Arthur Lawrence called it (i. 513) – would have been an immediate talking-point. As a result, Lawrence's earliest writing was done furtively at home, under the pretence of study: 'writing in the kitchen where all the household affairs were going on'. Like Paul Morel in *Sons and Lovers*, 'He would never have got so far in the direction of sentimentality as to read poetry to his own family.'[7]

One reason, of course, was that there had been very few genuinely working-class writers who had made names for themselves in British literary history. Robert Burns – a figure to whom Lawrence himself returned more than once – stood out: but John Clare was probably unknown to Lawrence. In Lawrence's own day, the career of H. G. Wells was a striking example of how a child with a working-class background might manage to make a name for himself as a writer.[8] But literature – particularly 'poetry' – as it was taught, sold and published, was generally a middle-class phenomenon. Lawrence's own early writing shows how he felt he needed to address a middle-class readership; all his life he knew how the tastes of the middle-class readership dominated the literary market. It is therefore particularly interesting, in the light of the poems his mother had written and of his own youthful reaction to them, that Lawrence's own ambitions should first have turned to '*poetry*': 'I remember the slightly self-conscious Sunday afternoon, when I was nineteen,* and I "composed" my first two "poems." One was to *Guelder-roses*, and one to *Campions*, and most young ladies would have done better: at least I hope so. But I thought the effusions very nice, and so did Miriam.'[9]

It was not only because working-class writers were so few, that Lawrence would have felt it unlikely that he could be one. To be a writer in early twentieth-century Eastwood meant one of three things. One could be a writer like Lydia Lawrence or her son Ernest (or her sister Lettie): the writer of religious and moral occasional poetry. Secondly, one could be the kind of writer, journalist and poet Willie Hopkin was, with his regular contributions and poems in the local paper, the *Eastwood and Kimberley Advertiser*: salty, ironical and 'impudent', intensely local in concern, his prose and poetry offering a kind of moral and social corrective.[10] The only alternative to these two kinds of local writing, to the young Lawrence, would have been the work of the professional 'artistic' writer, as alien to the mentality and concerns of the colliery village as if it had descended from Mars. But such an alienation from Eastwood was, of course, exactly what Lawrence and Jessie had felt during their reading and discussion of literature. Jessie remembered how 'When we were alone together we were in a world apart, where feeling and thought were intense, and we seemed to touch a reality that was beyond the ordinary workaday world. But if his mother or sister returned, bringing with them the atmosphere of the market-place, our separate world was temporarily shattered . . .'[11] To be 'a poet' in that sense was explicitly to set oneself apart from the place and its concerns: apart, too, from one's family, in so far as the latter lived in the kitchen, belonged to the place and participated in its intellectual and moral life, in its chapels and newspapers. 'A collier's son a poet!' To be the writer of 'Campions' and 'Guelder-Roses' was actually to model oneself on Wordsworth or Tennyson: to announce not only one's difference from one's father and from the whole male community, but also from the ambitions,

---

* DHL misremembered his age when he started to write: he was 20, not 19. The earliest versions of the poems in question have survived in drafts written out in the summer of 1908 (see Appendix II and – for 'Campions' – Illustration 24): it is impossible to say exactly what the 'effusions' of 1905–6 were like.

hopes and plans of one's mother; the things for which she had been slaving, over the years.

Such differences from both his parents were something Lawrence had no desire to advertise. His very decision to be 'a writer' of the artistic kind (and the phrase 'It will be *poetry*' shows that it *was* such a writer he wanted to be) involved him in an act of separation from his community, from his family and, for quite different reasons, from both his parents. It was a genuinely momentous decision – not just the adoption of an interesting hobby; it affected the way he embarked upon his career as a teacher and the kind of career he meant it to be. In spite of some pressure (presumably from his mother) he did not take a degree course in college – a course which might have opened up for him a career in higher education: as early as 1906 he knew that 'His real interest centred on his writing and not on his studies'. That meant an assertion within his family of his loyalties: and of his lack of loyalty, at the deepest level, to his mother. Everyone was proud of the scholarly books and prizes on the shelves: but Lawrence would tuck away the exercise book containing his own writing where he believed no-one would look for it, not even his poetry-writing mother: between the prize volumes in the glass-fronted bookcase.[12]

II   Pictures

And yet another art preceded writing as his first love. It was not an accident that he made his autobiographical hero Paul Morel a painter rather than a writer: painting had fascinated him since his teens. The whole group of friends painted; still lifes by George Neville, Ada Lawrence, Jessie Chambers and Lawrence himself survive. Indeed, one contemporary from Eastwood remembered Lawrence entirely for it: 'Quite good at painting. I don't know what he did after that as a trade.'[13] Though Lawrence later insisted that he had had 'only one real lesson in painting', around 1904 he attended evening art classes given in the Albert Street Schools by a local designer, George Leighton Parkinson – a relation of the famous painter Lord Leighton. He was 'thoroughly drilled in "drawing"'; yet fairly quickly he decided he 'couldn't draw', meaning that he 'could never do anything on my own. When I did paint jugs of flowers or bread and potatoes, or cottages in a lane, copying from Nature, the result wasn't very thrilling.' A number of his still lifes have however survived, and they are actually among the best of his early pictures.[14]

However, Lawrence discovered in himself a genuine gift for copying designs, drawings and paintings. He decorated fire screens and plaques, illustrated the autograph albums of friends and recreated numerous copies of pictures which he gave away as presents. These were nearly always water-colour copies from reproductions: 'I worked with almost dry water-colour, stroke by stroke, covering half a square-inch at a time, each square-inch perfect and completed, proceeding in a kind of mosaic advance, with no idea at all of laying on a broad wash. Hours and hours of intense concentration, inch by inch progress, in a method entirely wrong . . .'[15] And yet his copies managed, he thought, 'to have a certain something that delighted me: a certain glow of life, which was beauty to me'. His first copies were drawings and paintings in autograph albums; it was the great age of the autograph album, and his circle of friends demanded verses, music, decorations, drawings and paintings from each other. May Chambers recorded one memory of the Lawrence family kitchen in Walker Street, some time before 1904:

the table littered with water-colours and autograph albums, and Bert in his shirt sleeves painting furiously, surrounded by an admiring group of half-a-dozen girls and one boy, who had presented each other with albums for Christmas. Mrs. Lawrence sat by the hearth, exchanging quips and cracks with the liveliest of the group, beaming as we praised her son's talent. Bert painted a child with a watering-can over the flower bed and an umbrella over her own head in a heavy shower on a page of my album from himself, and wrote:

> His 'prentice han' he tried on man
> And then he made the lasses 'O'.

Each of us wanted a painting done for every one in the group, and Bert ran his fingers through his hair excitedly.

'I tell you what, you'll have to have them, and I'll do them one by one. You won't mind what I choose, will you?'

He was assured his choice would satisfy everyone.

'Just so long as there's a bit of colour will suit me,' said several, all of us accepting his kindness without any sense of obligation.

Bert was the centre of the gay crowd, and we took it for granted that he liked to do us such favors.[16]

Three albums survive with Lawrence's contributions in them: but there must have been dozens.[17]

Like others in the group, Lawrence moved on from these small-scale pieces to independent copies. He gave two little water-colours to his sister Emily as a wedding present in 1904; and there followed a stream of copies given as presents, up to 1912. His aunt Ada Krenkow received paintings in 1908 and 1911; three landscapes went to his landlord and landlady in Croydon, 1908–9; around 1909–10 he gave two paintings to his friend Alice Dax in Eastwood; two paintings went to his sister Ada in 1910, two more to his Croydon friend Agnes Holt when she married in 1911; at least one each to his fiancée Louie Burrows and to his Croydon headmaster Philip Smith in 1911; a painting to Arthur McLeod in December 1912.[18] At a time when good reproductions – like the oleographs which hung in the Lawrence family parlour – were expensive, a carefully hand-made water-colour copy could be a fine present, as well as an inexpensive one for the giver: 'a gift of a day of his life', as Lawrence put it to Jessie Chambers around 1906 (i. 28) and (in the same words) to Louie Burrows in 1911 (i. 235).

But the range of Lawrence's sources for his copies was very limited, so that he rarely ventured outside the English water-colour school. Carl Baron has pointed out that the young Lawrence's almost exclusive use of later Victorian and Edwardian paintings meant 'a high admixture of the theatrical and the banal . . . an earnest and "sweet" world presents itself'.[19] The adolescent and man who was experimenting with words and language – 'I can juggle with words' (i. 87) as he put it in 1908 – was carving out his own style and subject, and challenging convention from the start. In the visual arts, however, he produced the equivalent of the poems by his mother and his brother: second-rate variants of the models of others: literally models, in his careful (if joyful) copying of other people's work. The painted copies are undistinguished; at best efficient and at worst amateurish. There is an absolute contrast between what he achieved as a writer between 1905 and 1912, and what he painted: really no comparison to be made. He continued to copy paintings throughout the period with which this volume deals, however: his copying of Maurice Greiffenhagen's *An Idyll* in 1910 and 1911 is discussed below.

It is significant that his painting was a very public activity; literally carried out in the family kitchen, with admiring friends and family around – and also public in his constant giving away to other people of the copies he made. His paintings were designed to please people, including his mother; and they won the admiration and approval of almost everyone who saw them.* His writing, in contrast, was from the start intensely private, seen at most by one or two other people and never by his family; he was extremely reluctant to send it to magazines and very cautious about subjecting it to anyone else's criticism. The writing was difficult, dangerous and independent: the painting was a social activity, involving and needing the approval of others.

III D.H.L.

We might, however, date Lawrence's idea of being 'a writer' even earlier than his composition of those poems in 1905. He was christened David

---

* Arthur Lawrence's reaction may however be judged from a remark Lawrence recalled late in life: 'My father always said that was the beautifullest picture on a wall – a flitch of bacon!'[20]

Herbert Richards Lawrence, though the 'Richards' was hardly ever used.*
He very rarely used his first name, David, always claiming that it was
abhorrent to him, something which got him into trouble with his first
headmaster, William Whitehead: '"David! David!" he raved. "David is the
name of a great and good man. You don't like the name of David? You don't
like the name of David!" He was purple with indignation. But I had an
unreasonable dislike of the name David . . .' Later on, a few people who
probably disliked or disapproved of 'Bert' called him David. But he was
nearly always 'Bert' to his family and close friends – or 'Bertie' if someone
wanted to annoy him: he signed himself 'H. Lawrence' in his High School
algebra book, and his surviving school report is also for 'H. Lawrence'.[21]

Yet neither 'Bert' nor 'Herbert' appears as his signature on a single one of
his surviving early letters and cards, even those written to his own family
and to close friends; not even on the surviving postcard written to his
mother, nor on the many letters and cards to his favourite sister Ada.[22]
From the very start of his correspondence, he is either 'D. H. Lawrence' or
'D.H.L.'; that was his signature even when he wrote love-letters to his
fiancée Louie Burrows during 1911 or to Frieda Weekley in 1912. It seems
that his initials or initialled name gave him a certain status, a certain refined
personality, very different in kind from 'Bert'. His father was 'Art' or
'Arthur' in Eastwood; his elder brother had been 'Ern' or 'Ernie' in the
family, and 'Ernest' when (for example) writing to his father; but 'D. H.
Lawrence' or 'D.H.L.' did not belong to the locality, were not the same as
Herbert or Bert or Bertie or 'our Bert' (with all the family possessiveness of
the pronoun).[23] It is as if he were signing his name as an author or as an
artist when he put his name to his first surviving postcard at the age of 18,
when he was neither author nor artist; formally signing himself as someone
more distant than son, or brother or friend, and testifying to the separation
of the artist from family and locality. Even on the most trivial occasion –
like subscribing to refill a children's painting box – he appeared under his
initials: 'Who will subscribe? I open the list. D.H.L., 1s.'[24] We become,
perhaps, what we name ourselves; Bert Lawrence became, quite consciously, D. H. Lawrence.

The history, however, of his early writing and publications tells us a good

* Herbert Beardsall was Lydia Lawrence's favourite brother: but Alice Hall (who heard the
  story from Lydia Lawrence) recorded what happened at the baptism: 'One of the sisters [of
  Lydia Lawrence] had lost her lover in early life, and she wished Bert to have the same names
  as he had . . . as his aunt handed him to the minister to be christened she added the surname,
  too . . .' She also noted that the 'lover' had been 'a minister who died'.[25] The aunt was almost
  certainly Lydia's sister Lettie, then 28: it is unlikely that a married sister would make such a
  request, and her only other unmarried sister – Ada – was only 17 in 1885. The deceased Rev.
  Mr Richards (if that was his name) has not, however, been traced. 'Richards' does not appear
  on DHL's birth certificate.

deal about the problems of being the figure behind the name. Before 1905, letters had been occasions for experiment. Those he wrote to the Haggs Farm family while convalescing in 1902 were read out to the whole family, as they were doubtless meant to be: nothing survives of them except Jessie's memory of their 'joyous abandon' – Lawrence knew that he always put 'quite a lot of *me* in a letter' (i. 86) – and a memory of a letter in which he said that he could stand in his aunt's drawing-room and 'watch the tide rolling in through the window'. May Chambers wrote back at once to say what an uncomfortable drawing-room his aunt's must be.[26] A surviving diary fragment, dating from the Lawrence family holidays in August 1906, suggests how self-consciously he was still, four years later, teaching himself to describe what he saw. The fragment (an account of a walk to Theddlethorpe and the launching of the lifeboat at Mablethorpe) is curiously deliberate: less a private diary than a conscious piece of craftsmanship. It ends:

Horses now reversed go dashing into the sea, splashing the bare feet of their drivers, and running on until they are up to the thighs – then turned round. The stays are loosed, and the boat glides beautifully on to the water, then rises and falls on the waves like a child in its mothers arms. Twelve oars stand out simultaneously and sweep the sea, – the wind fills the brown sails and away she glides like a live thing, the sun burning on her red sails.[27]

What he means by 'now reversed' is quite unclear; the 'child in its mothers arms' is thoroughly literary, while the change from 'brown sails' to 'red sails' in the last two lines seems an attempt to particularise something observed, but reads more like a mistake than an observation. The passage is, however, part of the earliest surviving piece of Lawrence's descriptive writing: it suggests some of the struggle for expression going on in the first version of his novel *The White Peacock*, written simultaneously with it. For all its weaknesses, it is nevertheless far more experimental than his contemporaneous paintings of water and boats.

IV Breaking the Ice

'To think that *my* son should have written such a story'.[28] Lydia Lawrence's withering comment on the first version of 'Laetitia', written between Easter 1906 and June 1907, can be explained (as Jessie Chambers pointed out) by the situation of its heroine Lettie: left pregnant by Leslie, marrying George and giving birth to Leslie's child. It was an interesting scenario for the first novel by a young man with a strictly religious upbringing and a strong family background. But like much Victorian pulp fiction, it was a combina-

tion of the outrageous and the utterly conventional, and like much else in
the first draft of *The White Peacock* it did not survive into the published
novel.

The story of the pregnant and abandoned woman remains, nevertheless,
tantalising. It suggests the way in which Lawrence seized upon the problem
(still dominant in the final version of the novel) which all the main characters have with finding the right partners. He also introduced from the start
the problems of class divisions: George, the working-class man, has difficulties with Lettie, the socially superior woman, from first draft to
published version. In the first draft, too, there was also a child unloved by its
father and abandoned by him, which in effect becomes the child only of its
mother. In such ways, like so much else in the novel, the elements of this
very first plot prefigured Lawrence's subsequent preoccupations as a writer.

It is important, too, that his 'talk of . . . writing' with Jessie so quickly
came to mean more than poems. Lawrence's choice of the novel form is
itself significant; not only was it one of the great nineteenth-century forms
but (outside journalism) it also looked like his only chance of making a
living as a writer. And where would a young writer in 1906 look for his
models? '"The usual plan is to take two couples and develop their relationships," he said. "Most of George Eliot's are on that plan. Anyhow, I don't
want a plot, I should be bored with it. I shall try two couples for a start."'
Jessie Chambers goes on to describe how, at Whitsun 1906,

> he brought the first pages to me. I had been away from home, and returned to find
> Lawrence waiting uneasily. Out in the fields he gave me the manuscript and asked
> me if I had any to show him. I shook my head.
> 'We've broken the ice,' he said in a tense voice. He told me to put the writing
> away and read it when he had gone . . .[29]

It is a transaction which, in her memory at least, is marked by a striking
nervousness in Lawrence, and by extreme secrecy: the manuscript is smug-
gled to Jessie like contraband. But the way in which it *was* thus handed over,
so soon after being written, tells its own story. Lawrence was making Jessie
his audience, and much more: 'I its creator, you its nurse' (i. 221) he said
about the novel's first version. It was not Jessie's criticism he wanted,
because her capacity for objective criticism at this stage hardly existed. It
was her uncritical encouragement and above all her love for books and
literature which made her the right audience. Lawrence badly needed some
feeling of a literary context in which he could work, and Jessie (truly a
'nurse' in the sense of one who nurtures and tends but does not possess)
gave him that with innocent but passionate eagerness. 'From now on he
brought some pages almost every time he came up. He would pass them to

me in secret and wait restlessly until we were out in the fields and he could begin to talk about his writing.'[30] Not, it should be observed, so that *she* could begin to talk about his writing, but so that *he* could. When he created versions of her and himself in *A Collier's Friday Night*, he indicated the nature of Maggie Pearson's response to Ernest's poems. She asks to see them '*betwixt supplication and command*'; then follows her immediate, unthinking response 'I think they're splendid'. Ernest is sceptical about her enthusiasm and says that one poem is far more complex than the other. She immediately adopts his word to '*vindicate herself when no vindication is required*': 'Yes, it is more complicated: it is more complicated in every way. You see, I didn't understand it at first. It is best, yes, it is. (*She reads it again* ...)'.[31] Years later, Lawrence recalled how Jessie 'never used to *say* anything' (i. 551). Her value as an audience for the first chapters of his novel in 1906 was in the receptive sympathy and loving admiration she brought to them.

In the 1930s, with the benefit of a good deal of hindsight, Jessie Chambers recorded her memory of the first version of the book; it is most unlikely that she had been so critical in 1906.

I had not a high opinion of the first version of *T. . White Peacock*, in which George married Letty [the novel included a description of their being married at Basford Registry office] ... The novel, apart from its setting, seemed to me story-bookish and unreal. The upright young farmer, hopelessly in love with the superior young lady (very conscious of her social superiority) who had been served shabbily by a still more socially superior young man, married her after a puritanical exposition of the circumstances by her mother, and a highly dubious conjugal life began in the melancholy farmhouse, with, one imagined, Letty always in the parlour and George in the kitchen.[32]

Lawrence's own opinion of the book, she reckoned, was shown by the fact that 'he immediately started to rewrite it.' It was more likely that he had realised, while writing the first version, what really *could* and should be done with such a theme. Jessie considered, however, that 'in spite of its sentimentality, a thread of genuine romance ran through the story'.[33]

Lawrence knew something of its limitations, even in 1906:

I'm afraid it will be a mosaic. My time's so broken up. In the morning when I should love to sit down to it I have to go to school. And when you've done the day's teaching all your brightness has gone. By the time I get back to the writing I'm another man. I don't see how there can be any continuity about it. It will have to be a mosaic, a mosaic of moods.[34]

There exists a fragmentary plot outline for chapters xiv–xx which shows, however, that the novel was by no means *simply* 'a mosaic of moods'; its second half, at least, was carefully planned.

Even in that splintered form, the plot reveals glimpses of the high points towards the end of the novel: the moments when fates are decided. Most interesting of all, however, is the way the last two chapters correspond to an actual surviving manuscript of the novel's conclusion. All the elements described in 'XIX' and 'XX' appear. The surviving ending, however, is not only suffused with sentimentality and romance but also by a strange, symbolic kind of melodrama. Lawrence is struggling to show, in vivid scenes (part of the mosaic), how people unconsciously respond to the deepest and most powerful forces in their natures. So, for example, Lettie – in the 'Autumn – birth – madness' section – begins to suffer from delusions. She has given birth to Leslie's child after being abandoned by him, but she cannot accept her own unconscious knowledge that he has left her; she falls back on the theory that her husband George and his mother are keeping him away from her and the baby:

"It is like him," whispered Lettie "Isn't it like him? I'm sure he wants to see her—how could he help, when she is such a lovely child. But they won't let him come—when he comes, they won't let him in. They hate him, and they hate this little sweeting. To think that they could have the heart to want to send her away from me!"36

Lettie's delusions, hallucinations and attempts to express her wounded feelings dominate the surviving fragment, which is reminiscent of Emily Brontë and Hardy rather than of George Eliot. In a desperate attempt to get Leslie back, Lettie walks out in her dressing-gown on to the frozen mill-pond with her child, to leave it on the island where it will cry and attract Leslie: he will respond to that, if not to her. On her way back, the ice cracks, and she falls in: George manages to rescue her and the adopted child Sam is sent out over the ice to rescue the baby. On another occasion, in the still ice-bound landscape (the symbolism endures as steadily as the winter), Lettie goes out into the woods at night, again in her dressing-gown, to attract Leslie. The narrator Cyril fancies he sees 'someone all in white turn up a dark riding', and follows the voice crooning the Giordani song ('Caro mio ben') which Lawrence used again in 'A Prelude' in October 1907: 'Turn once again, heal thou my pain, / Parted from thee, my heart is sore.' In the centre of the wood, at the frozen well to which Cyril's instinct leads him as it leads Lettie – a well now no longer bubbling as when Lettie 'had listened to Leslie's passion' – Cyril finds Lettie, again with her baby, in the act of showing it to Leslie, who has incomprehensibly arrived at the right place at the right moment. 'Look closely. What a pity it is dark! But the stars shine fair on her face, don't they', Lettie croons.[37] Cyril escorts her home, Leslie is taken away by his sister: there has been a symbolic confrontation of the child-carrying, vulnerable and Ophelia-tragic Lettie with the hard-hearted, socially superior and materialist Leslie – something which seems to cure her of the madness of her longing for him, and of her delusions about his real nature. It also provokes the arrival, a day or two later, of a cheque for five hundred pounds from Leslie. The last chapter, narrated by Cyril in reminiscent mood, shows the subsequent emptiness of the farm around which so much passion has spent itself. George and Lettie with the baby (and little Sam) have gone to Canada; George's love for Lettie is fulfilled at last, as she writes her mother a letter which probably formed the conclusion of the novel: 'But George is magnificent. Nay, mother, I cannot praise him even to reassure you, I respect him too deeply. All of me which belongs to the past yearns for you, mother; but this of me that lives today and for to-morrow is full of him, full to exaltation.'[38] And so the novel ends with the triumph of unshown, unseen but reassuring love between George and Let-tie: the right couple are fulfilled, and the baby of the wrong couple (together with the fatherless Sam) will be growing up with the right parents.

Its surviving fragment reveals a strikingly non-realistic novel. The con-frontations of the mad Lettie with her fears and aspirations are intensely artificial and literary: the pre-Raphaelites are never far away, as her dress-ing-gown flutters and glimmers through the trees. Lawrence was also intensely alive to the melodrama tradition in which Dickens and Wilkie Collins – and Hardy – wrote. Having predicted a tragic outcome to its story of blighted relationships, the novel (like melodrama) finally turns against such an ending. Yet the first 'Laetitia' shows how Lawrence's interests, even at this stage, were directed towards the revelatory moment which naturally but mysteriously releases the instincts of his characters. And the past – both of mother-love and of love for the wrong man – is left behind: love which belongs to independent adults wins through, and children at risk will grow up properly parented.

V '... she doesn't like what I write ...'

Lydia Lawrence's withering remark in 1907 about the plot of 'Laetitia' was not her only response. In 1908, Lawrence reported another very similar reaction – '"Laetitia", of whom my mother will say nothing except "I wish you had written on another line"' (i. 49). Although both remarks show how coolly she distanced herself from his novel, they also show her knowledge of it. However, Lawrence would later claim that 'I never showed anything to my mother. She would have had an amused feeling about it all, and have felt sceptical', and gave an account of how she 'came upon a chapter of *White Peacock*—read it quizzically, & was amused. "But my boy, how do you know it was like that? You don't know—"'[39] Lydia Lawrence's amusement and seemingly accidental discovery of a chapter apparently demonstrate her ignorance of her son's writing. Another late essay, however, describes the occasion in detail:

At last, when I was twenty-two [*c.* 1907], and going to college in Nottingham ... when my mother loved me to come home and we were two together and alone, she took the exercise-book in which I had re-written the scene in the *White Peacock* where the bride runs up the church path. She put on her spectacles, and read with an amused look on her face.[40]

This account at least shows that she knew where the exercise book was hidden, and that her discovery of it was not accidental; but her sceptical amusement at what she reads is the same as in the other account.

In fact she read a good deal more than one chapter of 'Laetitia'. Lawrence's memory was certainly at fault (the passage he remembers her reading actually occurs in the first chapter of *Women in Love*,[41] written long after her death); but his late essays frequently reinterpret the facts of his early life. Willie Hopkin claimed that when Lawrence 'was writing *The White Peacock*, he and his mother criticised it together, and he rewrote parts of it until it satisfied them'; we do not need to accept that account to realise that she must have known what he was doing. Her August 1907 remark – 'To think that *my* son should have written such a story' – reveals not only her detachment but her knowledge of the plot, at least.[42] In June, Lawrence had only just finished the book in the form in which Lettie gives birth to Leslie's child. But Lydia Lawrence knew about it within two months. She must either have read it or Lawrence must have told her about it.

In spite of Lawrence's later denials, she was actually proud of his success as a writer and knowledgeable about what he wrote. In February 1910, she told her sister Ada Krenkow a great deal about her son's financial arrangements with Heinemann, for the publication of the novel; she also noted that the *English Review* was about to publish his short story 'Goose Fair'; she was sorry that Ford Madox Hueffer had resigned as editor, but recorded that Austin Harrison, however, had 'written Bert that he hopes he will continue sending his work'. But she also knew that he wouldn't actually be doing so, because 'revising his novel will take all his time'. All these details must have come from letters Lawrence had written to her from Croydon, but she shows herself both informed and interested. She also remarked to her sister Ada, after hearing about Heinemann's acceptance of 'Nethermere', the penultimate version of 'Laetitia', 'How the children grow beyond us. Who would ever think of Bert being what he is.' In July 1910, she told her sister Lettie more details of the arrangement with Heinemann; but she also said she was unable to find 'that story I promised to send you'.[43] The story was 'Odour of Chrysanthemums', at that stage unpublished; she must have had a manuscript of it. That alone suggests that she may have been a constant reader of Lawrence's unpublished work. She certainly knew the story and the genesis of 'The Saga of Siegmund' – the first version of *The Trespasser* – almost as soon as it was written. She told Louie Burrows about it no later than October 1910, while still at her sister's house in Leicester: 'She said how she disapproved of the theme – of the m[arried]. man & girl going away together. It was she who told me that Bert had written the story from an actual incident that had happened to a Croydon acquaintance.'[44] The evidence strongly suggests that Lydia Lawrence read what her son wrote, or at least was told all about it while he wrote it.

And yet, being the person she was, Lydia Lawrence would not have refrained from criticising her son's writing. Nearly everything we hear of her reaction is critical: she disapproved of the 1907 and 1908 versions of 'Laetitia' and of 'The Saga of Siegmund' in 1910. However proud she was of her son's success, she could not have helped seeing it as a distraction from the real business of his life: getting out of the small mining town by building a career as a professional man: 'she hoped her son, who was "clever", might one day be a professor or a clergyman or perhaps even a little Mr Gladstone'. It was also true that what he wrote shocked her. Her ambivalent reaction to his work probably accounts for her response to the arrival of his first book, *The White Peacock*, in December 1910. She was fatally ill, and

Willie Hopkin believed she was 'feverishly anxious to see "our Bert's first book"'.[45] And yet she showed not the smallest trace of enthusiasm when it arrived. She glanced at it, and – Lawrence noted in a letter – 'has said no more of it' (i. 194). May Chambers reports Lawrence's comments made no more than a day or so after his mother's death, which suggest just how unsatisfactory the book and the authorship had been to her. Lawrence described how, while she was dying, he had no comfort to give her: 'No comfort at all.'

'Well, she saw your book,' I offered. 'It must comfort you to have achieved that while she could have pride in it.'
    But he was shaking his head.
    'No, no,' he said sadly.
    'No?' I echoed.
    'No, she didn't like it.'
    'Why?' I demanded.
    He shook his head sadly.
    'I don't know. She didn't like it. Even disliked it.'
    'Still,' I protested, 'she must be proud of you, of your ability to write a book. You've given her that. It can't help but be a source of pride.'
    'No,' he insisted miserably, 'she doesn't like what I write. Perhaps if it had been romance. ... But I couldn't write that.'[46]

The reaction 'She didn't like it. Even disliked it' incidentally confirms that Lydia Lawrence had a reasonable knowledge of her son's writing. Her opinion of 'Laetitia' had clearly not changed much. But then – what would she have thought of the gamekeeper Annable, with his motto 'Be a good animal'? What would she have thought of Annable's account of his marriage; or of Lawrence's account of the sexual relationship between Lettie and Leslie? We have seen what she thought of 'The Saga of Siegmund', which even a man of the world like Ford Madox Hueffer judged 'erotic' (i. 339). What would she have thought of 'Odour of Chrysanthemums'? Lawrence's rather sentimental revisions to the story's ending in 1911 may even contain traces of her reaction to the 1910 version, as he tried to elevate (and succeeded in sentimentalising) the wife's feelings about her husband.[47] Lawrence's belief that his mother would not have minded his writing 'romance' is a clear indication of her predisposition to polite literature. The 1911 'Paul Morel' shows Mrs Morel disgustedly ripping the opening pages of *Tristram Shandy* out of the book; and Lawrence later characterised his mother's taste in fiction as being 'thrilled by *East Lynne*'. Her surviving poem also suggests how conventional her taste in writing was. Her son felt, at any rate, that what he wrote was too much concerned with the actualities of feeling (and the abandonment of reticence) for her; while she (linking

Jessie Chambers with everything he wrote) would have been predisposed to dislike it. To her, writing was a waste of time and energy for someone in his position: 'Flights of genius were nonsense—you had to be clever & rise in the world, step by step.'[48] And – anyway – such writing!

Lawrence's friends and family shared her attitude: George Neville describes them.

We all saw the danger of a literary career for Lawrence. The Little Woman [Lydia Lawrence] had sniffed, Ada [Lawrence] had 'pshawed and rubbished' times without number, 'Injun Topknot' [Emily Lawrence] had talked of prospective disappointments, 'Beat' [Alice Beatrice Hall] had angered him, as usual, by ruffling his hair and clinging on to him while she said, 'Why David lad, tha' knows it's nobbut rubbish.' (Beat could be very annoying when she dropped into our local dialect.) Franky and Grit [Cooper] had asked him what was the good of bothering, serious Alan [Chambers] had looked upon the prospect with alarm and I, in secret agreement with the 'Little Woman', had adopted an attitude of sheer contempt and often refused even to look at his manuscripts and advised him to do something useful.[49]

Arthur Lawrence tried reading the published *White Peacock*:

my father struggled through half a page, and it might as well have been Hottentot.
   "And what dun they gi'e thee for that, lad?"
   "Fifty pounds, father."
   "Fifty pound!" He was dumbfounded, and looked at me with shrewd eyes, as if I were a swindler. "Fifty pound! An' tha's niver done a day's hard work in thy life."
   I think to this day, he looks upon me as a sort of cleverish swindler, who gets money for nothing: a sort of Ernest Hooley.[50]

Both anecdotes demonstrate the awful problems Lawrence had in being a writer in Eastwood. No wonder he disguised and later even forgot what it had been like. His writing would have been the focus of a good deal of his family's *angst* over what it spent its money on and what the children should be doing with their lives. It was not even a matter of Lawrence's being more his mother's son than his father's (or vice versa, as his late essays suggest): both parents, for different reasons, were against the idea of writing. Both as man and as writer, Lawrence was carrying the burden of his family's conflicts within him, and was accordingly inhibited from striking out for the new realities in which he was coming to believe.

The figure of the writer in Lawrence's letters, too, is subject to some most uneasy humour, particularly in the letters he wrote to Blanche Jennings (a Liverpool woman he had recently met) between 1908 and 1910. The writer there is presented as absurd, foppish, the work he does ridiculous. 'I have pretty well decided to give up study; and to comfort my poor soap-bubble of a soul with writing' (i. 85), Lawrence tells his correspondent:

'Where could I send short stories such as I write? . . . I will take to writing frivolously and whimsically if I can – if I could but write as I behave!' (i. 81). 'Give a man that damned rot "Laetitia"? I'm not such a fool' (i. 71). 'It goes without saying, of course, that a fool with my variety of follies should have turned his capering wits to the trapeze of verse' (i. 63). The artificiality of Lawrence's manner here is oddly appropriate to his problem of writing about writing: his style becomes facetious, allusive, self-conscious, defensive. This man knows (with a vengeance) about being an Artist; that is, a trifler, an elegant turner of words and epigrams. When however he writes to the poet Rachel Annand Taylor in October 1910, self-confessedly 'on[e] degree from sober', he enacts a commoner role: the writer as reprobate, empty glass at his elbow (i. 181). Both roles are uneasy: Lawrence can not feel relaxed in them, however useful they are as poses.

VI Writer as Artist

There is, however, a striking brief account of 'the artist' in one of the drafts of 'Paul Morel' written late in 1911; it suggests the temperament which Lawrence had come to associate with both artists and women, and also the idea he had adopted of the artist's supposed capacity for staying outside events, 'uncaught by life', watching but uninvolved. Mrs Morel is at home, while her husband is out with his friend Jerry:

Nine o'clock passed, and still the "pair" had not returned . . . Mrs Morel sat at home churning her bitterness. As she sewed the baby-clothes, she cast her thoughts backwards and forwards, like a shuttle across the years of her life, weaving her own philosophy ⟨from the yarn of⟩ ⌈from⌉ her experience. She was able to do this the more, as she was not identified with her own living, but remained a good deal outside it: a good part of herself was left, like an artist, uncaught by life, watching. ⟨In this she was very different from most women, who are the subject matter of life, therefore, 'in esse', not philosophers or artists . . .⟩[51]

It is doubtful whether many women in Mrs Morel's position would have thought themselves 'uncaught by life': Lydia Lawrence, for one, would probably have said that being 'caught' was exactly how her life and her marriage should be described. And yet it is also perhaps true that Lydia Lawrence's reserve, which at times gave people the impression of 'stand-offishness', was another aspect of the behaviour Lawrence is here analysing; that Lydia Lawrence, too, for all her anger at being 'caught', also had the capacity to sit 'watching', looking very coolly at herself and others. It is certainly something the character Mrs Morel does: the woman who sits and feels 'What have I to do with all this' in chapter 1 is the same person who, after the drawer flung by Morel has caught her on the brow, is 'cold and impassive as stone, with mouth shut tight'.[52]

It is very doubtful, however, whether Lydia Lawrence would have gone on to postulate the link which her son makes between that kind of reserve, and the attitude of the 'artist'. Such an idea of 'the artist', of course, is hardly original, particularly coming from a man who had been an adolescent at the end of the 1890s. But it occurs a number of times elsewhere in Lawrence's early writing, too.[53] He was tempted to see such 'artistic' detachment as the way in which many sensitive people respond to the pressure of their experience.

What is particularly significant is that such a version of the artist – and of the reserved human being – takes us to the heart of what Lawrence later recognised had been one of the deepest traumas of his young life. Whether his mother truly felt that passion of detachment cannot be known for certain; the most we can say is that she had a rather cool and frequently astringent attitude to the emotions of others. May Chambers remembered her 'iron caustic wit'; and her counterpart Mrs Lambert in *A Collier's Friday Night*, observing young people in love, remarks: 'I can't understand myself how folks can be such looneys. I'm sure I was never like it . . . I was born with too much sense for that sort of slobber.'[54] Her son would echo those sentiments: 'I do *not* believe in love: mon Dieu, I don't, not for me: I never could believe in anything I cannot experience or, which is equivalent "imagine"' (i. 141). We know how the young Lawrence also experienced a feeling of being detached from his own feelings: 'in the moments of deepest emotion myself has watched myself' as he put it memorably in 1907 (i. 39). This often led to his adopting the role of the coolly self-possessed and self-controlled onlooker; as he put it in 1911, 'It is a thing I rather pride myself on, my control' (i. 333). Many different people commented on this, often in a rather puzzled way. How could the cheerful, lively and outgoing person they knew also be so controlled, detached and unmixing? Even his brother George found it mysterious, remembering how Lawrence 'couldn't and didn't mix with people much' and that 'he didn't make friends in Eastwood very much' – and yet also recalling how 'he was very good company, you know, when he was in the mood'. The Lawrences' neighbour Blanche Bircumshaw also remembered him like that: 'he could keep the whole party going the whole of the night, entertain them'. But another neighbour, Polly Goddard, remembered just the opposite; she found him 'very quiet . . . I never knew him to be very friendly'.[55] This clearly has something to do with the context in which you met Lawrence: the private person was very different from the public one. But it is also clear that – even more than most adolescents – he was a tremendous role player, as he struggled to find out who he was. And 'in the moments of deepest emotion myself has watched myself': his distance meant that he was not often caught up in experience, however sharply he was observing it: probably for the very reason that he *was* so sharply observing it. We can see both his desire for abandon and his watchful self-consciousness in his extraordinary description of the 64-year-old Sarah Bernhardt in *La Dame aux Camélias* in June 1908.

She opened up the covered tragedy that works the grimaces of this wonderful dime show. Oh, to see her, and to hear her, a wild creature, a gazelle with a beautiful panther's fascination and fury, laughing in musical French, screaming with true panther cry, sobbing and sighing like a deer sobs, wounded to death, and all the time with the sheen of silk, the glitter of diamonds, the moving of men's handsomely groomed figures about her! She is not pretty – her voice is not sweet – but there she is, the incarnation of wild emotion which we share with all live things, but which is gathered in us in all complexity and inscrutable fury. She represents the primeval passions of woman, and she is fascinating to an extraordinary degree. I could love such a woman myself, love her to madness; all for the pure, wild passion of it. Intellect is shed as flowers shed their petals. (i. 59)

The day after seeing la Bernhardt, he told Jessie Chambers that 'the play had so upset him that at the end he rushed from his place and found himself battering at the doors until an attendant came and let him out ... "I feel frightened. I realize that I, too, might become enslaved to a woman"' (i. 56). A woman could be wild: a man might be enslaved by such a woman: he was fascinated by the idea of being enslaved, and of having his own intellectual detachment stripped from him. And he did not know if he wanted it, or if he wanted to run away from it. That was the excitement of Bernhardt. There is more than a trace of self-congratulation as he tells Jessie how uncontrollably moved he was. His prose is both luscious and extraordinarily controlled, as it hymns primeval passion: he could hardly have helped comparing himself with Lucy Snowe in Charlotte Brontë's *Villette* when she (another controlled and eternal looker-on) is confronted by a great actress.[56]

In his search, however, to understand himself and his feelings – because he always used his writing, like his roles, to create and explore versions of himself, exactly as we can see him doing in his description of Sarah Bernhardt – Lawrence filled his early fiction with figures who, without being writers, view life with what is almost a parody of the cool detachment of the artist. Cyril Beardsall, the narrator (and in some ways central character) of 'Laetitia' – whom Lawrence on one occasion referred to as 'myself' (i. 141) – dabbles with 'verses' at the start of the novel but later we hear three times about his painting. He is, however, not actually a painter or a poet, though he dabbles in both arts, and is 'writing' the novel with sensibility enough for a dozen. He is not 'actually' anything. He appears to have no job: he can be 'kept indoors by a cold' for 'some weeks' without suffering money or job difficulties. At one stage he mysteriously goes away for 'a year of absence in the south'; he has gone to live in Norwood.[57] But while Lawrence himself went to South London to work as an elementary school teacher, Cyril has no such occupation.

Cyril hardly changed in the course of the book's many rewritings, remaining – as Jessie Chambers saw him in the book's first and second versions – 'old-maidish': sensitive and sympathetic, an intensely aesthetic observer, but detached to the point of helplessness. Lydia Lawrence objected: 'is annoyed that he portrays himself in Cyril as a colourless character'.[58] Cyril is a figure who plays hardly any part in the lives of those around him. He makes wry comments, feels lonely and detached. When Lawrence revised the ending of 'Laetitia' in the autumn of 1909, he noted that 'I . . . have married Lettie and Leslie and George and Meg, and Emily to a stranger and myself to nobody' (i. 141). It is inconceivable that Cyril – himself damaged by a parental conflict – could do anything so positive as marry anyone; his role is entirely to comment, and (like so many heroes with their roots in the 1890s) to feel sensitively and sympathetically. Lawrence's other early autobiographical heroes like Cyril Mersham in 'A Modern Lover', Edward Severn in 'The Old Adam', Bernard Coutts in 'The Witch à la Mode', John Adderley Syson in 'The Shades of Spring' and the Doppelgänger Hampson in *The Trespasser*

are incapable of tragedy themselves, though they are close observers of the tragedies of others; they present the Artist as brilliant entertainer, as word-magician, as the person of incisive but unfulfilling insight . . . As artists, or potential artists, what capacities for sensitive observation they have! But they are deprived of all context, and have nothing in which their perceptions might be rooted; they are incapable of relationship, except with inanimate nature and (above all) with words.[59]

The autobiographical hero Paul Morel is employed as a clerk and is a part-time painter and designer. But none of Lawrence's autobiographical figures is a writer; few of them, in fact, have any kind of job. The narrator of 'The Fly in the Ointment' is a schoolteacher, Hampson in 'The Saga of Siegmund' a musician and Moest in 'New Eve and Old Adam' apparently a businessman; Mersham in 'A Modern Lover', Coutts in 'The Witch à la Mode', Severn in 'The Old Adam', Syson in 'The Shades of Spring' and the narrator of 'Once—!' are all without visible means of support. They tend to spend their time imagining, rather sadly, the kind of relationship which Cyril yearns to have with George Saxton – warm, tender and intimate – or which Severn momentarily imagines having with Mrs Thomas in 'The Old Adam': passionate, eager.

Each of them, without being anything so definite as a self-portrait, is clearly an experiment Lawrence is making with the role of the detached, self-controlled man and aesthete; and they are an intensely depressing commentary upon it. Man and aesthete alike are condemned to nullity, to aimlessness, to experiencing only their own sensitivity.[60] The self-consciousness of Lawrence's description of his loss of detachment on the Bernhardt evening suggests how frequently he felt himself to be imprisoned within such detachment.

But such imprisonment was an experience about which Lawrence wrote continually and convincingly; and he eventually wrote about how it makes men incapable of forming lasting relationships. Women violently object to it. Clara, in *Sons and Lovers*, will complain about yet another detached hero, Paul Morel – and Paul actually *is* an artist – 'you've never come near to me. You can't come out of yourself, you can't.'[61] Peter Moest in 'New Eve and Old Adam', written in 1913, will remember his wife's accusation that

he did not love her. But he knew that, in his way he did. In his way—but was his way wrong? His way was himself, he thought, struggling. Was there something wrong, something missing in his nature, that he could not love? He struggled madly, as if he were in a mesh, and could not get out. He did not want to believe that he was deficient in his nature. Wherein was he deficient? It was nothing physical. She said he could not come out of himself, that he was no good to her, because he could not get outside himself. What did she mean? Get outside himself! It seemed like some acrobatic feat, some slippery contortionist trick. No, he could not understand.[62]

The charge was very close to that which Frieda Weekley would lay at Lawrence's door when she wrote, in one of his poetry notebooks, 'sadly I proved to myself that *I* can love, but *never* you . . .' 'Not being able to love' is something which Lawrence himself feared; and it is a state to which these artist figures of the early fiction are utterly condemned. When Severn in 'The Old Adam' feels that he and his landlady, Mrs Thomas, are starting to experience something like mutual sexual arousal, fear and shock overwhelm him; he is 'highly civilised' and will never submit simply to what he calls 'blind emotion'.[63] Cyril Mersham in 'A Modern Lover' is on the one hand a languid and elegant word-spinner; on the other, he proposes to Muriel that they should sleep together. But love for Cyril is a very conscious business. 'I shall never be blindly in love, shall I?', he says rather proudly to Muriel. She replies, 'You won't be blindly anything.' And when – in spite of his reassurance that she need not be afraid of getting pregnant – she expresses doubts about his proposal, he insists '"There need be no ifs . . . you *do* know," he exclaimed. "I have given you books—."' It is entirely appropriate that Cyril should believe that 'books' are his best way of reassuring her. It is also significant that the story should end not with commitment, or passion, but with Cyril's wandering over the fields feeling that he 'had played a difficult, deeply-moving part all night' and that he has now 'lost hold'.[64] Cyril is never abandoned to his feelings and desires, because he is always fatally conscious of his role: can never lose himself, and can never fall in love.

In all these stories Lawrence is using his fiction to explore the possibilities, and to discover or uncover the limitations and the ultimate emptiness, of this kind of role and this kind of artist. Such a role seems first to have fascinated and then to have horrified him; but his early fiction shows him unable to leave it alone for very long. Against such a character he came deliberately to oppose a range of others, like the gamekeeper Annable in *The White Peacock*. When Jessie Chambers objected to Annable, Lawrence 'shook his head decisively, and said: "He *has* to be there. Don't you see why? He makes a sort of balance. Otherwise it's too much one thing, too much *me*," and grinned.'[65] Annable is emotion incarnate: a man who has learned to live entirely through his feelings. Another kind of opposition is formed by the man of limited intellectual and artistic abilities, the profoundly sensual man who is also hardly aware of his own feelings: George Saxton in *The White Peacock* is such a man. And Lawrence is intensely aware of how limited such a man is, in spite of his sensuality.

Lawrence's main way of avoiding the character of the artist who cannot love was, eventually, to write a different kind of fiction – about the industrial communities of the English Midlands. In stories like 'Odour of Chrysanthemums', 'Love Among the Haystacks', 'Daughters of the Vicar', 'Strike-Pay', 'Her Turn', 'A Sick Collier' and 'The Miner at Home', the only traces of such a figure appear in the Mrs Morel-like Mrs Bates in 'Odour of Chrysanthemums' – detached from community by experience, language and habit. There are no artistic narrators or artist-figures. The division of the early fiction into such separate categories marks, however, one of the divisions Lawrence feared existed within himself; a division into a person who, like Arthur Lawrence and Mr Morel, felt in and of his place and community, and found that it naturally supplied the material of his writing; and an artist who, like Lydia Lawrence and Mrs Morel and Mrs Bates, felt outside it, detached from it, condemned to observation and feeling terribly (and at times terrifyingly) afflicted by the pain of self-awareness.

Writing, for the boy from Eastwood, was thus an extraordinarily courageous and potentially crippling choice. It intensified (because it focused upon) the profoundest problems of his background and his class. It continually exposed him to the danger of being a man hopelessly cut off from the actualities of his world. But it was also his best way of articulating the realities and complexity of his experience of being divided: of enacting the roles with which his experience had presented him. Writing was a way of coming to the end of his adolescent roles, of sharing his experience, of learning that his problems (however acute) were representative: and of actually breaking down in himself the barriers to experience which his upbringing had created.

CHAPTER SIX

◆

1906

SPIRIT LOVE

I   Sex and Love

'Delayed adolescence' is probably the best way of describing Lawrence's maturing between 1904 and 1908. Looking back from 1911, he reckoned that he had been 'very young' (i. 233) at 20 – in 1905: he thought he had lost his 'mental and moral boyhood' (i. 50) only when he went to college in 1906, and had 'changed from boyhood to manhood' during 1906–7 (i. 72). However, in April 1908 he still believed himself 'very young – though twenty two; I have never left my mother, you see' (i. 45); and less than a month later he wrote 'I ⟨am⟩ ˹was˺ a born boy, cut out for eternal boyish-ness' (i. 50). The man who thought that 'my youth was the most acute and painful time I shall ever see, I'll bet' (i. 119), and who knew how his child-hood had involved him in his mother's distressingly adult confidences about her marriage, was also aware that his youth had, paradoxically, continued far longer than most other people's – especially in an age when 12-year-old boys and girls often went out to work. In spite of his assertion in May 1909 that 'I am tremendously grown up' (i. 128), his final confrontation with adulthood would not happen until his mother's death at the end of 1910, when he was 25.

His relationship with Jessie Chambers during his teens had been his first close relationship with a woman outside his own family, and it had devel-oped into an enduring partnership. And yet for years it remained totally sexless; according to Jessie an 'unconscious period' when 'no instinct of sex was awake in either . . . it was all spiritual'.* When Lawrence suggested – in the spring 1912 version of 'Paul Morel' – that on one occasion during this early period Paul's fingers had significantly touched Miriam's, Jessie was quick to insist that 'There was no question of it at that time.'[1] Lawrence had to agree; he had recalled in the spring of 1910 that, in spite of having known

---

* The quotations from Jessie Chambers are taken from comments she made between Novem-ber 1911 and March 1912 upon Lawrence's novel 'Paul Morel' and in additional notes. These comments and notes specifically refer to the characters Miriam and Paul; yet they record facts and feelings Jessie thought Lawrence had ignored about their own young lives when he wrote the novel. They are thus evidence, from Jessie Chambers's viewpoint in 1911–12, of what had happened to her and to Lawrence between 1902 and 1906.[2]

Jessie for ten years, he 'had hardly kissed her all that time' (i. 154). An Eastwood contemporary who knew them both very well, Alice Hall, was once asked if Lawrence and Jessie would walk to the Haggs hand in hand, and replied emphatically 'No, no . . .' The same non-physical behaviour seems to have been also true of Lawrence's relationships with other women. Alice Hall recalled that although 'He was very friendly with the girls next door [the Cooper sisters] . . . he was more like a brother to them than anything. I never saw him make love to anybody or kiss them or anything, he wasn't, he wasn't . . . No, no, nor with any girl. I never saw him kiss anybody at the Coopers', girls or anyone.'[3] He was also friendly with the daughters of his Eastwood headmaster, George Holderness, in particular with Edith ('Kitty'); he visited the family more than once after they moved to Eakring in 1909. But when Kitty's younger sister once innocently asked 'So when are you two going to get married, then?' Lawrence was terribly embarrassed: there was no question of it. Alice Hall also remembered how 'he and Jessie, always when they were together, always seemed serious subjects they discussed. There didn't seem any love-making or anything like that'. In the autumn of 1912 Lawrence added to *Sons and Lovers* a passage describing how Paul and Miriam 'were late in coming to maturity, and psychical ripeness was much behind even the physical'.[4] The period of 'innocence' up to 1906 was a natural consequence of Lawrence's puritanical upbringing, his late maturing and his particular kind of self-possession. George Neville and others had noticed how Lawrence in his mid-teens had been physically very reserved and shy; another friend remembered how Lawrence 'was innocent of the facts of life when he was fourteen or fifteen years old'. According to Neville, discussion at the Haggs Farm about serving the sow and taking the cows to the bull had at first bewildered and then disgusted Lawrence. Neville also records an incident suggesting that until some time after 1904, and probably nearer 1907 – when he was 22 – Lawrence remained ignorant of the existence of female pubic hair, and violently refused to believe in it even when Neville told him about it.[5]

But Neville found no difficulty in accounting for such innocence. To him, Lawrence had never been a normal Eastwood boy at all:

had never 'knocked around' with any crowds of fellows, never played football or cricket, and I think I am correct in saying that at this time he had never indulged in a bathe . . . And there had been no one to give him any real introduction to matters of sex, save what I had done, and what he had gleaned from his mother . . .[6]

That is very probably true. Furthermore, in May 1908 Lawrence told Blanche Jennings that he had only started to write when his prolonged period of youth was drawing to an end – when boyhood 'began to drop from me as the grains drop one by one from a head of oats, or ten at a time when rudely shaken ... Consequently I wrote with crude sentimentality, being sick, having lost the health of my laddishness, all the humour that was the body of my mind's health dead' (i. 50). He thus linked his writing – started in 1905–6 – with the end of what he mythologised as his youthful 'body of my mind's health'. That points to a new and painful awareness of the body, and hints at the start of sexual behaviour; his later writings would be very expressive about the compulsions of masturbation.[7] He continued to show a deep nostalgia for that mythical, untroubled boyhood; maturity, in contrast, meant illness. When he heard, in 1906, that his old friend Neville had 'got a girl into trouble', he was 'very distressed', 'sounded sick with misery' and finally startled Jessie by 'bursting out vehemently: "Thank God ... I've been saved from that ... so far."'[8] Sexuality appeared to be something which attacked with the ferocity of a dangerous disease. Masturbation, shameful as he felt it to be, was better than 'that': but in many ways he would have preferred to keep his boyish 'health'.

It can be no coincidence that the period around 1906 also marked the end of his early relationship with Jessie Chambers: a relationship which had been wholly companionable and intellectual, but which could never be untroubled again. The violent outbursts of emotion which Lawrence seems to have begun to experience around the age of 21 conflicted as strongly with his old youthful high spirits as they did with the continuing gentleness and asexuality of much of his behaviour. Jessie Chambers recalled three such outbursts, the first at Mablethorpe during the family holiday of August 1906:

In the evening he and I wandered along the beach waiting to see the moon rise over the sea. We set off light-heartedly enough, but gradually some dark power seemed to take possession of Lawrence, and when the final beauty of the moonrise broke upon us, something seemed to explode inside him. I cannot remember now what he said, but his words were wild, and he appeared to be in great distress of mind, and probably also of body. In some way I was to blame. He upbraided me bitterly, and when I protested he blamed himself, and poured himself out in a torrent of passionate words.[9]

The passage as Jessie Chambers first wrote it made the sexuality of the exchange still more overt by reading 'spent himself upon me' rather than 'poured himself out'. There were two subsequent similar occasions: one at Robin Hood's Bay in 1907, 'when the combined beauty of moonlight and sea, together with whatever effect my presence had upon him, seemed to make him distraught ... he stalked some distance from me like a strange, wild creature, and kept up a stream of upbraiding, or something that sounded like it'.[10] The worst of the three came, however, at Flamborough in 1908:

Lawrence skipped from one white boulder to another in the vast amphitheatre of the bay until I could have doubted whether he was indeed a human being. I was really frightened then – not physically, but deep in my soul. He created an atmosphere not of death, which after all is part of mortality, but of an utter negation of life, as though he had become dehumanized. And always, somehow or other, it was my fault, or partly my fault. They were unforgettable experiences. I never spoke about them, for I was at a loss to describe them.[11]

These outbursts of demonic physical and verbal energy, with Lawrence 'beside himself', are akin to something that David Chambers once saw at a farm near the Haggs, when Jessie Chambers may well have been the cause:

he terrified me by jumping backwards and forwards across a millrace at Felley Mill farm. The water poured in a swift green avalanche down a shute about a yard and a half wide: too wide to step across but by no means easy to jump because of the sloping sides; but Lawrence jumped repeatedly backwards and forwards across it like an antelope, as though defying death itself, while I stood holding my breath with fear. I have seen the shute since and I still cannot see how it was done.[12]

Lawrence was as a rule self-possessed and unable to 'come out of himself'. But this demonic anger and physical violence, which sound increasingly like sexual feelings almost unwittingly directed at Jessie Chambers, seem to have been the first time his tightly-controlled and still adolescent emotions had been allowed to show themselves. They dramatically suggest what had been building up during that prolonged 'unconscious period'.[13] Lawrence's refusal of sexuality in his extended period of 'youthful innocence' had also been a continuing rejection of the very possibility of sharing or expressing emotion; the man who in 1913 at last confessed himself 'so damnably violent, really' had spent years behaving 'with decent restraint' and sitting 'so tight' on 'the crater' of his 'passions and emotions' that he hardly ever exploded. 'I have a good old English habit', he remarked, 'of shutting my rages of trouble well inside my belly, so that they play havoc with my innards' (ii. 73). But it had not just been his 'rages of trouble' which he had succeeded in shutting up: his emotions and his sexuality had been tightly reined in. There is just a single reference, transmuted into the fiction of *Mr Noon*, to childhood anger at the age of thirteen: 'horrible rages' which his sister could 'taunt' up in him: 'And he knew he could have murdered her.'[14]

But he had managed to sit tight on such feelings for years: had become, indeed, an expert in self-control. He had been a child who, for many years, had remained under the sway of his mother's personality: who had accepted her valuation of (and attitude towards) his father: who had adopted her religion, her standards, her code. As his mother would have wished, he was going to college to become a teacher, not a journalist or writer: and (very much against his own inclination) he would stay a teacher as long as she was alive. Loving Lydia Lawrence meant not only remaining a responsible son and becoming a salary earner; it meant inhibiting his own carelessness, impulsiveness, anger and (in particular) sensuality.

And yet, in the period 1906–8, his new awareness of sexuality became linked with a frequently expressed inability to fall in love: with Jessie or with anybody else. This seems to have been conditioned as much by his habitual self-awareness and detachment as by the love for his mother which he (and Jessie) would later use to explain it. He complained in June 1908 that 'I would give a great deal to fall in love' (i. 58), but a month later ruled out as 'impossible ... magnificent love between a woman and me' (i. 66); he referred during 1908 to his 'grain of sense' which 'prevents my falling in love – it prevented my becoming "converted" to religion' (i. 51). His love for his mother, and his sympathy with her, grew together with his ability to remain outside his own emotion, aware of himself in the same way as he was sharply aware of others. Lydia Lawrence hated shouting, violence and physical demonstrations of feeling. Hers was a marvellously understanding bright sympathy in which her son joyously participated: but it was not a physical warmth. What she provoked in her children was loyalty, under-standing and belief. Lawrence had grown up with a good deal of childhood rage bottled up inside him, and with fewer outlets for his feelings than most people; his love for his mother consisted in knowing her, through and through, and in being known and accepted by her.

To the adolescent and puritanical Lawrence, too, love for another person probably seemed safer – even more natural – between men than between men and women. Love for another man sublimated disturbing sexual feel-ings which (as Jessie saw) seemed dangerously akin to violence; he was ignorant, somewhat in awe and at times scared of women and their dif-ference from him. Furthermore, love for a man (and time spent in his company) aroused no storms of resentment at home. Given the kinds of inhibition with which his background and upbringing had equipped him, Lawrence had grown up strikingly sensual in his response to male beauty; and aesthetic appreciation of the male body was one of the few ways in which a writer could embody a heavily charged sexual meaning and still evade censorship. His early writing is full of such appreciation: George and Leslie in *The White Peacock*, Tom Vickers in 'A Modern Lover', Maurice Wookey in 'Love Among the Haystacks', Siegmund MacNair in 'The Saga of Siegmund'. There is a strongly narcissistic streak in the writing about some of these, too. In the summer of 1908 Lawrence told Blanche Jennings how, after working for a fortnight in the Chambers family hay harvest,

My hands are brown, hard, and coarse; my face is gradually tanning. Aren't you glad? I have really worked hard; I can pick alongside a big experienced man; indeed I am fairly strong; I am pretty well developed; I have done a good deal of dumb-bell practice. Indeed, as I was rubbing myself down in the late twilight a few minutes ago, and as I passed my hands over my sides where the muscles lie suave and secret, I did love myself. I am thin, but well skimmed over with muscle; my skin is very white and unblemished; soft, and dull with a fine pubescent bloom, not shiny like my friend's. I am very fond of myself. I like you because I can talk like this to you. (i. 65)

It is the self-consciously artistic chat of a man who did not often feel 'complacent as a god' in physical well-being, in spite of his dumb-bell practice; but who is proud, for once, of having a body like other men; and whose fondness for his own beauty is here offered in a quite unerotic but extraordinarily naive way to a rather older and thoroughly distant woman. His detachment would usually have inhibited the expression of such feelings to closer friends, however much he might have liked to express them.

But such appreciation of himself, and of unthreatening and undemanding male beauty, flowed naturally into love for other men: in particular for his friend Alan Chambers, and perhaps too for George Neville, in the period 1906–8. Chambers and Neville, who also worked in the 1908 harvest, were (Lawrence wrote) men 'whom I really love' (i. 67): Chambers was probably the man whose shiny skin seemed so different from his own. In *The White Peacock*, in the scene where George towels Cyril dry after swimming, Lawrence lovingly recreated the kind of aesthetic appreciation and homoerotic tenderness which he felt towards such men.[15] Cyril experiences a thoroughly envious sensual appreciation of a male physique which is attractively rounded and solid but which – to such a finely aesthetic observer – feels just a little limited. The novel also very compellingly suggests Cyril's attraction, when he looks at George's beauty, not just to the beauty of George's body but to an ease and unthinkingness which he himself never experiences.

There was also in Lawrence, however, a continuing and very powerful inhibition – not only a sexual inhibition – against 'any demonstration' of his feelings. Reading aloud Schopenhauer's 'Metaphysics of Love' to Jessie, in 1906 or 1907, he came 'to the passage "Accordingly, everyone in the first place will infinitely prefer and ardently desire those who are most beautiful" ... he looked up and said, "But that's just the trouble, I *don't* ardently desire, I see what is most beautiful but don't desire it".'[16] He would not himself have reached out and caressed another man any more than he would have allowed himself to be caressed, or any more than he would have caressed Jessie Chambers. His love and tenderness for both sexes were confined to observation, and to writing about what he saw. He remarked in 1913 how 'one is kept by all tradition and instinct from loving men, or a man' (ii. 115): and, as always, 'instinct' is a powerful word for Lawrence. We can be quite certain that, during the period covered by this volume, Lawrence never had any sexual relationship with a man.

We should see him, therefore, not as a 'repressed homosexual', nor as a 'latent homosexual', or indeed as a homosexual at all, but as a man caught between his habitual, torturing detachment, and his passionate longing for attachment: between the self who, like his mother, looked on and coolly understood and appreciated things – and the self much closer in sympathy to the more immediate, warmer and less articulate Arthur Lawrence. He certainly experienced homoerotic feelings, and he expressed them in his writing. But that is not the same as being a homosexual. He seems to have been particularly haunted by an acute nostalgia for being a man simple, sensual and whole: one who loved, and who was loved, physically and undemandingly in a way which he found, in his adolescence, more characteristic of his father than of his mother, and of men than of women. It was men with whom he could – just occasionally in reality, but mostly in imagination – be physically close and uncomplicatedly happy, and to whose beauty he was unthreateningly attracted. His attraction to men seems also to have corresponded to a reaction against and fear of women, and to emotional and psychic needs rather than sexual ones, just as his feeling for Jessie Chambers was – in fictional retrospect – 'only a fondness, a sort of sacred love, as for a sister',[17] while his love for his mother responded to his knowledge of her watchful jealousy.

II Easter Monday 1906

In the spring of 1906, Lawrence found himself subject to strong pressure from his mother and from his sisters (Emily in particular) over his relationship with Jessie. By then he had been going to the Haggs for four and a half years, and Jessie had also been coming to Eastwood; they had been sharing books, ideas and hours of talk. Lately they had also been sharing his writing; it had been at the Haggs Farm, Lawrence remembered, that 'I got my first incentive to write' (v. 592). Writing his poems and prose, and showing them to Jessie, were things that went naturally together. 'Whenever I've done a fresh bit I think to myself: "What will she say to this?"' – a process he summed up in 1928 as: 'I would . . . do a bit, show it to the girl'. That meant that he was involved in a closer (and more time-consuming) relationship with her than ever. For her part, innocently but certainly she loved him: 'At this time her love for Paul had not grown beyond herself—nor beyond her control'.[18]

At Easter 1906, Lawrence was approaching his 21st birthday; Jessie was 19. It had been a satisfaction to Lydia Lawrence that he had not taken up with a particular girlfriend, as both his elder brothers had: George getting married at 21, Ernest being engaged at 22. May Chambers remembered Lydia Lawrence's complaints: 'Look at my eldest [George]. "I shall never leave you, Mother." Many a time he said that, and there he was, arming a girl around almost before he was out of knickerbockers. And the next one [Ernest] soon cast off the old one for the young ones.' '"There's safety in numbers,' though, isn't there, mother?" Bert would say with a wink at us.' And, on another occasion, '"Everyone likes our Bert," Mrs. Lawrence liked to beam, "and there's safety in numbers."'[19] To make matters worse, the Lawrence family had never liked Jessie; but what made the spring of 1906 especially significant was that Lawrence's college career was approaching: he was going to Nottingham University College in October. It was probably becoming clear to his family that his writing (and especially the way it took him so much to Jessie Chambers) was not only absorbing a great deal of his spare time, but was something to which he was starting to pin his hopes. Lydia Lawrence, with her particular needs and ambitions, would have wanted to warn her son not only that he was behaving in a potentially compromising way to Jessie – but that he would not be being fair to himself, or to the sacrifices his family had made for him over the years, if he let either his writing or Jessie jeopardise his college career. Marriage to Jessie in 1906 would have meant no better future for him than that of the uncertificated elementary teacher.

It was certainly true that he and Jessie were getting themselves talked about. In the telling words of one of the Lawrence family neighbours, who had no axe to grind, 'She used to come to Sunday tea and sit at chapel with him. If you did things like that, you were spoken for.' According to local manners and mores, Lawrence and Jessie were engaged: the only other explanation would be that Jessie had no respect for herself. For Eastwood folk, nothing else, apart from the boy being touched in the head – and some people *did* say 'Summat's wrong, somewhere!'[20] – would have accounted for the way in which Jessie and Lawrence not only went to Chapel together but went for long walks in the fields, with Lawrence coming home late at night afterwards.

That, too, had been causing problems in the Lawrence household. *Sons and Lovers* is full of the quarrels which ensue because Paul (in his mother's words) goes 'trapseing up there miles and miles in the mud, coming home at midnight, and got to go to Nottingham in the morning . . . Is she *so* fascinating, that you must follow her all that way—?'[21] Paul starts to say that he likes Miriam, but his mother interrupts: '*Like* her! . . . It seems to me you like nothing and nobody else. There's neither Annie, nor me, nor anyone now for you.' Paul then tries to insist that he does not love Miriam: it is just that

'I *do* like to talk to her—I never said I didn't. But I *don't* love her.'
'Is there nobody else to talk to?'
'Not about the things we talk of . . .'[22]

Something very like that exchange must have occurred more than once in the Lynn Croft house between 1905 and 1906. It is the common pattern of an educated and sexually latent child growing beyond the bounds and understanding of a loving but possessive parent: but none the less painful for being common.

What his mother thought of Jessie in 1906 is unknown. What she thought in 1910, in a rather similar situation, is on record. In a letter to her sister Lettie which mentioned her son, she gave it as her opinion that Jessie 'certainly will not let him slip if she can help it. Though he is fond of her it does not seem to me like the real love he ought to have if he intends to marry her.'[23] There is, too, Lawrence's own testimony, given just after his mother's death in December 1910, that she had 'hated J. – and would have risen from the grave to prevent my marrying her' (i. 197).

In *Sons and Lovers*, however, the adolescent Paul Morel's mother says 'I can't bear to lose you—I can't bear her to have you. I could let another woman—but not her—she'd leave me no room, not a bit of room—'[24] It is not at all certain that this is something Lydia Lawrence would ever have felt, or said: certainly not before 1906, when the relationship between Lawrence and Jessie was so obviously unsexual. Once again, *Sons and Lovers* is a misleading guide to the events of real life. Lawrence was tremendously important to his mother, and it must have been profoundly disappointing and irritating to her to find him, with that important college course looming, giving so much time and attention to a girl she distrusted: to feel him evading her own watchful love of him, and to know that he was showing Jessie the writing which she feared would be a distraction from the real business of his life. Lydia Lawrence also knew that, however emotionally detached her son might be, Jessie was in love with him and hoped to marry him one day: was determined not to 'let him slip if she can help it'. Lydia was savagely opposed to Jessie and hated her devoted self-sacrifice to the dominant male; she would probably have disliked her even if Jessie had not loved her son or put his career at risk. But her jealousy of Jessie was not that of a woman threatened by a rival. Lawrence, too, would (much later) decide that his mother had been right to judge Jessie severely: like his mother, he grew to think Jessie's peculiarly self-sacrificing devotion both dangerous and destructive, because it never allowed a real and creative conflict to develop between her and another person.

For a number of reasons, therefore, Lawrence's family decided to try and put an end to his association with Jessie. It is perhaps significant that Emily Lawrence – now married – seems to have been Lydia's main helper in the attempt to prise Lawrence and Jessie apart. There is evidence that Ada also found it hard to take Jessie sympathetically, and one contemporary remembered how Ada 'wasn't very keen on Jessie: I've heard Ada say, when Jessie used to walk home from church on Sunday night with Bert, "Hm. Here comes Jessie again."' In *A Collier's Friday Night*, 'Nellie' – Ernest's sister – is notably contemptuous of Maggie Pearson: in the 1909–10 'Nethermere' draft of *The White Peacock*, where a character based on Jessie is called 'Emily', Cyril Beardsall's sister 'did not love Emily, and for several reasons'.[25] Of the two daughters, Ada was the more possessive of her brother. But she would also probably not have approved of interfering. Of the four surviving children, Emily was easily the most conventional – her brother thought her 'blind to the tragic issue' of their parents' marriage (i. 262) – and she was also the most responsive to local manners and morals. It is probable that she would have been genuinely puzzled, and a little shocked, at her brother following a girl over the countryside simply for the sake of talking philosophy and books to her. Characteristically, Emily had once made the experiment of going out to the Haggs 'to see what was the great attraction'; but was impressed most of all by 'that awful walk'.[26] It is impossible to believe that, knowing her brother as she did, Emily really thought that there was anything morally dangerous in his relationship with Jessie; nor (knowing her dislike of Jessie) can she have been much worried about Jessie's prospects being damaged by her friendship with Lawrence. However, George had got married at 21, and Ernest engaged only a year later: her brother Bert *was* behaving oddly: and the argument about Jessie's chances of finding another partner was a good one, because it did something to spare Jessie's feelings.

The Lawrence women therefore took their chances. Lawrence was told in no uncertain terms that he was being unfair to Jessie, and that they 'either ought to be engaged or else not to go about together'.[27] What he and Jessie had started doing when they were 16 and 15, back in the spring of 1902, was not now permissible.

Jessie later gave her version of the attack: she felt that 'the delicate fabric of our relationship had been mutilated deliberately'.[28] She also related the events of 1906 to Lawrence's own later comment (which survives only in her own recollection of it): 'They tore me from you, the love of my life . . . It was the slaughter of the foetus in the womb' (i. 268). Jessie was right to feel that she had been the target of Lydia Lawrence. Whether the attack amounted to a 'slaughter', or to deliberate mutilation of the 'delicate fabric of our relationship' is another matter. So far as Lydia Lawrence and Emily King were concerned, it was less a 'delicate fabric' than an immature but potentially dangerous entanglement.

When Lawrence told Jessie about his family's ultimatum on Easter Monday, 16 April 1906, she immediately put her finger on what had happened: 'Ah – I always thought your mother didn't like me.' Lawrence protested: '"It isn't that, you mustn't think that; mother has *nothing* against you," he urged. "It's for your sake she spoke. She says it isn't fair to you . . . I may be keeping you from getting to like someone else."'[29] It was on those grounds that Lydia Lawrence had put pressure on her son: he ought to end the relationship if he did not love Jessie – or if he was not sure whether he loved her or not. Accordingly, 'painfully' Lawrence told Jessie, 'I've looked into my heart and I cannot find that I love you as a husband should love his wife. Perhaps I shall, in time. If ever I find I do, I'll tell you.'[30] The similarity of the wording with the phrase Lydia Lawrence used in 1910 – 'Though he is fond of her it does not seem to me like the real love he ought to have if he intends to marry her' – is probably not a coincidence. Whether Lawrence or his mother were first responsible for them, the words became the formula which summed up why Lawrence could not marry Jessie. It was also what decided him to go along with his family's demands.

The fact that he did not love her 'as a husband should love his wife' was also horribly clear to Jessie. She was hearing again, now in deadly seriousness, what she might have heard at any time during the previous four years – how 'his feeling for me was entirely intellectual and spiritual, and had nothing to do with the physical side of life'. At some stage around 1907, however, Lawrence would go further still: '"It comes to this, you know," he said. "You have no sexual attraction at all, none whatever."'[31] The cruelty of the words (and of the Schopenhauer devotee who spoke them) was something she never forgot. Lawrence doubtless believed he was being the cool, dispassionate man and thinker when he spoke: but they reveal his desire to blame Jessie for his failure to feel. His suggestion, therefore, that he might one day love her – 'Perhaps I shall, in time' – was not only more cruel than out-and-out rejection would have been, but revealing of his own radical uncertainties. Jessie was thus encouraged not to give him up.

Between 1902 and Easter 1906, she had probably never thought of a future which did not somehow involve Lawrence: he had become incomparably the most important person in her life. Though they had never shown any affection towards each other, she had loved him and assumed that they would one day marry: for her, a relationship found its 'natural' form in 'love and marriage'. Her memory of the moment certainly suggests so: 'I saw the golden apple of life that had been lying at my finger tips recede irretrievably'. She had grown up isolated in attitude and inclination from the rest of her family, and the 'sense of understanding' between her and Lawrence had been 'a rare prize' for her.[32] She had, over a period of four years, helped him with extraordinary loyalty in their mutual self-education; she it was who had ensured that he could fulfil his potential as an intellectual. She was, in her own right, a most remarkable person, who did many things which a person with her background could never have been expected to do. But what Lawrence did to her in the spring of 1906 marked (she felt) the end of her hopes of a richer and more fulfilled life.

III The Intercourse of Talk

The decision taken at Easter 1906, however much its strictness was later relaxed, at first meant that Lawrence and Jessie would not be alone together; a third person would have to be present if they walked back from chapel to the Haggs, for instance, or when they were reading together at Jessie's home. When they went out into the fields, they would take a younger brother or sister of hers with them.

Jessie Chambers later intimated that she would have preferred to end their relationship completely, rather than accept the imposition of such terms. But she also remembered the extraordinary vehemence with which Lawrence insisted that they must not end their relationship.

No, we shall *not*. We shall not give everything up. It means too much to us. We can't give it all up. There's the question of writing, we want to talk about that. And there's the French, we can go on reading together, surely? Only we'll read in the house, or where they can see us. And chapel, that's important . . . We needn't let people think we're on a different footing from what we are, that's all. Only we *must* go on talking to one another.[33]

In one way – his way – the arrangement Lawrence was now proposing made no difference at all to his desire to go on reading with her, discussing books and showing her his writing. He went on showing her his work for another six years after 1906. We may even suspect that he looked forward to a 'cooler' relationship with Jessie, one which did not subject him so much to the 'overwrought feelings', 'unbalanced by strife', he was starting to be so critical of in her. She remembered how, around this time, 'He developed a highly critical tone.'[34]

But why did he insist so strongly that they '*must* go on talking to one another'? Why, too, did he insist so strongly on her reading what he wrote?

In the first place, it is obvious that Lawrence – having devoted himself to Jessie for four years – knew no-one else who could possibly fill her place. At Easter 1906, he actually remarked – 'pathetically' – that 'this is the only friendship that's ripened',[35] which suggests a little of his isolation in Eastwood (though college would widen the circle of his friends). Jessie, too, was exceptionally thoughtful and well-read, and knew him through and through; and, above all, she viewed his writing with love and admiration, and without any of the inhibitions and problems which would arise in discussion of it with his own family.

Lawrence also distinguished sharply between what Paul Morel, in *Sons and Lovers*, gets from his mother when he is painting, and what he gets from Miriam. When Paul is working at home, with his mother near him,

he, with all his soul's intensity ⟨. . .⟩ directing his pencil, could feel her ⟨warming his heart,⟩ ⌜warmth⌝ inside him like strength. They were both very happy ⟨,⟩ so, and both unconscious of it. These times, that meant so much, and which were real living, they almost ignored.

He was conscious only when ⟨some fret interfered.⟩ ⌜stimulated.⌝ A sketch finished, he always wanted to take it to Miriam. Then he was ⟨fretted⟩ ⌜stimulated⌝ into knowledge of the work he had produced unconsciously. In contact with Miriam, he gained insight, his vision went deeper. From his mother he drew the life warmth, the strength to produce; ⟨f⟩ Miriam urged this warmth into intensity like a white light.

The talks with Miriam, in the novel, serve the same function.

There was for him the most intense pleasure in talking about his work to Miriam. All his passion, all his wild blood went into this intercourse with her, when he talked and conceived his work. She brought forth to him his imaginations. She did not understand, any more than a woman understands when she conceives a child in her womb. But this was life for her, and for him.[36]

The novel, however, suggests that this talk does more than simply educate Paul into 'knowledge of the work he had produced unconsciously'. With an almost Dostoevskian relish, Paul responds to 'fret' or 'stimulus': it is significant that the one word should have replaced the other in revision. But he finds that he is urged into a 'white intensity' when he is talking to Miriam: he becomes 'quite ghostish, disembodied . . . A sort of disseminated consciousness, that's all there is of me. I feel as if my body were lying empty, as if I were in the other things—clouds and water—' It is not actually anything

Miriam says or does which provokes this reaction. It is the attitude she adopts – of being the eager audience for his spiritual outpouring, of being the chosen one who hears – which Paul finds so intensely stimulating. Her receptivity is why he goes back to her, time after time: her desire 'to draw all of him into her . . . urged him to an intensity like madness. Which fascinated him, as drug taking might.'[37] He loses himself, and loves losing himself, in his spiritual outpouring. He likes the feeling of bodilessness, although he also feels he becomes abnormal when he is with her, and he blames her for making him like that; though it is clear that he is every bit as much to blame as she. He also hates her because her listening to him (which is what he wants) makes him feel she is possessing him.

It is impossible to say how much of this relates directly to Lawrence's own experience. Probably a great deal. It suggests how the young Lawrence 'talked and conceived his work' when with Jessie. He wanted stimulus to understand it and to see beyond it. To talk about it with – or, more accurately, to – Jessie enabled him to realise what he had done and what he was after: he *had* to understand, as well as to create instinctively. He was not only an intellectual but also a very spiritual young man: which is why he found Jessie Chambers's spirituality so sympathetic. In that sense they were made for each other, as she was so very certain they were. The fact that it was also a very 'mental' process, at this stage, was something he reacted passionately against later in his life: but *Sons and Lovers* suggests how prone the young Lawrence was to spiritual ecstasies of the kind which his mature writing denounced.

In the novel there is, however, a good deal of sublimated sexuality in the description of a man lying bodiless, and of a woman wanting to 'draw all of him into her', of 'all his wild blood' going 'into this intercourse with her'. Jessie and Lawrence successfully inhibited each other's sexuality for years: but the fictional versions of their relationship in *Sons and Lovers* suggest that sexuality was always an element. This is partly because Lawrence conflated very different periods of his relationship with Jessie when he wrote about Paul and Miriam; and partly because he rewrote the novel while sexually involved with other women, and believing that his years with Jessie Chambers had had a sexual element too. They probably had, after 1906: but not of the kind which *Sons and Lovers* suggests. His sexual interpretations of Paul and Miriam's early behaviour have very little to do with what he and Jessie experienced, at least up to 1906 and perhaps as late as 1908.[38]

But as well as continuing to devote herself to his writing, Jessie also remained totally and (at the time) uncritically loyal to a man who had made it clear that he was not going to marry her. For her 21st birthday, in January 1908, he went out of his way to redefine his feelings towards her; he wrote a letter which survives both in her recollection of it, and in the version which he himself recreated in 'Paul Morel':*

I can give you a spirit love, I have given it you this long, long time: but not embodied passion. See, you are a nun. I have given you what I would give a holy nun—as a mystic monk to a mystic nun: surely you esteem it best. Yet you regret—no, have regretted—the other. In all our relations, no body enters . . . do you understand now why I only kiss you under the mistletoe. Do you understand?—and do I?—and is it better, think you? I think I am too refined, too civilised. I think many folk are . . .

I might marry in the years to come. It would be a woman I could kiss and embrace, whom I could make the mother of my children, whom I could talk to playfully, trivially, earnestly, but never with this dreadful seriousness.[39]

Between 1906 and 1910, Jessie not only had to cope with such explanations from Lawrence, but to go on standing up to pressure from his family to see less of him, to take up less of his time and (ideally) to break off the relationship. She also had to put up with the objections of her own family to what she was doing. Her sister May was very critical, as she often was of her younger sister: but the whole family showed its disapproval. When Jessie went to London for a weekend to see Lawrence in May 1909, at the age of 22, and planned to stay at his Croydon lodgings, 'mother told me with great seriousness that she and father did not approve of my going . . . Later, Lawrence told me that mother had written to him and warned him that they placed absolute trust in him'.[40] Besides all this, Jessie had had to put up for years with Lawrence's relationships with other women: in particular his friendship with and attraction to Louie Burrows, who was 'my girl' in college (i. 193): his lively and frequently flirtatious relationship with Alice Hall, in Eastwood: his interest in the married woman Alice Dax, also in Eastwood: his unofficial engagement to Agnes Holt in Croydon in the autumn of 1909: and his friendship there with Helen Corke in the spring of 1910. He also insisted on discussing with Jessie whether he should marry Louie Burrows or Agnes Holt since they were, unlike her, women he could 'kiss and embrace' (i. 43). It was an extraordinary devotion which depended so much upon her own fortitude; it suggests her need to hold on to what she could (and, incidentally, the unlikelihood that she had seriously wished to end things at Easter 1906).

It is wrong to imagine that Jessie in some perverse way must have welcomed the suffering imposed on her by her relationship with Lawrence after 1906. There is no evidence that she enjoyed it, and a good deal that she hated it. But she saw Lawrence, both now and later, as someone imposed by God, or fate, as a duty or a task, or – in a compelling way – by her own love

* See the Use of Sources for a discussion of the text of the letter in the two versions.

for him. And she responded to her love according to that half-religious, half-secular puritanism which characterised the background they shared. She was by nature an independent woman who decided upon her own career against the wishes of her family, and who conscientiously worked her way into it. But her code also demanded, in a way that did not conflict with her feeling of independence, that she must accept what the man she loved – the man of her choice – gave and demanded. Independent woman as she was, when confronted by Lawrence she felt not only an emotional but a moral, even a religious responsibility to him. She wrote late in 1911 that 'To Miriam, Paul was God's vessel: more than that she did not allow herself to think.'[41]

But what she herself took from the relationship with Lawrence was, beside the satisfaction of a loving duty – and the pain of a dreadful series of rejections – the charm, brilliance and stimulus of a most remarkable and unusual mind and man. Though it led her into despair, her association with Lawrence between 1902 and 1912 paradoxically also gave her the richer kind of life she had always dreamed of. She was close to his thought, and closer still to his developing writing. No-one else in her circle or family could give her anything like it. Nothing in the rest of her life ever did.

But, in 1906, one phase of their life came to an end. Lawrence duly went to college in October, and Jessie took up her duties in the Mixed section of Underwood National School, after three years in the Infants' section. Their lives were changing in externals, at least, and growing apart. With a rather hateful casualness, Lawrence told Louie Burrows a month after college started that he and Jessie 'do not know much of each other nowadays': but, he went on, 'I do not like to lose her intimate acquainta[nce]' (i. 32). He went on for years not wanting to lose it.

CHAPTER SEVEN

◆

1906–1908

COLLEGE

I Disillusion

Lawrence went to college, according to Jessie Chambers, 'in a mood of wistful anticipation. He felt it might be a step into a fuller life'.[1] Lawrence himself knew he was going to college primarily in order to qualify himself as a certificated teacher; not perhaps quite so sanguine as Jessie, he would have regarded college as an opportunity to continue the education he had been getting only part-time at the pupil-teacher centre, and which had been interrupted by his year's teaching.

As it turned out, college was not only disappointing as an education but – exactly as school had been – was 'a progress in isolation'. He was thoroughly disappointed: 'Later on, Lawrence told me that if he had known what College was like he would never have made the sacrifice of those two years and all the expense . . .'[2] Shortly before his college career ended in 1908, he summed it up to Blanche Jennings:

You know when I first went to Coll., I was in the Normal Classes, taught by a woman and one man whom I could teach myself with excellent advantage . . . three parts of my time I was bored till college boredom became a disease . . . College gave me nothing, even nothing to do – I had a damnable time there, bitten so deep with disappointment that I have lost forever my sincere boyish reverence for men in position. (i. 49)

He found the subject hard to keep away from in 1908, telling her very much the same four months later: 'College disappointed me painfully . . . one of the cruellest shocks I ever had was to find that half the pro's [professors] in college were not superior to me in intellect or character' (i. 72). It was this which hit him hardest: not the course, nor the work, nor his fellow students, but the unimpressiveness of those who taught him. 'I came to feel that I might as well be taught by gramophones as by those men, for all the interest and sincerity they felt' (i. 72).

This certainly shows his disappointment that college had not brought the intellectual stimulus he lacked in his home town (and which without Jessie Chambers would have been acutely deprived of); but, too, it reveals how much – and perhaps how naively – Lawrence had expected his teachers to be

168

wise about what he was coming to think were the real problems of the twentieth century: questions of faith and belief, of nature and science. He was shocked to realise that he would have to go on breaking new ground for himself, as a man coming to terms with the modern world, as he had been doing (for example) with Carlyle, and as he was to do with Schopenhauer during his college career. However, very naturally, his dissatisfaction with the teaching staff associated itself with his simultaneous loss of other loyalties; and that reveals his situation most painfully. Not only did he doubt the intellectual capacities of his teachers at Nottingham but 'I began to despise and distrust things; I lost my rather deep religious faith; I lost my idealism and my wistfulness ...' (i. 72). What he had come up against at college was a change taking place within himself. His loyalties, at the age of 21, remained bound to the world of his upbringing: to the religion of the Congregational chapel, a still profound respect for authority, a distrust of the fallible individual and a belief in the value of restraint and the suppression of instinct. During his college career, his religious faith, full of moral certainties and moral restraint, gave way to reactions distinctively individual and modern. We need to return to Lawrence's past to make sense of his reaction to college.

II Loss of Faith

During Lawrence's adolescence, chapel had continued to be the major source of the 'outer life' it provides for Alvina Houghton in *The Lost Girl*, where Lawrence recreated the chapel-oriented life of the Midlands adolescent in the early 1900s. Alvina has gone, of course, to chapel and Sunday school as a child; but when she is in her teens,

Chapel provided her with a whole social activity, in the course of which she met certain groups of people, made certain friends, found opportunity for strolls into the country and jaunts to the local entertainments. Over and above this, every Thursday evening she went to the subscription library to change the week's supply of books, and there again she met friends and acquaintances. It is hard to overestimate the value of church or chapel—but particularly chapel—as a *social* institution, in places like Woodhouse. The Congregational Chapel provided Alvina with a whole outer life, lacking which she would have been poor indeed.[3]

The adolescents who attended the Congregational chapel not only had the regular morning and evening services on Sunday to attend; they had choir practices, Christian Endeavour Meetings, Pleasant Sunday Afternoon (P.S.A.) gatherings and Bible classes, as well as socials on Saturday nights.[4] And a group of friends gathered together after the Sunday services, frequently in the Lawrences' house. Lawrence vividly remembered those days when writing to Gertrude Cooper in 1927:

I suppose they're warbling away in Eastwood Congregational Chapel at this minute! Do you remember, how we all used to feel so sugary about the vesper verse: Lord keep us safe this night, secure from all our fears –? Then off out into the dark, with Dicky Pogmore and the Chambers and all the rest. And how Alan [Chambers] used to love the lumps of mince-pie from the pantry? And Frances [Cooper] did her hair up in brussels-sprouts, and made herself a cup of ovaltine or something of that sort! Sometimes it seems so far off. And sometimes it is like yesterday. (v. 634)

For adolescents and adults in Eastwood there was, too, the Congregational Literary Society on Monday evenings in the winter months, October to March. The Rev. Robert Reid kept up the tradition of intellectual stimulus within Congregationalism by founding the rather misleadingly named Society in 1899. Its speakers (mostly clergymen) lectured on a wide range of topical subjects; out of the ten lectures in the 1905–6 session, for example – Lawrence's last year in Eastwood before going to college – four were on travel and geographical subjects, two theological, two scientific, two politi- cal and only one – on Thomas Chatterton – literary. Lectures were nor- mally followed by discussions. Jessie Chambers remembered how in her family 'we all paid our shilling for a membership card', and how disap- pointed she was at missing a lecture she had looked forward to 'with extra- vagant anticipation'. There were too, in 1905–6, a further eight meetings of the society taking the form of slide-shows, socials, debates, concerts and recitals. Chapel attendance with friends, social life after chapel, Literary Society, excursions and walks with the same friends (to the Hemlock Stone at Bramcote on 22 April 1905: to Matlock, Wingfield Manor and What- standwell two days later: to Dale Abbey on 14 April 1906) – these were the everyday experience of the young Lawrence and his circle.[5]

   Yet the Sunday evening services (with extended sermon) in chapel remained the real focus of discussion for an intelligent individual and his friends. The group including Lawrence, as it existed between 1902 and 1906, was originally formed mainly of the young teachers and pupil- teachers who went to Ilkeston at around the same time; George Neville and Steve Bircumshaw called them the 'Pagans', though there is no evidence that they ever called themselves that, and it seems rather unlikely that they would have done. There were Lawrence and his sister Ada, Jessie Chambers and her elder brother Alan, Louie Burrows, George Neville, Richard Pog- more – and the Cooper sisters Mabel, Frances and Gertrude, though the Coopers were neighbours rather than discussion partners. May Chambers knew them all, but did not count herself as a member of the group: Alice

Hall was a Lawrence family friend who called at the house for 'gossip between ourselves' but specifically not for the 'philosophical discussions'⁶ which others (like Louie Burrows) attended (i. 42). Flossie Cullen was also a family friend rather than one of the group: Alice Dax was an intelligent married woman who came to Eastwood in 1905 and who left her mark on the discussions at the Literary Society, but – several years older than the others – she was not one of the group either.

As the group grew up into adolescence and beyond, the more serious ones among them (Lawrence, Jessie and Alan) not only went to – and discussed – the sermons in their own chapel in Eastwood but regularly visited local preachers (i. 23), and went to Nottingham to hear sermons too, again discussing them afterwards: the Lawrence home was the centre of such gatherings, as of so many other occasions (Lydia Lawrence always enjoyed the company of young people). A finely-crafted imaginative account of the group's behaviour was provided by Ford Madox Hueffer from what Lawrence told him several years later, though Hueffer pretended he had actually been to visit Lawrence in the Midlands. Before chapel, the group would be 'talking about Nietzsche and Wagner and Leopardi and Flaubert and Karl Marx and Darwin': at chapel, the sermon would discuss the same figures. At home afterwards,

I asked one of Lawrence's friends if that was not an unusual sort of sermon. He looked at me with a sort of grim incredulity.
'What do you suppose?' he said. 'Do you think we would sit under that fellow if he could not preach like that for fifty-two Sundays a year? He would lose his job.'
I asked him if the elder generation liked it. He said that of course they liked it. They wanted their sons to be educated people.⁷

Even allowing for Hueffer's invention and exaggeration, the account is not simply ridiculous. A few years later Lawrence wrote how 'We are *not* conventional. Our set is a bit astonishing' (i. 69). At Nottingham High Pavement Congregational Chapel, where they went regularly, the Rev. J. M. Lloyd Thomas – a notable worker for the Suffragist cause, and a contributor to the *Hibbert Journal* – 'frequently preached on contemporary social and intellectual issues'.⁸ And although in Eastwood the Rev. Robert Reid would not have preached such a sermon as Hueffer describes, being primarily concerned with exposition of the Bible, Jessie Chambers remembered that even Reid's sermons were 'more lectures than sermons'. On 3 February 1907, for example, he took on the so-called 'New Theology' – a great topic of the day – with a sermon on 'The New Theology and the Atonement'; while, starting on 1 December 1907, he gave a series of four sermons on 'Religion and Science'. His topic on 8 December 1907 was

'Evolution and Traditional Views of Creation'; the local newspaper noted that 'the ground covered was so extensive that a listener in order to follow intelligently was obliged to concentrate his utmost attention on the subject, and even then some elementary ideas of science in general was [sic] requisite to a thorough grasp of the matter under consideration'. The third talk, 'The Ascent and Fall of Man', 'was listened to with rapt attention by an unusually large congregation'; the local paper commented after the fourth of the series, 'The Evolution of Revelation':

It is a noteworthy fact that by this course of addresses on what is admittedly a difficult subject to lay before an audience of all sorts and conditions of men, Mr. Reid has proved conclusively that there are large numbers of people who are anxious to hear sermons of intellectual depth dealing with facts which all men of education accept but which too many ministers fear to teach for fear of arousing doubt and unrest in the minds of their hearers, evidently not realising that in large numbers of cases the doubt exists already, and the only reasonable way of allaying this mental unrest is to face the situation by placing the results of scientific research in their true aspect before their congregations.[9]

What Lawrence's group could not hear in sermons, it would bring to discussion when the service was over: and what Reid could not do in his sermons, he contrived to promote in the Literary Society. In such ways he specifically attempted to cater for the intellectual interests of people like Lawrence and his friends, and for those parents who in Hueffer's words 'wanted their sons to be educated people'. Combine Lawrence's conformity (at this stage) to the habits and values of home and chapel with his outstanding intellectual and academic gifts, and it is not surprising to find him, in his late teens, considering the ministry as a profession. It would have been odd if he had not. Around 1903–4 he 'hinted' at the idea to Jessie: 'he took up a Bible and said with a defiant look: "If the Bible gives me a clue, then I shall enter the ministry." He opened the Bible at random but the message was inconclusive.'[10]

It was also utterly natural that young people so much influenced by religion, brought up with it as so large a part of their lives, should in the end spend a good deal of time and energy questioning it. The process started for Lawrence when he was about 17, and found that Jessie Chambers was someone he could talk to seriously about such things; though, two years later, an essay written for the Ilkeston Pupil-Teacher Centre shows how orthodox he remained; he referred to 'awe at the majesty and wisdom of the Creator'.[11] The process of questioning for Lawrence, as for so many others in his generation, was helped on its way by Fitzgerald's *Rubáiyát of Omar Khayyám*. Today it is hard to realise the potency and daring for Lawrence's generation of this hedonistic and cheerfully nihilistic poem. First published in 1859, it was rediscovered and became immensely popular in the late 1890s and early 1900s: as a contemporary of Lawrence noted, copies appeared 'in every bookseller's shop window'. It clearly produced a kind of spiritual liberation in many people. Lawrence gave Jessie Chambers a copy for a Christmas present, either in 1904 or in 1905, but Jessie's mother paid tribute to the poem's reputation when she reacted strongly on behalf of her younger children: 'I won't have their faith destroyed. You grieve me by reading such things, but you shan't take the children's faith.'[12] What she would have objected to were stanzas like these:

XLVIII

A Moment's Halt – a momentary Taste
Of BEING from the Well amid the Waste –
And Lo! – the phantom Caravan has reach'd
The NOTHING it set out from – Oh, make haste!

LXXII

And that inverted Bowl they call the Sky,
Whereunder crawling coop'd we live and die,
Lift not your hands to *It* for help – for It
As impotently moves as you or I.[13]

But Fitzgerald was at most only a provocation to non-Christian or materialist thought. Rather more serious than *Omar Khayyám* were the books which around 1906 Lawrence and Jessie (and possibly others in the group) were starting to read. Lawrence was showing an interest 'in the question as to how the old religious ideas stood in relation to the scientific discoveries that were sweeping away the familiar landmarks ...'[14] That process of questioning had begun almost a century earlier; but Lawrence was one of those people who came to consciousness in the earlier twentieth century with their Christian faith still untroubled. Religion in Eastwood's chapels was still an unassailable fact of life, its faith unquestioned and often unquestioning. Jessie Chambers, however, remembered Lawrence around 1906 describing to her 'the nebular theory of the universe' and being 'troubled by the discrepancy between such a hypothesis of the origin of things and the God postulated by the Congregational chapel'. The discussion may sound sixty or eighty years late, in the process of the breaking down of orthodoxy – George Eliot had given up her orthodox views by January 1842, for example; but it was the natural first step for someone of Lawrence's background, and we should not underestimate its daring.[15] It was also characteristic of Lawrence that he should confront his problems head on. The boy his Beauvale headmaster remembered as being 'a note of interrogation – he was always wanting to know why' applied himself with typical zest and seriousness to the new problem. May Chambers remembered 'Darwin's theories and then Schopenhauer's essays breaking into the pattern of our life, "filling our heads with rubbish," as we women put it'.[16]

This would probably have been during Lawrence's first year at college, 1906–7, when he read Schopenhauer for the first time, in a version extensively filtered and adapted by its translator. Lawrence's copy of Mrs Dircks' version survives, with some marginal comments by Lawrence on 'Metaphysics of Love'. Jessie Chambers tells us that 'This essay made a deep impression upon him ... He followed the reasoning closely, as always applying it to himself, and his own case.'[17] The essay is a lengthy insistence upon the primacy of the sexual urge in the affairs of the affections, and cuts clean across any idea of love as romantic or selfless. Schopenhauer insists that what men and poets call 'love' is really the working of the 'will of the species', which ensures that human beings are attracted to each other so as to reproduce in ways that will safeguard the finest qualities of the species. Jessie Chambers remembered how 'Schopenhauer seemed to fit in with his mood. He thought he found there an explanation of his own divided attitude and he remained under the influence of this line of reasoning for some time.'[18] He was confronting, even in the bowdlerised form in which he read it, a clear statement that love of the beautiful was sexual, and therefore inevitable: yet he knew in his own case that 'I see what is most beautiful, and I *don't* desire it.' He could see, for example, that Jessie was beautiful: and yet he felt no sexual desire for her. His reading of 'Metaphysics of Love' would have told him that the reason was the lack of sexual appeal in Jessie: he could not himself love a woman until he was sexually attracted. Schopenhauer both posed the problem and helped provide 'an explanation of his own divided attitude'. We can see how, like Thomas Hardy in the 1890s reading Schopenhauer and finding support for ideas of tragedy to which his own work had already led him, Lawrence *used* Schopenhauer: adapted what he read to what he wanted to find.[19] The philosophy of Schopenhauer is less important than the process of absorption it was subject to in Lawrence's synthesising and creative mind.

But Schopenhauer was only one revolution. According to Jessie, Lawrence also unwillingly felt 'compelled to take up a rationalistic standpoint with regard to religion, although it made him miserable'.[20] This first specifically non-Christian position was a reaction against his final and desperate attempts in 1906 to believe in the religion in which he had been brought up. He had, in that last stage of faith, felt 'sore, frightfully raw and sore because I couldn't get the religious conversion, the Holy Ghost business, that I longed for ...' (i. 49). He explained what he meant in a letter the following year to the Rev. Robert Reid. He had been 'brought up to believe in the absolute necessity for a sudden spiritual conversion; I believed for many years that the Holy Ghost descended and took conscious possession of the "elect" – the converted one; I thought all conversions were, to a greater or less degree, like that of Paul's' (i. 39). But Lawrence found himself unable either intellectually or emotionally to experience such a conversion: and sometime between 1906 and 1907 he abandoned his 'rather deep religious faith' (i. 72). The arguments of science and materialism were strong, and – as he put it to Reid – something else was even stronger: 'in the moments of deepest emotion myself has watched myself and seen that all the tumult has risen like a little storm, to die away again without great result' (i. 39). He could not simply or passionately *believe*; the watching and questioning characteristic of Lawrence's highly developed youthful self-consciousness was, as usual, an inhibitor of passionate emotional – or spiritual – experience.

III   Religious without Religion

In the first phase of his rebellion against Christianity he acted as a kind of spokesperson for his group. Alan and Jessie Chambers challenged him, during 1907, to write to Reid about materialism and the agnostic authors they were discussing. In October 1907, Lawrence took up the challenge.[21] He told Reid that 'Reading of Darwin, Herbert Spencer, Renan, J. M. Robertson, Blatchford and Vivian ... has seriously modified my religious beliefs' – as well it might. But, to start with, Lawrence simply asked Reid for clarification of 'the attitude of the nonconformist Churches to such questions as Evolution, with that the Origin of Sin, and as Heaven and Hell' (i. 36–7). Reid was capable of responding sympathetically to the demands and criticisms of such a group in his congregation as Lawrence and his friends. His reply no longer exists, but Lawrence's subsequent letter shows that Reid took him seriously, argued with him and recommended books. And six weeks later, Reid started his series of four evening sermons on religion and evolution. They were the best reply he could give to Lawrence and his friends, and were almost certainly directly intended as such. On 3 December Lawrence thanked Reid for the books and for 'your late sermon': 'There seems some hope in a religion which will not answer one with fiats and decrees' (i. 41).

But in that same letter Lawrence went further than before in defining his unbelief; he declared outright to the minister that 'I do not, cannot believe in the divinity of Jesus', or in a *'personal, human* God': 'Men – some – seem to be born and ruthlessly destroyed; the bacteria are created and nurtured on Man, to his horrible suffering ... I do not wage any war against

Christianity – I do not hate it – but these questions will not be answered . . .'
(i. 40–1). Lawrence may well have had in mind such mysterious challenges
to faith as the fact of his sister Emily's baby being born dead on 30 September 1907: May Chambers recalled his being particularly upset by it.[22] And
he was certainly influenced by the writings of Robert Blatchford, in spite of
his declaration that he 'could not read *God and My Neighbour* with patience'
(i. 39) and that 'I care not for Blatchford or anybody' (i. 41). He may well
have objected to Blatchford's tone, but Blatchford's arguments were
extremely useful: Lawrence's point that the continued existence of slums
and human misery is 'not compatible with the idea of an *Omnipotent*, pitying
Divine' (i. 40) is taken directly from Blatchford's 'I cannot discern the hand
of a loving Father in the Slums . . .'[23] Lawrence's declaration that 'for the
present my religion is the lessening, in some pitiful moiety, the great human
discrepancies' (i. 41) is, too, exactly the 'argument from Socialism' which
Blatchford employs.

Although he went out of his way to tell Reid that 'I do not hate it' (i. 41),
Lawrence's quarrel with Christianity could also issue in a more personal and
less intellectual rebellion. It was towards the end of his time at college –
probably in the early summer of 1908, six months after his correspondence
with Reid – that an incident recalled by David Chambers took place, which
gives the other side of the coin to Lawrence's deference to the minister.

We were returning from Chapel on a summer evening: his mother, my mother,
various members of the family, with Lawrence and perhaps one or two of his friends.
It was a beautiful evening, and we chose to return through the field paths and
through the Warren. Lawrence was in a dark mood and by the time we had reached
the Warren he began to inveigh against the Chapel and all it stood for and especially
against the minister, the Reverend Robert Reid, for whom we all had a great respect.
Lawrence poured a stream of scorn and raillery upon the poor man, made fun of his
ideas, and mimicked his way of expressing them: it was a fierce, uncontrollable
tirade, an outpouring of long pent-up rage that left us all silent and rather
frightened. We had never seen him in such a mood before. He seemed to be beside
himself. His mother was as shocked as the rest of us, and perhaps she had the most
reason.[24]

Chambers intelligently links Lawrence's savage attack on Reid with his
rebellion against the authority of home and of Lydia Lawrence. That Reid
was not the only target is confirmed by Lawrence's later statement that 'at
the bottom, I like him: and I always respect him' (i. 243). But it was to just
this period that Lawrence subsequently dated his own emotional leaving of
home: 'I had a devil of a time getting a bit weaned from my mother, at the
age of 22' (i. 527). The year 1907–8 was 'the year that I changed from

boyhood to manhood' (i. 72); it had been, David Chambers goes on, Lydia Lawrence

who had fastened the Chapel bonds around him; he submitted, but with a bad grace. He told his friend, Mrs. Collishaw [i.e. Mabel Thurlby], that he hated the Chapel, even as a boy, and only went to please his mother. He was now in open rebellion. He was giving notice to his mother that the days of her reign over him, at least in this respect, were numbered.

He continued to go to chapel with his mother, however, 'up to the end'; but only because he cared for her.[25]

His rebellions against his mother, Reid, chapel and college, and his rebellion against Christianity, all seem to have been aspects of each other. It was, after all, his mother who had been so keen that he should go to college and take a degree course, and who had hoped he would qualify himself for the profession of clergyman or academic.[26] That would not happen; in part, because Lawrence did not want it to happen. His had been an intellectual disappointment with college; but, even more, it seems to have been an emotional disappointment. His college years were not giving him anything to fill the gap left by the breaking of ties with his home and by the loss of his religion. He was not finding himself the inhabitant of an advanced, intellectual community, a community of scholars: like Ursula in *The Rainbow*, he was angered by his 'long service at the inner commercial shrine', as he worked for still more qualifications to ensure a successful career. Jessie linked his anger and disappointment with something she once heard him say 'in a tone of deep chagrin, "I've never really had a father."' She thought that 'What he was asking perhaps unconsciously of the University was that it should partly make up for his lack of a father ...'[27] There may be a little truth in that: as he grew up, his position caught *between* his parents continued to trouble him, and he may well have been starting to feel it as a loss, rather than as something for which his love for his mother could compensate. Yet he knew a very great deal about authority and the weight it could bring to bear upon him: and at this point he was rather desperately cutting free from authority, not searching for it. His life-long habit of using authorities – philosophers, for example – as sources of ideas which he wanted, rather than as writers or thinkers to believe in or to follow, is an indication of his attitude towards 'authority'.

But college did nothing to free him from his increasing sense of loneliness. It is to this period that we can date an anecdote told by May Chambers about Lawrence trying to 'take some of us a little way along the path he was treading', by giving a little talk 'about the empyrean, at the home of a mutual friend'. It turned out to be a humiliating experience:

He had some sort of sketch or diagram on a big sheet of paper pinned to a chair back. We were ashamed not to understand him and sorry for his increasing humiliation at this failure to make us understand . . .

'I've been a silly ass,' he said savagely on the way home.

I tried to reassure him that nobody else thought so but only felt hopelessly ignorant.

'That's just it,' he cried. 'Don't you see it makes a gulf? It leaves me lonely.'[28]

From 1907, in spite of the support of Jessie and Alan Chambers, that loneliness was habitual: he was increasingly out on his own. Jessie never followed him into materialism or unbelief; and though Alan had adopted a 'sceptical materialism', Lawrence saw far less of him after 1908.[29] He found almost no-one else in his home circle or at college who could share his new thinking, however much he tried to explain it. Louie Burrows, for example, remained a Christian believer – Lawrence thought of her as 'churchy' (i. 343). It is significant that, around this time, he began to see more of Willie Hopkin and his sympathetic wife Sallie – people to whom he later paid tribute for having 'led me over some frontiers' (iv. 327); his sister Emily linked his friendship with them to the time when he 'was getting into a psychological set at the University, who ridiculed religion'. Lydia Lawrence naturally did not approve, remarking 'I hope he doesn't get too friendly with Willie Hopkin': Hopkin was a noted socialist who, though once secretary of the Eastwood Sunday School Union, had broken away in 1900 and was now a notorious agnostic.[30] But the Hopkin house became one where Lawrence felt himself welcomed: it was an important substitute home in these years when (Hopkin remembered) Lawrence 'was restless mentally and spiritually', 'delving deep into his mind and bringing up a strange mixture of ideas and beliefs'. Most of what we know of Lawrence's interest in politics is linked with this particular friendship, too; it was at a meeting of the 'Eastwood Debating Society' in the Hopkin house on Devonshire Drive, on 19 March 1908, that Lawrence gave his speculative paper 'Art and the Individual', which began: 'These Thursday night meetings are for discussing social problems with a view to advancing to a more perfect social state and to our fitting ourselves to be perfect citizens—communists—what not.' The next meeting of the society was devoted to a discussion of the paper. With the Hopkins, Lawrence was able to say what he really thought, and argue things out with people able to understand him.[31]

And although his rebellion against the Congregational chapel might be, in part, a rebellion against his mother and his own one-sided upbringing, he also discovered that the problem of religion remained with him long after the debris of chapel Christianity had been cleared away. As he moved into his twenties, he found himself to be a man whose mind and conscience were imbued with the habits of religious thought, although he lacked the context and support of any particular faith. He found himself wanting to develop his religion for himself.

IV Materialism, Monism, Pragmatism

What had come to a head in Lawrence betwen 1906 and 1908 was, in fact, a most complex and far-reaching change. Having begun to question Christianity, and not being satisfied with his answers from the Rev. Robert Reid, he had (characteristically) done a thorough demolition job. Jessie Chambers remembered how violent and assertive his new opinions became, and how, to begin with, materialism 'came in full blast with T. H. Huxley's *Man's Place in Nature*, Darwin's *Origin of Species*, and Haeckel's *Riddle of the Universe*'. There is actually little trace of Darwin and Huxley in Lawrence's subsequent writing; a reference to Darwin in 'Art and the Individual' turns out, perhaps revealingly, to come from a secondary source.[32] Haeckel's work, however, certainly left its mark. *The Riddle of the Universe* advances the belief (as a provable scientific fact) that there is only one substance in the Universe, which is both 'God and Nature', body and spirit. This 'Monistic' belief – what William James called 'materialistic monism' because of its insistence upon the 'law of substance' – asserts that all life has a cellular basis, and that upon such a basis all structures – animal, plant, social – are founded. Haeckel's book, which was frequently reprinted in cheap editions, produced in Lawrence what he later described as his own temporary adherence to 'a torturing crude Monism' (i. 147).[33] But Monism was an important stage to Lawrence because it helped him abandon the Christian divinity and the Christian schema: it offered him his first insight into beliefs which might supplant the religion in which he had been brought up.

And yet Monism, even of Haeckel's pantheistic kind – 'pantheism is *the world-system of the modern scientist*', Haeckel wrote, to be met by James's retort that Monism was an 'unintelligible pantheistic monster' – was never satisfying, however enthusiastically Lawrence embraced it.[34] It offered only a rarified form of materialism; and, as Lawrence told Reid at the end of 1907, 'I cannot be a materialist' (i. 40). What we know of his intellectual progress during these years comes mostly from a letter he wrote in December 1909 to Ernest Alfred Smith, a lecturer in botany at Nottingham University College, and one of the two members of staff he genuinely admired. (The other was the Modern Languages Professor, Ernest Weekley.) It was 'Botany' Smith, Lawrence declared, who was his 'first live teacher of philosophy': who showed him the way out of Monism, 'past

Pragmatism, into a sort of crude but appeasing Pluralism . . .' (i. 147). It is interesting that Lawrence should have learned his philosophy from a botany teacher; but Smith also had academic competence in philosophy, sociology and ethics (he was a successful extra-mural teacher in these subjects). And his botany classes were probably unique in Lawrence's college studies not only because – in a very practical way – they confronted Lawrence with the cellular universe of Haeckel, but because they were intellectually demanding and provocative, and linked directly with his own feeling for natural life.

If Smith was the teacher who mattered, however, William James was the philosopher. It seems likely that Smith recommended – and may even have lent – James's *Pragmatism*, first published in June 1907 and reprinted three times before the end of the year. It was not a book Lawrence could have bought, but Jessie Chambers's recollection of his enjoyment of it shows that he read it. In conjunction with Smith's teaching, it probably did more than anything else to steer Lawrence away from Haeckel. Pragmatism was a concept inextricably linked with James, who defined it as 'the doctrine that the whole meaning of a conception expresses itself in practical consequences, either in the shape of conduct to be recommended, or of experiences to be expected': pragmatism was James's way of attacking idealism, absolutism and Monism. It obviously helped free Lawrence from the latter. Pluralism, in turn – again linked with James, who argued for it in *The Varieties of Religious Experience* in 1902, in *Pragmatism* in 1907 and in *A Pluralistic Universe* in 1909 – was a system of thought directly opposed to Monism, and recognising more than one ultimate principle. It allowed for a God, though a God very different from the traditional Christian deity: 'It need not be infinite, it need not be solitary'. It is probable that Lawrence came to know *A Pluralistic Universe* from the review which appeared in the *English Review* in October 1909; he wrote his letter to Smith only two months later.[35]

Smith was surprised at the passion Lawrence showed in his pursuit of ideas – 'Botany Smith says I'm not *possessed* with an idea, I'm *obsessed* with it',[36] Jessie heard – but Smith was probably unaware of the particular battles Lawrence was fighting. For Lawrence had realised that he was engaged not just in one battle but in several. He was warring against the influence and power of upbringing, chapel, Robert Reid, his mother, and indeed everything that 'home at Eastwood' came to represent; but to assert his freedom to believe in a materialistic universe was only a very partial answer to his problems. He had quickly discovered that he had on his hands a battle not only against home and Christianity, but against the very philosophy of scientific materialism which had destroyed his Christianity. This accounts for the odd fact that Lawrence possessed both a deep distrust of scientific conclusions, and a thoroughly scientific vocabulary – a vocabulary which reveals his intellectual origins and background. Both are brought into sharp focus in *The Rainbow*. There, Lawrence experiments with the technical vocabulary of laboratory science for describing human relationships. When Ursula and Skrebensky kiss, the 'dark kiss . . . subjected them, knitted them into one fecund nucleus of the fluid darkness': and this is 'the nucleolating of the fecund darkness'. Ursula 'vibrated like a jet of electric, firm fluid in response': Skrebensky 'felt himself fusing down to nothingness, like a bead that rapidly disappears in an incandescent flame'.[37] The language is one to which Lawrence's own scientific training had accustomed him; he finds it appropriate for describing, in a novel set in the first decade of the twentieth century, reactions taking physical form which cannot be outwardly seen or observed. They are, so to speak, the felt life of physical experience.

On the other hand, it cannot be a coincidence that in the same novel Lawrence went a long way towards charting the very progress away from scientific materialism which he himself had undergone. This progress had been almost completely omitted from the life of Paul Morel in *Sons and Lovers*; Paul does not go to college, and though aware of a thinker like Herbert Spencer,[38] he is emphatically not an intellectual. Written 1914–15, *The Rainbow* goes well beyond the period of Lawrence's early life; yet although its comprehensive and articulate account of Ursula's development plays down the struggle of Lawrence's own inner life at college, the novel subjects Ursula to many of its author's formative intellectual experiences.

For a start, she discovers a necessary opposition between the scientific advances and certainties of the nineteenth century, and the needs and experience of the early twentieth-century individual. When Ursula and Skrebensky start their last relationship, she feels that the 'normal world' – the scientifically explained world of the late nineteenth century in which she has grown up – has now had its true nature revealed to her. It is no more than an 'inner circle of light in which she lived and moved', where 'the trains rushed and the factories ground out their machine-produce and the plants and the animals worked by the light of science and knowledge . . .'[39] What has changed for Ursula is that she has become aware of another context in which she also lives: a 'vast darkness that wheeled round about, with half-revealed shapes lurking on the edge'. This darkness contains not only a suggestion of mysterious savagery in the 'grey shadow-shapes of wild beasts', but also of 'dark shadow-shapes of the angels, whom the light fenced out'. And such angels 'in the darkness were lordly and terrible and not to be denied, like the flash of fangs'. Lawrence is symbolising the classic dilemma of early twentieth-century materialist man, learning from his scientific education (as he himself had done) to believe in 'the eternal light of knowledge' and the 'fire of illuminating consciousness';[40] but also finding the scientifically explained and ordered universe utterly inadequate in its understanding of man's emotional needs and beliefs, his fears and particularly of his religious experience. What place for reverence or awe, for humility, for guilt and responsibility in such a universe? The concept of evolution, in the mid-nineteenth century, had become the focus for (and justification of) a great deal of liberated thinking; but for Lawrence it quickly came to symbolise the tyranny of a scientific version of progress. It attempted to impose mechanical laws of behaviour upon the frequently non-materialistic experience of the individual creature or soul; it attempted to define an individual's potential as limited to mechanical development or regression.

Hence Lawrence's creation, in Ursula, of an individual who although fascinated (as he had been) by science and botany, and particularly by the microscope's revelation of the lives of unconscious organisms, nevertheless comes to a totally non-scientific understanding of the unicellular creature she observes through her microscope. Whereas, for a Haeckel, such a creature is only one of the multitudinous examples and types of animal, plant and social forms which make up the All, Ursula – and Lawrence – seize on it as an ideal focus for their discontent with scientific materialism. That materialism is personified by Ursula's teacher – a thorough-going Haeckelian materialist, Dr Frankstone. She argues, as a Dr Frankenstein must, that life is only 'a complexity of physical and chemical activities', without any 'special mystery'; it could, for example, be created in the laboratory. When Ursula herself observes the living organism through her microscope, she is led to a very different sequence of thoughts:

If it was a conjunction of forces, physical and chemical, what held these forces unified, and for what purpose were they unified? ... What was the will which nodalised them and created the one thing she saw? What was its intention? To be itself? Was its purpose just mechanical and limited to itself?

It intended to be itself. But what self?[41]

And as she watches the unicellular creature, Ursula has a vision of life. The creature is 'not limited mechanical energy, nor mere purpose of self-preservation and self-assertion. It was a consummation, a being infinite. Self was a oneness with the infinite. To be oneself was a supreme, gleaming triumph of infinity.'[42] Ursula thus marks her break not only with the theory of evolution – which she dismisses as 'mere purpose of self-preservation and self-assertion' – but with the scientifically explicable universe governed by 'mechanical energy'. 'Infinity' interests her far more than 'energy', 'will' more than 'conjunction', 'self' more than 'forces'; she will henceforth replace 'progress' with 'fulfilment' as her goal.

It is in such terms that the important end results of Lawrence's college experience eventually rose to the surface. We can see him moving, during his college studies and the years immediately following, from an unassaulted and absolute faith in Christianity to a position in which he began to oppose the very stress upon progress and scientific advance (and a scientific under-standing of self and the world) which his nineteenth-century thinkers had taught him. By 1908 he knew he was no longer a believer in the Christian God (i. 72), no longer a believer 'in a Godhead even – not a Personal God' (i. 99), but felt he had 'still some religion left' (i. 58): was sure he could not be a materialist (i. 40). It had taken him two years and more to start coming to terms with the muddle and conflict that he had experienced; all he had had was perhaps the occasional moment of revelation like that of Ursula in the laboratory.

He ended up between 1908 and 1911 as non-Christian and non-material-ist, but as a William James Pluralist with a philosophy which included 'a God, but not a personal God' (i. 256). He was also strongly influenced by scientific thinkers like Spencer; Helen Baron has pointed out how frequently the young Paul Morel's thinking in *Sons and Lovers* touches on Spencer. Paul's remarks about 'shimmering protoplasm' in chapter VII are probably influenced by Spencer's remarks on 'living protoplasm' in his *Principles of Biology*; Spencer's influential analysis of society as 'social organ-ism' lies behind Paul's remark 'people matter. But *one* isn't so very import-ant', while when Paul describes 'the force of gravitation' as 'the great shaper' he echoes Spencer's *System of Synthetic Philosophy*, and when he insists on nature's 'correct geometrical line and proportion' he repeats Spencer's *Principles of Biology*.[43]

Yet nevertheless Lawrence was also convinced that it was one of his tasks as a writer to rescue human consciousness (and in particular the idea of human individuality) from the clutches of merely scientific understanding, be it evolutionist, materialist or pantheist. He found himself wanting to argue for man's religious nature and experience, but not from a Christian standpoint. We might more accurately say that it took him until the very end of his writing life to realise and to convey what his double break, with Christianity and with the scientific revolution, really meant. Towards the end of his college career, he was more likely to explain his non-scientific but religious concern for human beings along socialist lines, as we see him doing in his letters to Robert Reid in 1907 when he emulates Blatchford or when he writes to Blanche Jennings during 1908–9 about the importance of knowing if 'the great procession is marching, on the whole, in the right direction' (i. 57). Friendship with the Hopkins would have encouraged such language. But socialism, or a belief in the equal rights of all human beings when freed from the tyrannies of religious or scientific systems, was only a useful intellectual staging post for Lawrence. As early as 1910 he had lost most of his interest in socialism. He flirted with aestheticism, remarking in December 1909 how 'Life seems to me barbarous, recklessly wasteful and destructive, often hideous and dreadful: but, on the whole, beautiful' (i. 147): Cecil Beardsall and Cyril Mersham, his self-portraits of the winter of 1909–10, show how aesthetic his own attitudes appeared to him to be. But he once remarked that he saw his life 'moving on phase by phase' (i. 239); after (in sequence) his materialist, socialist and aesthetic phases he became increasingly concerned less with the needs of 'the great procession', or with beauty as a compensation for pain, than with realising his own non-Christian religion. 'It is a fine thing', he would write to his sister Ada in April 1911, 'to establish one's religion in one's heart, not to be dependent on tradition and second hand ideals.' She too had suddenly found herself going through 'the torment of religious unbelief': he tried to help her with his own idea of religion.

Jehovah is the Jew's idea of God – not ours. Christ was infinitely good, but mortal as we. There still remains a God, but not a personal God: a vast, shimmering impulse which wavers onwards towards some end, I don't know what – taking no regard of the little individual, but taking regard for humanity. When we die, like rain-drops falling back again into the sea, we fall backward into the big, shimmering sea of unorganised life which we call God. We are lost as individuals, yet we count in the whole. (i. 255–6)

The religion is pluralist: Buddhist in its language (it is strongly influenced by the poetry of Edwin Arnold's 1879 *The Light of Asia*) but non-Buddhist in its belief in a God and in being purposive and moralist. It is a stage, a phase, on the way towards the revelation of individual life and significance which Ursula experiences in *The Rainbow*.

V Study

We can now put Lawrence's disillusion with college into some perspective. Older than most of those students following the Normal course, Lawrence had had the incomparable advantage of having been engaged since 1902 in that 'strenuous' course of serious reading and discussion with Jessie Chambers, which had culminated in the scientific and religious thinking of the years 1906–8. He told Jessie Chambers, however, that at college he felt treated 'like a school-kid'; letters to Louie Burrows written just after the course started in 1906 show how one of his first essays (perhaps that on 'Autumn' which Jessie also recalled) had been 'crushed' by his English teacher, 'Madame'.[44] Not only was she severely critical, but she 'has asked me now to write the essay she wanted':

She told me some of my phrases are fine, but other[s] ludicrous; that I was not entirely incapable of writing, but mixed up some sense with a great amount of absurdity. Therefore I must restrain myself to writing just what other people think, and are therefore willing to accept.

Bien – I consent – I am merely a pupil, therefore I must work by rule. I only wish Madame were not so ready to laugh at us as silly infants. (i. 31)

It was the demand for the conventional – 'just what other people think' – combined with the dismissal of his rather precious prose style which Lawrence found galling; and this, within four weeks of the start of his course. We know that more than once, during college, he felt snubbed by small-minded expectations: 'when in his writing a paper he had used the word "stallion," his English professor had taken him aside and said: "My boy, that is a word we do not use."' A contemporary at College also recalled that English teacher, for whom 'We had no very great respect'; they had to write a fortnightly essay, 'and Lawrence and I put our heads together, and we used to imitate the style of various writers. He'd write one, an imitation of Macaulay, and I would write one in the imitation of Bart Kennedy . . . We had a lot of fun with that, we used to get about 6 marks out of 10 each . . .'[45] Lawrence must have been surprising and in some ways awkward to teach; he had read much more than most of his fellow students, had certainly written more and was more confident of his writing. He was also energetic and serious in argument, while remaining extremely sensitive to criticism. Confront him with a conventionally-minded teacher, used to run-of-the-mill students and not prepared to go outside the safe boundaries of style or syllabus – let alone speculate intelligently about the nature of God and the universe, in the light of Haeckel or Herbert Spencer or William James –, and disappointment was bound to follow.

Lawrence's deliberately casual and mannered writing style also invited the attentions of his teachers. On 22 February 1907, informality in a test on Duncan in *Macbeth* – 'the majority, thank heaven, smile when they are glad' – had 'thank heaven' crossed through and the instruction 'omit' added (the essay all the same got 8+ out of 10). Similarly, on 1 June 1907, the sentence 'the mind is master, and, happy mind, it commands' in an essay on 'The Character of Theseus' (in *A Midsummer Night's Dream*) had 'happy mind, it' marked for omission: the essay got 9 out of 10. On 22 March 1907, another essay on *Macbeth* (presumably on a set passage) had received the note 'Don't add to the original – too free'; it got 17 out of 20.[46] His surviving written college work reveals an intelligent and (in expression) ambitious, but thoroughly literary student. He was happier writing fine phrases than in answering the question: probably a sign that, deep down, his course work bored him.

Following the advice of his Head of Department, Professor Amos Henderson – the man he reckoned he could teach himself 'with excellent advantage' – Lawrence had, early in his studies, considered changing to the degree course in Arts; his mother supported the idea. The establishment of the day-training Colleges (and their association with Universities or University Colleges) had always been seen as marking a distinct upgrading of the students trained there, and had made available to them the previously unattainable opportunity of taking a degree; in the words of an educational historian, 'although the number who obtained their degrees in this way was not large, the fusion of some teacher training with university education was a step towards the fulfilment of a long-cherished dream of the teaching profession'.[47] A degree would, of course, immediately qualify a student for secondary rather than elementary teaching. To follow a degree course, however, Lawrence needed Latin, which he had never learned; and he asked the Rev. Robert Reid, back in Eastwood, for help: this was before he ventured on his correspondence with Reid about religion. After Reid had given him four months' assistance, Professor Henderson – much to Lawrence's surprise, and probably rather to his relief – offered to take over (i. 34). Latin vocabulary and a number of translations from Horace's *Odes*, Book 1, appear in one of Lawrence's surviving College notebooks.[48] But even that plan went wrong, in a way that seemed characteristic of his teachers as Lawrence felt he was now coming to know them: 'the professor at College was unable to give him the extra help he had promised. "He can't spare the time for it," Lawrence said. "I know he can't pull it in with all he has to do, but why did he promise?"' According to Jessie Chambers, Lawrence then 'dropped the degree course': she probably meant 'dropped the idea', as there is no evidence of his ever having formally taken it up.[49] Thereafter he simply followed the two-year day-training course leading to the teacher's certificate. This involved studies in English, Maths, History with Geography, Music and Teaching (the last two studied during the second year): he also followed two optional subjects, French and Botany. There were several weeks of required teaching practice; the Certificate exams took place in June–July 1908.

There were good times, of course. There were friendships with fellow students, in particular with the scientist Tom Smith, whom Lawrence was still seeing in 1911 (i. 296) and who appeared under his own name in *The White Peacock* 'quietly looking over his spectacles with his sharp brown eyes'.[50] The Botany course was very important to Lawrence: he enjoyed the Music course; lectures on poetry by the Principal, the Rev. J. E. Symes, were worth attending and he persuaded Jessie Chambers to go to some, on Saturday mornings: he admired the style of Professor Ernest Weekley, who gave French lectures. 'He really *is* a gentleman. He's quite elegant. He leans back in his chair and points to the blackboard, too elegant to get on his feet. And he addresses us as "gentlemen". He's sarcastic, of course.' But Lawrence's general boredom with college – and the fact that he stayed with the non-degree course – meant that he was able to spend far more time on his reading and on his own writing than he had expected. He wrote 'poems & patches of *The White Peacock* during lectures': a draft plot for the novel appears at the front of one of his college notebooks.[51] The novel was, he remarked cynically, 'almost the sole result of my coll. career' (i. 50). This does not seem to have had much effect on his marks. He was the kind of bright student who makes a show of casualness, while actually getting through the relatively undemanding work very easily; he ended up with the best course marks of any male student of his year. The report on his academic and teaching work, unsigned but probably written by Professor Henderson himself, is a remarkable document:

Well-read, scholarly, and refined Mr L. will make an excellent teacher if he gets into the right place. His work at present is uneven according to the ordinary standards owing to his lack of experience of the elementary schoolboy and his management. He would be quite unsuitable for a large class of boys in a rough district; he would not have sufficient persistence & enthusiasm but would become disgusted.

Mr L.'s strong bias is towards the humanistic subjects, and at times boys interest in such lessons is intense. Intelligence however is cultivated in lessons on all subjects by the treatment, especially the questions, the defect being a want of that persistent driving home and recapitulation which are necessary – like many intelligent teachers Mr L. tends to teach the best pupils exclusively. Though very fluent, he sometimes has an obvious difficulty in finding words sufficiently simple. He is emphatically a teacher of upper classes.

Mr L. is fastidious in taste, and while working splendidly at anything that interests him would perhaps easily tire amid the tedium and discouragement of the average classroom. With an upper class in a good school or in a higher school he could do work quite unusually good, especially if allowed a very free hand.[52]

The report is rather longer than for most students in Lawrence's year, and more divided between strengths and weaknesses. If we compare it with reports written on other students by the same assessor, it is clear that Lawrence is by no means the 'exceptionally good teacher' or 'one of the best teachers this year' which, for example, J. J. Clarkson and C. P. Simpson are: nor, like Simpson or W. T. Haslam, can he 'be unreservedly recommended to any school authority' or 'recommended to any school authority, as a man and as a teacher'. Just the opposite: Lawrence comes over as rather a risk as a potential teacher, and is made to sound suitable only for an exceptional school. The problem is, simply, his 'fastidious' nature and his lack of resilience: no other student in his year is described with adjectives like 'refined', 'well-read' and 'scholarly': no other student has his strikingly individual 'taste' recorded, nor is made to sound either so sensitive or so easily put-off. Nor is any other student, with the exception of Lawrence's friend Tom Smith (who 'teaches upper classes much better than young children') so 'emphatically a teacher of upper classes'; two other students (T. Collins and W. H. King) are actually singled out as teachers of 'middle and lower classes'.[53] Lawrence may have found his teachers second-rate, but this report is full of insight; it points out just how highly cultivated he had become, and how bad that was for his prospects in 'the average classroom'. As a child at school, he had utterly failed to fit in with a 'large class of boys in a rough district': the report now reckons that, as a teacher, he would become 'disgusted' with such a group. In 1908, he would indeed find himself struggling in the very rough surroundings of Croydon, and he then projected a self-image identical to that in the report: 'Think of a quivering grey hound set to mind a herd of pigs and you see me teaching . . .' (i. 85). In the judgement of his assessor, Lawrence is quite unlike the son of Arthur Lawrence of Eastwood: he is far closer to those sensitive, over-cultivated and uneasy superior souls who regularly appeared as his autobiographical heroes in his writing before *Sons and Lovers*. Lawrence could, at times, enact them himself. Louie Burrows remembered, of a period between 1906 and 1908,

Once when we were lost in Annesley Park I suggested that we walk towards the house for directions. The rest were very afraid & timid. When however we saw a keeper approach I moved towards him, urging Bert to ask the way. Bert did so in a very superior manner and the man thinking we were from the House directed us politely calling Bert 'Sir'. It was remarkable how he took it. Digging his hand into his pocket with a grand movement he gave the man what I *know* was his only sixpence. 'Did you notice that he called me "Sir". It is interesting' he ruminated 'that people instinctively call me "sir".' I could wonder in silence though I liked him too well to be supercilious with him.[54]

The fictional heroes had that much truth: they were genuine possibilities.

He sat the final Certificate exam in the summer of 1908 and again, in spite of his attention to his own writing during the year, did very well; his results were by far the best of any man in his year. He got distinctions in his two optional subjects French and Botany, as well as distinctions in Mathematics and History with Geography. No other man got more than one distinction (Gilbert Noon, for example, got one in Music). Lawrence failed, however, to get a distinction either in Education (as Louie did) or in English (as Jessie Chambers did). Jessie recalled him being 'a little piqued' about it.[55]

VI Writing in College

But the real achievements of his college years were his intellectual struggles and his writings. By the end of his first year, in June 1907, Lawrence had completed a draft of his novel, but at this stage appears to have made no effort to publish it. His first reaction to the College magazine *The Gong* was to reject it as 'a very mediocre publication. I do not think I shall try to be admitted as a contributor' (i. 31). In spite of this, he sent them his poem 'Study', 'but they returned it' (i. 31 n. 5).

Publication was something he was extremely cautious of; and his first appearance in print was not even the product of his own ambition. In August 1907, the *Nottinghamshire Guardian* announced the details of its annual Christmas competition: three categories of stories ('OF WHICH THE SCENE MUST BE WITHIN NOTTINGHAMSHIRE, DERBYSHIRE, LINCOLNSHIRE, LEICESTERSHIRE'):

£3 FOR THE BEST STORY OF AN ENJOYABLE CHRISTMAS
£3 FOR THE BEST STORY OF AN AMUSING CHRISTMAS
£3 FOR THE BEST LEGEND OF SOME HISTORIC BUILDING[56]

The winning stories would be published in the newspaper. Making it clear why he was entering, Lawrence told Louie Burrows on 20 October 1907 that he had written two stories 'just for fun, and because Alan [Chambers] and J[essie] asked me why I didn't, and so put me upon doing it to show I could. I may write a third' (i. 38). As an author, he had to be able to show that he could write; but such writing was not to be taken too seriously. He entered stories in all three categories, but as no competitor could be awarded more than one prize, Louie entered the first version of his story 'The White Stocking' in the 'Amusing Christmas' section for him, he himself entered the 'Historic Building' with an early version of his mediaeval story 'A Fragment of Stained Glass' called 'Ruby-Glass', and Jessie Chambers entered the third category for him with 'A Prelude'. The last – a skilfully crafted 'sentimental little story' (as Jessie was later to call it)[57] containing a version of the Haggs Farm family – shows little sign of his college teacher's criticisms of his style having had any effect. The writing remains intensely literary, and the story is primarily interesting for showing what the contemporary version of 'Laetitia', the early *White Peacock* – also recreating the Chambers family – was probably like. 'Ruby-Glass' is that rare thing in Lawrence's output, a piece of historical romance: it offered him a chance to write pastiche mediaeval English (he had studied Chaucer and Langland at Nottingham),[58] and to explore the difference between historical account and lived reality. And yet it has no time to develop its themes of sexual attraction and the flight from the country to the town. The third and extremely slight story, 'The White Stocking', has almost no connection with the story Lawrence rewrote six years later; it is simply an anecdote (drawn from the girlhood of Lydia Lawrence) about a young woman at a dance who pulls a white stocking out of her pocket in mistake for a handkerchief.

Nevertheless, 'Ruby-Glass' was given an honourable mention in the competition report, while 'A Prelude' won its category and was published under Jessie's name. The three stories – given the nature of the competition – must have been composed especially for it; another story Lawrence wrote around the same time, 'The Vicar's Garden', draws upon the Lawrence family holiday in Yorkshire in the summer of 1907; it would therefore not have been eligible for the competition.

But Lawrence appears to have made no further effort to publish 'The Vicar's Garden' or the stories which did not win. By the summer of 1908, he had at least twenty-four poems in a finished and polished form (he entered them in clean drafts at the back of one of his college notebooks); he had completed the second draft of his novel; he had at least two essays in some state of completeness; he may well have had more short stories than the four so far mentioned. And yet he still made no effort to publish any of his work. The reason is not hard to find. In the spring of 1908, he had sent what Jessie Chambers remembered as most likely an essay to 'an author, whose weekly article in the *Daily News* we often read and discussed, asking him if he would give his opinion as to its merit'.[59] It is significant that Lawrence should have approached another writer – in this case, G. K. Chesterton – for his approval, rather than sending his work to a magazine or a publisher. At this stage, he was more anxious about being accepted as a writer than about getting his writing into print. However, 'Some weeks or even months had passed since he sent it, and now he was telling me that the author's wife had returned the manuscript, saying that her husband regretted his inability to give an opinion, owing to pressure of work.' Jessie Chambers recognised 'the chagrin that lay behind his casual words' when he described what had happened; but, remarkably, Lawrence continued: '"I've tried, and been turned down, and I shall try no more. And I don't care if I never have a line published," he concluded in a tone of finality.'[60] This was not just pique: Lawrence meant it. He was always obdurate in his decisions; the experience of rejection (another version of the feeling of exposure which had always upset him) was something he found particularly hard to bear. In 1908, at the end of his college career, he remarked that he was refusing to send in any more job applications: 'I cannot bear to advertise myself' (i. 58). The pride and the self-conscious touchiness of his maternal grandfather were very strong in him. He could not bear the experience of humiliation; an angry, self-lacerating feeling of helpless exposure is followed by a resolve never to be so humiliated again. For more than another year, Lawrence does not appear to have approached a single magazine or publisher; and this in spite of doing more work on his novel, writing a large number of new poems into his poetry notebook (a sign that they were in something approaching a finished state) and doing a second and much fuller draft of his 'Art and the Individual' essay. He did not want to be rejected: would rather not try than be exposed to his own self-contempt, and what he imagined was the amused reaction of others. The writing was necessary to him: it was his way of understanding what he was feeling, it was his breakthrough into another world from that of his upbringing. But whether he could actually do anything with it was another question altogether, and he had no idea of the answer.

Shortly after finishing the second draft of his novel in April 1908, he offered it to an entirely new reader. He had met the socialist and suffragist Blanche Jennings through his Eastwood friend Alice Dax, but hardly knew her; nevertheless he asked her to 'read and criticise some writing of mine that purports to be a novel' (i. 43). The fact that she lived outside his immediate circle of friends made her easier to approach; she was 'a cold stranger, and not my mother or my bosom friend' (i. 49). She was also interested by writing and writers, she was personally sympathetic to him and – what was important to Lawrence's sense of his audience – she was genuinely middle class. The very first sentence of his first letter to her reveals it: 'Since you belong to a class which I conceive of as scorning conventional politeness – don't ask me "what class?" – I am going to be just natural, which is to be rude . . .' (i. 43). And, further on in the letter – which he was writing on unusually fine paper – he gets entangled with the problem again: 'Oh dear, I am not accustomed to writing to ⟨ladies,⟩ women of your class – I wish you'd let me be really shamefully polite, or the opposite' (i. 45). All Lawrence's letters to Blanche Jennings reveal his attempt to adopt the style appropriate for addressing a middle-class woman; when he writes to her, he is very decidedly the David Lawrence ('pray continue to call me David – since it suits me so well') he would be to Helen Corke, too, a couple of years later.

But as he told Blanche Jennings in May 1908, he was condemned to 'be an elementary school teacher ... unless I can do something with that damned damnation of a Laetitia' (i. 50). He asked her not to apply 'the tests of artistic principles' to his novel, but to tell him simply 'whether it is bright, entertaining, convincing – or the reverse' (i. 44): he clearly wanted to know if it was publishable. To her, he was witty, sharply critical and (just as often) self-defensively denigrating about his novel.

In the first place it is a novel of sentiment – may the devil fly away with it – what the critics would call, I believe, an 'erotic novel' – the devil damn the whole race black –, all about love – and rhapsodies on spring scattered here and there – heroines galore – no plot – nine-tenths adjectives – every colour in the spectrum descanted upon – a poem or two – scraps of Latin and French – altogether a sloppy, spicy mess. Now madam – I offer you the dish. (i. 44)

When Lawrence writes like that, he reveals how much he hopes to be loved for his comic insight as well as criticised for the faults which (defensively) he shows himself so perceptive about. He shows striking insights into the book's weaknesses, as we can see from the final version of the novel, let alone from the solitary fragment of the second version to survive. The second paragraph of that runs:

There the daffodils were lifting their glorious heads and throwing back their wanton yellow curls to sport with the sun. At the foot of each sloping, grey old tree a family of these healthy happy flowers stood, some bursten with overfulness of splendour, some raising their heads slightly, modestly showing a sweet countenance, others still hiding their faces, leaning forward from the jaunty cluster of grey green spears; many were just venturing timidly out of their sheaths, peeping about. I felt inclined to hug them, I wanted desperately to know their language perfectly so that I might talk out my heart to them. They had a rich perfume as of oranges; they laughed to me, and tried to reassure me. So I looked up, feeling my spirit triumph again, and I saw betwixt me and the sky the trees with lifted fingers shaking out their hair to the sun, decking themselves with buds as white and cool as a water-nymph's breasts. Why should I not be glad? For even where the ground was hard by the paths the colts foot discs glowed in merry company. Oh spring gold is not like autumn gold; it is full of vigor, dazzling with vitality, it thrills through the blood like a first con-sciousness of love long felt but not known. Stooping to stroke the velvet face of a foal-foot I smelt again the black-currant spice, odour of fruits that always clings round the dark stems of the currant bushes. Nothing can bring back more memories to me than the smell of black-currant bushes.[61]

The 'nine-tenths adjectives', the 'poem or two', the 'rhapsodies on spring scattered here and there', 'every colour in the spectrum descanted upon'; above all, the dreadfully self-conscious sensitivity of the writing and its cloying concern with beauty – all are characterised in Lawrence's own criticism. The prose is frequently archaic, like a Pre-Raphaelite version of the mediaeval world; Pre-Raphaelite, too, in its flowers and nymphs and loving detail, though laden with the self-conscious significance and rhetoric of a piece by Richard Jefferies. What is also clear, however, is Lawrence's desperate problem with his narrator Cyril, whom he clearly wishes (in spite of his criticisms) to be the sensitive focus of his 'novel of sentiment'; yet cannot help making a fool of too, as Cyril expresses his wish to hug the daffodils and talk out his heart to them.

Blanche Jennings must have replied that she would read the book; but by the time he heard from her, the manuscript was already in the hands of Alice Dax. The latter, however, was also slow with her criticisms of the novel: 'Of course she thinks I don't care many damns about Laetitia . . . but as a matter of fact my mind is sore, and it waits for the ointment of somebody's sincere criticism' (i. 50). We cannot be certain whether Alice Dax actually read the whole book or just 'the first four chapters' (i. 48); Lawrence at first gloomily reported that 'she is not impressed, or ill impressed' (i. 55). But he was already certain that he would have to rewrite the book yet again – or at least 'great pieces of it' (i. 49); and Blanche Jennings's criticisms after she finally got the manuscript in July 1908 confirmed his intention: 'I will write the thing again' (i. 69).

She supplied some notes on the book when she had finished it, and Lawrence accordingly affirmed his intention to 'give Lettie a few rough shakings': she must have been getting her own way too easily. Yet the criticism of Cyril which both Alice Dax and Blanche Jennings voiced, and which made Lawrence vow to 'stop up the mouth of Cyril – I will kick him out – I hate the fellow . . . I *will* leave out Cyril, the fool' (i. 69), actually had little effect. Cyril was still necessary to Lawrence, here as elsewhere. Cyril is helpless in many ways, dependent (like an orphan) upon chance or friendship or nature. He is also a scientist and the heir of modern unbelief: in the largest sense, fatherless. But, like his substitute father the gamekeeper Annable, if rather less obviously, Cyril too ensures 'a sort of balance'[62] in the complex network of attachments making up the book. Being unable to act, he sympathises with George: being detached and superior, he knows what it is to be Leslie: he is Lettie's brother and shares some of her cynicism: while Annable treats him like a son.

Yet Blanche Jennings's silence about 'the Annable part' was a disappointment and made Lawrence ask her if she genuinely had nothing to say: 'Is it really coarse (Mrs Dax says it is)?' (i. 69). At some stage, Blanche Jennings must also have remarked that the Father incident (presumably a version of the brief appearance of Cyril's actual father surviving into the final version) was 'ugly and superfluous' (i. 92) – only to find Lawrence rather surprisingly insistent that 'The Father incident is not unnecessary – there is a point; there are heaps of points; I told you there would be, but you have not bothered to find them' (i. 72). Lawrence's writing style is so mannered in his letters to Blanche Jennings that it is often impossible to tell where he is seriously responding to criticism, and where fashioning a piece of flippant and defensive repartee. In this case, he hastily retreats from his own rudeness: 'you have not bothered to find them; quite rightly, too. I will re-write some time, and your suggestions will be valuable' (i. 72). The impression left by his response, however, is that nothing said by either Alice Dax or Blanche Jennings, or by the friend to whom the latter also showed the manuscript, made much impression upon this 1907–8 version of the novel; that Lawrence's writing remained a private matter, which he took far more seriously than his self-denigrating tone suggested.

In the course of his first winter in Croydon, in 1908, Lawrence reread the novel himself, and then he told Blanche Jennings what he could not have said back in May.

You can none of you find one essence of its failure: it is that I have dragged in conversations to explain matters that two lines of ordinary prose would have accomplished far better; I must cut out many pages of talk . . . secondly, one is cloyed with metaphoric fancy; thirdly, folk talk about themes too much . . . fourthly, I don't believe Lettie ever did break her engagement with Leslie – she married him. (i. 92)

This letter – especially its final perception – marked a real breakthrough. Lettie, whose female dangerousness was one of the few features of the novel Lawrence still liked – 'Lettie herself is not bad' – would after all reject George and marry Leslie: but unlike her marriage to George in the first two versions of the novel, her marriage to Leslie would not be fulfilling. Nor would George's marriage be. The one-sidedness of the two central male characters would lead to tragedy, not to romantic and unexpected fulfilment. It would be a novel about female power and self-image, and about wasted lives; things Lawrence really knew much more about than he did about romantic fulfilment. He knew he would have to write it all over again.

VII The Feminine

Another of the things lacking in the biographical records is any real source for the attraction Lawrence felt towards the fictional woman like Lettie. Immensely sophisticated, strikingly good-looking, high-spirited, discon-

1. The Lawrence Family 1897
Ada, Emily, Lydia, George,
Bert, Ernest, Arthur

2. Lydia Lawrence c. 1900

3. Arthur Lawrence c. 1875

4. D. H. Lawrence *c.* 1886

5. Ernest Lawrence 1901

6. Gipsy Dennis 1901

7. Emily Lawrence c. 1905

8. Eastwood 1900

9. Brinsley Colliery

10. 8a, Victoria Street

11. 57, The Breach

12. D. H. Lawrence March 1905

13. D. H. Lawrence September 1906

14. D. H. Lawrence September 1906

15. D. H. Lawrence *c.* summer 1908

16. D. H. Lawrence *c.* December 1908

17. D. H. Lawrence *c.* December 1908

18. Walter Lawrence *c.* 1903

19. Harriet Lawrence *c.* 1900

20. The Chambers Family *c.* 1898
May, Bernard, Mollie, Edmund, Ann, David, Jessie, Hubert, Alan

21. The Chambers Family *c.* 1906
May, Mollie, Alan, Edmund, Jessie, David, Hubert, Ann, Bernard

22. Jessie Chambers *c.* 1908

Last Words to Muriel

His You have borne the shame and sorrow
    But the disgrace is mine;
Your love was innocent and thorough,
Mine was the love of the Sun for the flower
    I loved to life in sunshine.

Yea, I was ~~diligent~~ - fine
    Yea, I was fine enough to ~~probe~~ explore you
        Blossom you stalk by stalk
Till the full-fed fire of curiosity bore you
Shrivelling down in the final dour
    Flesh-anguish, then I suffered a balk.

I heard thy cries of pain, and they broke
    My fine, craftsman's nerve,
Flawed my delicate courage in its stroke,
And I failed ~~from weakness~~ in my Cowardice to give thee the last
    Bright torture thou didst deserve.

Thou art shapely, thou art adorned
    But opaque and dull in the flesh,
Whom if but I had pierced with the thorned
Fire-threshing anguish, had been fused and fast
    In a lovely illumined mesh

23. 'Last Words to Muriel'

Campions

The _{green clouded} unclouded seas of bluebells have ebbed and
passed
And the pale stars of forget me nots have climbed
to the last
Rung of their life's ladder fragile height
Now the trees with interlocked hands
uplifted hold back the light

Though the purple dreams of the innocent Spring have
gone
And the glimmering dreamlets of the morning are pallid and
wan
Though the year is ripening like a woman who has conceived
And the wood, like a manly husband, spreads softness and
silence, thick-leaved:

The Campions drift in fragile, rosy mist
Draw nearer, redden and laugh like young girls
kissed
Into a daring, short-breath'd confession
Which opens earth and heaven to Love's fugitive, _{glowing} triumph
progression

24. 'Campions' and 'Last Words to Muriel'

25. Ada Lawrence and Frances Cooper *c.* 1900

26. Ada Lawrence *c.* 1907

tented and witty, independent and tough-minded, Lettie flirts with the heavier-footed and duller-witted men who surround her; she makes love to all and finally to none. She remains one of the few things still vital in *The White Peacock*, and seems to represent an amalgam of the qualities Lawrence would most have liked to define as feminine and to have found in women. However, she is perhaps even less attractive than he thinks she is. It would take him a while longer as a writer to combine her dislike of sex, her manipulative power games, her overpoweringly conscious (and self-conscious) reaction to experience in the creation of a character like Hermione Roddice in *Women in Love*. Yet in Lettie's direct and forceful opposition to the masculine temperament which Lawrence gloomily predicates in men like Saxton, Beardsall and Tempest, Lettie perhaps presents, more than anything else, her creator's version of his own receptive, dynamic and what he would call feminine temperament. She remains a trifle androgynous: a shade too much in her author's shadow, still.[63]

VIII From a College Window

Apart from Ursula's college experience in *The Rainbow*, and the brief references to Cyril Beardsall's and Ernest Lambert's college studies in *The White Peacock* and *A Collier's Friday Night*, there is nothing in Lawrence's fiction about the experience of higher education. Paul Morel in *Sons and Lovers* experiences neither school nor higher education: but nor does Paul have problems with chapel, religion or scientific materialism.

Lawrence did, however, write three poems about his period at college. The first, called 'The Worm Turns' and completely deleted in manuscript, reads in its first version:

> There is no passion in my life,
> There is no action, it is almost a sleep.
> Oh for a delirium of love or of strife
> Or sorrow to weep!
>
> I am quite sick of books
> Give them to the old
> My chafed curbed blood no longer brooks
> Such saprophyte mould.
>
> No readings and writings
> While the blood is alive
> But lovings and hatings, struggle and fightings—
> I'll work and I'll wive.[64]

The same rather ostentatiously romantic impatience is also felt in 'Study', the poem rejected by the College magazine. This time, the contrast is between the student whose 'exams are near' and who is 'making friends of the brainy dust / Of ancient swotters long since dead', and the life going on around him:

> Close by the wood's edge there's a girl hovers
> Looks through the hazel screen out on the meadow
> Where, wheeling and screaming the petulant plovers
> Wave frighted. Who comes?—A labourer with still tread.
> Oh, sunset swims in her eyes' swift pool!
> (I curse myself for a studying fool)[65]

For years Lawrence had been the 'studying fool' rather than the man looking for his girl: but his self-consciousness about it does not make a poem.

The third poem, 'From a College Window', however makes explicit the nature of the contrast between the life of the student at college and the world around him. It is not just that the student is wasting his time studying when he should be out living – working, loving, wiving. The original 1907–8 version contrasts the student, aloof in his college, with the world going on beneath him: 'And there a beggar slouches through the heat / And all remote from me in my high window seat.' The student's college life turns him, however, into a mere observer: distant, rather absurd. The third stanza runs:

> Remote although I hear the beggar's cough
> See the lady's rose-lit fingers hold him a coin:
> These are fragments of an incoherent play, and we scoff
> As we look at the actors, and say in our souls we will never join
> Their ill-played drama, we, like gods in the window seat
> Uplifted in wisdom, half amused by the play in the street.[66]

The complexity comes from the fact that the superiority of 'uplifted in wisdom' is bitterly ironical. The students look down 'like gods', 'half amused' by the little incoherent drama going on beneath them. But their certainty of never participating in such 'ill-played' drama is undermined by the irony. They may say 'in our souls' that they won't be joining in: but before long the gods will be cast down, their tinpot 'wisdom' seen for what it is. The poem does not say it: but they will shortly be out teaching Standard IV in tough schools. College does not really make them superior, in spite of its pretence at academic work; the students are deeply deceived, not to say co-operators in a lie. Lawrence had learned enough about himself by 1907 to know that he was no 'god' looking down, however tempting the pose was. He was going to have to earn his living: he could not be cut off from the world.

When Lawrence turned to write fiction on the subject of college and what it meant, he used precisely the same symbol. Ursula in *The Rainbow* goes to college after a year's teaching; and, very shortly after she starts, she is seen viewing the world outside – literally 'From a College Window'.

Looking down, she saw the lime-trees turning yellow, the tradesman's boy passing silent down the still, autumn-sunny street. There was the world, remote, remote.

Here, within the great, whispering sea-shell, that whispered all the while with reminiscence of all the centuries, time faded away, and the echo of knowledge filled the timeless silence.

The 'echo of knowledge', the 'reminiscence of all the centuries', is what fascinates her, when she starts at college; the professors are 'the black-gowned priests of knowledge, serving forever in a remote, hushed temple'.[67]

After a year there, her attitude to college has changed completely: 'This was no religious retreat, no seclusion of pure learning. It was a little apprentice-shop where one was further equipped for making money.' Her Botany studies are the only ones which interest or stimulate her. Once again Lawrence describes her sitting at the back of a lecture hall, looking down at the world outside:

Down below, in the street, the sunny grey pavement went beside the palisade. A woman in a pink frock, with a scarlet sunshade, crossed the road, a little white dog running like a fleck of light about her. The woman with the scarlet sunshade came over the road, a lilt in her walk, a little shadow attending her. Ursula watched spellbound. The woman with the scarlet sunshade and the flickering terrier was gone—and whither? Whither?

In what world of reality was the woman in the pink dress walking? To what warehouse of dead unreality was she herself confined?[68]

Lawrence no longer needs to use the situation of the woman giving money to a beggar to bring out his sense of the unreality of the student's situation. A distinctly wretched kind of remoteness is Ursula's lot, as she looks down at the street. The writing in *The Rainbow* is far more accomplished, far richer and more evocative than that in the poem. But, like the poem, it suggests Lawrence's frustration, loneliness and mordant irony towards the end of his student days. These were the years in which he left home (in several senses) for the first and last time; he would never be thoroughly at home anywhere again. They were also the years in which he lost his faith and his respect for the authorities he had so far known; years of a new, lonelier and newly modern self-sufficiency.

PART TWO

◆

*Croydon
and
London*

◆

CHAPTER EIGHT

SUCCESS

I   Croydon Teacher

Just before his final college examinations, we find Lawrence declaring that although 'I have not got a job . . . They will give me a place at Nottm. when there is one' (i. 58). But no place at Nottingham was offered him, and on second thoughts he was also determined not to work there: 'No more Notts. C[ounty] C[ouncil] for me' (i. 78). The reason, according to Jessie Chambers, was that 'At the end of his arduous and expensive training he could command in his home county a wage of slightly over thirty shillings a week': rather less than his father had earned in the pit when young. Accordingly, Lawrence 'refused to offer his services to any education authority that would pay him less than £90 a year.'[1] But although both Professor Amos Henderson and George Holderness had written him good testimonials, both stressed his 'promise' as much as his ability: and Henderson's emphasis in particular upon Lawrence's intelligence, and his 'taste for, and appreciation of literature', did not make him sound an ideal candidate for the post of elementary teacher in a tough school. It took him three months of copying out his testimonials and writing applications to find a job: Jessie Chambers recalled that 'Lawrence out of work was a sardonic figure. He spent much of his time at the farm, handing his manuscript over to me, and accompanying my brother about the farm work.'[2] He considered trying for a job in Liverpool (i. 63), was unsuccessfully interviewed at Stockport (i. 77), and even wrote to Egypt (i. 69): he used 'pounds of paper in applications' and could 'recite two long testimonials by heart' (i. 73). His family were perhaps more anxious than he about his prospects; after all, this was the culmination of six years training: 'Post time is a period of painful suspense – about 8.30 a.m. and 7.0 p.m. – when the postman should come. He brings me a letter – the house holds its breath – "We beg to inform you that your application was not successful" – the devils!' (i. 73). Not until 26 September was he interviewed in Croydon, 9 miles south of London. There was a post at the Davidson Road School, which had only been opened in 1907; its headmaster Philip Smith (according to one of his colleagues) was 'a wiry, impetuous man of middle age but youthful enthusiasms' and an advocate of the 'experimental lesson'. Around Smith had gathered a group of 'young men all of about Lawrence's age, and one woman, Miss Agnes Mason, who was considerably older'; two of the staff had come from Smith's previous school in Croydon to work at this brand-new school in a difficult area. Smith had little influence upon new appointments; 'At that time teachers were posted to schools directly from the Central Authority without reference to the wishes of the Head Master.'[3] But clearly someone thought Lawrence was a risk worth taking as a teacher, and the kind of person who would get on with Smith and his staff. And Lawrence was offered the post of assistant master at a salary of £95 a year.

He spent a few days back in the Midlands, packing and saying goodbye. 'Seven girls are coming to tea today to weep a farewell tear into our best saucers with fragile fleeting poppies on them' (i. 79), he told Blanche Jennings – but it really was the end of an era. He went out to the Haggs Farm:

He was pale and his eyes looked dark with pain.

'Well, Bert, you're going to leave us then,' father said, and much feeling lay behind the casual words.

'It looks like it,' Lawrence replied in the same way. He set off for home soon after supper. I walked with him to the last gate, where we stopped. He leaned towards me.

'*La dernière fois*,' he said, inclining his head towards the farm and the wood. I burst into tears, and he put his arms round me. He kissed me and stroked my cheek, murmuring:

'I'm so sorry, so sorry, so sorry.'[4]

It was the end of his six-year love-affair with the farm and the Chambers family: for Jessie, one of the repeated conclusions of her loving intimacy with him. Lawrence travelled to Croydon on Sunday 11 October, and started work there the following day.

Croydon in 1908 was a growing and, in one sense, thriving town. Lawrence found himself in a place utterly unlike Eastwood: much more like Nottingham in its size, but with London itself only a short bus or train journey away. In Croydon during his first week he could have gone to see the musical *Dare-Devil Dorothy* at the new Theatre Royal, or *Raffles* at the Grand Theatre: he could have heard 'Madame Amy Sherwin with her Ladies Choir and Operatic Quartette' in George St (Thursday 15th, Balcony 1/-). He actually went to hear W. P. Ker, Professor of English at London University, speaking on 'Criticism' at the Croydon branch of the English Association (Thursday 15th, tickets 1/-) in Whitgift Grammar School; and hated it. 'I went to a literary society conversazione and nearly discovered the North Pole – such poor fools' (i. 84), he reported. But

Croydon offered a range of entertainment and excitement worlds away from the Congregational Literary Society in Eastwood.

He had found his lodgings on the east side of the town, in streets only built during the previous two years. 12 Colworth Road was a small terrace house, the newly acquired home of Marie and John Jones: she a former teacher, and he a Schools Attendance officer. His room cost Lawrence 18/- a week, including 'good and copious' food. It was not the cheapest lodgings in the area, which cost only about 14/-, but clean and comfortable: 'not half bad', Lawrence told Louie Burrows (i. 83). The Jones family had two small children: Lydia Lawrence is reported to have remarked 'austerely' that 'I was glad when I knew there was a baby. It will keep him pure.'[5]

It turned out that John and Marie Jones were after all 'people who jangle' (i. 271) and not particularly happy together: 'Pa is really a bit gênant. There are rather rotten rows occasionally' (i. 254). Both made a confidant of him; Marie Jones told him 'things . . . marital and faintly horrifying' (i. 298) and 'took every possible opportunity of describing to him the wickednesses and infidelities of her husband – in all probability more imaginary than real', while John Jones 'told him that his wife had no more warmth for him than a bag of mud would have had'.[6] And yet Lawrence stayed with the Jones family until December 1911. Life with them was comfortable and easy-going lower middle-class life, with a piano and a canary in the living room, and a char to help with the housework. Lawrence became very much one of the family; Marie Jones gave him handkerchiefs for his birthday (i. 302), while he painted on Sunday mornings with his landlord, played chess with him (i. 89, 86) and discussed women – 'Such a pretty tart in the "Crown", Mr Lawrence – really warm and fruity' (i. 450), he remembered Jones saying once. Lawrence and Jones sometimes went out drinking together: 'Mr Jones particularly remembered an evening when they went to the Greyhound after a visit, cut short by Lawrence, to a billiard saloon. At the Greyhound Lawrence asked for absinthe . . .' And even if his landlord's opinions and opinionatedness often bored him – 'He is an inflated frog' (i. 89) Lawrence commented in 1908 – then Marie Jones was 'a splendid woman' (i. 86) ('I like his missis best' (i. 83)), and he always loved the children. As at home, he took his share in the woman's role of child care: 'he bathed the two small children of the house and put them to bed after suitable devotions, thus permitting the parents to take an evening off at the pictures'.[7] He described in a 1911 letter how the younger girl, Hilda Mary (born in March 1908), 'makes a praying stool of me. She kneels on my knee and says "Ph-Peh-Ph Ph" – then suddenly, very loudly "Amen", where-upon she opens like the sun looking over the end of a cloud, laughs, and the racket begins. Her prayer pleases me immensely. She's begun at the right end' (i. 227). In his first months in Croydon, Lawrence even took the 5-year old Winifred ('Freddy') up to London with him, to see the shops; 'we went into a great draper's where there is a Father Christmas Cave, and bears, and – and paradise all in one nook. The bairnie pays threepence, and the Real Father Christmas gives her a bundle of toys. We did enjoy ourselves, Freddy and I' (i. 97). In April 1911 he described how

Having been larking with the kiddies in the garden I am in a breathless and careless mood. Winnie is behind my chair getting undressed, peeping over my shoulder and when I turn round to look at her she croodles down to hide her dishabilly state . . . Mary is anxiously awaiting the finish of this to fly down to post with me. She loves to go out and see the dark and the stars and the moon.
'What are they?', she asks of the stars.
'Little girls going to bed with their candles,' I tell her.
'Where do they go to?'
As I can't answer that – 'Look!' I say 'the wind's blowing 'em out.' She clings close round my neck, and puts her cheek on mine, looking up in wonder –
. . . Now I've got a bracelet of red wool and tape to wear. There's no peace in this life. (i. 257)

The Davidson Road School was about ten minutes' walk from Lawrence's lodgings, across 'a piece of wild waste land . . . where the grass is wild and trodden into mud – where the brick-layer's hammer chinks, chinks the funeral bell of my bit of waste land' (i. 121). The school was part of that development,

a great big new red-brick imposing handsome place, with a fair amount of open space – looking across in front over great stacks of timber, over two railways to Norwood where the musichall folk live in big houses among the trees, and to Sydenham, where the round blue curves of the Crystal Palace swell out into view on fairly clear days. Inside all is up to date, solid and good . . . floors are block wood – thirty dual desks for forty five boys – all very nice. (i. 83–4)

And yet never had Lawrence taught children who came from such poor families. Eastwood, for all its grime, was not a poor place; the 'collier lads' at the British School had come from families with enough to eat, at least. Nor had Lawrence previously had boys from institutions in his classes. The Davidson Road School included in its catchment area the thirty boys at the Gordon Home for Waifs and Strays at 24, Morland Road, Croydon: such children always being referred to, another Croydon teacher remembered, as 'the "home" boys',

from a nearby institution for illegitimate and unwanted children. The 'home' is run on humane lines . . . But the house in which they live is too small to provide scope for the activities of forty healthy children, all kept on a full, stodgy diet, and the restless 'home' boys are not welcomed in any class, nor by other children less well-nourished. These latter, often thin and threadbare, nevertheless maintain a caste superiority which isolates the unfortunates.[8]

The boys struck Lawrence, in his first term, as 'of insolent, resentful disposition; that is only superficial, owing to training, I think' (i. 97). His first writing about school mentions both the 'home' boys and children 'less well-nourished'. Parental poverty is vividly revealed when the weather is cold or snowy: on the one hand 'Lads in their warm, light slippers bound down the hall to the measure/Of their dancing blood . . .' But, on the other, 'Clinging to the radiators, like numbed bees to the drenched grass/The boys from the Home, blue and inanimate.' Yet not even the Home boys can be compared with the children from really poor families:

> Like sad processions of exiles you could have seen them shivering, pass
> Down the glad streets, pinched waifs in ill-assorted clothes.
> —Shuffling his ragged boots, there comes one boy late
> —When he lifts his foot I see the folded pad of his stocking soaked under his
>   toes.

> "Please sir, I was sweeping snow, an' I never heard the bell
> I didn't know it was so late. No Sir—I 'ad to—because my father
> He—he's in prison. Yes sir—one and six—with my sister's as well."
> We all march out to prayers, soft slippered feet and clattering soles
> And shuffle of broken, sodden boots; yet singing goes rather
> By nature than by boots, and wet feet often carry merry souls.

On his own way home, the narrator meets the ragged boy again, with his shovel and brush: '. . . "But please Sir, my movver said I could—an'—/—We ain't got no farver—only a movver, an' she 'as ter go/Cleanin'—Yes Sir—a shillin, by myself—all right Sir." '[9] The narrator is simultaneously shocked by things like 'the folded pad of his stocking soaked under his toes', amused that 'singing goes rather/By nature than by boots', charitable in giving the ragged boy 'a shillin, by myself', an experimenter with the urban ballad and, in a slightly Dickensian way, sentimental about the very boys he sympathises with ('We ain't got no farver'). The uneasy combination suggests Lawrence's problem of tone, a problem exacerbated by Croydon. He was, as teacher and professional man, concerned and sympathetic, but he remained very much in the position of the narrator of his poems: an outsider. We can, indeed, see just how callow he was capable of being in a letter he wrote to Blanche Jennings on 9 October 1908, just before leaving for Croydon. Daisy Lord had recently been sentenced to life imprisonment for murdering her child; the case had become a *cause célèbre*.

Concerning Daisy Lord, I am entirely in accord with you. If I had my way, I would build a lethal chamber as big as the Crystal Palace, with a military band playing softly, and a Cinematograph working brightly; then I'd go out in the back streets and main streets and bring them in, all the sick, the halt, and the maimed; I would lead them gently, and they would smile me a weary thanks; and the band would softly bubble out the 'Hallelujah Chorus'. (i. 81)

It may be a pose, but it is a particularly nasty one; he does not know how much he is revealing the precariousness of his own sense of class superiority.

His relations with his colleagues at school, too, were initially difficult. Agnes Mason told a friend that 'he avoids, or is avoided by, the other men on the staff (Arthur McLeod excepted) and looks lonely and unhappy'.[10] Arthur McLeod was a bookish and studious man who eventually became Lawrence's best friend in Croydon – Lawrence, writing to him later and remembering school, recalled especially 'walking talking books with you' (i. 446). (Lawrence struck his headmaster Philip Smith, indeed, as knowing 'more about books than about boys'.) But the men on the staff – Smith, Robert Henry Aylwin (who had also been Class 1, division 1 in the 1904 King's Scholarship exam) and Ernest Arthur Humphreys – had, to begin with, little time for their quiet, unathletic and inexperienced colleague. Lawrence 'failed signally to pass their tests of capacity both for sport and school discipline, so that they first extended to him a contemptuous patronage; and later, when they had had some experience of his intellectual fearlessness and power of passionate argument, paid him a grudging respect and kept out of his way'. As time went on, he got on better with them, 'for he was always friendly, and gay and eager in discussion'. Smith, in particular, came to enjoy his company, and invited him to call at his hotel in Brighton at Christmas 1910, where Lawrence felt that the 'proceedings were somewhat languid and should be accelerated. This he proceeded to do . . .' Smith 'heard then, for the first time, Lawrence's peculiar laugh' of 'exuberant gaiety'. He had obviously not heard it at school. Lawrence also visited Smith at home in Croydon, and showed himself cultivated in exactly the way he had educated himself to be: 'My wife, like Lawrence, was interested in French literature. They read French verse and we sang French songs. Lawrence translated some French verse into English. He also attempted some verse in French.'[11]

However, Lawrence began his school career in Croydon by having exactly the problems predicted for him by Professor Henderson. George Holderness, at the Albert Street School, had been 'sometimes very aggressive with the stick': had never been slow to punish, or to take that problem away from his juniors. And although Lawrence had had 'to fight bitterly' for his authority in Eastwood (i. 39), Holderness had supported him and his pupils had in the end 'liked me nearly as much as I loved them' (i. 89). When he left in 1906, his class clubbed together to collect half a crown to buy him 'a silver coloured propelling pencil'. The pupil who organised the presentation retained an elegiac memory of it: 'giving Bert Lawrence that, the last day he was at school; and the sun was . . . slanting . . . through the school windows, so I gave it to him, I could hardly see for the sunshine coming through, hazy, a rainy kind of sun; and that was the last time I remember Bert at school.'[12] Croydon was very different. Lawrence found the children 'rough and insolent as the devil' (i. 93), and was aggrieved at the way in which Smith 'shifts every grain of responsibility off his own shoulders – he will not punish anybody; yourself, when you punish, you must send for the regulation cane and enter the minutest details of the punishment in the Pun. book – if you do. Discipline is consequently very slack and teaching is a struggle' (i. 84). It got worse: within a fortnight of starting, he described to Blanche Jennings how 'School is a conflict – mean and miserable – and I hate conflicts . . . the lads and I have a fight, and I have a fight with my nature, and I am always vanquished . . . I struggle with my nature and with my class, till I feel all frayed into rags' (i. 85). That exactly coincides with Professor Henderson's estimate of him as fastidious and easily discouraged: teaching was 'trying to tame some fifty or sixty malicious young human animals' (i. 93). All he could do in Croydon, like Ursula in her teaching career in *The Rainbow*, was to learn to overcome his 'nature': 'it only needs that I gird up my loins, and take to arm me for the fight the panoply of a good stinging cane – and me voilà!' (i. 94). Before the end of term in December, 'I have smitten the Philistines with the rod, and they are subdued' (i. 100): and in February 1909 he could announce that 'I have tamed my wild beasts – I have conquered my turbulent subjects, and can teach in ease and comfort' (i. 117). Ursula's experience should remind us that Lawrence, in spite of his exuberant tone, probably found it a violation of himself to behave as he did. Smith seems to have been astute in leaving Lawrence 'at liberty to work out his own salvation': it was his only hope in such a school.

But Smith was a remarkably intelligent and forward-looking headmaster (McLeod characterised him as 'discerning', 'enlightened' and 'kindly');[13] and after Lawrence had settled his problems with discipline, he grew to appreciate the freedom his headmaster gave him. Having dismissed Smith as a 'weak kneed windy fool' and his enlightened ideas as 'much pretence of high flown work' in October 1908 (i. 84), in November Lawrence described him as 'nice, but very flabby' (i. 93): a month later Smith had become 'a delightful man (a bit of a fathead sometimes, but kind as an angel!)' (i. 97). And that was how Lawrence continued to think of Smith: in 1927 he recalled how 'he treated me always very decently' (v. 641).

For his part, Smith from the first 'recognized his quality and gave him free scope to follow his bent':[14] and his enlightened approach enabled Lawrence to teach in a way that not surprisingly astonished a visiting School Inspector who one day walked into his classroom.

The intrusion was unexpected and resented. A curious wailing of distressed voices issued from a far corner. The sounds were muffled by a large covering black-board. The words of a familiar song arose from the depths:

> Full fathom five thy father lies;
> Of his bones are coral made.

The class was reading *The Tempest*. The presentation expressed the usual thorough-ness of Lawrence's attitude to the exercise in progress. It must not be spoiled by even official comment. Lawrence rushed with outstretched hands to the astounded visitor: 'Hush! Hush! Don't you hear? The sea chorus from *The Tempest*.'[15]

He had his pupils act out *As You Like It* 'as if the front of the class were a stage'; and as a result of the acting, 'the boys enjoy it: only they do want to caper round in a dance while Rosalind delivers the epilogue, and there's not enough room. Poor Orlando forgot to take the duster off, so he was married with his arm in a sling' (i. 245). The rest of his English teaching was also, according to his headmaster, 'for the time, unorthodox'. In poetry for example,

He would have none of the 'We are seven etc' category. Nor would he tolerate any with what he called 'a sniff of moral imposition.' I found entered in his records such selections as 'The Assyrian Came Down' (Byron), 'The Bells of Shandon' (Mahony), 'Go fetch to me a pint of wine' (Burns). He considered that the best approach to poetry for young people was through rhythm and the ring of words rather than the evasive appeal of an unreal and abstract morality.[16]

And some years later Lawrence gave his wife Frieda an idea of how he had taught history: 'arranged the boys in two sides and they *fought* the battle of Agincourt over schoolforms and all'. In Art, too, his ideas were regarded by the authorities as 'somewhat suspect': Philip Smith recalled how

While I was conferring with another Board of Education inspector, a boy brought a large pastel drawing, still life, for inspection. After a glance, I made an ineffectual attempt to suppress the sketch. The official eye had, however, anticipated my effort. 'Is this sent for any particular reason?' I inquired. 'Mr. Lawrence thought it was rather good,' the boy replied. The artist returned to his class leaving his masterpiece with us.

'Are you by any chance an artist?' inquired the wary dictator. 'No,' I replied. 'Neither am I,' he commented. 'We had better be careful about this man. After the session, without his knowledge, collect a sample of these drawings. I will send them to the Art Department at Kensington for an expert opinion.'[17]

Later the inspector himself returned the pictures, with the news that the Department 'highly approves'. A colleague of Lawrence's remembered his success as an art teacher: 'the whole class acquired his own free, vigorous style and painted boldly and with huge enjoyment. It was almost his one regret on leaving that his successor might cramp that freedom of handling. For enlightenment on "child art" was then only feebly dawning.' His teaching remained, however, 'always a strain to him'; a 'wearing, nerve-racking business' (v. 479) which wore him down over the next three years. He worked with 'untiring industry' and 'shirked none of the drudgery of the details which hamper the routine of a teacher's life'; he took charge of the school library, and painted scenery for the school play (i. 246). Smith found him extremely conscientious – 'just as conscientious as in his writings' – but Lawrence suffered badly at times from the strain of enforcing discipline during the day, and marking and writing in the evenings.[18]

Things were not so bad in his first year, 1908–9, after he had overcome the worst of his discipline problems and while his health was still good; his literary work consisted mostly in the writing of poems and in doing yet another revision of 'Laetitia'. After an initial time of 'loneliness and despair' (i. 84) – one of the reasons why the Jones children were probably such a comfort – he also found time to enjoy London, and to explore the country to the south of Croydon. He toured Surrey on his bicycle – 'a most sweet and lovely country' (i. 91); he also described it in a way that shows how naturally he practised his writing: 'The masses of gorgeous foliage, the sharp hills whose scarps are blazing with Autumn, the round valleys where the vivid dregs of Summer have collected – they have almost intoxicated me ... I've come thro Epsom to Dorking – am going on to Reigate' (i. 90). He frequently went to London by bus: saw the Royal Academy winter exhibition, stared at the shops. While waiting for the bus in Croydon one Saturday in December 1908, he had his photograph taken: 'I did not smile, for, somehow, I felt ridiculous' (i. 100). Two poses survive: he already looks less plump than in his Nottingham University College photo: even a little haggard, in a becoming way, as he stares into the camera (see Illustrations 16 and 17). He went to Barnet, to Wimbledon, to Richmond Park, to Dulwich to visit the Art Gallery: he may have gone to the Derby at Epsom in June 1909. But 'life is very still. Even here near London – life is a still pool – or a puddle' (i. 120). He still mainly lived for the holidays, when he returned to his Midlands circle of friends; in February 1909, seeing flower sellers in town, he recalled with desperate nostalgia 'snowdrops from under the hazel brake in the steep dell in the woods of Strelley ... still I long for the country and for my own folks' (i. 117).

His social circle consisted mostly of other teachers: to start with, Agnes Mason, fourteen years older than he, 'a very able, almost over-conscientious teacher' who 'rather "mothered" him'. But they became friendly and he 'had soon persuaded her to try her hand at little stories and sketches and at water-colour painting'. As time passed, he grew closer to Arthur McLeod and shared books and thoughts about books with him; by March 1909 Lawrence was reading Conrad, Wells and Tolstoy – 'I love modern work' (i. 118). He struck his headmaster as, compared with McLeod, 'always too busy to read greatly'; but this may well have been Lawrence, as usual, disguising the range of his intellectual and literary interests.[19]

It was in Croydon, for example, that he discovered both Nietzsche and Wagner. Although he made no reference in his letters to Nietzsche until April 1913 (i. 545), he had known about him from at least early 1910. In the manuscript of his story 'A Modern Lover', probably written in January that year, he referred to 'Nietzche' as the most recent reading of his autobiographical hero Cyril Mersham; on the back of a page of his 1910 novel 'The Saga of Siegmund' appears the note 'Nietzche Lamp and cock', while Helena takes an unnamed volume of Nietzsche with her to the Isle of Wight in *The Trespasser*, the 1912 version of the novel. The two mis-spellings may well indicate that Nietzsche was new to Lawrence in 1910.[20] Croydon public library, however, contained a number of Nietzsche's work in translation. From 1903, they held *The Case of Wagner*, *The Dawn of Day*, *A Genealogy of Morals* and *Thus Spake Zarathustra*: in 1908 they added *Beyond Good and Evil*. But it was, too, the great age of Nietzscheans in England: of Havelock Ellis, H. G. Wells, W. B. Yeats and George Bernard Shaw. The socialist weekly the *New Age* to which Lawrence subscribed for a while in 1908–9 (it cost 1d a week), was committed to Nietzsche, and its editor A. R. Orage had published a little book of extracts and explanations called *Nietzsche in Outline and Aphorism* in 1907.[21] Nietzsche, too, was thoroughly unacademic and appealed to English writers and artists rather more than to English philosophers.

As with his discovery of Schopenhauer, however, what is important is how Lawrence turned Nietzsche to his own advantage. In Nietzsche he experienced the force and conviction of a writer very unlike himself who was brilliantly formulating things which he himself increasingly wanted to express. He was always less concerned with what Nietzsche actually said or meant than with how he could be used. On the one hand, Nietzsche was good for supplying a way of characterising what Lawrence disliked about the mentality of individuals like Leslie Tempest in *The White Peacock*; the phrase 'Will to Power' was extremely useful shorthand, and Lawrence used it in 1916 about Gerald Crich in *Women in Love*.[22] When he gave Helena her volume of Nietzsche in *The Trespasser*, he was probably suggesting how a philosophy of ideas of power would attract a woman seeking to dominate herself and her partner. On the other hand, Lawrence would have found Nietzsche useful in confirming him in an active rejection of Christianity. More than anyone else, Nietzsche had convinced his contemporaries 'that they were living "at the end of the Christian era"'; and it was this Nietzsche to whom Lawrence referred in February 1913 when he described modern times as 'years of demolition', with Nietzsche responsible for demolishing 'the Christian Religion as it stood'.[23]

Nietzsche would also have confirmed Lawrence's growing sense of the opposition between spirit, mental will and mental knowledge on the one hand, and body, instinct, blood and self on the other. In particular, he provided a language for the almost inexpressible area of 'blood-knowledge' which, as a writer, Lawrence already inarticulately knew to be crucial to him. Even in the poor translations available to him in 1910, Lawrence must have found Nietzsche's description of the body's 'rationality' extremely useful:

An instrument of thy body is also thy little rationality, my brother, which thou callest 'spirit' – a little instrument and plaything of thy big rationality . . .

Behind thy thoughts and feelings, my brother, there is a mighty lord, an unknown sage – it is called self; it dwelleth in thy body, it is thy body.

There is more rationality in thy body than in thy best wisdom . . .

Of all that is written, I love only what a person hath written with his blood. Write with blood, and thou wilt find that blood is spirit.[24]

As a man fascinated by the power of 'spirit', and very well aware that he had himself habitually ignored the 'blood' which Nietzsche hymned and celebrated, Lawrence would have found Nietzsche particularly important. Nietzsche became one of the most powerful of those multitudinous subterranean influences upon him: one of the figures who helped make modern a mind and consciousness educated by the nineteenth century.

Jessie Chambers remembered how Lawrence never mentioned Nietzsche directly to her, 'nor suggested that I should read him', but all the same she 'began to hear about the "Will to Power", and perceived that he had come upon something new and engrossing . . .'[25] It was unusual for Lawrence not to pass on his discovery: it may partly have been because the books he read were public library copies, not his own. But by 1909–10 his reading habits had grown apart from Jessie's. Although their period of serious reading between 1902 and 1908 had been for them both an extraordinary breakaway from the confinements of the lives they might have expected to lead, it is hardly surprising that the very seriousness eventually started to feel a strain. It is the strain which dominates Lawrence's first fictional account of this shared education, in 'A Modern Lover' (written 1909–10). Many of the books and authors mentioned in the story also appear in Jessie's account (though, notably, he does suggest that 'Muriel' read Nietzsche). Cyril Mersham thinks, years on,

How infinitely far away, now, seemed "Jane Eyre" and George Eliot. These had marked the beginning. He smiled as he traced the graph onwards, plotting the points with Carlyle and Ruskin, Schopenhauer and Darwin and Huxley, Omar Khayyam, the Russians, Ibsen and Balzac, then Guy de Maupassant and Madame Bovary . . . Since then had come only Nietzsche and William James. They had not done so badly, he thought, during those years which now he was apt to despise a little, because of their dreadful strenuousness, and because of their later deadly, unrelieved seriousness.[26]

The autobiographical hero Mersham is however not only describing his intellectual development, but starting to denigrate it. This is a process visible in a good deal of Lawrence's fiction about the experiences of his autobiographical heroes with Muriel and Miriam. By 1910, too, Lawrence may well have felt that Jessie would find Nietzsche so unsympathetic that there was no point in trying to pass on his discovery. That feeling would have been strengthened if he had been reading the anti-Christian polemic of, for example, Part Three of the Croydon library copy of *Beyond Good and Evil*.

We do not know if McLeod encouraged Lawrence to read Nietzsche; if he did not, then a woman Lawrence met in the spring of 1909 probably did; Helen Corke had herself begun reading Nietzsche in 1908. Lawrence was starting to meet and make woman friends in Croydon: by March 1909 he described himself as 'having one or two delightful little flirtations – quite little, but piquant' (i. 121). Helen Corke was a former colleague of Smith, McLeod and Agnes Mason, who still taught at Smith's old school and who had an enormous appetite for discussion, walks, reading and music. She was the first person Lawrence met in Croydon who influenced him to any marked degree: but during his first year there he knew her only slightly. Smith thought of her as an 'extremely attractive and accomplished young lady'; small, red-haired and with a very pale skin, the daughter of working-class parents, she had – like Lawrence – made her way into the professional classes.[27] When Lawrence met her she was having a troubled relationship with her music teacher Herbert Baldwin Macartney, a married man in his forties who was strongly attracted to her. She admired Macartney and in a way loved him, but found herself unable to respond to him in spite of his appeals and advances. She generally loved women rather than men; she had had a long and possessive relationship with Agnes Mason which was just coming to an end, and she would later fall in love with Jessie Chambers. When she met Lawrence at the house of Agnes Mason, he gave her the impression of 'a tall, slim, lank figure, of thick, straight, ruffled hair, of keen, deep-set blue-grey eyes under a high forehead and heavy brows': he was 'seated on the floor . . . telling fortunes with cards, chattering clever nonsense in three languages'. One Saturday morning in April 1909, again with Agnes Mason, she heard him reading out loud Swinburne's 'Chorus from Atalanta' 'with a restraint that intensifies its exultation': she linked the memory with the suggestion which Macartney had made that same morning, that in August he and she should spend a week's holiday together in Freshwater, on the Isle of Wight. For the time being, her attention was turned fully towards Macartney; Lawrence was only 'this young Midlander, whose intuition is so strangely acute'.[28]

Another Croydon teacher Lawrence got to know well during his first year was Agnes Holt: 'you know my kind, a girl to whom I gas' (i. 141). She was 'rather a striking girl with much auburn hair . . . alert, prompt, smart with her tongue, and independent in her manner' (i. 153); she may well have been one of those he was flirting with in the spring. He found her most attractive; and in the autumn of 1909 they would consider getting married.

II   Ford Madox Hueffer

Throughout his first year in Croydon, Lawrence worked on his revision of 'Laetitia', turning it into 'Nethermere': 'Sometime, I hope, it will be finished. I have to do it over and over again, to make it decent' (i. 118). Although this must have been the rewriting which, in outline at least, gave us most of the book we now have, we know very little about its process or progress. In January 1909, we find Lawrence determined not to be such a 'sentimentalist' in it (i. 106); and in May 1909 he must have been re-imagining the eventual destinations of all the characters in part III, because he asked Jessie Chambers – the model for Emily – 'Do you mind if, *in the novel*, I make Emily marry Tom?' He also showed the manuscript at some stage to McLeod, 'with the anxious demand to let him know if it was good'.[29]

Friends came to see him: Jessie Chambers visited in May 1909, on the trip her parents were so concerned about; Louie Burrows followed in July (and Lawrence wondered if she would be 'improper' like Jessie, and stay at Colworth Road). Both were given tours of the London shops and art galleries, with concerts or operas in the evening. With both, too, Lawrence corresponded about writing; interestingly, given his own reluctance to publish, he encouraged Louie to publish the stories she was writing: 'Send me them, please, and I'll see if I can put a bit of surface on them and publish them for you. We'll collaborate, shall we? – I'm sure we should do well. At any rate send me the tales at once, and I'll send em to the publisher some time or other in your name' (i. 130–1). He continued simply to send his own poems to Jessie Chambers, as well as to consult her about 'Nethermere', and made no attempt to publish his work in spite of her urging. His reluctance to submit his writing to magazines probably still had a good deal to do with his fear of rejection.[30] Jessie Chambers had told him that he ought to send some contributions to the *English Review*, the new and prestigious literary magazine edited by Ford Madox Hueffer which had made its first appearance late in 1908 and to which Lawrence had introduced the Chambers family in the winter of 1908–9: 'It is the best possible way to get into touch with the new young school of realism' (i. 139). Hueffer had founded the magazine to publish the very best of contemporary writing: its first issue consisted of a quite extraordinarily impressive line-up: Hardy's poem 'A Sunday Morning Tragedy', Henry James's 'The Jolly Corner', Joseph Conrad's 'Some Reminiscences', John Galsworthy's 'A Fisher of Men', W. H. Hudson's 'Stonehenge', Tolstoy's 'The Raid' and the first of a four-part serialisation of H. G. Wells's *Tono-Bungay*. Lawrence had read the Wells serialisation from the start: it was 'the best novel I have read for – oh, how long?' (i. 119). Hueffer's ambition was quixotic: 'I am running a philanthropic institution for the benefit of the better letters' he told Arnold Bennett in 1909, when Bennett quarrelled with him over payment for a short story. 'I am perfectly resigned to bankruptcy and the sooner you bankrupt me the sooner my troubles with the *Review* will be over.'[31] He had hoped for a sale of 5,000 copies a month, got only 2,000, and had been losing £300–£400 per issue: his money ran out at the end of 1909. But during the period of his editorship (the last number he put together was probably that of February 1910), the magazine was an extraordinary forum of publishing. Jessie Chambers remembered her family's reaction to it:

We were delighted with the journal. The very look of it, with its fine blue cover and handsome black type, was satisfying. Father thoroughly appreciated it, and we decided to subscribe to it amongst us [2/6 a month or £1-5-0 a year]. The coming of the *English Review* into our lives was an event, one of the few really first-rate things that happen now and again in a lifetime.[32]

And it was to this magazine that, very naturally, Jessie suggested Lawrence should send some of his own work.

I soon noticed that the Editor was prepared to welcome new talent. I drew Lawrence's attention to this and begged him to submit some of his work, but he refused absolutely . . .

'I don't care what becomes of it,' he said stubbornly. 'I'm not anxious to get into print. I shan't send anything. Besides they'd never take it.'

He then suggested that Jessie should send in something of his: 'Send some of the poems, if you like.' When she asked which, he replied 'Send whatever you like. Do what you like with them . . .'[33] The consequences would be *her* responsibility.

Jessie looked through the poems Lawrence had sent her in letters since October 1908, picked out those she thought the best and, 'one beautiful June morning', copied them out. She sent four poems: two with school as their setting, two inspired by the 2-year-old Helen Mary Jones. 'I was careful to put the poem called "Discipline" first, not because I thought it was the best, but hoping that the unusual title might attract the Editor's attention.' And, astonishingly, early in August she had a letter from Hueffer, asking to see Lawrence in London and saying that 'perhaps something might be done'.[34]

Lawrence, his mother and father, and a number of friends (but not Jessie, this year) had gone on 31 July 1909 for the last of the family holidays together; they spent a fortnight of blazing sunshine on the Isle of Wight. When Lawrence returned, Jessie gave him Hueffer's letter. ' "*You* are my luck," he murmured. Then he said with suppressed excitement, "Let me take it to show mother." And I never saw it again.'[35] The anecdote is yet another of those used by Jessie Chambers to demonstrate Lawrence's sub-servience to his mother; it suggests just as strongly, however, Lydia Lawrence's interest in her son's writing.

Lawrence's 1928 description of how he broke into print, gracefully com-plimentary though it is, completely ignores the stresses of the moment:

It was while I was at Croydon, when I was twenty-three, that the girl who had been the chief friend of my youth . . . copied out some of my poems, and without telling me, sent them to the *English Review* . . . The girl had launched me, so easily, on my literary career, like a princess cutting a thread, launching a ship.[36]

In 1909 it had by no means been so unproblematic; 'without telling me' suggests a surprise which had little to do with what had actually happened. Hueffer, too, had shown the most extraordinary judgement in singling out Lawrence's work: he used to receive 'on average twenty manuscripts a day from the first day I started the periodical to the day when I gave it up'.[37] It was also lucky that Jessie wrote when she did. A few months later, Hueffer was no longer running the magazine.

Hueffer later told the story of his first sight of Lawrence's writing in some detail; his account is unfortunately misleading, being based on the conviction that Jessie first sent him the story 'Odour of Chrysanthemums' (not in fact written until some months later, in the winter of 1909). Hueffer saw Lawrence's poems before he saw his prose, printed his poetry first in the *English Review* and had read 'Nethermere' before he saw 'Odour of Chrysanthemums'. (He also printed Louie's and Lawrence's story 'Goose Fair' long before 'Odour of Chrysanthemums' was included in the magazine.) However, his anecdote provides a striking account of the impact Lawrence's work could make:

'The small locomotive engine, Number 4, came clanking, stumbling down from Selston,' and at once you know that this fellow with the power of observation is going to write of whatever he writes about from the inside. The 'Number 4' shows that . . . 'With seven full waggons.' . . . The 'seven' is good. The ordinary careless writer would say 'some small waggons.' This man knows what he wants. He sees the scene of his story exactly. He has an authoritative mind.

'It appeared round the corner with loud threats of speed.' . . . Good writing; slightly, but not *too* arresting . . . 'But the colt that it startled from among the gorse . . . outdistanced it at a canter.' Good again. This fellow does not 'state.' He doesn't say: 'It was coming slowly,' or – what would have been a little better – 'at seven miles an hour.' Because even 'seven miles an hour' means nothing definite for the untrained mind. It might mean something for a trainer of pedestrian racers . . . But anyone knows that an engine that makes a great deal of noise and yet cannot overtake a colt at a canter must be a ludicrously ineffective machine. We know then that this fellow knows his job.

. . . You are, then, for as long as the story lasts, to be in one of those untidy, unfinished landscapes where locomotives wander innocuously amongst women with baskets. That is to say, you are going to learn how what we used to call 'the other half' – though we might as well have said the other ninety-nine hundredths – lives. And if you are an editor and that is what you are after, you know that you have got what you want and you can pitch the story straight away into your wicker tray with the few accepted manuscripts and go on to some other occupation . . . Because this man knows. He knows how to open a story with a sentence of the right cadence for holding the attention. He knows how to construct a paragraph. He knows the life he is writing about in a landscape just sufficiently constructed with a casual word here and there. You can trust him for the rest.[38]

It seems likely that Hueffer hoped to find in Lawrence the working-class writer he was 'after': the *English Review* had a strikingly left-wing bias, and Hueffer may well have been impressed, in the first instance, with the facts of Lawrence's origins rather than with the poems which (after seeing their author) he accepted. The fact that he later made so much of a story written months after he had got to know Lawrence certainly suggests so. Lawrence went to see him – 'fairish, fat, about forty' (i. 138) – when he returned to Croydon at the start of September 1909; but having talked to Lawrence, not only did Hueffer accept the poems but said 'he will be glad to read any of the work I like to send him' (i. 138).

However it had been achieved, here at last was a breakthrough: Lawrence had both encouragement and an experienced reader for his work. His first job was to revise the poems, whch were still 'all in the rough, and want revising, so this week and so on I am very hard at work, slogging verse into form. I shall be glad when I have finished: then I may get on with the prose work' (i. 137–8). The latter was almost certainly 'Nethermere', which he gave to Hueffer less than eight weeks later, at the end of October, after doing what he could to get it into a presentable form (he enlisted the help of Agnes Mason and Agnes Holt to make fair copies of the most heavily revised passages).

On seeing the novel, however, Hueffer felt 'inclined to prescribe' Lawrence 'a course of workingman novels'. He was probably irritated that Lawrence was not quite the working-class writer he had expected. Such a person (as Hueffer said of 'Odour of Chrysanthemums') would write 'of whatever he writes about from the inside', would know intimately 'the life he is writing about'. But 'Nethermere' had almost nothing to do with working-class life.

However, it can hardly be a coincidence that, in the autumn of 1909, Lawrence wrote first his play *A Collier's Friday Night*, then his short story 'Odour of Chrysanthemums' and then, in December 1909, two sketches of school life in Croydon which can also be linked with Hueffer.[39] The play and the story were unique in Lawrence's writing up to that point; they were drawn directly from the everyday life of the mining community, with the local dialect playing a significant part in both. Lawrence probably wrote them specifically because Hueffer suggested he should do something of the kind. There had been only one thing in the least like them in his output before: a single dialect poem, 'Violets for the Dead', finished before the middle of January 1909. But that was the very poem another London editor, Ernest Rhys, remembered as most characteristic of Lawrence's output; and it so impressed yet another London literary specialist, Edward Garnett, when he saw it more than two and a half years later, that he got it into print almost immediately.* This was the kind of work people expected from the son of a coal-miner, and it helped make Lawrence's reputation. The dialect

---

* Lawrence's other three dialect poems were actually written in Garnett's house some time after September 1911, almost certainly at Garnett's direct instigation (he discussed at least one of them with Lawrence).[40]

speech in 'Nethermere' had, in contrast, been confined to minor, genre characters.

It is significant, then, that this new work about the Midlands was written only after Lawrence had got to know his London literary editors. It was by no means easy, or natural, for him to write about the colliery community; he was not so simply a product of it as Hueffer wanted to believe. Even when he came in 1910 to start his 'colliery novel' 'Paul Morel', set in a fictional version of the community in which he had been born, the novel would still be strikingly literary. It was actually more natural for him in 1909 to write 'Nethermere' than 'Odour of Chrysanthemums'.

III Devotion

To gauge a little of what Lawrence's life was like at this point, just as he was breaking into print, we can turn to Jessie Chambers's account of a day she spent with him in November 1909; and we can see both what Lawrence demanded, and what she most willingly (though not without effort) gave.

On Saturday 27 November 1909, the same month as Hueffer had printed the poems by Lawrence she had sent him, she got up at 6 o'clock, and travelled (from Langley Mill station, after a 3-mile walk) to Nottingham; there she caught a train to King's Cross Station in London. Lawrence met her, and as soon as she arrived told her what he had not dared tell her before she came (for fear she would not have come): the following day, they would be having lunch with people from polite society – Ford Madox Hueffer and his companion, Violet Hunt. As she wrote in her memoir, 'My heart sank, for I dreaded meeting strangers.' But, too, 'I banished all thought of it, lest it should cast a shadow on the day.' She was to have her Saturday with Lawrence first, and 'the joy of being with him' overshadowed everything else. In the afternoon, they went to the National Gallery; after that, to Waterloo Bridge, observing what she called 'the human wreckage preparing to spend the night on the Embankment';[41] then to the theatre in the evening; finally down by train to Croydon, where the Jones family had gone to bed. And then, supper (they would not have eaten much since lunch). ' "I'm awfully sorry, it's macaroni again," he said. We had had macaroni at lunch. But it didn't matter. We could have banqueted on a crust. Supper over, he cleared the table and began to show me his writings.' The real business of the day thus starts: it cannot have been earlier than eleven at night. There were new poems, and *A Collier's Friday Night*, just completed; they spent two hours over them. As usual, Lawrence demanded Jessie's immediate response: ' "Do you like it?" he asked.' She said she would take it home.

He swept the papers together.

'Now we'll talk,' he said. 'But perhaps you want to go to bed?' It was one o'clock. I had left home at six the morning before. 'Can you stay up a little longer? Can you give me one hour?' he said.

'Yes, I can stay another hour,' I answered.

And the serious talk of the day began, with Lawrence asking

– What did I expect from life, what did I hope for in the future? I bent my head and the tears ran down into my lap, because in my heart was no hope at all, but only fortitude. So I said:

'I don't know. I can't tell. I don't hope for anything much. But I shall get along somehow. I'm not afraid.'[42]

Only four days later, Jessie gave a month's notice to her school authorities; she was moving from Underwood to the Musters Road School in Nottingham, and at least one of the reasons was the continued strain of living at home with her family at the Haggs. As well, she was not being treated as a certificated teacher at Underwood School, but would get the promotion she deserved – and a salary increase – if she moved to Nottingham. All this must have been very much on her mind as she considered her lonely future in Nottingham.

Lawrence in his turn then began to tell her how the strain of London, of work, and of his new literary success, affected him; how, too, he wanted a woman to sleep with. ' "But I've no money," he went on. "I shan't be able to marry for ever so long. I think I shall ask some girl if she will give me . . . that . . . without marriage. Do you think any girl would?" ' Jessie's reply demonstrates how much her own subsequent sexual relationship with Lawrence conflicted with the sort of woman she was: ' "I don't know," I answered. "The kind of girl who would, I think you wouldn't like." '

And so the discussion continues: until Jessie reminds him that it is two o'clock. ' "*Must* you go to bed?" "Yes, I must go now," I said, getting up from my chair. "Very well. I'll let you go. You shall go," he said.' An early version of her memoir recorded how 'When I was in my room I was surprised to heard [sic] what seemed like a knock on the door, and listened, but heard no more, so I was sure I had been mistaken.'[43]

Lawrence's demands on Jessie to read and to talk and to respond to his talk were extraordinary; he was also trying to summon up the courage to ask her to sleep with him – an appeal he made less than a month later, on Christmas Eve 1909. But Jessie's practical devotion is utterly clear. She accepts his right to demand not only her attention to his writing – he seems to have passed it on to her almost compulsively: he *had* to have someone reading it; but she also accepts his demand for the most serious concentration and thought from her. She is driven to tears of pain, as she realises the consequences of her devotion. But she loves being with him, and life is an adventure for her when they are together – they can banquet on a crust, let alone twice on macaroni. Above all, she *listens* to him and encourages him to explain himself to her. In a word, she takes him seriously, both in word and deed, regardless of the cost to herself.

It was a quite extraordinary and rather frightening kind of devotion. It left her vulnerable, at every point; it confirmed the hopelessness of her prospects even as Lawrence made his demands on her; while the object of her devotion might well feel, as the Lawrence character in Helen Corke's *Neutral Ground* feels about the Jessie character, 'as if she'd rolled a blessed *Federdecke* round you and tied you in'. As Lawrence remarked in October 1910, probably thinking of Jessie, 'There is nothing more tormenting . . . then to be loved overmuch.'[44] He had told Blanche Jennings in 1908 how 'one woman . . . yearns to nurse me and soothe me. But I will not have it' (i. 62). He nevertheless went on having it, on his own terms. Being with Jessie was not often a joy for Lawrence – she was not the kind of person to lift the heart; but at this stage of his life he badly needed her support, her companionship, her appreciation – the 'taking seriously' which she was so extraordinarily good at. He was also an expert in the secret satisfactions of self-sacrifice; he had seen them in his mother, all his life, and also in Ann Chambers. He probably disliked himself and Jessie, even while accepting her devotion.

IV 'The makings of a very considerable novelist'

The following morning, Jessie went with Lawrence to visit Hueffer and Violet Hunt: the latter 'rich, and a fairly well-known novelist' (i. 144). This gave Jessie just a glimpse of the metropolitan literary world in which Lawrence was starting to move; it also, incidentally, introduced her to a couple who lived together without being married. Lawrence had had lunch with Hueffer and Violet Hunt a fortnight earlier, and in the afternoon Hueffer had taken him to tea in Hampstead with Ernest and Grace Rhys, both successful writers and editors (Rhys had invented and edited the Everyman series of books for Dent); they had then called on H. G. Wells and met his family (i. 144). Two days after that Lawrence had met Ezra Pound for the first time, at Violet Hunt's; he stayed with him in Kensington at least once, in December 1909, and never forgot him 'in an attic with some pliers and a patty pan heating frankincense over a candle "to recover some of the aroma of the East in your filthy London"'. In the company of the exotic Pound he had also met W. B. Yeats. 'Aren't the folks kind to me: it is really wonderful', he had remarked to Louie Burrows (i. 145). Now, with Jessie beside him and 'the spectacle of London's opulence' before them on their way to Hueffer's flat in Holland Park, Lawrence exclaimed: 'I'll make two thousand a year!'[45] Jessie however was not impressed: she thought Lawrence could do more interesting things than make money.

Lunch with Hueffer and Violet Hunt passed off well; 'a young American poet', almost certainly Pound, was there as well and kept the conversation going. The meal was excellent, and Jessie noted 'how the gravy ran down into the dish when Violet Hunt carved the joint, and brussel sprouts I had never seen so perfectly cooked – each one sound and whole'. Such were the advantages of polite society. Jessie's only awkward moment came, Violet Hunt recalled, when 'she turned ... and asked my maid, who was handing the potatoes, in a speaking whisper whether she should keep her gloves on'. Kensington was a long way from the midday meal in the Haggs kitchen, and Jessie had no experience to guide her. But Violet Hunt was kind and reassuring, and told her after lunch that 'Mr. Hueffer would do all he could for Lawrence, and they would both talk about his novel to their friends.'[46] Jessie could be confident that, with such patrons, Lawrence was fairly launched.

And Hueffer was also engaged in the most important job of all: reading 'Nethermere'. On 1 November 1909 Lawrence told Blanche Jennings how he had just sent him up the book – 'much altered. I have added a third part, have married Lettie and Leslie and George and Meg, and Emily to a stranger and myself to nobody. Oh Lord – what a farce' (i. 141). Hueffer immediately read the great mass of manuscript (over 700 pages of small blue-lined paper) 'with the greatest cheery sort of kindness and bluff'. By 20 November, a few days before Jessie came to London, Lawrence knew that Hueffer thought it 'good' (i. 144) in spite of his predisposition against it: and, as Lawrence later remembered, 'in his queer voice, when we were in an omnibus in London, he shouted in my ear: "It's got every fault that the English novel can have ... But," shouted Hueffer in the bus, "you've got GENIUS." '[47] And on 15 December 1909, Hueffer – 'the kindest man on earth' Lawrence had called him in September (i. 138) – wrote Lawrence a letter to introduce him and his book to a publisher:

84 Holland Park Avenue W.

Dec. 15 09

Dear Mr Lawrence,

I have now read your novel, and have read it with a great deal of interest, which, in the case of a person who has to read so many MSS as I do, is in itself a remarkable testimonial. I don't think I could use it in the 'E[nglish] R[eview]' for several reasons, the chief of them being its inordinate length. As you know, I like to publish a serial in four numbers, and a quarter of your book would take up almost half the Review. But I don't think that this great length would militate against its popularity with the public, for both the public and the libraries like long books. Properly handled, I think it might have a very considerable success, and I don't think that in these matters I am at all a bad judge; but a great deal depends on its being properly handled, and if you are sending the MSS to a publisher, I should advise you to try one of the most active – that is to say one who already has the ear of the public. As you must probably be aware, the book, with its enormous prolixity of detail, sins against almost every canon of art as I conceive it. It is, that is to say, of the school of Mr William de Morgan – or perhaps still more of the school of Lorna Doone. But I am not so limited as to fail to appreciate other schools than my own, and I can very fully admire your very remarkable and poetic gifts. I certainly think you have in you the makings of a very considerable novelist, and I should not have the least hesitation in prophesying for you a great future, did I not know how much a matter of sheer luck one's career always is. With this in view I should advise you in approaching a publisher to promise him at least the refusal of several of your future works. This means that he will be encouraged to make efforts with your first book with some confidence that if it succeeds you will not immediately abandon him for another firm.

Yours sincerely
Ford Madox Hueffer[48]

Although the letter makes no mention of a particular publisher, Hueffer had advised Lawrence to try the firm of William Heinemann – and his reference to 'the school of Mr William de Morgan' would not have been lost on Heinemann, De Morgan's publisher.[49] The same day as Hueffer wrote his letter, Lawrence sent Heinemann a copy of it, 'to offer you the novel of which he speaks' (i. 149). Heinemann very naturally asked to see the manuscript; only a month later, on Friday 21 January 1910, Lawrence was called up to London to see William Heinemann in person; 'he read me his readers crits: mostly good. I am to alter a bit in parts, then the thing will come out, and I shall have royalties' (i. 152). Heinemann – or, to be exact, his editor Sidney Pawling, a 'clever man behind the sleepiest features in London' – though accepting the novel, thought it should be shorter; Pawling also requested the removal of some offensive language. But, as Jessie Chambers put it, 'A kind of transfiguration from obscurity and uncertainty had taken place . . . And it had all come about so simply, almost without effort. There was a glamour about those days, even something of a glitter.'[50]

In the early spring of 1910 Lawrence had some assistance from his friend Helen Corke to help him meet Heinemann's criticisms of the book's length. As she wrote later, he asked her in February to 'read the manuscript and make suggestions, especially marking passages that show prolixity'. She should also look out for 'split infinitives and obscurities of phrase' (Heinemann had presumably objected to them too). Lawrence himself tried to expurgate his manuscript to make it suitable for (as he called them) 'the old ladies of Croydon', and by 9 March he thought he had 'nearly finished the novel ready for the publisher' (i. 156). However he continued to work hard at it during the Easter holidays (25 March–3 April), finishing it 'in a rare sunny mood', Jessie remembered.[51] He submitted the manuscript to Heinemann for the second time on 11 April 1910. Characteristically, in view of the revisions he would subsequently make in his novel-writing career, he had done far more than Heinemann had asked for.

It has been a new labour of Hercules. A good deal of it, including the whole of the third part, I have re-written. To be sure, it needed it. I think I have removed all the offensive morsels, all the damns, the devils and the sweat. I hope nothing of the kind remains . . . I am sorry, also, that I could not compress it any further. It is a pity, but I could not cut my man to fit your cloth. I have snipped him where I could, and have tried to make him solid. (i. 158)

Although Lawrence professed himself 'the most docile, the most amenable of pens', his politeness attempted to disguise the fact that he had actually done very little about Heinemann's requests for cuts. He now anticipated a further attack on the book's length. As early as November 1908, he had remarked that 'I will defend my construction throughout' (i. 92); he had a strong sense of what the book was like, of the oppositions it set up; and although its construction is certainly unconventional (most critics attack it much to their own satisfaction), Lawrence knew how it consciously and sometimes laboriously establishes its themes, both in detail and over the novel as a whole. He had, after all, spent four years working on it.

Pawling, at William Heinemann, after going through the book between 11 and 25 April, wrote back (as Lawrence had expected) to point out that he had expected cuts. Lawrence replied almost immediately:

I think the novel is complete and final in its form as I have sent it you; also I think you will not find it actually so lengthy as the weight of the M.S. might lead one to suppose . . . I will delete as much as I can in phrases and perhaps here and there a paragraph from the proofs, but there are now no passages of any length that I could take out. (i. 159)[52]

Pawling gave in. 'Heinemann was very nice: doesn't want me to alter anything' Lawrence told Helen Corke on 1 June (i. 161). The only problem remaining was that of the book's title. It had originally been 'Laetitia', and then – as submitted in December, perhaps on Hueffer's advice – 'Nethermere'. But the publisher was unhappy with that title too, and from 1 June to 15 July Lawrence discussed alternatives with Heinemann's reader Frederick Atkinson. Lawrence suggested – 'to give a truly rural odour' –

'Lapwings', 'Pee wits', 'The Cry of the Peacock' and 'The White Peacock': or – 'take a parable to explain a parable' – 'The Talent in the Napkin' and 'The Talent, the Beggar, and the Box' (i. 163). A little later he offered 'Tendrils', or 'Tendrils Outreach', or 'Outreaching Tendrils' or 'Outreach of Tendrils' (i. 167). At some stage 'Crab-apples' was also a possibility (i. 169). Although Lawrence was certainly responsible for the final title – he included it in a list on 14 June – who actually selected it is unclear, since Lawrence firmly rejected it on 24 June: 'That "White Peacock" must be shot: it is a bird from the pen of Wilkie Collins or of Ibsen' (i. 166). It may well have been Atkinson who finally adopted it: it was perhaps just as well that he did.

V   *The White Peacock*

Three months after the publication of the novel in January 1911, Lawrence remarked that not only is 'the tragic' the 'most holding, the most vital thing in life', but that, in literature, 'all great works' are tragedies: 'Tragedy is beautiful also. This is my creed' (i. 261–2). He had been reading Gilbert Murray's translations of Euripides' tragedies in 1909 and 1910, and had read the *Bacchae* of Euripides in May 1910, immediately after finishing the last draft of 'Nethermere'. In the final version of the novel, choruses of natural beings in the storm utter their commentary upon life: the lapwings

> seemed to seek the storm, yet to rail at it. They wheeled in the wind, yet never ceased to complain of it. They enjoyed the struggle, and lamented it in wild lament, through which came the sound of exultation. All the lapwings cried, cried the same tale "Bitter, bitter the struggle—for nothing, nothing, nothing"—and all the time they swung about on their broad wings, revelling.

As early as March 1909 Lawrence had been convinced that 'great sympathetic minds are all overwhelmed by the tragic waste, and pity, and suffering of it' (i. 120); and his first novel might easily have been a celebration of tragic helplessness: as Lettie says, in dismay, 'If we move the blood rises in our heel-prints!'[53]

Yet the characters of *The White Peacock* are tragic not because they are helpless, or because they live in a brutal and dehumanised world, but because they work out the consequences of their natures. George's love for Lettie, for example, however compelling it is at moments, can never master his tendency to inertia. His struggle is only intermittent; it is transmuted into an undemanding marriage, an energetic but brief and cynical involvement in politics, a sloppily run business. Finally, after a last meeting with Lettie (now married to Leslie), any desire to struggle he may still have is swallowed up in the hopeless self-contempt of a drunkard. A dreadful, decaying kind of inertia characterises George at the end of the book: 'Like a tree that is falling, going soft and pale and rotten, clammy with small fungi, he stood leaning against the gate, while the dim afternoon drifted with a sweet flow of thick sunshine past him, not touching him.'[54] George's life suggests that the worst fate of all is not to be touched by one's experience.This was the conclusion Lawrence came to about George, over the years between 1906 and 1910: that his struggle was not, in the end, heroic, or fortunate, or even unfortunate or tragic, but given up: abandoned. In one sense, George *has* realised his nature, because he is not a struggler; he is an accepter who finally accepts his own decay. Perhaps his situation is the more terrible because he partly realises, partly dare not realise, what has happened. When, on the penultimate page of the novel, Cyril rather brutally reminds him of what he might have been, George's 'momentary agony of fear and despair was frightful'.[55]

It is at such moments that *The White Peacock*, for all its extraordinarily period quality, shows its links with Lawrence's subsequent work. Never again would Lawrence write so extensively to please the taste of his contemporaries; never again would the social world of his fiction create such an uneasily middle-class version of family life. Everyday problems and realities are evaded almost completely; a fantasy world is substituted in which versions of his own favourite people (Lydia and Ada Lawrence at 'Woodside', Edmund, Alan and Jessie Chambers at 'The Mill') live untouched by real problems – and in the case of Lydia and Ada, without the particular problems of husband, father or money. No other of Lawrence's books would be so allusive, so intellectual, so playful, so sententious, so extensively a memorial to the extent of an intelligent man's captivation by the second-rate and the second-hand.

But although Lawrence wrote in an essay on 1 September 1925 that 'I have never read one of my own published works', a month earlier he had told a visiting journalist, Kyle Crichton, how

Last year in Mexico I reread *The White Peacock* for the first time in fifteen years. It seemed strange and far off and as if written by somebody else. I wondered how I could have thought of some of the things or how I could have written them. And then I'd come on something that showed I may have changed in style or form, but I haven't changed fundamentally.[56]

Lawrence may well have just looked through *The White Peacock* in Mexico, rather than have reread it; but his commentary is characteristic. In George he had described a kind of response to oneself, and to the world, to which as a writer he had returned time after time: the response of a man for the most part almost unconscious of his own feelings; a man much simpler than the over-refined, conscious Leslie character, yet also clumsier; passionate, exemplifying 'the brute in man' (i. 88), instinctive where Leslie is self-conscious – but unable to take firm hold on his life and eventually trapped within it.

Against such a man, Lawrence set Leslie Tempest: the man both passionate and refined, but with too much breeding and self-awareness ever to be entirely himself, fearful of his own feelings, standing back from and vividly aware of his experience, while simultaneously sensually pressing ahead into it. Leslie is split, partial, intensely aware of his predicament; more open to satire and to the savage alienation of caricature than to tragedy. Lawrence returned to him time after time, too.

On the other hand, in Lettie he first described the special type of woman with whom he would constantly confront such men. She is wilful, predatory, dominant, intelligent, fearful of sexuality but desiring above all else to exert her power. She denies men their independence; she prefers to turn them into children. She despises them as a result; and tends to despise herself, too. That is precisely imaged when we see the married Lettie, at the end of *The White Peacock*, combing the hair of the disappointed George. She can only cope with him when he is both her child and her amusement, only lightly touched (as a plaything might be), and never allowed real contact in return. Her actions trivialise him, and her pun on 'parting' is deeply unfeeling: ' "I believe you *would* have a parting," she said softly . . . She continued combing, just touching, pressing the strands in place with the tips of her fingers.' The moneyed, upper-class pointlessness of Lettie's own life is the price she has paid for her power: our last vision of her is as a woman who 'dropped herself on the settee, and lay with her bosom against the cushions, looking fixedly at the wall'.[57] Her achievement of independence deprives her of human contact. There is also a strong feeling that her sexuality – at first diverted into playful power games – is later stultified and thwarted. She cannot in the end be a sexual being, because that would mean admitting the human contact she finds herself unable to bear.

While it is rather too simple to see in the two male characters an opposition simply true of Lawrence's own personal experience, there can be no doubt that in such divisions he felt he was portraying something of the very first importance, both to himself and to his contemporaries. Leslie and George offer parallel but opposed kinds of twentieth-century experience: the sophistication of the townee supplanting the instinctiveness of the countryman: the modern and permanently rootless confronting the old and gradually unrooted. There are obvious connections with the opposed roles taken by Lawrence's own parents; but when, for example, he insisted upon his own commonplaceness to Blanche Jennings, he was showing how aware he was of an exactly similar division within himself: 'Did you like my photo? It is not bad. It represents me in gross; it has no subtlety; there is no insight in it; I like it exceedingly: I like myself bluff, rather ordinary, fat, a bit "manly"' (i. 104) (see Illustration 15). Against that, we can set his description in 'A Modern Lover' of a photograph on the mantelpiece in the farmhouse of Muriel's family, just as Lawrence's photograph occupied the place of honour in the farmhouse of the Chambers family: 'the photo, which had been called the portrait of an intellectual prig ... was really that of a sensitive, alert, exquisite boy'[58] (see Illustrations 13 and 14). Both the bluff and the exquisite were possibilities in self-portraiture for Lawrence; the dangers of being the exquisite boy lay in being an intellectual prig: the bluff and resilient person, however, ran the risk of dullness and insentience. Both types, in the long run, were painfully condemned to separation of one form or another. And neither is a match for Lettie. What power the book retains comes largely from the combination of her manipulative sexuality with her regret that she has to use it.

But, rereading *The White Peacock* in 1924, Lawrence would have found in the narrator Cyril another permanent possibility: the damaged and father-less child remaining on the sidelines as an observer, and growing into an adult who longs to be comforted; and who, in spite of an extraordinary artistic sensitivity, never belongs anywhere. In one sense, the character mediates between George and Leslie; yet he has the strengths (and there-fore possibilities) of neither, because he hardly operates on the plane of the everyday at all, being in no way engaged *with* people, or surroundings, or possibilities, or fulfilments. Lawrence may well, in 1910 and again in 1924, have said to himself that although he feared to be like George and knew what it was like to be Leslie, of this range of life's possibilities he would fear most of all to be like Cyril. Even George, pappy with inertia and unfulfil-ment at the end of the novel, is capable of moments of poignant realisation; even Leslie has his moments of passion and possession. Cyril can only observe and feel nostalgic.

Above all, the figure of Annable stands as the first in a line of opponents and outsiders in Lawrence's fiction. Annable is, appropriately, a gamekeeper: a man with the actual social role of an outsider. Gamekeepers, as Lawrence had seen them on the estates around Eastwood and Under-wood,[59] preserved the game of the landowners against the predations of the industrial working class who lived in the towns and villages; but most gamekeepers would themselves originally have been from the working class.

The gamekeeper is thus distrusted by both his employer and by his original class; although knowing his region and its inhabitants intimately, he will have almost no recognisable social role among them. He is déclassé: an employee, yet curiously independent, living the nearest thing to the wood-land lives of James Fenimore Cooper's characters which can be imagined in twentieth-century England. Annable is also a stunted and thwarted man, the tragic materialist which at one stage Lawrence also feared to be; Haeckelian in his rejection of anything except the material, Schopenhauerean (as Lawrence understood Schopenhauer) in his insistence upon sex, Nietzs-chean in his nihilism, Spencerian in his edict 'Be a good animal'.[60] He haunts Cyril's commentaries on the lives of George, Meg, Leslie and Lettie; his children sprawl with the fecundity of symbolism, and with a liveliness Lawrence borrows from Dickens.

But he hardly balances the book, or makes up for the contrasting presence of Cyril. Annable is dead before the middle of the book; is at best a literary device, an idea of something other and dangerous and necessary. And Lawrence's versions of sexual appeal in the novel are limited to flagrant sexual allure and motherly acceptance. Like his narrator Cyril, he seems both fascinated and appalled by most sexual behaviour. For all its themes, its richness, its cleverness, the book successfully *refuses* the adult world; it remains locked within the confines of its local and mostly adolescent prob-lems. It very strongly suggests what Lawrence had to work through, as a young man; it cannot go much beyond that.

And, appropriately, *The White Peacock* borrows more than any other novel by Lawrence from literature and art; it is, in its very essence, an artistic creation. Michael Black has pointed out how

The literary ancestors might be George Eliot's pairs of young people in *Mid-dlemarch*, or Tolstoy's pairs in *Anna Karenina*; or one might see George Saxton as a failed version of Hardy's Gabriel Oak in *Far from the Madding Crowd*. More strik-ingly, the strong rustic pair at the farm (George, Emily) set against an overbred pair from a cultivated drawing room (Lettie and Cyril) may remind the reader of *Wuthering Heights* – Lettie's wilfulness and charm and her disastrous choice are very like Catherine Earnshaw's.

H. M. Daleski has pointed out, too, the extraordinary parallels between the novel and George Eliot's *The Mill on the Floss*.[61] The literary and philosophical content of *The White Peacock* is the surest indication of the intellectual and artistic climate in which Lawrence was brought up, and of the readership for which he designed it. It reveals his original idea of what a novel was, as it charts his progress from the man who in the spring of 1906 had published nothing and written only a few poems, to the man who –

when the book was published – while remaining a suburban schoolteacher moved in advanced circles, had met Wells and Yeats, stayed with Pound, impressed Hueffer and was published by the most prestigious literary review in England.

CHAPTER NINE

◆

1909–1910

STRIFE

I The Literary World

Lawrence received proofs of *The White Peacock* at the end of August 1910, but it is hard to convey how much his life had changed by then, compared with his situation when he had submitted the novel to Heinemann.

Apart from Hueffer's habit of introducing him as 'a genius' – 'I wish Hueffer wouldn't' (i. 171), Lawrence commented, but Conrad too noted how 'H. loves to manage people'[1] – Lawrence seems at first mostly to have relished his first experience of literary life in the autumn of 1909, and to have enjoyed the 'glamour' Jessie Chambers remembered. He sounds, however, another note for the first time in a letter of 11 December 1909, when he explains that he is going out 'to meet various poetry people. I am to take some of my unpublished verses to read. I do not look forward to these things much. I shall feel such a fool' (i. 147). To people in the literary world, he continued to be an oddity: Violet Hunt, who liked him very much, could not help thinking of him as 'a board-school boy grown to man's estate', and was surprised to find him 'gentle, modest, and tender, in a way I did not associate with his upbringing'. She obviously expected a man from the working class to be coarser-grained, and she felt her opinion confirmed when she heard his 'brusque way of discoursing about intimate things'.[2] A reminiscence by the literary editor Ernest Rhys of a poetry evening in Hampstead (internal evidence shows it to be a composite reminiscence) suggests how easily Lawrence could be pigeonholed as provincial. When asked to read, according to Rhys,

He rose nervously but very deliberately, walked across to a writing desk whose lid was closed, opened it, produced a mysterious book out of his pocket, and sat down, his back to the company, and began to read in an expressive, not very audible voice. One could not hear every word or every line clearly, but what was heard left an impression of a set of love-poems, written with sincerity and not a little passion, interspersed with others written in dialect not easy to follow . . .[3]

The oddity and bad manners Rhys recalls – Lawrence reading 'on and on' with his back to the company and boring people till Rhys told him 'he must want a little rest' – is called into question by Rhys's memory of having heard a number of dialect poems. In November 1909 Lawrence had copied only one dialect poem into the 'black book' Rhys remembered him using (the first of the two college notebooks in which he kept copies of his poems). But Lawrence was 'provincial', and Rhys's reminiscence is devoted to creating a distinctively regional impression of the man and his work. Lawrence met the Scottish poet Rachel Annand Taylor a little later, at the Rhyses' house, and went to dinner with her in October 1910; he never forgot 'a frail little dinner-party where the china seemed to crack if one spoke aloud' (iv. 304). She, too, thought him best defined by his class orientations: 'He was a terrific snob, he was definitely a cad, yet in this early period he was touching, he was so artlessly trying to find his way.'[4] The 'artlessly' once again shows that Lawrence struck the memoirist as essentially ignorant of the literary world. The creator of Cyril Beardsall was both a self-conscious artist, and naive by metropolitan standards. In March 1910, just before another evening at the Rhyses 'to meet some celebrities, and to read some of my own verses', Lawrence confessed 'I am not very keen, and not very much interested. I am no Society man – it bores me' (i. 156). He had learnt that such events were primarily social rather than literary, and the people he met there made him feel 'clownish' (i. 491), though he was capable of producing a brilliant vignette of society manners, as in his description of Violet Hunt's social display: 'She is very dexterous: flips a bright question, lifts her eyebrows in deep concern, glances from the man on her right to the lady on her left, smiles, bows, and suddenly, – quick curtain – she is gone, and is utterly someone else's, she who was altogether ours a brief second before' (i. 170).

We know a good deal about his life on the fringes of literary circles at the end of 1909 through his correspondence and meetings with Grace Crawford. The latter was the daughter – with artistic ambitions – of wealthy American parents living in London. She had got to know the émigré Ezra Pound; and through Pound she had 'heard, for the first time, the name D. H. Lawrence' and about 'his coal-mining background, his defensive touchiness'. Pound introduced them, though only after she had specially asked: 'Ezra said he was too shy and difficult, would probably dislike me and my background and that a meeting between us could not be a success.'[5] Even Pound thought Lawrence was a 'difficult' outsider in such circles.

Grace Crawford's first impression of Lawrence was of a somewhat lower-class man tidied to meet the middle classes: 'a very "everyday young man", with a small, drooping moustache, carefully brushed hair and heavy clumpy boots'. The boots were doubtless Lawrence's own old and embarrassing 'button boots', of which he was always very conscious; in 1910 he complained to her that he hadn't enough money 'to buy a decent pair' (i. 171), and by July 1911 those same boots had finally become 'not presentable' (i. 286). But although Grace Crawford thought that every now and then Lawrence would bring in some reference to his background 'just to see how I would react',[6] Lawrence's first letter to her, written the day after he met her, shows how capable he was of holding his own in artistic circles. The language of his letter is beautifully turned, to the point of being thoroughly pretentious; it is quite the reverse of artless.

> Here is the 'morceau' of Francis Thompson: no 'Hound', but an exquisite little thing written as most of Thompson's are on a dim sad day when the dew stays grey on the grass. Poor Thompson! Poor me and my rhetorics . . .
> It is a shame to break the moment from its stalk, to wither in the vase of memory, by thanking you.
>
> Addio   D. H. Lawrence
>
> What an ass I am! (i. 145–6)

It is not a new tone in his surviving correspondence, but it is even more mannered and poetic than the tone he had adopted to Blanche Jennings in 1908. It tells us a good deal about what he thought of his correspondent. Again and again, writing to Grace Crawford, he launched into apologies: for his 'rotten paper' (i. 148) – he no longer had any of the superior writing paper he had used for Blanche Jennings; for his verses (i. 149), his failure to return a book and his reluctance to call (i. 164–5), his shyness (i. 165), his failure to answer a note (i. 170), his description of the family kitchen in Eastwood: 'You may as well know what it's like: even though you may not be interested' (i. 174). But, as that last remark suggests, the artistic manner originally adopted for her benefit (which he could mimic to perfection, but which always radiated unease) gradually changed to a more cheerful camaraderie.

He knew, nevertheless, that certain of his writings and experiences were not for the likes of Grace Crawford, or the circles of the polite middle and upper-middle class in which her family moved. He had no intention, for example, of sending her the manuscript of 'The Saga of Siegmund', written during the spring and summer of 1910, and categorised by Hueffer as 'erotic' (i. 339): 'it would not, I am afraid, interest you much' (i. 183) he told her. Writing a letter during his mother's last illness in the autumn of 1910, and feeling 'as miserable as the devil', as usual he apologised for his feelings: 'you are the last person to whom I should pen my jeremiads' (i. 183). Grace Crawford was bright, young, shiningly 'artistic' – what had *she* to do with sexuality, death or real life? When he sent her the manuscript of his play *The Widowing of Mrs. Holroyd*, his customary apology involved some sarcasm at her expense:

Here is the MSS. I shudder to think of its intruding like a muddy shaggy animal into your 'den', sacred to the joss-stick and all vaporous elegantly-wreathed imaginations of literature. I like something in which the outline is fairly definitely laid. I like corporeality. You have a weakness for spirits – not bottled, but booked . . .

Don't let Mrs Crawford read the thing – it's too common. Mothers like stuff to be decently high-falutin. (i. 188).

Such a play was decidedly not for Cyril, not for the drawing-room, nor for the parent, nor (perhaps) for the unmarried woman; the Crawfords had their artistic inclinations, but art as they understood it was 'decently high-falutin'. The appearance of an ear-ring in Ezra Pound's right ear had made Grace Crawford's father tell his daughter she 'had better drop him entirely', and shows how little time the Crawfords had for the really unconventional. Although Lawrence was happy to move occasionally in their circle, and Grace Crawford herself was more than happy to shine in his company and her parents (devoted to her) very pleased to encourage the young genius they understood Lawrence to be – yet they also actively discouraged the friendship when they felt their daughter was getting too fond of the young man from the Midlands.[7] Their conception of the artist's life would not have included an alliance with a working-class elementary schoolmaster.

Lawrence's correspondence with Grace Crawford not only reveals his shrewdness in understanding the expectations and hesitations (as well as the language) of those middle-class 'artistic' circles. It also shows the pleasure he took in such language. He may, truly, have preferred what he called 'corporeality': but 'Odour of Chrysanthemums' and his plays apart, most of his writing in 1910 – the new third section of 'Nethermere' and almost all of 'The Saga of Siegmund' – was 'artistic' in a way he developed in London, according to his conception of an audience which – though not 'polite' quite as the Crawfords were – was at least appreciative of the poetic qualities of prose.

This is strikingly obvious in the paper on the poet Rachel Annand Taylor which he delivered to the Croydon branch of the English Association in November 1910. On the one hand, he shows himself fascinated with the romanticism and luscious decadence of the poetry and poet he describes. On the other, he looses a devouring irony on it and her – she with her 'long white languorous hands of the correct subtle radiance. All that a poetess should be.' When he says that, as a child, 'She lived apart from life, and still she cherishes a yew-darkened garden in her soul where she can remain withdrawn, sublimating experience into odours',[8] it is genuinely hard to distinguish the irony from the fascination. He writes the prose of a man who has seen through a falsity and can now judge it to a hair's breadth – and yet remains nostalgic for it, and will defend it against the philistines.

Mrs Taylor, in her second volume, "Rose and Vine" published last year, makes the splashes of verse from her spilled treasure of love. But they are not crude startling bloody drops. They are vermeil and gold and beryl green. Mrs Taylor takes the "pageant of her bleeding heart," first marches it ironically by the brutal daylight, then lovingly she draws it away into her magic, obscure place apart, where she breathes spells upon it, filters upon it delicate lights, tricks it with dreams and fancy, and then re-issues the pageant.[9]

Her 'art' is that of sensual music. Lawrence has abandoned the socialist positions he tried out in 'Art and the Individual' in 1908; he demands that art be emotionally sufficient, sensual, actual. It makes him sound defensive, not to say evasive.

In his reminiscences of Lawrence, Hueffer – probably irritated that his protégé had refused to conform to his own conception of the working-class genius – attributed the change in Lawrence's writing which he saw in 'The Saga of Siegmund' in 1910 to Lawrence's having 'come under the subterranean-fashionable influences that made for Free Love as a social and moral arcanum'.[10] Lawrence was certainly influenced by fashion, but he had always written about 'Free Love': the very first version of 'Laetitia' had revolved around its consequences. What Lawrence remembered Hueffer saying about 'The Saga' in 1910–11 is more revealing. He called it 'a rotten work of genius. It has no construction or form – it is execrably bad art, being all variations on a theme. Also it is erotic – not that I, personally, mind that, but an erotic work *must* be good art, which this is not' (i. 339). Hueffer made the crucial word 'art': and his ideal post-Flaubertian art is a product of 'construction' and 'form'. To Hueffer, Lawrence had stopped writing his 'naturally' artistic 'sort of long book'[11] when he wrote 'The Saga' – the word 'artless' is not far away – and was now experimenting with a form he was not equipped to handle. But, as Lawrence himself knew, the problems of 'The Saga' had little to do with its construction (which he admitted to be 'gorgeous tableaux-vivants' – i. 229). Its faults were its 'fluid, luscious quality' (i. 351), the way it was 'too florid, too "chargé"' (i. 358): ' "chargé" as a Prince Rupert's Drop (if you know that curiosity): its purple patches glisten sicklily' (i. 229). Far from not being 'artistic' enough, it was (as Lawrence well knew) 'artistic' with a vengeance. And it shared with those letters to Grace Crawford, and his analysis of Rachel Annand Taylor, a special language for 'art', although its 'erotic' quality disqualified it from the Crawfords' drawing-room.

Lawrence's work in the period 1909–10 was torn between the 'artistic' as he understood it (and was attracted by it), and the working-class realism which people like Hueffer expected of him; while what he wanted to write was some combination of both – something 'corporeal'. His first poems about school demonstrated the problem his own standpoint as onlooker, as detached artist, caused for him when he was writing about an actual situation; the problem is still more clearly visible in a story first called 'A Blot' which he wrote in the early months of 1910.

II Class and Selfhood

The schoolmaster narrator of 'A Blot' (later 'The Fly in the Ointment') goes down to the kitchen of his London lodgings late in the evening, when the rest of the family is asleep; he has been writing to·'Muriel', who has sent him buds and flowers and who sounds very like Jessie Chambers. In imagination he has been 'keeping the atmosphere of Strelley Mill close round me'[12] – Strelley Mill being the Midlands farmhouse he loves so much, where Muriel lives (and where Emily and George live in *The White Peacock*).

In the suburban kitchen, however, he disturbs a youth who has just broken in: the youth threatens him with the poker. 'I was not unaccustomed to displays of the kind in school, and I had not the least alarm, only intense scorn and disgust. He dared not, I knew, strike, unless by trying to get hold of him I terrified him to a frenzy, to a momentary madness such as the depraved slum type is subject to.'[13] The narrator's suavity is remarkable; he *knows*, almost without looking, the 'depraved slum type' of the youth: 'He was not ugly, nor did he look ill-fed. But he evidently came of the lowest class.' The narrator questions him: what would he have taken? It is obvious that the house has not much worth stealing. ' "I might 'a took some boots" he said simply.' The narrator rounds on him: 'You dirty swine – How many times have you done this before?' Considering the condition of the feet (peeping through the holes in his boots) of the boy in 'A Snowy Day in School', such a tone is extraordinarily unsympathetic. The youth explains that he 'never could get a job'; his father does not work, his mother is 'in the laundry', his sisters work 'at the ginger place': and he himself confesses that 'I never have a hae'penny. It's sometimes three months, an' I never touch sixpence.'[14]

The youth's problems do not, however, interest the narrator; what concerns him – while not worrying the youth at all – is 'what's going to become of you?' The narrator is morally repelled at the thought:

"Get a laundry girl to marry you and live on her?" I asked, sarcastically.
He smiled sicklily, evidently even a little bit flattered. I felt very disgusted.
"And loaf at the street corners till you drop rotten?" I said.[15]

The narrator questions the boy from the position of one who works hard for his own living, and who knows what it is to be rewarded for work: he lectures the boy about it.

"But remember that, if you bucked up, and tried to make yourself decent and smart, you could get a carter's job, or a tram conductor's, very soon. But if you won't make yourself worth a job . . . you can never expect to have one given you. We don't give a cow a fiddle to play, because we know it isn't any use."

He grinned at me.

"And *you're* no use."

The animal comparison adds point to the narrator's earlier observation that the youth's voice had 'an incredibly animal mongrel sound'.[16] The narrator, however, gets no response: and, rather helplessly abandoning his role as Beatrice Webb, gives the youth a glass of beer and some food, then (treating him like a servant or a schoolboy) 'dismissed him'.

In the story as Lawrence rewrote it in 1912, to create 'The Fly in the Ointment', the narrator goes upstairs thinking that the youth 'was a blot, like a blot fallen on my soul'. But in the 1910 story it is he himself who is the blot:

I stood quite still for some minutes, up against the unpassable rock face of this man, which seemed to utterly bar the outward movement of my thought, even of my life. Then I climbed the stairs, numbed with a peculiar intense misery. It was like a nightmare. I thought I was a blot, just a blot of ink on a page, a black, heavy, disfiguring blot, with no meaning. That was one of the most dreadful nightmares I have ever suffered. It vanished when I switched on my bedroom light.[17]

The nightmare is the more extraordinary because, throughout the encounter, the narrator has been so confident in his judgement, so superior in manner and language. But his confidence now seems the frailest of bridges over swirling and unplumbed waters; the youth so utterly outside his experience and conceptions has created in him a feeling of meaninglessness and individual worthlessness. What does his *own* life add up to?

It is a peculiar, inarticulate story in its first version: but it conveys very powerfully the limits of the narrator's confidence when he is faced by someone not only poor and without a job, but without any desire to better himself. The narrator is confronted by an impassable barrier: his own sense of himself depends utterly upon his belief in his professional role; without a sense of meaning, work, prospects and progress, he is starkly terrified. Helen Corke described, with some feeling, the ill-paid situation of the elementary Croydon schoolteacher of Lawrence's generation: 'The world of wealth is remote, completely removed from mine. Much nearer is the world of extreme poverty. It is rather as if I am walking firmly along a low dyke which crosses a morass.'[18] But Lawrence's sensitivity to the peculiarity of his situation is much sharper. As was clear in the lives of his grandparents and parents, it is the person nearest the border of class who often has the intensest feeling about it: such a person is conscious not only that the dyke is low and the morass near, but that their own status and language are the most fragile of constructs. For Lawrence, from the industrial working class himself, working in a poor suburb like Croydon, conscious of his own comparative poverty, sharply aware of his status as educated and professional man, but aware too of the much intenser poverty and black hopelessness breaking in upon his cultivated (relative) security every day at school – for him, the achievement of his own life of 'getting on' sometimes felt like nothing at all, and the confident language of progress and moral certainty could strike him as a humourless and ignorant façade. London was a test on him too, not just on Jessie's table manners. His awareness of class divisions had at one stage driven him towards socialism; it might have pushed him towards entrenched superiority, of the kind the story's narrator demonstrates and which he was certainly capable of himself; but it actually drew him to think of other people according to how far they were individual, independent, proud and capable of fulfilling themselves. Such a pattern of thinking, as was natural for one of his background, tended to be religious rather than moral or social. He was drawn to insist on the primacy of inner qualities, and developed a violent distrust of status and respectability.

It was natural that this process should have started in Croydon rather than in Eastwood. It was in Croydon that Lawrence started to grapple with his awareness of his own strangely ambivalent situation, belonging as he did both to the working class and to the educated middle classes; and it was in Croydon that he first began to write poems, stories, plays and a novel not only about the lives of the working class, about poverty and alienation and about the conflict of the educated with the communal, but about the gulfs between people.

This is vividly revealed by two surviving sketches of school life which he had written by December 1909. In 'Lessford's Rabbits', the schoolteacher narrator is in charge of the free breakfasts provided at school for the really poor pupils. He knows that the free breakfasts do not really deal with the situation:

We could never get many boys to give in their names for free meals. I used to ask the Kelletts, who were pinched and pared thin with poverty:

"Are you sure you don't want either dinners or breakfasts, Kellett?"

He would look at me curiously, and say, with a peculiar small movement of his thin lips,

"No Sir."

"But have you plenty—quite plenty?"

"Yes Sir,"—he was very quiet, flushing at my questions.

The reason the boy refuses is that 'Not many parents would submit to the indignity of the officer's inquiries'; boys 'prefer to go short rather than to partake of charity meals of which all their school-mates were aware'.[19]

The story hinges, however, upon the breakfasts eaten by a boy called Lessford, who 'would have five solid pieces of bread, and then ask for more'. Lessford is actually stuffing the bread down his trousers, not eating it. When detected he refuses to explain, but 'Next day, when asked why he was absent from breakfast, he said his father had got a job.' It turns out that, with another boy, he has been fattening up rabbits to sell.

"For how much?"
   "Eightpence each."
   "And did your mothers know?"
   "No Sir." He was very subdued and guilty.
   "And what did you do with the money?"
   "Go to the Empire—generally."[20]

Like 'A Snowy Day at School', 'Lessford's Rabbits' is apparently a story about poverty; the narrator is very conscious of the 'great holes at the elbows' of Lessford's jersey. But, unlike the poem, the sketch is about a child who – although poor – does not earn to help his family. He goes to the Music Hall; he and his friend Halket are enterprising (if very small) business men who one day lose their business. Their rabbits are stolen: ' "My rabbits has all gone!" he cried, as a man would announce his wife and children slain. I heard Halket exclaim ... He was half out of the desk, his mercurial face blank with dismay.'[21] These astute, street-wise children are not victims of poverty, but of someone even more astute and street-wise than they. They are simply pathetic figures in the competitive townscape of South London; a sketch which began as if it would be about the narrator's attitude to poverty turns into a finely observed parable of commercial struggle.

The other sketch, 'A Lesson on a Tortoise', is more complex. It shows the teacher-narrator, at the end of his week, giving a Nature Study lesson to a class which includes some boys – the Gordons – from the local charity home, some boys 'from a fairly well-to-do Home for the children of actors', some really poor children and some comparatively well-off whose shoes reveal their background: they bring 'soft, light shoes to wear in school on snowy days'.[22] The class has to draw the tortoise. The narrator feels peaceful and happy: it is the last lesson on Friday afternoon, and he looks out of the window at 'a great gold sunset, very large and magnificent ... I lifted my hands, to take the sunlight on them, smiling faintly to myself, trying to shut my fingers over its tangible richness'. Somebody asks for an eraser: and although (after thefts) the narrator has said that his class will not be allowed

238

erasers again, he feels indulgent and goes back on his word. And then it
turns out that 'There's only eleven, Sir, and there were fifteen when I put
them away on Wednesday—!'[23]

The aesthetically pleasing and slightly unreal atmosphere is destroyed in
a second: 'Another of the hateful moments had come.' Poverty and meanness replace the teacher's imagination of 'richness', and he launches an
onslaught on his class:

"Again! I am sick of it, sick of it I am! A thieving, wretched set!—a skulking, mean
lot!" I was quivering with anger and distress.

"Who is it? You must know! You are all as bad as one another, you hide it—a
miserable—!" I looked round the class in great agitation. The Gordons, with their
distrustful faces, were noticeable.[24]

It is striking that the teacher should be so upset by the theft. Like the
narrator of 'A Blot', he is thoroughly, even unnaturally distressed: the
stealing touches him with disgust and repulsion. It does not belong to
human nature as he wants it to be; it demonstrates human behaviour which
he *knows* is depraved. But his language is characteristically unsure and
inadequate, behind his attempt at a robust, manly put-down.

He accuses first one, then another of the Gordon Home boys of the theft.
One of the Gordons, Wood, accuses him in turn of being 'always on to
us—!' The narrator is sure that this is 'manifestly untrue', but we have seen
the speed with which (because they have stolen in the past) he has accused
the Gordons. He threatens Wood with the cane for impudence; then, to his
chagrin, hears from the boy that 'We know who it is. Everybody knows who
it is—only they won't tell.' Some of the other boys deny knowing the
culprit, but as Wood himself remarks, 'they won't own up . . . I shouldn't 'a
done if you hadn't 'a been goin' to cane me.'[25] The teacher appeals to the
class to tell him, but they will not answer. The resourceful Wood sees a way
out and suggests a ballot: each boy must write down on a piece of paper the
name of the person he suspects.

A few papers were blank; several had 'I suspect nobody';—these I threw in the paper
basket; two had the name of an old thief, and these I tore up; eleven bore the name
of my assistant-monitor, a splendid, handsome boy, one of the oldest of the actors. I
remembered how deferential and polite he had been when I had asked him, how
ready to make barren suggestions . . .

And thus the teacher learns that Ségar, one of the boys from the 'fairly well-
to-do' actors' home and thus 'more or less gentlemanly',[26] is his thief. After
class the boy denies the charge, but the teacher nonetheless dismisses him as
monitor.

". . . You will not come into the class room, until the class comes in—any more. You understand?"

"Yes Sir"—he was very quiet.

"Go along then."

He went out, and silently closed the door. I turned out the last light, tried the cupboards, and went home.

I felt very tired, and very sick. The night had come up, the clouds were moving darkly, and the sordid streets near the school felt like disease in the lamplight.

The teacher still links the theft (and his own sickness over it) with the 'sordid streets' rather than with the 'fine, handsome lad' who is actually his thief.[27] He makes the crime a 'disease' of the streets and feels isolated in a vile and alien environment. Like 'A Blot', the story finally leaves its readers with the not-quite-articulated problem of the narrator's reaction to what disgusts him. The narrator's crisis, in both cases, is caused by his desire to believe in the fine rather than the sordid, in the gentleman rather than the lout; and by his knowledge that he himself – professional, sensitive, understanding – is wholly on the side of the gentleman. But his experience baffles him. Who really deserves his sympathy? Who is *he* in these conflicts? What should his language be, in his judgements of people? He is certain only of his violent disgust with the sordid, and of his own lack of confidence.

Such experiences were, we can guess, among the painful discoveries which Croydon brought Lawrence, as he endeavoured to chart in his writing what was happening to him. He came into close contact with poverty; but also into experiences which rocked his confidence in himself. Who and what was he? What should his attitude be to those around him? Superiority? Artistic distance? Intimacy? His social situation, his very language (like the narrator's) cuts him off from ordinary people. He is actually better at portraying his inner trouble than at judging others. Deep down, he needs to exercise another kind of judgement than the easy moral superiority with which his early experience has equipped him. He wants, too, to find a language in which to write about what people *really* are.

There are numerous other examples of such an ambivalence in Lawrence's writing and experience during this period. When Jessie Chambers came to visit him in London in November 1909, one of the things he insisted on showing her was 'the human wreckage preparing to spend the night on the Embankment', while he also wanted her 'to see the bridges at night, with the lights of the trams reflected, as he had described them in his poems'.[28] The city at night seen with the eye and language of the self-concious artist had an odd glamour about it, as did boys with broken boots, or the boy encountered in the snow. This is reflected, too, in the third part of *The White Peacock*, which draws on what Lawrence saw of London in

1908–10. The detachment and aesthetic raptures of such passages are, however, only a step away from insufferable moral superiority. As with his attraction to the poetry of Rachel Annand Taylor, we cannot be sure whether it is love or irony which guides him; the aesthetic position is also clearly febrile, over-bred, self-satisfied, incapable of dealing with fundamentals; at best only a strategy for keeping deeper conflicts at bay.

The best example of this comes in the very first of Lawrence's Midlands stories, 'Odour of Chrysanthemums'. This did in part what Hueffer wanted Lawrence to do – convey the ordinary life of a Midlands family. But having in the first part of the story written an incomparable account of the tensions in the lives of ordinary people in the mining community – Lawrence described it as 'a story full of my childhood's atmosphere' (i. 471) – he turned its ending in the 1909 and 1910 versions of the story into a lugubrious moral epistle about drunkenness and death. Mrs Bates's husband is killed at work; her hatred and disgust for him and his drinking are instantly transformed into a sentimental preference for him dead: 'She loved him so much now; her life was mended again, and her faith looked up with a smile; he had come home to her, beautiful. How she had loathed him! It was strange he could have been such as he had been. How wise of death to be so silent!'[29] Lawrence is having huge problems dealing with Mrs Bates's moral superiority to her husband. In effect he shares her superiority and sentimentality. Writing which had begun by presenting lives intimately and with complexity took on, instead, a deadly commentator's voice which, in Lawrence's 1911 revisions, would speak even more distinctly *de haut en bas*. Mr Bates, we hear, 'betrayed himself in the search for amusement. Let Education teach us to amuse ourselves, necessity will force us to work. Once out of the pit, there was nothing to interest this man. He sought the public house, where, by paying the price of his own integrity, ⟨ . . . ⟩ he found amusement . . .'[30] Lawrence made room for such interpolations by cutting out many of the earlier details of the family's life: the playing of the children, and what is revealed about the divided family, were considerably shortened. The moralism is proclaimed without the kind of context which allows a narrator's uneasy position to be part of a story's meaning, as in 'A Blot'. Phrases like 'the recreant maimed and destroyed himself' can only be read as simple and unironic: the narrator is not only artistically detached, but deeply absurd in his moralising about the sordid lives of the drinking classes.

We must remember however that Lawrence had previously written nothing equivalent to such a story: had never attempted to set out his intimate knowledge of the working class in the full glare of an 'artistic' creation for the middle-class reading public. He would not do so again until the first version of 'Paul Morel' in the autumn of 1910; and even the second draft of that novel would be distinctly uneasy in its narrative commentary on the working class. The bulk of Lawrence's fiction in 1909–10 (his continuing work on 'Nethermere', the story 'Goose Fair' – which he wrote jointly with Louie Burrows between the summer and winter of 1909 – and 'The Saga of Siegmund', begun in April 1910) was more conventionally 'literary', oriented towards a middle-class readership, rather accomplished and rather less interesting: it does not get itself entangled with the problems seen in 'A Blot', 'A Lesson on a Tortoise' and 'Odour of Chrysanthemums'. Even his 1910 poems about school are more conventionally literary and more rhapsodic than those of 1909: the boys who caused the problems in his first poems and sketches are addressed idealistically, as in 'A Still Afternoon in School': 'Oh my boys bending over your books/In you is trembling and fusing the creation/Of a new-patterned dream, dream of a generation'.[31] Lawrence appears to have kept his troubled awareness of his own status as man and artist so far as possible out of his fiction in 1909–10. As a result, his fiction was impoverished, except where he could overcome the problems of narrative stance in another genre altogether: drama.

III Plays

Lawrence showed Jessie Chambers his play *A Collier's Friday Night* when she visited Croydon in November 1909:[32] by the end of 1910, he had also completed the first version of *The Widowing of Mrs. Holroyd*, and had begun *The Merry-Go-Round* in 'the interminable watches of the bedroom' (i. 200) during his mother's last illness, November–December 1910. It is impossible to discuss *The Widowing of Mrs. Holroyd* as work of 1910, because its only surviving text is the revision Lawrence made in August 1913, when he was convinced that he had made it 'heaps better' (ii. 58). If it altered as much as its companion piece, 'Odour of Chrysanthemums', then it must have changed enormously.

The other two plays, however, show how successfully Lawrence could write in 1909–10 outside the literary genres of 'Nethermere' and 'The Saga of Siegmund': and although he later described *A Collier's Friday Night* as 'most horribly green',[33] he was quite wrong. Its very subject sets the play in stark and ironical contrast with the Burns poem ('The Cotter's Saturday Night') which provokes its title. Burns had celebrated the unity and harmony of a family at its Saturday night meal and its pre-Sabbath devotions. But Friday night in the English Midlands around 1909 is not remotely pre-Sabbath: it is pay-night, baking-night, market-night, courting-night, the night when you go out on the town if you can afford to, when (if you cannot) you envy those who can. For many people it marks the end of the working week, and the arrival of the pay-packet: but for housewives, it simply means the continuation of work. These tensions are extremely likely to issue in family rows. For example, the educated son, Ernest Lambert, wants money for college textbooks; a college education which is pointedly unrelated to the problems of his everyday world (the books he wants are *Piers the Ploughman* and two books of Horace). They will cost 7/6 – 'And in the middle of the term too',[34] his mother points out; they wreck her budget. But she accepts his need for them without thinking. She has already been seen economising against such unexpected needs by offering her daughter Nellie potted meat for tea; only when Nellie protests are the tinned apricots (reserved for Ernest) opened. For Mr Lambert, hearing that *Piers Ploughman* is 'sheer rot' from Ernest, the problem is simply one of having ordered something you don't really want:

Father: I should non get 'em then. You nedna buy 'em unless you like — —dunna get 'em then.
Ernest Lambert: Well, I've ordered them.
Father: If you 'anna got the money, you canna 'a'e 'em, whether or not.
Mother: Don't talk nonsense, if he has to have them, he has. But the money you have to pay for books, and they're no good when you've done with them!—I'm sure it's really sickening, it is![35]

Mrs Lambert is caught between her desire to see Ernest get his college education – to her, a passport out of the slavery of the mining village to which she herself feels condemned – and the budget problems posed by books. Mr Lambert's attitude is interestingly complex. He does not pronounce on the validity of the education; he *is* shocked at the cost of unnecessary objects like books which will be no use in the future (nor in the present, so far as he can see). And he is unhappy about Ernest being given the money. It is, after all, *his* money, because he earned it: and the boy does not earn.

Ernest is thus a focus for his father's anger and his mother's defences: until, that is, Maggie Pearson (very much in the role of Jessie Chambers) arrives for her Friday evening French lesson with Ernest. Then it is Mrs Lambert who keeps her distance from her son. She goes shopping with the money from her husband's pay-packet, angry with what he has given her – only twenty-eight shillings. We have seen the men dividing the money up, and know that Mr Lambert will go out drinking on what he reckons is his share. To his wife he simply says 'I know it's a bad wik':[36] he can go out, however, because – it being Friday night – he has money too. The daughter Nellie Lambert, too – a recreation of Ada Lawrence – can go out, though not with her young man Eddie (Eddie Clarke in real life), who must work in his father's shop on Friday nights. They must wait until he has finished, after ten o'clock; and until then she has to go out with her friend Gertie Coomber (Gertie Cooper in real-life), who is also waiting for her young man to arrive. The only prospect Nellie and Gertie have ahead of them is marriage: Friday night means going out with the men who might relieve them of the pressure of life in this particular place and who might (ideally) excite them with other prospects. In fact Gertie finds her man thoroughly boring. Maggie Pearson, who loves Ernest, sees things differently; she is learning French from him. Where other girls look for boys and marriage, she looks for self-improvement. Yet, although intelligent, she is priggish and self-deceived.

Lawrence is creating a complex of attitudes; his art is that of observation, of selection and arrangement; for the man who has the wit to use it and who wants to 'get the hang of it', the material grows naturally out of the situation of an Eastwood family; he battles away at it with what Frieda later called his 'hammering energy'[37] until its potential is fully revealed. It may well be that exactly these conflicts occurred in the Lawrence family. It is extremely likely. But in *A Collier's Friday Night*, Lawrence transformed one family's tensions into an action which kept them all in play without judging them. Writing a play, he is unable to introduce the kind of moralising commentaries which interfere with the 1909–11 versions of 'Odour of Chrysanthemums'; nor does he have the problems of his uncertain fictional narrators. Instead, having to construct the entire action in realistic dialogue, he reveals a most remarkable talent for it. The whole pattern of interdependent lives in a small community is economically and precisely established. The play develops into a study of the relationship between mother and son; in particular, the mother's jealousy of Maggie Pearson, and the son's growing away from his mother.

Ernest Lambert: But I can't help it: I can't help it. I have to grow up—and things are different to us now.
Mother (*bitterly*):   Yes, things *are* different to us now. They never used to be. And you say I've never tried to care for her—I have—I've tried and tried to like her, but I can't, and it's no good.
Ernest Lambert (*pathetically*):   Well, my dear, we shall have to let it be then, and things will have to go their way. (*He speaks with difficulty*): You know, Mater—I don't care for her—really—not half as I care for you—Only just now—well I can't help it, I can't help it—but I care just the same—for you—I do.[38]

The conflict, however, has been located in the middle of the Friday night tensions. We know that Mrs Lambert is particularly worked up and unhappy over her husband's earnings: and we can see that Ernest's relationship with Maggie Pearson is also in many ways awkward and unhappy, for all that he needs her to read his writing and to talk to. She is, however, the one person who understands his intellectual needs: and those needs appear in the context of a family which naturally underrates them, which feels that other things – like earning money, and spending it wisely – are more to the point.

Lawrence uses a lot of stage directions throughout the action; at the very end, he has only stage directions to create a conclusion, as Mrs Lambert and Ernest say good-night:

Ernest Lambert: Goodnight, my dear.
Mother: Goodnight!—Don't you want a candle?
Ernest Lambert: No—blow it out,—Good night.
Mother: Goodnight (*very softly*).
>   (*There is in their tones a dangerous gentleness—so much gentleness that the safe reserve of their souls is broken. Ernest Lambert goes upstairs. His bedroom door is heard to shut. The mother stands and looks in the fire: the room is lighted by the red glow only. Then in a moment or two she goes into the scullery, and after a minute—during which running of water is heard—she returns with her candle, looking little and bowed and pathetic, and crosses the room, softly closing the passage door behind her.*)[39]

The 'dangerous gentleness' of their tones, like the 'safe reserve of their souls', reminds the reader of what a novelist can do which a dramatist cannot; the dramatist can only trust to his director and actors to carry out his ending faithfully. And yet the details save the ending from mawkishness: the mother's rinsing her husband's pit-bottle, if that is what it is, reminds the audience that life must go on, that even overwrought feelings exist within the context of ordinary life.

Such a play shows something of Lawrence's extraordinary ability: he had been writing for less than five years when he finished it. 'Nethermere' had been growing into a great mountain of ideas, experiences and styles, though its appeal was specifically to a literary and middle-class audience: Lawrence's earliest short stories had tended to be conventional and derivative, his poems rather wordy expressions (rather than explorations) of emotion. Only in the occasional poem or story – or in drama – would he risk using, directly, the language of his own background: the directness and immediacy of another kind of language altogether from the literary style he affected. In his plays that language is combined with his extraordinary understanding of and sympathy with the problems of a family in the Midlands community. It is not surprising that the play is so often reminiscent of *Sons and Lovers*; Lawrence is experimenting with many of the situations and the conflicts which he would not risk using in his fiction for another two years. Only the novel realises anything of the same directness in his writing; yet the presentation of, for example, the father in the play is arguably both clearer and less one-sided than in the novel. The character is not imposed upon to *make* a point: the drama forces the characters to respond to each other, rather than to the conceptions of them in which the novelist wishes to believe.

IV The Haggs as Myth

When Lawrence left the Midlands in October 1908 to go south to Croydon, it had been with a particular unhappiness that he had left the Haggs. He knew it marked the end of a whole phase of his life. May Chambers, often antagonistic to Lawrence, gave a striking account of what he had meant to her family over the years:

Why need fate have taken him so far away? we wondered. Why need he go to London? And yet it seemed right that he should go to London. He had sometimes hinted that he feared the world would drag him away its whole width from the valley he loved so deeply. Having become accustomed to the fret of his going, to us it seemed very fit that his brilliance should have a London polish. He left a blank that no other could fill, and there was envy of those who had gained him.[40]

She remembered how 'Everyone of the group watched for a letter signed with the magic initials D.H.L.' But as with all his significant experiences, Lawrence did not get to the end of them until he had written about them. He created two quite separate stories – 'A Modern Lover' and 'The Harassed Angel' (later 'The Shades of Spring') – about the experience of the man who leaves a farm family in the Midlands and goes south, but who pays them a return visit; and, of course, the experience of coming back to the Midlands after an absence is also shared by Cyril in Part III of *The White Peacock*. Lawrence wrote very little (indeed nothing before *Aaron's Rod* in 1917–21) about the experience of the man who leaves a small mining town and goes to London. Also remarkable is the fact that he wrote two stories rather than one. 'A Modern Lover' – its title doubtless influenced by Meredith's poem sequence 'Modern Love' – was written in the winter of 1909–10, after one of Lawrence's last visits to the Haggs (the Chambers family left in March 1910); but he forgot all about it (i. 372–3) and wrote the rather similar 'The Harassed Angel' in the winter of 1911, when he was a very long way indeed from his actual experience of the farm and its family.[41]

What was constant between the two stories was the continuing problem of his relationship with Jessie Chambers. But, in so far as they deal with the farm family, both stories are melancholy memorials to loss and change. Lawrence writes in 'A Modern Lover' about the family

who, a few months before, would look up in one fine broad glow of welcome whenever he entered the door, even if he came daily. Three years before, their lives would draw together into one flame, and whole evenings long would flare with magnificent mirth, and with play. They had known each other's lightest and deepest feelings. Now, when he came back to them after a long absence, they withdrew, turned aside. He sat down on the sofa under the window deeply chagrined.[42]

Though this is not straightforward autobiography, it is interesting for its description of how the precious memory of a country and family idyll is shattered by the middle-class lives represented by Cyril Mersham here and by John Adderley Syson in 'The Harassed Angel'. Both men are, however, as off-putting to the farm family as the family is to them; they are acutely conscious of country manners, and feel desperately aware of their own altered position. Mersham becomes 'extremely attentive to the others at table, and to his own manner of eating. He used English that was exquisitely accurate ... His nicety contrasted the more with their rough, country habit.'[43] As Mersham becomes more middle-class than Lawrence ever was, so the family becomes coarser and more crudely working-class than the Chambers family had ever been. Exactly the same happens in 'The Harassed Angel'; Syson is aware of the women not wanting him to join the family at table, and declines the midday meal: 'It is early for me', he remarks gently.

"Why, what time *do* you reckon to have your dinner?" asked Frank, the second son, rather insolently.
    "Dinner?—usually at half past seven."
    "Oh—ah!" sneered the sons all together.
    They had once been intimate friends with Syson. Now they disliked him.[44]

The idyll of the place remains – 'To his last day, he would love this place more than any other place on earth' – but Syson finds contact with the family impossible.[45]

    This version of the end of the idyll may be true of some aspects of Lawrence's own experience (his 1928 letter to David Chambers confirms his continuing love for the place); but what we know of his return to the Chambers family in 1909, for example – a year after going away – suggests that it is quite untrue of their reaction in general.[46] What is significant is that Lawrence is taking elements from the real-life situation in order to dramatise the experience of déclassé isolation in the central character. To do that, from his memories of the Chambers family and the Haggs, meant a considerable revision and alteration of his own actual experience.

    But the isolation from human warmth which we see in Mersham and Syson, their good-mannered incapacity to feel, their sharp and ironical perceptiveness coupled with cool detachment – coupled with a desperate need for warmth, intimacy and belonging: these were things which ran as a deep rift through Lawrence's emotional life. And he used his writing to explore the pain they caused him. As always, places like Eastwood and the Haggs were on the one hand realistically recreated in his writing – and, on the other hand, transformed into symbols which he could use to help enact and work through his own needs and divisions. He could re-experience the pressures and conflicts he knew so well, sharpened and made acute as they were in his writing; he could fully realise them, as he made his own experiences the centre of his fiction. He did this at the cost of rewriting as fiction what he himself (or others near to him) had actually experienced. We are thoroughly mistaken if we think we learn 'the whole truth and nothing but the truth' about Lawrence and the Chambers family from such stories.

V 'The great experiment of sex'

Lawrence's unease of tone in so much of his writing during this period was accompanied by a similar unease in his everyday life. This had been exacerbated rather than relieved by his literary success at the end of 1909. He was pulled in many ways at once; was simultaneously the hard-working elementary schoolmaster and the poet associating with Pound and Yeats: the creator of finely-crafted works of poetic literature, and the writer whose imagination and memory were filled with the life of the Midlands mining town: the dutiful son whose job it was to send money home, and the man whose sister 'complained that he went about too much and did not send money home'.[47] He was still attached to Jessie Chambers, but was drawn to other women, despite the fact that 'I do *not* believe in love . . . I never could believe in anything I cannot experience' (i. 141). Worst of all, he was the writer whose work had the uncomfortable habit of reminding him of all his most difficult problems.

In the autumn of 1909 he started going out with a woman in London who particularly interested and attracted him, the teacher Agnes Holt, 'an erect, intelligent girl' with 'grey eyes and auburn hair';[48] but the relationship failed to bring either of them any real happiness. We know almost nothing about her or what happened between them, though Lawrence would later characterise her as 'a jolly nice girl' (i. 208). At first she struck him as 'a person of great capacity, being alert, prompt, smart with her tongue, and independent in her manner' (i. 153); he went out with her 'a good bit' (i. 153) in the autumn of 1909 and found her 'very nice', though she 'takes me seriously: which is unwisdom' (i. 141). As a celebration of his first prestigious publication, she copied his first poems in the *English Review* into his poetry notebook, to form the first entries in his second volume of poems in finished forms. She also helped him prepare 'Nethermere' for Hueffer by making a clean copy of the beginning of the manuscript;[49] she appeared in its pages as Agnes D'Arcy.

But remarks about her which he made when their relationship was over – when he was feeling both sore and self-righteous – described her as 'utterly ignorant and old fashioned, really'. She thought (Lawrence claimed) that 'men worship their mistresses' – something he declared 'sickly sentimentality' (i. 153). He had tried to present their relationship to her as no more than an exciting game – 'I can't help it . . . I play it, and the girl plays it, and – what matter what the end is!' (i. 141). What is, however, highly significant is that he had made sexual advances to her – the very first time we can be sure he did. Sexual awareness had been creeping into his poetry; in the summer of 1909 he had fantasised about seeing a woman in the street 'who shall set me free/From the stunting bonds of my chastity'.[50] Agnes Holt, however – according to him – thought that 'A man is . . . not an animal – mon dieu, no!' He had, he informed Blanche Jennings, 'enlightened her, and now she has no courage. She still judges by mid-Victorian standards, and covers herself with a woolly fluff of romance that the years will wear sickly' (i. 153). It is impossible to do Agnes Holt justice without knowing more about her – and Lawrence is obviously an unreliable witness. But the important thing, so far as Lawrence was concerned, was that he had clearly been trying for a relationship in which 'kisses are the merest preludes and anticipations' (i. 153): he wanted a sexual relationship and, interestingly, assumed that that meant either marriage (Agnes Holt was described by Jessie Chambers as 'his possible fiancée'[51]) or else a relationship which avoided (if possible) both commitment and love. His final and certainly unfair judgement on Agnes Holt was that she was 'frightened' (i. 153; she may well have been the girl his landlord remembered giving him up 'because she was morally frightened of him'[52]). But she may have found his demands as much absurd as dangerous. In January 1910, at any rate, he announced 'Now I'm tired of her' (i. 153). He gave her two of his paintings when she got married and left Croydon in 1911; but he abandoned all thoughts of relationship with her, ostensibly because she was not prepared to enjoy an uncommitted relationship with him or to sleep with him. It was not an auspicious start to his sexual life; he remained held within the 'stunting bonds'.

The really distressing thing, however, was that immediately after his disappointment with Agnes Holt, Lawrence asked Jessie Chambers to become his mistress. After their a-sexual relationship between 1902 and 1906, and then the literary and intellectual intimacy which they had shared between the spring of 1906 and the autumn of 1909 – with any sexual component firmly refused – during Jessie's late November 1909 visit to London Lawrence had told her he wanted a woman to sleep with; and left her to realise that he meant her. Since Easter 1906 he had encouraged her to feel at best sexually neutral, and at worst positively unattractive; although he had told her that 'Some part of me will *always* want you', it had explicitly not been 'the purely animal side'. But on Christmas Eve 1909, he went up to the Haggs Farm:

and from his first glance I was aware of a difference. When I went with him over the fields he told me he had found out – he had really loved me all along and not realised it. He had told Agnes Holt that he belonged to me, everything was over between them ... He said that all our long association was in reality a preparation for this 'une intimité d'amour'. It came as a shock to me, very disturbing, yet at the same time inevitable ...[53]

They began to kiss and to embrace; up to now, kisses had been rare and special events. Lawrence declared that marriage 'for the moment is inexpedient', only necessary if Jessie should become pregnant. And he intended using a contraceptive, so that should not happen.[54]

Jessie agreed to take him as her lover at a considerable risk to her reputation (she would have lost her teaching job if it had become known), obviously without any kind of support from her family and against her own deepest instincts. She must have known that, in spite of what he was now saying, Lawrence did not love her. He wanted what in November he had hesitantly described to her as 'that ... without marriage' and would later describe as 'the great experiment of sex'.[55] And, just as with Agnes Holt, he went on insisting upon his independence from the woman whose lover he wanted to be. Only Jessie's devotion to him could ever have brought her to accept him.

How can we account for this sudden and violent reversal of what Lawrence had been saying, and of how he had been behaving, for years? Hurt pride had something to do with it: he had failed to persuade Agnes Holt to sleep with him and, in turning to Jessie, he was turning to the one woman in England likely to say 'yes'. Yet, characteristically, he was continuing to fantasise about such a relationship not being binding on its partners; he was instinctively not going to allow himself to depend upon a woman or to allow her to feel committed to him; he would, if he could, keep his crucial detachment. Jessie, because she loved him, would accept that.

Yet to turn to Jessie, of all people, was to be thoroughly exploitative of her. Even George Neville (himself the father of an illegitimate child) thought it rather dreadful: before knowing whom Lawrence was sleeping with but guessing it was Jessie, Neville remembered saying to his friend: 'Instead of getting away and buying yourself a woman, my guess is that you're trading on somebody's regard for you, when there is not the least regard on your side.'[56] Jessie was only the first of a number of women to whom Lawrence would go for sex in the next two years. He was attracted to Helen Corke: to Alice Dax: probably to Marie Jones: and there was at least one relationship in London with a woman he called 'Jane' of whom we know nothing.

But however exploitative he was being, Lawrence felt excitingly kindled by the prospect. The image of fire is his own: he described how, at Christmas 1909 with Jessie, 'an old fire burned up afresh, like an alcohol flame, faint and invisible, that sets fire to a tar barrel': he presumably being the blazing tar barrel and Jessie the 'faint and invisible' alcohol flame. That realistically (if depressingly) describes the differences between their feelings. But Lawrence had been joyous and triumphant: in the same letter in which he disparaged Agnes Holt, in January 1910, he described how Jessie

has black hair, and wonderful eyes, big and very dark, and very vulnerable; she lifts up her face to me and clings to me, and the time goes like a falling star, swallowed up immediately; it is wonderful, that time, long avenues of minutes – hours – should be swept up with one sweep of the hand, and the moment for parting has arrived when the first kiss seems hardly overkissed. She is coming to me for a week-end soon; we shall not stay here in Croydon, but in London. The world is for us, and we are for each other – even if only for one spring – so what does it matter! (i. 154)

However, in the heartrending words of the first draft of Jessie's own memoir, 'The times of our actual coming together, under conditions both difficult and irksome, and with Lawrence's earnest injunction to me not to try to hold him, would not exhaust the fingers of one hand'.[57] They managed a weekend together in London at the end of March 1910, but it is not clear how or where; naturally, 'my people and hers' (i. 154) had to be prevented from suspecting anything, and Jessie now thought it ' "not honourable" to take advantage of Mrs Jones's hospitality' at Colworth Road. They may have gone to a hotel: they may not have made love at all. Lawrence wrote to Jessie during the week after their meeting how 'You have done me great good, my dear. Only I want you here with me. It is as if I cannot rest without you near me, you goodly thing, good to be near, to touch and to hold . . .'[58] Touching and holding, physical gentleness and warmth, and time going 'like a falling star', were utterly new to him: previously only imagined with men: every bit as important as the longed-for sex. Jessie as an active sexual partner may still have been unimaginable, even if in theory what he most ached for.

But it is also clear that, after years of repression and sublimation, Lawrence was now sexually motivated for the first time in his life. In March 1910, when his old Eastwood friend Alice Dax also came to London – the

week before Jessie – he found himself on the very verge of making love to
her instead: 'I was very nearly unfaithful to you' (he told Jessie): 'I can never
promise you to be faithful. In the morning she came into my room, you
know my morning sadness' (i. 157). A month later, in April 1910, it was
Helen Corke who attracted him irresistibly. His years of enforced virginity
had given way to a kind of compulsive arousal, divorced as far as possible
from the claims of relationship; he would later refer to a partner as his 'bed-
rabbit', and when Clara in *Sons and Lovers* asks Paul 'is it me you want, or is
it *It*?', the Lawrence of 1910 would have to have answered 'it'.[59]

During the Easter holiday (from the end of March to the beginning of
April), Lawrence – Jessie told Emile Delavenay – 'donne beaucoup de son
temps à sa mère; ils n'ont que des promenades et des conversations'.
However, Jessie remembered it as 'Beau temps; ils sont heureux.'[60] They
may well have been happy precisely *because* they were not able to sleep
together. Their brief sexual relationship, according to Jessie, reached what
she called its 'height' during the Whitsuntide holiday (14–21 May), which
they spent in the Midlands. They solved in the usual way the age-old
problem of couples with no house to go to and too little money: Lawrence's
two poems about their love-making both describe it as out of doors, among
the marsh marigolds, cowslips and dead leaves. In the first, 'Scent of Irises',

> Me, your shadow in the bog-flame marigolds,
> Me full length in the cowslips, muttering you love:
> You upon the dry, dead beech-leaves, in the hair of the night
>
> Invisible – but the scent of you –   night irises
>   scent of irises in the grove!

In the other poem, 'Lilies in the Fire', totally rewritten in 1928 but recoverable to a 1913 version, 'The ground is a little chilly underneath/The leaves
...'[61] Unlike Easter, Whitsuntide was wet: 'Pouring all morning, and every
morning' (i. 161).

But it was not just the weather which made things difficult: the experience
itself, recreated in that 1913 poem, was intensely depressing.

> I am ashamed, you wanted me not tonight –
> Nay, it is always so, you sigh with me.
> Your radiance dims when I draw too near, and my free
> Fire enters your petals like death, you wilt dead white ...
>
> Tis a degradation deep to me, that my best
> Souls whitest lightning which should bright attest
> God stepping down to earth in one white stride,
>
> Means only to you a clogged, numb burden of flesh ...[62]

If Lawrence found the experience degrading, Jessie found it numbing, clogging and 'like death'. She had never wanted nor desired him; she wrote later how 'the tension was greater than I could bear . . . I could not conceal from myself a forced note in L's attitude, as if he were pushed forwards in his sensual desires – and a lack of spontaneity.' Even Lydia Lawrence was aware of something momentous happening between her son and Jessie at Whitsuntide 1910. She wrote to her sister Lettie: 'Bert is still about the same – one hardly knows what to make of him. He made a tremendous fuss of Jessie Chambers while here at Whitsuntide & yet I could see at the end of the week, he was tired.'[63] Bearing in mind Lawrence's feeling that pregnancy would be the only reason for him and Jessie to get married, a remark he made in a letter of 24 June (five weeks after Whitsuntide) that his love relationships 'go a bit criss-crossy' and that 'It is very probable that I shall have to return in September to home, to a little mining village in the midlands' (i. 166) may indicate that Jessie feared she was pregnant. Luckily she was not.

VI   Enter Helen

But even before he and Jessie became lovers, Lawrence was turning away from her. To understand the events of the spring of 1910, we have to go back to Lawrence's finishing of his novel between January and April.

The two 'Laetitia' drafts and 'Nethermere' had so monopolised his novel writing between 1906 and the end of 1909 that we have no idea what he had originally planned as his second novel; if indeed he had made any plans. Some time early in 1910, he tried to write a novel about his mother's early life called 'Matilda' but quickly abandoned it. In the early spring of 1910, anyway, he had committed himself to extensive revision of 'Nethermere' as well as to rewriting its third part: this took from 21 January to 11 April. His Easter holidays (from 24 March to 4 April) were probably largely occupied with the revision – another reason why his relationship with Jessie may have got no further forward then. However, Jessie Chambers recalled that 'Towards the end of the same holiday', when at last he had leisure to plan 'his next novel', he told her he 'would write a "bright" story and take one of my brothers . . . as hero'. This story was perhaps written in 1911 as the long tale 'Love Among the Haystacks'. However, almost simultaneously with Lawrence's resubmission of the manuscript of 'Nethermere' to Heinemann on 11 April – exactly a week after term had started in Croydon – he wrote to Jessie Chambers, 'apparently very much disturbed, saying that he found he had to write the story of Siegmund . . . It was in front of him and he had got to do it. He begged me to go to Croydon and make the acquaintance of "Helen".'[64]

He had known Helen Corke for well over a year; but in 1909 she had been wrapped up in her feelings about her music teacher Herbert Baldwin Macartney. In August 1909, hearing that she was going on holiday to the Isle of Wight simultaneously with his own family, Lawrence had suggested that they might travel down together from London. What he did not then know was that she was holidaying with Macartney, a married man: and, although the Lawrence family party was on the island at the same time, in the same blazing heat, Helen Corke and Macartney were in a different part of the island and the two parties never met. Following their week's holiday, and after Helen Corke had gone on to Cornwall with her friend Agnes Mason and another friend, Macartney killed himself. Helen Corke travelled back to London to be greeted by the news, which devastated her. Throughout the autumn of 1909 she wrote a diary in the form of a letter to Macartney ('Siegmund' to her: he had called her 'Sieglinde', after characters in Wagner's *Die Walküre*). She also wrote 'The Freshwater Diary', a detailed account of their five days together in August.

Lawrence learned about what had happened from Agnes Mason, and had been doing what he could during the winter of 1909–10 to draw Helen out of what she later called her 'living-death' and 'to revive the zest of life in her'. They exchanged books; he taught her some German; he showed her his poetry and his play *A Collier's Friday Night* (she modelled the beginning of her own play about her experience with Macartney, 'The Way of Silence', upon it).[65] He also asked for her help with the correction of 'Nethermere' for Heinemann in the spring of 1910. She was impressed and intrigued by Lawrence, but was still deeply withdrawn emotionally; he was struck by 'the wall you have built about you'. However, he was also insistent that 'You cannot cover yourself under "the snows of yesteryear" ' (i. 157).

Helen Corke was a strikingly individual and self-possessed person, with some range of reading and a suppressed desire to be a writer. The 'prose poems' which made up her 'Freshwater Diary' show her style at its happiest in the purple-patch. To be fair to her, the 'Diary' – the product of a long, painful and loving gestation, and laboriously worked over – shows her writing at its worst. But she is unable to mention the most commonplace object without including her ideas about the nature of the universe and man's place within it. She looks at seaweed, and characteristically exclaims: 'Torn, shrivelled, seaweed, beyond reach of the tide! the life-tide in which we exult, in whose infinity our self consciousness is lost.' An hour passes: but many more than sixty minutes of fine feeling go by, 'fleeting before us in sea-woven blue and gold': the hour may actually be 'three sister hours, playing on the edge of the foam; or maybe none of these, but a Life, in sheen of countless softened hues. Our eyes are sun-dimmed, and we can scarcely trust our vision.'⁶⁶ In her 'Diary', Helen Corke turned her experience on the Isle of Wight into an exercise in waking-dream, full of symbolism and the haunting beauty of transcendent life, disturbed only by the vision of imminent death.

Wagner's operas successfully brought her and Lawrence together. As early as December 1908, Lawrence had confidently remarked to Blanche Jennings 'Surely you know Wagner's operas – *Tannhäuser* and *Lohengrin*. They will run a knowledge of music into your blood better than any criticisms' (i. 99). Croydon and London had given him far more chance for hearing music and going to opera than Nottingham had; and in October 1909 he had been able to extend his knowledge of Wagner by going to see *Tristan und Isolde* at the Grand Theatre, Croydon. But he was 'very disappointed . . . *Tristan* is long, feeble, a bit hysterical, without grip or force' (i. 140). What made the difference to his feeling about Wagner was Helen Corke. Her relationship with Macartney had led her to attend *Walküre* (sung in English for the first time) at Covent Garden in 1908, and one of Lawrence's fictional recreations of her shows her 'fingering the piano from the score'. She then heard the *Ring* cycle later in the year.⁶⁷ She passed on her enthusiasm to Lawrence when they began to see each other during the autumn and winter of 1909; he certainly learned about Siegmund and Sieglinde from her, and why she had identified Macartney with Siegmund. By November 1911 he could refer to *Siegfried* as 'one of the *Ring* cycle that I had not heard' (i. 327), implying that he had been to more than one part of the cycle.

Some time between the start of the spring term in Croydon on 10 January 1910 and the end of term, Lawrence – still worried about the state Helen Corke was in – asked if he could see 'The Freshwater Diary'. Eventually she lent it to him.

There is a new urgency in his voice when he returns it. 'What are you going to *do* with these prose poems?' he asks. I reply, nothing. They are written; it is enough . . .

He returns to the subject later – comes with a request that he take the diary and expand its theme – use the poems as basis for a more comprehensive rendering of the story. He will bring me his work as it grows; nothing shall stand with which I am not in agreement.

A couple of years later, Helen Corke wrote (and repeated to the end of her very long life) that what she wanted was 'clothing for the soul of Siegmund and voice for his silence'.⁶⁸ A talented and published writer was now asking her help in creating a memorial to him. She lent Lawrence 'The Freshwater Diary' again (he may have worked at least some of the time with it beside him): she also helped from her own recollections and her knowledge of

Macartney and his family. She encouraged Lawrence to immerse himself in the operas she could help him explore; the novel, even in its rewritten 1912 form, is still thoroughly Wagnerian in motif, reference and atmosphere. Her own writing of the 'prose poems' had been silent, rhapsodic, personal; Lawrence's version, written by a 'sensitive, impersonal artist' – a man capable of deep insight and extending a 'healing' and 'comprehending sympathy'[69] – such a text, unlike her own, might one day be published, and stand in place of the music she believed Macartney should have written. Clothing and voice, indeed.

Thus 'The Saga of Siegmund', the first version of *The Trespasser*, was born. Lawrence accidentally included the name 'Siegmund' three times in the final manuscript of 'Nethermere', which suggests that he had begun to write about the predicament of Siegmund before finishing the other novel, particularly as the three occasions are all in the first two chapters of Part III of 'Nethermere', which he probably rewrote in March 1910.[70] Siegmund came to Lawrence's mind when he was writing about Leslie Tempest, and particularly about Leslie's relationship with Lettie: it is she who mistakenly calls him 'Siegmund', as she exerts power over him. It is another confirmation of the fact that Lawrence continued to work on the same predicaments and problems over and over again, and suggests one of the reasons why Helen Corke's experience had attracted him. He probably started to write 'The Saga' shortly after reading 'The Freshwater Diary' in February or March 1910, as a break from the continuing revision of 'Nethermere': and then had to abandon the second novel temporarily when he realised that he wanted not only to revise 'Nethermere' as Heinemann had asked but also to rewrite Part III. However, he carried in his imagination the name and the situation of Siegmund, and clearly found Lettie's power games with George and Leslie illuminated by those of Helena with Siegmund. With the first novel finally despatched, he was able to continue with 'The Saga' and on 27 April 1910 told Heinemann about it: 'I have written about half of another novel' (i. 159).

Not surprisingly, Jessie Chambers – in spite of her closeness to Lawrence in the spring and summer of 1910 – knew less about the writing of 'The Saga' than any other of his works up to this point. She thought that he wrote it 'in feverish haste' between Whitsuntide and Midsummer;[71] but it was begun a good deal earlier and finished rather later than she thought. Lawrence was still working on the death of Siegmund on 9 July ('I have just hanged my latest hero: after which I feel queer' – i. 168), and hoped to finish on 15 July (i. 169), though he probably went on for another fortnight (i. 172, 175). For a man in an exhausting full-time job, it was still a miraculous outpouring.

But there is an obvious reason, too, why Lawrence might deliberately have left Jessie with the impression that he did not begin 'The Saga' until the early summer of 1910. The novel was intimately concerned with Helen Corke: he was reimagining the situation of her former lover and writing extensively about her sexual experiences: and very often found himself writing out of a deep sympathy for Siegmund. 'I feel often inclined, when I think of you, to put my thumbs on your throat', he told Helen Corke, while working on the novel: 'You don't know how inimical I feel against you' (i. 160, 162). It may well have been this reaction which produced his extraordinary and prophetic remark to Jessie Chambers in March 1910: 'I have always believed it was the woman who paid the price in life. But I've made a discovery. It's the man who pays, not the woman' (i. 155). He had 'always believed' what his mother had told him about her marriage, and the price she had 'paid'; now he was becoming vividly aware of what a man – he himself, for example – might (like George and Leslie and Siegmund) end up paying to a woman in devotion and self-sacrifice.

But Helen Corke was a very special kind of challenge. She may – as she herself thought – have been sexually neutral; but Lawrence was stimulated and perhaps excited by her having lived through the experience with Macartney, and knew that he had a lot to learn from her about women's power over men. He was also probably fascinated by a man being so overwhelmed by his feelings as Macartney had been – and as he himself had never been. We can imagine him looking at Helen Corke rather as Siegmund looks at Helena on the way back from the Island:

he knew nothing of her life, her real inner life. She was a book written in characters unintelligible to him and to everybody. He was tortured with the problem of her till it became acute, and he felt as if something would burst inside him. As a boy he had experienced the same sort of feeling after wrestling for an hour with a problem in Euclid; for he was capable of great concentration.[72]

Writing the novel was Lawrence's way of trying to break out of his own version of that state. But he would also have wondered whether, although he was a man, he was actually more like Helena than like Siegmund: the Helena who, in 'The Saga' makes Siegmund feel 'she had left him and gone alone, as the sea withdraws itself into solitariness'.[73] Was he, too, fatally unable to give himself, or to love?

While writing the novel he was, however, also engaged in his new relationship with Jessie Chambers; and for a time he felt polarised between the two women, obsessed by them both in different ways. With one consciousness, he told Helen Corke, he was reading Jessie's letters to him (she was writing 'very lovingly, and full of triumphant faith'), and was longing to be with her at Whitsuntide, when they would sleep together. Yet the writing of the new novel was also a passion: and he told Helen Corke, in the same letter, two days before Whitsun,

I have a second consciousness somewhere actively alive. I write 'Siegmund' – I keep on writing, almost mechanically: very slowly, and mechanically. Yet I don't think I do Siegmund injustice ... You see, I know Siegmund is there all the time. I know you would go back to him, after me, and disclaim me. I know it very deeply. I know I could not bear it. (i. 159–60)

For the writing of the novel, he needed Helen Corke and her peculiar sympathy. He was probably not sleeping with her: he probably never did, though he tried hard to in 1911. But – according to his own later account – for a time he was 'more or less in love' with her, while knowing he couldn't love her 'altogether, nor really': so 'what shall one do but take the moment – Carpe diem, if you can't gather an eternity in your fist' (ii. 91). On Saturday 7 May, a day when he and she had been wandering in the Kent countryside, and only four days before he wrote that letter about Siegmund, they had run down a slope together and he had caught her as she ran: 'David clasps me longer than is necessary, and when we move, holds my hand fast, protectively and possessively'.[74] Exactly a week later, he would be with Jessie in the Midlands. He wanted to believe that when 'The Saga' was finished he would simply go back to Jessie, and that she would – he told Helen Corke – 'take me as she would pick up an apple that had fallen from the tree when a bird alighted on it' (i. 159). He ignored how much he would resent being as passive as a fallen apple. In July, too, while working towards the end of the novel, he very probably went with Helen Corke – like Cecil Byrne in the novel – to see the larch wood where a year before she had gone with Macartney.[75] Helen Corke was probably never again as close to him as when he was writing the novel, and while he was trying to imagine what she had experienced. It must have been both flattering and disturbing to find this peculiarly perceptive and intelligent man concentrating so totally upon her, writing a book about her, repeating the experience of her lover and falling in love with her, while simultaneously involved with another woman. But it would have been far more distressing to Jessie if she had known what Lawrence was doing.

For her part, Helen Corke was now increasingly playing Jessie Chambers's traditional role: reading with Lawrence, discussing and lending books, talking ideas through. Lawrence lent her Wells, Bennett, E. M. Forster and Walter de la Mare: and either in May or June, she lent him Olive Schreiner's *The Story of an African Farm*, which in turn Lawrence recommended to Jessie Chambers (i. 161); the two 'Stranger' chapters of

Part II of that novel directly accounted for Lawrence's own device of 'the Stranger' in chapter VII of 'The Saga', written in June. He continued to find Helen Corke extraordinarily stimulating, as she did him: in her novel about Macartney and Lawrence, she even has the Lawrence character say to the Helen Corke character: 'I'm pure stimulus to you, so you've often said, and you're much the same to me.'[76] Such words may well have been exchanged in real life.

Lawrence was for a long time thoroughly attracted to her, as he frequently was to women who were serious, independent, unconventional, tauntingly a-sexual and seeking some kind of fulfilment in their lives – and refusing to accept that marriage might be their fulfilment. Yet, like the 'Stranger' Hampson in 'The Saga', he also knew that 'These deep, interesting women don't want *us*: they want the flowers of the spirit they can gather of us. We, as natural men, are more or less degrading to them and to their love of us. Therefore they destroy the natural man in us—that is, us altogether.'[77] This particular insight was developed to an extreme degree by Lawrence's writing of 'The Saga'. At some stage he must have realised that the book was actually as important to him as to Helen Corke; his conclusions about himself as a man (and her as a woman) would in the end come close to Hampson's.

And during the exact period of his writing of the novel, Lawrence's sexual relationship with Jessie Chambers pursued its painful and eventually humiliating course. It was not only a coincidence that he should simultaneously have been creating a failure in sexual relationship in 'The Saga', in the story of a sensual man who is attracted to a woman who cannot bear his overt sexuality. 'The Saga' is not the story of Jessie Chambers and Lawrence; but just as all Lawrence's experiences fed into his writing, so his writing was his immediate and best way of understanding what was happening to him and to those around him. The writing of 'The Saga' at such a moment must have helped him 'get myself free' (iii. 522), as he would later put it.[78] His sexual relationship with Jessie Chambers ended within a fortnight of the ending of 'The Saga', and may actually have been ended *by* it, as Lawrence began to dread the power of the loving woman and the helplessness of the frustrated man, the 'man who pays'. Writing about Helen Corke's experience enabled Lawrence to imagine the ways in which both she and Jessie Chambers were alike. He found both of them stimulating and (he came to feel) antagonistic, as they tried to make up for their own unhappiness by loving men and encouraging men to love them. Lawrence, however, believed that such love was calculated to break down his self-possession: both women, in different ways, drove him into extreme defensiveness.

VII 'The Saga of Siegmund'

But 'The Saga' was also important to Lawrence as a writer. Chance had supplied him with a tragic story centring upon the very subject which most deeply fascinated him: the sexual power and potential dominance of the independent (and sexually ambiguous) woman, and the helplessness of the sensitive man attracted to her. The problems of relationship in 'Nethermere' could be pushed still further in this new novel: Lettie remained a worrying problem even when the first novel was finished. Where Leslie's tragedy had been in his submission, and George's in his decay, Siegmund's lay in his frustration and his despair: and in 'The Saga', Lawrence could find out what happened when Leslie, not George, became the tragic hero.

Having finished his first draft of the novel by the start of August 1910, Lawrence felt 'inclined to be rather proud of it; but those who belong to the accurate-impersonal school of Flaubert will flourish large shears over my head and crop my comb very close: so I will not crow' (i. 169). He was thinking in particular of Hueffer, upon whose patronage he still felt dependent: and Hueffer did indeed react violently against the book. He recalled how Lawrence 'one day . . . brought me half the ms. of *The Trespassers* [sic] – and that was the end'.[79] Believing that 'prose *must* be impersonal', he found 'The Saga' 'execrably bad art' (i. 178, 339). But that reaction, which the previous year would probably have compelled Lawrence's compliance, could now be parried: and Lawrence's pride in his book outweighed his doubts about it, which he had begun to express as early as June 1910: 'It is horribly poetic: Covent Garden market, floral hall' (i. 167).

His main problems with it were, firstly, that it needed thoroughly revising after 'one or two of my people' had had a chance to read it (probably Jessie Chambers and Helen Corke, certainly Hueffer): he told Atkinson, at Heinemanns, that 'I will overhaul it rigorously: then I will send it to you' (i. 169–70). Secondly, he had probably agreed with Helen Corke not to publish it until she was willing; and although we know she approved of it in its first draft, we do not know whether at this stage she would have wanted it published.

But, most of all, the problem of 'what the world will say to it' (i. 172) worried Lawrence. Even Hueffer's criticism of its 'bad art', however painful – and Lawrence 'suffered badly' from it (i. 417) – mattered less than the word 'erotic' Hueffer used about it in September 1910 (i. 339). The word was almost the novel's death blow. Hueffer told Lawrence that, if he published it, the novel 'would damage your reputation, perhaps permanently' (i. 339), and as late as the winter of 1911 Lawrence was determined that 'I don't want to be talked about in an *Anne* [sic] *Veronica* fashion' (i. 339). H. G. Wells's novel *Ann Veronica* had been attacked in 1909 for being 'capable of poisoning the minds of those who read it' (i. 339 n. 4), and for its demonstration of the power and attractiveness of the sexually active and independent woman. In 1910 Lawrence was too scared of damaging his fledgling reputation to publish such a book; and though he sent 'The Saga' to Heinemann in September, a month later he declared himself 'not in the least anxious to publish that book. I am content to let it lie for a few years' (i. 184).

His reaction against it got stronger, as time went by, quite independently of his fears of its eroticism. In October 1910 he felt sure 'It contains . . . some rattling good stuff'; but it was also 'a decorated idyll running to seed in realism': he contrasted it with his brand new novel, only one-eighth written, 'Paul Morel': 'a restrained, somewhat impersonal novel' (i. 184). 'The Saga' – even its title now struck him as 'idiotic' – was exactly the opposite: overwritten, dreadfully personal, quite unrestrained. Helen Corke had encouraged him in the very worst writing he was capable of, so that the novel had become a kind of bathetic Wagnerian drama: 'Damn Wagner, and his bellowings at Fate and death' (i. 247), Lawrence remarked in April 1911. Very often he felt himself revealed by his writing, 'vulnerable, naked in a thickly clothed crowd'; but 'The Saga' (like *The Rainbow*, *Women in Love* and his play *David*) produced a particularly violent reaction in him. As early as June 1910, while still at work on 'The Saga', he had been sure that 'I shall never do anything decent till I can grow up and cut my beastly long curls of poetry. I look at the clouds go past, and I say to myself, of this new book: "Now, by the stamp of Heaven, that's rather fine" ' (i. 167). Learning not to admire his own prose was one of the lessons of 'The Saga' and of 1910. Elegant and poetic writing like his letters to Grace Crawford had doubtless been greeted with admiration: and he might well feel 'that's rather fine' as he contemplated his prose poetry and his finely turned metaphors. But, as he also noted in 1910, such writing was not marked by what he called 'corporeality' (i. 188). It was not real, and of the body; and one of his own demands upon himself, now that his own bodily awareness was so much more acute, was that it must be. It had been in part his need *not* to be ordinary, not to be the 'board-school boy grown to man's estate', which had encouraged his poetic prose and his self-conscious eloquence; though, of course, the distinction between the 'ordinary' and the 'sophisticated' in his own background and make-up was one to which he had been accustomed from his very earliest years. In the end, the pretentiousness of a voice whose mannerisms had been learned but which was never really his own, never issued out of his own past and his own self, made him feel 'a naked fool' (i. 167).

It was, too, while he was writing 'The Saga' that he had had his first violent reaction against the literary world for which, in one sense, the novel was precisely designed. On 1 June 1910 he wrote to Helen Corke that

I assure you, I am not weeping into my register. It is only that the literary world seems a particularly hateful yet powerful one. The literary element, like a disagreeable substratum under a fair country, spreads under every inch of life, sticking to the roots of the growing things. Ugh, that is hateful. I wish I might be delivered. (i. 162)

The fact that he wished that he 'might be delivered' is a sign not only of a new distaste for the literary world, but shows that he knew that the 'literary element' was sticking to the roots of the 'growing things' which he himself was trying to create. He felt that the novel was not as good as he had hoped ('I am rapidly losing faith in it'), and was also annoyed at the waywardness of the new editor of the *English Review*, Austin Harrison, for not publishing 'Odour of Chrysanthemums': 'I expect he's forgotten – mislaid it' (i. 162). It must have struck Lawrence as significant that the editor of a literary magazine had managed to lose his first non-literary story. 'The Saga' would best stay unpublished: and that was how it remained from September 1910 to December 1911.

VIII Ending with Jessie

The writing of 'The Saga' nevertheless seems to have been one of the reasons why Lawrence's relationship with Jessie foundered in the summer of 1910: partly because of his attraction to Helen Corke, partly because of what he had learned from the novel about the power of the loving woman. He had been strongly attracted to Alice Dax that spring, too, but had told Jessie about it, and how his feelings for her were 'all finished' (i. 157). It was much more difficult to continue not telling Jessie about his feelings for Helen Corke, especially as his attraction to her showed no sign of dying away. By not telling Jessie, Lawrence knew he was 'deceiving/Her who never yet in speech or silence lied to me', and his solution came at the end of the same poem, 'Sigh No More', written in the early summer of 1910: 'I will tell her, though it set her heart grieving, grieving/Better that, than as I am, bereaving/Her of faith in me, who have been her great believing.'[80] As so often, his experiences were hammered out in poetry almost as they came to him. It was Jessie's 'faith in me' which he felt he could not take, and that suggests the acuteness of his understanding of her. Even more than she wanted him faithful, she needed to believe in him.

Accordingly, he confessed to her that 'Between you and Hélène I am torn like a garment', and insisted to Jessie that ' "he must have" Hélène', though 'It is only for the writing of the book, I shall always return to you.' Her published memoir added the words 'only you must always leave me free'. Jessie, as well she might, had then suggested 'la rupture': she had always threatened 'all or nothing'.[81] In July, he still refused to break with her; he still clung to his need of her as intelligent companion, and to Helen as partner for the experience of this book.

But in his understanding of Jessie's 'great believing', Lawrence had realised something fundamentally important. Following their experiences as lovers in May, he had not only begun to react against the very idea of their sexual relationship: he had also started to blame her for loving only the ideal man she wanted him to be: 'the best of me'.[82] Her idealisation put a pressure upon him which he had come to hate and fear. She now loved her ideal of him 'to madness', he wrote in December 1910; her love was of a kind which 'demands the soul of me' (i. 190). Above all, he felt that her devotion was terrifyingly possessive: it prevented her sympathising with, or even seeing, the 'prostitute man in him'. Such a conclusion was perhaps even more disturbing than his own lack of feeling for her. And there was still, of course, the matter of his family's reaction to Jessie, in particular his mother's: she was convinced that Jessie was exactly the wrong person for Lawrence and had made very clear how much she hated the power Jessie could exert over him. Lawrence was now starting to realise the nature of that power himself.

After the Whitsuntide week, Lawrence and Jessie probably saw each other only once more before the end of the summer term: Jessie came to London for a weekend (probably 16–17 July) and on the Sunday Lawrence introduced her to Helen Corke, just as he had introduced her to Agnes Holt in November 1909. Helen Corke was struck by Jessie's gentleness and by the way she treated Lawrence: 'rather as Mary of Bethany might have treated Christ. He reacted irritably . . .'[83]

Lawrence saw Jessie briefly in Nottingham when he arrived home by train from Croydon on Friday 28 July, and he saw her again the following day; they had planned to go out properly together on Monday 1 August, and had arranged that Lawrence would then go on to stay some days at the Chambers family's new farm at Arno Vale, which he had scarcely seen. They had a room ready for him; Jessie was looking forward to their first holiday together. However, when she met him on the Monday, 'instead of returning with me as he had planned to do, he broke off our engagement completely'. Her word 'engagement' is a public word for the sexual commitment which to her felt 'binding and sacred'.[84]

In her 1935 memoir, Jessie Chambers implied that Lawrence's decision was a result of his mother's influence on him that weekend.[85] But in 1935 she blamed Lydia Lawrence for almost everything Lawrence did: and although Lawrence's mother would certainly have been glad to hear that her son had broken off from Jessie, Lawrence's decision seems to have been provoked entirely by what he feared in Jessie and in himself. A remark he had made a week earlier to Louie Burrows suggests how much he wanted his friends to be aware of the distance between Jessie and him. He had told Louie, ingenuously, that 'I do not know what J[essie] is thinking of doing this holiday, not having heard from her to that effect. Do you know?' (i. 172). A letter Lawrence wrote to Helen Corke on Sunday 31st, the day before he broke with Jessie, suggests very clearly why he did it, and how like Helena in 'The Saga' he feared Jessie was.

She is very pretty and very wistful. She came to see me yesterday. She kisses me. It makes my heart feel like ashes. But then she kisses me more and moves my sex fire. Mein Gott, it is hideous. I have promised to go there tomorrow, to stay till Thursday. If I have courage, I shall not stay. It is my present intention not to stay. I must tell her. I must tell her also that we ought finally and definitely to part: if I have the heart to tell her. (i. 173)

It was not anything as simple as love for his mother or even for Helen Corke which made him want to end with Jessie. He knew he did not love her, and could not make a life with her; he had perhaps always known that. But what was new was his fear of the way she could encroach upon his sexuality. He found it 'hideous' to be aroused by her when he did not want her: that was even worse than her devotion because it was still more of an assault upon the castle keep of his independent self. What, however, made it particularly difficult to break with her just then was her situation, which Lawrence described as 'forlorn'. He had heard how 'at home, at her home, none of them care for her, for Muriel, not much: that they did not want her to go back home: that she asked them, could she go?' (i. 173).

But all the same, on Monday 1 August he ended their relationship. He knew that 'I have been cruel to her, and wronged her,' but – he insisted, several months later – 'I did not know' (i. 190): did not know, perhaps, quite how upsetting Jessie's claim to him and his physical response to her could be. Jessie, as ever, stood 'for complete union or a complete break . . . all or nothing'. Lawrence said 'Then I am afraid it must be nothing.' They agreed 'not even to correspond'. Jessie 'se sent presque devenir folle'.[86]

Within a week of the break, he went back on their agreement and wrote to her again; but only to tell her to read J. M. Barrie's *Sentimental Tommy* and *Tommy and Grizel* if she wanted to understand his position – 'I'm in exactly the same predicament.'[87] In the latter novel, Tommy tells Grizel that 'I want to love you, you are the only woman I ever wanted to love, but apparently I can't': he now feels 'A madness to be free' of his long relationship with her, in spite of 'all that was adorable and all that was pitiful in her'. He also demands her sympathy by asserting that 'I am as pitiful a puzzle to myself as I can be to you'. Tommy is a highly self-conscious, frequently role-playing man, full of fine feelings; he is also an author who has now moved to London. One can see why he was so useful to Lawrence. And Tommy cannot love. Not just Grizel: but anyone.[88] In one way, Lawrence was offering Jessie an explanation of his conduct which put all the blame on himself: although she was adorable, he was unable to love her. It was not only a saving lie; it contained elements of truth. Tommy is a man too conscious of himself ever to feel anything directly or unconsciously; and Tommy's was one of the fates which Lawrence was particularly frightened of, and about which he wrote again and again. (As late as 1920 he had a fictional character comment that *Tommy and Grizel* was 'a study of a man who can't get away from himself'.[89]) Just as Lawrence had to go on breaking with Jessie, time after time – in 1906, again in 1908, in August 1910, again in the spring of 1912, again in the writing of *Sons and Lovers* in the autumn of 1912 – so it would be a kind of painful but belated tribute to Jessie's haunting influence that his fiction should have continued to work on the subject of the woman like her (and in particular the attraction to her of the man like himself) for so many years after 1910. His experience with her had not only taught him about the power of a woman over him, and his increasingly powerful resentment of it: it also revealed him to himself in very sharp relief. Whereas, after *Sons and Lovers* and *The Daughter-in-Law*, written between September 1912 and January 1913, he did not again take up the subject of possessive mother-love until *Fantasia of the Unconscious* in 1921, he continued to write about the experience of a man loved by the 'Miriam' woman. He had done so in *The White Peacock* with Emily, and again with Muriel in 'A Blot': did so in the various 'Paul Morel' versions with Miriam, over and over again: did so in his poem 'Last Words to Muriel' around December 1910* and with Hilda in his story 'The Shades of Spring', first written in December 1911: did so again in extensive revisions to the story in the spring of 1913, and then again in the summer and once again in the autumn of 1914. Each time, he rewrote or revised the hero's conclusions about his relationship with Hilda. He revised his 1910 story 'A Blot' in 1912, too, together with the narrator's reactions to Muriel; but in April 1916, he wrote nearly thirty pages of the 'Prologue' chapter to *Women in Love* about a very similar relationship between Birkin and Hermione.[90]

---

* See Illustrations 23 and 24 for the original version.

When in May 1913 he received Jessie's own account of their relationship, written in the form of a novel (which she herself later destroyed), it made him 'so miserable I had hardly the energy to walk out of the house for two days' (i. 551); as late as 1921, the 'Miriam' figure was still disturbing him: 'I dreamed of her two nights ago', he recorded (iii. 720). What perhaps most worried him about Jessie – and Emily, and Miriam, and Muriel, and Hilda, and Hermione – was not only the way in which he had come to feel that their devotion was dangerous, but also the fact that he himself was so attracted by it. They offered, in their bodiless demands, desires and ecstasies, something he knew very well and responded to in kind: the pleasure of a bodiless and 'uncorporeal' relationship which ignored the 'other' of another person as well as the demands of the passionate self: which encouraged the self-conscious, detached and observing self to remain within its enclosing envelope. Early in his life, Lawrence had very much wanted such relationships; he ended up positively loathing his capacity for them. Whereas the ghost of Lydia Lawrence could at least be confronted in *Sons and Lovers* and *The Daughter-in-Law*, the ghost of his own past self (with its self-consciousness and its spirituality) was terrifyingly persistent.[91] The man who, as he grew older, increasingly and at times stridently insisted in his writing on the vital importance of experience of 'the other', did so out of a very fearful knowledge of what the opposite experience was like. That was something for which he might eventually be as grateful to Jessie as for her original 'launching' of him and his career, and for her years of devotion to his work. Nonetheless, he knew he had behaved 'rather disgracefully' (i. 187) in August 1910; he left her devastated.

THE BITTER RIVER

I The Death of Lydia Lawrence

On 1 August 1910 Lawrence's break with Jessie had ended the formative relationship of his early years. A fortnight later, Lydia Lawrence collapsed while visiting her sister Ada in Leicester. Less than four months later, at the age of 59, she was dead.

She had been troubled by illness on and off over many years; on the Isle of Wight during the holiday of August 1909, for example, although she completed a 4½ mile walk from Shanklin to Ventnor, it was something of a surprise to her son ('even mother managed it' – i. 133): and it was while there that, like Mrs Morel, she probably had fainting bouts. Lawrence's comment, five days after the holiday, that 'I am beastly disappointed about one thing and another' (i. 136) may well relate to his realisation that his mother was feeling much older, and was not getting better. Ironically, in February 1910 she had declared 'I am glad to say that I am better now than I have been for the last few years. Dr Michie did me so much good.'[1] As proof of her good health, in May 1910 she had been to visit her sister Lettie in Harrow, and had stopped off on the journey to see Ada in Leicester; she had then arranged to go back to Leicester in August. Letters she wrote in February, May and July 1910 show her full of energy, even though she was unhappy about the miners' strike which started at the end of June: 'things are very bad here, and one gets depressed'. In February and in July she had expressed her particular gratitude to her daughter Ada for her help at home – 'She is very good to me. I do not know what I should do without her' – but without any sense of not being able to cope herself: Ada was simply 'as good as gold, only one does hate to take so much'.[2]

The last image of Lydia Lawrence at home comes ten days before her illness. Lawrence – rather unexpectedly in Eastwood at the start of August, because he had not gone to stay with the Chambers family at Arno Vale – described to Grace Crawford what his home was like:

I am writing in the kitchen, or the middle parlour as it would be called if my mother were magniloquent – but she's not, she's rather scornful. It is cosy enough. There's a big fire – miners keep fires in their living rooms though the world reels with sun-heat – a large oval mahogany table, three shelves of study-books, a book-case of reading books, a dresser, a sofa, and four wooden chairs. Just like all the other small homes in England.

My mother, who is short and grey haired, and shuts her mouth very tight, is reading a translation of Flaubert's *Sentimental Education*, and wears a severe look of disapproval. (i. 174)

Arthur Lawrence was out, 'drinking a little beer with a little money he begged of me' (i. 174): Ada was at the theatre in Nottingham with Eddie Clarke. Only the American Grace Crawford, however, might have believed that the book-lined living-room was typical of 'all the other small homes in England'. The 'study-books' and many of the 'reading books' in the kitchen were Lawrence's and Ada's: the *English Review* had printed two sets of poems and a story: he had finished his second novel: and he was waiting for proofs of what was now *The White Peacock*.

But there was no family holiday this year, as there had been every summer since 1906. Arthur Lawrence was no longer working as a butty: he had stopped between April and September 1909, and thereafter worked only as a dayman in other butties' teams, not always full-time – which was why he needed to borrow money from his son.[3] And there was his impending retirement to be thought of. The Lawrences could not afford a holiday in 1910, in spite of money coming in from both Ada and from Lawrence. Lydia Lawrence was going to her sister in Leicester; and instead of staying at Arno Vale, Lawrence (he told Grace Crawford) arranged to go to Blackpool instead: 'It is a crowded, vulgar Lancashire seaside resort. I am going with a man friend: I shall enjoy it: you would think it hideous' (i. 175). He had been glad at having escaped 'the annual feminine party this year. The old clique is broken . . .' (i. 172).

The friend was George Neville, who provides a long and lively account of his days with Lawrence in the boarding house at 77 Talbot Street. Lawrence exuberant, Lawrence dancing, Lawrence laughing and others sharing his infectious laughter, Lawrence polished and graceful in company, Lawrence flirting happily with a Yorkshire girl: it is a very different account from those of his London circle. The girl

was a lovely little sport, that Yorkshire lass, full of fun and *joie de vivre*, and she just loved playing up to the grace and bubbling sparkle of Lawrence. Those two simply kept the house uproarious with laughter by their fun and 'love-making foolery', but there was one object that Clara was never able to achieve. On the second night she invited us along to their room 'to help lower the level of the whiskey bottle' as she put it. We excused ourselves . . .[4]

In spite of their restraint that night, another house guest noted rather grimly that Lawrence's 'temperate habits, which his mother had tried to foster in him, had now almost gone . . . they seemed to go out and have a really good time while they were there'. Lawrence could be an exhilarating companion, full of mockery and fun, particularly when away from home, literary circles and Jessie. 'I remember quite clearly, in the visitors' book, they drew themselves as this tall man, Lawrence, and Neville, this little fellow, and put underneath "the arrival"; and then, before they left, they drew themselves later [as] two bloated people as had had a good time . . .'[5] Lawrence and Neville spent a week in Blackpool, c. 6–13 August, and then went on to Leicester. But when they arrived at the Krenkows' house, 20 Dulverton Road, they found Lydia Lawrence ill: 'a tumour or something has developed in her abdomen. The doctor looks grave and says it is serious: I hope not' (i. 176). Lawrence hoped it was a non-malignant tumour; but it was actually a carcinoma, or cancer.

Poor Ada Krenkow. In March 1908 her sister Ellen ('Nellie') had come to stay with her for a holiday, and had gone down with kidney disease: within a month, she had died in the Krenkow house.[6] Lydia, on holiday, was now also fatally ill. Lydia Lawrence stayed in Leicester for about a month, with her family coming over from Eastwood when they could. On 28 August, Lawrence had to go back to Croydon for the start of term; Lydia Lawrence was however still capable of writing letters, and Lawrence had (for example) 'a little note' from her on Saturday 17 September in which 'she says she is better again this week end than she was on Monday and Tuesday'. But, he went on, 'she would never let me know how bad she was' (i. 179). Two photographs of her sitting up in a chair with a rug over her knees and a book in her hand, taken in the back garden of Lynn Croft, show that she was taken back to Eastwood while the weather still remained good and before she was confined to bed (see Illustrations 27 and 28).[7]

There was little the doctors could do. Lawrence himself simply came up to Eastwood from Croydon every weekend he could manage. He was correcting the proofs of *The White Peacock*: Helen Corke remembered his face 'set with pain' as he worked on them.[8] One unforeseen result of his frequent visits to Leicester had been that he had seen more of Louie Burrows (currently working just outside the town) than for a couple of years. She also visited Dulverton Road, and was able to help keep him informed about his mother's condition. She it was, therefore, who received his spare set of the proofs of *The White Peacock*: 'Mother may not read them, may she?' (i. 178) he asked, obviously hoping that she might nevertheless want to see them. Louie always remembered Mrs Lawrence, wearing 'a little rose pink dressing gown', talking not about *The White Peacock* but about 'The Saga of Siegmund' in the library of the Dulverton Road house: 'She spoke with a tiny breathlessness as though emphatic speech would be physically painful to her.' Even after Lydia Lawrence was taken back to Eastwood, Louie's warmth and concern were a great stand-by; she visited Eastwood and sent flowers (i. 189), and Lawrence's elder brother George particularly remembered her as 'very kind when mother was ill'.[9]

Meanwhile, Lawrence's life in Croydon continued its usual round: with the exception that he did not go out as much as he used to, as he had to pay for so many extra train journeys to the Midlands. He did not go up for Alan Chambers's wedding to Alvina Reeve on 15 October, which suggests his difficulty. He told a friend on 30 September that 'I have not been into any literary society: – indeed, not in London at all, for months and months' (i. 180). He had, in truth, little inclination: on 3 October he was feeling 'as miserable as the devil' (i. 180) and he used the same words nine days later, when accepting an invitation for an evening out. But, he added, 'It behoves me to be gay, I am so sick inside' (i. 182). *The White Peacock* was also taking far longer in production than had been expected; and, as Lawrence remarked on 18 October, 'I *do* want that book to make haste. Not that I care much myself. But I want my mother to see it while still she keeps her live consciousness' (i. 184). In fact, in spite of Heinemann's efforts, no copy was available before early December. It is a proof of the publisher's embarrassment over the delay that, in September, they agreed to give Lawrence an advance on royalties which was unwarranted by their contract with him:[10] he received a cheque on 15 September 'for £15 on account of general royalties to be earned' (i. 177 n. 2). But it was the expenses of his mother's illness for which he needed the money; it may have paid for the specialist's visit to Leicester to see her, though Ada Krenkow herself paid £3 for treatment from her local doctor, Dr James Eddy (i. 283). A good deal of the £50 which the book earned him must have been spent on railway fares, doctors' fees and funeral expenses. Like *Rasselas*, which paid the costs of the funeral of Dr Johnson's mother, *The White Peacock* became inseparable from its author's loss.

By 9 November, Lawrence knew they were simply waiting for an inevitable end: 'My mother gets rapidly weaker' (i. 186) he told Grace Crawford, and the Eastwood doctor H. M. Gillespie informed him that his mother had only a fortnight longer. His sister Ada was allowed leave of absence from school from 11 November 'on account of the very serious illness of her mother':[11] Lawrence, too, requested leave of absence, and on Wednesday 23 November travelled back to Eastwood to be with her and to help Ada with the nursing. There he waited: sat with his mother: saw friends: went over to Leicester. But, more than anything else, waited. 'I sit upstairs hours and hours, till I wonder if ever it were true that I was at London. I seem to have died since, and that is an old life, dreamy' (i. 189). Lydia Lawrence was often in fearful pain; and when the pain left her – 'Oh the weariness', she moaned on 3 December, so quietly that (Lawrence went on) 'I could hardly hear her. I wish she could die tonight' (i. 189). Yet she kept her hold on life. May Chambers remembered Lawrence describing those last days:

'Just watch and wait, watch and wait. There's nothing more to do. She doesn't talk to us at all now. She hardly speaks. She's hardly conscious and yet,' he paused and looked at me, 'at the exact right time she says, "Have they got your father's dinner all ready for when he comes home?"' His eyes and voice were soft and questioning. 'Why does she think of that? How does she know the time? . . .'[12]

The Eastwood miners' strike, which had started at the end of June, ended on 25 November: the detail in *Sons and Lovers* of the dying Mrs Morel asking if the men were complaining of sore hands, now they were back at work, is probably taken from life.[13] Ruling and running her house, and providing for the money-earner in it, had been Lydia Lawrence's life-work.

The days dragged by, snowy and stormy in December (i. 192). The advance copy of *The White Peacock* promised by Heinemann came at last, on 2 December – for months Lawrence had been 'day by day anxious to receive a copy for my mother. Will there not soon be one ready?' (i. 187). Its arrival, though, was an anti-climax: 'Mother just glanced at it. "It's yours, my dear," my sister said to her. "Is it?" she murmured, and she closed her eyes. Then a little later, she said, "What does it say?" – and my sister read her the tiny inscription I had put in. Mother has said no more of it' (i. 194). The inscription ran: '2nd Dec 1910. To my Mother, with love, D. H. Lawrence' (i. 194 n. 3) – the initialled signature designating the published author which at last he properly was.

Arthur Lawrence went to work as usual; Lawrence sat with his mother, talked to her, painted, wrote his play *The Merry-Go-Round*, visited a few friends: was outwardly controlled, but – his sister Ada wrote when it was all over – 'suffered tortures during these long weeks of her illness'. His sister Emily remembered him saying 'Why should his mother, that had never done anyone any harm, have to suffer like that? Oh yes, he did . . .' He never forgot it:[14] in 1927, shocked at the lingering illness of his old friend and next-door neighbour Gertrude Cooper, he commented: 'It starts Lynn Croft all over again' (v. 631). He saw a good deal of May Chambers and her husband Will Holbrook over at Moorgreen, enjoying the atmosphere of their cheerful and plain-speaking marriage: there was an irony in that, of course. But May Chambers was one of the very few people with whom he could share what he was feeling. She remembered his saying, a few days later still,

'She's barely conscious now. I doubt if she knows us.'

Bert pressed his back against the high armchair and lifted his head as if bracing himself to say it:

'And Father never goes up to see her.'

I said, 'But he asks.'

'Oh, he asks. Every day as he gets in from the pit, he asks, "How's your mother today?" and we tell him.' His voice fell to a shocked, almost horrified tone. 'But he never goes up to see her.'

'He knows without seeing,' I said.

'But he *ought* to go up,' he insisted softly. 'He ought to *want* to see her. He should go up.'

'He can't,' I ventured. 'Things have happened between them.'

'But he was once her lover,' he protested with wide eyes.

'That doesn't matter,' I said.

'Then what does matter?' he demanded in a voice that broke as if strangled.[15]

'Then what does matter?' was the question he would come back to, over and over, as he watched his parents' marriage end, during these days.

Lydia Lawrence grew weaker and weaker: 'and still she is here, and it is the old slow horror' (i. 192). Life in Lynn Croft, such as it was, went on. 'My heart winces to the echo of my mother's pulse. There is only one drop of life to be squeezed from her, and that hangs trembling, so you'd think it must fall and be gone, but it never will – it will evaporate away, slowly. And while she dies, we seem not to be able to live' (i. 195). The night watches seemed endless: Lawrence 'got a cold with going to sleep on the floor in the midst of my watch' (i. 198). Part of his agony was the feeling that, after her punishing life, 'this is the conclusion – no relief' (i. 195): 'She has had a bloody hard life, and has always been bright: but now her face has fallen like a mask of bitter cruel suffering. She was, when well, incredibly bright, with more smile wrinkles than anything: you'd never know that this was the permanent structure on which the other floated' (i. 192). Her dying made Lawrence articulate about his feelings for her in a way he had never been before, as we saw in his remarks to May Chambers. He wrote about her to Louie Burrows: 'She is my first, great love. She was a wonderful, rare woman – you do not know; as strong, and steadfast, and generous as the sun. She could be as swift as a white whip-lash, and as kind and gentle as warm rain, and as steadfast as the irreducible earth beneath us' (i. 195). But now all he wanted for her was for her to die. Paul Morel, in *Sons and Lovers*, asks the doctor to give his mother something to make her die: her will to live is so strong. The doctor refuses, but Paul takes things into his own hands. In December 1913, Lawrence told an acquaintance made in Italy, Lina Water-field, that – just as described in *Sons and Lovers* – he and his sister Ada finally gave Lydia Lawrence an overdose of sleeping draught. He wrote into the novel's proofs how 'On top of all their horror flickered this little sanity.'[16]

Lydia Lawrence died the following day. Lawrence commented: 'I think this is finally the bitter river crossed. It certainly feels like one of the kingdoms of death, where I am. It is true, I have died, a bit of me' (i. 199). He registered her death himself, the day she died. They buried her on 12 December: 'and there is gone my love of loves' (i. 199). On the gravestone they had the words 'It is finished' inscribed, to commemorate her exemplary, even Christ-like life and suffering.

This account of the autumn of 1910 has left out two extremely important facts: that Lawrence asked Louie Burrows to marry him on 3 December, and she accepted; and that it was also the moment when he began to write the novel which eventually became *Sons and Lovers*. It is time to retrace our steps and consider the larger perspective of the year.

II Biography, Autobiography

Lawrence started his autobiographical novel 'Paul Morel', which would one day become *Sons and Lovers*, not long after finishing 'The Saga of Siegmund'; and from the first it seemed to its author to be a reaction against the earlier novel. However, ideas for the novel – and for related projects – can be dated back at least to the early part of 1910, and some of them even earlier.

That is not surprising. As early as *The White Peacock* he had been experimenting with portraits of his mother, his sister Ada and himself. Cyril and Lettie's mother is named 'Beardsall', had long brown ringlets as a girl, is addressed as 'Little Woman', uses the Puritan 'child' in addressing her children, is 'fifty odd years' old, smiles 'sardonically' and within a page of first appearing launches an attack on her son for spending so much time with the farm family (while blaming the family's daughter for attracting him): all exactly like Lydia Lawrence.[17] Mrs Beardsall's background as a young wife who 'revolts from' her husband is very similar indeed to what Lydia Lawrence had told her children about herself; while the ex-husband of *The White Peacock* is dismissed as 'of frivolous, rather vulgar character, but plausible, having a good deal of charm. He was a liar, without notion of honesty, and he had deceived my mother thoroughly. One after another she discovered his mean dishonesties and deceits, and her soul revolted from him ...'[18]

However, the history of Mrs Beardsall's marriage, and her current situation in life, are utterly different from Lydia Lawrence's. Lawrence had drawn for his fiction on what his mother had told him of her youth and her family; and he had started to look at her marriage. But everything which related to recent times had been completely altered: in *The White Peacock*, Frank Beardsall abandons his wife when their children are quite small. The complicated problem of children growing up in a divided home is therefore evaded: there have been no family quarrels, no money problems either (all these characters are middle-class). That was characteristic of the use to which Lawrence put his prose fiction – and his family – before 'Paul Morel': the extraordinary thing about his play *A Collier's Friday Night* in 1909 was that it had actually created a tension-ridden working-class family, and was thus different from anything else he had written.

But there survives another, and stranger, description of the life of a character drawn from Lawrence's mother. By November 1909 Lawrence had drafted a sequence of nine poems he called 'A Life History In Harmonies and Discords'. He had actually referred to it in *A Collier's Friday Night*;[19] and he copied it into his poetry notebook sometime before February 1910. It is a peculiarly inaccessible sequence of poems because at some stage Lawrence heavily deleted parts of it in his notebook, and obliterated very nearly the whole of one poem; the final poem may also be unfinished. On the other hand, two of the poems (in revised form) are well-known in their own right, having become 'Twenty Years Ago' and 'Discord in Childhood'.[20]

However, Lawrence remembered as late as 1928 that 'Discord in Childhood' had originally been part of a longer poem. He wrote how 'I must have burnt many poems that had the demon fuming in them. The fragment *Discord in Childhood* was a long poem, probably was good, but I destroyed it.'[21] Fortunately he did *not* manage to destroy it completely, and many lines are perfectly legible; it contains some of his most inventive early poetry.*

It starts with two extraordinary poems (written rather as if Blake had been influenced by Whitman) about birth and patterns of opposition. The whole sequence 'A Life History', with its contrasted 'Harmonies' and 'Discords', is constructed out of such oppositions. But the first two poems together suggest (on the one hand) the necessity of contraries and (on the other) the violence that inevitably accompanies their co-existence.

The third poem presents the speech of an unhappy woman. Like the Lady of Shalott in Tennyson's poem, only in her mirror can she find eyes and lips which (narcissistically) respond to her unhappiness. But then two other very blue eyes and two little hands (which must be those of a baby) bring her joy and 'Plant my heart like a garden,/Grow lilies in brackish sands'. Harmony is here seen growing out of discord; but its sudden growth

---

* Because of the particular interest of this poem-sequence, it is printed in full – so far as it can now be recovered – as Appendix III.

makes us unsure about a mother who is so clearly using her child to help her escape her own unhappiness. Mrs Morel's love for Paul, and the way she sees him as a way of making up for her marriage, are the obvious parallel in Lawrence's writing.

The fourth poem is heavily deleted, and only a little less than half is recoverable; but that shows the conflict of two opposites (who seem, in the fragments of the third and fourth stanzas, to be parents): like Night and Day they oppose each other – and between them 'went tramping the panther of scorn,/Skulked the hyaena of spite'. The poem can be seen as the counter-part of the third poem; again we are aware of the precarious position of children at the centre of the opposition, caught as they are between the scorn and the spite.

The fifth and six poems, focusing upon the children, explicitly contrast scenes 'Round the house' and 'Outside the house'. The first is idyllic, with pain and trouble soothed by the mother – 'Between a mother's knees, a trouble/Lost all its little meaning': the second (which became 'Discord in Childhood') parallels the lashing of the ash tree in the wind outdoors with the 'booming dreadful sound' of the man's voice and the 'swift thin lash' of the woman's voice, as they quarrel indoors. Lawrence described his mother in 1910 as 'swift as a white whip-lash' (i. 195). The woman's voice is drowned by a 'fearful ominous silence' in the quarrel: the 'spell of blood' dominates the silence. This, again, precisely parallels those scenes in *Sons and Lovers* where the children hear the howling of the ash tree and the raised voices of the parents in the room below where they sleep.

The seventh poem is a consciously artificial patterning of colours and shapes, as the narrator constructs a harmony. However, in the last stanza, a partnership between two people is also suggested – 'an intimate joyous connection' – which parallels the harmony revealed in pattern and colour and shape.

Against this, the eighth poem – sadly, no more than a few fragments – uses flowers to suggest its 'discord': 'One by one the fingers of love loosened the petals/from off the rose'. The third line, with its 'fallen chrysanthemum petals', brings to mind Lawrence's story 'Odour of Chrysanthemums', drafted almost simultaneously in the early winter of 1909, with its account of a marriage surrounded by symbols of death; *A Collier's Friday Night*, written, too, late in 1909, also mentions the jar of 'ragged pink chrysan-themums' in its fictional version of the ornaments of the Lawrence household.[22]

But the Hardyesque last poem is in a way the most fascinating of all. Suddenly, a narrator speaks: 'I trace a pattern', he says, and that exactly describes the whole poem: a consciously patterned piece of art. But, he says, the pattern he traces – which to a casual eye might be no more than a random pattern of feet on a pavement 'With broken curves and faltering lines' – can also be seen as 'mine or thine'. It is as if he shared some kind of identity with the woman whose story has been told in the previous eight poems.

He recognises that his job is to find out what the pattern is, and to 'over-line' it – that is, as artist (and word-artist) to bring out the shape of the pattern he has managed to distinguish. Yet he is also conscious that the pattern of the 'blindly stepping kindly feet' has become entangled with his own pattern: 'The curves waver and meet and intertwine/Twisting and Tangling mine and thine'. Using the image of a graph of plotted points, he attempts to distinguish the 'part of my graph' which 'was plainly plotted' – and which he can therefore dispassionately 'over-line' – from the part 'Where the curves were knotted'. His problem is, somehow, to 'define/Pains that were clotted over mine'. And he knows that 'clotted' pains confuse 'her' pattern with his own; he may attempt to 'define' the pains by 'over-lining' them on his graph, but the fact that they are 'clotted over mine' (with their pain transmitted to and shared by him) suggests the near impossibility of finally distinguishing between the 'mine' and the 'thine'. Yet it is his job as an artist to try to do so.

This last poem describes an artist confronting the patterns made by the lives and conflicts of others: he declares that his role is that of definition, even when the conflicts touch him very nearly – so that he can hardly tell whether the patterns he can see are those in his 'material', or those surviving within himself. It is a striking poem for the incipient author of 'Paul Morel' to write. As well as being a work of art in its own right, it is an author's instruction to himself about what his job should be when he deals with material such as the story of his mother.

So when we find him, a few months later, starting a novel which began with an extended treatment of the early life of Lydia Lawrence, the project would seem to be one for which he had been consciously preparing himself. He and Louie Burrows had started to send each other writing to criticise and revise in the summer of 1909 (one product of their collaboration had been 'Goose Fair'). They were still sending each other work in January 1910 (i. 152); and Lawrence had sent Louie a manuscript (hereafter called 'Matilda') some time before he remarked on 24 July 1910, presumably in response to a query from her about what had happened to it since she had seen it: 'As to "Matilda" – when I looked at her I found her rather foolish: I'll write her again when I've a bit of time' (i. 172). The forty-eight page fragment is, like the manuscript of *The White Peacock*, divided not only into chapters, but into subsections within chapters; something rather rare in

Lawrence's writing.[23] That perhaps suggests the fragment's proximity in time to the earlier novel; the manuscript of 'The Saga of Siegmund', his next full-length work (finished in July 1910), had no such divisions. Seeing that Lawrence was fully engaged between late January and July 1910 first on revision of the second 'Nethermere' for Heinemann, then on starting 'The Saga', then on further revision of 'Nethermere', and then on finishing 'The Saga', it would seem at least possible that he had drafted 'Matilda' in early January 1910 – shortly after 'A Life History'; on 23 January he excused himself for not writing to Louie on the grounds that 'I scribble so much' (i. 152).

As it now exists, 'Matilda' is only a fragment: a fictional account of events in Lydia Lawrence's childhood. It is set in the Norwood of the 1860s: Lawrence transfers the setting there, from the real-life Beardsall home of Sheerness. Matilda Wootton is a child of 10 at the start of the story, the eldest of six children; she, her mother and father are in the same social situation and described in exactly the same way (and even in some of the same language) as Gertrude Coppard, her father and mother in *Sons and Lovers*. An account of Robert Wootton's career exactly parallels that of George Coppard in the later novel; his pride, his 'overbearing manner' to his wife, his religion, are identical. Even the way 'Matilda' ends parallels a development in *Sons and Lovers*; Matilda is working as the assistant to an old woman who runs a private school – and Gertrude Coppard in *Sons and Lovers* 'remembered the funny old mistress, whose assistant she had become, whom she had loved to help in the private school'. The fragment of chapter II of 'Matilda' suggests that it might also have continued in parallel with *Sons and Lovers*; Matilda Wootton has made the acquaintance, in Norwood, of a young man, Arthur Murray, rather as Gertrude Coppard gets to know John Field when she is young; and although 'Matilda' stops before the relationship really starts, the fact that John Field in *Sons and Lovers* also ends up in 'Norwood' confirms the parallel.[24]

Although 'Matilda' is written with occasional sharpness, it is in general a rather unwieldy collection of childhood memories and anecdotes from the history of the Wootton family. Presumably Lawrence meant to go on to describe the young life – and the marriage – of Matilda Wootton. But it is striking that, sometime before July 1910, Lawrence had started to do what six months later – when Lydia Lawrence was dying – he said would be the most 'awful' piece of writing he could imagine – 'a biography of my mother' (i. 195). 'Matilda', as he had begun it earlier in the year, was by no means such a daunting project, and his thinking in 'A Life History' had helped prepare him for it.

Both 'A Life History' and 'Matilda' suggest that one route of access to the

Sons and Lovers material was directly through 'a biography of my mother'; though it is doubtful whether such a book could have been balanced, or fair, when it came – if it came – to describing Matilda's marriage to a collier. The kinds of rather sanctimonious approval of Mrs Morel still bubbling up in the 1911 'Paul Morel', and even occasionally in *Sons and Lovers* itself, in 1912, suggest the dangers for Lawrence of an approach from the point of view of a main character. The 'biography' Lawrence eventually came to write would not separate Mrs Morel's life off from that of her husband, nor from the children whom she herself influences.

At all events, Lawrence – finding 'Matilda' 'rather foolish' – abandoned its manuscript; there is no evidence that he ever started to 'write her again', as he suggested to Louie that he might (i. 172). In July 1910 he was however fully occupied with 'The Saga of Siegmund'. But he could not let the project rest completely: and within a month and a half of finishing 'The Saga' he had started 'Paul Morel' – a very different kind of novel from 'Matilda'.

Two lines in the last poem of 'A Life History' are worth a moment's further notice: 'With pain did I carefully overline/What part of my graph was plainly plotted'. When Lawrence wrote to his publisher in October 1910 to tell him about his new novel 'Paul Morel', 'plotted' was the very word he used about the part not yet written, but 'plotted out very interestingly (to me)' (i. 184). Perhaps that is merely a coincidence. And yet a draft 'Plot' for a good deal – perhaps all – of Lawrence's third novel survives.[25] It must be an early version of the 'Plot' which he mentioned to his publisher in 1910; it certainly is not an outline of the second draft of the novel, written in 1911. A good deal of that novel survives and it is quite different.

The 1910 'Plot' fragment, however, shows a novel as far from 'Matilda' as it is possible to go. Worried perhaps about the 'foolishness' of the 'Matilda' material, and about the weighting of a book written from her point of view, not only does Lawrence cut the material out – but he practically omits the Matilda character as well:

I

i. Introduction – he pushes her out of the house before the birth of their son.

ii. Tears without cause – watching the engines on Engine Lane – young sister ⌐Aunt Ada⌐ ⌐playing in Breach house⌐

iii. Sent to school – ⌐long lane⌐ young brother – ⌐Sunday school – super. Cullen⌐ Miss Wright – visit to Cullens – ⌐Newcombe lives there⌐ ⟨Jess⟩ ⌐Floss⌐

iv. Move from Breach – Mrs Limb – Father hospital – ⌐Miss Wright⌐ making toffee in evening.

V. Return of Father – walks with Mabel – filling straws – visit to Aunt Ada

vi. Band of Hope – Fred strikes father – father blacks eye – Miss Wright – Fred in office – horse manuring – Mabel – painting

vii. Fred dancing – quarrels with father – Gertie teacher – Wm. learns from her – ⟨J⟩ Flossie friends – Mabel jealous – Wm. ⟨with ⟩ ⌜at⌝ Mr Bates' school – painting. – visit Aunt Ada

viii. ⟨Death of Fred.⟩ Death of Fred – Wm ill – Mabel – death of Walter Morel – Aunt Ada superintends

II

i. ⟨Fred⟩ ⌜Wm.⌝ begins at Haywoods.

ii. Goes to Miss Wright for painting – meets Flossie much ⌜& Newcome⌝ – reads & learns – neglects Mabel – she becomes engaged.

iii. Advance at Haywoods – Miss Haywood & painting (red-haired Pauline) – Newcome very jealous

iv. Flossie passes high – renewed attention of Wm. – great friendship after painting in Castle – death of Miss Wright.

v. Flossie in College – death of Miss Wright[26]

Part I starts almost where the final version of the novel starts: it probably remained a common beginning to all the intermediate drafts. But this reference to 'her' in the 1910 'Plot' is the only certain appearance of the mother. The son is named 'William', so the novel plotted here could not have been 'Paul Morel' – but 'William' and 'Billy' were among his family's pet names for Lawrence himself.[27] Instead, the character 'Aunt Ada' is given a crucial role. She enters the 'Plot' at the end of chapter ii (about William's childhood), she is visited at the end of chapter vii, and when 'Fred' – apparently William's elder brother – dies along with the father Walter Morel in chapter viii (probably in a version of the Walter Lawrence manslaughter followed by prison sentence used in the 1911 revision of the novel), she 'superintends'. Mrs Morel simply vanishes; it looks as if she has either left her husband, or has died. Whatever else was included in this idea for the novel, the marriage of the Morels cannot have been its central subject. In an attempt to cut out the superficiality of 'Matilda' – and also, perhaps, out of sensitivity to Lydia Lawrence's actual desperate illness – Lawrence's intended novel would, like *The White Peacock*, have completely ignored the problem of the unhappy working-class marriage.

A good deal of Part I is concerned with material which Lawrence reused in subsequent drafts of the novel: 'Tears without cause ... young sister ... filling straws ... quarrels with father ... painting' all stayed in the book until the end. But the book seems preoccupied with violence at home (as in chapter vi when 'Fred strikes father – father blacks eye') set against a middle-class environment outside it. This is created by 'Aunt Ada', by the 'visit to Cullens' and by 'Wm. at Mr Bates' school', which sounds like a private school quite unlike Beauvale Board School. Like the 1911 'Paul Morel', the first part of the book climaxes with the traumatic events of the death of a brother and the death of a father.

Part II is concerned with the hero's subsequent career: he works 'at Haywoods' (this parallels Paul at 'Jordans' in subsequent versions). But instead of Miriam, his most important relationship appears to be with 'Flossie': and as many names in the 'Plot' are not changed from their real-life originals, this was quite probably a version of Flossie Cullen, the daughter of the grocer George Henry Cullen, whose family Lawrence would describe in 'Paul Morel' in 1911, and whose own career he would later sketch out in 'The Insurrection of Miss Houghton' of 1913 and *The Lost Girl* of 1920. But she also seems to be amalgamated (as the character Clara would later be) with a version of Louie Burrows: she is academically successful and goes to college. The draft 'Plot' ends with 'Flossie in College – death of Miss Wright'. Miss Wright, the Cullen family governess and in effect Flossie's substitute mother, died on 9 October 1904; and though we do not know if the 'Plot' is complete, Lawrence may have planned to make the death of Miss Wright the climax of his novel. It is striking that, after the death of his own mother, Lawrence would specifically express his sympathy with Flossie Cullen: 'I often think of Flossie. If I don't write to her – well – she will understand. But I know what she's had to go through, and has: and I think of her very often, with sympathy' (i. 234). In 1910, before Lydia Lawrence's illness and death, Flossie Cullen's was the experience of loss which Lawrence was most impressed by, and which he was apparently planning to draw upon for his own fiction. She had been deprived first of a beloved guardian, Miss Fanny Wright, and then very shortly afterwards of her mother (who died in November 1904): at the age of 25 she too had been left to cope with a difficult and demanding father. One explanation of the absence of Mrs Morel in the 'Plot', and of the book perhaps ending with the death of 'Miss Wright', would be that Lawrence could not bring himself in September or October 1910 to 'plot' such an ending for Mrs Morel. 'Miss Wright', another 'mother', took her place. Using 'Miss Wright' and 'Flossie' in such a way would however throw the book's emphasis upon another family, another child and parent altogether. That might account for the book's curiously broken-backed structure in the 'Plot', and the absence of relation between the opening chapter and the rest of the novel. The idea of writing 'a biography of my mother' (i. 195) was actually terrifying to Lawrence: he almost certainly did not want to make the first 'Paul Morel' such a book.

Not a page of the first 'Paul Morel' survives, only the 'Plot'; as the novel Lawrence began to write in September or early October 1910 was 'Paul Morel', it must have differed from the surviving 'Plot' in many respects. By late September Lydia Lawrence was seriously ill; by early October, Lawrence reported that she was 'very ill' (i. 181); by 18 October, she was 'really horribly ill' (i. 185). On the same day, he told Heinemann that 'about one-eighth' of the novel was written (i. 184). He had apparently promised them his second novel for August 1910, but Hueffer's condemnation of 'The Saga of Siegmund' had decided him not to press for its publication. So although Hueffer had forwarded the manuscript of 'The Saga' to Heinemann, Lawrence told Pawling 'we can let the thing stay, and I will give you – with no intermediary this time – my third novel, Paul Morel'. 'Paul Morel' was thus a substitute for 'The Saga'.

Lawrence also made it sound the complete opposite of 'The Saga'. It was 'a restrained, somewhat impersonal novel. It interests me very much. I wish I were not so agitated just now, and could do more' (i. 184). For a manuscript five to eight hundred pages long, 'one-eighth . . . written' could mean anything between sixty and one hundred pages.[28] On 11 February 1911 he declared that the 'Paul Morel' manuscript 'sticks where I left it four or five months ago, at the hundredth page' (i. 230), which suggests that he did not do very much to it after describing it to Heinemann.

Having abandoned the writing of 'Paul Morel', Lawrence was also able to realise what kind of a novel he might have written instead. We can even see him starting to compose that 'new' novel when he wrote an extraordinary letter to Rachel Annand Taylor on 3 December 1910. With his mother still alive, Lawrence launched himself into an account of the history of her marriage: the past tense of his writing showing how close to death he thought she was, and also revealing the distance which his objective narrative style was giving its subject.

I will tell you. My mother was a clever, ironical delicately moulded woman, of good, old burgher descent. She married below her. My father was dark, ruddy, with a fine laugh. He is a coal miner. He was one of the sanguine temperament, warm and hearty, but unstable: he lacked principle, as my mother would have said. He deceived her and lied to her. She despised him – he drank. (i. 190)

And so on: sentences that, in almost any other circumstances, would have been turning themselves into a fiction, not a letter. Lawrence went on to include his relationship with Jessie Chambers, his break with her and his sense of his mother's love having made him 'in some respects, abnormal' (i. 190). He describes his sudden proposal (that very day) to Louie Burrows, on the train to Quorn, and the way in which that fitted into the pattern of his mother's love for him and his love for his mother. Like the character Clara in the novel, Louie would never be like Jessie Chambers (or like Miriam); 'She will never plunge her hands through my blood and feel for my soul' (i. 191). And, in the middle of all this, 'I look at my father – he is like a cinder.' A novel is there, in embryo: blurted out almost uncontrollably, under intense pressure, to a woman who was almost a stranger – and yet sympathetic, at such a moment.

The illness and death of Lydia Lawrence irrevocably changed the direction of a novel which was (at most) one-fifth written. The 'Paul Morel' novel, in its second writing, would after all concern itself with the worst aspects of the Morel marriage, which Lawrence had begun to describe so tellingly in his letter to Rachel Annand Taylor. This would certainly account for Lawrence's remarks at the time when he restarted the novel, during the weekend of 11–12 March 1911: 'I am afraid it will be a terrible novel' (i. 237) – because it would, after all, be the 'awful' biography: and, as he said to Helen Corke, 'glory, you should see it. The British public will stone me if ever it catches sight' (i. 239). It would do what other novels had never done: describe the complex pain and tragedy of a working-class marriage which had gone wrong.

However, during the final course of his mother's illness, when he was home from Croydon and helping to nurse her, all that Lawrence wrote were some poems and his comedy *The Merry-Go-Round*. The novel – which he knew 'belongs to this' (i. 195) – could be restarted later; Lawrence decided that he was 'not going to write or read till January – not much, at any rate' (i. 201).

But *The Merry-Go-Round* – 'candidly impromptu' (i. 477) as Lawrence himself admitted it – was all the same a remarkable thing to have written at such a moment: remarkable for its linguistic vitality, and for the light it throws on one of the most poignant events of his life. As he remembered, 'When things get too intolerably tragic one flies to comedy' (i. 200). The dying Mrs Hemstock in the play, as Keith Sagar pointed out, is 'unambiguously harmful to her whole family, especially to her thirty-year-old son Harry, who is "nowt but a baby" and "scared to death of a wench" '.[29] But although this provides an extraordinary sidelight upon Lawrence's relationship with his mother – and suggests that, as in *A Collier's Friday Night*, he risked things in plays that he would not risk in other genres – the very realism of the dialogue compelled a kind of honesty for which he had as yet no narrative voice. Yet Mrs Hemstock herself is actually very unlike Lydia Lawrence. She is a working-class woman with the potential for satire and the dialect inventiveness of her background. She may do a lot of damage to

her family, but her directness is wonderful. The nurse offers to lift her on to
the couch:

Mrs Hemstock: No, tha wunna. I non want droppin' an' smashin' like a pot. I'm
    nowt but noggins o' bone, like iron bars in a paper bag. Eh, if I wor but the
    staunch fourteen stone I used to be.
Nurse: You've been a big woman.
Mrs Hemstock: I could ha' shadowed thee an' left plenty to spare . . .[30]

The play (a deliberately complex formal comedy, a Midlands *As You Like It*
with a contrived ending) is scrappy, uneven and too long – not surprisingly,
given the conditions of its writing. But compared with the artificiality of so
much of Lawrence's writing during 1910, it is a revelation. Emotional taste
and distaste are handled wittily and directly; ordinary lives are not occasions
for artistic self-communing on the part of a narrator, but for direct and lucid
exploration. When Harry Hemstock talks with the baker, Job Arthur
Bowers, he cannot help mentioning Rachel Wilcox, a girl he dislikes but
who fancies him: and to whom, in a way, he is attracted in spite of his
distaste.

The Baker: . . .—But what hast got against Rachel?
Harry: Nowt—but I heave wi' sickness at the thought of 'er.
The Baker: Hm! I like one as'll give as much as she takes.
Harry: A sight more.
The Baker: It depends who's who.
Harry: I can never make out why she went in service at the vicarage.
The Baker: Can't you?—I've had many a nice evening up there. Baron an'
    Baroness go to bed at nine o'clock and then—. Oh, all the girls know the
    advantage of being at the vicarage.
Harry: Oh—an' does she ha'e thee up in th' kitchen.
The Baker: Does she not 'alf.
Harry: I thought she wor so much struck on me—!
The Baker: You wait a minute. If she can't feed i' th' paddock she'll feed at th'
    roadside. Not but what she's all right, you know.
Harry: I do know.[31]

The baker's pragmatism is beautifully caught: while Harry, wanting to be
loved, shows his need for Rachel's admiration while simultaneously realising that she makes him sick. The dialogue is sharp, funny and economical:
and it is a thousand pities that, although Lawrence could write like this,
publishers and producers neither believed in nor accepted such a craft.
Lawrence was encouraged to go on believing that his future was as a writer
of fiction and poetry; and he adopted for them the literary style he believed
appropriate.

III *An Idyll*

Although he was not yet going to restart his novel, during the last days of his mother's illness he was also active as a painter: and the final work we can link to the death of Lydia Lawrence is Lawrence's water-colour copying of Maurice Greiffenhagen's celebrated painting *An Idyll*. It is not known when he first saw the painting reproduced; but he knew it by August 1908, when he singled it out for conveying passionate emotion.[32] His attention was drawn to it again at the end of the year, when Blanche Jennings sent him a reproduction; the original still hangs in the Walker Art Gallery in Liverpool, her home town. He replied to her:

As for Greiffenhagen's *Idyll*, it moves me almost as much as if I were fallen in love myself. Under it's [sic] intoxication, I have flirted madly this christmas; I have flirted myself half in love ... it is largely the effect of your *Idyll* that has made me kiss a certain girl till she hid her head in my shoulder; but what a beautiful soft throat, and a round smooth chin, she has; and what bright eyes, looking up! Mon Dieu, I am really half in love! But not with the splendid uninterrupted passion of the *Idyll* ... By the way, in love, or at least in love-making, do you think the woman is always passive, like the girl in the *Idyll* – enjoying the man's demonstration, a wee bit frit [frightened] – not active? I prefer a little devil – a Carmen – I like not things passive. The girls I have known are mostly so; men always declare them so, and like them so; I do not. (i. 103)

At that stage he was 'reading' the painting primarily from the point of view of the male figure and his 'uninterrupted passion'; the passive role of the female both fascinated and disappointed him. By the autumn of 1909, and possibly rather earlier, he had included in 'Nethermere' a passage in which George Saxton is also first shown the *Idyll* by Lettie. George exclaims 'There! ... Wouldn't it be fine?' What he means quickly becomes clear: 'a girl like that—half afraid—and passion!' He is one of those men who prefer the woman 'a wee bit frit'. But he has great difficulty saying any more: ' "But," ... "it would be—rather—" ... "But I shouldn't—" ... "I don't know whether I should like any girl I know to—" ' [33] That is, George also prefers his women conventional: it hardly matters whether he means 'I wouldn't like any girl I know to behave like that' – embracing the passionate, half-naked Arcadian shepherd – or 'I wouldn't like any girl I know to look at such a painting'. However passionate he is made by the painting, he would *not* like a woman willingly to abandon herself to passion. But his excitement also embarrasses Lettie, who had herself once been enthusiastic over the picture. Characteristically, she evades him (and it) by accusing him of 'studying just how to play the part' of the passionate man, when he is actually 'breathlessly quivering under the new sensation of heavy, unappeased fire in his breast, and in the muscles of his arms'.[34] Both are actually fascinated and excited; but while George is unable to do more than simply contain his feelings, Lettie runs away from hers into game and role playing. Lawrence uses the painting to suggest George's potential – that of the inarticulate but instinctively passionate man – and also his limitation within instinct: while the painting also shows Lettie scared of her own sexuality. The painting continued to fascinate Lawrence because it provided a strong visual analogue of what he was struggling to do as a writer: create both the power and the danger of instinctive feeling.

But in 1908 and 1909, in spite of his regular copying of other paintings, Lawrence does not yet seem to have copied the *Idyll*. His copying was devoted to less controversial material; so that, when he finally did begin to make a copy of the *Idyll* in December 1910, it stood out as something unique in his output. During his mother's illness he had at first been copying Frank Brangwyn's *The Orange Market* for Ada. But 'the night mother died' (i. 243) he began to sketch the *Idyll*: and within seven months he had produced three copies of it; he even began a fourth in December 1911. No multiple versions survive of any other of his copies. He finished two *Idylls* in March 1911, one for Louie and the other – the copy he had started the night his mother died – for Ada. He made a third copy for Agnes Holt in July; it had been she who had copied for Lawrence those pages in the first 'Nethermere' in which George and Lettie look at the painting together, and she especially asked Lawrence to make her a copy as a wedding present (i. 282).[35]

It is impossible to ignore the coincidence of Lawrence making his first copy of the painting simultaneously with the death of his mother, and immediately after starting his engagement. It may have been that he felt released into copying it; his painting had previously always been uncontroversial and something of which Lydia Lawrence had thoroughly approved. But even more significantly, the way he was starting to think about his parents' marriage, as his mother lay dying, links directly with the painting. He had described his father to Rachel Annand Taylor as 'dark, ruddy' in the letter containing that abortive account of the marriage: Lawrence was now starting to see his father symbolically, as representing the less conscious aspect of man's nature, just as he was beginning to see the potential of the 'dark, ruddy' figure in the painting. Again, one can compare the account of his mother in the letter – a strangely plastic description of a 'clever, ironical delicately moulded woman' – with the delicate flesh tints and modelling of the woman in the painting. Copying the painting in December 1910 could be a way of doing what his letter to Rachel Annand Taylor had done, and the 1911 'Paul Morel' would do: contemplating the

285

tensions of the relationship of Lydia and Arthur Lawrence. It could also, like so much of his work, be a work of autobiography: because the questions he was asking about his parents' marriage were the same as those he was asking about his own engagement, six days after getting engaged to Louie Burrows.

The previous simplicity of Lawrence's readings of the painting – 'splendid uninterrupted passion' – 'passive, like the girl' – could now be replaced by the much more complex questions of the marriage and the engagement: and they made it a work worth copying again and again. He now saw himself in both the figures; both possibilities were his own. Painting a copy of *An Idyll* for Louie Burrows was a way of saying that he was like his father as well as like his mother. He would have liked to be 'pagan' himself, immersed in his feelings: in contrast with the role he assigned Louie, potentially passionate but actually constricted by her religious background, he would himself have liked to be the unconscious and passionate man.

He feared, however, that he was always likely to be self-conscious: and he was extremely reluctant to accept commitment to another person. As in the 1911 'Paul Morel', he now had to ask: is the instinctive man a brute, as he traps the woman who is different and tries to bring her down to his level? He also had to ask whether the girl in the picture was really superior, as she turns away from the passion her partner shows, endures his embrace and looks out towards the spectators with a look which emphasises her entrapment. The only major difference between all three of his copies, and the original, is that Greiffenhagen's girl has her eyes turned away from the spectator; while the slight awkwardness in Lawrence's handling of her figure further stresses her unhappiness in the embrace she suffers.

Painting a copy for Louie was also a way of encouraging her *not* to be the 'passive' girl, 'a wee bit frit', which he feared she might be. In March 1911, he made the link explicit between her reluctance, and what he wanted the painting to say to her, by complaining how 'You know, Lou, you make me ashamed of passion – I've finished the *Idyll*, by the way' (i. 242). In all his copies of the painting, he made the red poppies scattered over the woman's dress, the man's legs and in the grass spectacularly vivid: they are the flowers of unashamed passion, suggestive of the crushed carnations which cover the ground and besprinkle Clara's dress like drops of blood after she and Paul make love in chapter XII of *Sons and Lovers*. The message to Louie would be clear: as it would be to Agnes Holt, about to marry. But the painting was also a message to Ada, in the first copy he began: it was a painting of the struggle and tension which as children they had both inherited, of the duality of their own upbringing.

IV   Rain on a Grave

On Friday 9 December, Lydia Lawrence died. Arthur Lawrence lived on another fourteen years; when asked why he did not marry again, he replied 'I've had one good woman – the finest woman in the world, and I don't want another.' There is a lingering irony in his determination not to marry another 'good woman'. Lawrence wrote 'little poems' to his mother, both before and after her death: 'She'd like that'. He met Jessie Chambers on the Sunday and gave her drafts of three of the poems: he also told her about his engagement to Louie Burrows (i. 197).[36] On Monday 12 December, with Lawrence in charge of the funeral arrangements, in pouring rain and a storm of wind, Lydia Lawrence was buried in the grave of Eastwood Cemetery where her son Ernest was already buried. Lawrence did not forget the rain. He was in New Mexico when his father died in 1924, and wrote to his sister Emily: 'And when did you bury him. I hope it didn't rain' (v. 124). On Tuesday 13th, after taking a wreath from Louie Burrows to the cemetery ('all maiden hair, and cold chrysanthemums, and a bunch of Neapolitan violets'), Lawrence caught the train back to London and to work. 'I wore one or two of the violets, and I kept catching their scent all the way down to London, in the warm carriage' (i. 202), he told Louie.

CHAPTER ELEVEN

◆

1911

THE SICK YEAR

I Louie Burrows

Lawrence's engagement to Louie Burrows lasted from 3 December 1910 to 4 February 1912. The idea of a close relationship with Louie had intrigued him for years; he had always found her attractive, and she had been drawn to him ever since they had first met in 1905. The Burrows family (inheritors of a tradition of yeoman farmers but not themselves working on the land) lived until 1908 in Cossall, only a couple of miles from Eastwood; Alfred Burrows taught woodwork and handicrafts. Louie, born in 1888 and the eldest of seven children, had gone to Ilkeston Pupil-Teacher Centre in 1904 or 1905, where she met both Jessie Chambers and Ada Lawrence. The latter introduced Louie to her brother: 'asked me to wait with her so that she could borrow his india rubber'. At that date Lawrence 'was already teaching so came on Wednesday & Saturday. He was slight & tall in blue serge – fair with blue eyes and the nicest smile. He became at once very interesting to me. Ada made us known – borrowed his rubber & we moved on.' He was lively and talkative, but Louie soon became aware of the link between him and Jessie Chambers; he was 'less sportive in J's presence because they conversed chiefly of more serious things'.[1] Their continual talk of art and artists had, to Louie, 'seemed strange & showy, all on the surface with much talk – of Rossetti of Carlyle':

> You didn't just read a poem gently to yourself – but you announced that you would read it – and would discuss it at such a-time, – and you read for uplift – criticising feverishly & for the sake of criticism . . . My own enjoyment of life was direct – less vicarious. They must imagine themselves as someone soulful – some character in a poem. It was enough happiness for me to be myself . . .[2]

From the start, Louie appealed to Lawrence's lively, carefree side: something in which Jessie Chambers had no interest. In 1908, for example, when Lawrence and Louie flirted outrageously at Christmas-time, Jessie was one of those who (very naturally, given her own feelings) disapproved: 'Lord, we were imps,' Lawrence wrote to Louie in January 1909: 'I know three or four folk who would love to shake me. Do you?' (i. 105). The following month he chose not to go to Louie's birthday celebrations: 'do you think J, you, and I make a happy triangle? . . . somebody has a bad time when we three meet. Do you not feel it?' (i. 112).

But in contrast with Lawrence and Jessie, Louie in 1905 felt much less well-read, and far less interested in books: 'literature for me was simply tales told and had precious little to do with life. I had not myself the slightest experience of life . . .'[3] She became, however, a friend both of Jessie Chambers and of the Lawrences. Notes she made around 1931 recalled her first visit to the Lawrences' house, probably just after Christmas 1905, and remind us of the Lawrences' difference from their neighbours: a choice of midday meals (even if Christmas left-overs) surprised the unexpected guest, as did the house's lack of ostentation: 'Later in Xmas holiday in snow I went there for the day – not expected – choice of stew or joint – a very delightful afternoon with Bert – the little bare parlour – cushion at back in window – sun on my hair at sunset'.[4] But while neither Jessie Chambers nor Ada Lawrence went to college, Louie Burrows went there in 1906, the same year as Lawrence: she was his constant companion, ' "my girl" in Coll' (i. 193), 'always been warm to me' (i. 190). She was physically 'about as tall as I, straight and strong as a caryatid . . . and swarthy and ruddy as a pomegranate' (i. 193); more than once he told her she was 'tawny' (i. 64, 114): another 'Gipsy' Louie. Around 1907, Lawrence made drawings of her which included imagined nude studies; he continued to see Louie, and to write her letters, from 1906 on. Jessie Chambers remembered his speculating about the possibility of a 'purely physical' marriage with Louie: he told Jessie 'I could marry X. from the purely animal side', and Jessie rather superciliously reckoned that two lines of his poem 'Snapdragon' – 'And there in the dark I did discover/Things I was out to find' – were 'a literal description of the situation'.[5] But Jessie's attempt to represent Louie as simply physically attractive, while she herself was necessary to what Lawrence called 'The writing, all that side of me', ignores the fact that by 1907 Louie, too – possibly because of Lawrence's influence – had ambitions to be a writer: we find Lawrence playfully fantasising about her 'years hence, . . . in your study as you sit writing your newest novel' (i. 42). Louie began with short stories; she and Lawrence exchanged pieces for criticism, and in the autumn of 1909 he rewrote one of her stories as 'Goose Fair', his first publication of fiction in the *English Review*. They shared the proceeds of its publication. After college, in 1908, she had gone straight into a teaching job in Leicester (i. 60 n. 1);[6] but after a bad time in her first school, in January 1909 she had become headmistress of the small Church of England school in Ratcliffe-on-the-Wreake, in Leicestershire. She continued to see a good deal of her family, even after setting up on her own: but with six younger brothers and sisters growing up, must have been glad of her independence from the family home – a home, Lawrence felt a couple of years later, which 'would be nice if there were not so many folk' (i. 316).

What made the crucial difference to their relationship was the accident of her living and teaching near Leicester in the late summer of 1910, when Lydia Lawrence fell ill at her sister's house there. Lawrence saw Louie regularly between August and October, on weekends up from Croydon; and on a visit to the Midlands between Thursday 6 and Sunday 9 October (he had permission from school to be away on the Friday), he arranged to see Louie on the Saturday evening. Late in life, she attached a note to the postcard in which he made the arrangement. It has the terse expressiveness of a poem by Emily Dickinson: 'I went – and we walked home by the canal & then to his train at Ilkeston. Our first knowledge of our love came on that evening – but it was unexpressed though both knew – it was communicated – as it were electrically by a handshake.'[7] Lawrence later told her that he had asked his mother 'carefully', late in October or early in November, 'Mother, do you think it would be all right for me to marry Louie – later?'; and that Lydia Lawrence had at first answered ' "No – I don't" – and then, after half a minute "Well – if you think you'd be happy with her – yes" ' (i. 197). The new relationship with Louie grew throughout the period of his mother's illness. A poem called 'Reminder' can also be dated to the 'unlit autumn' of 1910: the poem's narrator is condemned to watching his mother dying, but in spite of 'great kisses' from the woman to whom he goes for release, she will not give him what he asks for:

> For you told me 'no'
> And cried to me not to ask you for the dour
> Communion: you would give me something better.
> So I lay on your breast for an obscure hour—
> Feeling your fingers go
>
> Like a rhythmic breeze
> Over my hair, tracing my brows,
> Till I knew you not from a little wind . . .

Lawrence may have written the poem thinking of Helen Corke; it may equally well have been provoked by what was now happening between him and Louie.[8] A number of times in his writing after 1910 Lawrence showed the violent attraction to a woman of a man whose parent is dying, or has died. It is as if the strong sexual attraction, and the torture of the parent's often long-drawn-out death, became locked together in the writer's imagination: as one love is torn away, so another is violently, even deliberately born. In *The Rainbow*, after his father-in-law's death, Will Brangwen feels that 'death and all seemed to gather in him into a mad, overwhelming passion for his wife';[9] that is something many writers have shown. But when Lawrence came to write about Gerald Crich in *Women in Love*, he would show him particularly attracted by Gudrun Brangwen while his father is suffering his long-drawn-out death agony: and in chapter XXIV going to her bedroom at night when his father is dead. In *Sons and Lovers*, chapters XIII and XIV, Paul Morel goes to Clara in exactly the same situation. And in 'Two Marriages', in July 1911, Lawrence showed a man attracted to a woman (incidentally called Louisa) upon the death of his mother. In each case the woman is at first less strongly attracted than the man: her initial response is not sexual but pitying, out of her desire to comfort the man.

Yet Lawrence stressed in both his surviving letters about the circumstances of his own actual engagement on 3 December 1910 that it had been 'quite unpremeditated' (i. 190), 'an inspiration ... What made me do it, I cannot tell' (i. 193). He had been in the train from Leicester to Quorn with Louie, five other women also in the compartment; obviously with his mother's impending death in mind, Louie had sympathetically asked him what he was going to do after Christmas. He had said that he would like to get married.

'Should *you*?' I asked. She was much embarrassed, and said *she* didn't know. 'I should like to marry you' I said suddenly, and I opened my eyes, I can tell you. She flushed scarlet. – 'Should *you*?' I added. She looked out of the window and murmured huskily 'What?'. – 'Like to marry me?' I said. She turned to me quickly and her face shone like a luminous thing. 'Later', she said. I was very glad. The brakes began to grind. 'We're at Quorn' I said, and my heart sank. She suddenly put her hand on mine and leaned to me. 'I'll go to Loughboro' she said. The five women rose. 'I can come back by the 8.10,' she said. The five women, one by one, issued forth, and we ran out among the floods and the darkness ... (i. 193)[10]

His insistence upon the suddenness and unexpectedness of the proposal may have been an attempt to explain something he knew his friends would find disconcerting, but it also revealed his commitment to impulse and spontaneity. Impulse had led him to surprise even himself: but he stood by his impulses – the engagement seemed suddenly, even miraculously, to answer a long-lasting problem in him, as his mother died. Louie was a woman both more straightforward and less demanding than Jessie Chambers, Helen Corke or any other of Lawrence's close relationships had been. She was very warm and lively; and although not an intellectual, was certainly intelligent. Like him, though only 20, she had emerged from her college course with a first class teacher's certificate. She was an independent woman who shared some of his own interests, like writing; she was also known as a suffragist.[11] Lawrence had written her a specially lengthy account of the Croydon by-election of March 1909, which was the scene of keen activity by the suffragists (i. 122–4). She must have left him feeling more his own man, and less possessed, than any of the other women in his life would have done: to that extent was an escape from the old patterns. And she could be 'jolly' into the bargain; she enjoyed parties, she loved clothes and being 'in the cream of fashion' (i. 212–13).

We can also see how Louie, with her yeoman farmer background – and her fantasy, which Lawrence gently mocked, of 'May I live to be a lady' (i. 213) – would have struck Lydia Lawrence. Helen Corke thought of Louie as 'a girl of his mother's world',[12] meaning that she was a woman Lawrence's mother would not have objected to. Lawrence told Louie the same on 6 December: 'I know she approves, and she always liked you' (i. 197), while Louie herself felt certain that Lydia Lawrence was 'very fond of me' (i. 197 n. 2). Louie, like everyone in Lawrence's circle, had for years been aware of Lydia Lawrence's feelings about Jessie Chambers. She remembered how Mrs Lawrence had been 'considerably upset' in the spring of 1906 because Jessie had got into the first class of the King's Scholarship exam (as Lawrence himself had done), while Ada Lawrence had only got into the third. Lydia Lawrence had put Jessie's result down 'to DHL entirely tho I knew that J was of a much more studious nature & had better health. Nevertheless there was increased jealousy of J and I was given a welcome even warmer than usual.' Jessie was always uneasy when in company with Lydia Lawrence; but Louie admired Lydia and naturally sided with her. In 1909, for example, when Jessie had 'enthused over Emily's baby and I didn't – his mother remarked "No Lou sees enough of babies at home" which was marvellously true and clear sighted of her. She didn't like J's intense enthusiasms . . .'[13] Nor, clearly, did Louie.

Louie also offered a marvellous contrast to the long-running conflict between spiritual companionship, intellectual need, possessive love and physical unhappiness which had plagued Lawrence's relationship with Jessie. Immediately after the engagement, what Lawrence stressed was Louie's handsome warmth and freedom from care – 'like a sunny happy day' (i. 190). She made him 'feel happy with a sort of warm radiation – she is big and dark and handsome . . .' But that in turn made him still more agonisingly conscious of his mother:

when I think of my mother: – if you've ever put your hand round the bowl of a champagne glass and squeezed it and wondered how near it is to crushing-in and the wine all going through your fingers – that's how my heart feels – like the champagne glass. There is no hostility between the warm happiness and the crush of misery: but one is concentrated in my chest, and one is diffuse – a suffusion, vague. (i. 190)

Lawrence's imaginative participation in his mother's state is vivid in the image of the crushed-in glass; the metaphor seems to start as one of her fragile life being crushed out of existence, but turns into an account of his own feelings. Six months later, Lawrence described (in 'Two Marriages') Alfred Durant's agony as he waits for his mother to die, 'feeling as if red hot iron were gripped round his chest'; his pain in direct correspondence with his mother's pain: 'a fierce, cutting *physical* fever of grief, that came on in bouts, as his mother's pain came on in bouts'.[14] Against such feelings, Louie offered the only possible kind of relief: a 'suffusion, vague'. But there could be no 'hostility' between the agonies he went through as his mother died, and the happiness he felt about Louie, any more than there was any connection between the simile of the 'sunny, happy day' and the 'crushing-in' of the champagne glass. What Louie offered seemed to be outside the old conflicts created by Lydia Lawrence.

And what Lawrence hoped Louie would give him was, above all, relief; from the start of their engagement he connected her with rest and sleep, which extended to fantasies of sleeping *with* her. A few months later he sent her a four-line fragment about sleep from his poem 'A Love Song', in which the relief turns directly into sexual fulfilment:

> To toss the troubled night long through for you
> To dream the bliss of your great mouth on mine
> To feel the bliss of your strong life lift through
> The weight of this my body, fallen on thine.[15]

The poetry is not Lawrence's best: but it is struggling to imagine a new experience: love with a self-reliant, vigorous woman. Lawrence also sent Louie an early version of his poem about sleep which he later called 'Martyr à la Mode': 'you, vast, outstretched, silent sleep,/Permit of no beyond'. His desire to sleep with Louie was, at least in part, precisely that: a longing, as he told her in December 1910, for 'Somebody to rest with – you perhaps don't know what a deep longing that may be – perhaps you do know' (i. 198). He would write in *Sons and Lovers* of Paul having 'ease of' his mother when he sleeps in her bed,[16] and he had told Jessie Chambers, at the start of their 1910 relationship, how 'It is as if I cannot rest without you near me, you goodly thing' (i. 157). But what he had tried to make Jessie into – warm, passionate, healing – Louie was naturally. He was more cynical but no less precise when, the day after expressing to Louie his need for 'Somebody to rest with', he told Violet Hunt that he would be 'daft as Dostoieffsky' if he couldn't soon 'stick my head in some hole – c'est à dire, a woman's bosom' (i. 199). He also told his old friend Sallie Hopkin ten days later how 'I could adore any maiden just now if she were sufficiently fruitful and reposeful in her being' (i. 211). Like sleep, Louie – in this fantasy, anyway – would 'permit of no beyond': would bring no complications with her, would be utterly relieving, 'fruitful and reposeful in her being'. He had written to her immediately after their engagement that

The more I think of you, the more I am glad that I have discovered the right thing to do. I have been very blind, and a fool. But sorrow opens the eyes. When I think of you, it is like thinking of life. You will be the first woman to make the earth glad for me: mother, J[essie] – all the rest, have been gates to a very sad world. But you are strong and rosy as the gates of Eden. We do not all of us, not many, perhaps, set out from a sunny paradise of childhood. We are born with our parents in the desert, and yearn for a Canaan. You are like Canaan – you are rich and fruitful and glad, and I love you. (i. 195)

In the middle of the cold and slush of those winter days, as his mother slowly died with her face 'grey as the sky' (i. 194) – she who had once been 'generous as the sun' (i. 195) – Lawrence made Louie paradise, the pro-mised land, light and flame, flowers and fruits and wine: 'pomegranate – that's your symbol' (i. 198): 'full-fruited and rash and open as a sunflower' (i. 197): 'bright and vital as a pitcher of wine' (i. 193). His love for his mother had been 'rather terrible' (i. 190); but the mutual possessiveness of that love, the frightening exclusiveness of the bond, was being replaced (he hoped) by 'a fine, warm, healthy, natural love'. For, unlike Jessie Chambers – and unlike his mother, too – Louie 'would never demand to drink me up and have me' (i. 191). Lawrence was making Louie a symbol of what would save him both from the death of his mother and from his attraction to Jessie. None of his later love letters is as direct and compelling as the very first one, of 6 December 1910, which – while his mother still lived – revealed his *future* hope for Louie: Louie as the promised land. She knew this: 'at the first he delighted in the experience of new love'.[17]

Even his 6 December letter, however, contains a significant reservation: 'Don't love me too much' (i. 197). He could not shut out that old fear, even from his new happiness. And implicit in his way of thinking about Louie was a most dangerous reduction of her to the person he most needed, and of himself to the person most suitable for her. He told her, for example, that after his mother had died, 'I am going to write romance – when I have finished Paul Morel, which belongs to this' (i. 195) – presumably to this death, this misery. But Lawrence was no more capable of being simply a writer of romance than he was of loving Louie for ever in a paradisal future, however genuinely he wished to. Just as the 'Paul Morel' novel 'belongs to this', so '*this*', however painful, was the local habitation of Lawrence's living and writing: and, from the very start, he attempted to exclude his engagement from it.

For Louie Burrows, too, far more than for Jessie Chambers or Helen Corke, the engagement was not a testing ground for relationship. It was a sensible and committed period of waiting; from the start it was her 'serious and settled conviction' that 'We cannot marry yet awhile for a long time' (i. 237). The first of Lawrence's surviving letters after their engagement mentions the financial basis for their future: 'Oh, I wish I could get some money. There was a money-spider on my hair this morning, dangling in front of my nose. I thought to myself "Oh, if only that meant £100 – we might be married after Christmas." Because all you want, if we had money, you could buy' (i. 197). £100 capital was to furnish a home, and his wish for it seems genuine enough. Yet even though the last sentence stresses to Louie that the money is to buy what she deems necessary as homemaker – she apparently had a hankering for 'black furniture' (i. 246) – Lawrence implicitly dissociates himself from it: 'all you want . . . you could buy'. They were to agree by January 1911 that marriage would need '£100 in cash and £120 a year income' (i. 223): his income, of course, because that was the expectation of a couple in their social and economic situation. She might even have kept her job when first married but have given it up shortly afterwards (as Ada Lawrence did in 1913). By the end of July 1911, either Lawrence or Louie had pushed their starting figure up to £150 a year (i. 293).

But the salary of an elementary schoolmaster permitted such savings or earnings only over a period of years; and Lawrence's agreement to those figures may even have been an unconscious strategy on his part to use financial circumstances as an excuse for not marrying. At any rate, as he told her in April, because 'you are not inclined to bolt through the hedge of circumstance – why, circumstance, like a hedged lane, will have to lead us where it will' (i. 248–9). When he went away with Frieda Weekley on 3 May 1912, he made an uncommon bolt out of the hedged lane (and his experience of the opposite with Louie must have encouraged him to make the break). But his engagement to Louie was an engagement to marry, not the desperate seizure of a necessary relationship.

Unfortunately, Lawrence was not the man to need the home Louie was planning. His mother's death had broken up the only home he had ever known. His sister Ada took over caring for his father, and they had moved on 9 March 1911 to share Bromley House in Queen's Square, Eastwood, with her sister Emily and brother-in-law Sam King (together with their 2-year-old daughter Margaret); but there is little sign in Lawrence's surviving correspondence that he regretted the loss of his old home. On the contrary, when Ada asked if he wanted anything from the Lynn Croft house, he replied: 'No, there is nothing I want – saving the woman, and, if you like, the black vases, which will always remind me of home: not, God knows, that one wants too much to be reminded thereof' (i. 233).[18] The Queen's Square house was never 'home' to him (i. 280). He was to travel remarkably light all his life, never owning property nor very much of anything: as he put it in 1910, 'Possessions all go under the heading "Impedimenta"' (i. 197). And he told Louie how inconceivable it was 'that I should own property: a house. It will have to be yours' (i. 302). Frieda would remark, about possessions, that he 'had no use for them. He used to say "They weigh you down, your movements are hampered. A trunk and two hand-bags are more than enough."' His capacity for remaining clear of 'the world's gear'[19] would stand him in good stead when he went away with Frieda in 1912; but it was in absolute contrast to what his engagement to Louie offered and demanded. His mother's death, his increasing impatience with and dislike for schoolteaching, his belief in his writing, all prepared him for homelessness and financial insecurity just at the time when the engagement demanded that he behave responsibly as saver and breadwinner.

II 'Paul Morel'

The engagement also directly affected his ambition to be a writer. If giving up a safe schoolteaching job were unimaginable to the potential wife, then the time Lawrence expended on his writing also became something he needed to justify to Louie in terms of results and (ideally) returns. According to Jessie Chambers's painful recollection, early in 1911 Louie was passing around a copy of The White Peacock 'as the work of the clever young author to whom she was engaged'; a congratulatory letter from a college friend on her engagement shows that Louie had not been slow in advertising the novel: 'I hope that Mr. Lawrence's book will be a success. I shall go to the library to read all the criticisms.'[20] But Louie's attitude towards the books may also have been provoked by how Lawrence wrote about it to her:

I shall be very sorry if I get no success . . . from the White Peacock: chiefly, because it will leave me miles further off from marrying you; also, because I want a measure of success, and the book deserves it . . . I cannot save £5 a year without descending into petty carefulness. When shall we marry then? We trust to luck and literature. I have worked hard enough at that damned mill to obtain a reward so insignificant in cash. (i. 223–4)

Money from 'literature' might be able to assist them where their regular incomes could not. The White Peacock actually made relatively little money, but the attitudes expressed in that letter help explain Lawrence's subsequent promise to Louie to write ten pages of 'Paul Morel' regularly – probably every week. Not only was the book promised to Heinemann and already overdue: but a £50 advance on royalties for it would take Lawrence and Louie half way towards their £100 lump sum. Lawrence probably restarted the novel during the weekend 11–12 March; but it cannot have been more than about eighty manuscript pages long when the Easter holidays began on 13 April. The promise to Louie must have been made during the holidays, and on 24 April Lawrence made his first progress report:

24 April   I am going to write a bit of Paul Morel, if I have any luck with myself. (i. 260)

28 April   I have done only about five pages of MSS, 'Paul Morel'; and that only from sheer pressure of duty. (i. 262)

1 May   At your behest I wrote yesterday fourteen pages of Paul Morel . . . (i. 264)

7 May   I have managed my ten pages of Paul . . . (i. 265)

9 May   The 112 pages of Paul are pages such as this on which I write. Am I a newspaper printing machine to turn out a hundred sheets in half an hour? (i. 266)

29 May   I'm going to do a bit of Paul. (i. 263)[21]

4 July   I've done a fair amount of Paul . . . (i. 281)

But by the middle of July he had probably abandoned the promise, the plan and the novel; his impatience on 9 May shows how irritated he felt with Louie's 'behest'.[22] She, however, probably felt that their future as a married couple depended upon his success as a writer; a future made possible not only by 'luck' but from earned and profitable success with 'literature'. Loving him as she did, what could have been more natural than that she should hope for success?

Some puzzling characteristics of the novel Lawrence wrote in such circumstances can be seen to be partly a consequence of his attempt to write a successful novel, at a steady rate, out of recalcitrant and painful material. Paul is really only half a person; his younger brother Arthur is his intelligent and over-sensitive other self. Mrs Morel is an heroic, self-sacrificing and almost saintly figure: 'the final lesson of life is honourable self-sacrifice', preaches the novel's narrator. Mr Morel, however, is a drunken, 'infinitely vulgar' character who actually vanishes from the novel for long stretches;[23] who is alone at fault in the family quarrels, even in a short-tempered family; and who finally kills his son Arthur. He has been, from the start, a rather ineffectual drunkard – his son Paul sees him from an upstairs window one day getting into a fight and being rolled in the dust – but the killing is a direct consequence of his drinking and his envy of his superior sons. 'He had drunk till his iron constitution was ruined: ruined by drink and moral despair, both. Now he was very inflammable, fiercely irritable, and in his rage there was a viciousness, a starting back of fear, as there is in the rage of a cowed mongrel.' Lawrence used many details of the Ilkeston manslaughter of 1900; exactly like Walter Lawrence, Walter Morel throws a carving steel, kills his son, is tried and convicted, but is 'scarcely in prison at all'.[24] He dies within a year of his return home.

This would apparently have left Paul at last living happily at home with his mother. But, as if recognising that he has severed many of the novel's tensions by killing off Mr Morel, Lawrence then causes Paul to fall ill with the pneumonia which in later drafts of the novel follows the death of William. And Paul's illness rouses Mrs Morel to life again: she has – astonishingly – been prostrated by her husband's death. Paul gets better, and talks reassuringly about being 'great'; Miriam reappears too, as a peripatetic music teacher. The novel is starting to fall to pieces. Lawrence attempts to revitalise it by beginning a new chapter, originally called 'Passion', about Paul's relationship with 'Frances Radford' (the Clara figure in this version).[25] This was the only part of the 1911 'Paul Morel' to survive into the final 1912 manuscript, where fifteen heavily revised pages appear; they suggest a rather desperate but none the less significant attempt to rescue the 1911 novel.

But just as vulgarity and brutality are injected into the character of Mr Morel for the sake of carrying off the murder episode, so there are other rather desperate attempts to *make* the book significant, striking and interesting. Lawrence's attempt to write his weekly ten pages – or at least, to write as much as he could – probably contributed to the fact that there are narrative homilies on, for example, Mrs Morel's genius at saving money to equip their dining table decently: 'It cost Mrs Morel a great struggle to win back taste and refinement into her home, that had grown so ugly during the bitter, weary times when her children were little. And ⟨it⟩ ˹there˺ was ⟨something heroic⟩, in her contrivance to get the table refined, something noble, a kind of divine intuition.'[26] In spite of Lawrence's distinction between 'romance' and 'Paul Morel' in December 1910, the novel itself is in danger of turning into romance, as when (for example) Miss May – to whom Paul goes for painting lessons – remarks about his painting of wallflowers that

". . . they have something about them—a ⟨sort⟩ ˹kind˺ of glisten in their darkness—quite a touch of genius, Paul."
Paul coloured, was very glad.
"If I am a genius," he thought, "what will my mother say. That will be the thing she'd like most, to have a genius for a son."

Whereupon he fervently hoped he were a genius, although he was convinced that, of himself, he was nothing 'of the sort'. Perhaps, though, he might be turned so as to catch the light of God at an angle sometimes, and the light would break into ⟨shad⟩ colours.[27]

It is, of course, extremely interesting that Lawrence should thus have defused or romanticised his early life's actual conflicts. This is not something we can put down entirely to the conditions under which he was writing in 1911. He was still reluctant to enter deeply into the tensions of his early life; he probably knew instinctively that the novel would take him into dangerous regions. (The painting of *An Idyll* was a far easier matter, for all that it suggested the outline of the Lawrence parents' marriage.) Mr Morel, in a more life-like version of the novel, might not be simply an object for criticism or condemnation; Mrs Morel, if looked at hard, might well appear less saintly than the 1911 version made her, and her attitudes might start to seem responsible for some of the pain of Paul's life. Paul's elder brother William is only a minor character in this draft of the novel, and what *Sons and Lovers* shows of his ambition (fostered by his mother) to 'get on in life' – and his resultant death – has no equivalent in the 1911 'Paul Morel': while the death of Paul's brother Arthur in the 1911 draft is entirely Mr Morel's fault and has nothing to do with Mrs Morel. Lawrence was writing the first part of the novel at the same time as doing his 1911 revisions of 'Odour of Chrysanthemums': but he showed no desire, in either piece, to investigate the tensions of a marriage which might have gone complicatedly, rather than simply, wrong.

For that was a direction which, so shortly after the death of his mother, Lawrence would not have wanted to take. He was still wearing mourning black in May 1911 and feeling that 'I daren't go out of black yet awhile' (i. 265): he used mourning notepaper as late as September 1911.[28] If we compare his rather desperate attempts to produce a regular batch of pages of the novel during the spring of 1911 with the way in which he wrote the two 1912 versions, it becomes clear that the very violence and romanticism of what he wrote in 1911 helped the novel cope with problems it could not solve. It also seems quite likely that Lawrence did not want to write either about the death of Mrs Morel or about the way in which she damages her children. The final version, written in the autumn of 1912, not only made him physically ill while writing it but elicited Frieda's comment: 'His courage in facing the dark recesses of his own soul impressed me always, scared me sometimes.'[29] In 1911 Lawrence could not reach such recesses in himself or in his family; and during the summer of 1911, probably around the point where Paul meets the Clara figure, he abandoned the novel completely. This suggests that he himself knew it was avoiding its real problems. When he remarked in October 1911 that 'I haven't done a stroke of Paul for months – don't want to touch it' (i. 310), he was probably admitting the compromised unreality of what he had written.

III Marriage Considered

The 1911 novel had shown a saintly woman trapped in a hopeless marriage with an unredeemable husband – until released by his death. Not for another year and a half would Lawrence come up with the apophthegm 'the cruelest thing a man can do to a woman is to portray her as perfection' (i. 549). His writing about marriage during the year of his engagement (the year following his mother's death) is particularly interesting. In the spring, he created new or heavily revised versions of his short stories 'A Fragment of Stained Glass', 'Odour of Chrysanthemums', 'The White Stocking', perhaps 'The Shadow in the Rose Garden'; all except the first focused upon marriages either at risk or breaking down. In June 1911, he wrote 'The Old Adam', with its account of the effect of a young lodger upon the married couple with whom he boards (a kind of urban 'Fox'); in July 1911, he wrote 'Two Marriages', the first version of 'Daughters of the Vicar', which showed a middle-class girl abandoning family and respectability for the sake of the working-class man she loves; it also shows her sister marrying a man she does not love, for the sake of financial security. 'Paul Morel', like 'Odour of Chrysanthemums', had showed a middle-class woman trying to minimise the effect upon herself and her children of her marriage to a working-class husband; to that extent 'Two Marriages' was doing radically new things with its sympathetic account of an inter-class marriage. It may have had a beneficial effect upon the writing of the 1912 'Paul Morel'. But 'Two Marriages' – which also owed a good deal to Lawrence's feelings at the start of his engagement – was for the moment kept from Louie Burrows. Lawrence told her as soon as it was finished that 'you can see it as soon as you come to Croydon: it's not worth sending by post' (i. 288) – though, the same day, he posted her a book. Quite apart from what she might have thought of her namesake's behaviour in the story, Louie always felt anxious about time which Lawrence was taking off from work on 'Paul Morel'. When he had told her about writing 'The Old Adam' in June, she must have expressed disapproval, provoking Lawrence to reply: 'Damn Paul. Why mustn't I write Old Adams?' (i. 279). But Louie was never a reader of Lawrence's work as Jessie Chambers had been; it is uncertain whether she even saw the end of the uncompleted draft of 'Paul Morel'. To complete this history of short-story writing in 1911, by November Lawrence had

completed 'Love Among the Haystacks' in its 1911 form; this, too, described the approach to marriage of two contrasted couples.

Such a range of stories with a common theme is not unique in Lawrence's
writing. But the stories of 1911 allow us to trace his loyalties to different
ideas of marriage. The 1911 revisions to 'Odour of Chrysanthemums' link
the story with the cripplingly one-sided account of marriage Lawrence was
offering in 'Paul Morel'; marriage is seen as a matter of the (superior)
woman maintaining home and honour at the expense of her (recreant)
partner. Both might remind us of Louie Burrows's remark that Lawrence
'set as high a standard for me as I for him. He had a very pronounced sense
of what was ladylike. His mother was a lady . . .'[30] But the marriages which
are at risk in the other stories refuse any such analysis; in particular, in 'Two
Marriages' and 'Love Among the Haystacks' Alfred Durant and Geoffrey
Wookey make successful alliances with women of very different social
classes from themselves. Marriages go wrong in these stories because
partners refuse to accept each other, or are obsessed (like the Lindley
parents) with ideas of the genteel; or (like Mary Lindley) marry simply for
security. That suggests a very different idea of fulfilment from anything
Lawrence had yet created in 'Odour of Chrysanthemums' or 'Paul Morel'.
And in particular it was significant that ideas of fulfilment should at last be
supplanting moralistic analysis in Lawrence's fictional accounts of marriage.
1911 was a year in which he was trying to come to terms with divisions in
his own nature and expectations; he had bound himself to a conventional
engagement while simultaneously coming to believe that those in love
naturally behaved unconventionally.

IV Helen and Louie

This was startlingly revealed in March 1911. When Louie had gone home
after having joined him in London for a weekend, Lawrence wrote her a
fiercely honest letter about his frustrations: the letter sounds a new note in
his correspondence with her. She was happy for the engagement to go
steadily forward; but, he wrote,

I cannot slowly gather flowers as I saunter. I wish to heaven I could. I cut straight
through like a knife to what I want. I cannot, cannot slowly enjoy watching the rose
open: I can't help it Louie, I can't. I am really dangerous in my fixed mad aim. I love
my rose, and no other: and when I can have her I shall want no other. But when I
have her not, I have nothing. Your pleasure, which you enjoy, in the thought of me,
is nothing to me. I am a nuisance and a trouble to everybody. Always I am cursing
myself, but it doesn't alter me what I am. (i. 237)

What had caused this? Our understanding of the tensions of the relationship is heightened by a knowledge of the context in which the visit had taken place. Lawrence's insistence 'I love my rose, and no other: and when I can have her I shall want no other' was made the day before he wrote a letter to Helen Corke which shows that, only a few days earlier (just before Louie had come to London) he had been urging Helen to sleep with him and that as usual she had refused. She had asked to be guaranteed his 'intimate company' (i. 239): he insisted that what they wanted was no different, in essentials.

After all, Helene – what difference is there between your arrangement and mine? You say – let us be together, because it stimulates you. – You know you would take my arm when we were alone: you know, when I was a bit tormented, you would put your arms round my neck. Now if you can tell me any difference between this and the ultimate, I shall thank you. (i. 238)

And he unrepentantly insisted that 'I genuinely believe I was *not* wrong in what I asked you' (i. 239).

The letter to Helen Corke gives point to Lawrence's warning to Louie that, as long as he did not have his rose, he felt he had nothing: and that he was dangerous in his fixed, mad aim. It also explains why the end of his letter to Louie had been so full of self-contradiction. He had been discussing an admirer of Louie's called Court, who was

less worthy of you even than I am – else I'd say have him. But he's got no understanding. But a man who causes sorrow by his deeds and yet has understanding is better than a righteous stiffnecked fool who gives disgust.
    Which is vanity on my part.
    And after all, I'm not doing anything wrong, so what am I talking about.
    You will never let me make you unhappy, will you? (i. 238)

He was well aware that he would be causing 'sorrow by his deeds' if Louie knew about them: so had to explain 'I'm not doing anything wrong' (which may technically have been correct, given Helen Corke's refusals). On the other hand, he warns her against himself: 'You will never let me make you unhappy, will you?' Lawrence was certainly in a position to make Louie very unhappy. Quite apart from the fact that she was in love with him, her family were rather against him – 'ne croit guère dans mon amour pour vous' (i. 290)[31] – and might have welcomed any revelations about moral laxity on his part. At one point they even demanded that Louie choose between them and him (i. 291 n. 1); and it was because of pressure from her father, among others, that Louie gave up her job at Gaddesby in July 1911, took a post in her home town of Quorn (i. 271 n. 1) and went back to living at home.

Louie was also quite capable of smelling a mouse, if not a rat: in 'a bit of verse to you' (i. 246) first drafted late in 1910, Lawrence had described how

> Over every single beauty
>   You have had your little rapture
> You have slain, as was your duty
>   Every sin-mouse you could capture.
>
> Still you are not satisfied,
>   Still you tremble faint reproach;
> Will you challenge me that I have beside
>   A key to the rooms you may not broach.[32]

'To my Usurper Love' – the poem's first title – was a pleasant, sardonic, friendly poem; Lawrence sent Louie a couple of stanzas from it in a letter. But, all the way through, it trembles on the edge of seriousness, as Lawrence's comic art tends to. Louie had been made thoroughly miserable by Lawrence's 'sin-mice' when, very early in their engagement, he had offered her 'a brief résumé of my life' (i. 205), and – when she took him up on the offer – had mentioned five serious relationships. He had had to backpedal hastily. She herself was, he told her, one of the five: Jessie was another: 'As for the other 3 . . . well, I lied. They only liked me and flattered me. I am a fool' (i. 208). Agnes Holt must have been one, Helen Corke another and Alice Dax the third. But, during her engagement, Louie was always distressed at the prospect of Lawrence seeing or even hearing from Jessie Chambers, and was (for example) alarmed when he had a letter from her at the end of January 1911 (i. 225–6). As late as mid-May the thought of his seeing Jessie for half an hour still worried her, though Lawrence tried to calm her fears: 'doubtless, soon or late, you will see me with J for half an hour: and doubtless you won't mind a scrap' (i. 269). He also had to allay her fears of other women: when at the start of April he went to tea with Helen Corke's friend Laura Macartney (H. B. Macartney's sister), he reminded Louie that 'she's 35 or 36' (i. 253).

A month later, in May, he also had to resist Louie's request to see his most recent poems. Early in the year, she had copied into his notebook three of the poems he had written on the death of his mother; she now wanted to see what he had written since. The subsequent poems included at least two poems provoked by Helen Corke in March ('Red' and 'Return') and one ('Meeting') inspired by Jessie Chambers. By May the notebook may also have contained 'A Love Song', an extremely erotic poem, only part of which he had sent to Louie. He had to refuse: 'If you will allow me, I will not give them to you. They are all very well dancing up and down the pages of my little note book, shut safely in the cupboard – but wandering, even as speech from me to you, as yet, "no", permit me to say' (i. 272). His difficulty saying 'no' politely is beautifully revealed in the circumlocution. We can again draw a comparison with Jessie Chambers, who seems to have read everything Lawrence was writing – even works like 'A Modern Lover' or 'The Saga of Siegmund' or 'Paul Morel'.

But before we simply condemn Lawrence for his behaviour towards Louie, we should consider what else was happening during 1911. In particular, his feelings for his mother were coming out slowly, like a bruise. From the distance of 1928, Lawrence would look back on 1911 as 'the sick year' after the death of his mother, the year of 'the collapse for me of Miriam, of Helen, and of the other woman, the woman of *Kisses in the Train* and *The Hands of the Betrothed*' – that is, Jessie Chambers, Helen Corke and his fiancée Louie Burrows: although, as he went on to say, it was he himself who actually broke down: 'for me, everything collapsed, save the mystery of death, and the haunting of death in life. I was twenty-five, and from the death of my mother, the world began to dissolve around me, beautiful, iridescent, but passing away substanceless. Till I almost dissolved away myself, and was very ill: when I was twenty-six'.[33] Lawrence did not carry the 1911 'Paul Morel' far enough to write anything about the death of Mrs Morel (if that was, indeed, the ending he had in mind). But when in 1912 he came to describe Paul Morel after his mother's death, he wrote how 'Everything seemed so different, so unreal'; people are only 'small shadows whose footsteps and voices could be heard' – but, like Paul, they are filled with darkness: 'in each of them, the same night, the same silence'.[34] Grief makes the world both vivid and remote. Paul Morel looks out 'at the lighted street. But he was not of it or in it. Something separated him. Everything went on there below those lamps, shut away from him. He could not get at them. He felt he couldn't touch the lampposts, not if he reached . . . he felt he should smash.' The light is haunting and unreal to the person outside it – who feels that 'the night' is the 'realest thing'. In the words of Lawrence's poem 'Troth with the Dead', written sometime in the spring of 1911, 'I enshrine/A dark within me'.[35] The core of darkness revealed at the core of existence, originally an image of death (as in 'Troth with the Dead') but actually revealing part of the true nature of the individual, has taken its place in Lawrence's basic language for the unconscious. This was a discovery of the year 1911, though it took him several more years to realise it fully.

But most vividly of all, Alvina Houghton's experience in *The Lost Girl* comes very close indeed to Lawrence in the spring of 1911. After her mother's death, Alvina is at first apparently 'completely herself again';[36] but then, in a way mysterious even to herself, she is drawn to visit her father's little coal-mine. And when she returns to the surface, she 'blinked and peered at the world in amazement. What a pretty, luminous place it was, carved in substantial luminosity. What a strange and lovely place, bubbling iridescent-golden on the surface of the underworld. Iridescent golden—could anything be more fascinating! Like lovely glancing surface on fluid pitch.'[37] It is of course possible that Alvina's vision was the provocation for Lawrence's 1928 description of his reaction to the 'beautiful, iridescent' world of 1911: the fiction may have helped him recreate the life, rather than the other way about. But both accounts illuminate his experience in 1911, when the world's beauty also seemed to float vivid but unreal over a void or underworld. In 1920, Lawrence stressed the 'golden' light, the 'lovely glancing surface': in 1911, it was golden bubbles of lamps at night and the blaze of green fire in the daytime which fascinated him. 'Troth with the Dead' described how

> This spring that has come bursts up in bonfires green
> Of wild, of puffing emerald trees like fires . . .
>
> I am amazed at this spring, this ⟨. . .⟩ conflagration
> Of green inflaming the soil of this earth, this blaze
> Of blossom, and puffing of sparks in wild gyration
> As the faces of people flash across my gaze.[38]

The same image of the trees' green fire occurs, too, in a letter of May 1911 – 'afire with the vividest green' (i. 266) – and in the short story 'The Old Adam', first written in June 1911: 'those oaks kindle green like a low fire—see!'[39] It was this spring's peculiar quality to be like a world on fire with hallucinatory brilliance, but utterly distinct from the narrator who observes it. The poem 'Drunk', written in the summer of 1911, describes the narrator's fear of a 'haunted road',

> Whose lofty roses break and blow
> On the night-sky bending to their load
>
> Of lights: each solitary rose,
> Each arc-lamp golden does expose
> Ghost beyond ghost of blossom, shows
> Night blenched with a thousand snows,
>
> Of hawthorn and of lilac trees,
> White lilac; shows discoloured night
> Dripping with many a golden flame
> Of laburnum glimmering back the light.[40]

This vision of the golden bubbles of light against the darkness offers another version of the iridescent-golden world, floating on darkness, which Alvina perceives.

For Lawrence in the spring and summer of 1911, the image of illumination floating on the surface of the dark offered a potent image of his own experience: golden bubbles of light – like the 'Tall, brilliant tram-cars' Paul Morel sees in *Sons and Lovers* – contrast with a night which for Paul, 'Out in the Dark' at the end of the novel, seems another and more powerful reality.[41] The experience stayed in Lawrence's consciousness for years, and re-emerged in his writing a little more sharply each time he returned to it.

V   Getting and Spending

A quarrel over money earned by his writing reveals the stresses to which Lawrence's engagement was subject by July 1911. He had just been paid £10 by the *English Review* for 'Odour of Chrysanthemums'; he told Louie about it on Tuesday 11th. The money had been more than he expected,

so that I shall be able to pay off all my encumbrances, get some boots and shirts and a suit, and have just a bit left. I want, when I come up, to bring Mrs Burrows something really nice . . . And if still there remains anything – I have such elastic ideas of £10 – then you and I we will not pinch a bit in the holiday, eh? – I've had to send a tidy bit to Eastwood, to settle matters there. (i. 284–5)

He had sent 30/- to Ada: 'Don't tell Emily . . . and don't tell Louie' (i. 284). But Louie must have replied the next day, Wednesday 12th, with the accusation that he was not even *trying* to save: it might be true, as he had said in January, that 'petty carefulness' would not save more than £5 a year – but a lump sum of £10 was important: and there was Lawrence, simply planning ways of spending it! Not to try to save was tantamount to saying that he did not want to get married.

Lawrence got Louie's reply on Thursday 13th, and wrote a scrappy and petulant reply the same day.

I am afraid you are falling out with me for not attempting to save. And does 10 quid seem much to you. Pah – it is nothing. Shall I make you out a bill of how I spend it? Shall I say how much goes to Eastwood, what I give to Agnes Holt for a wedding present, et cetera. No, my dear – we won't quibble about the money for 'Chrysanthemums'. (i. 286)

But the rest of his letter does little except quibble. '–I don't chuck money about – ten quid doesn't seem to me a lot of money – but a scroddy bit. I went to Dover yesterday alone – trainfare 2/6 – tea 1/- – oddments, 1/-. I suppose it *was* extravagant. No matter, it's done' (i. 286–7). The sardonic catalogue of expenses shows his irritation at the charge of 'chucking money about'. And, in spite of dismissing the money problem for a second time –

'No matter, it's done' – the letter returns to the subject yet again. 'But listen; – if I don't make money in a fairly large sum, I can never save: I have too many calls. So beware – chuck me if you're going to be sick of my failures: but they may be successes' (i. 287). His letters very rarely brought up the idea of ending their engagement; the fact that he did so here suggests how close to the surface lay his irritation.

Louie must have replied by return, in a way which left Lawrence feeling foolish, as well as both rude and petty.

How horrid of me! – I'm awfully sorry. And the tone of your letter in answer was really beautiful, and I love you for it. My dear, it was the answer of a gentlewoman, I fairly rejoice over it. The artist in me rejoices in sympathy with the man. I love you profoundly at this minute. – The profundity of love is a thing that varies, eh? (i. 287)

The 'artist in me' – 'the second me, the hard, cruel if need be, me that is the writer . . . the impersonal part of me – which belongs to nobody, not even to myself' (i. 214) – could rejoice because Louie wrote so sharply and directly. But three days later he was again telling her that 'Je ne te donnerai que des chagrins' (i. 290);[42] he was warning her against himself, without telling her why. Her letter had reminded him, for a moment, how direct and independent she could be: which must have made his own conduct all the more reprehensible to him.

For what gives the exchange its peculiar poignancy is the way it coincided with – and to some extent may have been provoked by – Lawrence's attraction to Helen Corke. The latter later declared that she found Lawrence in 1911 'a changed man, whose prevailing mood was ironical and bitter': very different indeed from the man she had so much admired in 1909 and 1910. She mourned, she said, 'the eclipse of those subtler perceptions which had distinguished him previously'.[43] But her superior tone is a way of expressing her anger with him for bombarding her with a battery of sexual demands. Jessie Chambers believed that some time in the autumn of 1910 – late October or early November – in spite of his developing relationship with Louie Burrows, 'H. C. devient sa maîtresse.'[44] Helen Corke denied that she ever did: but Jessie Chambers was the one person in whom Helen Corke would have confided. Whether or not they actually went to bed together at any stage, it is clear that during 1911 Lawrence was furiously attracted to Helen Corke, and that things came to a head between them at least twice; the first occasion being in March, and the second being the second week of July, when – Lawrence remarked to Louie – 'This sultry weather makes one burn like a fire that wants feeding. I wish you were nearer' (i. 282).

On Wednesday 12 July – a school holiday, for Sports, and the day Lawrence went to Dover – he wrote Helen Corke a letter about what had happened the previous weekend.

What is between you and me is sex. I was good on Saturday [8 July] so long as I remained just sufficiently dimmed by alcohol. But in the end comes the irony that you know is stultified passion. And on Sunday, when I hadn't been able to get a drink because like a fool I had come without money, then I was a nuisance. It is wearying.

On Sunday night, after I left you, I threw away, over St James' railway bridge, the two little articles Jones gave me months back, and which were my articles of temptation. It is no use saying that was another little death I died. I am sick of talking.

But I will never ask for sex relationship again, never, unless I can give the dirty coin of marriage: unless it be a prostitute, whom I can love because I'm sorry for her ... (i. 285–6)

The 'two little articles' must have been condoms. The same letter to Helen Corke helps us understand why Lawrence went on that small and expensive jaunt to Dover the following Wednesday:

I have been extraordinarily happy by myself at Dover. There has been nothing to push back, nothing to get ironic over. The moon rose close against my breast. I think I can manage to live alone body and soul as long as must be. Never, never, – and I *can* keep my soul's vows – never never will I ask a woman for anything again: I will pay her market price.

Note that I write at twenty to one, after an excursion: and so discount a great deal of this as sentimentality. (i. 286)

His trip to Dover seems to have been a deliberate assertion of his self-sufficiency, of doing without women, and of his determination not to be hurt by Helen Corke's rejection. Some of his anger with her (and his tone shows that he was wounded) would have been directed at the fact that she was at least in part lesbian.[45] On the rebound, he was determined 'to live alone body and soul as long as must be'. He could also have looked at the steamers and thought about France and his 'old desire' (i. 215) to escape there: Cyril in *The White Peacock* often goes to France, Bernard Coutts (the hero of 'Intimacy', the 1911 version of 'The Witch à la Mode') has just returned from France, while the hero of 'The Old Adam', Edward Severn (first written in June 1911) was educated there.

The letter from Louie which arrived the day after his Dover excursion, accusing him of not even trying to save for their marriage, brought into cruel focus the extent to which he was *not* 'alone body and soul', however much he might desire to be. It would also have reminded him, rather rudely, that he was (literally) paying someone 'the dirty coin of marriage' – or at least, he was supposed to be paying it, by dint of careful saving. In his poem 'Drunk', probably written during July, the narrator complains that 'she is my love for whom I wait/And serve and wearily save'.[46] Were the serving and saving really only to pay the 'dirty coin' and be rewarded with marital sex? Before July 1911 he probably thought he had more chance of sleeping with Helen Corke than with Louie – especially if she had (even if briefly) been 'sa maîtresse' the previous autumn. Now he felt forced to abandon the idea; was determined to live alone: affirmed rather high-mindedly to Helen Corke, in his renunciatory letter, that 'I love Louie in a certain way that doesn't encroach on my liberty, and I can marry her, and still be alone. I must be so, if I marry – alone in soul, mostly' (i. 285). He was, however – in a horribly comic way – confronted in the next post by his fiancée encroaching on his liberty (in this case his liberty to buy boots, shirts and presents), while simultaneously asserting her claim as fiancée upon him and criticising him for not saving. He had insisted, the previous night, that 'I *cannot* marry save where I am not held' (i. 285), and he had presented Louie as the ideal person *not* to hold him; but here she was, holding him down firmly to his responsibility. All the time he must also have known that the individual aloneness he was proposing was mixed with self-pity: was a way of evading the problems of his life, not of answering them. The man who had recently been writing so sternly and moralistically about the 'recreant' married man in 'Odour of Chrysanthemums' cannot have felt particularly happy about his own behaviour, either.

Finally, when Louie replied to his petty and irritable letter of Thursday 13 July with what he called her 'answer of a gentlewoman', the compliment – though real – was also double-edged. With his 'very pronounced sense of what was ladylike', he also enjoyed the girl 'of his mother's world' being a gentlewoman for him, even if that meant only her ability to be both fair and selfless. Yet he had increasingly felt depressed by what seemed to him her inability to respond to her own feelings – or to his – and to stay aloof in what (with the dismissiveness of hindsight) he crudely and most unkindly called her 'time-long prudery'.[47] Anger would have been more satisfying – even more loving – than wise forgiveness. He had more than once pleaded with her 'do say you love me – and don't be so restrained' (i. 206). He had painted her an *Idyll* as an object lesson. Now – probably within a fortnight of the episode of the *English Review* money – he wrote a poem which summed up his frustrations:

Your Hands

> Her tawny eyes are onyx of thoughtlessness,
> Hardened they are like gems in old modesty,
> Yea, and her mouth's prudent and crude caress
>   Even, means more than her many words to me.

Though her kiss betrays to me this, this only
That in her lips her blood at climax lifts
Like a wild creature up two wild paws for the lonely
Fruit of my heart that with over-ripeness rifts.

I know from her full red lips that hungry her heart is
For me, whom yet if I place my hand on her breast
She thrusts aside as a woman of stall in the mart is
Rude to the pilferer who starves, yet is no-one's guest.

But her hands, her large, strong, generous hands,
Heavier than mine, yet like leverets caught in steel
At my grasp; my baffled spirit understands
Their dumb confession of what her soul does feel.

For never her hands come nigh me but they lift
Like partridges toward the morning stubble, & settle
Timid as these birds on me, timidly shift
Inch by inch across me, melting my mettle.

How furtively she lays her hand on my knee,
How hard she tries to withdraw it, the timid, craving
Gluttonous bird that on my thigh softly
Stirs for the pulse of my flesh, sensations worth having.

And often time she clenches her fingers tight
Oftimes she thrusts her fists in the folds of her skirt,
And sometimes, how she grasps her arms with her bright
Big hands, as if her arms did surely hurt.

And I have seen her stand all unaware
Pressing her spread hands over her breasts, as she
Would crush their mounds in on her breast, and kill there
The anguish, the ache that is the ache for me.

Her strong hands play my part, the part of the man
For her; she crushes them into her bosom deep,
Where I should lie, and with her own strong span
Enfolds herself, that should fold me to sleep.

Ah, and she puts her hands upon the wall
Presses them there, and kisses her white hands,
Then lets the black hair loose, the black coils fall,
And shakes the night for herself from its thick black bands

And sits in her own black night of her bitter hair
Dreaming—ah God knows what, for her speech is the same
Current loose cash she handles everywhere,
And her eyes are like onyx, her lips are tame,

Her bearing is English, modest and reserved,
False as hell; God, what have I deserved
Thus to be tortured, thus to be consumed
Like a covered fire, choked, and bitter fumed.[48]

The poem – to Jessie Chambers 'the terrible poem' in the most fearful sense[49] – is an extraordinary study of repression, focussed upon the body-language of the person studied; it expresses the contradiction between what Lawrence felt was potential but repressed in Louie's nature and what she permitted herself (and him). But the poem expressed anger not only because she would not sleep with him; it looks for realisation of self in relationship, for fulfilment, for language beyond the commonplaces of everyday speech, for the discovery and enactment of sensual possibility – and finds nothing. Lawrence did not often reveal such feelings, but they were the other side of his dutiful submissiveness to Louie and his silent rage at his own confusion.

VI Flames

His short story 'Intimacy' – an early version of 'The Witch à la Mode' – drawing upon the events of March and July 1911, and written no later than August, gave him an opportunity to explore in his writing exactly that complexity of feeling: ideas of loneliness and loyalty, of freedom and bond, reactions of passion and hatred. Bernard Coutts – returning from France – decides to stay overnight in South London before returning to his fiancée Constance in Yorkshire. He goes for the evening to friends in Purley, hoping to meet his old companion Margaret Varley. When they meet, 'they dovetailed into a rare, if combative intimacy'. Coutts, the engaged man, remarks

"I should like to be nailed to something, if it was only a cross."
    She laughed sharply.
    "Is it so difficult to nail yourself to a cross? —I thought the trouble lay in wrenching free."[50]

The sharpness is very much Margaret's *forte*. When they go back to her house, Coutts thinks in contrast of Constance's house, 'where he must always be strictly "comme il faut"'. With his fiancée,

he felt the old, manly superiority, he was the strong creature, she the beautiful dependent. He stroked her hair, he softened his tones for her, he selected his speech for her, he put aside many thoughts, leaving for her only a pleasant little theatre for speech. All this he did lovingly, longing to caress, to make much of her, to humble himself to her, to make her his wife and his queen, who should rule him. His heart softened towards her, slumbering as she would be in the northern rectory. He bit his lip, holding his breath because of the strain of the situation.

It was all so different in Margaret's house. Here he was, as it were, naked, unclothed like a leopard. She also, Margaret, naked as a panther seemed to run before him. In her house, he did nothing, assumed nothing. The two creatures, Coutts and Margaret, fronted each other almost divested of all the clothing of convention. Saying nothing, betraying nothing, yet immediately they were betrayed one to the other, exposed in all their secrecies. Each shuddered, each, defenceless, hated the other by turns, yet they came together, as flames converge, leap, and are lost then with a faint snap in the chimney. Coutts had something of the fear of a leap into the dark, into extinction, when he thought of Margaret.[51]

Constance and Margaret are clearly selective versions of Louie Burrows and Helen Corke: Lawrence is taking elements from his own situation in 1911 and experimenting with them. He once described Louie as 'good, awfully good, churchy' (i. 343), while she was happy that he 'never in any way spoke against my faith. He was possibly glad that I had it.'[52] In 'Two Marriages', Louisa is a vicar's daughter while Coutts's fiancée sleeps 'in the northern rectory'. By contrast, Margaret is untamed, panther-like, unconventional and questions Coutts's engagement: Helen Corke (who had had an affair with a married man, who seemed predatory on men and who rejected the very idea of marriage) thought it 'utterly wrong' that Lawrence, 'complementary to Muriel, should marry a girl whose quality of mind he appears to despise' – though that phrase also rather unpleasantly suggests how Lawrence talked to her about Louie. Coutts also ignores his 'troth' and the 'pledges that claimed him':[53] in September 1911 Lawrence would tell Helen Corke that 'as for Louie's claim on me it is I who discount it, not you' (i. 303).

However, Coutts is finally as repelled by Margaret's kind of sexuality – her 'swooning on passion' – as he is by his fiancée's distance from sexuality. In Margaret's house, his body aching 'with heavy intensity, like a swollen vein', he finally breaks free from 'the heavy, hanging form of the woman upon him' by kicking over the oil lamp; he burns himself putting out the flame on her dress, and escapes from the house, 'running blindly with burning red hands stretched before him, down the street'.[54] The fire is a punishment (Coutts actually and metaphorically gets his fingers burnt) as well as a metaphor for tormented and tormenting sexuality. Sometime later in 1911 or early in 1912, Lawrence's poem 'And Jude the Obscure and his

Beloved' further described a woman's dislike of masculine desire. In Hardy's *Jude the Obscure*, Jude Fawley accuses Sue Bridehead of leading him on, but of really being sexless; Sue, like Helen Corke, feels responsible for the suicide of a man in love with her. Masculine desire, to a Sue – or a Helen –

> Comes licking in flame through the bars of your lips,
> And over my face your stray fire slips
> Leaving a burn and a smart
> That must have the oil of illusion: Oh heart
> Of love and beauty loose no more
> Your reptile flames of passion: store
> Your beauty in the basket of your soul,
> Be all yourself one bonny, burning coal,
> That steady stays with joy of its own fire,
> But do not seek to take me by desire,
> Oh do not seek to thrust in me your fire.[55]

When Coutts knocks over the lamp in the story, he is demonstrating to Margaret a little of what he really feels: he sears her with a momentary touch of desire. But he also hates her and feels guilty about being sexually attracted to her; angry and frustrated, he punishes himself.

The story is really concerned with Coutts's experience with Margaret; his fiancée is simply a moral pawn in the game, and Lawrence's revisions of the story in 1913 reduced her role still further. But it is typical of Lawrence's problems in 1911 that a story drawing so much upon real life should refuse to acknowledge the full complexity of an emotional impasse; should reduce a lively and demanding Louie Burrows to a sleeping Constance, simplify the feelings of a Lawrence to those of a Coutts and replace the sexual complexity of Helen Corke with Margaret's mannerisms and provocations. The surviving letters from Lawrence to Louie Burrows and Helen Corke reveal a far more complex drama than the created fiction; the imagined interchanges of 'Intimacy' are cruder than the subtle interplay of guilt, need and desire between the three real people. One of Lawrence's problems with Louie Burrows, for example, was that she was only in part the object of his 'gentlemanly love'. Far from slumbering on her pillow in a distant rectory, her tangible and tawny presence in the holidays and during the occasional weekend excursion disturbed, aroused and thoroughly excited him. Her 'churchy' quality may have suggested the rectory – but was not what attracted him to her. After a weekend in the Midlands in October 1911, he wrote to her from Croydon:

I've now got to digest a great lot of unsatisfied love in my veins. It is very damnable, to have slowly to drink back again into oneself all the lava and fire of a passionate eruption ... It is just the same with you I guess – perhaps worse: but it can't be worse, or you wouldn't keep your presence of mind ...

The most of the things, that just heave red hot to be said, I shove back. And that leaves nothing to be said. All this, you see, is very indelicate and immodest and all that ... and I always want to subscribe to your code of manners, towards you – I know I fail sadly. (i. 321)

That combination of suppressed sexuality and apology represents one of the unhappy patterns of their relationship. Later on, Louie was extremely tart about the way Lawrence 'wallowed in the miseries of continence';[56] but for his part Lawrence always saw her as confused about her own instincts, using the 'code of manners' to hide her own feelings from herself. He had described in 'Hands' how the betrothed's actions betray her: in 'Intimacy' he attempted to simplify the emotional impasse by denying any such complexity to the fiancée or to Coutts's feelings. Coutts's attitude to Constance is a parody of the real-life Lawrence wanting 'to subscribe to your code of manners'. And while in 1931 Louie could be very cutting about Lawrence, in 1911 she seems simply not to have known what to do about his feelings, or hers. One of the things she stressed in her memoirs of Lawrence was how immature she had been in 1911.

But in 1911 it was exceptional for a young woman of lower-middle-class background to be able to discuss sex or even to acknowledge her sexuality before marriage. Yet again, it is clear what an unusual (though also complicatedly unhappy) person Jessie Chambers was, by contrast.[57] For Louie, love naturally led to marriage, and nothing less: and until then – and it might well be 'a long time' (i. 237) – to nothing more.

VII   The 'Jeune Fille'

Such episodes as that of mid-July do not, however, only make us see Lawrence as immature, duplicitous and untrustworthy; they reveal the gulf which lay between him and Louie. His own letters often reveal how, like Coutts in 'Intimacy', he tended to select 'his speech for her, he put aside many thoughts, leaving for her only a pleasant little theatre for speech': at times he was prepared to sum up her language to him as 'the same/Current loose cash she handles everywhere'.[58] His letters often show Lawrence starting to say what was on his mind – then rounding on himself for being outspoken, or foolish, and apologising. In that way he was able to communicate to Louie things which – according to the code of manners he had adopted towards her – were unsayable. They clearly both enjoyed the game in which he was wicked, or daring or satirical about her 'standards', and she shocked, or blushing or reproving; he told her in April 1911 that 'I'm always trying to avoid doing things you'd reproach me for. I don't always succeed to my thorough satisfaction: but then, who would' (i. 250). But it was also true that he sometimes fell back on telling her his dreams – and his feelings – in French, though this may also have been a precaution in case anyone else in her large and tight-knit family saw his letters. He dreamt of her in childbirth, and of sleeping with her lying awake beside him; and told her about it in French (i. 272). He also told her 'je te cherche, bouche et gorge, pour t'embrasser': 'Hélas, que vous êtes loin d'ici, que votre corps loin du mien': 'Un baiser à la bouche' (i. 259, 263, 265).[59] French allowed him to write, and her to read, what was otherwise impermissible.

But if, for very good reasons, he was unable to tell Louie what his emotional and sexual life in Croydon (with her or without her) was like, neither could he share much of his past or his present with her. As always with inhibited speech, it is hard to tell the extent to which he is, a little patronisingly, being careful not to say things which she might take amiss – and how far he is sensitively allowing for her genuine difference from himself. For example, he described his continuing grief for their mother to his sister Ada, and remarked 'No one understands but you. Lou doesn't understand a bit – and I never say anything. I'm afraid she's one I shan't tell things to – it only seems to bother her. But it's just as well. In the things that matter, one has to be alone, in this life – or nearly alone' (i. 243). Yet again, Jessie Chambers appears to have been the one person (before Frieda) to whom Lawrence told almost everything: about himself, about Helen Corke, about Agnes Holt, about Louie too. He told Louie that although he still dreamed of his mother, 'You do not know. If I told you all, it would make you old, and I don't want you to be old' (i. 212). That, however, was perhaps less patronising than it now sounds. Louie knew very well that 'if he suffered I had no experience to help me understand it'. She had always been much younger, in every way, than he or other members of his circle; in 1905, for example, when she was 17, he had remarked about books that 'what people like best is erotic'. Louie was puzzled: 'What exactly is erotic? I questioned in ignorance. Oh – about a love motive you know. Oh! I subsided modestly [and] we spoke of other things.'[60] Lawrence obviously had no wish to enlighten her: in 1909 he remarked cheerfully, in passing, 'Louisa, my dear, thou art a century or so behind' (i. 124). But her naivety in 1911 must have remained shocking to him, as in her response to a remark he made at the end of October. She had gone with him to Eastwood for the weekend; when he saw her off at the station, on Sunday 29th,

he said unexpectedly & sombrely 'After all you must not be surprised if I give you up'. A few minutes before I had been happily in his arms. I looked in surprise – not understanding at all. In the train going home alone I reconciled myself completely then to the thought that in marrying him I must not expect happiness but only love. – That I was content to have – I could see no further. I wish I had known more of life to have understood things better.[61]

Her final comment, from the perspective of twenty years later, is sadly perceptive; her belief that she could have love, but could do without happiness, is frightening.

Lawrence had his own explanation of her difference from him: he reminded Ada how 'When she is a bit older, she'll be more understanding. Remember she's seen nothing whatever of the horror of life, and we've been bred up in its presence: with father. It makes a great difference' (i. 230). He was reassuring Ada that she need not be jealous of Louie: 'She hasn't any share in *your* part of me', he told her: 'there is more *real* strength in my regard for you than there is for Louie' (i. 231). Ada had also been dreadfully hurt by the death of her mother, and Lawrence needed to reassure her of his continuing love; and it was characteristic of him that what he said to one person was absolutely meant for that person's ears. But it was not only his love for Ada which made her special to him – and so unlike Louie. He knew that he and Ada had both been through the same difficult and damaging childhood, and he now felt 'I never want Lou to understand how relentlessly tragic life is – not that' (i. 261). He liked, instead, the idea of Louie – he told her – as 'a "jeune fille", you know. Well, I like you so' (i. 214). Saying that, of course, helped keep her so: though it didn't stop him complaining about her, too.

VII   Keeping Faith

We must not underestimate, however, the way in which Louie's youthfulness, high-spiritedness, straightforwardness, 'fine, warm, healthy, natural love' (i. 191) and lack of a sense of tragedy in her life, continued to be a consummate relief to Lawrence after years influenced by his mother, by Jessie Chambers and latterly by Helen Corke. He had told Louie in December 1910 how she would be 'the first woman to make the earth glad for me'; the others had been 'gates to a very sad world' (i. 195). Lydia Lawrence's frequent grimness, sardonic ironies, contemptuous sniff of sarcasm and sense of injustice had all been dominant factors in her children's lives; even when miserable himself (as on first going to Croydon in 1908) Lawrence had felt obliged to hide his feelings from her and 'to smile when I write to Eastwood' (i. 86). Before condemning his engagement to Louie as a mistake, we need to understand why it lasted so long (fourteen months), given the pressures upon it and Lawrence's dissatisfaction with it. Distraught as he was during December 1910, Lawrence had sufficient self-knowledge and native wit not to do something utterly wrong for himself. Louie was lively, warm, straightforward and refreshing: 'When I think of you, it is like thinking of life' (i. 195) he told her. But, given the 'inspiration' (i. 193) of the engagement's beginning, and the continuing relief given by Louie's difference from his other women, the very conventionality of the relationship reveals something important about Lawrence himself.

The first surprising thing about his engagement to Louie was that it actually was an engagement to marry. Lawrence had never been officially engaged to Jessie Chambers at any time in their 'betrothal of six years standing' (i. 187); their intimacy, their partnership, their final sexual relationship, all occurred outside the boundaries of engagement or marriage. At Whitsun 1910, Lawrence had told her 'This (our relationship as lovers) is what holds us together; this is the bond between us. Others have a ring and an outside token, but we have this – this inner bond.' The fact that they ignored the conventions so completely provoked some of the Lawrence family's hostility to Jessie. Lawrence never seems to have been engaged to Agnes Holt at the end of 1909, in spite of his expressed intention of marrying her (i. 143); Jessie knew of her only as 'his possible fiancée'.[62]

But the only way in which he could have had a close relationship with Louie Burrows was as a fiancé; neither she nor her family would have stood for anything else. And not only was Louie the girl his mother did not object to: she drew out of him qualities his mother would thoroughly have approved of – prudence, loyalty, devotion, ambition to succeed in his profession. In spite of his desire to be a writer, Lawrence's profound sense of his obligations to home and family (especially financial obligations) ensured that he knew how to be financially resourceful, prudent and far-sighted; his letters reveal that he was still sending money (including some of the disputed £10) 'home' during 1911 (i. 223, 234, 285, 286). In many ways it would have been natural for the provident son to have become the provident husband.

It is also significant that Lawrence not only chose to be engaged in December 1910; he continued to stick to his engagement even when trying to make other women his mistresses. He knew what it was to want to be conventional, 'ordinary', and to seek in the ordinary at least some of the person he was: such a desire was (in part) a deliberate inhibition of his resources of sarcasm, anger, passionate denunciation and frequently demonic energy. His 1911 story 'The Old Adam' shows how – as with 'The Prussian Officer' ['Honour and Arms'] in 1913 – he was full of insight into violence and violent behaviour. His stress on his ordinariness can be seen as a kind of deliberate compensation; of reassurance to others and himself. The child and adolescent who had obviously *not* been ordinary was now declaring how well he fitted in. The creation of Paul Morel in *Sons and Lovers* is a good example of this process. 'Ordinariness' was a quality Lawrence associated with men rather than with women: 'I wish I were just like ordinary men' (i. 208) he remarked in 1910.

> My greatest happiness, I am sure, lies in being coarse, strong, not easily vulnerable; in a word common-place, like the rest of the dull blades and flat muddy pools … Hurrah for a sluggish, dormant soul – (i. 54)

> I am a real jolly animal – thorough as you like; I could continue so for ever, if folks would let me; and be rid of the disease of soulfulness. (i. 71)

> The common everyday – rather superficial man of me really loves Louie. Do you believe that? (i. 240)[63]

The rather old-fashioned care and courtesy he extended to Louie is another example of that 'common everyday' self in action; the role was one he could easily adopt, because it corresponded to a need already within him. To Louie he offered a further distinction: between 'the second me, the hard, cruel if need be, me that is the writer', and 'the pleasanter me, the human who belongs to you' (i. 214). The division was artificial but convenient; Lawrence could 'belong' to Louie by offering her a self he knew she could accept, and which he was quite prepared to enact; he could remain to some extent detached, freed by the role he was playing. As well as convenient, the division (like the engagement) was in line with troubling divisions within Lawrence himself. The writer and the thinker – according to this convenient self-analysis – was not socially responsible, was thoroughly selfish and took no care for the morrow: sounding remarkably like the wilder spirit of Arthur Lawrence. However, the 'pleasanter me', which accepted attachments like engagements, was decent, responsible, unselfish: the counterpart of an idealised Lydia Lawrence. It was a sign of Lawrence's continuing insecurity that he should have divided himself up in such a way.

But his engagement to Louie was undeniably a way of keeping faith with his mother and what she had stood for. With the death of Lydia Lawrence, he instinctively took on the responsibility of loyalty to a woman she had approved of. And that loyalty was not something he could easily give up, however much he was attracted to other women and chafed at his engagement. In 'Two Marriages' Alfred Durant tells Louisa Lindley about his dying mother's approval of her: the July 1911 first draft runs:

> "I feel as if she knew, and was glad. I don't feel disloyal to her," he said, gravely, asking for Louisa's opinion.
> "She asked me to—to accept you, if you wanted me," Louisa blushed. They both thrilled at the suggestion of the unknown working round them.

It was a black night. Durant felt as if there were accord between him and his two women. He sighed with relief . . .[64]

Almost as soon as he had written that, Lawrence began to modify it – so that Louisa only says 'She said you'd ask me' in the revised version, with Durant only feeling 'in accord with life' rather than with 'his two women'. But Lawrence's experiment with the idea suggests how close to the surface it may have lain in real life.

IX   Running Away

Louie and he spent a fortnight of their summer holidays together, in August 1911: compared with the time he had spent with Jessie in the old days, or could now spend with Helen Corke in Croydon, Lawrence could see Louie only infrequently: and holidays were correspondingly important. Ada went with them as chaperone to Prestatyn, in North Wales, where they had lodgings 'with relatives of a Methodist clergyman', Louie reassured her mother (i. 294 n. 2): it sounds impeccably respectable. The unrespectable George Neville joined them there however, and wrote later how they 'managed to cover the whole coast of North Wales, together with Snowdonia and a considerable portion of the hinterland. We scarcely saw a cloud for the whole of the time we were there . . . we had a holiday never to be forgotten.' That impression of joyful but ceaseless activity is, oddly enough, confirmed by what Jessie Chambers later heard (almost certainly from Ada); but Jessie's narrative attempts to throw a very different light on it. 'I heard later that Lawrence was never still for a minute, that he ran up and down the crags like a man possessed; that he absolutely refused to be left alone with Louie and insisted on Ada accompanying them wherever they went.'[65] It is a thoroughly spiteful reminiscence, by someone very conscious of not having been there; but we can compare it with a remark Lawrence once made to Jessie about Louie: that, although strongly attracted to her, as soon as he was alone with her he wanted to run away (i. 238): in part probably *because* he was so attracted.[66]

For all that, he stuck to his engagement. There was no-one he wanted to run away to: but the summer holiday seems to have marked a turning point. It may well have been in August 1911 that he started his affair with his old Eastwood friend Alice Dax (now living in Shirebrook, 10 miles north of Eastwood); in fact he went to see her and her husband exactly a week after getting back from Prestatyn.

X Breakdown

By the early autumn of 1911, his situation had finally grown intolerable. He felt 'rather, – very – sick of teaching when I want to do something else' (i. 303), and his sense of being trapped came out as a feeling of being literally asphyxiated. Lung trouble was never very far away, and school 'makes me feel as if I can't breathe' (i. 302). 'Rush, rush, its one big struggle, nowadays, to get things done' (i. 311). He remained both the engaged man, and the man wanting sex with other women. If ever he did have an affair with his landlady Marie Jones, it was probably in the second half of 1911; there was Alice Dax; and, of course, on 29 October he told Louie that 'you must not be surprised if I give you up'.[67] We might remember his insistence to Helen Corke in July that, in future, he would pay women their 'market price'; he imagined loving a prostitute 'because I'm sorry for her' (i. 286). In December 1908, Lawrence had felt an innocent in London: 'I cannot tell a "femme perdue" by the look of her, as most men seem to be able to do' (i. 101). But his landlord, John William Jones – who provided Lawrence with his condoms (i. 286) – had an eye for prostitutes, and instructed Lawrence: ' "Such a pretty tart in the 'Crown', Mr Lawrence – really warm and fruity." "Oh," ' said Lawrence, ' "and didn't you cotton." "No", ' replied Jones, ' "I'd rather have a good dinner any day" ' (i. 450–1). His friend George Neville had advised him in 1910 on 'buying yourself a woman'; Alfred Durant in 'Daughters of the Vicar' and Tom Brangwen in *The Rainbow* – sensitive, working-class men at odds with themselves – both go to prostitutes, and may well have had some origin in Lawrence's own experience; there is, for example, a mysterious 'Pauline' in his address book, with an address near the Midland Railway Station in Nottingham.[68]

He was also suffering the loss of the encouragement and support for his work of Jessie Chambers, who for more than six years had been the pivot of his artistic and intellectual life. He was working with exasperation as a teacher while being unable to concentrate for very long on his writing, when he knew that such concentration was exactly what he needed. At the start of June 1911 he had been approached by the publisher Martin Secker for a book of short stories, but because he had written too few had had to put Secker off; hence the production of 'The Old Adam', the early 'Daughters of the Vicar', 'Second-Best' and 'Love Among the Haystacks', in the summer and autumn of 1911 – at the expense of his work on his novel. None of them got into print, however, and the short-story volume remained a vague and distant project. In August, he had made his second crucial contact with the literary world, when the publisher's reader Edward Garnett (acting as English agent for the American magazine the *Century*) had got in touch with him and asked him for stories. Lawrence tried

'Intimacy' and 'Two Marriages': but both were rejected as insufficiently commercial. The manuscript books at Lawrence's elbow remained, for the most part, school-books to be marked rather than stories being written. 'How's that for MS? – it is awful: it'll be the death of me one of these days' (i. 319) he told Garnett ruefully and prophetically, as he surveyed his marking. And Garnett, for all his efforts, was unable to help get more than two poems into print before the spring of 1912. 'Paul Morel' had been at a standstill since July, and there seemed little prospect of its escaping the impasse into which it had struggled. Lawrence's attempts to publish his work in magazines, too, had still got no further than the appearance of an occasional poem or story in the *English Review*. He had tried a little journalism at the end of August, sending a piece about the riots and strike in Lincoln to the *Daily News*: it was not printed (i. 298–9). The relative success of *The White Peacock* was growing steadily more distant, and 'The Saga of Siegmund' remained unpublishable. Worst of all, his depression following the death of Lydia Lawrence was deeper than ever. The unreality of his experiences in 1911 are movingly expressed in his poem 'Elegy', which probably dates from early in 1912 and is addressed to his mother.

> Still, you left me the nights,
> The great dark glittery window,
> The bubble hemming this empty existence with lights.
>
> Still in the vast hollow
> Like a breath in a bubble spinning
> Brushing the stars, goes my soul, that skims the bounds
>   like a swallow!
>
> I can look through
> The film of the bubble night, to where you are.
> Through the film I can almost touch you.[69]

The vision of the bubble night shows how the appeal of darkness and death remained strong and recurring.

He was, in spite of all this, living a characteristically complicated social life which pulled him in many different directions: and he felt obliged at least to appear cheerful. 'Folk hate you to be miserable, and to make them a bit miserable' (i. 243). His last week before illness finally overtook him in November 1911 was typical. On Monday 13th, he went to Covent Garden to hear Wagner's *Siegfried*; the author of 'The Saga of Siegmund' probably felt obliged to. On Wednesday 15th, he worked at home on his writing; on Thursday 16th, he went to the theatre in London again, with a friend of his brother George. On the Friday evening he went to a 'glee-singing party' at his headmaster's house;[70] he went down to Kent on Saturday 18th to stay with Edward Garnett at his home 'The Cearne' till Sunday night. Such a week suggests how hard Lawrence was forcing himself, how little he was able to 'live his own life' as he wanted to (i. 328). And, like Siegmund in 'The Saga', he had already had a strong presentiment of things working to a crisis. On Wednesday 15th he had written to Louie: 'My mouth seems to be lifted blindly for something, and waiting, puzzled. It is shocking how I curse within myself' (i. 328).

The breakdown came on the Sunday night, in the form of a physical collapse. He had got caught in the rain on the way down to Garnett's on the Saturday, did not change his wet clothes, spent some time outdoors watching Garnett chopping logs, developed a chill and got back to Croydon on the Sunday evening looking (according to his landlord) 'as if he was suffering from a frightful hang-over. The next morning he tried to get up for school, but was unable to, developed double pneumonia and nearly died.' Just as ten years earlier Lydia Lawrence had hurried south to Ernest, so Ada Lawrence this time left her teaching and travelled to London; a nurse was also needed.[71] Louie was not allowed to go, because the doctor was supposed to have said that it would excite Lawrence too much; it is difficult not to suspect, however, that either Lawrence or Ada deliberately kept her away. Ada's letter to Louie of Tuesday 28 November survives:

My Dear
    Doctor says Bert is no worse – tomorrow or next day is the crisis and please God all may be well – the disease in the left lung has not spread further. Last night he had a morphia injection and therefore had a fairly good night. He wanders a great deal but when sensible talks of you often. Don't write to him my dear until he's passed the crisis for he hasn't been able to read anything for over a week. I've told him little bits of his letters & even that has excited him. So Louie just for a time put phrases specially for him in mine. About Sat. if he passes the crisis early I will ask doctor or nurse, but if you have to wait until next week I know you will be willing to abide by their decision. We are all fighting hard for him – nurse is so good, and the doctor says he thinks he will go on alright now if we keep his heart something like – so my dear keep a brave heart for his sake and try not to worry or when he sees you he will know, as soon as ever he can bear I shall send for you. You know he will be in bed for weeks & weeks if he gets through so I shall make arrangements for you to spend Xmas here with us.

                                                                Your Sister   Ada

That evening she sent Louie a further note:

Doctor just been – says Bert's strength is keeping up wonderfully and now says he will get over the crisis alright. I only wish it were over.

                                                                        Love
                                                                          Ada

Had an injection and sleeping well.[72]

Lawrence survived 'the crisis', but it had been a desperate time. It was another ten days before he was even allowed to be propped up in bed. And still Louie was not allowed to visit: 'the Doctor is emphatic' (i. 331) was still the official word. It was perhaps just as well Louie had not been there before. According to Ada, it was 'when sensible' that Lawrence had talked of Louie, and he might have said things when delirious that Louie should not have heard. It was this perhaps which made Ada say, a couple of months later, that she wouldn't marry a man like her brother, 'no, not if he were the only one on the earth' (i. 361 n. 2). It was arranged that Louie should come to Croydon only when school ended for Christmas.

Lawrence had written his first note to Louie on 2 December: a week later, he was a little petulant about her tender care: 'Do not tell me so often to be patient. Do I complain so much?' (i. 332). He was also irritated when she took too seriously a remark he made about drinking cold water to make his temperature go down; but illness frustrated and irritated him. 'I hate to be waited on, and to be treated gently' (i. 343), he told Garnett; he was 'By nature . . . ceaselessly active' (i. 337) and extremely independent – not to say untouchable. 'If ever I'm ill again I shall die of mortification' (i. 343), he remarked; and, all his life, treated illness as something entirely personal and incidental, not something which gave others any rights over him. To make up to Louie for his bad temper, he was planning a joint Christmas holiday for them, when he got on his feet again. He had grown his first beard: but (propped up in bed with pillows) shaved it off again on 11 December. He was sitting up out of bed – 'a weird experience' (i. 336) – on 15 December, but two days later still could not stand: 'I hate my legs, miserable defaulters' (i. 343). But Ada told Garnett, that same day, how

He has really made wonderful progress the last week.

The report concerning the expectoration was very satisfactory. No germs were discovered, and since then both lungs have almost completely cleared up.

Of course my brother will be very liable to consumption and as the doctors say will always need great care.[73]

The sputum analysis had proved negative: he did not have tuberculosis. But to go on as a teacher would be extremely unwise. On the 20th Ada wrote to Louie that he 'actually made a short journey down the passage this morning, hanging on to my shoulder'[74] – Lawrence's own more spectacular version being 'This morning I strolled into the bathroom, prancing like the horses of the Walküre, on nimble air' (i. 341). He went downstairs for the first time on Christmas Eve, the day Louie arrived. 'She rubs her cheek against me, just like a cat, and says "Are you happy?" It makes me laugh. But I am not particularly happy, being only half here, yet awhile. She never understands

323

that' (i. 343). But he was now recuperating fast: together with Ada and her fiancé Eddie Clarke, Louie and he spent Christmas together in Croydon. On 4 January 1912 Lawrence and Louie left Croydon for a couple of days together at Redhill with an old friend with whom Louie had stayed more than once when visiting Croydon: and then Lawrence travelled on to Bournemouth by himself on Saturday 6 January, to convalesce.

Just when it seemed as if he could do nothing to change his situation, his illness had succeeded in changing everything. His pneumonia had been a strange counterpart of that childhood pneumonia to which he had succumbed almost exactly ten years earlier, after the death of his brother Ernest. That earlier illness had freed him from the factory, and had made very special the bond between him and his mother. The later illness seems to have been a corresponding rite of passage away from school, and away from that old bond; in 1928, he wrote about his sense of the change as 'slowly the world came back: or I myself returned: but to another world'. He came back as a 'resurrected man':[75] it was important to him that he had so nearly followed his mother, but had not done so. At the end of *Sons and Lovers* (see Illustration 50), Paul Morel also feels the possibility of following *his* mother into death, but in the end finds he cannot: 'On every side the immense dark silences seemed pressing him, so tiny a speck, into extinction, and yet, almost nothing, he could not be extinct.' Lawrence's assertion of surviving (or resurrected) self made him feel more free of his old attachments and bonds than he had ever been. He later stated how certain he was that, 'when I have been ill, it has been sheer distress and nerve strain which have let go on my lungs' (ii. 73). It was as if his own illness had this time released him from the power which his mother's dying and death had exerted over him, and he could start to confront the world afresh. Paul walks 'towards the faintly humming, glowing town, quickly';[76] Lawrence knew a less dramatic but no less definite return to everyday life. But while his novel could end at that point, Lawrence would have known that his own life must change.

CHAPTER TWELVE

◆

1911–1912

BREAKING OFF

I The End of School

Lawrence returned to different kinds of freedom. For one thing, as he told Garnett on 17 December 1911, 'The doctor says I mustn't go to school again or I shall be consumptive' (i. 337); he never taught in school again, though he did not actually submit his resignation from Davidson Road until 28 February (i. 369 and n. 2.). Without a job, and without any more than occasional payments for his writing, he had – after convalescence in Bournemouth – to return to the Midlands, where his sisters could support him. He was anyway, eager to leave Colworth Road and apparently linked it with his breakdown and illness: 'I want to leave Mrs Jones and Mr Jones, and the children. It is queer, how I have turned, since I have been ill' (i. 332). Ada's remark to Louie just before the latter arrived for Christmas – 'If only the Jones will leave us to ourselves what a splendid time we shall have' – suggests the awkwardness of a small and crowded house during Lawrence's illness. Jones himself said that he told Lawrence 'to clear off',[1] which is probably untrue, though it perhaps reveals some lingering suspicion of his wife's feelings for Lawrence. But Lawrence was putting his past behind him, deliberately cutting himself free.

Although he told Louie Burrows about wanting to leave the Joneses, his surviving letters to her from December 1911 do not once discuss school, teaching or career, although he told Grace Crawford (now a comparative stranger) how 'I shall not stay in the South. For at least six months, I shall be away from London, staying with my sister and other friends in the north' (i. 335). That sounds like a plan to write. He went still further when, towards the end of December, he told Helen Corke that 'he would try to make a living by writing'.[2] He seems to have saved up the discussion of these things with Louie until she came to Croydon for Christmas. Nevertheless, he knew – and she must have suspected – that he would be giving up teaching; and that would call into question all the assumptions upon which their engagement rested.

II Miriam Again

It was also significant that, just before Louie came down to Croydon, a short story Lawrence called 'The Harassed Angel' (later 'The Shades of Spring') forced itself upon him with such precipitation that he wrote it (he told Garnett on 30 December) 'last week in bed – before I could sit up much' (i. 343); he first sat up in a chair around Friday 15 December, so the story must date from between then and Christmas. His sudden need to write it corresponds to a remark in his late essay 'Getting On': '. . . if I had never written, I probably should have died soon. The being able to express one's soul keeps one alive.'[3] 'The Harassed Angel' was like the dawn chorus in winter, an assertion of survival against the odds. The writer commenced his new life, however, with an attack on the old self – and a return to the problem of the Miriam figure.

Such a return looks strange, on the face of it. Lawrence had seen very little of Jessie Chambers since August 1910; had met her briefly 'on fewer occasions than I could count on the fingers on one hand'. She had sent him a cake for his birthday in September 1910, and he had had occasional postcards from her (i. 243). He had, however, continued to write to her and to send her books: J. M. Synge's *The Playboy of the Western World*, with a Baudelaire poem copied on to its fly-leaf in the autumn of 1910,[4] and at Christmas 1910 'Leon Daudet's *Le partage de l'enfant*, saying it would help me to realize the position of the child in a home where the parents do not get on well together'. The book survives, inscribed simply 'Christmas 1910. To J from D.H.L.' Some time after August 1910 he also wrote to Jessie about *Crime and Punishment* and passed on to her Israel Querido's *Toil of Men*, while at Christmas 1911 he gave her a book – *Contemporary Belgian Poetry* – which Louie Burrows had wanted, but which Lawrence was extremely reluctant to post to her family home because of some of the poems' sexual subjects: 'I really hesitate to send the *Belgian Poetry* into Coteshael' (i. 325).[5]

He had gone on feeling guilty about what he had done to Jessie in August 1910. 'I have been cruel to her, and wronged her' he wrote in December 1910 (i. 190): and at times during 1911 he had been very conscious indeed that he was still, in part, the man who had been her spiritual and intellectual companion all those years. In the spring of 1911 he had written in his poem 'Meeting' how 'Long have I waited, never once confessed/E'en to myself how bitter the separation.' But personal contact between him and Jessie had effectively ended. She had not even known, in the autumn of 1910, that he had started his autobiographical novel; she only heard about it from Helen Corke.[6]

However, on Saturday 7 October 1911 he had gone to the theatre in London with his brother George, and had there met Helen Corke and Jessie, who was on a visit to Helen Corke for the weekend. The meeting is unlikely to have been a coincidence. And some time shortly afterwards Lawrence sent Jessie the unfinished manuscript of 'Paul Morel', just as he had always given her his manuscripts to read in the old days. Louie Burrows had read the earlier part of the novel, but we have no evidence that she even saw the later part – and her reading was not a critical one.[7] The fact that Lawrence approached Jessie Chambers again, and thus reverted to the former pattern of his creative work, does not necessarily mean that he wanted to renew the old relationship with her; but just as 'Paul Morel' had defined Miriam as 'a wonderful medium' to the young Paul – 'a medium to him rather than a force directing him' – so Lawrence probably hoped that renewed contact with Jessie would renew in him the old self she had been so good a medium for.[8] He had spent a year trying to be another kind of person altogether. He was desperate with the novel and could not finish it: there were still knots in him which would not come free.

Twenty years later, from memory, Jessie gave an account of what she read:

He had written about two-thirds of the story, and seemed to have come to a standstill. The whole thing was somehow tied up. The characters were locked together in a frustrating bondage, and there seemed no way out. The writing oppressed me with a sense of strain. It was extremely tired writing. I was sure that Lawrence had had to force himself to do it. The spontaneity that I had come to regard as the distinguishing feature of his writing was quite lacking. He was telling the story of his mother's married life, but the telling seemed to be at second hand, and lacked the living touch.[9]

She attempted to define its 'sentimental' quality: 'A nonconformist minister whose sermons the mother helped to compose was a foil to the brutal husband. He gave the boy Paul a box of paints, and the mother's heart glowed with pride, as she saw her son's budding power ... It was story-bookish.'[10] The incident of the box of paints does not occur in the surviving manuscript, but Jessie's account gives a fair impression of how Miss May treats Paul's growing powers as a painter. Mr Morel's murder of his son Arthur, too, something not at all story-bookish in essence, constitutes an evasion of the reality of such a family. Jessie Chambers concluded:

I told him I was very surprised that he had kept so far from reality in his story; and I thought what had really happened was much more poignant and interesting than the situations he had invented. In particular I was surprised that he had omitted the story of Ernest, which seemed to me vital enough to be worth telling as it actually happened. Finally I suggested that he should write the whole story again, and keep it true to life.[11]

Dislike for work produced without her, and pride in her contribution to its rewriting, led her to denigrate the 1911 novel: although it was flawed, it was not the disaster her account makes it.

But such criticism was exactly what Lawrence needed. It cut clean through his tendency to evade the problems of family life by resorting to melodrama and romance. As a result, he determined at the start of November 1911 to begin the book again, 'for the third and last time . . . It is a book the thought of which weighs heavily upon me' (i. 321). He also decided that Jessie could also give him some practical assistance with the novel's next draft. He asked her to write for him what she could remember of their early days, 'because, as he truthfully said, my recollection of those days was so much clearer than his. I agreed to do so, and began almost at once'.[12] She remembered this request having been made immediately after she read 'Paul Morel' in October, but it is possible that Lawrence did not actually ask her until he saw her again in December. At all events, what he wrote of the new version of the novel between 3 November and falling ill on 19 November would not have taken him up to the point where her memories would have been useful; he wrote only seventy pages.[13]

He had a contractual obligation to supply his publisher Heinemann with a novel; in October 1911 he had promised one for March 1912. But quite apart from that – and his own increasing desire to start carving out his own independent career as a writer – what emerges most strongly from his renewed attack on the novel is his *need* to write it. Not only was it the book 'the thought of which weighs heavily upon me', not only was it the 'biography of my mother' which 'belongs to this' (i. 195), but it had become the book he needed to write so as to explore the self (and selves) he had become through the tensions of his upbringing and adolescence. It was a way of looking through the membrane of the bubble into the darkness: though not 'to follow her'. If the artist hero was emotionally handicapped – as the sensitive artist heroes of his previous fiction had always been – it was now time to find out why; and what could be done about it. This would have been particularly obvious to the man who felt himself, in November 1911, sliding into the kind of despair and hopelessness which preceded his breakdown. The 1911 'Paul Morel' had effectively bypassed the essential problems of Paul's life, his parents' marriage, and those posed by his relationship with Miriam. The rewritten novel would have to do all these things.

A short story Lawrence had written in the summer of 1911, 'Second-Best', might have started the process. Set in the Friezeland, just north of the

Haggs Farm, 'Second-Best' had investigated the situation of Frances, a woman recently abandoned by Jimmy Barrass, her lover of five years standing – a 'far-off' lover who had never given her more than 'his half-measures'. Barrass – the connection with 'embarrass' seems inescapable – is now engaged to another woman. Frances's younger sister exclaims: 'Engaged! Jimmy Barrass! Well of all things!! I never thought *he'd* get engaged.'[14] People had probably said very much the same about Lawrence. However, just as Emily in *The White Peacock* turns to Tom Renshaw, and Muriel in 'A Modern Lover' turns to Tom Vickers, so Frances – though no Miriam-figure – finds her Tom in Tom Smedley (the 'second-best' of the title); and the 1911 story ends with their low-key but mutual acceptance of each other:

"Do you care for me?" he asked, in low, shamefaced tones.

She nestled her face on his bosom, with a shaky little laugh. She badly wanted fondling, caressing, soothing. He caressed her very tenderly.

Their married life was "very comfortable":—it is the term of approbation the common people prefer.[15]

The woman troubled and abandoned by the ambitious and sophisticated man turns to 'the common people': 'Second-Best' had been yet another exploration of the territory between sophistication (Jimmy is a Doctor of Chemistry) and nature which had been the subject of so much of Lawrence's writing from 'Laetitia' onwards. And yet the provision of another man for Frances – as if Lettie had, after all, gone back to George – did nothing to explain why Barrass abandoned her, or what *he* was now like. Lawrence was not yet willing to make any fundamental analysis either of the sophisticated man or of his fear of the desiring and loving woman. A hymn to male dependence on women in the first pages of the rewritten 'Paul Morel' in November 1911 suggests that he still preferred to write about exactly the opposite:

No man can live unless his life is rooted in some woman: unless some woman believes in him, and so fixes his belief in himself. Otherwise he is like a water plant, whose root is detached: floating still, and apparently flourishing, upon the river of life, but really decaying slowly. Morel decayed slowly.

It was a great tragedy, and it is the tragedy of many a man and woman.[16]

There is an enormous difference between this and the final version of the novel, which only a year later Lawrence thought was also a 'great tragedy', 'the tragedy of thousands of young men in England' (i. 477), because it showed how much Paul had been damaged by his dependence on his mother and by her love for him.

Lawrence's writing about the Miriam figure in 'The Harassed Angel' in

December 1911, however, was a genuine preparation for writing about Miriam in 'Paul Morel' and was probably the direct result of his instinct to take his understanding of them both back to its origins. He began the story almost simultaneously with seeing Jessie again in December: Jessie (on another visit to Helen Corke in Croydon) went to see him either on Saturday 16 or 23 December: 'He asked me if I had written the notes I promised to do, and I told him I had begun to write them before he was ill and just went on . . . This was our first real talk since his mother's funeral. Some of the old magic returned, the sense of inner understanding which was the essence of our friendship.' But while she – at least in memory – was conscious of the 'old magic', 'The Harassed Angel' shows that Lawrence was looking at something very different. Where 'A Modern Lover'[17] had described a new start in the relationship with the old lover, 'The Harassed Angel' initiates a post mortem enquiry into the old one. The story has nothing to do with engagement or marriage, in spite of the fact that its hero is married; his marriage is insignificant. 'The Harassed Angel' once again saddles the 'Miriam' figure (here called Hilda) with a non-intellectual (gamekeeper) lover who has replaced the hero – but there its parallel with the 'Tom' scenarios ends. At moments, Syson apparently starts to recognise what his habitual reaction to Hilda does to him: 'He felt a quick change beginning in his blood.'[18] But Hilda's new relationship prevents the hero from renewing his spiritual relationship with her, much as he would like to. The autobiographical hero Syson withdraws 'to count his losses', and to come to terms if he can with his understanding of Hilda. Lawrence wrote this part of the story over and over again between 1911 and 1914. In 1911, Syson's analysis of what had gone wrong between him and Hilda ran:

She always knew the best of me, and believed in the best I might be. While she kept her ideal 'Me' alive with her, I was sort of responsible to her: I must live somewhere up to standard. Now I have destroyed ⟨her . . .⟩ Myself in her, and I am alone, and purposeless. I have ⟨murdered⟩ destroyed the beautiful 'Me' who was always ahead of me, nearer the realities. And I have struck the topmost flower from off her faith. And yet it was the only thing to do, considering all the other folk . . .[19]

That was at best only a very partial version of what had happened to Lawrence in August 1910. But elsewhere in the story, the analysis of the bodiless, sublimated, bloodless self which he loves to be, but which he also hates Jessie for drawing out in him, is a breakthrough in Lawrence's realisation of what he had always gone back to Jessie for, and what he hated in her. It must have helped him write the story of Paul and Miriam in 'Paul Morel' in the spring of 1912, with such speed and point – and to the utter distress of Jessie Chambers as she read it.

Both the story and the novel, however, were returning him to the early period of his adolescence: a past before Louie Burrows had mattered. And the way he had constructed the novel allowed no place for Louie in his significant life-history. Paul's sexual relationship with Clara, after Miriam, would concentrate upon what Lawrence only shared with Louie in fantasy. In that way, as well, we can see how Lawrence's writing of the winter of 1911–12 was starting to exclude Louie.

III Edward Garnett

In December 1911, too, a piece of sheer good luck prepared the way for Lawrence's career as a writer: a career which was almost certainly going to mean the abandonment of Louie. His second novel, 'The Saga of Siegmund', written back in the summer of 1910, had remained with Heinemann after being read (and severely criticised) by Ford Madox Hueffer. Lawrence cannot have seen it since October 1910. He had originally waited 'with some curiosity' to hear Heinemann's 'opinion of the work' (i. 184), but he had received no definite answer. He had wondered in November 1910 whether 'you have temporarily forgotten the matter' (i. 187), but in February 1911 decided 'to suppress the book, and beg you to return the MSS to me' (i. 229). But in March 1911 the book had still not come back. 'Haven't you yet waded through the Siegmund MSS?' he asked Heinemann's reader, Frederick Atkinson (i. 240); and although Lawrence heard that Heinemann were prepared to publish the book (i. 276), it was not until December 1911 that – at the instigation of Garnett, who had said he wanted to see it – Lawrence at last 'extorted' the manuscript from Heinemann, and sent on the parcel (without even opening it) to Garnett (i. 330).

The only good reaction the novel had so far received had been Helen Corke's admiration – 'The intuition it shows, the tense concentration, the rare symbolism, fill me with wonder': and that did not count for very much. Jessie Chambers's response 'seems to have disappointed' Lawrence, Hueffer had condemned it outright – and all Lawrence had had from Heinemann was Atkinson's remark 'I have read part of the book. I don't care for it, but we will publish it.' Atkinson had never actually finished it, he told Lawrence: ' "It's your handwriting, you know." – a sweet smile "Perfectly legible, but so *tedious*" – a sweet smile' (i. 339).[20]

Now, however, Garnett – a man with a considerable knowledge of the literary world – turned out to be most enthusiastic about 'The Saga'. That was, to Lawrence, 'very exciting'; but, in December 1911, it was also extraordinarily important. If Lawrence were to earn his living by writing, he needed another novel to publish – a novel which would enhance his reputation – and without 'The Saga', his career would have to wait until he at last managed to finish the recalcitrant 'Paul Morel'. Garnett was now not only reassuring him that Hueffer had been wrong, but telling him to offer the book to Duckworth, the publisher he read for. He also offered Lawrence advice on how best to revise the book. Lawrence finally saw the manuscript of 'The Saga' again late in December, and began work on it at once, while still in Croydon with Louie, Ada and Eddie Clarke. He felt he was making it 'heaps, heaps better' (i. 344), and took the manuscript with him when he went to convalesce in Bournemouth, in January.

In Bournemouth, within sight (on clear days) of the Island whose blazing summer weather he was recreating in January cold and wet, Lawrence managed fairly quickly not only to rewrite nearly all of the first part (he only reused three old pages of the manuscript of 'The Saga' out of the first hundred), but to continue with a combination of new writing and the reuse of old pages. Two sisters in his Bournemouth boarding house (Margaret and Irene Brinton) contributed their name to a character in chapter v. The further he got, the more of the old manuscript he kept: forty-four pages from the second hundred pages of 'The Saga', forty-nine from the third hundred, and then all but four of the last two hundred and four.[21] The last three-fifths of the book were thus a straightforward revision of 'The Saga'.

The book – later rechristened *The Trespasser* – surprised him, he told Garnett, 'by its steady progressiveness': but 'At the bottom of my heart I don't like the work, though I'm sure it has points' (i. 351). In November Lawrence had begun turning 'Paul Morel' into something similar to the *Sons and Lovers* we now know; to go back to 'The Saga' was to step back into the kind of fine writing he had been doing nearly two years earlier, and to confront the kind of poetic taste for which he had then been writing. He could certainly improve 'The Saga', commenting after rewriting the first chapter that 'There was room for improvement, by Jove!' But he also felt that 'I was so young – almost pathetically young – two years ago' (i. 344); and although he could modify the most embarrassing things in the novel, and let the good ones stand out more clearly, it was still 'too florid, too "chargé". But it can't be anything else – it is itself. I must let it stand' (i. 358). That was a wise and pragmatic decision: the novel depended so much upon its origins in the prose poems of Helen Corke, upon the accumulating symbolism working up to the suicide of the hero, that essentially it could not be rewritten: only revised, or discarded.[22] In January 1912, with the new 'Paul Morel' hardly started but with Lawrence's immediate prospect of having to live by his writing – then *The Trespasser* was too important to abandon.

His revisions succeeded in considerably reducing the number of its embarrassingly over-written passages; a comparison of the two drafts of the 'Stranger' (or *Doppelgänger*) chapter, in its first and second incarnations, shows how – following Garnett's advice – he vastly improved it, though he knew it was 'probably still too literary' (i. 353). No longer does the 'Stranger' spin Siegmund didactic fables about the nature of human existence: no longer does he pursue, paragraph after paragraph, his tedious metaphor of the 'house of life'. He no longer apologises for his horrendously literary metaphors by explaining that he was drunk the night before: his 'brilliant' smiles vanish. Instead, Lawrence does exactly what Garnett told him to do in one of the notes he scrawled on the manuscript in December (see Illustration 43):

Something is wanted to carry off this passage with the Stranger, i.e, – you must intersect his talk with little realistic touches to make him very *actual*. He must not spring quite out of the blue & disappear into it again. He's too much a *deus ex machina*, for your purposes. Make some of his talk more ordinary & natural & slip in the pregnant things at moments.[23]

It may seem elementary criticism, but it is exactly what the chapter needed, and what Lawrence now did. On another occasion, Garnett noted 'not so good, this imagery', and Lawrence responded 'by crossing out nearly a page and a half of extended images, replacing them with a few lines'.[24] His whole treatment of Helena in the early part of the book was made sharper than it had been in 'The Saga'; his recreation of her suggests what he had slowly and painfully learned since creating Lettie in *The White Peacock* about 'the dreaming woman' who becomes sexually aroused but who does not want either sex or men.

Lawrence did not, however, have to change very much of the section about the return of Siegmund and Helena from the Island, nor the passage about Siegmund at home on his return. This last part – wholly imagined – remains the most impressive part of the book. The guilt Siegmund can do nothing about: his wife and family's silent criticism of him: his love for his youngest children, and the way they ignore him because of their mother's influence – such things drew from Lawrence his deep understanding of the tensions in a divided family. It is as if we were being taken inside Mr Morel in *Sons and Lovers* when his wife rejects him and his children are being induced to despise him.

The extremely florid writing before Siegmund's actual suicide is oppressive: but the dramatic control of the immediate aftermath is again astonishing, with its oddly comic (and choric) window cleaner brought in to find out what has happened in the upstairs room. Lawrence also experiments very oddly in the chapter after the suicide, when he creates a kind of comic antimasque in the description of Siegmund's wife Beatrice as lodging-house keeper, with recreations of three fellow-teachers at Davidson Road as lodgers – much to the annoyance of one of them (i. 465 and n. 1). The final chapter, paralleling the first, shows Helena with her new partner, Cecil Byrne: but there is no sign that this particular C.B. knows, any better than Cyril Beardsall or Siegmund, what is happening to him. Helena has not changed, and Byrne clearly needs to read *The Trespasser* if he is to escape the fate of his predecessor.

Such was the book Lawrence finished early in February 1912; he made one further effort to rid the text of its overwritten quality during proof correction in April, when he promised Garnett to 'wage war on my adjectives. Culpa mea!' (i. 381); and indeed '121 adjectives were removed, and many adjectival phrases . . . as well'.[25] But the rest had to stand: 'it is itself'.

The book had, however, one further role to play. By the time it was published, on 23 May, Lawrence had abandoned caution, planning and England, and was expecting to settle down shortly with Frieda Weekley in Bavaria. And although he finished 'Paul Morel' for William Heinemann in the summer of 1912, it was rejected and not published until the middle of 1913. What kept Lawrence and Frieda alive were the royalties of *The Trespasser*. Almost his last reference to the book in his correspondence came in a letter to Hueffer, who in the winter of 1912 had written his 'full opinions on the *Trespasser*'. 'I agree with you heartily', remarked Lawrence: 'I rather hate the book. It seems a bit messy to me. But whether it injures my reputation or not, it has brought me enough money to carry me – so modestly, as you may guess – through a winter here on the Lake Garda. One must publish to live' (i. 485). It was a nice irony that Lawrence's most literary book should have financed the writing of *Sons and Lovers* and the making of his career as a writer.

IV   The Casting Off of Louie

For Lawrence as man and professional writer, his engagement to Louie Burrows had become strangely irrelevant. But it remained for him to break it. He told her almost a year later that 'I only knew towards the end we couldn't make a good thing of it' (i. 480), but no correspondence between them survives for the crucial period 24 December to 6 January, because they were together, first at Croydon and then at Redhill. The only indication of what passed between them is a rather surprising note Louie made twenty years later that 'he made me the offer of immediate marriage in Jan. 1912 – which I as quickly accepted'.[26] As there is no such 'offer' in Lawrence's surviving correspondence to her between 6 January and 2 February, he must have made it before he went to Bournemouth. It was probably an offer made in the expectation (and hope) of her refusal; Lawrence knew that his financial state and his health were much worse than a year before. But a letter he wrote within a week of getting to Bournemouth shows that they had agreed that he should get on his feet physically, and financially, before they married or settled down: 'Have you heard from Auntie that Hannah Krenkow wants me to go to Germany, to Waldbröl near Cologne, in Spring. And I want to go in April or May. Won't it be just all right. If I get a living knowledge of German and French, then any time, if necessary, I can go into Secondary teaching' (i. 350). The fact that he expected her to find the idea 'just all right' shows that they were not going to get married at once, though the reference to Secondary teaching certainly postulates a common future. His surviving letters to her for the rest of January did not, however, discuss the future. He fell into a comfortable routine in his boarding house:

One gets up at 8.30, and breakfasts at nine – very prolific breakfasts – bacon and kidney and ham and eggs – what you like. I chatter in the smoke room till about 10.30 – then work in my room where I have had a fire made – until 1.30, when we have lunch – which is a bigger meal, or as big as our usual dinners. In the afternoon I go out, or if its wet, like today, I just stop in the recreation room and we play cards and games. After tea I went out with a man for a stroll, then a gin and bitters, then dinner. When I've done this letter I'm going up to the rec. again for games. It is really rather jolly. (i. 347)

By the end of the month he was capable of walking 'six miles – *now* am I not a garçon solide' (i. 358). He came to enjoy the company enormously, just as he had done in the Blackpool boarding-house in 1910; he also got on very well with *The Trespasser*.

And yet he knew that 'at the bottom I am rather miserable' (i. 358–9). His letters to Louie were becoming rather desperately casual; that of 28 January begins: 'I don't in the least know when I last wrote you, but I suppose it's my turn' (i. 357). Louie had been planning a couple of excursions for his return to the Midlands, but Lawrence's main desire was to put her off: it is not a pleasant letter.

Your questions trouble me considerably.

I do *not* want to go with a bushel of maidens to the castle. I shall be delighted to accompany you to Bingham, but don't fix the date yet. What else? Oh, I will remember the 13th [Louie's birthday, the date of which he had 'forgotten again' (i. 355)] – what an unlucky date.

Was that all I had to answer? My memory's really gone to pot since I've been crocky. (i. 357)

It cannot have escaped Lawrence, as he turned 'The Saga' into *The Trespasser*, how easily its central dilemma could apply to himself. He had always feared to 'become enslaved to a woman' (i. 56): Siegmund is a man trapped in a hopeless marriage, who goes away for an equally hopeless holiday romance with a young woman to whom he is strongly attracted, but who is an extremely reluctant sexual partner. During 1911, there had been times when Lawrence had contemplated his projected marriage with just the kind of irritable realism with which Siegmund contemplates his. Lawrence, too, had tried to escape the responsibilities of his engagement in the company of Helen Corke (Helena's original), who had (in turn) refused to sleep with him. As he now worked to create the dilemma of a man who loves life, but who is reduced to hopeless despair, Lawrence also reached a decision about his own life. He told Edward Garnett on 29 January that

I can never decide whether my dreams are the result of my thoughts, or my thoughts the result of my dreams. It is very queer. But my dreams make conclusions for me. They decide things finally. I dream a decision. Sleep seems to hammer out for me the logical conclusions of my vague days, and offer me them as dreams. (i. 359)

Unlike Siegmund (married and 38), Lawrence (unmarried and 26½) felt that he was standing on the threshold of a new life: and he was unwilling to evade what he called, in that letter to Garnett, 'one's own – what? – self – daemon – fate, or something' (i. 359). He would no longer compromise his sense of himself for the sake of a loyalty which he no longer acknowledged. Fourteen months after the death of Lydia Lawrence, he was prepared to overrule that part of himself which turned towards security, responsibility and prudence. And his own illness had helped him overcome the process of grieving with which Louie had always been linked, and with which she had helped so much. His only real problem now was how to hurt Louie least when he broke with her.

It was not until he left Bournemouth on 3 February and had gone to stay with Garnett at the Cearne, incidentally writing to Helen Corke while there and making one last proposal that she should sleep with him – Siegmund, as it were, continuing to claim Helena – that Lawrence finally told Louie what he had decided. He had taken Garnett into his confidence, and it would have been characteristic of the latter to advise an artist needing his freedom to break an engagement. Lawrence wrote the crucial letter to Louie on 4 February; he was not sure he could resist her appeal in a confrontation, and (anyway) the 'cruel me' had always been the writer.

In the letter he told (or possibly reminded) Louie that 'the doctor at Croydon and the doctor at Bournemouth both urged on me ... that I ought not to marry'. His health was genuinely 'precarious' and he could not be relied upon to support a family. And he went on to stress that he should not 'undertake the responsibility'. 'Responsibility' was a crucial word, the word which had dominated the engagement, and with which in some ways Lawrence had sought to dominate himself.

Then, seeing I mustn't teach, I shall have a struggle to keep myself. I will not drag on an engagement – so I ask you to dismiss me. I am afraid we are not well suited.

My illness has changed me a good deal, has broken a good many of the old bonds that held me. I can't help it. It is no good to go on. I asked Ada, and she thought it would be better if the engagement were broken off; because it is not fair to you.

It's a miserable business, and the fault is all mine. (i. 361)

It is painfully clear that Lawrence was determined both to produce sensible reasons, and to end the engagement with or without reasons. The first paragraph quoted is reasonable, responsible, and far-sighted – and almost ends with the gentlemanly request 'I ask you to dismiss me'. But then it adds – an ill-concealed afterthought – 'I am afraid we are not well suited' – as if Lawrence dare not trust solely to the power of politeness and reasonableness, but had also to say a little of what he felt. The first sentence of his second paragraph tells some real truths, though it is questionable whether Louie much needed to hear, or would have understood, what Lawrence had to tell her about 'bonds'. The word suggested the whole complexity of his attachment to his mother, to responsibility, to the idea of a career as a professional man. But, once again, Lawrence is unable to trust his tone of measured truth-telling, and interrupts himself with the brutal dual statement: 'I can't help it. It is no good to go on.' The last sentence of the paragraph, about Ada, certainly reproduces something of what Ada thought,[27] but the appeal to fairness is pure rationalisation. His very last sentence is a confession of muddle and guilt, but – in spite of the guilt – he knows that the end of the engagement is 'a miserable business': something too complex to be resolved by guilt. Louie later referrred to the document as 'the dreadful Cearne letter': it is not humble, and though it tries to be kind it is the letter of a man determined to be free.

Louie responded by begging him not to make a hasty decision, and asking him to reply by telegram. Lawrence wrote back from Eastwood, where he now was:

I'm sorry I could not wire back as you wished. But I do really feel it would be better to break the engagement. I dont think now I have the proper love to marry on. Have you not felt it so?

But I will see you next week – I will think out a time and a place. (i. 363)

His increase in honesty about the fact that he did not love her enough to marry her must have been dreadful. However, although Lawrence was ending the engagement, he was not capable of stopping Louie being attractive to him. He reported his final meeting with her to Garnett:

I saw Louie yesterday – she was rather ikey (adj. – to be cocky, to put on airs, to be aggressively superior). She had decided beforehand that she had made herself too cheap to me, therefore she thought she would become all at once expensive and desirable. Consequently she offended me at every verse end – thank God. If she'd been wistful, tender and passionate, I should have been a goner. I took her to the castle, where was an exhibition from the Art School – wonderfully good stuff. She stared at the naked men till I had to go into another room . . . (i. 365–6)

It is rather shocking to discover that Louie herself read that letter fifty years later, in the 1962 publication of Lawrence's *Collected Letters*. In her copy, she crossed out that last sentence, adding in the margin: 'He was already in evening clothes & kept his overcoat buttoned up. This is not at all a true statement'.[28] Lawrence went on:

– she gave me a disquisition on texture in modelling: why clay lives or does not live; – sarked me for saying a certain old fellow I met was a bore: could not remember, oh no, had not the ghost of a notion when we had last visited the Castle together, though she knew perfectly: thought me a fool for saying [Louie crossed out the last six words] the shadow of the town seen faintly coloured through a fog was startling – and so on. I took her to a café, and over tea and toast, told her for the fourth time. When she began to giggle, I asked her coolly for the joke: when she began to cry, I wanted a cup of tea. (i. 366)

Louie also crossed out 'when she began to cry', and added in the margin: 'I said Is there another girl He said Yes, if you'd *call* her a girl'. She also added, in the opposite margin, 'I was simply dumb with misery'. But Lawrence must be allowed to end his performance:

It's awfully funny. I had a sort of cloud over my mind – a real sensation of darkness which lifted and trembled slightly. I seemed to be a sort of impersonal creature, without heart or liver, staring out of a black cloud. It's an awfully funny phenomenon. – I saw her off by the 5.8 train, perfectly calm [Louie crossed out 'calm' and inserted 'dumb']. She was more angry and disgusted than anything, thank God. (i. 366)

The 'cloud over my mind' Lawrence describes here is both alarming and characteristic. His division of himself into 'the second me, the hard, cruel if need be, me that is the writer' and 'the pleasanter me, the human who belongs to you' (i. 214) had this much truth in it: he had a real and sometimes frightening capacity for obduracy, in the face of almost anything, as well as a marvellous capacity for sympathising with and identifying with the feelings of others. Both were characteristics of the artist he was, not only the second; and the letter shows him withdrawing from what he had determined not to feel. The letter also shows his defensiveness: it reveals more about him than he imagines. Yet, too, the letter has an odd feeling of being a demonstration of emotional and verbal control: a *tour de force* from Lawrence's developing literary armoury. Louie's marginal comments are the more poignant because, in comparison, they are so simple. She puts in exactly the things which Lawrence is determined neither to allow nor to imagine.

However, a writer who used the details of the inner and outward lives of his contemporaries in Eastwood and Croydon the way Lawrence did, in his fiction: the man Jessie Chambers remembered declaring 'With *should* and *ought* I have nothing to do'[29] – such a man was not going to let tender-heartedness stand in the way of his future life, as he saw it at the beginning of 1912. When he wrote to Louie later in 1912, and especially when he wrote to her in November, his letters show the kind of sympathy which his desire for escape had inhibited in February. 'I want to say that it grieves me that I was such a rotter to you. You always treated me really well . . . the wrong was all on my side. I think of you with respect and gratitude, for you were good to me – and I think of myself in the matter with no pleasure, I can tell you' (i. 479–80). But he could probably tell that Louie was still in love with him, and perhaps waiting for his return to England. So: 'now all I can do is just to say this. I am living here with a lady whom I love, and whom I shall marry when I come to England, if it is possible . . .' (i. 480). The letter contains only a single scrap of self-justification, which is obliterated the moment it shows itself: 'I feel a beast writing this. But I do it because I think it is only fair to you. I never deceived you, whatever – or did I deceive you – ? I may have done even that. – I have nothing to be proud of. – ' (i. 480). He had of course effectively deceived her with Helen Corke, as well as with Alice Dax. But, for her sake as well as for his, he glosses over that; he has said enough to allow his closing advice – 'The best thing you can do is to hate me' – to be more than a self-regarding gesture; he is giving her grounds for hatred.

If we compare her situation with that of Jessie Chambers when Lawrence ended their 'betrothal' in 1910, Louie looks far less capable of understanding what had happened. She was more completely deceived, and she did not have the history of Lawrence's behaviour over the previous nine years to help her understand him. On the other hand, that may actually have helped. She had no spectre of Lydia Lawrence to brood over as the cause of Lawrence's emotional incapacities; and she could blame his illness for the change in him, as Ada Lawrence encouraged when she wrote to Louie shortly afterwards: 'Its surprising how very much changed Bert is since his illness, and changed for the worse too, I think' (i. 361 n. 2). Later on – and quite wrongly – Louie blamed Frieda as the person for whom Lawrence had left her, and as the cause of Lawrence's shocking behaviour: her 1931 notes refer more than once to 'the seducer'. She came to believe that an episode on 11 June 1911, when Lawrence behaved coldly to her, marked the beginning of Frieda's influence upon him:[30] and she thought that Frieda was the 'girl' ('if you'd *call* her a girl') he mentioned on 13 February, when it was probably Alice Dax he was referring to.

What follows is the longest of her accounts of her engagement, which allows her own voice to be heard distinctly; it demonstrates her sense, her intelligence, her insight: also the desperate sadness of devoted and in many ways ignorant love. The sentence 'Love took away all selfishness & I had no life apart from him' is a heartrending epitaph for her.

Bert seemed to change suddenly when we had become engaged – as though he must impress me from the beginning as Lord & master. He made it a point never to relent – never to repent and in every way displayed his pride in the family will power.

I who had been born with an instinct to show a complaisance in ordinary affairs – gave way always & constantly – except in the things that mattered. My traditions were deeply planted. He was aware of this and never challenged them – but these were the rock upon which the wreck came, probably – (apart from the seducer) – for he realised that there were principles or standards that were part of my make-up, part also of what he admired in me, which I was unable at that time to shed – nor have I ever lost them, however inadequately the adherence has been.

He paid all he had, for his impatience, and he knew very early that he had made a big mistake in leaving me so dreadfully, though the phrase 'She was as well off without me' was a piercing bit of intuition which probably had much to do with his going – there the real soul I knew, the humility and consideration beneath the egotism spoke, – I felt at the time that he thought there was something of that in his desperate action, that it might be best for me. If only he could have lowered his pride sufficiently to discuss with me our two happinesses. I told him plainly enough that I would wait – ten years – always – Love took away all selfishness & I had no life apart from him. Time made no difference to me – but the thought of waiting only enraged him & increased his desperate impatience. Was he already committed to her when he made me the offer of immediate marriage in Jan. 1912 – which I as quickly accepted – before the dreadful Cearne letter came?[31]

Lawrence was *not* committed to Frieda in January 1912 when he made the offer of marriage Louie remembered, though in the long run it was probably easier for her to believe that Frieda was to blame.

Lawrence seems never to have written a harsh word about Louie after he broke their engagement, in contrast with the verdicts he uttered on both Jessie Chambers and Helen Corke. On the contrary, as he remarked in 1919, 'I was fond of her, and have always a good feeling for her in me' (iii. 353); the way he drew on her life and career for Ursula in *The Rainbow* shows that. For her part, Louie never forgot Lawrence; she kept his letters all her life, and let no-one else see them; in 1930, as she told Ada, she even 'went to Vence and saw the poor lad's grave'. Sir Herbert Read, who met her there, was impressed by the way she 'obviously had never renounced her love and devotion for Lawrence' although she felt ill-treated by him.[32] She did not marry until she was 53; her family always regarded her life as having been ruined by Lawrence.

But it is almost impossible to imagine any future she could have shared with him. The only chance, perhaps, would have been in that 'country school' (i. 202) which Lawrence fantasised about, right at the start of their engagement. If he had given up the idea of a career as a writer, and had kept his writing to spare-time work: if they had gone as teachers together, husband and wife, to that school on the north Cornish coast about which he wrote for job particulars on 19 December 1910 – then, perhaps, 'Think of us, by the brawling ocean in a land of Cornish foreigners blowing out our lonely candle as the clock quavers ten' (i. 207). But he never even sent in the application forms. Years later, at the end of the autobiographical novel *Mr Noon*, Lawrence wondered what the future for Gilbert Noon would have been like 'If he had married some *really* nice woman', and concluded: 'then he would never have broken out of the dry integument that enclosed him. He would have withered with the really nice woman inside the enclosure.' It is a hard saying, but probably true of Lawrence after 1911; and Louie was (as he confessed) 'good to me'. As he remarked towards the end of his life: 'she would have given too much – it wouldn't have been fair'.[33] When he eventually went to the north Cornish coast five years later, in December 1915, he went as the husband of Frieda – by no means a '*really* nice woman' – and as the author of *Sons and Lovers, The Prussian Officer* and *The Rainbow*: he would write *Women in Love* on that coast. It is impossible to imagine that life, that future, for the husband of Louie Burrows.

PART THREE

◆

Eastwood Again

SPRING

I On the Margin

If for a moment we step out of the narrative history to take stock of where Lawrence had got to in that life he felt 'moving on phase by phase' (i. 239) – then, in spite of the emotional and sexual disasters which had blighted the years 1909 to 1912, and the fact that he had ended up with a career neither as a teacher nor as a writer, yet all the same a great deal in his life and career had been the story of an extraordinary success.

He was 26½: not particularly young. At that age, James Joyce had already lived in exile on the continent for four years, having (at the age of 22) found the woman he loved and made his break with Ireland; Joyce had gone away to live his life and to write, with the confidence of a man who knew exactly what he wanted to do. Ezra Pound, born the same year as Lawrence, had left America and published his first book *A Lume Spento* in Italy at the age of 23; he had had a reputation on two continents before he was 25, and at the age of 26 he was one of the most influential figures in literary London. And, again, he had known almost all his life what it was he wanted to do.[1]

By comparison, Lawrence looks both undecided and a late starter. And yet that is not really true. He had published a long first novel in 1911, finished a second and drafted a third, written a number of short stories and many poems – all during full-time employment in a time-consuming and exhausting job. In becoming a published writer he had combated the prejudices of his own family and circle of friends. He had applied himself remorselessly to his writing: and had finally overcome both his own deep inhibition about exposing himself and his work to publication, and the problem of being a writer from a colliery village. As his mother had remarked as early as February 1910, 'Who would ever think of Bert being what he is.'[2]

Even more impressively, he had overcome the most extraordinary odds not only against achievement and success, but against education itself. He had had two years in a training college which were not of much use to him; but he was wonderfully self-educated. He had a wide knowledge not only of the English writing of the past three centuries but of contemporary poetry, drama and fiction. He was also well aware of contemporary Continental writing: had read Ibsen, Chekhov, Tolstoy, Turgenev and Dostoevsky in translation, and Stendhal, Balzac, Verlaine, Baudelaire and Maupassant in French, as well as German poetry in the original. He also read theology, history and philosophy with particular interest: he knew what had been said by Schopenhauer, Darwin, Spencer, Haeckel and Nietzsche, and knew what was being said by contemporaries as different as Henri Bergson and William James. His writing shows him engaging with their arguments: and all this by the end of the year 1911. While never having had access to large or academic libraries, and lacking the money with which to buy books, he had managed to extend his reading by borrowing books from smaller libraries and from friends and relations, and by judicious second-hand buying. He read omnivorously, but books and ideas were never solitary experiences for him: he continually challenged the ideas he met, and discussed books and their ideas with others. He had thus come into full possession of his reading. At first there had been Jessie Chambers to share his intellectual pursuits and discoveries: later, Arthur McLeod and Helen Corke: back in Eastwood, Sallie and Willie Hopkin: in London, Edward Garnett. Mentioning his new girl friend in 1909, Lawrence had typically described Agnes Holt as 'my kind, a girl to whom I gas' (i. 141).

A man with very little formal or academic training – or money – had thus learned that he was the contemporary of Hardy and Yeats, of Wells and Bennett, of William James and Henry James, of Conrad and Pound, of Ibsen and Turgenev: and that he was the heir to the nineteenth-century thinkers. He had grown an immeasurable distance from the expectations and standards of the colliery village – and had paid the price for it too, in loneliness and self-conscious difference. He had come to inhabit a kind of intellectual border country between what Ford Madox Hueffer called 'the high things of culture'[3] and the realities of the everyday which he knew so well: a life cramped and pinched in outlook and expectation. Scholarship, education, reading, career and language had cut him off from ever being fully at home anywhere. He was a man on the margin, in the border country: at the place where the cultivated land becomes the untilled wild.

Characteristically, he made this a source of strength. He knew he was at the rapidly shifting confluence of the nineteenth and twentieth centuries; and if he had nowhere he could really call home, he could assert as a belief and philosophy the isolate individuality which he had grown to realise was his fate. He saw with piercing clarity and a very cool eye: saw himself, too, with the frequently inhibiting eye of self-consciousness. Yet he was also the kind of companion with whom people loved to be: sharp in insight and observation, warm in understanding and exhilarating in company – even if he was destined to be the kind of companion by whom people tended to feel abandoned, as he went his own way. He actually cared very deeply about the things which interested him: was naturally a concerned and worrying person. This he frequently attempted to hide under the light-hearted manner of a person who took nothing seriously and many things cynically.

At the start of 1912, he had two novels on his hands: the rewritten *Trespasser* to publish, the worryingly complex 'Paul Morel' to carry through to its conclusion. But at last he had time to pursue his writing. He had no idea if he would survive as a professional writer; he would (after the experience of 1911) probably have reckoned it unlikely. But he was going to take the chance which had suddenly been offered him. Above all he believed in his writing: which was why he had been so reluctant to risk publication in the first instance and had spoken and written so deprecatingly of his work to almost everybody, while simultaneously agonising over it and continually revising it.

He was going back to Eastwood and was planning to see more of Jessie Chambers than for some time. But not because he believed they had a common future: he thought she could help him understand the processes which had made Paul Morel what he was. He showed no sign, however, of escaping the old pattern of splitting himself into two kinds of men (the sophisticated and the non-intellectual) and opposing himself to a loving and (he felt) threatening woman. He was not in love except – in a very special way – with his mother: she had been the only person who had ever really succeeded in breaking down his reserve and getting a whole-hearted loving response from him. His experience suggested that that was unlikely to happen with anyone else. He knew women who would sleep with him, but he felt no desire at all to embark on a serious relationship. He was actually as likely to denounce women as run after them.

His illness had set him the far side of a gulf from his previous life. He was going to spend a few months at home recovering – and would then go abroad. When he came back, he might be earning enough to continue as a full-time writer: but he knew he could always return to teaching if he had to. He knew that the past no longer held him quite so tightly as it had: but he had no real direction forward.

II 'Paul Morel' in Eastwood

Ironically, the first move in his new life was back to Eastwood. He returned on 9 February 1912; it was his niece Margaret's third birthday, and his married sister Emily wanted 'to give a party in honor thereof, and of my homecoming' (i. 354). After Bournemouth he was feeling 'very decent in health: just the little twists and turns of ordinary convalescence. I think I get fatter – I think I look better than I did six months ago. I feel about all right – have odd bad days . . .' (i. 367). He had nearly died; and for the rest of his life, would rarely be absolutely well again.

But, in February 1912, the way was clear – and the need considerable – for him to start earning. As if to confirm his potential, a second payment of royalties (£49-15-1) for *The White Peacock* arrived from Heinemann – though just as the first royalties had helped pay for the expenses of his mother's illness and funeral, this second batch was immediately eaten into by the expenses of his own illness and convalescence. Lawrence had hoped that the money would last him six months, living at home (i. 339), but he remained unable to pay back Garnett the 7 guineas he owed (i. 364). He also felt let down by Croydon Education Committee, who had reduced his December salary because he had been away 'more than the number of times allowed by the Standing Orders' (i. 368 n. 1). He must have felt that his illness – however useful in one way – had nonetheless precipitated him too quickly into being a full-time writer. He had still very few contacts with magazines, and indeed told his one real contact – Austin Harrison at the *English Review* – that 'It is a nuisance I should have to come to depend upon literature' (i. 378). But he was sure he was not going back to teaching, at least for a while: 'no, I'll be a tramp rather' (i. 367). Creating *The Trespasser* for Duckworth in Bournemouth had been an important step; now he was going to work full-time on his long delayed and twice abandoned colliery novel for Heinemann, 'Paul Morel' (now due for submission in June 1912). But the fact that he was soon going abroad suggests how cautious he still was about his prospects as a writer.

He was also restless, rootless and unattached. Although 'at home' in Eastwood, for the first time in ten years he was close to no woman apart from his sister Ada. Of his male friends, Arthur McLeod was still in Croydon, his old friend George Neville had got married in January and was now living in Staffordshire, and Alan Chambers was married and living in Nottingham. 'Home at Eastwood' was no longer what it was, as he made clear to Neville when he saw him in March and insisted that he join the old group of friends if they had a summer holiday together. Lawrence was sure that, if he went without Neville, he would feel 'Just stranded by myself with all the crew'; for 'the old days have gone; gone altogether; gone beyond recall'.[4]

With the national miners' strike of February 1912 starting almost simultaneously with his return to Eastwood, however, he would have seen a good deal more of his father than he would have expected. The Queen's Square house contained Ada, little Peggy, Emily (with her husband Sam

King) and Arthur Lawrence. Lawrence was thus living for some weeks in the same house as his whole family, for the first time since he had gone to Croydon. Sam King and Ada were out at work all day, but Emily would have been at home, as would Arthur Lawrence, on strike (at the age of 66) from his job, albeit only part-time, at Brinsley colliery. Lawrence was fond of his family: yet he was by no means happy to be back so squarely in the middle of them. He told May Chambers how 'A.'s quite ready to step into mother's shoes. If I go to Nottingham in the evening it's – "Where have I been? Whom have I seen? What was my business?" I say to her "Ask me another." A. mustn't think she's mother.'[5] Ada had remained close to Eastwood, compared with her brother; her name appears regularly in the columns of the local paper, recording her singing, her playing the piano at school recitals and her acting with a group from the chapel, where she was also a member of the choir. Unlike her brother she had kept her Christian faith: she had only 'dipped into disbelief' in 1911, following her mother's death (i. 248). Her six-year engagement culminated in marriage; her brother's one-year engagement had collapsed. And when, shortly after that collapse, she found him kissing a girl friend of hers after a dance – 'we were kissing like nuts', Lawrence admitted – she was indignant (i. 369). Like her brother, Ada was lively minded and alert, so that people often thought of them as alike: 'he was a comic. Their Ada was too, they had us in stitches'.[6] But Ada was also strict and respectable in a way that Eastwood appreciated.

It is therefore particularly striking that, during February, March and April 1912, Lawrence should have been engaged in writing 'Paul Morel'. He was actually 'at home' while doing it; not only observing the sometimes oppressively intimate life of the mining community and its surrounding villages – like Jacksdale, where the scandalous dance took place – but actually living with his sisters and father. He thus created the early married life of the Morels in the very kitchen where the 3-year-old Peggy King was the child growing up, Arthur Lawrence still sat beside the fire in his wooden armchair and Ada (25 in June) very consciously shared the role of the young woman of the household with Emily (30 in March). The sisters were furious about the strike and rather too like their mother for comfort: Lawrence noticed how 'every evil that could be urged against a working man is urged by his woman-folk ... They would murder any man at any minute if he refused to be a good servant to the family' (i. 379).

Lawrence wrote four sketches of mining life during his first five weeks in Eastwood; he had particular local knowledge which he hoped would help him find a magazine market during the coal strike. Only one piece, 'The Miner at Home', got into print immediately.[7] But all four show Lawrence's talent for recreating the everyday details and tensions of Eastwood life:

particularly the inevitable quarrels over money during the strike. They are extraordinarily compact and brilliant sketches: a proof that Lawrence was now prepared to create working-class life in his fiction without any overlay of moral commentary. They are also the first sign that he could write about Arthur Lawrence's world without subjecting it to Lydia Lawrence's disapproval.

But in spite of an active family and social life in Eastwood, he must have felt a good deal isolated; and, as he expected – given the way she was helping him with 'Paul Morel' – he started seeing Jessie Chambers again. Jessie was now living in Nottingham and teaching at the Musters Road School. Sometime in February 1912, probably only four days after getting back to Eastwood, Lawrence went to see her, to collect the notes about their early life which she had been writing. In the fictional version of the meeting in *Sons and Lovers*, Paul notices that Miriam's 'face was much older, the brown throat much thinner . . . A sort of stiffness, almost of woodenness had come upon her.'[8] But she was almost the only person with whom he could speak frankly about what concerned him most; still the person closest to him, the one who knew him best. He had told Jessie more than once that, if she wanted him to marry her, he would; he felt he had taken advantage of her and he was determined to be honourable. Now he told her that if, after he had been abroad for a year, 'neither of us had found anyone we preferred, then we would marry . . . He concluded rather dismally as though it were the only alternative.' The idea rather repelled Jessie; but she felt she saw, once again, 'his intense loneliness, his separation, as it seemed, from the rest of life'. She slipped her hand 'into his empty one. His arms closed round me in a moment, he drew me to him, begging me to "come to him".'[9]

Was it a new start? He also told Jessie 'I want to be free': he was by no means simply offering himself to her. But he was turning back to her. She went with him to Nottingham station: 'On the tram he seized my hand: "I wish we could run away on this," he said. But I did not see why we needed to run away . . .'[10] For Lawrence, a relationship with Jessie now would only be possible if they could manage a mutual and spontaneous break away from their old patterns, like the one he had glimpsed on the train with Louie Burrows. He believed it possible; at least, he hoped it was. Jessie did not. Her very natural cynicism stifled the chance they might just have had of breaking free from the past.

Lawrence gave the manuscript of 'Paul Morel' to Jessie as he wrote it, exactly as he had that of 'Laetitia', six years before. To start with, Jessie was deeply impressed and delighted with what she read. 'The break', she wrote, 'came in the treatment of Miriam'. This time, Jessie Chambers watched Lawrence recreate their relationship in great detail, in fictional form: compressing it, restructuring it and in two respects making it unbearable to her. In the first place, Lawrence largely omitted what was to her still the most marvellous part of their life together, what she later called 'D.H.L.'s Golden Age':[11] their very earliest years, up to the break forced by his mother and sister at Easter 1906. Secondly, he represented their 'experiment with sex' of 1910 in a way she found repugnant. In the 1911 'Paul Morel', the externals of Miriam's life had borne little resemblance to Jessie's. In the 1912 'Paul Morel', they became both startlingly alike and terribly different. But of all the things which distressed Jessie Chambers about 'Paul Morel' as Lawrence wrote it in the spring of 1912, perhaps the worst was the absence of anything equivalent to all those years of intellectual effort and shared reading. She was both bewildered and horrified: 'to give a recognizable picture of our friendship which yet completely left out the years of devotion to the development of his genius – devotion that had been pure joy – seemed to me like presenting *Hamlet* without the Prince of Denmark'. The imbalance – as Jessie saw it – of the novel's account was incidentally later made worse by some of the deletions which Edward Garnett introduced when he cut the novel for publication in 1913. A four-page account of the young Paul meeting Miriam at the library of the Mechanics' Institute, and of their common love of books, was cut, as was the sentence in Paul's letter at the end of chapter IX: 'You have played a fundamental part in my development.'[12]

But the 'damage' was really inevitable following Lawrence's decision to make Paul Morel a painter rather than someone interested in words, or an intellectual, and to cram together the years between 1902 and 1910 into a single space. Paul talks a great deal, but he and Miriam hardly ever read books together. Herbert Spencer and *Tartarin de Tarascon* are mentioned; but the moment in 'Strife in Love' when we hear 'they read Balzac together, and did compositions, and felt highly cultured' is unusual. Revising 'Paul Morel', Lawrence cut out the word 'together' after 'Balzac', thus limiting still further the possibilities of Paul and Miriam's mutual enjoyment. Again, we hear that Miriam – on a visit to the Morel household – 'talked books a little. That was her unfailing topic.'[13] The novel thereby suggests that books were not such a topic for the autobiographical hero. Only relatively late in the novel, and rather strangely (given what has gone before), do we find Paul and Miriam 'talking books: it was their unfailing topic. Mrs Morel had said that his and Miriam's affair was like a fire fed on books—if there were no more volumes it would die out.' But that has not been the account of their lives which in general the novel presents; and the radical lack of sympathy for the youthful literary couple would eventually suffer a positively goblin transformation into Mellors's account of his early life in *Lady Chatterley's Lover*.[14]

We also regularly hear in the 1912 'Paul Morel' that Miriam is a stimulus to Paul's thinking, but we get very little of that thinking or much mention of the intellectual advances Lawrence and Jessie – and then Lawrence on his own – had made, except for occasional descriptions of Paul considering Michelangelo, or making remarks about his own paintings. We are told that Miriam stimulates Paul; but his thinking tends to be abstract, not much connected with literature and hardly at all with words. There is very little reference in the novel to the years in which the conversation of Lawrence and Jessie was the most important thing in the world to them both: nothing to compare with Lawrence's sense of Jessie as 'the anvil on which I have hammered myself out' (i. 112). We hear that Paul is teaching Miriam – algebra, for example, and French; but never that they are studying together. Miriam is an unintellectual woman; the real-life Jessie Chambers, as we know from her reading and from her writing, was determinedly intellectual. And at no stage until the very end of the novel is Miriam allowed to get free of the farm, or of the way in which (exactly like the young Jessie Chambers) 'she drudged in the house'. Even in *The White Peacock* Emily had been a teacher.[15] This means that Paul's company becomes Miriam's only opportunity of escape, or of education which might help free her from her home. Jessie Chambers's actual struggle over many years for independence of the family farm, and her work as pupil-teacher and teacher, are omitted from the fiction; and while it is true that Paul, too, participates in none of Lawrence's own education or teaching work, the consequent difference in his situation – as employed man and potential artist – matters far less than it does in Miriam's. Jessie's years of struggle for career and self-fulfilment are reduced to Miriam's rather foolish failure to learn algebra. Her years with Lawrence, from 1902 to 1910, were the great and formative period of Jessie's life; not just because of him, but with his active participation.

'Paul Morel' thus offered an extraordinarily one-sided recreation of the early years of Lawrence and Jessie; but it was a novel written at a time when Lawrence was more interested in the non-intellectual hero than he could possibly have been between 1902 and 1910, and at a time when the intensely literary and intellectual youth who had 'rushed with such joy to the Haggs' had become the object of his own puzzled cynicism. As he compressed his relationship with Jessie into a few years, Lawrence also crucially altered it by making it a matter of *love* from the start; Paul and Miriam experience 'First Love' (the original title of the 'Lad-and-Girl-Love' chapter) almost at the start of their time together. This continued what he had done in the 1911

'Paul Morel', where Miriam had showed Paul 'a tree covered in yellow hazel-catkins ... he had looked at her so brightly that she felt giddy and leant against him—that he enjoyed, but when she put her hand on his arm he drew away'.[16] In the spring 1912 'Paul Morel' what was suggestive is made explicit; the episode of the rose tree is used to emphasise the sexual nature of Miriam's feelings from the start. When Jessie read what Lawrence now wrote she found comments such as 'when Miriam had made it impossible for him to kiss her, she wanted his mouth'. She was horrified: she crossed it through, together with the paragraphs around it, and remonstrated: 'Astonishing misconception. Miriam was sixteen – as pure and fierce in virginity as Paul.' She also insisted that 'In this chapter Paul and Miriam are *each* unconscious, undesirous even of love'. She added annotations to the novel's manuscript all the way through (see Illustration 41). Lawrence took Jessie's criticisms to heart; he rewrote part of the chapter in May–June and again in September, making some significant changes.[17]

But as Lawrence was now conceiving and writing his novel, Paul and Miriam's final sexual relationship (which in the autumn of 1912 he called 'The Test on Miriam') is inevitable from the outset – whereas in real life it had been an unexpected and in most ways unlooked-for end to eight years of non-physical partnership. Jessie repudiated the idea that in real life their relationship had culminated in a 'Test' which she had failed. But she felt utterly hopeless as she watched Lawrence recreating the story of their early life together:

I tried hard to remind myself that after all *Sons and Lovers* was only a novel. It was not the truth, although it must inevitably stand for truth. I could hear in advance Lawrence's protesting voice: 'Of course it isn't the truth. It isn't meant for the truth. It's an adaptation from life, as all art must be. It *isn't* what I think of you; you know it isn't. What shall I put? What do you want me to put . . .?' in a mounting crescendo of irritation and helplessness.[18]

In the spring of 1912, Lawrence was less concerned with what *had* been than with what he wanted his hero Paul Morel to experience. The working-class boy – his relationship with his mother apart – is a far more ordinary and far less complex person than Lawrence himself had ever been: he is an artistic and sexual being, but not an intellectual one. It is Miriam who is the emotional and spiritual misfit. Jessie thought she recognised what Lawrence was doing: giving Miriam 'his own failing, namely, inability to make a normal adjustment to life'.[19] Lawrence may well have thought it unwise to try and give a realistic acount of his years with Jessie: the partnership had been so very unusual, its intellectual concerns so extraordinary, its sexual commitment so desperate. But, as a result, the only role Miriam can really fulfil in the novel is as Paul's first and unsuccessful partner in love.

For the first time in Lawrence's writing about the 'Miriam' figure, too, there enters some rather ruthless analysis of her, which turns at times into an almost jubilant denunciation of her weaknesses. Lawrence probably felt he was now starting to understand what Jessie had been, and what – in particular – he had been, with her: and what he was now determined *not* to be any more, and would rather not allow Paul to have been either. Miriam's concentration upon the spiritual, the bodiless ecstasies in which Paul engages at times – Lawrence was now starting to turn against these as some of the worst excesses of his years with Jessie. The novel allowed him to write them out as an act of exorcism, but at the expense of the woman who had shared in them with him, and who remained devoted to the memory of those early days.

Jessie's pain and sense of betrayal were overwhelming. It was impossible for her to say it was 'only a novel', or for her to recognise or understand the nature of its focus and selectivity. Continually, in detail and at large, the picture of Miriam drew on her habits, her speech, her home and family, and recreated episode after episode which had really happened. 'The Miriam part of the novel is a slander, a fearful treachery', she wrote in 1913: 'I was hurt beyond all expression', she added in 1934: 'I didn't know how to bear it.'[20] It took her the rest of her life to come to terms with the novel and with the loss of Lawrence.

III Jessie Chambers and Lydia Lawrence

There was another reason, too, why Jessie may have been particularly hurt by the spring 1912 'Paul Morel'. We have no idea how Lawrence ended the novel in its early drafts: the first 'Paul Morel' was never more than a fragment, the spring 1911 version was never finished and none of the ending of the spring 1912 version survives. But Lawrence's particular distress in November 1912, when he wrote about Mrs Morel's death at the end of *Sons and Lovers*, suggests that he may not have written quite that ending before. It is even possible that the spring 1912 'Paul Morel' ended with its hero abandoning Miriam and Clara, but with Mrs Morel still alive; it is rather more likely, however, that Mrs Morel's death occurred, but not as the haunting and significant event it would become in *Sons and Lovers*.

If Jessie had found Lawrence presenting the failure of the relationship between Paul and Miriam, but not ending with or making much of the death of Mrs Morel, she might well have felt that he was presenting Mrs Lawrence with (as she put it in the 1930s) 'the laurels of victory': 'instead of a release and a deliverance from bondage, the bondage was glorified and made absolute'. It is hard to see how that description could be applied to the finished novel, a novel in which Mrs Morel dies after Paul gives her an overdose, and Paul is left having to cope with the awful aftermath of her death; far easier to see it how it could be the reaction of a Miriam to a novel in which the death of Mrs Morel either did not occur, or occurred in a far less significant form.

Jessie also developed the belief – in which, paradoxically, she may have been assisted by the completed *Sons and Lovers* – that both Paul and Lawrence were unable to love anyone because of their love for their mothers. She came to see it as axiomatic that what was true of Paul in the novel had also been true of Lawrence in real life: that because he had always been loyal to Lydia Lawrence, he had not been able to be loyal (or loving) to anybody else. At every turn in her 1930s book, Jessie showed herself sensitive to what she called Lydia Lawrence's 'repeated assaults' upon her, and Lydia's baleful influence upon her son.[21] Lawrence himself knew that his love for his mother – 'We have been like one, so sensitive to each other that we never needed words' – had 'made me, in some respects, abnormal' (i. 190); he also knew that his mother 'hated J.' (i. 197). But all that can be true without the simple conclusion which Jessie drew from it – that Lawrence was unable to love her because Lydia Lawrence forbade it and because he loved his mother. He may well, however, have tried to convey that idea to Jessie, as his sister Emily also tried when she said to May Chambers, after her brother had gone away: 'Our Bert can never love any woman. He could only love his mother.'[22] Both Lawrence and his sister were trying to save Jessie from the more hurtful truth that he did not love her and could not bear her love for him.

But by the early 1930s, Jessie had decided that – after drafting the novel in the spring of 1912 – Lawrence abandoned her yet again because he still loved his mother. What she says about this in her memoir is rather agonisingly self-deceived, and indicates the extent to which she forced her interpretation of Lawrence's overpowering love for his mother upon events. She wrote how, in the spring of 1912, 'We were together again, and outwardly there was nothing to keep us apart, but his mother's ban was more powerful now than in her lifetime.'[23] In no sense were Lawrence and Jessie, in 1912, 'together again'. In spite of his closeness to her, and the ending of his engagement to Louie, there was an enormous amount to keep them apart. Their sexual relationship in 1910 had been a disaster; Lawrence's feelings of August 1910 had not changed; he feared and at times hated Jessie's intensity and what he later knew had been her possessiveness; he deeply distrusted that part of himself which responded to her; and he was having an affair with Alice Dax while remaining involved with Helen Corke. Jessie may well have seen her role as that of recalling Lawrence to a proper understanding of his past. But she overrates her importance when she says that, having read the 'treatment of Miriam' in the novel, 'I began to perceive that I had set Lawrence a task far beyond his strength.'[24] It was not 'a task' set by her which had made Lawrence rewrite the novel, and it was not according to her prescription that he rewrote it. However, by the early 1930s Jessie had grown certain that Lawrence's novel 'burked the real issue. It was his old inability to face his problem squarely. His mother had to be supreme, and for the sake of that supremacy every disloyalty was permissible ... He had to present a distorted picture of our association so that the martyr's halo might sit becomingly on his mother's brow.'[25] Her memoir is incomparably important; but, in these passages, it is not trustworthy, and has done some damage to the understanding of Lawrence's life.

Her memoir also confirms her seriousness, her self-destructive devotion, her inflexible will and the intensity of her tunnel vision. She herself told Helen Corke that her forebears had passed on to her 'a terrible degree of intensity ...'[26] A good deal of this seems to have been the result of her relationship with her own mother, who was a possessive, self-sacrificing and often deeply unhappy woman. Her brother David wrote sensitively about this, and about the effect upon Jessie of her additional confrontation with Lydia Lawrence:

It should be remembered that she [Jessie] entered into the whole gamut of the sorrows of two intensely self-centred women [Ann Chambers and Lydia Lawrence] while she was still a child, and an exceptionally sensitive and gifted child at that. This premature plunge into the vortex of adult experience may have overstimulated her sensibilities while thwarting growth in other directions.

She once referred to herself as 'unbalanced by strife'.[27] An anecdote about Ann Chambers is the more revealing because Jessie wrote so little about her. Around 1907, at the age of 20, Jessie had decided to leave home: she could not bear not being loved by Lawrence while seeing him so often.

I told mother I should like to get a post away and she made no objection until she saw me filling in a form of application. Then she said she could not bear the thought of my going away. She began to cry and begged me to stay at home.
    'It's on account of Bert that you want to go away,' she said. I acknowledged that it was, and she replied accusingly:
    'You would leave *me* because of him.'[28]

Jessie had been horribly torn between her mother and the man she loved with such devotion and such unhappiness. In 1906, and then again in 1908, in 1910 and yet again in 1912, she felt abandoned by Lawrence, and wanted to blame his mother; in her 1930s memoir, she presented her whole relationship with Lawrence as counterpointed by her own struggle with Lydia Lawrence. Helen Corke, who always remained sympathetic to Jessie, was struck by her 'possessive love for Lawrence's adolescent self' and wrote how, in the memoir, 'Though utterly unconscious of the fact', Jessie 'was repeating the error of Lawrence's mother, who with similar insistence had claimed the boy as she herself was now demanding the youth.'[29]

IV   Ending with Jessie

Lawrence stopped going to see Jessie to talk about the novel sometime in March 1912, but went on sending her the manuscript by post. She believed that his avoidance of her was significant. 'I felt it was useless to attempt to argue the matter out with him. Either he was aware of what he was doing and persisted, or he did not know, and in that case no amount of telling would enlighten him.' It is difficult to imagine that Lawrence did not know what he was doing: but he had the bit between his teeth and was pursuing his novel to a new and particular end. By mid-March he was also likely to have stopped going to see Jessie not because he was ashamed about what he was doing (as she suspected) but because he was now involved in his relationship with Frieda Weekley. The 'Test on Miriam' section of the novel was, nevertheless, one of the most ruthless things he ever wrote. Jessie thought it 'brutal and false', and Frieda too would realise 'the amazing brutality of *Sons and Lovers*'.[30] Jessie gave Lawrence her few final comments in written form, and only saw him twice more before he left England at the start of May; on those occasions they were always together with others. On Easter Monday, 8 April, she saw him by chance at the railway station:

I had a view of Lawrence for a full moment before he was aware of my presence. The misery I saw depicted in his face was beyond anything I had ever imagined. Utterly lonely, he looked as if his life had turned to complete negation. His expression at that moment was the direct development of the face that he used to turn towards the dark fields when he would declare, in agony of frustration: '*Nothing* matters.'[31]

He was just finishing 'Paul Morel' and may have been creating the death of Mrs Morel. He was not, however, suffering the agony Jessie imagined ('Utterly lonely . . .'), but her reference to the agony of frustration is suggestive. He felt, after all, that he had discovered in Frieda 'the finest women I've ever met' (i. 384), the woman he wanted to marry. And she was married to somebody else.

The last time Jessie saw him was two weeks later, on 21 April 1912, during a visit to her sister May. This must have been the worst occasion of all for her; she knew he was very soon going away for a long time – and they had almost nothing to say to each other. At last she prepared to leave: 'We shook hands and said goodbye like casual acquaintances'. The Chambers family trap set off down the road: 'and when I turned round he was still standing in the road looking after us. I waved my hand and he raised his cap in just his old way. I never saw him again.'[32] Lawrence saying goodbye 'in just his old way' was Jessie's final vision of him; the very last in the sequence of 'last words' he had been saying over the past six years.

That same afternoon, Lawrence suddenly exclaimed to May's husband William Holbrook: 'Bill, I like a *gushing* woman.'[33] Lawrence must now have been thinking of Frieda Weekley and of emotional honesty and immediacy. Before going away with Frieda a fortnight later, however, he wrote and told Jessie what he was doing; told her so as 'to leave her a chance of ridding herself of my influence' (i. 440). She was almost the only person he told; but his influence was not so easily escaped. Nor was hers: he would write about it for years.

V Alice Dax

Jessie Chambers naturally dominates our understanding of Lawrence's growth from the youth who wrote her his first poems in 1905, to the man who created 'Miriam' in 'Paul Morel' between 1910 and 1912. What is more, her book *A Personal Record* assures her immortality; she was one of the few people who knew him well when he was young who wrote very much about him – and she wrote both sensitively and intelligently. If, nevertheless, we place her for a moment beside Lawrence's old Eastwood friend Alice Dax, it is not in any attempt to lessen Jessie's importance, but to see even more clearly how significant Lawrence's relationships with both women were, and how common were some of the problems which both women endured.

At first sight Alice Dax offers a huge contrast with Jessie Chambers. She was utterly dissimilar in character, being outspoken and aggressively straightforward; but there is, too, an extraordinary difference in the amount we know about the two women, and in how we know it. Against Jessie's careful, loving and detailed book and her numerous surviving letters to others – as well as her accounts of Lawrence's letters to her – there exists just one lengthy letter from Alice Dax, written to Frieda Lawrence in 1935, together with a number of references to her in Lawrence's correspondence, two postcards from him to her and some accounts of her by those who knew her.

She was a remarkable woman. Born Alice Mary Mills in Liverpool in

1878, one of the seven children of a Harbour Board clerk, she attended Liverpool Central School and then worked in the post office. Her background was that of the impoverished lower middle class and sounds rather similar to that of Lydia Lawrence: in her 1935 letter to Frieda she expressed her feelings about her childhood unforgettably:

> the poverty of my life was shut in behind clean faces and gloved hands; a father's silk hat and frock coat, and a table which carried fair linen and crochetted doyleys even though every cake on it had to be halved or quartered to make them go round – a damnable crippling poverty, bare and dishonest which had no room for thought or books or recreation, but which demanded that every moment must be devoted to mending and making and scraping to keep up an appearance.
>
> *I* happened to be the most unlucky bird of the brood – damned from before my birth and doubly damned after it. I was conceived during a long period of unemployment, and the sordid story of those pregnant months, as well as those which followed, I heard time after time after time repeated by my mother throughout my childhood with tears of thankfulness to the good God who had always provided her with *bread* – she seemed to have had little beside![34]

That anger on behalf of the slaving and self-sacrificing mother – 'for years the bread-winner' – is something Jessie and Lawrence also felt about their mothers. As Alice Dax grew up, she developed a formidable hatred for her father and for men in general: 'I swore vengeance on his sex when I should myself be married and since *everyone* said that no man would ever marry me, I took the first who offered lest I should be cheated.' Her sisters had always jeered at her looks – '*You* won't get married. What would any man see in *you*?' – and when a man was eventually attracted to her 'because she *knew* more than other women of his acquaintance', her family 'more or less railroaded her into the marriage'. Luckily for her husband, however, she had 'developed a rather strong sense of justice before the marriage day', so that 'he didn't suffer so much as he might have done'. At the age of 27, in 1905 – a girl 'from away' as Eastwood thought of her – she married a man born and educated in Liverpool, but now running a shop in Eastwood: the dispensing chemist and optician Harry Richard Dax.[35]

She was 'no beauty – even when young . . . thin, angular, with large hands and feet, straight awkward and wispy hair and a strange mouth. But her eyes were wonderful . . . She had a wide, generous forehead and those eyes, deepset and steadily penetrating, looked at you directly with a long, wide stare that was disconcerting . . .'[36] Gap-toothed beneath the bright eyes and the long hair done up in a bun, in a 1915 photograph her smile looks both direct and vulnerable (see Illustration 31): the one flaw in the otherwise bright competence of a wife and mother of two. In Eastwood she quickly became prominent, involving herself energetically in local affairs. She had been a leading socialist and active suffragist in Liverpool; her activities had led to her being transferred from her post office job to one on the Isle of Man. A friend of hers, Enid Hilton (daughter of Willie Hopkin), recorded how Alice Dax gradually 'became a NAME in the district, a person to whom people turned in trouble, and who initiated all the good community enterprises . . .' She began one of the earliest Nursing Associations 'by a door to door subscription scheme': she was also involved in the Workers Educational Association. As that suggests, she was widely read; as a child she had escaped into books, 'giving herself a general knowledge far beyond her home and her surroundings'.[37] She read Ibsen (i. 50) as well as the serious magazines Lawrence passed on to her, such as the *English Review* (with its serialisation of H. G. Wells's *Tono-Bungay*) and the religious quarterly the *Hibbert Journal* (i. 128, 359); a progressive article about Bergson attracted her in the latter. She apparently had the works of Edward Carpenter on her shelves, too – as might be expected for someone of her interests – and lent them to Jessie Chambers and Lawrence. She was a writer herself of poems and plays (none of which survives) and an active member of the Congregational Literary Society, her 'frequent contributions to discussions' being noted in the local newspaper (i. 4). And she had naturally also been at the meeting of the 'Eastwood Debating Society', run by Willie Hopkin, which on 19 March 1908 had heard Lawrence read his paper on 'Art and the Individual'. In the 1930s she introduced A. J. Cronin, the Brontës and Jane Austen to the daughter of her husband's partner, who also remembered being given 'an appreciation of the English language'.[38] Alice Dax – 'Dax' to her friends – was 'advanced' in dress, and in a small town where respectable married women like Lydia Lawrence always wore black, her 'grey costumes' caught the eye (i. 88). She was

almost completely uninhibited in an age when you just weren't . . . Part of her fight against the 'clutter' of her generation showed itself in her refusal to have one unnecessary article or item in her home. There were few pictures, only one rug, no knickknacks collected over the years, no items of beauty or arresting interest, but lots of *tidy* books. The furniture was good, modern (then) plain oak and served its purpose with-no-nonsense. There were no little mats under the clocks, or the cookie jar, no 'hangings'. The floors were linoleum-covered or of polished wood. It reflected Alice – clear, direct, uncluttered in thought and action, to the point of harshness.[39]

She was unsentimental on principle – Lawrence once mentioned the way she found 'photos a sentimental folly' (i. 100). She was deeply interested in the Women's Movement, and feared by 'most of the men of her generation' as a formidable opponent, articulate and scathing; although – to Enid Hilton – she was 'one of the kindest persons I have ever met'. She disapproved of conventionally polite behaviour; Alice Hall recalled how 'she said to me once, "I wish young Lawrence would sit down and not open the door when I get up." She didn't like it.' And her '*loud* laugh', a 'sudden explosion into laughter', was 'particularly offensive to local people'.[40] She was also 'an agnostic' – Lawrence saw her as a type of the non-believer (i. 256) – and 'very advanced for her time in those days ... really more advanced than Willie Hopkin was in her views'. By Alice Hall's standards, Hopkin was 'about the only intellectual man in Eastwood at that time'; Alice Dax, therefore, stood out as still more remarkable. Hopkin's daughter, however, suggested that her father was actually frightened of Alice Dax: 'subconsciously feared the impact of her personality and beliefs on my mother, and on me. As with most reformers he could change the world but liked his home intact ...'[41]

Lawrence's attitude towards Alice Dax seems often to have been like that of Paul Morel towards Clara Dawes and her suffragist beliefs; amused and ironical, insinuating that her opinions and 'sweeping general interests' (i. 44) were a consequence of her own unhappiness. Paul suggests that if Clara were happier in herself, she wouldn't have the opinions she does; and it was with delight – and wicked unfairness – that Lawrence wrote in May 1909, when Alice Dax's first child was a year old, how she 'has lost all that dam-foolery of faddishness about this that and the other – chiefly the ethics of society and women – and come to her senses as an ordinary woman, 'cause she's married and got a child and 'll have more sometime!' (i. 126). It is the very accent of Paul Morel, and quite untrue of Alice Dax.

However, Lawrence made her the second reader of 'Laetitia' in its 1908 state (assuming Jessie Chambers was the first); and that shows how high his opinion of her really was. It had been at the Daxes' house, after a rally for women's rights in Nottingham, that Lawrence had met Blanche Jennings; and almost all his subsequent comments about Alice Dax appear in letters he wrote to Blanche Jennings. As a result, it is often hard to estimate what he really thought of Alice Dax and of her comments on his book. His letters are written with the characteristic mixture of whimsicality and metaphorical stylishness in which he addressed Blanche Jennings; at times with the dry, ironic tones of Paul Morel – at other times with the voice of a languid aesthete, dismissing Alice Dax's opinions as earthbound and unimaginative.

Confined to bed in anticipation of the birth of her first child, Eric Cunningham Dax, Alice Dax (having previously read the first four chapters of 'Laetitia') was given the whole manuscript to read (i. 48); but Lawrence also explained how reluctant he had been to let her see the book. It was 'remarkable how sensitive I am on her score': 'You know ... my fondness for playing with the "Fine Shades", for suggesting rather than telling, for juggling with small feelings rather than dashing in large ones – this Mrs. Dax would at one time entirely have scorned, and even now I am not sure of her' (i. 44). Alice Dax was normally astringent, and scornful of artistic subtleties: Lawrence expressed surprise when she read L'Abbé Prévost's *Manon Lescaut* 'without a smile, a scoff, or an upheaval of the nose' (i. 55). And 'even now' – that is, almost eight months pregnant – she might well subject 'Laetitia' to scathing criticism.

Lawrence went on to ask Blanche Jennings whether she had noticed any change in her friend –

– a softness, an increasing aesthetic appreciation of things instead of mere approval on utilitarian grounds, or because of appeal to a strong, crude emotion? – do you remark an increasing personal, individual, particular interest which takes the place of her one-time sweeping general interests – in Woman, for instance, instead of in a woman and some women; in humanity rather than in men . . . She is a much gentler, broader woman; she is broader because she is not so broad, not so general, not so sweeping . . . I attribute it to maternity – she attributes it to me. (i. 44–5)

The letter is, of course, designed to poke fun at the social conscience of Blanche Jennings as well as to satirise Alice Dax. But it is also clear that Lawrence liked Alice Dax; and his last phrase suggests that she liked him too. He told Blanche Jennings in July 1908 how, after the birth of her child, Mrs Dax now had 'no interest in anything but "Son"': 'As you have prophesied, my nose is out of joint at Mrs Dax's – the nose of my interest is knocked off. Mrs Dax asks me to go, and then she is quite hopeless. She has no mind left . . .' (i. 69). It was a characteristic piece of mockery, but also suggests how flirtatious he could be with Alice Dax. Her reaction to his novel might have been more scathing had it not been for her liking for Lawrence himself; when Blanche Jennings suggested to Lawrence that he had 'a sane critic' in Alice Dax, he responded: 'a sane critic in a woman who is fond of me! – and you know human nature! She is careful of me' (i. 53).

Mrs Dax's criticisms of the novel were naturally slow in coming. In mid-June 1908, Lawrence at first gloomily reported that she had 'expressed her opinion in some half-dozen laughing lines of amused scoffing' (i. 55). But her criticisms struck him, he told Blanche Jennings, as those of 'a woman whose feelings flow in such straight canals', 'like a mother who reads her son's school essay'. Like his teachers at Nottingham, she criticised his English: 'She does not know that I must flaw my English if I am to be anything but a stilted, starched parson' (i. 53). Lawrence felt that his novel contained 'such a lot of crude sentimentality . . . and youthful gusty sighing, bungling insupportable. Nevertheless, there is some real good stuff – a good deal that Mrs Dax never sees, for she only cares about whether such people could really exist, and live like other folk in the midst of neighbours, chapels and mothers-in-law ...' (i. 55) She provoked Lawrence's first defence of himself as a non-realistic writer: 'I don't care a damn whether they live or whether they don't – there are some rather fine scenes and effects' (i. 55). But given the novel's poetic extravagances, Alice Dax's uncompromising concern 'whether such people could really exist' was exactly what Lawrence and his novel needed – even if he obstinately refused to recognise it. Certainly her criticism that the novel 'is too full of moods' (i. 61) was to the point, though (again) Lawrence made light of it: 'the moods disquieted Mrs. Dax; they were unfamiliar pages to her; they were therefore affected, not genuine; at any rate something was the matter. "Too suggestive of moods"' (i. 61).

Since Lawrence's correspondence with Blanche Jennings came to an end in the course of 1909–10, our knowledge of Alice Dax and her relationship with Lawrence diminishes too. We know he gave her two paintings around 1910: he also gave her a print of a van Gogh.[42] But Lawrence had gone to Croydon as a teacher in October 1908, and saw his Eastwood friends only during the school holidays. Alice Dax must however have kept up the relationship through letters written to him in Croydon; in November 1908 we find him once again reacting against a judgement of 'Laetitia' which must have come by letter: 'Mrs Dax told me her opinion – she is wrong – she is no judge of style – she likes style as she likes *not* people – well-bred, accurate, carefully attired – she dresses herself in grey costumes – she is like the whole world, she likes things "superior"' (i. 88). Lawrence both refuses to accept criticism of his self-proclaimed 'poor stuff' (i. 87–8) – and insists that conventional readers underestimate it; he deliberately turns the 'advanced' Alice Dax into a conventional reader. But his letters to Blanche Jennings show how full of mockery and flirtation his letters to Alice Dax would have been. 'When you see Mrs Dax give her my – my – regards' (i. 104), he wrote to Blanche Jennings in December 1908; he could make the matter a joke. But the relationship almost certainly remained an innocent one. Eastwood was a small town, his mother was still alive and anything untoward between Alice Dax and Lawrence would not have gone unremarked. Their friendship was that of a clever and articulate man of 23 sparring and flirting with an unconventional and intelligent woman seven years older than himself. When Mrs Morel asks her son Paul, in chapter IX of *Sons and Lovers*, what he likes in Clara Dawes (he is 'going of twenty-three', and Clara is seven years older), he replies: 'I don't know—a sort of defiant way she's got—a sort of angry way'.[43] That was certainly what Lawrence liked in Alice Dax.

By most people's standards however – be they those of an intellectual like

Willie Hopkin, or of a woman like Lydia Lawrence or of the ordinary collier's wife – Alice Dax could easily be seen as eccentric, rather shocking, and still something of an outsider: the girl 'from away' whom Henry Dax had perhaps unwisely married. Eastwood – which 'wasn't prepared for anyone like that' – eventually found its own way of dealing with her. She and Sallie Hopkin both refused to festoon their windows with traditional Nottingham lace curtains, and local people threatened to stone the windows; but Alice Dax upset local morals too. When the milkman called, 'he found her wearing sandals without stockings, he was horrified, but she didn't care anything for anyone and finally the trade went away from them, and they went Shirebrook way to live . . .'[44] 'The trade went away from them': against that, it was impossible to protest. The Daxes were bought out by Boots the Chemists in the summer of 1910, and left their shop in Nottingham Road, Eastwood; they moved to Shirebrook, ten miles to the north. Lawrence and other of their Eastwood friends kept up the contact; but we know comparatively little of their subsequent lives, except that in their seventies they both emigrated to Australia.

VI 'Morphia'

And that might have been that: Alice Dax might have been simply the early reader of The White Peacock, the unconventional woman and pioneer social reformer who left her mark on Sons and Lovers. In fact, the reality of events gives her a special importance not only in a biography of Lawrence, but in any understanding of the period.

How Lawrence first made love with Alice Dax was described more than once by Willie Hopkin; the story was perhaps his unconscious revenge upon her. His fullest version, recorded by a journalist friend, told how

Lawrence called one morning on an Eastwood lady with whom he was on friendly terms. Lawrence was in a restless mood . . . 'There's a poem I want to write.' 'Well,' says the lady, 'there's pen and ink and paper in the next room. Go and write your poem, and then, perhaps, you'll be a bit more sociable.' Lawrence went on walking as he said 'That's just the trouble. I can never work until after I've had sexual intercourse.' 'Too bad,' says the lady, disappearing from the room. Ten minutes later she reappeared in a dressing gown, saying 'All right, Bert. You can use me.'[45]

That was a full but rather crude version of the story. Hopkin's more cheerful version described Alice Dax telling his wife 'Sallie, I gave Bert sex. I had to. He was over at our house, struggling with a poem he couldn't finish, so I took him upstairs and gave him sex. He came downstairs and finished the poem.' The proper response to both versions is probably that of Frieda Lawrence, who reviewed a biography which included the second story in a version with the names left out: 'I don't believe the story of the mystery woman who says she "gave Lawrence sex". Lawrence was a fastidious and sensitive man, who would not go like a lamb to the slaughter with a woman who expressed herself so unfortunately.'[46] That sounds convincing. What seems to have happened is that Alice Dax – capable of appearing before a milkman without stockings on, and clearly fond of Lawrence – would, particularly after she left Eastwood, have been an easy target for such stories. And since Lawrence later really did have an affair with her, doubtless her poetry-loving reputation prospered.

In the early spring of 1910 began the sequence of events which led to their affair; according to Jessie Chambers, Alice Dax had already 'given Lawrence plenty of provocation, of which he had taken no advantage'.[47] But the spring of 1910 was, of course, the period of Lawrence's new relationship with Jessie Chambers, before he broke with her in August. Perhaps significantly, in *Sons and Lovers* Paul is attracted to Clara before he finally breaks with Miriam; and his affair with Clara follows the break. Alice Dax went to London to see Lawrence in March; itself a sufficiently unconventional thing for a married woman to do. She refused to stay in his lodgings, as Jessie had done; she went to a hotel. She and Lawrence probably attended a performance of Strauss's *Elektra* together, which would give a *terminus ad quem* for the visit of 19 March, when the opera ceased performance. Lawrence wrote to Jessie Chambers a few days afterwards: 'I was very nearly unfaithful to you. I can never promise you to be faithful. In the morning she [Alice Dax] came into my room, you know my morning sadness. I told her I was engaged to you. But it is all finished now with her – there is no more sitting on the doorstep' (i. 157). 'Later on', Jessie recalled, 'Mrs Dax gave me her account of what happened, which tallied with Lawrence's'.[48] It sounds as if Lawrence had been staying in the same hotel – something he had planned to do with Jessie. The fact that Alice Dax told Jessie what had happened is characteristic of her straightforwardness and of her sympathy with another woman. But it also left Jessie needing 'to talk about her, for relief', while Alice Dax was left in what Jessie called 'a molten state'. Jessie told Helen Corke that Lawrence would currently be unwise to write to her: 'let him give her time to cool and crystallise: to regain the normal'.[49] Things cooled down, even though Lawrence appears to have been left angry (the faithful man who did not *want* to be faithful) and certainly humiliated: he may have had Alice Dax in mind when he told Louie Burrows, in December 1910, about an ex-lover who was 'a little bitch, and I hate her: and she plucked me, like Potiphar's wife' (i. 208).

But 'the normal' was never recovered: it was by no means 'all finished now with her'. Most of what is known about their subsequent relationship comes in Alice Dax's 1935 letter to Frieda, from the traces left by Alice Dax upon Clara in *Sons and Lovers* and from the memoir by Enid Hilton. The names 'Dax' and 'Dawes' are not far apart, and the name of Clara's husband – Baxter – actually bridges the gap. The feminist commitment of Clara Dawes, her pride, her angry dismissal of men and her married status are all probably influenced by Alice Dax: while Jessie Chambers herself recorded that, of the three women whose lives she thought contributed to the character, the 'external resemblance to Mrs Dax is the strongest'. In an effort to reassure Jessie Chambers, Alice Dax once wrote to her that 'I have read *Sons and Lovers* and I *swear* it is not true.'[50]

Yet, even if not 'true', it certainly came close to the truth. Lawrence began to create the character of Frances Radford, a 30-year-old married woman (renamed Clara in later versions), between pages 330 and 353 of 'Paul Morel', around June–July 1911. The appearance of the character in the novel may be an indication that Lawrence and Alice Dax were viewing each other with particular interest around then. It is also possible that a sudden alienation from Lawrence which Louie Burrows experienced on 11 June 1911 – which she subsequently put down to Lawrence meeting Frieda Weekley – was actually provoked by Lawrence's relationship with Alice Dax.[51]

What is certainly true is that Alice Dax's child Phyllis Maude, born 6 October 1912 – and given a name chosen by Lawrence in 1908 (i. 48) rather than the 'Emmeline' (after Mrs Pankhurst) originally planned – would (Alice Dax asserted) 'never have been conceived but for an unendurable passion which only *he* had roused and my husband had slaked'. According to Enid Hilton, she actually hoped that the child was Lawrence's; but since Lawrence had gone down with pneumonia on 19 November 1911, and did not return to the Midlands until 9 February 1912, that would seem impossible unless Alice Dax visited Bournemouth during January. The conception of the child nevertheless strongly suggests that Alice Dax was suffering her 'unendurable passion' for Lawrence during the second half of 1911, when his sexual frustration with Louie Burrows was at its most intense, or in February 1912. Enid Hilton confirms, from what Alice Dax told her, that Alice 'became pregnant with the girl either just before the D.H. period, or early in that time'.[52] Lawrence had gone to stay with the Daxes in Shirebrook in August 1911 (i. 296), and after leaving probably wrote one of his two surviving postcards to Alice. It was a picture of the *Laocoon*, and he subsequently sent her two other pictures (now lost), telling her 'Arrange these as I number them' (i. 137 and nn. 1–2); the postcard promised 'Will write you later, from London' (i. 137).[53] The struggle of Laocoon was the beginning of some kind of sequence; that is all which can now be inferred.

Alice had originally married Henry Dax out of the belief that it 'might be her only chance ... She never really knew what she felt about Harry. She didn't know what one was supposed to feel. She liked him and thought that was what one *did* feel. No one informed her otherwise.' And she told Enid Hilton that she had 'never found sex exciting, or thrilling, or even very pleasant until D.H. came along.' Lawrence however awoke 'for a brief time all the deep feelings of which she was undoubtedly capable'.[54] Their relationship was, nevertheless, radically unbalanced. Alice Dax could never dare disagree with Lawrence:

the probable truth being that I felt unsure of him and feared to lose him, whilst he in turn, I suppose equally unsure of me, rarely quarrelled with me, but when he became extremely angry would turn and walk out. It was not honest – I know it, and I know too how much sooner I should have achieved myself had I given vent to the feelings I had, *when* I had them. And then I expected of him an honesty which I myself did not render, which was impertinence, so that always between us there were under currents which we could not cross.[55]

Their affair must also have been spasmodic and clandestine, with Lawrence in Croydon from late August 1911 onwards, ill from mid-November and then in Bournemouth from early January 1912. He planned to meet Alice in Nottingham on 14 February 1912, exactly a week after getting back to the Midlands (i. 365). However, when he saw Louie Burrows in Nottingham on the 13th, he was 'in evening clothes': it is tempting to link what was probably a visit to the theatre that night with the episode in chapter XII of *Sons and Lovers* in which Paul – also wearing 'an evening suit' – goes to the theatre with Clara and makes love to her afterwards. Something certainly happened the evening after his meeting with Louie; there was a 'sequel – which startled *me*' (i. 366).[56] Lawrence had yet another 'rendez-vous' on the 14th (i. 366), which may also have been with Alice Dax.

However, a short time later – perhaps only a fortnight – Lawrence met Frieda Weekley; and 'the day after the event' told Alice Dax about her. Alice Dax was immediately convinced 'that he would leave me'; it is quite likely, in fact, that she never saw Lawrence again. She subsequently went through a period 'suffering in body and sick in soul'; all through the summer of 1912, pregnant and ill, she experienced what Enid Hilton called 'a hell of the sort we can barely imagine'.[57] She wrote to Lawrence at least once: he 'told her I was with another woman – but no details. I am sorry for her, she is so ill' (i. 440).

Alice Dax was impelled to write to Frieda by reading *"Not I, But the Wind ..."*:

I had always been glad that he met you ... I was never *meet* for him. What he

367

liked was not the me I *was*, but the me I might-have-been – the potential me which would never have struggled to life but for his help and influence. I thank him always for my life though I knew it cost him pains and disappointments. I fear that he never even enjoyed 'morphia' with me [i.e. alleviation of pain] – always it carried an irritant – we were never, except for one short memorable hour, whole: it was from that one hour that I began to see the light of life.[58]

It is an extraordinary letter; she is uncritical of Lawrence without being in the least submissive or self-abnegating, and her ascription of her personal liberation to him is, in the circumstances, marvellously selfless. It is significant that she thought of the Lawrence of 1911–12 as someone in need of 'morphia', in confirmation of his own longing for 'a woman who loved me to rest me' (i. 311). He actually told Frieda in May 1912 – probably thinking of Alice Dax – how 'sometimes one needs a dose of morphia. I've had many a one' (i. 404). But Alice Dax is also perfectly sure, as she writes to Frieda, that Lawrence 'needed *you*'. Although Lawrence 'had set her free and given her something she scarcely knew existed', she did not feel free or liberated enough to leave her husband and son, or to saddle Lawrence with the responsibility of her and her children. She had to let him go.[59]

In retrospect, at least, Alice Dax felt that she had been fighting with so many demons of her own past, had been struggling so hard to 'achieve herself', that she could not actually get free. Considering her younger self with all its predicaments and desires, she was certain that she could never have been 'the vessel from which D.H. might drink to his joy and wellbeing'. She felt condemned to marriage, children, domestic life and joylessness: Jessie Chambers, who continued to visit her at Shirebrook, was struck by a comparison of her with Emma Bovary. Alice Dax knew that it was precisely the quality of freedom in Frieda which Lawrence found so attractive; the first time he had mentioned Frieda to her, he had remarked 'You would like Frieda – she is direct and free . . .' Alice told Frieda in 1935 how 'Alas! I loved him. But now I think you will understand why I was glad that you loved him too – you who could give him so much'. Nevertheless, she suffered horribly when Lawrence wrote to her in the autumn of 1912 'in the richness of fulfilment. How bitterly I envied you that day! How I resented his snobbery and his happiness . . .'[60] That letter from Lawrence no longer exists: all that survives is a brief postcard to her dated September 1912, hoping that she was 'going on decently' in the last weeks of her pregnancy, describing the beauty of the Lago di Garda, and ending 'love' (i. 457).

VII   The Limits of Liberation

Jessie Chambers, Louie Burrows and Alice Dax all felt that Lawrence left them for Frieda: Louie thought of her as 'the seducer'. In *A Personal Record*,

Jessie never mentions Frieda by name; all she says is that, in the summer of 1912, she received a letter from Lawrence which 'contained a hysterical announcement of the new attachment he had formed'. The word 'hysterical' shows how little time Jessie had for *this* Lawrence – and 'attachment' indicates her refusal to believe that Lawrence was, or ever could be, in love. She further wrote that his letter showed 'an intense *will* to love, but it carried small conviction to me'. She chose for the rest of her life to ignore Lawrence's relationship with Frieda; it had, she wrote, nothing to do with 'the man I wanted'.[61] Twenty-three years after Lawrence's life and writing had clearly been deeply influenced by Frieda, the obduracy of Jessie's attitude is very revealing. Alice Dax's outburst in 1935 has a generosity Jessie did not and could not feel.

But the comparison of Jessie Chambers with Alice Dax can go further than a contrast of their attitudes towards Frieda. Both women were highly intelligent, and had a great capacity for achieving what they wanted; but both, quite independently of their relationships with Lawrence, were deeply disappointed by the lives they found themselves leading. Alice Dax, married with one child and expecting a second, exemplifies – even more than Frieda Weekley did – the problem of the intelligent woman in a narrow-minded provincial society who knows that her life is lacking, but knows nothing which can be done to change it – except by changing the very society in which she finds herself. Her suffragism, her work in the W.E.A. and in the Nursing Association were designed to do just that, and made her, in the words of one of her contemporaries, 'a kind of ramrod, forcing the future into their present'. Her struggles for independence, for fulfilment, and her gratitude to Lawrence for his 'help and influence'[62] also have their direct parallel in Jessie Chambers's resolute self-education and uncompromising rigour of thought, feeling and behaviour: again, assisted and influenced by Lawrence. Both women adopted strategies to deal with situations which women in their position could not control: Jessie saw Alice Dax paying the price for it, and wrote a striking account of Alice's 'melancholy' and 'egoism' in 1913; yet, Jessie concluded, 'After all, how can she help it? I should think that she really has more of what Alan [Chambers] used to call "superfluous" sense than anybody in Shirebrook, and all powers that run to waste raise a crop of weeds.'[63]

But both women, very differently, had hoped to find in love – love outside marriage in each case – a fulfilment which would make up for their disappointment with their lives. Both trespassed, by the standards of the time. And both were desperately and lastingly hurt by their failure to keep the man to whom they committed themselves, as well as by Lawrence's abandonment of them for another woman – a woman prepared not only to leave her husband and children, but to give up all social respectability. We can see in Jessie Chambers and Alice Dax not only the inevitable problems of intelligent women in their society; we can see how their dreams of fulfilment arose as solutions to dilemmas arising in their social lives and in their families – and how (with almost equal inevitability) they failed to find the fulfilment they had glimpsed.

This is particularly striking in the light of how Lawrence was to write about women. One of his major aims as a writer after 1912 was (he told Sallie Hopkin in December) to 'do my work for women, better than the suffrage' (i. 490). That is, he would commit himself to writing about how women managed to break through the social and emotional barriers hemming in their existence. This was certainly very different from how he had previously written about women. But from 1912 onwards he almost always linked such a breakthrough with erotic liberation; he wrote the novels and stories which the partner of Frieda Weekley would most naturally write. Work which was 'better than the suffrage' also ignored the suffrage, as Frieda ignored it.

But Lawrence was, by background and experience, also extraordinarily qualified to write about women who failed to make that breakthrough; women who did not think that sex was very important, however much it gratified the men who demanded it. Those were novels which, after *Sons and Lovers*, he did not attempt to write. In his novel *The Lost Girl* (1920), he explicitly made sexual liberation the only thing which really frees the woman trapped in the small provincial town. Even in *Sons and Lovers*, Miriam is left helplessly unfulfilled, while Clara Dawes, in a burst of conventional feeling, goes back on her achievement of female independence and returns to her brutal husband.

But what about the woman like Alice Dax, who remained intelligent and independent, but who went on living with her husband and bringing up her children, and who had no chance of sexual liberation? Or the woman like Jessie Chambers who, abandoned by the man she loved, married another and lived a decent life in spite of everything? Or the woman like Louie Burrows, who settled down to her career? Lawrence's passionate writing about the liberation of women through the active realisation of their own sexuality would ignore the continuing predicaments – and solutions – of women like Alice Dax and Louie Burrows and Jessie Chambers.

But Frieda Weekley, who certainly believed in sexual liberation, was an extraordinary being; Lawrence's meeting with her, in the spring of 1912 was the making of him as the kind of writer he became.

CHAPTER FOURTEEN

◆

1912

FRIEDA WEEKLEY

I Wedded Wife

We had so many battles to fight out, so much to get rid of, so much to surpass. We were both good fighters.[1]

That was part of Frieda Lawrence's conclusion about her quarrels with Lawrence, in the introduction to *"Not I, But The Wind . . ."*. Their early life together involved, for both, a process of attempting to break with the patterns of the past. It is easy to forget that Frieda – Frieda Weekley as she was in 1912, born Frieda von Richthofen in 1879 – had as much to 'get rid of', to 'surpass', as Lawrence had when they met. Partly because of her own upbringing, she had made apparently irrevocable choices for herself very early in life. When she was 20 – an age when Lawrence was still living at home and teaching in the Albert Street School – Frieda was getting married to a Professor of modern languages, and was committing herself (with very little spoken English) to spend the rest of her life in a foreign country. Before her 21st birthday, she had given birth to her first child: Lawrence, at that age, had only just started *The White Peacock* and had not yet begun college; he was, in his own words, 'almost pathetically young' (i. 344).

Or, to put it another way: six years older than Lawrence, Frieda had had her first child on 15 June 1900 – when Lawrence was still at Nottingham High School. Before he sat the King's Scholarship exam, in December 1904, she had had her third child; and even then she had more than seven years of married life ahead of her before she met Lawrence. It is actually rather likely that Lawrence saw her long before his crucial visit to the Weekley house in Nottingham in March 1912. Between 1906 and 1908, while he was at Nottingham University College and frequently going to his brother George's house for lunch, he would have walked up the Wood-borough Road and turned right into Sycamore Road, directly opposite the entrance on the left to Vickers Street, where the Weekleys were then living. George Lawrence himself remembered seeing Frieda Weekley while she was living there (the Weekleys moved up the hill to Private Road in 1910): she would have been a striking figure in the locality.[2] If Lawrence had seen her in the street, she would quite likely have been pointed out to him as the young wife of the Professor at college whose lectures he admired.

But that they actually met for the first time on a Sunday during March 1912 is certain: rumours that they knew each other long before then, or that Lawrence paid visits to her while at college, are disproved by independent testimony from them both.[3] Since the middle of January 1912 Lawrence had been planning to go to Germany: his uncle Fritz Krenkow had relations in the Rhineland, and his German cousin Hannah Krenkow had suggested he go 'to Waldbröl near Cologne, in Spring. And I want to go in April or May' (i. 350). He told Jessie Chambers in February 1912 (after breaking his engagement to Louie Burrows) that eventually he might 'go further afield, and remain abroad probably a year'.[4] The idea of trying to get a teaching place in Germany – perhaps as a 'Lektor' in a University – seems to have developed a little later, and may well have come from his uncle and his aunt; they probably did not believe in Lawrence's chances as a full-time writer.

The person they turned to for advice about the 'Lektor' plan was the same Professor at Nottingham University College, Ernest Weekley, who had himself been a Lektor at Freiburg University in 1897. One Sunday in March 1912, probably the 3rd, Lawrence found himself asked to lunch with the Weekleys; it is impossible to be certain of the date. He had told Jessie Chambers 'I shan't go; I don't want to. I've written and told him so': which very much suggests that it was a Krenkow plan rather than his own. But it seems that a second invitation came, and that Lawrence felt that after all he had to go – 'I can't refuse the lady', he told Jessie. And he went to lunch with the Weekleys after all.[5]

Ernest Weekley, born in 1865, was 47 years old: an etymologist, the author of a number of scholarly books and just about to publish the book which gave him his national reputation for witty erudition, *The Romance of Words*. He had been Professor of modern languages at Nottingham since 1898; he had the chair there until 1938. He died in 1954. His early life, as one of the nine children of a middle-class couple in London, had been a struggle: he had started work as a schoolteacher at 17 to pay for his studies, had taken an external degree at the University of London and got a scholarship to Trinity College, Cambridge. There he won an athletics blue and studied Middle English and modern languages (he had already spent a year at the University of Bern). He then spent a year at the Sorbonne, and subsequently took up a post as Lektor in English at the University of Freiburg between May and November 1897. Here he acquired a reputation for learning, for commanding skill at tennis and billiards, for being a most amicable companion in the town's cafés and taverns – and for never getting up earlier than eleven o'clock in the morning.[6] It was while at Freiburg that he gained his Chair at Nottingham.

In the summer of 1898, he went back to Freiburg, revisiting friends, playing tennis and enjoying himself. And at Haus Eichberg in the village of Littenweiler, a few miles outside Freiburg, he met Frieda von Richthofen, who was staying there with the Misses Camilla and Julie Blas, old friends of her family. The wife of Professor A. Schröers was apparently initially responsible for bringing Frieda and Weekley together, and actually carried Weekley's proposal of marriage to Frieda's parents. As Frieda wrote the following day to her sister Else, 'er liebte mich und kann und will mich heiraten; es hängt jetzt nur noch von mir ab [he loved me and can and wants to marry me; it now only depends on me]'. Frieda intended to say yes, 'denn er gefällt mir wie mir noch keiner gefiel [because I like him as I never liked anyone before]'. Weekley was 34, 'greying at the temples', on the crest of a wave after his success at Nottingham; tall, elegant, witty, a good sportsman and genial companion.[7] Frieda was 19 and strikingly good-looking. She remembered a rendezvous in the Black Forest that summer: in her memoir she called herself 'Gisla' and Weekley 'Vernon'.

Gisla got more excited as she neared the fountain. She was conscious of her pink and white frock with the pink and white sunbonnet that Vernon loved so much. She thought more of her effect on him than of himself. At last she saw him standing in the entrance of a sombre pinewood, the trees forming a deep archway behind him. He was like a man lifted out of ordinary life. He did not know anything; he was nothing by himself, his sole being was in that approaching pink and white girl. His emotion almost paralysed him. Gisla felt slightly uncomfortable; she went up to him. He took her in his arms. Gently, tenderly, repressing his passion, so as not to frighten her. 'My sunflower,' he said.[8]

In Frieda's own, very simple words, 'He was no longer in his first youth, but of the age when a man falls head over heels or not at all. He asked her to marry him and she said yes.'[9] He never ceased to marvel at Frieda as his beautiful child bride: he was 14 years older than she.

Frieda had been born on 11 August 1879 in Metz, the German Garrison town in Alsace Lorraine: her father had a reserve commission and a desk-bound job as civil engineer for the city. A forefinger shattered in the Franco-Prussian war of 1870–1 had ended this young career officer's military hopes: had resulted in his being retired from active service, and condemned to the far slower (and less prestigious) promotion which went with an administrative post. A photograph from the 1890s shows him bristling with determination, while self-consciously concealing his damaged hand behind his back (see Illustrations 33 and 34). His gambling and womanising (he had a mistress and probably an illegitimate child) had a lot to do with his sense of having failed in his career.[10] Frieda's accounts of her childhood are rich in the details of family life: in particular, the mixture of affection and competitiveness which existed between her and her elder sister Else, and the estrangement between her parents: 'nothing but convention and the children kept them tied together. They lived the life that is so destructive to the best in people, is murderous in its fierce hatred, always newly roused by the contact of daily life.'[11] The parental estrangement had occurred before Frieda was 12 years old; her love for her father touches almost all her memories of childhood; her feelings for Else are a recurring theme up to the point when Else left home, leaving together Frieda and her even more beautiful younger sister Johanna.

Frieda was brought up as the child of parents who, while far from rich, preferred to be seen as aristocrats rather than as the gentry they really were; her father made his appearance on her birth certificate with his full name of Friedrich Ernst Emil Ludwig Baron von Richthofen.[12] They belonged to a social class and the kind of family where the daughters would not be expected to work or make their way in the world; that was for the male members of the family, for the uncles and cousins who found their way into political circles in Berlin or – like Frieda's father – into the army. But Anna and Friedrich von Richthofen had no sons; it was up to their daughters to marry well, securely and (ideally) rewardingly. To the outward eye, all three did this; the youngest, Johanna, marrying a successful career officer in the army when she was just 18, Frieda meeting her English Professor when she was 19 and marrying him when she was only just 20. The eldest daughter, Else, most remarkably (and quite unlike her sisters) had insisted on education; she went to University and took up a career as a sociologist and political scientist. Her eventual marriage – when she was rather older than either of her sisters – was outwardly equally successful, to the University Professor and economic theorist Edgar Jaffe, who became Finance minister to the short-lived revolutionary government of Bavaria in 1919.

It is probably not a coincidence, however, that the marriages of all three daughters came to grief. Their upbringing had encouraged them to see their father as both despicable and pitiable, despite his demonstrations of anger and forcefulness: they all came under the influence of contemporary ideas about free love: and they all married men whom they could dominate. Else's marriage (in 1902) lasted the shortest time: within five years, she was regularly living apart from her husband and having extended extra marital affairs, including a child by another man. She and Jaffe never divorced, and at times continued to form a family unit with their children, together with

Else's child Peter (see Illustration 40). In this, too, by English standards they were remarkable, though less so by those of German intellectual circles. Johanna's marriage lasted, technically, for twenty-three years, though she and her husband (the officer Max von Schreibershofen) had separated long before that. Frieda married Ernest Weekley in Freiburg on 29 August 1899;[13] her marriage lasted nearly thirteen years, although she too was having extra marital affairs long before it ended.

Frieda's marriage was in many ways the most conventional and certainly the least spectacular of the three. Unlike her sisters, she was condemned by marriage to a life of bourgeois respectability; on her very first visit to England she had felt how 'Like something heavy England came down on the lightness of her heart.' The dullness of her Nottingham life eventually enraged her:

Was hier so unerträglich ist: es giebt keinen lebendigen Menschen, Dickhäuter, Schlafhauben, Gänse Enten sind es und ich wünsche oft, ich wäre ein gewaltiger Fußtritt. [What is so unbearable here: there are no living human beings, they are pachyderms, sleepy-heads, geese, ducks and I often wish I were an enormous kick.]

She wrote to another friend pleading to be remembered 'in meinem scheusslichen England [in my ghastly England]'.[14] The dullness and loneliness were the price she had paid for her security: 'Ich leide unter der Einsamkeit, aber wer tut das nicht? [I suffer from loneliness, but then who doesn't?]' And though her husband loved her devotedly – she remembered how 'He used to kiss my feet in stupid boots' – and though he could impress her as a 'simple, strong man' and as a self-made man, he hardly ever excited her. Rather the opposite: the honeymoon (at the Hotel Schweizerhof in Lucerne) had been a disaster. Frieda had gone up to the bedroom first, and – typically – thought of climbing up on a cupboard behind the door to surprise her husband when he came in. She did not: he would have found it too upsetting. Instead, 'when Ernst came in, I threw myself naked into his arms. He was horrified and told me to put on my nightdress at once.' Weekley – 'strung to an unbearable pitch' – then made love to her and reduced her to 'an unspeakable torment of soul. It had been so horrible, more than horrible.'[15] Lawrence would later tell her 'You never got over your bad beginning with Ernst' (i. 404).

But she had married Weekley because he had fallen in love with her, and because he had seemed – to her adolescent self – able to free her from her family. 'I had been reading Tennyson, and I thought Ernst was Lancelot!' And after the first trauma and anguished disappointment she came to accept the advantages of her new state. She felt 'firm ground under her feet for the first time in her life. Here was something different from her own home life

... Her own home had been such a scattered thing.'[16] Weekley's stability was utterly different from what she had known in Germany: utterly different from her father's recklessness. Her own memoirs show, too, how much in spite of her disappointment she sometimes enjoyed the role of the young wife. She always enjoyed floating round at home dressed in almost nothing – something which could be especially satisfying on a Sunday evening in pious Nottingham. 'Gestern bin ich in meinem Zimmer nur mit einem Shawl angethan herumgetanzt, während die braven Philister in die Kirche gingen! [Yesterday I danced around in my room clothed only in a shawl, while the well-behaved Philistines were going to Church!]'[17] Her son Montague's recollection of her 'when I was about five, and she was about twenty-six' was of 'a tremendously vigorous, high-spirited wench': he thought her 'very much a creature of impulse' and believed that 'there was a great streak of childish impulse in her nature'. There speaks the very accent of his father. Marriage to Weekley did not, however, dampen Frieda's spirits. A close friend of later years, Maria Huxley, explained the Lawrences' relationship: 'Lawrence likes her *because* she is a child'.[18] Frieda went on attracting men, all her life, because of the way she combined spontaneity and freshness with sexual directness and uninhibitedness: she would look at men with admiration while simultaneously displaying her own sensual *savoir-vivre*.

During her Nottingham years, too, she was never buried under the cares of domesticity or child raising. Montague Karl Richthofen Weekley was born in 1900, Elsa Agnes Frieda in 1902, Barbara Joy ('Barbie') in 1904; but Frieda had the servants who went with middle-class life, including a German nurse for the children: at first a girl called Paula, later Ida Wilhelmy who 'made life easy for me'. Frieda always remembered 'the Sunday mornings, when the three [children] had come to her bed, when she had pillow fights with them in spite of the disapproving nurse, when they rode on her raised knees and she made them tumble down'.[19] She loved her children, loved playing with them and being loved by them and retained her exuberance and youthfulness and charm; she was, after all, not yet 21 when Monty was born, only 23 when Elsa was born, only 25 when Barbie was born. And to Weekley she went on being the young bride he had married. Lawrence still saw this in her when she was 33 and a woman 'glowing with zest and animation, her grey-green eyes laughed and lighted, she laughed with her wide mouth and showed all her beautiful teeth ... She was full-bosomed, and full of life, gleaming with life, like a flower in the sun, and like a cat that looks round in the sunshine and finds it good.' People always associated her with sunshine. Her sister Else, thinking back from 1966 to Frieda's birthday celebrations in the 1880s, wrote how 'Wir feierten ihn in dem grossen Garten in Sablon/Metz, der voller Blumen & Früchte war. In meiner Erinnerung schien an diesem Tag immer die Sonne ... [We celebrated it in the large garden in Sablon, Metz, which was full of flowers and fruit. In my memory the sun always shone on that day ...]'[20] Her lover Otto Gross wrote to her 'Du Sonnige [you sunny one]' and described her 'goldene Leuchten [golden shining]'. Sunshine, carelessness, spontaneity: this was Frieda, so that even Ernest Weekley 'became a youth again under her laugh'.[21]

Her reading, too, could provoke violently adolescent loyalties in her: she remembered an exchange with Weekley.

'Do you remember,' she laughed, 'when I had my Plato fit on and I began at breakfast, "Socrates says". You banged the table as if it were Socrates and said, "Curse Socrates."'

'Yes,' he said, 'you get your measles late, most people have done with Plato at your age, but your fits!' And he sighed wearily, comically ...[22]

Frieda had *never* 'done with Plato': that was part of her charm. She was fearless in argument, had an inexhaustible appetite for ideas and for people, a warmth and readiness in acquiring the ideas of others and in talking about deeply serious subjects. She had always read a lot, and – as befitted the wife of a Professor – she edited two little books for pupils of German: of Schiller's ballads and of German fairy-tales. She wrote at the time how 'it fills me with great pride to produce something "brainy" ... My little book about Schiller has given me tremendous pleasure'. She also helped with the translation of a German play upon which one of Weekley's colleagues was engaged.[23] (It was characteristic of her that her own memoirs of her life with Weekley mentioned none of these). Without anything beyond a young lady's education, either – certainly nothing like the education of her sister Else, or Lawrence or Weekley – and without ever being bookish (her staple reading was fiction rather than Plato), she had grown up an independently minded and thinking woman. On visits to Else in Munich she entered the circles of the Schwabing intelligentsia; met and talked with academics, artists, doctors and writers. On her very first encounter with Lawrence, they 'talked about Oedipus and understanding leaped through our words'.[24] They may have been discussing psychoanalysis or they may have been discussing Sophocles; few Nottingham wives would have been able to do both, and fewer still would have been prepared to do so in the sitting-room before Sunday lunch.

However, in a gesture revealing her boredom and her feeling of being stifled, Frieda would sometimes throw off her respectability as wife and mother – and not only in the privacy of her own room:

in the evening she put on an old hat, ran out of the house, tore up the Mapperley hill. The lanterns gave a cheerful light; in rhythmic distances the burring noise of the trams as they toiled up the hill came near and passed again, and she had a glorious feeling of escape, of freedom as she ran on and on the dark road where the wind was catching the trees on the top of the plain. Then she would go back to her house quietly, sane again.[25]

It was an interesting sanity which depended upon such releases. But Nottingham did not demand much of her; her job was simply to love her children and her husband, and to relieve him of the cares which lay upon him; to be a source of charm and youthful warmth and cheerfulness within the family circle. She clearly did this very well indeed. She also escaped Nottingham through extended visits to her family in Germany, sometimes taking the children with her: a couple of months a year to be with her mother, to visit her sister Johanna in Berlin or Dresden and to visit Else in Munich.

Nevertheless, she felt increasingly stultified by her marriage: 'cut off and alone in a world of millions, living her inner life unrelated to the outer one'. In 1907–8 she had a serious affair with the Austrian psychoanalyst Otto Gross (see Illustration 44), who lived in Munich and who had married Else's old school friend Frieda Schloffer. Gross, while remaining on reasonable terms with his wife, was already having an affair with Frieda's sister Else and was the father of her son Peter, born in 1907. Gross and Frieda fell for each other in the spring of 1907, in Munich, and saw each other again in the early summer, on Frieda's journey home to England; they wrote extensive letters to each other for about a year, Gross's being sent via Frieda's brother-in-law Edgar Jaffe. Gross made Frieda feel marvellous and admired and wanted; and gave her the incidental satisfaction of being preferred to her intellectual elder sister. He went so far in the winter of 1907–8 as to suggest that Frieda might leave Weekley, first taking her children to her mother in Germany so as to be able to retain them in her care after Weekley learned she had gone.[26]

Frieda loved being loved, but she also retained a strongly practical streak; and while Gross was an extraordinary lover and marvellous talker, he was in the grip of his own campaign for erotic and personal liberation: for breaking with the past, for inscribing sexuality at the centre of our experience as the sole measure of our authenticity as human beings. But he was also a drug-addict, constantly starting cures and failing to complete them (he died in 1920 in consequence of his addiction): for all his insistence on the new and on the future, he remained, in a way, trapped within the patterns of his life and his rhetoric even as he tried to break free. Frieda would later feel that 'he did not have his feet on the ground of reality'; and though her future looked 'so grim and miserable', she did not leave Weekley. One of her arguments was that she didn't have '*das Recht* die Existenz eines guten "Menschen" auf's Spiel zu setzen! [*the right* to gamble with the existence of a good "fellow"!] Between 1910 and 1912 she had an affair with the German painter Ernst Frick (who had previously lived with Gross's wife Frieda).[27] At some stage she had yet another affair, with the Nottingham lace manufacturer William Enfield Dowson, an old friend of the family and Barbie's godfather: 'Then she felt alive again; there weren't only dull teas and servants and grimy towns.'[28] Weekley continued perfectly ignorant of his wife's affairs, which he would not have forgiven her; according to Lawrence in 1912, he loved Frieda 'in a jealous monogamistic fashion' (i. 388). There was an extraordinary contrast between Weekley's entrenched respectability and Otto Gross's capacity to have relationships with three women simultaneously.

But everyone who knew Frieda noticed how adaptable she was. Her third husband, Angelo Ravagli, wrote that 'as [Middleton] Murry said: "No woman ever demanded less to make her happy" and he is so right.' She could easily adapt to the compromises and lies entailed by her affairs, to momentary (but passing) envy of her sisters and their marital arrangements. She continued to enjoy the role of respectable wife and mother which her upbringing had made important for her; Weekley always admired and loved her, while she relied on him as, if unexciting, 'uranständig [fundamentally decent]'.[29] In spite of Gross, Frick and Dowson, in spite of Weekley, she was capable of living with her own discontent. She had good friends in Nottingham, and she could play the role of the Nottingham wife even though it bored her. It bored her particularly after 1907, when (with Gross) 'The world had suddenly become a large growing place with endless possibilities'. She did not forget how Gross had told her that she was 'the woman of the future':

Ich *weiss* jetzt, wie die Menschen sein werden, die nicht mehr befleckt sein werden von allen Dingen, die ich hasse und bekämpfe – ich weiss es durch *Dich*, den einzigen Menschen, der *heute schon* frei geblieben ist von Keuschheitsmoral und Christenthum und Democratie und all' dem gehäuften Unrath – *freigeblieben durch seine eigene Kraft* – – – wie hast Du nur dieses Wunder zustande gebracht, Du goldenes Kind – mit Deinem Lachen und Deinem Lieben den Fluch und Schmutz von zwei verdüsterten Jahrtausenden von Deiner Seele fernzuhalten? [I *know* now what those people will be like who keep themselves unpolluted by all the things which I hate and fight against – I know it through *you*, the only person who *already, today*, has remained free from the code of chastity, from Christianity, from democracy and all that heaped-up filth – *remained free through her own strength* – – – how on earth have you brought about this miracle, you golden child – managed with

379

your laughter and your loving to keep your soul free of the curse and dirt of two gloomy millennia?]³⁰

She was left with a good measure of Gross's belief in her erotic potential. Her husband's attitude towards such modern ideas may be judged by his advice to his son and daughter-on-law on their wedding in 1930: 'I wish you both all happiness. In married life this depends less passionate devotion than on such old homespun qualities as unselfishness and considerateness.'³¹ But Frieda had always believed in passionate devotion: and now she believed in her capacity for erotic fulfilment. However, she remained 'living her inner life unrelated to the outer one': dreaming of liberation but outwardly living entirely conventionally. She stayed married for another four years after her affair with Gross and in spite of her other affairs.

II 'The most wonderful woman in all England'

Lawrence arrived in late morning for his March 1912 visit to the Weekleys in Private Road. He was noticeably dressed up for the occasion: Ida Wilhelmly, the children's nurse, remarked after he had gone that 'a person like that should not wear patent leather shoes'. Frieda later wrote how 'I see him before me as he entered the house. A long thin figure, quick straight legs, light, sure movements. He seemed so obviously simple. Yet he arrested my attention.' To the end of her life she remembered that morning: in April 1954, forty-two years later, she spoke of how 'At first he came to me in the sitting-room. I can remember the pure red velvet curtains blowing out of the French windows before lunch.' They talked for half an hour about Oedipus and about women – 'I was amazed at the way he fiercely denounced them.'³² Frieda's children were playing in the garden on that brilliant and spring-like day; to the eye of hindsight, those playing children form a poignant backdrop to the drama about to be played out. We do not know what was said at lunch with Weekley. Lawrence never made any serious attempt to become a Lektor in Germany; without a degree, he would have had almost no chance. He never saw Weekley again.

But that same afternoon, by cruel irony, Lawrence had arranged to meet Jessie Chambers at her family's home in Arno Vale, only a couple of miles from the Weekley house in Mapperley. He instantly told Jessie that

it would do me good to know Mrs Weekley. I am afraid I replied that I was not very anxious to be done good to by Mrs Weekley ...
After tea we gathered round the piano as in old days, with my younger sister playing and my two brothers singing. We sang Folk songs and Hymns, and my sister turned the page and began 'We are but little children weak' ...

I was about to turn the page, saying, 'We don't want that,' but Lawrence stopped me impulsively.

'It's true, we *are*. Let's have it,' and he joined in the singing with gusto.

Later he watched my brothers getting ready to go out.

'Are you going courting?' he asked them, half enviously.

'We're supposed to be,' they replied, laughing at his strange question.[33]

Not really such a strange question; except that the man who would later create Tom Brangwen in *The Rainbow* going out to see *his* foreign woman – 'Bit of courtin', like' – was unable to court his own, except clandestinely. But Frieda remembered how, shortly after his first visit – probably some time the same week – he wrote to her 'You are the most wonderful woman in all England', to which she characteristically replied 'You don't know many women in England, how do you know?'[34] But her fearlessness, her emotional warmth and unconstraint, appealed instantly to one of Lawrence's careful, 'intense and concentrative' and in many ways constrained nature (i. 332): the product of a puritanical upbringing in what he called a 'weedy creek of life' (i. 247). As soon as he met Frieda he found himself like Lydia Beardsall attracted to Arthur Lawrence back in 1874; drawn to the exciting, sensual and highly unsuitable partner who, because of their utter difference, offered the promise of freedom.

Frieda, too, although married and living an outwardly conventional life in an English provincial city, amazingly believed after her affair with Gross 'that if only sex were "free" the world would straightaway turn into a paradise'. It was only a theory, born of Gross's liberating talk: but for a woman in the English Midlands, it was astonishing.[35] And Frieda was revelation for Lawrence.

He could only pay the occasional visit to Private Road: a houseful of servants and children meant that he had to be discreet. On one occasion, on the maid's afternoon off, he found to his ironical amusement that Frieda had no idea how to light the gas to make tea. Doubtless he showed her. They managed to see *Man and Superman* together one evening in Nottingham during the week 18–23 March. Frieda, however, could use her two younger children as an excuse for going out. They visited May and Will Holbrook at Moorgreen at least once, and the girls, Elsa and Barbie, saw the farm animals.[36] On another (or perhaps the same) day, they

came to a small brook, a little stone bridge crossed it. Lawrence . . . put daisies in the brook, and they floated down with their upturned faces. Crouched by the brook, playing there with the children, Lawrence forgot about me completely . . .

He also made them paper boats and put burning matches into them; 'this is the Spanish Armada, and you don't know what that was.' 'Yes we do,' the older girl said promptly. I can see him now, crouching down, so intent on the game so young and quick, and the small girls in their pink and white striped Viyella frocks, long legged like colts . . .[37]

Frieda added that the girls were 'in wild excitement over such a play-fellow'. Barbie, at least, was not. She recalled how

We were out with my mother for the day, my sister and I, and we got out at a little station near Nottingham and in a lane, a country lane, was a tall, pale, tense looking young man whom I remember clearly. I didn't like him, children don't like that sort of young man, they like somebody genial, like a doctor, and some of the professors at the University College that we knew . . .[38]

Lawrence must have been especially tense to provoke such a reaction. But Frieda never forgot the vision of him with her daughters. She recalled it in 1930, when he was dying, as the moment 'when I knew I loved him, when a tenderness for him rose in me that I had not known before'.[39] But the recollection not only shows us that Frieda was falling in love with Lawrence. It reminds us that she had no intention of abandoning her children when she went to Germany with him at the start of May: she had every intention of returning to her family.

So what were they to do? Frieda's past experience of affairs would have taught her to be discreet, to deceive her extremely busy and frequently absent husband, and simply to enjoy the affair as long as possible. Willie Hopkin maintained that Lawrence and Frieda were in bed together within twenty minutes of their first meeting. That cannot have been true; but the version of the meeting between their fictional counterparts Gilbert and Johanna in *Mr Noon* should make us reflect on the probability that they did go to bed together very soon indeed; Frieda's doctrine of 'free' sex and her 'theory of loving men',[40] combined with Lawrence's belief in acting on impulse, would have ensured that they did.* Frieda had affairs with men all her life; they became natural to her and she loved the excitement (and the

---

* *Mr Noon* is a remarkable guide to much that happened to DHL and Frieda in 1912: its second part not only contains a great deal of direct recreation of the events of the months May–September 1912, but is valuable as a counterbalance to the idea of the romantic elopement which Frieda perpetuated in her memoirs. Yet the novel *is* a comic novel; we know it amalgamates some actual episodes and heightens others; and it is much too deeply satirical of 'uplift' and even at times of love, as well as being too concerned to say things which to DHL in 1920–1 needed saying, to be very sympathetic to what DHL and Frieda experienced in 1912. Gilbert Noon, too, is unaffected by any attachment to a mother (never having had one to speak of), and although Johanna worries about her children, she experiences no agonies at being cut off from them. The couple are picaresque, not confessional, and are always seen with far more detachment than either DHL or Frieda could manage in 1912. I shall quote a good deal from *Mr Noon* – a biography of DHL which did not draw from it would be absurd. But only occasionally shall I rely on it to supply something not confirmed by other sources: and I shall make very clear when I am using it as a source.

lack of commitment) in such relationships. The Holbrook cottage at the lane end in Moorgreen seems to have been the one place Lawrence could go safely with women; the pear-blossom next to the window in April provoked at least two ecstatic poems from him, both probably about Frieda.[41]

But one Sunday when Weekley was away and Frieda said to Lawrence 'Stay the night with me', rather frighteningly he replied: 'No, I will not stay in your husband's house while he is away, but you must tell him the truth and we will go away together, because I love you.' That was not what Frieda expected – or wished. But Lawrence wanted more than an affair. According to Enid Hilton, he had once suggested to Alice Dax that they should go away together, but she had refused to abandon her husband and children. This time, Lawrence refused any such compromise. He insisted that he wanted a life with Frieda, and he wanted commitment and honesty, truth and love. He was writing 'Paul Morel' with desperate urgency at the same time: he showed Frieda some of it.[42] Characteristically, he was able to keep on with the writing throughout the tormenting and astonishing weeks between the middle of March and the middle of April. As he had told Helen Corke back in 1910, while simultaneously writing 'The Saga' and waiting for Whitsuntide and Jessie Chambers, 'I have a second consciousness somewhere actively alive ... I keep on writing, almost mechanically' (i. 159).

By 23 April, Lawrence knew he was 'most awfully fond of her. Things are getting difficult' (i. 386). But in one way they were marvellously lucky. Frieda was about to go to Germany, and they could combine the plans Lawrence had made as early as January for a visit to Germany 'in April or May' (i. 350) with her visit to Metz for the celebrations on 6 May of her father's fifty years in the Prussian army. They were also able to spend two whole days together without the children in London at the end of April. Lawrence had – as usual – told Edward Garnett about his new woman: 'Mrs Weekley is perfectly unconventional, but really good – in the best sense. I'll bet you've never met anybody like her, by a long chalk ... she is the woman of a lifetime' (i. 384). Garnett, as Lawrence had hoped, invited them to the Cearne. Lawrence's poem 'At the Cearne' commemorates the visit. He was acutely conscious of the 'crazed machinery' in which he was caught, while Frieda remained confined 'to that hell/Which you call home'. But, all the same, 'you and I, you and I/On the little bank where bluebells droop/Sit and make love to each other.'[43]

But however 'splendid' Frieda was (i. 384), she did not go back to Nottingham and do the one thing which Lawrence really wanted her to do: tell Weekley she was leaving him. She did so, with considerable reluctance, only after Lawrence himself had told Weekley what had happened and had thus forced the issue. However much in love Frieda was, she had – a friend remembered her saying – 'no intention whatever of leaving my husband and children and the comfortable & respectable life I knew to go off into certain social exile and most probable poverty'. She was happy to be Lawrence's lover 'while I continued to live with Prof. W.'; she would doubtless have preferred the affair to go on like that. Her book *"Not I, But the Wind . . ."* remarked that, after the episode when she had watched her children playing with Lawrence, 'things happened quickly'. But they did not.[44] There was no elopement, no passionate rushing away together. Frieda was going to Germany for her father's celebration; Lawrence was also going to Germany. Good, they could go together, and they could continue their affair. But Frieda was not leaving her husband or her children. Lawrence, too, was under no illusions about what to expect: only ten days before leaving, his main hope was that, in Germany, 'we could have at least one week together' (i. 386). But a week with Frieda was better than nothing: 'I feel as if I can't breathe while we're in England', Lawrence told her (i. 389).

III *The Married Man*

We have one further insight into how Lawrence was thinking about Frieda in April 1912. By 23 April he had finished his comedy *The Married Man*, in which a woman fluent in German with the name of Elsa Smith appears as the fiancée of the character closest to Lawrence himself, Billy Brentnall. Elsa is highly unconventional: a striking and superb *dea ex machina*, she descends upon the last act of the play and sorts out the characters' lives. George Grainger (based upon George Neville, also recently married and with a small child) has been running after other women while separated from his wife, but Elsa remarks: 'It's not *very* dreadful . . . I, who am a woman, when I see other women who are sweet or handsome or charming, I look at them and think "Well, how can a man help loving them, to some extent. Even if he loves *me*, if I am not there, how can he help loving them?" '[45] She speaks for emotional honesty as against conventional feeling; and according to Brentnall, her openness is 'better than subterfuge, bestiality, or starvation and sterility' ('Yes—yes', she says). When it is pointed out to her that George is, after all, 'a married man', she replies: 'I think a man ought to be fair. He ought to offer his love for just what it is—the love of a man married to another woman—and so on. And, if there is any strain, he ought to tell his wife "I love this other woman." ' The first of those opinions – altered to 'the love of a woman married to another man' – sounds exactly like Frieda's own, even if the last is certainly Lawrence's, and what he was urging Frieda to do. But Elsa Smith is presented as remarkably honest, direct, womanly and sympathetic, if a little naive: 'with a little love, we can help each other so much', she says: 'Each should live his own life.'[46] These are the very accents of the 'perfectly unconventional, but really good' person Lawrence had told Garnett about: 'She is ripping – she's the finest woman I've ever met' (i. 384).

IV 'Sort of freedom'

How had Lawrence so quickly recognised his 'woman of a lifetime' (i. 384) in Frieda, after struggling so unsuccessfully with relationships for so long? Like his creation Tom Brangwen in *The Rainbow* saying 'That's her' to himself on glimpsing Lydia Lensky,[47] Lawrence seems to have known at once that he wanted to marry Frieda Weekley.

The 'Stranger' in *The Trespasser*, Hampson, had described how men of his type are always attracted to the wrong kind of women. ' "The best sort of women—the most interesting—are the worst for us," Hampson resumed. "By instinct they aim at suppressing the gross and animal in us. Then they are supersensitive—refined a bit beyond humanity. We who are as little gross as need be, become their instruments ..." '[48] Lawrence had spent most of his adult life trying to be 'as little gross as need be' with interesting but refined women like Agnes Holt, Jessie Chambers, Helen Corke and Louie Burrows. But he had begun his pre-lunch conversation with Frieda, that March day in 1912, with a Nietzschean insistence that he would no longer be an instrument: she remembered hearing how 'he had finished with his attempts at knowing women. I was amazed at the way he fiercely denounced them. I had never before heard anything like it. I laughed, yet I could tell he had tried very hard, and had cared.'[49] Provincial sitting-rooms are not accustomed to such denunciations, nor to young men who make them to hostesses to whom they have only just been introduced. But nor are provincial sitting-rooms used to women who lack any desire to suppress the 'gross and animal' in themselves or in the men they know. After Otto Gross in 1907, Frieda never did. Neither her intelligence nor her self-confidence depended on a separation in herself between the 'higher' and the 'lower'. In no sense was she 'refined ... beyond humanity'.

The intelligent and independent English women of Lawrence's acquaintance had, for very good reasons, acquired their independence by forcibly reversing the traditional roles of working-class or lower-middle-class women; they had devoted themselves to their careers rather than to men or marriage or children. They knew that love and sex were liable to condemn them to marriage, pregnancy and children, and men to marrying them; and they tended to be sexually inexperienced into their middle or late twenties.

They wanted to be independent: and that meant work – as teachers, for all of them. Sex, as their upbringing had made clear, was not only a 'lower' instinct, but particularly dangerous to women attempting to make their way through the dangerous territory of the 'Man's World' which Ursula experiences in *The Rainbow*. Helen Corke, who had had her affair with Macartney when she was 27, remembered how her

early religious training had divided soul and body, and presented the body as the inferior, rightly subordinate to the soul. The literary patterns of the period mostly enhanced this teaching. They tended to exhibit physical passion as a gross manifestation, linking man with the animal, but, in the case of man, properly controlled by reason and the will.

Her conclusion had been that 'mind must control bodily instincts, or human beings sink to animal level'.[50] Such was the code which in general dominated the independent-minded women Lawrence had known. It was probably true of Agnes Holt, certainly true of Helen Corke and Louie Burrows and even true of Jessie Chambers (though Jessie was exceptional in many ways, and would 'sacrifice herself' to the man she loved by sleeping with him). Alice Dax got married at the age of 27 but only (according to her own account) because '*everyone* said that no man would ever marry me'. Helen Corke never married: Louie Burrows did not marry until her fifties: at the age of 28, Agnes Holt married Walter Blanchard: Jessie Chambers's marriage, also at the age of 28, confined her – in a way she seemed at least in part to want – to the role of a wife assured of the devotion of a straightforward, good man.[51] The woman who wanted to continue making her way in the world had in general to reject any connection with sexuality. The 'Man's World' was exactly the world in which Lawrence had seen and known women rejecting the role of the marrying and childbearing woman.

Frieda had had none of these experiences. She had never suffered the dreadful struggle for independence which characterised and cramped the lower-middle-class upbringing of Helen Corke and – in different ways – Jessie Chambers and Alice Dax. She had never worked for her living: she had married at 20. At the age of 33, with her children growing up fast, she struck Lawrence as 'young, so young!'[52] A minor aristocrat by birth, she still retained some of her aristocratic sense of carelessness in spite of her years in Nottingham – years in which she herself tried to be '*bourgeoise*'. She would shock Lawrence, in Germany in the summer of 1912, by her attitude towards possessions:

One day I bathed in the Isar and a heel came off one of my shoes on the rough shore; so I took both shoes off and threw them into the Isar. Lawrence . . . was shocked at my wastefulness.

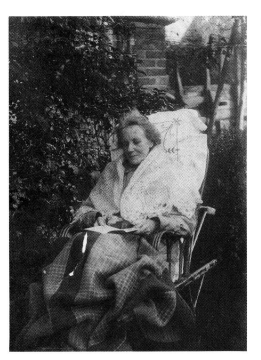

27. Lydia Lawrence *c.* September 1910

28. Lydia Lawrence *c.* September 1910

29. Helen Corke *c.* 1906

30. Louie Burrows *c.* 1910

31. Alice and Harry Dax with Phyllis and Eric 1915

32. Marie and John Jones c. 1906

33. Friedrich von Richthofen 1870

34. Friedrich von Richthofen *c.* 1895

35. Anna von Richthofen
c. 1895

36. Frieda von Richthofen and Ernest Weekley 1898 or 1899

37. Agnes and Charles Weekley, Ernest and Frieda Weekley *c.* 1900

38. Frieda Weekley with Montague and Barbara 1905

39. Ida Wilhelmy with Barbara, Montague and Elsa *c.* 1910

40. Edgar and Else Jaffe with Friedel, Peter and Marianne 1907

Oh dear no: the conversation ~~then~~ was Paul's.
at Nether Green. She wanted from him ~~a~~ some sort
of acknowledgement of his love. She knew he loved
her, but she wanted him to acknowledge it himself.
Men are so blind, and they run so to futility, in their
blindness. The second self that watches things was beginning to rouse
in Paul: these remarks were some kind of justification of himself.
"You know," he was saying ponderingly, "I
think if one person loves, the other does."
"Ah!" she ~~cried~~ said, "like mother said to me when I
was little 'Love begets Love.'"
"Ye—es—something like that.—I think it
must be" he said. ~~His hesitance hurt her.~~ She
No, Miriam merely noted again: you see, at this time, the balance of strength was
~~knew it was a personal question between them~~ her love for that
on the side of Miriam, so that she had great reserve strength. At this time had not
"I hope so—because, if not, love might be
grown beyond herself—, nor beyond her control. It was not until it became
very terrible" she replied. invested with holmes like religion
and not behind it the whole force of the will to live that the denial of it was
"Yes, but it is: at least with most people terrible
to her.
he answered. And ~~not reading his reservation~~
~~aright, she was assured~~ Nay—Miriam knew that Paul spoke for
his own assurance.
She always regarded that sudden coming
upon him in the lane as a discovery. It revealed to
her a part of him that she ~~thought, with some justice, nobody~~
had never seen, and that he himself did not suspect.
She held it very precious, thus finding out that he
was lonely, as she termed it. He had so many
friends, such a rattling host of affections, that
to make Paul very human
it seemed a splendid paradox ~~for her~~ ~~that~~ knowledge
alone, that he was lonely. There was a suggestion

41. Jessie Chambers and 'Paul Morel' p. 220

42. Frieda Weekley and 'My Love, My Mother'

43. Edward Garnett and 'The Saga of Siegmund'

44. Otto Gross *c.* 1914

45. D. H. Lawrence and Margaret Brinton 26 April 1912

46. Frieda Weekley *c.* 1912

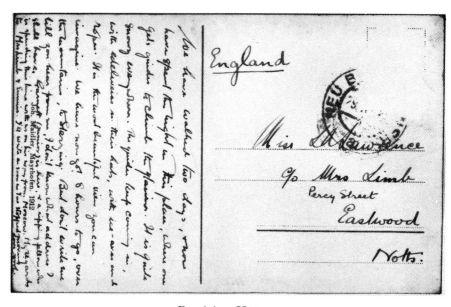

47. Dominicus-Hütte *c.* 1912

48. Villa and Gargnano *c.* 1912

Villa di Gargnano. — Villa de Paoli.

49. Villa de Paoli (left) and Villa Igea (centre), Villa *c.* 1930

foolish, so wasteful, never at peace with himself. And now where would he go? And what did he care that he wasted her? He had no religion - it was all for the moment's attraction that he cared, nothing else, nothing deeper. Well, she would wait and see how it turned out with him. When he had had enough, he would give in, and come to her.

He shook hands and left her at the door of her cousin's house. When he turned away, he felt the last shelter for him had gone. The town, as he sat upon the car, stretched away, over the bay of railway, a level fume of ~~many~~ lights. Beyond the town the country, little fuming spots for more towns - the sea - the night - on and on! And not a place for him! Whatever spot he stood on, there he stood alone. From his breast, from his mouth sprang the endless space - and it was there behind him, everywhere. The people hurrying along the streets offered no obstruction to the vast space in which he found himself. They were small ~~shadows~~ whose footsteps and voices could be heard, but in each of them, the same night, the same silence. He got off the car. In the country all was dead still. Little stars shone high up, little stars ~~spread~~ far away below, in the floodwaters, a firmament ~~down~~ deep down. Everywhere the vastness and terror of the immense night which is roused and stirred for a brief while by the day, but which returns, and will remain at last eternal, ~~...ng~~ everything in its silence and its living gloom. There was no ~~Time~~, only ~~e.~~ Who could say his mother had lived and did not live? She had been in one place, and was in another, that was all. And his soul could not lean, wherever she was. Now she was gone abroad into the night, and he was ~~they were together~~ her still. ~~she was there~~ But ~~they~~ there was his body, his chest that leaned the stile, his ~~to~~ hands on the wooden bar. They seemed ~~forsaken~~ something by ~~himself~~. Who is he? - one tiny upright ~~thing~~ ~~speck~~ of flesh, less than ~~a grain~~ an ear of wheat lost in ~~vast, left standing when everything else is gone, and the night~~. He could ~~it. On every side~~ the immense dark silence seemed pressing him, ~~so tiny a speck~~ ~~tion, and yet, tiny speck?~~ almost nothing, he could not be extinct. ~~there was the~~ Night everything was lost, ~~went~~ reaching out, beyond stars and sun. Stars and ~~...~~, a few bright grains, ~~went~~ spinning round for terror and holding ~~in~~ each other's embrace, there in a darkness that outpassed them all and left them tiny and daunted. So much, and himself, infinitesimal, at the core, ~~crushed out~~ a nothingness, and yet not nothing. ~~It was too much~~

"Mother!" he ~~gasped~~ whimpered, "mother!"

She was the only thing that held him up, himself, amid all this. And she was gone, intermingled herself! He wanted her to ~~touch him, have him alongside with her~~ ~~along side with her.~~

But no, he would not ~~consent~~ give in. Turning sharply, he walked towards the low ~~broad~~ fuming of the city's gold phosphorescence. His fists were shut, his mouth set fast. He would not take that direction, to the darkness, to follow her. He walked towards the faintly humming, glowing town, quickly.

He lectured me: 'A pair of shoes takes a long time to make and you should respect the labour somebody's put into those shoes.'

To which I answered: 'Things are there for me and not I for them, so when they are a nuisance I throw them away.'[53]

While shocking, the carelessness was also invigorating; and it applied to men as much as to shoes. Frieda immediately convinced Lawrence of something in which he had always wanted to believe: that 'women are more passionate than men, only the men daren't allow it' (i. 468).

Frieda could not only encourage Lawrence to overcome the constraints which had become part of his very nature. Still more important, with her he found he no longer had to play the dual role of either the sensitive, brilliant but withdrawn man (safe with women) or the sensual and outrageous one, dangerous to women but (of course) limited in intellect and spirituality. He could be all the selves he was: sensitive *and* outgoing, intellectual *and* ordinary, spiritual *and* sexual. Frieda's independence made her, of course, in some ways a threatening woman to a man who had grown up terribly aware of the power of women. But she was honest and uncompromising about her demands and desires; she was not devious, did not withdraw herself into moral superiority. Her independence and confidence were not won at the price of being untouchable. Just the opposite: her confidence lay in her awarenesss of herself as an intelligent and sensual woman.

Lawrence in turn was drawn 'to form the woman in whom one can be free' (ii. 115): it was not just a matter of discovering her. He wanted to *make* her his partner; to help her recover the self she had lost during her years in Nottingham. She recalled how 'All the exuberance of my childhood came back to me'; how 'he was a sort of new element to me and though he bullied me, I also felt free to be myself'.[54] To some extent, Lawrence mythologised her as soon as he got to know her; she was the sleeping beauty whom he could release from imprisonment.

This starts to answer the question how a 33-year-old woman, wife of a distinguished Professor, settled in a domestic life and deeply fond of her children, should have found herself listening to a jobless man six years her junior who wanted her to give it all up and live with him instead. If she was, for Lawrence, the 'woman of a lifetime' – then he constituted for her perhaps the one way she might break with her past. She found herself commanded to leave it by an extremely determined man who was serious about marrying her, liked children, was highly intelligent and also thoroughly practical and down-to-earth: 'so obviously simple', she thought him. She had said exactly the same about Weekley: it was one of her touchstones. Gross too had wanted her to leave her husband, so as to fulfil her nature, but Gross ignored 'The everyday life ... He hardly knew whether it was night or day . . . On visions alone you can't live.'[55] Lawrence was absolutely different; he was a man 'at home in both worlds, the material and the adventurous spiritual one', and 'in spite of his lots of unrealities he is simple and real underneath' (i. 449). His coming from the working class further fascinated Frieda and gave her the feeling that here at last was an authentic man. And it was very clear to her that he needed her more than Weekley did: he told her so. 'He was trusting with her, completely generous. "Take me, all of me, I am yours." It almost frightened her. He forced the responsibility of himself on to her; she did not want to take it.'[56] His love for her excited and thrilled her: while his emotional tangles, his self-consciousness, his isolation and its struggles were a tremendous challenge to her.

He was also an artist. Weekley was a Professor, and – in the words of Frieda's sister Else – had 'opened to her the access to another world'.[57] As a young woman living in Metz she had almost exclusively met army officers. As a young woman she had had, too, a kind of rivalry with Else and something of the traditional respectful German attitude towards Professors: that had certainly helped Weekley in his successful pursuit of her in 1898. But, as an artist, Lawrence appealed to something else. The artist was the one person she could immediately respect and be fascinated by, and who could give her the role of the woman behind him: she would expect there to be a woman behind an artist. She wrote happily about Lawrence's ability: 'I am sure he is a real artist, the way things pour out of him, *he* seems only the pen, and isnt that how it ought to be?' (i. 479). Late in life, her daughter Barbie commented on Lawrence's difference from Weekley. The latter

was a scholarly, not a very vital-type of man and she always had this reckless, and also something of a sort of missionary thing about her, Frieda; and in that she was utterly fulfilled, because as soon as she met Lawrence she said to friends of ours in Nottingham, a lace-manufacturer who was my god-father, he'd lent her some Galsworthy, and she had only just met Lawrence who was then, of course, quite unknown and she said to him: 'I've met somebody who's going to be much more than Galsworthy' to this man.

She had a kind of . . . that German quality of great reverence to the artist, which is not always to be found in this country . . .

Her son Monty remembered 'my mother lying in bed, devouring sheets of manuscript by Lawrence' shortly after she met him.[58] As Monty surmised, this must have been 'Paul Morel'; we know she was reading it before the end of April (i. 388). Lawrence's discussion of Oedipus with Frieda pointed to what she might have looked for in the novel.

When Lawrence wrote his story 'New Eve and Old Adam' in the summer of 1913 however, he himself described the fascination felt by Paula Moest, a married German woman, towards the literature-soaked young man who comes to visit her and her husband Richard: she 'absorbed herself in this dazed, starved, literature-bewildered young German'. To her husband's anger, she sees in the young man 'her mission—"Just as," said Moest bitterly to himself, "she saw her mission in me, a year ago." ' The mission is to save the young man from himself and his complexes. ' "Oh, but he makes me so miserable, to see him!" she cried. "Self-conscious, can't get into contact with anybody, living a false literary life like a man who takes poetry as a drug.—One *ought* to help him." '[59] Lawrence's denunciations of women fascinated Frieda, on the first day they met: but his isolation, his detachment and his self-consciousness would have made him exactly the same opportunity Paula sees in the young man. She cannot resist missionary work; to her husband she remarks, 'half contemptuous', 'Did *you* get off your miserable starved isolation by yourself?—you didn't. You had to be fetched down, and I had to do it.' The fact that Lawrence chose to dramatise the idea so compellingly in 1913 suggests that, by then, it was one of the things he had learned (and also learned to fear) about Frieda's potential.[60]

Frieda was often possessed by her sense of her womanly role: but in Lawrence she found someone who, though she could help him, knew how entangled in theories she was, how much trapped in lies and with how little opportunity for change. To a large extent she had hidden her own loneliness behind exuberance and charm. But Lawrence, in his writing and by temperament, was fundamentally opposed to the bourgeois life in which she felt trapped: and particularly when she and he began their nomadic existence, she could once again feel a sense of liberty from ordinary constraints. She wrote, later in life, how with Lawrence 'all the misery of loneliness, of unconnectedness, was gone'.[61] She could feel herself to be a child again, and could also recover a sense of her lost aristocracy: she would have 'an aristocratic fit' in Munich in the summer of 1912, buying handkerchiefs identical with her father's 'with a . . . little crown on them'. Wandering Europe, as she and Lawrence were to do that summer of 1912, in spite of her sheltered past she often turned out better at coping with change, poverty and ignominy than Lawrence was. Many years later, a friend described her as 'one of life's natural "squatters", a gypsy and totally impractical'.[62] She was sustained by her sense of her own untamed aristocratic nature and by her status as liberated and liberating woman: both being qualities obscured by her bourgeois life but which, in the company of the wandering artist, might once more flourish. When he met her, Lawrence made her look at herself and what she wanted: 'taught me the feel and the understanding of things and people' (i. 439). And he made her realise that none of her missions to others – to him, perhaps to Dowson and Frick, certainly to Gross, and later to men like Udo von Henning and Harold Hobson – could ever be a substitute for a new life for herself.

We must not ignore their differences. Lawrence was very clear about them. He told Edward Garnett, for example, how 'I hate her when she talks to the common people. She is not a bit stuck-up, really more humble than I am, but she makes the *de haut en bas* of class distinction felt – even with my sister' (i. 502). She could be infuriating in all kinds of ways, driving Aldous Huxley to realise (he said) why the Buddha thought stupidity the greatest sin of all. Late in 1912, she sent Weekley a copy of Tolstoy's *Anna Karenina*: in October Lawrence said she was studying it 'in a sort of "How to be happy though livanted" spirit' (i. 463). Weekley can hardly have enjoyed finding himself cast as the rigid, unfeeling, unappealing husband. But Frieda had left in the book a letter from Dowson saying 'if you had to go away with someone, why didn't you go away with me?' – probably Weekley's first inkling of the relationship. He returned the letter to Lawrence, presumably hoping it would be news to him too.[63] But Lawrence would have hated being caught up in such a mess: in his turn he was unforgiving and horribly self-contained. And yet, in spite of everything, they realised that they identified 'remarkably the same thing in life' as what they wanted: 'sort of freedom, nakedness of intimacy, free breathing-space between us' (i. 439). Frieda's life up to 1912 had conditioned her to believe that the chance of such things was probably over for her; that they were at best only theories. Lawrence's life had never made such things seem even remotely possible. Together at the end of April 1912, they had a chance – however briefly – to make the freedoms neither of them had previously found.

PART FOUR

◆

Germany
and
Italy

Metz, Trier, Waldbröl

I Metz

On Friday 3 May 1912, at 2.00 p.m., Lawrence met Frieda outside the 1st Class Ladies Room at Charing Cross railway station; they had travelled to London separately, Frieda first taking her two daughters to 40 Well Walk, Hampstead, to stay with their Weekley grandparents. She and Lawrence caught the 2.20 boat train to Dover and crossed to Ostend: a single fare to Metz would have cost them £2-1-9 (2nd class).[1] It was the first of many journeys away from England which they made together, and was the proto-type of a number of Lawrence's fictional characters' journeys: the journey taken by Birkin and Ursula in *Women in Love* – 'deuxième classe' – by ferry and train via Folkestone, Ostend, Bruges, Ghent, Brussels and Luxembourg towards Metz, almost exactly parallels the journey Lawrence and Frieda made in May 1912.

What better subject for a biography than the passionate elopement of the hero with the heroine? But their journey was very far from being an elope-ment. Lawrence and Frieda both knew that Frieda would be going back to Nottingham after her holiday in Germany (i. 391). As late as Tuesday 30 April Lawrence had had no idea which day Frieda would even be travelling: he wrote pleading with her to make up her mind and tell him (i. 388–9). She then decided to travel on Thursday 2nd, but he could not get ready in time and had to ask her to change to Friday 3rd. On the Thursday, he was still beset with uncertainties because he did not know what she was actually feeling: 'If I knew how things stood with you', he wrote, 'I wouldn't care a damn. As it is, I eat my blessed heart out' (i. 390). They made their separate ways to London; then, as Frieda described it in 1934, 'crossed the grey channel sitting on some ropes, full of hope and agony. There was nothing but the grey sea, and the dark sky, and the throbbing of the ship, and ourselves.' The 'nothing but ... ourselves' was a gloss given by Frieda's subsequent imagining of their history; in 1912 she was still married, still had children and had every intention of going back to them. A month later Lawrence was still wondering 'Where it'll end, I don't know' (i. 418). When Ursula and Birkin make their journey in *Women in Love* – even sitting where 'a great rope was coiled up' and seeing the Metz train at Ostend – they are married, and certain of each other.[2]

Things were still more disjointed in Metz. Their train would have arrived at three minutes past six in the morning on Saturday 4 May; Lawrence got a room at the Hotel Deutscher Hof, only 2 km. away from the von Richthofen family home at Montigny.* The von Richthofens were extremely well known in Metz, and Frieda's father would have made life impossible for her if he had known that she had a man with her; Frieda could not afford to seem to know Lawrence too well. He could only be acknowledged 'as a distant friend', and this involved him in a 'thousand baffling lies' (i. 392). He was stuck in what *Mr Noon* called 'a semi-religious kind of family hotel',[3] cut off from Frieda for most of the day and all night; his spoken German was weak, and he found life as depressing as being in a monastery (i. 391). He and Frieda had also to be more discreet than was natural to either of them. *Mr Noon* describes an occasion when Gilbert and Johanna are very nearly discovered in bed together by the hotel-keeper. It may have been exciting but it was certainly humiliating to Lawrence to have so little chance either of seeing Frieda when he wanted or (in particular) of affecting her decision about what she was going to do next.

Although Friedrich von Richthofen could not be told about Lawrence, Frieda immediately told her mother she had a man with her, and that she was thinking of leaving her husband for him. It may not have been the first time such a thing had happened: the Frau Baronin does not seem to have been surprised. She was mainly curious about what Frieda's new man was like. To judge by *Mr Noon*, Lawrence was speedily introduced to her, on the Saturday afternoon, and also met Frieda's sisters when they arrived: Frieda greeted Else with the whispered words 'I have brought someone with me. You must help me.'[4]

Lawrence hung around Metz on the Sunday, and apparently saw Frieda just once. Being with her in Germany was as bad as being back in Nottingham. He had hoped she would come to his hotel first thing on the Monday morning, but she didn't, so he wrote to her – the fact that he had to write her a letter shows how bad the situation was – advising her to 'count your days in Germany, and compare them with the days to follow in Nottingham' (i. 391). They still had no hope of spending more than a week

---

* Frieda's book *"Not I, But the Wind . . ."* says that she also stayed in the hotel: she may have been there for a night, but Lawrence's letter to her of Monday 6th, hand-delivered after he had decided to 'venture forth' in the rain – 'I don't know where you live exactly – so if I can't find you I shall put this in number 4' (i. 390) – shows that at least some of the time she was not under the same roof as DHL but living at home, probably at 4 Kronprinz-Wilhelm Strasse, Montigny.

or two together – but even that precious time was vanishing away, as Frieda spent time with her family rather than with him. 'I don't mind', Lawrence told her: 'At least, I do, but I understand it can't be helped.' The festive day itself was Monday 6th – 'the last day I let you off', Lawrence told her (i. 391) – with bands playing in honour of the baron. Like Gilbert Noon in *Mr Noon* Lawrence 'rambled round the attractive but to him hateful old town' and explored some of the country round it; he described what he saw in three newspaper articles he wrote a few days later.[5] There was a fair on in Metz, where by accident he ran into Frieda and her sisters – and at once had to make himself scarce, because her father was coming along behind. He had his hair cut, which for a man rather short of money suggests the time on his hands. Like Gilbert Noon, he doubtless felt 'wretched, and not in his own skin. He felt thoroughly humiliated, and now knew he was embarking on a new little sea of ignominy. He writhed under all the ignominy.'[6] The experience of humiliation had all his life been very significant to Lawrence; his experiences in Metz and during the months following brought him a good deal of it. That is one of the ways in which *Mr Noon* is at times a more reliable – or differently reliable – source for understanding Lawrence than his surviving letters. The novel continually stresses the uncertainties and humiliations which Gilbert suffers: the wounds to his sense of pride, the helplessness of having nothing to do, the ignominy of being surrounded by women deciding his and Johanna's future. Lawrence's letters to Frieda, naturally enough, rarely admit to any of that; and Lawrence was not open enough to anyone else to be able to express such feelings to them.

What made matters particularly bad for Lawrence was that Frieda was supposed to have told Weekley about him on Monday 29 April, five days before leaving: but had not done so. The most she had told her husband was that she had been unfaithful to him with 'two *other*, *earlier* men' (i. 409): she named Frick and Gross. She seems to have started to tell Weekley about Lawrence, but had got scared: she was frightened of what Weekley might do to her or to her children. She had not previously told him about her affairs (though like Johanna in *Mr Noon* she may well have tried to). She knew that he wanted her to remain for him a perfectly beautiful, untouched 'sunflower'; on 11 May he would, indeed, announce that he had been 'insane for ten days' following her disclosures about her previous lovers, the news having hit him like 'ein Blitz aus klaren Himmel [a bolt from the blue]'.[7]

Before doing anything further, let alone committing herself to Lawrence, Frieda wanted to listen to the advice of those of her family she could trust: her mother and her two sisters. Lawrence met all three of the von Richthofen women; the image of him in his 'cap and raincoat' meeting the 'handsome, ultra-fashionable' Johanna von Schreibershofen, 'who had daring dark eyes and looked like a cocotte', is one that Frieda treasured. They all liked him: even the fashionable Johanna said 'You can go with him. You can trust him.' He struck Else as 'a very young, sensitive, gentlemanly English-man, quiet but not shy, who gave an impression of self-reliance'.[8]

But it is also plain, especially from *Nr Noon*, that all of them (even Johanna), however much they liked Lawrence and in general approved of their sister's affair, were utterly opposed to the idea of Frieda giving up her marriage for him. Both Else and Johanna had remained married and attached to their children, while simultaneously living the lives they wanted to lead, to the extent of living with other men. Else had even had a child by another man. Lawrence was amazed by them and their totally non-moral attitudes; they were so utterly different from any women he had previously known. He told Garnett, on 9 May, that

You should see the Richthofens at home – three sisters – one, the eldest, a professor of psychology and economics – left her husband, gone with two other men (in succession) – yet *really* good – good, the sort of woman one reverences. Then there's Frieda. Then the youngest sister, very beautiful, married to a brute of a swanky officer in Berlin – and, in a large, splendid way – cocotte. Lord, what a family. I've never seen anything like it. (i. 395)

Twelve days later, he added that 'They are a rare family . . . mother utterly non-moral, very kind' (i. 409). Johanna – 'Nusch' – was also, according to Frieda's daughter Barbie, 'the only woman whom I ever heard Lawrence describe as "desirable"'.[9]

But, apart from Frieda, all the other female von Richthofens had reached understandings, or accommodations, with husbands they no longer loved. Why, they now asked each other, was Frieda being so absurd as to refuse to do the same? The general opinion seems to have been that Frieda should have her affair with Lawrence, discreetly; and that if she were genuinely unhappy with Weekley, she should ask for a London flat or even (for the moment) stay with her parents in Germany. She and her family could then take their time either in pursuing a reconciliation with Weekley, or in constructing an arrangement by which she would continue to have her children. The one thing she must not do was compromise herself, and ruin her chances of recovering her children in a divorce settlement, by publicly acknowledging Lawrence ('an unknown young fellow of the lower classes' as Lawrence rightly thought he must have appeared to them) who was not only, as Else sharply and characteristically said, 'very young' but – even more important – unable to provide for Frieda financially after a divorce. It was the 'afterwards' which Frieda's family stressed: 'Afterwards! It is this we must think of.'[10]

Although Lawrence himself was well aware of how sensibly he too had to plan for the future – he wrote to Frieda later in the month how 'One *must* be detached, impersonal, cold, and logical, when one is arranging *affairs*' (i. 401) – the only future he was prepared to consider was a future with Frieda. (When Gilbert Noon plans his life with Johanna, he also is absolutely sure that Johanna 'was predestined to stay with *him*, and there was no thinking to be done'.[11]) Lawrence hated the idea that Frieda's family were interfering in what was not their business; he felt particularly helpless while Frieda's family rained down advice upon her while he hardly saw her.

What made matters more pressing still was the fact that Weekley suspected that Frieda had not been alone when she left on Friday 3 May; what she had told him about her previous affairs had aroused his suspicions. He apparently sent a telegram to Metz as soon as Frieda left, asking whether she was with a man. On the advice of her family – and in the teeth of Lawrence's demands that she tell Weekley the truth and announce that she was not coming back – Frieda replied ambiguously, probably on Monday 6th, saying she was writing.[12]

By the morning of Tuesday 7th, Lawrence was growing desperate: desperate with being cut off from Frieda, and with being excluded from the decisions about her future which she and her family were making. An accident finally brought things to a head. That Tuesday morning, Frieda and he – at last managing to spend time together away from her family – went for a walk and entered a forbidden area of Metz's military fortifications. Lawrence described what then happened in his essay 'How a Spy is Arrested', in which Frieda appears as 'Anita':

We lay together in the ⟨gr⟩ still sunshine. I was twisting Anita's ring, an old square emerald, full of green life

. . . Anita started, and looked round.

"Oh!" she exclaimed.

I looked over my shoulder. A young fellow in uniform was 'standing behind us,' looking at us from the under the ledge of his helmet. 'He had evidently been listening to, without understanding, our most interesting conversation, which had been carried on in English.'

"What are you doing here?" he asked in German.

"Nothing," said Anita. "Why?"

"It is forbidden to come here," he said, with quiet, authoritative tones, almost threatening.

'Verboten!' One is not in Germany five minutes, without seeing or hearing this word: only it is usually, 'Strengstens verboten.'[13]

Their names and addresses were taken, and they were told that 'inquiries' would be addressed to Frieda's father. The female von Richthofens must have been enraged with them for getting into such a mess; the incident precipitated the introduction of Lawrence to Freiherr Friedrich von Richthofen, at tea in Montigny that afternoon.

It was the only time they ever met: 'my father, the pure aristocrat, Lawrence, the miner's son'. Gilbert Noon, introduced to the various friends and family, feels 'like an image of the Virgin being wheeled round': he finally talks briefly to the Baron, who offers him a cigarette.

"Merci," said Gilbert, taking a cigarette and getting most hopelessly entangled with it and his tea-cup. The Baron gave him a match, and with tea-cup shivering nervously in his left hand our young friend lit his cigarette.

"Vous êtes longtemps en Allemagne?" asked the Baron.

... Gilbert stuttered hopeless French. He *sounded* a hopeless fool: he behaved like an unmitigated clown ... the Baron was impatient.

"Vous êtes à Munich, ma fille m'a dit. La Bavière vous plaît?"

"Oui! Oui! Beaucoup. Et la peuple est très interéssante."

"*Le* peuple—oui," said the Baron.

And that put the stopper on it. Our friend stood corrected, and not another sound would come out of him.[14]

The account in *Mr Noon* gives one a good idea of what Lawrence's own self-mimicry (which his friends all admired) must have been like. But it also records a humiliating experience, as such experiences in foreign languages are particularly likely to be. At this stage, Lawrence's spoken German was even worse than his French. Probably that evening, he wrote an angry letter to Frieda, demanding that they put an end to the pretence that he was just a friend, and insisting that she tell no more lies to Weekley or to her own family, and no longer attempt to put off what was – to him – the inevitable final decision:

No more dishonour, no more lies. Let them do their – silliest – but no more subterfuge, lying, dirt, fear. I feel as if it would strangle me. What is it all but procrastination? No, I can't bear it, because it's bad. I love you. Let us face anything, do anything, put up with anything. But this crawling under the mud I cannot bear. (i. 392–3)

He felt the ignominy of duplicity as keenly as filth. And he enclosed a letter to Weekley for Frieda to send: 'You needn't, of course, send it. But you must say to him all I have said' (i. 392). Frieda did not, apparently, either send it or say what Lawrence wanted. *Mr Noon*, however, describes Gilbert Noon writing and posting his own letter: and since the letter which Lawrence undoubtedly did write to Weekley had on it the date '8th May', it was almost certainly sent direct by Lawrence on Wednesday 8th and not via Frieda.[15] 'Don't curse my impudence in writing to you', Lawrence wrote:

'In this hour we are only simple men . . . I love your wife and she loves me
. . . To me it means the future. I feel as if my effort of life was all for her'
(i. 392).

This, of course, was the irrevocable step which Lawrence had been pressing Frieda to take, and which she had deliberately not taken. Weekley may
have respected Lawrence for being honest – he called him 'ehrlich' later in
the summer (i. 424) – but Lawrence's letter became, as a matter of course, a
main item of evidence in the divorce proceedings a year and a half later.
Frieda would later accuse Lawrence of having mishandled things and
Lawrence would reply 'I did not do wrong in writing to Ernst' (i. 401); but
the law as it then stood was sure to award custody of Frieda's children to her
aggrieved husband, and to make her access to them entirely dependent
upon his good will. Lawrence, however, wanted to prevent Frieda's retreat-
ing once again – after a little more 'subterfuge' – to her husband. He did *not*
want an affair with her: a non-moral relationship of the kind her family
favoured, even specialised in. He was quite determined on marriage: Frieda
was 'predestined to stay with *him*'. In spite of her later belief in her commitment to Lawrence from the start, at this stage Frieda seems to have been
very uncertain indeed about what she wanted.

Back at his hotel on the Tuesday evening, however – according to the
essay 'How a Spy is Arrested' – Lawrence heard that 'still everything was
not certain' concerning him: 'in official quarters' he was considered to be an
English officer. 'That finished me off. I forgave them everything, stood in
front of my long mirror, turning this way and that. An English officer! It
was *such* a compliment to my figure, as to feel like a sarcasm.' It is very
strange that Friedrich von Richthofen was not able to clear up the matter.
But he may well have preferred not to. (Louise – the Else figure in *Mr Noon*
– reports that, following his meeting with Gilbert, her father 'asks so many
questions, and it is difficult to make him quiet'.)[16] The Baron doubtless
thought it best to get Lawrence out of Metz and to rescue his daughter's
reputation as far as was now possible; the indiscretion gave him the chance
he needed.

On the morning of Wednesday 8th, Lawrence packed his bags. His only
satisfaction was that he had been mistaken for an English officer in the
fortifications – '*I – I*!!' (i. 395); but he had at least managed to precipitate
things with Weekley, in the letter which that day started on its way to
Nottingham. And, for better or worse, his relationship with Frieda was out
in the open. He was not expected at his relations in Waldbröl until Saturday
11th, in another three days: nor would he have wanted to leave Frieda
sooner than he had to. Else advised him to go to Trier, some eighty miles
down the Mosel river from Metz, 'only two hours in the train'. Accordingly,

on the Wednesday morning Lawrence went to Trier, fully expecting to see Frieda there. He never saw Frieda's father again, but that night Frieda dreamed 'they had a fight, and that Lawrence defeated my father'.[17] Freud's *Interpretation of Dreams* had been published in 1900, and Frieda had a smattering of psychoanalytic theory; but she would have been able to understand her dream without it.

II   In Fortified Germany

Lawrence enjoyed Trier, though he was only there briefly and it was very hot: 'like a perpetual Turkish bath' (i. 399). It was not a military base like Metz, and even though he still could not see Frieda, he must have felt a little more assured about the future now that he had written his letter to Weekley. It was while in Trier that he took his chance to get back to his work as a writer. He had to publish to live, particularly to make a life with Frieda: and the past few days had given him lots of material. Before leaving England, he had arranged to send Walter de la Mare – who had become a reader for Heinemann – some essays about Germany for the *Westminster Gazette*, where de la Mare had contacts; and while at Trier he wrote three articles drawn from his first impressions. Two got as far as being set up in type, but Lawrence feared that the third was a piece 'that nobody on earth will print, because it's too plain and straight' (i. 396). It was called 'How a Spy is Arrested' and described Tuesday's experiences in the fortifications of Metz: as he predicted it was rejected by the pro-German *Westminster Gazette* as 'too violently anti-German'.[18] The first essay, entitled 'In Fortified Germany' and mostly about the military in Metz, got as far as proof before it too was turned down: it was also probably thought to be too hostile to Germany. But the third essay, 'French Sons of Germany' (about a visit to Scy, just outside Metz) got into print, together with a fourth article which Lawrence wrote in Waldbröl a week later. The four pieces together give us an idea of Lawrence abroad, making his first attempt at being a professional travel writer.

His first experience of Germany had been in the second largest military centre of the Reich, and the essays continually focus upon soldiers and the military. Frieda was used to Metz's soldiers: they had been the background to all her early life. As a child she had gone into the barracks and sung with the young soldiers: as an adolescent she had flirted with them and had first fallen in love with a young officer.[19] Lawrence was quite unused to what he had seen in Metz, where 'there seem to be four soldiers to every civilian' – and that had increased his sense of not belonging:

A German officer, in a flowing cloak of bluey-grey—like ink and milk—looks at me coldly and inquisitively. I look at him with a "Go to the devil" sort of look, and pass along. I wonder to myself if my dislike of these German officers is racial, or owing to present national feeling, or if it is a temperamental aversion. I decide on the last . . .

Over the river, all is barracks—barracks, and soldiers on foot, and soldiers on horseback. Everywhere these short, baggy German soldiers, with their fair skins and rather stupid blue eyes! I hurry to get away from them.[20]

Although he describes in some detail his sympathy with the French people he meets in Metz – his barber, an innkeeper and his wife – and also writes in a very detailed way purely about what he sees in the streets, he is not afraid to speculate and to generalise. Each of the first three essays focuses on the nature of the German spirit, split between 'his animal nature and his spiritual', upon Lawrence's dislike for the militarism he sees and upon England's deliberate ignoring of instinct and desire: 'nowadays it is easier not to live than to live. It is easier to suffer than to insist. It is easier to submit than to conquer.'[21] He knew from his own experiences during 1911 how very often it had been 'easier to suffer than to insist'. But now, in May 1912, he could not resist using his own situation – without explaining what it was – as an example of the English malaise. 'I know a certain woman wants to love me, I know I want to love her. I can do without loving her, she can do without loving me—just as I can deny myself of something I need. But love is life, both to her and to me. Is it better to live or to forgo life? The English answer is always "to forgo life."' Some people, he knows, might accuse him of simply wanting 'licence':

There are plenty of well-shaped women in England or in Germany who would love me enough in a licentious fashion. But I don't want them. They are *not* life to me: they would brutalise me. This woman mates my soul. Yet if I love her I shall be no longer respectable, whereas if I loved the other women I should lose no caste. This feeling is stronger in England, I believe, than anywhere else, the insistence on formal respectability.[22]

It is hard to imagine Lawrence writing like this before meeting Frieda or hearing Frieda talk: but, away from England, he felt the old inhibitions and constraints within himself losing their accustomed power.

III Trier

Frieda had promised to come to Trier to stay with him on the Saturday and he had probably (like Gilbert Noon) arranged for her to share his hotel room; he would then go on to his Waldbröl relations on the Monday or Tuesday. In fact she came on Friday 10th for only half a day, accompanied by her mother and Johanna: she had had to promise her father to return to Metz the same night. The Baronin harangued Lawrence: the tone – but not the impeccable English – of Lady Charlcote pleading for the return of her daughter Barbara in Lawrence's autumn 1912 play *The Fight for Barbara* suggests that *Mr Noon*'s version of the encounter is close to the truth of what was said.

"Her father is a gentleman and an officer. Hee [sic] fears very much for his daughter's name and all the trouble and shame. Ah, you do not know. You have not thought of it all. Ah, you must think much more. You cannot begin this thing in such a way, like a glass of wine . . . You are young, ach, so young! You do not know the world, you do not know how to keep a woman. Ach, you have all your life before you, and you would take a woman who has two children and a husband! Oh yea! Oh yea! Think what you do. Think what you do! You will spoil your life. You will spoil your life. And also Johanna's life! Oh no! Ach, nein, es ist zuviel. Better you should go back to England."[23]

But the Baronin did not know, of course, about Lawrence's letter to Weekley: she thought the situation could still be rescued. Eventually Lawrence and Frieda were allowed to go off by themselves. Almost certainly in response to Frieda's ambiguous telegram of Monday, a letter had come from Weekley demanding a half-English and half-German (thus slightly coded) confirmation that she had gone off with another man: 'If it is true, wire to me "Ganz [very] recent"' (i. 409). Away from Frieda's family, Lawrence persuaded Frieda not to temporise any longer, but to wire back just that: 'Ganz recent'. His own crucial letter to Weekley had arrived in England that morning, anyway.

In the hectic muddle and confusion of these days, Lawrence had one single advantage: he was the only person who knew exactly what he wanted. He wanted the woman who 'mates my soul'. In spite of the pressure he was putting Frieda under, that continued to be his attraction (Johanna in *Mr Noon* feels about Gilbert that 'In a world of floating straws he seemed for the moment solid'). Her family were being reasonable and realistic, trying to safeguard her reputation and her children and to defend her future prospects. But Frieda found that Lawrence simply 'wanted her, he needed her, and that was bliss'; *her*, not her reputation or her future. *Mr Noon* describes Gilbert and Johanna, out in the country away from Trier, making the best of a dry ditch under a beech-tree for their love-making during their afternoon together: 'This was not the matrimonial bed Gilbert had prepared. But still, it was something. And that is always better than nothing.'[24]

There was no point in Lawrence's staying in Trier; the hotel bills were making deep inroads into the money (from her sister Else) Frieda had probably given him before he left Metz, to supplement the £11 he had brought from England.[25] He travelled on to Waldbröl on Saturday 11th, with at least the next step in his relationship with Frieda planned; Frieda was eventually going on to Wolfratshausen, near Munich, to stay with her sister Else, and he would join her there. Else, though not approving of what Lawrence and Frieda were doing, would at least not put the obstacles in their way which her mother and father presented. In the card he sent Frieda from Hennef (his last changing-place on the nine-hour train journey to Waldbröl), and in the poem he wrote about his experience there ('Bei Hennef'), Lawrence made her feel how much he loved her. Like Gilbert Noon, Lawrence was becoming 'unEnglished';[26] he had previously had difficulty in simply saying 'I love you': 'I always have to bite my tongue before I can say it. It's only my Englishness' (i. 391). Now, in Hennef, 'for the first time during today, my detachment leaves me, and I know I only love you. The rest is nothing at all. And the promise of life with you is all richness. Now I know' (i. 398).

Life together was still only a 'promise': but at least they knew what they would be doing next. An ironical aside, written into *Sons and Lovers* towards the end of October 1912, remarked 'It is not easy to estimate exactly the strength and warmth of one's feelings for a woman, till they have run away with one.' That was probably true for Lawrence: fighting for Frieda had revealed to him how much he loved her. Frieda, late in life, wrote very simply that 'Lawrence believed in his destiny, and his destiny included me as his wife.'[27] Going to Germany with her had been a little like jumping over the edge of a cliff, but it had at last focused his determination, his ambition to *make* his life and his marriage.

IV Frieda under Pressure

Just when Lawrence must have hoped that things were starting to settle down, a storm of letters and telegrams from Weekley and the English relations burst on Metz. In response to Frieda's 'ganz recent' telegram from Trier 'came back a wire "kein moeglichkeit" . . . i.e. all is over' (i. 409) from Weekley. Weekley had had Lawrence's letter on Friday 10 May and had written to Frieda 'I bear him no ill-will and hope you will be happy with him'; but he had also raged at Frieda, asking her if she wanted 'to drive me to suicide to simplify things'. He announced, dramatically, that he had asked his sister Maude to break the news to his parents: 'They have to know it but I am afraid it will kill them; if they had only died earlier.' Frieda must herself have written to him at some stage: he wrote in a melodramatic fury to Frieda's mother on 13 May that he could not see Frieda's handwriting 'without trembling like an old cripple – to see her again would be my death.

I would kill myself and the children too. It is terrible when one so longs for death and still must live for others. I will not kill myself, but she *must* leave me in peace.'[28]

At least one of Frieda's communications to Weekley – almost certainly that written under the influence of her family, around Monday 6 May – had suggested 'a compromise'. On receipt of Lawrence's Metz letter, however, Weekley abandoned any such idea: he wanted nothing except an admission from Frieda herself of her guilt, so that he could arrange a divorce; unless he got that, he hysterically threatened her, 'it might cost me my post here and our children could starve'. He rejected her suggestion of 'a compromise' out of hand: 'All compromises are unthinkable. We are not rabbits.'[29] That presumably meant that although *she* was sexually promiscuous (three previous affairs and now Lawrence), *he* was not. Another letter from Frieda offered to come and help with the removal of the children and the family home to London, where a new establishment would be set up consisting of them, their grandparents and Weekley's brother George and sister Maude. This suggestion was also firmly rejected. Weekley's sister Maude wrote a long, maudlin and savage letter to Frieda: the *Titanic* had gone down on the night of 15 April.

It is possible that you cannot see the mischief any more than the Titanic Iceberg did. I know that you have strange views of life, selfish views as you know I think, and I am sorry that you have collapsed.

... You have somehow missed the best in life and the best in love, for love that cannot suffer is unworthy of the name of love.

Poor Frieda make the best of the wreck and make for the light.[30]

Frieda's father and mother must have felt their worst fears confirmed, as these letters arrived. Weekley was going to keep the children to himself, and he was going to make Frieda no financial settlement: as he wrote to her mother, 'She must understand that she has no more rights but she knows I am honourable.' He would not blacken her name and reputation: but that was the full extent of his obligation to her. When he wrote to her father he referred, ominously, to the children as wholly his own: 'I have only two goals – to make Frieda free so that she can marry the man, and to provide for the future of my children.'[31]

Frieda's position was dreadful. Her parents were accusing her of making a mess of things (or of allowing Lawrence to); she must have felt that, in a way, she had; the man for whom she had caused all this hysteria and misery was hundreds of miles away, enjoying himself in Waldbröl; Weekley was now threatening suicide and infanticide; and quite apart from her own desperate feelings for her children, she was also the recipient of letters like the following, from the wife of one of Weekley's closest Nottingham friends:

Dear, do come home. I am sure you will regret it all your life if you don't. I have just been up to Private Rd. I think if you could have looked in you would have come back. Not a word of reproach in any way, only a broken hearted man. Do think of the children – the dear little girls and Monty – if you don't think quickly remember you ought never to see them again . . . don't spoil your own life and the lives of all the others – the little girls without a mother, no mother's love, and Monty, he *must* have a mother to protect him . . . the children you brought into the world can't be cast off like this. Don't you remember the night Monty was born? Don't you remember when E. was so ill and you thought you would never see him again? Come back. No one knows. The children would rush to meet you . . . Don't say I am old fashioned or anything like that: only be quite quite sure from me that when you are my age, 44, you will bitterly regret it if you don't come back.[32]

How could Frieda resist such appeals? Johanna in an identical situation in *Mr Noon* 'declared she would go mad', while the whole household 'began to go off its head'. Around 13 May Frieda wrote a letter to Lawrence saying he must come back from Waldbröl and support her; she also took comfort in the consolations offered by her old friend the army officer Udo von Henning. She probably had a brief affair with him, using him (as Lawrence put it) as 'a dose of morphia' (i. 404), though Lawrence also reckoned that she made von Henning 'more baby-fied' (i. 406). Johanna in *Mr Noon* then escapes from her parents to her sister in Munich, 'Where she took to her bed and would not stir for two days.'[33] At some stage before 21 May Frieda too went to Wolfratshausen, to stay with Else.

Lawrence had got to Waldbröl on the 11th, and had thus escaped the barrages from the Weekleys and the von Richthofens; but this was the visit which had been his original reason for coming to Germany, and the Krenkow family were very kind to him. His cousin Hannah, he reported, began to fall in love with him, which probably means no more than he enjoyed being found attractive, and wanted to counter Frieda's relationship with von Henning. The relief from the pressures and humiliations of Metz, Trier and the von Richthofens was wonderful; he felt he was starting to grow 'solid again' (i. 401). The Waldbröl family took him out into the country, on visits to a local fair and – one Sunday – over to Bonn and up the Rhine by steamer to the Drachenfels. He also had work to do; 'Paul Morel' needed its final revision before being submitted in June. He probably knew that when he rejoined Frieda it would not get done very fast; but that was the book he was counting on for their financial future.[34] He finished the revision, 'all but 10 pages' (i. 411), in Waldbröl. He also wrote another newspaper article for the *Westminster Gazette*, 'Hail in the Rhine-Land', in which he described a walk to the village of Nümbrecht and extensively fictionalised his relationship with Hannah Krenkow: on the way back they had taken a horse-driven omnibus to avoid a storm which ravaged the Waldbröl area on 15 May 1912, and Lawrence fantasised about starting a relationship with her.[35] But fantasised flirtation with Hannah Krenkow was a writer's device: he wanted to sell his essay. He needed to be certain about money for the future, and at one point even suggested to Frieda that they should not live together until he was in a position to support her. 'I have got about thirty pounds due in August ... Can we wait, or not, for that?' (i. 401). Louie Burrows would have been proud of him. The suggestion also shows how shell-shocked Lawrence was, after Metz, and how much he enjoyed the rest from heroics and (as Edward Garnett put it) 'making history' (i. 408). Waldbröl he told Frieda, 'restores me to my decent sanity' (i. 402). But Frieda must have said that of course they could not wait.

However, Lawrence also told Frieda, on 14 May, that – in spite of her letter demanding that he come back – he was not going to, just yet. 'Look, my dear, now the suspense is going over, we can wait even a bit religiously for one another. My next coming to you is solemn, intrinsically – I am solemn over it – not sad, oh no – but it is my marriage, after all, and a great thing – not a thing to be snatched and clumsily handled' (i. 401). Frieda's reply naturally accused him of leaving her 'in the lurch' (i. 406), of abandoning the ship with the rest of 'the rats'. Lawrence responded '"Rats" is a bit hard, as a collective name for all your men – And you're the ship?' (i. 406). But it is wrong to see the relationship of Lawrence and Frieda as a matter of love and desire drawing two people irresistibly together. The letter shows that Lawrence was not going to rush things now he could be fairly sure that Frieda would not (at least for the moment) be going back to Weekley. It was not the continuation of an affair that he wanted, but a commitment.

... it is a great thing for me to marry you, not a quick, passionate coming together. I know in my heart 'here's my marriage'. It feels rather terrible – because it is a great thing in my life – it is *my life* – I am a bit awe-inspired – I want to get used to it. If you think it is fear and indecision you wrong me. It is *you* who would hurry who are undecided. (i. 403)

He also felt (very sensibly) that it might be good for them both to get over the awful hysteria of the last ten days before settling down together: 'I'm not going to risk fret and harassment', he told her: 'I will not come to you unless it is safely, and firmly' (i. 402, 401). It was a new kind of relationship for him, utterly unlike anything he had had with Alice Dax or Louie Burrows or Jessie Chambers: he announced to her that 'I'm not coming to you *now* for rest, but to start living' (i. 404). Frieda herself wrote how she, too,

406

found their relationship turning into something serious: it was 'Not a sort of love affair' of the kind she was used to.[36] Lawrence had chosen her, and pursued her remorselessly: and she had finally had to accept him.

But it is also interesting that 'There had sprung up no grand passion between them'. *Mr Noon* is particularly helpful in stressing how Gilbert and Johanna make 'a curious couple'; how their first love-making is often unhappy, perhaps as Lawrence's poem 'First Morning' suggests: 'I could not be free, / not free myself from the past, those others—' – probably the other women in his life rather than the men in hers. The patterns of their lives could not easily be broken. Rather than being 'in love' at the start, however, Gilbert and Johanna are 'happy just being together . . . They were delighted like two children at being together.'[37] Lawrence and Frieda's relationship began not only as an affair, but – like the relationship of Gilbert and Johanna – as 'an infinite joy of living and sharing all that life had to offer': 'Without noticing one another, they gave each other a strange ease in the midst of a life that was alien to them both.'[38] Frieda had what Lawrence called 'a genius for living', and he now began to share a little of her kind of ease and warmth and acceptance. That was a new experience for the intensely conscious and detached person he had always been before and – 'free from oneself' (ii. 115) – could at last begin to feel relieved from being. Just as Gilbert's 'old closed heart had broken open', so Lawrence was 'realising things I never thought to realise' (i. 403): 'I never knew what love was before' (i. 414). And in a sentence reminiscent of Otto Gross, he told Frieda 'You make me sure of myself, whole': as Frieda later commented, 'that is what he needed'. Gross had written to her in 1907, more rhapsodically, how

Weisst Du denn auch, Geliebte, was Du mir *Grosses* gegeben hast – weisst Du, welch' unvergleichliche Kraft Du mir geschenkt hast in diesen Tagen, als ich mein Zukunftsideal als lebende Wirklichkeit schauen durfte und als es sich noch viel schöner erwies als ich mir je geträumt – weisst Du, wie Du mich stark und froh gemacht – dass Du mich auch das Lachen gelehrt hast – – dass mir seit Deinen Tagen die grosse *Sicherheit* geblieben ist, wie ich sie bisher noch nie gekannt? [Do you know then, my Love, how *great* the thing is which you have given me – do you know what incomparable strength you bestowed upon me in those days when I was permitted to behold my ideal of the future as a living reality and when it proved even more beautiful than I had ever dreamed – do you know how strong and happy you have made me – that you have also taught me how to laugh – – that since the days with you I have known a greater *security* than I have ever known before?][39]

It was Frieda's great gift to make her men feel like that, some of the time. Lawrence, however, found that his feelings towards her were 'no longer a sort of wandering thing, but steady, and calm'. He wrote to her about it in a way calculated to minimise her erotic potential: 'I think, when one loves, one's very sex passion becomes calm, a steady sort of force, instead of a storm. Passion, that nearly drives one mad, is far away from real love ... I shall love you all my life. That also is a new idea to me. But I believe it' (i. 403). (With Johanna in *Mr Noon*, Gilbert feels 'rested within her presence, and looked out from the little inaccessible conning-tower of his submerged spirit upon the world, as if the world were some endless stream-ing phenomenon'.[40]) Lawrence later summed up his discovery when he wrote to a married friend how the security given by love in marriage 'will leave you free to act and to produce your own work' (ii. 191).

If this is what Frieda gave Lawrence, then – in spite of the catastrophes of the past ten days – he too gave her the certainty that she was loved, needed and longed for; and he gave her, as well, a clear direction forward, such as had been missing from her life for years. 'His love wiped out all my shames and inhibitions, the failures and miseries of my past.'[41] The battery of letters from Weekley, his family and friends and the opposition of her own family, may also (paradoxically) have helped to drive Frieda towards Lawrence. She needed someone to help her overcome her guilt at having made such a dreadful mess of her husband's life – and of her children's lives.

Frieda was now in Wolfratshausen with Else, and Lawrence was drawing to the end of his visit to Waldbröl. By Tuesday 21 May, 'The soles of my feet burn as I wait' (i. 409); on Friday 24 May he travelled to Munich. Frieda met him, and they spent the night there either in a hotel or in her brother-in-law's flat at 1 Dillis Straße, in the suburb of Schwabing. On the Saturday they wandered round Munich; then took the yellow-green no. 10 tram down to the Isartalbahnhof, and the Isartal railway south. They were going – as man and wife of course, 'down here in Bavaria' (i. 428) – to the tiny village of Beuerberg, to an old Gasthaus zur Post which Edgar Jaffe had recommended to them.[42]

V Beuerberg

They must have spent a long day in Munich; they arrived in Beuerberg by the last train at night, in pouring rain, and followed the station porter across the fields to the Gasthaus. Peasants were drinking beer at tables in the hall downstairs; for 2/- a night – Whitsun prices – Lawrence and Frieda acquired a rather bare corner bedroom, with a great horse-chestnut tree outside the window and the sound of the river below. They went down, had a meal – doubtless watchfully observed by the locals – and retired to bed, partners at last.

Their week at Beuerberg 'in the wonderful meadows at the head of the Loisach' (i. 417–18), with the Alps gleaming in the distance, was something neither of them ever forgot. They breakfasted in the garden under the chestnut trees, the mornings 'a dream of beauty'. There is a wonderful and unironical recreation of it all in *Mr Noon*.

The mountains in the distance sparkled blue with snow and ice. The foot-hills were green-golden, and the wonderful meadows, a sea of blue and yellow flowers, surged nearer in the pure, transcendent light. The magic of it! A few great trees by the road, and two farm-houses with enormous sweeping roofs, white gables and black balconies! And then a pond, and a bridge downhill, and most lovely birch-trees standing translucent and gleaming along the wet, white way between the river-meadows. And everything crystal-pure, having the magic of snow-Alpine perfection . . .

Gilbert and Johanna would sit together in the sun, talking, watching the flash of the mountains, hearing the magical tong-tong of the cow-bells, and finding themselves outside the world, in the confines of a northern heaven. Johanna wore a smoke-blue gauze dress and a white hat, and was like the landscape. Gilbert watched and wondered, with his soul unfolded and his mind asleep. A wonderful deep peace flowed underneath his consciousness, like a river.[43]

They saw Else Jaffe in Wolfratshausen at least once; they went to a Passion-play in a nearby village; they went to the Kochelsee by train one afternoon. Lawrence wrote to Garnett, when the week was over, how 'The world is wonderful and beautiful and good beyond one's wildest imagination . . . Life *can* be great – quite god-like' (i. 414).

But *Mr Noon* also suggests that, however wonderful their time in Beuerberg, it was while there that Lawrence began to realise how much of a struggle his partnership with Frieda (whom he grew to think of as his 'complementary opposite'[44]) would be. Lawrence had a violent and irritable temper, and Frieda relished a quarrel. In Waldbröl he had admired 'the way you stick to your guns', though at that stage he thought 'We won't fight, because you'd win, from sheer lack of sense of danger' (i. 406). But even at the Kochelsee, during their honeymoon week, they walked in different directions, lost each other and got 'rather angry' with each other in a way that surprised them both: Frieda insulting Lawrence and him fighting back.[45] Disagreements, outbursts of rage and anger – about almost anything, but arising out of the difficult balance struck between two strong-minded and implacable individuals – these became everyday facts of life. Politer or better-mannered friends were frequently shocked. Edward Garnett's wife Constance observed them quarrelling a year later, and told Lawrence how 'I didn't believe their relation could survive these conflicts &

as a sensible man he ought to see it & part before he makes things too hard for her.'[46] It was impossible for Constance Garnett – indeed, for almost everyone – to believe that the public rows between Lawrence and Frieda were not going to end with them splitting up as a couple. But the arguments were the outward manifestation of what Lawrence realistically called 'the inner war which is waged between people who love each other' (i. 419). He tried to explain it to Constance Garnett, who noted: 'he says I don't understand – that his love is of the permanent sort – & that's it's all [sic] that F. only *half* loves him – but he'll *make* her love him altogether'.[47] He wanted absolute commitment, the abandonment by both of them of their old enclosed selves. Frieda accused him of preaching and theory. But in pursuit of his goal of 'permanent love', and with Frieda doubtless rejecting the very idea of such a goal, Lawrence insisted on his need always to say what he felt at the moment, spontaneously. *Mr Noon* gives us several representative rows between Gilbert and Johanna:

And as they came home, the fire-flies were threading in and out of the tall, tall dark rye, carrying their little explosive lanterns in their tails.

"I love you! I love you, you dears, you dears!" she cried to the fire-flies. " I *wish* I was a fire-fly."

"Don't gush," said he.

"You—who are you?" she cried at him.

"And what are you, for a fire-fly?" he said.

"Go away, you spoil everything.—You dear, you dear fire-flies, I love you. I wish I was one of you, to swim through the tops of the rye. Oh, I do! I should love it. I should love to be a fire-fly, and not bother with tiresome men and their pettiness any more."

"You might be less of a fool, if you were a fire-fly," he said to her. "You're too big a fool to be a human being."

"Oh God! Oh God!" she cried, lifting her hands to the deity. "Why am I persecuted by this person at my side."

"Because you ask for it," said he.

"Go away! Go away! I want to be happy. I want to be happy with the lovely fire-flies."

"Yes, you might ask *them* first, before you go butting in."

"*They'll* be glad of me," she said.

"By God, then they're welcome."

"Go away! Go home, you hateful thing."

"Come away, you ass. Don't slobber any more."

"Slobber! If you weren't a dried English stick, you'd know it wasn't slobber."

"And being a dried English stick, I just know it is."

"You would. There isn't a drop of sap in you."

"And you're going squashy and over-ripe."

"Oh, but isn't he a *devil*! Now he's spoiled my fire-flies."

And she went home in a dudgeon, and spent the rest of the evening making a marvellous painting on brown paper, of fire-flies in the corn.[48]

There is apparently nothing too serious in this: yet the charges they hurl at each other (Gilbert's failure to feel or to admit feeling: Johanna's gushing 'over-ripeness') could easily become very serious indeed. A remark in a letter of late June 1912 shows it – and demonstrates that Lawrence reversed the cause of the quarrel in the novel: 'F. raves over glow-worms, I over fire-flies, and we nearly murder each other' (i. 420). A very serious quarrel is recorded in one of Lawrence's poetry notebooks, which had been sent on to him from England. In the notebook, Frieda came across the poem 'My Love, My Mother' (later published, with an additional three stanzas, as 'The Virgin Mother'). The poem had originally been written in December 1910, reverently shown to Jessie Chambers before Lydia Lawrence's funeral and copied into Lawrence's notebook by Louie Burrows at the start of their engagement. Louie Burrows probably revered the poem's declaration of love for the dead mother. Frieda did not. She wrote into the margins of the notebook, and underneath the poem, exactly what she thought of it, and of Lawrence for it (see Illustration 42): it cannot have helped that the poem was in the handwriting of an ex girlfriend (Frieda was always quick to launch attacks on Lawrence's other women).

My little love, my darling
You were a doorway to me,
You let me out of the confine   *I hate it*
Into a vast countrie,
Where people are crowded like thistles
Yet are shapely and lovable to see.

                    You love it, you say!!!!

My little love, my dearest
Twice you have borne me,
Once from the womb, sweet mother.   *I hate it*
Once from myself to be
Free of the hearts of people
Of each heart's home-life free.

You sweet love, my mother
Twice you have blooded me,
Once with your blood at birth-time   *Good God*
Once with your misery.   *!!!!!*
And twice you have washed me clean,
Twice-wonderful things to see.

And so, my love, Oh mother
I shall always be true to thee.
Twice I am born, my mother   *I hate it*
As Christ said it should be,
And who can bear me a third time?
—None love—I am true to thee.

Yes, worse luck – what a poem to write! yes, you are free, poor devil, from the heart's homelife free, lonely you shall be, you have chosen it, you chose freely, now go your way. – Misery, ⟨an⟩ a sad, old woman's misery you have chosen, you poor man, and you cling to it with all your power. I have tried I have fought, I have nearly killed myself in the battle to get you into connection with myself and other people, sadly I proved to my self that I can love, but never you – Now I will leave you for some days and I will see if being alone will help you to see me as I am, I will heal again by myself, you cannot help me, you are a sad thing, I know your secret and your despair, I have seen you are ashamed – I have made you better, that is my reward –[49]

It is impossible to date these comments exactly; they might have been added as early as May 1912 or as late as June 1913, though May–July 1912 is most likely. But the poem is a startling expression of feelings which Frieda hated in Lawrence, and which he had by no means outgrown by the summer of 1912: the four stanzas appeared almost unchanged in the 1916 volume *Amores*, with another three added. Frieda's comments reveal how devastating she could be when roused: how sure of herself, how ready to dismiss him and his love, how wounding. She was a mother too, but not (she insisted) *this* kind of a mother, or one who wanted this kind of a son (or this kind of lover). She would 'leave him for some days': doubtless to go and stay with Else in Wolfratshausen. We know that they were apart 15–17 June (i. 418) and again in July (i. 421).[50]

In these first weeks together Lawrence and Frieda were both gaining the courage to abandon self-sacrifice, and to assert their needs and demands (as Frieda's comments certainly do); and they were committed to distrusting reserve. As Frieda put it, a little later: 'I am never *quite* sure whether I love or hate L, I only know I would rather die than do without him and his life along of mine' (i. 467). The point about the quarrels, even ones as devastating as that over the poem, was that they were *expressed*: part of the process of making a life together. Just as Lawrence's writing life was a search for expression, for finding the words for the experience so as to bring it to consciousness, to make it actual, to master it – so the anger and the quarrels were ways for them both to bring their differences and their needs out into the open. They both had a lot 'to surpass', to get over, from their past lives;

the newly liberated anger, like the love they shared – and like Lawrence's writing – were vital ways of shedding 'sicknesses' (ii. 90) for them both. Their quarrels helped define them to each other, and to themselves: helped them build a partnership which, although in one sense still desperately insecure, was continuing to develop. Every week that went by without Frieda returning to England was, for Lawrence, something gained; every week that passed without her going back was a proof to Frieda of how much more the new life fulfilled her than the old one had done.

VI Icking

From Beuerberg, after their week, they moved back up the Isartalbahn to Icking. One of the results of Frieda's sister Else's way of living (and not living) with Edgar Jaffe was that the region south of Munich was full of places where they both might live, separately or together. Edgar had his flat in Munich, and was currently building a little house in Irschenhausen (where Lawrence and Frieda would stay in 1913 and again in 1927). Else had her own house, with the children, in Wolfratshausen, just seven miles up the Isar–Loisach valley from Irschenhausen; but her lover Alfred Weber had a small flat in Icking, half-way between the two, where he could spend time with Else. With such a choice of houses and flats, there was bound to be somewhere for the homeless sister and her lover; and Lawrence and Frieda were given the Icking flat rent free. The second-floor flat had a balcony looking over the road and down the long slope to the distant river Isar. On the ground floor was the shop belonging to Herr and Frau Leitner – Herr and Frau Breitgau in *Mr Noon*: Walburga Leitner 'like a round, shiny, rosy sausage that has been dipped in hot water', Josef Leitner 'with a long grey brown-fringed moustache which looked as if it had grown into a long grey weed hanging over the rim of a beer-pot'.[51]

Behold then Frau Breitgau beaming in the door with the milk, and Gilbert in pyjamas and Johanna in her blue silk dressing-gown. Behold Gilbert running down to Frau Breitgau's shop, for liver-sausage, or a cutlet of Ripperle, or Schnapps, or whatever it was, and struggling with a conversation in strong Bayrisch, with the happy Frau or the beer-dim Herr. Behold our couple living in a land of milk and honey and joyful abundance, for fifteen shillings a week for the two of them.[52]

The idyll was however regularly interrupted by letters from England, and by half-comic, half-shocking episodes such as an unexpected visit on Friday 2 August from Frieda's mother, who spent an hour abusing Lawrence 'like a washerwoman':

'Who was I, did I think, that a Baronesse should clean my boots and empty my slops:

she, the daughter of a high-born and highly-cultured gentleman . . . No decent man, no man with common sense of decency, could expect to have a woman, the wife of a clever professor, living with him like a barmaid, and he not even able to keep her in shoes.' – So she went on. (i. 429–30)

And then she told Else that Lawrence was 'a lovable and trustworthy person. – You see I saw her off gracefully from the station' (i. 430). The version in *Mr Noon* is significantly different from that in the letter (or that in *The Fight for Barbara*): it leads to a scene between Gilbert and Johanna in which she taunts him for being scared of her mother, and succeeds in successfully humiliating him; and he gets into a murderous rage. 'He had almost forgotten, forgotten these horrible rages. When he was a boy of thirteen his sister could taunt them up in him . . . Now suddenly the black storm had broken out again.'[53] For all its later and very different perspective, *Mr Noon* may once again be a more honest reflection of events than Lawrence's writing of the time. It suggests how Lawrence's life with Frieda was also important in making him show (not control) his feelings, and in making him come to terms with bottled-up rages by being violently angry.

What, however, the account of these months in *Mr Noon* ignores is Frieda's growing and dreadful realisation that she had given up her children. In the novel, Johanna gets a 'little scrap of a note from her son' which is distressing: 'But she backed away—she fought off her realisation.'[54] Frieda Weekley never fought off the realisation; and Lawrence never found a way of coping with her misery. Earlier in the novel, during its recreation of the week in Beuerberg, Johanna had become nostalgic:

"Think of my little boys!" she said.
    "Why think of them!" he said. "They are all right."
    "Are they! Without their mother!"
    "But you wouldn't go back till August, anyhow. You weren't due to go back till August."
    There was a pleading in his voice . . .[55]

Johanna punishes him by insisting on sleeping in the other bed, that night, though the following morning they are reconciled. '"Ha—I suppose one can't always be happy," she sighed. And she sighed rather bitterly, as if against fate.'[56] But those are the only two references in the novel to Johanna's loss of her children. In Icking, Frieda was sometimes quite desperate. 'She lies on the floor in misery', Lawrence told Garnett. Weekley first used the children as a lure to try and get her back; he wrote to her that they were 'miserable, missing her so much' (i. 421). He then tried the opposite tack: as she had not come back, 'she must forego the children' (i. 424). Frieda told her sister Else how her feelings tortured her so much that 'sometimes I must get up in the night, and go out into the garden, because I can't bear the pain'.[57] The fact that Weekley had dismissed the children's nurse Ida made matters still worse; Frieda knew how her children were being deprived of the love and affection they had been used to. In different ways they all grew up bearing the scar of their loss.

Frieda was very aware of how her feelings also tormented Lawrence; her unfinished memoirs describe how he 'felt helpless, her grief was something beyond him, he could not cope with it. His oversensitive, oversympathetic nature could not bear the suffering imposed on her and on him. He shut himself off from her.' That was his old, habitual technique. In the memoir, he starts to get 'beside himself' and actually falls ill. She pleads with him to 'see what it means to me': '"No," he said quickly, "no man can understand it."' In her biography, Frieda tried to come to terms with what she always felt was a strange reluctance or gap in Lawrence. Her agony over her children, she felt, 'was my worst crime in his eyes. He seemed to make that agony more acute in me than it need have been. Perhaps he, who had loved his mother so much felt, somewhere, it was almost impossible for a mother to leave her children.'[58] It is an interesting and partly convincing idea; these, after all, were the months when Lawrence was torn by recollection of his mother and rethinking 'Paul Morel' (he turned it into *Sons and Lovers* in the autumn).

And yet Frieda's attitude towards her children was probably one of the clues which led to his insistence, in the novel, on how destructive a possessive mother love – as opposed to love for husband or man – could be. In a poem in *Look! We Have Come Through!* actually designated 'Beuerberg', Lawrence wrote angrily against 'mothers who fortify themselves in motherhood', accusing them of 'devastating the vision': 'the curse against you is still in my heart / Like a deep, deep burn. / The curse against all mothers.' In March 1912 he had angrily equated 'mother' with 'manage' (i. 377) while a passing reference to the 'true maternal instinct' in December 1912 claimed that it 'kicks off an offspring as soon as it can go on its own legs' (i. 492). Far from believing that a mother should not abandon her children, Lawrence was on the road to believing that she could do nothing better.[59] But, like Weekley, he had realised that Frieda was effectively faced with a choice between him and her children. If Frieda wanted him, she would have to give up her children until they were grown up. If she wanted the children, she must leave him and go back.

This was made quite explicit in the crisis of July 1912, when the offer of a new settlement arrived and Frieda was tempted as never before to go back. Weekley now proposed what he had previously refused: that if Frieda would return to England without Lawrence, he would install her in a flat in

London – with her children – and would not divorce her. He would not, of course, live with her. Such a settlement would have struck Frieda's sisters as the ideal solution; it was exactly what they had both managed. (*Mr Noon* records an evening immediately after the offer arrived, when Louise – the fictional version of Else – insists on Johanna's staying with her and not returning to Gilbert: '"Tonight," said the officious Louise, "Johanna will stay here. Because there is much to talk about, which we must say ALONE."') The narrator of *Look! We Have Come Through!* is, like Gilbert Noon, devastated:

> Oh my God, how it aches
> Where she is cut off from me!
>
> Perhaps she will go back to England.
> Perhaps she will go back,
> Perhaps we are parted for ever.[60]

That was Lawrence's main fear during June and July: he told Garnett 'she won't leave me, I think' (i. 421), but it was an ever-present and terrible possibility.

Yet he refused to try to persuade her to stay. She was 'fearfully angry' in Icking 'because I won't say "stay for my sake" . . . she almost hates me, because I won't say "I love you – stay with me whatever happens." I *do* love her. If she left me, I do not think I should be alive six months hence . . . God, how I love her – and the agony of it' (i. 421). He was trying desperately to steer clear of a solution in which she gave up, for his sake, what she most deeply longed for. He was sure that self-sacrifice – in some ways the most seductive policy for them both – would make them hate each other: they had both known enough of it in their lives. He had told Louie Burrows in 1911 how 'damnable' was the 'eternal cultivation of the habit of going without what one wants – needs' (i. 322). He would have no more of it. He would not, could not give up his love for Frieda, any more than he would expect her to abandon her own feelings: but neither would he plead with her. 'I say "decide what you want most, to live with me and share my rotten chances, or go back to security, and your children – decide for *yourself* – Choose for yourself"' (i. 421). He would put her under no obligation to anyone, not even to him. His pride, his independence and his new belief in how a relationship should be carried through, would none of them allow it. It was a thoroughly dangerous (and to Frieda infuriating) attitude, but he stuck to it. And it laid down a powerful model for him of the forces which govern – and which to him should govern – the relationships between men and women. He was coming to regard the independence of both partners within a relationship as a necessary precondition of its survival.

Sometime around 8 July, Frieda wrote to Weekley 'definitely she could never come back': this provoked a 'cyclone of letters' (i. 424) from Weekley, yet paradoxically left Lawrence no more certain that Frieda would stay. It meant that she was now faced not by the potential loss of her children but by their actual loss. 'I shan't let F leave me, if I can help it' he told Garnett on 22 July (i. 427); but he still did not know whether he could stop her.

VII First Round

There is no point in attempting a reasoned explanation of Lawrence's attitude towards Frieda's love for her children. Frieda's sympathisers will always say that he was, quite simply, jealous of the children; his sympathisers will accuse Frieda of refusing to accept that she had decided against the children by staying with him.

But part at least of Lawrence's anger with Frieda for agonising over her children, and for pleading with Weekley, was a characteristically violent reaction to humiliation. How could Frieda give herself away so much to someone she had come to despise – to the person he characterised at the start of August as 'Weekley whining bullying threatening' (i. 430)? Lawrence suffered for Frieda where she did *not* suffer: experienced the tortures of her humiliation as her appeals were rejected, her pleas ignored. He himself would have gone to the stake before getting into such a position. It was also the case that Frieda's children were already being alienated from her. They were effectively being brought up by Weekley's sister Maude, who hated Frieda; and Lawrence knew a great deal about the estrangement of children from a parent whose character is systematically blackened. Frieda could never accept that that might be happening.

And yet the matter goes deeper still. In the first place, Lawrence had some agonised sympathy with Weekley's love for Frieda: 'He's rather fine – never, for one moment, denies his love for F, and never says anything against her herself' (i. 424).* In his poem 'Meeting Among the Mountains', first written in August 1912 when he and Frieda were both especially conscious of Weekley's sufferings (i. 439–40), he created a vivid imaginative version of Weekley's 'frozen breath of despair, / And in his heart the half-numbed agony', as he ponders 'the frozen memory of his wrong' and feels 'in / His belly the smouldering hate of me'. Lawrence's own guilt about what he and Frieda had done to Weekley meant that he wanted to bottle up

* In 1952, when Frieda was in England for what she guessed would be the last time, she was persuaded by her children not to go to see Ernest; but when he died in 1954 a tiny photograph was found of Frieda and him together in the Black Forest, in 1898 or 1899: cut into a rough circle, it had probably been kept in a locket or a watch. See Illustration 36.

his feelings and forget Weekley, the children, everything. As Frieda put it, 'he denied all the suffering and suffered all the more – like his mother before him . . .' (ii. 151). Frieda characteristically felt less guilty than he did (Weekley would complain about her failure to feel any 'Gewissensbisse [pangs of conscience]'; but her longing for her children ensured that Lawrence's guilt was unappeased.[61]

But above all it was Lawrence's belief in himself which brought him to believe in a life without the children. 'I suppose I'm so damned conceited in my belief in myself – it doesn't seem to be myself, really' (ii. 73), he would write rather disarmingly in 1913. His sense of his own mission and destiny, as man and writer, was something he only rarely referred to, except when anger or excitement betrayed him. But indications of an extraordinary certainty about himself surface regularly, like bubbles revealing submerged life. He had told May Chambers before leaving for Germany in May 1912 that he 'had a strong feeling of destiny',[62] while he would tell Garnett a year later that 'I *know* I can write bigger stuff than any man in England' (i. 546): 'I think "here you are, I tell you the truth"' (ii. 73). His body was frail, his life potentially short: but he had a passion to understand and – through his writing – to alter people by bringing them to self-realisation. He wrote of the British public, in the summer of 1912, 'I should like to bludgeon them into realising their ⟨real⟩ 'own' selves' (i. 424). He would eventually write, early in 1913, how 'I think, do you know, I have inside me a sort of answer to the *want* of today: to the real, deep want of the English people, not to just what they fancy they want. And gradually, I shall get my hold on them' (i. 511). Life with Frieda and his developing writing were rooting that confidence in him. He knew himself gifted and exceptional: when 'Paul Morel' was turned down, his response was: 'my cursed, rotten-boned, pappy hearted countrymen, *why* was I sent to *them*' (i. 422).

Frieda was 'the woman of a lifetime': but her love for her children was a 'drawn sword' between them (i. 551) because he knew that if she were ever to get her children – or (more likely) were to accept that London flat – then their own exceptional life together would be at an end. He would have to earn much more as a writer: would have to be commercial in a way he profoundly did not want to be.[63] If Frieda meant what she said about loving him, then from his point of view she had no business betraying their vital new partnership with a fruitless (and humiliating) longing for children for whom she – and he – could no longer care. Without her children, she would help him carve out his own new territory of writing: he could learn from her what someone utterly different could give him. He wanted her for that; he was now feeling that that was his life's work. But it was a need which he was reluctant to explain or to articulate. He refused, for example, to allow it into *Mr Noon*.

There was something else that *Mr Noon* could not recreate, either: Lawrence's actual writing. In Icking, on the little balcony over the quiet country road, with its marvellous view on clear days out to the 'great blue wall of mountains' (i. 415) in the distance, and down to the pale, milky-green river Isar, Lawrence had at last a place to sit and work. And in spite of the 'great war . . . waged in this little flat' (i. 419), it was here that he finished the revision of 'Paul Morel'. The novel had been started back in the dark days of Croydon in November 1911; only seven months earlier, but an impossible world away from Icking in June 1912. The revision took only another week, and on 9 June Lawrence posted the novel off to Heinemann (i. 416); in the next three weeks, he revised three short stories: 'The Fly in the Ointment', 'Delilah and Mr Bircumshaw' and 'The Christening'.[64]

But, just as he finished the stories – and coinciding with the most dangerous (because the most tempting) mail from Weekley – out of the blue arrived potentially disastrous news. Of all that he had so far written, Lawrence was most proud of 'Paul Morel'; and, equally important, he believed it was the novel which 'may get me onto my feet' (i. 417). He had been uneasy about the firm of Heinemann ever since their lukewarm response to 'The Saga of Siegmund'; yet this new novel was, he felt certain, 'a good thing, even a bit great' (i. 416). But almost exactly three weeks after Lawrence had sent off the manuscript, William Heinemann wrote in person explaining that he was turning it down.

I feel that the book is unsatisfactory from several points of view; not only because it lacks unity, without which the reader's interest cannot be held, but more so because its want of reticence makes it unfit, I fear, altogether for publication in England as things are . . . one has no sympathy for any character in the book. A writer must create interest in his characters. Even, after a while, one's interest in Paul flags, – while, in the early part, the degradation of the mother, supposed to be of gentler birth, is almost inconceivable. (i. 421 n. 4)

Lawrence's response – in a letter to Garnett he wrote the day Heinemann's rejection arrived – was wildly angry and derisory, and shows what he thought of Heinemann's phrase 'its want of reticence': 'Curse the blasted, jelly-boned swines, the slimy, the belly-wriggling invertebrates, the miserable sodding rotters, the flaming sods, the snivelling, dribbling, dithering palsied pulse-less lot that make up England today' (i. 422). It was not only Heinemann's rejection of the novel for its 'want of reticence' which angered him: the reference to the 'degradation of the mother' would have reminded him of the practically insuperable gap between what he knew of working-class life, and the expectations of middle-class readers and publishers. And he simply had to publish the novel to live. Up to now, he had frequently written and revised with an eye to the sensibilities of his readers: he had toned down the sexuality of *The White Peacock* when asked, and only two of his pieces of fiction about the working class ('Odour of Chrysanthemums' and 'The Miner at Home') had ever got into print: the former after extensive changes. In 'Paul Morel', however, he had not paid enough attention to the susceptibilities of middle-class readers, or to those of publishers worried about offending (and losing) the lucrative library market: he could see, through his anger, that 'Heinemann . . . is quite right, as a business man' (i. 422).

But, for a rejected author, Lawrence was in an extremely fortunate position. He knew that the publisher's reader for another firm admired his work in general and the rejected manuscript in particular. Edward Garnett had stepped in to rescue 'The Saga of Siegmund' and had seen 'Paul Morel' when Lawrence took it to the Cearne at the end of April. Garnett had also heard from Heinemann's reader Walter de la Mare that 'Paul Morel' was being turned down. His letter to Lawrence offering to read it for Duckworth arrived the day after Heinemann's rejection. The bulky parcel of manuscript (it had cost Lawrence 2/9 to post it first time) went back to England the day it arrived, with Lawrence hoping that Garnett would write notes as he had done for *The Trespasser* (i. 423). By 22 July, not only had Duckworth accepted the novel, but Garnett had sent Lawrence two batches of comments, together with the manuscript; Lawrence started revising it immediately.[65]

He and Frieda were happy, too, in visits from Garnett's son David ('Bunny') in late July; outgoing, full of youthful bounce, Bunny was an undemanding companion who seems to have fallen in love with them as a couple, and whom – in their still shocked and uncertain state – they found very cheering. Lawrence described him to Garnett *père*: 'You should see him swim in the Isar, that is effervescent and pale green, where the current is fearfully strong. He simply smashes his way through the water, while F. sits on the bank bursting with admiration, and I am green with envy' (i. 429). Much later, David Garnett characterised Lawrence's appearance when he first met him as 'incredibly plebeian, mongrel and underbred', especially when compared with the aristocratic Frieda and her 'magnificent shoulders'. Lawrence was

slight in build, with a weak, narrow chest and shoulders, but he was a fair height and very light in his movements. This lightness gave him a sort of grace . . . His forehead was broad, but not high, his nose too short and lumpy, his face colourless, like a red-haired man's, his chin (he had not then grown a beard) altogether too large, and round like a hairpin – rather a Philip IV sort of chin – and the lower lip, rather red and moist, under the scrubby toothbrush moustache.

In contrast, Frieda's 'head and the whole carriage of her body were noble':

Her eyes were green, with a lot of tawny yellow in them, the nose straight. She looked one dead in the eyes, fearlessly judging one and, at that moment, she was extraordinarily like a lioness: eyes and colouring, and the swift power of her lazy leap up from the hammock where she had been lying.[66]

The descriptions, however, reveal as much about what the later Garnett wanted Frieda and Lawrence to be like as what he actually saw in 1912; he always admired Frieda, but preferred to typecast Lawrence.[67] Although, like others, Garnett was fascinated by the partnership between an aristocrat and a miner's son, he enjoyed the security of his own class judgements when distinguishing what he liked from what he did not.

The time Lawrence and Frieda could spend in Icking was, however, running out (Alfred Weber probably wanted his flat back); and Lawrence was only able to do a limited amount to his novel. Even that was important; the novel remained the one piece of writing with which, in the future, he might hope to earn a substantial sum of money. But the novel was still primarily concerned with making sense of previous relationships and experiences; and Lawrence wrote a good deal else besides, some of which allowed him to explore what was currently happening to him. He wrote over twenty poems between his arrival in Germany and leaving Icking on 5 August; all but three of them were printed in *Look! We Have Come Through!* in 1917, in the sequence from 'Ballad of a Wilful Woman' to 'Fireflies in the Corn'. Very few of them survive, however, in their 1912 form; the notebook in which Lawrence probably originally collected them and revised them is no longer extant. Many of them exist only in the form of 1917 revisions, and we can be reasonably certain that they record not the experiences of 1912, but the experiences into which poetry took Lawrence during the next five years. Like *Mr Noon*, the poems were revised to demonstrate how 'we' have 'come through': how a relationship had been more than grounded or sustained, but had also released its partners into fulfilment. This is the history which in the end Lawrence felt his life during these months could tell; but it was not the original history.

But he wrote at least one new short story – 'Once—!' – which can be set beside the poems describing the beginning of the new relationship. The story's first-person narrative uses yet another version of the slightly lang-uorous and middle-class artist-hero, who is in Germany having an affair with an older woman called (like the woman in 'How a Spy is Arrested')

Anita, but drawn in part from Frieda's sister Johanna. A good deal of the tale consists of an anecdote about a love-affair with an army officer which 'once' the woman had. But surrounding the anecdote, there exists a frame-work in which the central relationship between a man and a woman starts to be explored; and it is a crucially new kind of relationship for the artist-hero – and also for Anita. Anita admits she has always loved men – '"but I have put them all in my pocket," she said, with just the faintest disappointment in her good-humour'. The narrator feels the temptation to follow them 'into Anita's pocket, along with her purse and her perfume and the little sweets she loved'. 'But,' he says, 'I loved her: it would not be fair to her: I wanted to do more than give her pleasure.'[68] In comparison with Paul Morel's simple fear of going into Miriam's pocket, this man's anger with his loving but just slightly disappointed woman is also his provocation to demand a new kind of relationship altogether. At the end of the story, after her anecdote has been told – very much an anecdote of the old, 'pocketing' self – Anita asks the narrator 'very low' what he is thinking. He answers:

"I was thinking, all you want, you get."
  "In what way?"
  "In love."
  "And what do I want?"
  "Sensation."
  "Do I?"
  "Yes."
She sat with her head drooped down.

The man – jealous of her past, and still a little absurd in his wounded pride – responds callously. 'Have a cigarette', he says. The commonplace remark is an insult: it means that, because she is incorrigible, there is nothing else which it is worth his while saying. Sensation is all she wants from a man and self-gratifying love all she will give. The narrator insists on his common-place – and thus on her incorrigibility:

"—You *won't* have a cigarette?"
  "No thanks—and what else could I take—?"
  "Nothing, I suppose—" I replied.
  Still she picked pensively at her chemise string.
  "Up to now, you've missed nothing—you haven't felt the lack of anything—in love," I said.

His peevishness indicates his jealousy but also shows how much he would like her to be different – would like her to be exposed to the *lack* of self which love is, to him. And at the very end of the story, she responds to his insistence that she has never felt such a lack:

She waited awhile.
   "Oh yes I have," she said gravely.
   Hearing her say it, my heart stood still.[69]

This is done too quickly: but it takes very seriously indeed the idea of the Frieda character being able to change: to admit her need, not just enjoy her healthy love for a while and pass on. It takes the study of relationship between independent and possessive people to the very threshold of *Sons and Lovers*.

   Lawrence may well have begun the story in Icking as a German travel sketch for the book he was thinking of putting together (i. 430); he finished it as a fully fledged story beside the Lago di Garda.[70] The moment of decision had come; he and Frieda had to leave Icking. It was also just the time when Frieda may well originally have arranged to go back to England. In a tone which sounds grim and relieved rather than joyful, Lawrence wrote to Garnett: 'I have at last nailed F.'s nose to my wagon. At last, I think, she can't leave me – at least for the present: despite the loss of her children' (i. 430). In the terms of the story, Frieda could no longer be a woman simply enjoying a new experience with a man she adored, but one who needed to recognise that her self-gratifying life was also unfulfilled. She threw in her lot – 'at least for the present' – with Lawrence. A further commitment was not yet to be expected.

   They had wretchedly little money, however, and knew they must live as cheaply as possible. *Mr Noon* records an exchange between Louise and Gilbert which probably recalls very much what Frieda's sister Else – according to Lawrence, 'a person who arranges other folk's affairs' (i. 530) – said to them in late July:

"Have you never been to Italy? Oh but it is lovely! Why not go there? Why not go, and walk some of the distance!"
   "But money?" said Gilbert.
   "Ach money! Money will come."
   Again she said it. And he was all his life grateful to her for the laconic indifference with which she said it. For some reason he believed her. "Money will come."[71]

Lawrence and Frieda had '£23 between us' (i. 430). Their three trunks went ahead by rail: on 5 August 1912, knapsacks on their backs, they set off towards Italy with the immediate destination of Mayrhofen, in Austria, but ultimately intending to go down to 'Lake Garda, or Maggiore' (i. 430): hoping that money would come, or at least follow them there.

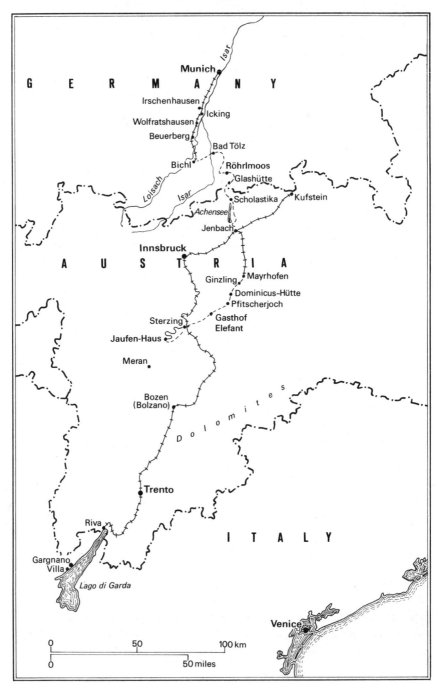

Icking to the Lago di Garda

VIII Over the Hills

The journey south became a high point of their early years together: a proof of their new freedom and a symbolic leaving of their old lives. In practical terms it was at last a journey away from England, Weekley and the children. There was for the moment to be no going back: Frieda had made her choice and – at least for this winter – was going to have to live with its consequences.

Lawrence wrote three essays about the journey and recreated it at length in *Mr Noon*. Frieda also described it lovingly in her 1934 biography, and yet again in 1954:

> It was a great day when we set out to walk from the Isartal over the Alps. We only had a rucksack each. Our great standby was a small spirit stove called the *kitchenino*, and we would cook a little meat by the roadside. We had bread, sausage, cheese and foods that we bought coming through the villages. We walked for six weeks; at night we slept in haylofts which I thought was wonderful . . .[72]

Memory is a great refiner of experience: they slept in hay-huts only twice, and although they were on the road from 5 August to 4 September they actually walked on only eleven of those days, and travelled on only thirteen. They took trains and buses for good stretches of the journey; all the way from Sterzing down to the Lago di Garda, for example. But it was still a marvellous adventure. Six months earlier, convalescing in Bournemouth after pneumonia, Lawrence had been proud of being able to walk 'six miles' back from Wimborne to Poole (i. 358). But now, accompanied by a woman whose exercise in Nottingham had probably been restricted to mad dashes up the Woodborough Road, he walked over the Alps.

They left Icking at 7.00 a.m. on Monday 5 August, 'in the dimmery-glimmery light . . . before breakfast-time, with blue chicory flowers open like wonder on either side the road';[73] they walked the 5 km. to Wolfrat-shausen, bought their little stove and went a few km. further on. But it looked like rain; they took the Isartal train a few stops down the line before walking on. It was still 15 km. to Bad Tölz, and it rained a good deal; they stopped at least once to eat and to dry off, and only arrived at half-past six in the evening. They found a cheap lodging; Gilbert and Johanna's need to save money does not deter them from paying 1/- each to see a play that night. On Tuesday 6th, Lawrence and Frieda walked all day up the valley of the Isar, covering 15–16 km., but – to save time, late in the afternoon – decided to take a short cut over the hills, down to the road towards the Achensee. Baedeker describes one such route, starting just behind Winkel, which they may have considered (though it took them over a considerable hill on the way); but – encouraged by a misleading map in Baedeker – they probably started out on a different path and, when that path petered out, crossed over to yet another path, going in quite a different direction.[74] Just at nightfall, and very tired, they ended up at a tiny upland wooden chapel at Röhrlmoos which fascinated Lawrence. It was dry and warm, and full of ex-voto pictures: he lit the candles to look at them, and – ever the journalist in search of material for his German sketches – almost certainly made some notes about them and their inscriptions. But the wooden floorboards of the chapel disappointed Frieda. She wanted to sleep in a hay-hut, and found one just over the saddle of the pass, down into the Alpine meadow. (In *Mr Noon*, Johanna is 'in ecstasies' because she has got away at last from her suburban villa, her provincial town, from civilisation, and was 'sleeping like a tramp. She wanted to be made love to there in the darkness of the hay: so she was made love to: and at length the two disposed themselves for sleep . . . "It's lovely, *lovely*!" said Johanna.'[75]) Lawrence remembered the dreadful, tickling discomfort, the intense cold and their failure to sleep.

Before dawn on Wednesday 7th, in pouring rain (which was turning to snow a little higher up the hills), they put on their ice-cold clothes and boots, made a miserable breakfast and in the first daylight made their way across the meadow to a hut where they got directions; they followed a stream down a steep and stony path to meet the main road to Austria they had been aiming for. After coffee and a real breakfast in a house on the road, they went to bed and stayed there till early afternoon. Sitting on the bed wrapped in his duvet, Lawrence – 'out of sheer exasperation' – began to draft his two sketches about the previous night's adventures.[76] In both sketches, he made himself a rather stiff, conventional person contrasted with the exuberant Anita: another tribute to Frieda and how good for him she was.

It was still raining when they got up; they took the post-omnibus (which stopped outside the door) over the Austrian border, down to the dark-green, mountain-bound Achensee. Here there was no room (they were told) in the rambling and grandiose Hotel Scholastika, with its 140 beds; they may well have been turned away because of their tramp-like appearance. But they found a farmhouse to take them in: Lawrence bought food and (as usual) they cooked and ate in their room. On Thursday 8th, which was fine again, they walked on beside the lake, and down the winding road to Jenbach (about 15 km. away) in the Inn valley; in the afternoon they took the train along the valley to Kufstein, where their trunks were waiting for them on the German side of the border. After taking things out of their trunks – and probably a quick change of clothes – they despatched the trunks to Mayrhofen, which was their immediate destination. They stayed overnight in Kufstein, under the shadow of the castle; travelled back to Jenbach by train next day and got themselves the 30 km. from Jenbach along the Ziller valley to Mayrhofen, just in the foothills of the Alps. They would have walked some of the way; it would have been odd if they had not also taken the little narrow-gauge railway which runs within sight of the road almost the whole distance. It was Friday night, 9th August: the journey from Icking had taken them five days of most energetic travel.[77]

In Mayrhofen they had arranged to meet David Garnett, and Garnett was expecting his friend Harold Hobson (i. 443 n. 4); while waiting for Garnett to arrive, Lawrence and Frieda stayed in a farmhouse at the end of the village, at the foot of the mountains, 'just by a lovely stream' – the Ziller itself – 'that tears along, and is as bright as glass' (i. 433). They spent their days walking up into the hills; Lawrence probably discovered the extraordinary crucifix in the Klamm gorge which he described in 'Christs in the Tirol'. He worked on his essays about the journey and wrote a couple of poems to which he gave local place names; he may even have done some work on 'Once—!' and 'Paul Morel'.[78] 'Sometimes we drink with the mountain peasants in the Gasthaus, and dance a little. – And how we love each other – God only knows' (i. 441). In the letters Lawrence was now writing we find a continual excitement about his new experience. In a letter to his old Eastwood friend Sallie Hopkin he remarked that

For ourselves, Frieda and I have struggled through some bad times into a wonderful naked intimacy, all kindled with warmth, that I know at last is love. I think I ought not to blame women, as I have done, but myself, for taking my love to the wrong women, before now. Let every man find, keep on trying till he finds, the woman who can take him and whose love he can take, then who will grumble about men or about women. But the thing must be two-sided. At any rate, and whatever happens, I do love, and I am loved – I have given and I have taken – and that is eternal. Oh, if only people could marry properly, I believe in marriage. (i. 440–1)

It was particularly important that he should have written that to Sallie Hopkin: 'my very close friend', as he described her in a presentation copy of *Love Poems* in 1913.[79] During his engagement of 1911 he had asked her for her thoughts about Louie Burrows: 'tell me where I am wrong – since you put your head on one side and close your eyes so shrewdly' (i. 261). Now he admits 'taking my love to the wrong women, before now'. And, as that letter also suggests, Lawrence's work would henceforth be addressed – like a true Pauline epistle – to the needs of his own generation, seen from a distance but known intimately. What his letters show better than anything else is how concerned Lawrence was to articulate what was happening to him. Like, perhaps, much of his experience, it was not wholly his own, certainly not capable of becoming (as he wanted it to be) anyone else's, until it had been written about. 'The being able to express one's soul keeps one alive . . .'

They stayed in Mayrhofen just over a fortnight, joined for the second week by Garnett, and Hobson a few days later still. Lawrence and Hobson got on very well, and indeed all four seem to have had a riotously happy time. On Monday 26 August, Lawrence and Frieda sent off their trunks to Bolzano, the first really Italian place they thought they would come to on the road south, and the four set off to trek over the Pfitscherjoch pass. After the first day's walk up the blue-and-white-marked path, they slept in a hay-hut somewhere beyond Ginzling, with Garnett the outdoor expert giving directions; the following afternoon they reached the Dominicus-Hütte (see Illustration 47 for the postcard of it Lawrence sent to his sister Ada) and stayed overnight, a couple of hours below the Pfitscherjoch.

That evening, Lawrence and Garnett went scrambling off up the mountain sides looking for flowers to go into the botanist Garnett's collection; while they were gone, Lawrence later learned, Frieda and Harold Hobson made love in a hay-hut. It had not been the first time that Frieda had exerted in practice her belief in free sex; in Metz she had had Udo von Henning, while Garnett believed that, during the weeks in Icking, Frieda had once swum over to an island in the Isar and made love to a woodcutter.[80] It is impossible to say whether this was really true, or a story Frieda invented to torment Lawrence (or excite Garnett). Bavarian woodcutters are canny, not to say superstitious folk, and probably not susceptible to the charms of upper-class women emerging from rivers. But at the Dominicus-Hütte, she wanted Hobson, he wanted her – and it was a certain way of proving that she might be walking to Italy with Lawrence, but was still decidedly her own woman. (*Mr Noon* provides a most amusing and bitter account of Gilbert – when he learns about Johanna's unfaithfulness – being extremely and unselfishly forgiving in a way which she finds most annoying: 'forgiveness is a humiliating thing to the one forgiven'.[81]) Lawrence had to come to terms with Frieda's belief in her erotic potential, both now and later; if he believed – like her – in the power and importance of instinct and the fulfilment of the self, then he had to accept it. It was, anyway, a change for Lawrence to find himself in the role of the partner having to forgive the other's unfaithfulness.

On the third day, the Wednesday, the party set off for potentially the hardest day's walk. It was eight hours to Sterzing, their destination, and there can be snow on the 2600-metre-high Pfitscherjoch pass even in August: none of them was equipped for mountain walking. But in spite of the snow and the cold, they had no problems. They ate out of doors at the summit of the pass, with the most wonderful view across to mountains beyond (the Grabspitze prominent) and down into the green valley below; then they scrambled down the steep path to Stein, where they rejoined the road and stopped in an inn to eat and drink. It was taking them longer than they had planned, however; there was a good deal to look at, including the extraordinary and bloody 'Christus im Elend' in the chapel at Wieden, which deeply impressed Lawrence and which he described in both 'Christs in the Tirol' and *Mr Noon*.[82] Baedeker reckons on $5\frac{1}{2}$–6 hours from the Pfitscherjoch to Sterzing, and Lawrence was keen to get there that night; but by nightfall they were probably no further than the lonely 'Gasthof Elefant', still 10 km. short of Sterzing. Here they stayed, and Garnett and Hobson walked on at three in the morning to catch the early train from Sterzing: Hobson was probably acutely aware of his guilty secret about Frieda (which he had not even confessed to Garnett), and happy to leave without seeing Lawrence again. At any rate, they left Lawrence and Frieda to make a more leisurely descent to Sterzing the following day. Lawrence and Frieda were particularly tired: they had had three consecutive days of hard walking since leaving Mayrhofen. After starting late and wandering slowly down the road towards Sterzing, past the wayside Christ which in 'Christs in the Tirol' Lawrence described as 'very elegant, brushed and combed', they arrived in the afternoon and decided to stay a few days.[83]

But, unlike Mayrhofen, Sterzing was no paradise. (*Mr Noon* describes the extraordinary W.C. and the mediaeval town which leaves Gilbert and Johanna 'never very happy' there.[84]) They arrived on the afternoon of Thursday 29 August: on the morning of Sunday 1 September they left again, heading for Meran and Bolzano, to collect their trunks. This meant going over the Jaufenpass (again over 2,000 metres high) and staying at the Sterzinger Jaufen-Haus; but Lawrence had worked out a route which – though not in Baedeker – looked both easier and quicker than the winding motor road.

It was on this stretch of the journey that things went seriously wrong. Lawrence wrote to David Garnett how they 'had the most terrific scramble here, worse by far than the Pfitscher Joch. Frieda lost her patience utterly' (i. 445). After a full day's fairly gentle walking up the valley of the Jau-fenbach from Sterzing, in late afternoon they faced a steep climb up to the last hamlet and then a further exhausting couple of hours up even steeper slopes to the top. They lost the path, and the route they took (probably beside the stream) went up even steeper than the proper track. Around half-past eight at night, 'Frieda dead with weariness, I furious for having come the wrong way, the night rolling up filthy and black from out of a Hell of a gulf below us, a wind like a razor, cold as ice' (i. 450), they faced the final climb. And according to the version in *Mr Noon*, Frieda chose that moment to break the news about Hobson and herself, in order to punish Lawrence and to assert her freedom from him. And he forgave her: much to her annoyance.

Worse was to come. Their final desperate and exhausted scramble on to the path at the top of the pass, half an hour later, brought them out with the lights of the Sterzinger Jaufen-Haus rather below them, over to the right; they staggered down to the hut, had a meal and went to bed. The following morning, coming out on to the road, Lawrence assumed that they had already come over the top of the pass itself to the Passierer Jaufen-Haus, and were now facing the way down to Italy on the far side. All day, accordingly, they followed the zig-zagging road downwards, into the valley which they imagined contained Meran. In fact they were walking back to Sterzing, down the motor road they had avoided the previous day. It was not until four in the afternoon that Lawrence realised that they had spent two hard days walking, and one desperate and shattering late-evening scramble, getting absolutely nowhere. It was bitterly disappointing: Lawrence would again have been furious with himself for having made such a stupid mistake. It was of a piece with Frieda's announcement: they were back where they started, no romantic heights had been scaled or sustained. They crept back into Sterzing, could not face returning to their old lodging, went on to the station and spent some of their carefully hoarded money on a fast train to Bolzano that same night. Lawrence was prime conserver of their money: but he could not now have resisted Frieda's demand for a train (and according to *Mr Noon* a meal on the train, too.[85])

The whole of this part of the journey turned out to be an anticlimax and a disappointment. They effectively gave up walking after the disaster of the Jaufenpass and the awful return to Sterzing; thereafter they took trains, though they knew they could not afford them. Lawrence's trousers (bought with Jessie Chambers long ago, and known as 'Miriam's trousers') were frayed, his old straw hat 'shapeless and puffed up' (i. 455); Frieda's red-velvet hatband had dribbled colour over her battered panama hat. (In *Mr Noon* Johanna is obliged to keep her thick Burberry raincoat on, in all the heat of summer, to hide the state of her dress.)[86] After disliking Bolzano – 'beautiful but beastly' (i. 450) – where their trunks had arrived, they tried the next main station down the line, Trento. This was the first really Italian place on their journey, though in 1912 still well inside the Austrian border. It gave them a horrible overnight lodging with bugs on the walls and a disgusting lavatory. The following morning, their tramp-like appearance and lack of Italian meant that they had at least one door slammed in their faces as they tried to find a room to rent. Frieda – 'much to Lawrence's dismay' – burst into tears by the statue of Dante in the gardens next to the railway station: 'He had seen me walk barefoot over icy stubble, laughing at wet and hunger and cold it [sic] had all seemed only fun to me, and here I was crying because of the city-uncleanness and the WC's.'[87] On such things depend futures; because Trento's privies were horrible, Lawrence and Frieda gave up the idea of staying there, went back to the station, saw a picture of Riva on a poster of the Lago di Garda and decided to return to their original idea of going there. It was too far to walk and they had – anyway – given up walking; on the evening of Wednesday 4 September they arrived by train in Riva, on the northern shore of the lake. And Riva, 'quite beautiful, and perfectly Italian' (i. 447), was the Italy they had dreamed of and longed for. The lake was wonderful, purple and emerald green, and in spite of their awful appearance they were rented a room by two little old ladies in a beautiful villa for 2/6 a day. Lawrence described the brilliance of the roses and oleanders and how everywhere 'the grapes are ripe – vineyards with great weight of black bunches hanging in shadow' (i. 448). The German name for Riva – *Reif*, ripe – was exactly how they found it. They got their trunks and Frieda's sister Johanna sent her some fashionable hats, which doubtless helped compensate for her initial weather-stained appearance. They had come almost as far as they needed and determined to settle for the winter.

But their money was now very short – 'The fear of money frets me a bit' (i. 448), Lawrence noted – and even 2/6 a day was too much. Further down the lake, actually over the border into Italy, was the village of Gargnano, accessible from the north only by boat. And the wife of the landlord of the Hotel Al Cervo in Gargnano was a Bavarian, Maria Samuelli. She sent them on to one of the local landlords, Pietro de Paoli. In Villa, a quarter of a mile beyond Gargnano itself, for only three guineas a month they could have a whole floor of the Villa Igea – just along the road from the Villa de Paoli – with rooms looking out over the lake (see Illustration 49). They moved down there on 18 September; and exactly when they needed it to pay the rent, £50 from Duckworth for *The Trespasser* arrived on 16 September – 'in notes – the angel!' (i. 453). They could settle, and Lawrence could once more start to write, in this place 'lovely as a dream' (i. 475).

And so began Lawrence's relationship with Italy. We must not romanticise it; to start with, he and Frieda were both utter strangers. Neither could speak Italian; they were extraordinarily isolated, even with German hotel-keepers in Riva and Gargnano. Nor could they get very far from the past, however much they felt it lay behind them, the far side of the Alps. Letters always managed to get through: 'yards and yards and yards' from Weekley to Frieda's mother were sent on. 'He writes', said Lawrence, 'that I am honest, but no gentleman, and when F. quarrels with me, she will find her mistake – that I am selfish etc etc' (i. 448); but he also wrote how Frieda should give up her children 'um ihr unschuldiges Leben nicht ganz zu verpfuschen [so as not to make a total mess of their innocent lives]'.[88] Frieda's despair over the loss of her children was perhaps never so acute as in the Villa Igea. In her unfinished memoirs (mostly written in the third person), she gave an account of so badly missing her children, during the winter, that she felt 'she could stand no more': she goes down to the lake, takes her clothes off and lets the lake water lap over her: 'Her arms and legs relaxed, she sank back in the water.'[89] If Lawrence was isolated, at least he had his work to occupy him. In spite of finding '2 woman friends, most eminently and superbly respectable' (i. 476) – one was a schoolteacher member of the local superior family, Signora Feltrinelli, the other probably Maria Samuelli – Frieda had very little but Lawrence, the parcels of books which English friends sent out to them and the tormenting letters. After four months in the Villa Igea, Lawrence knew that he must not 'bury Frieda alive' in their next home (i. 501).

Yet that autumn and winter were tremendously important for them as a couple, and for Lawrence's work as a writer. At last they were a couple, planning a future; the past was both acutely present and oddly distanced in such a place and in such isolation: it was a distance which was crucial for *Sons and Lovers*. They could both look back on the past; and once again ask whether they had indeed grown beyond its patterns. The final creation of *Sons and Lovers* out of the 'Paul Morel' drafts constituted Lawrence's final break with the past: his own past and his past as a writer. Yet the novel had to be more than a simple break; he needed to overcome what belonged to the past within him. Perhaps he could have found nowhere better to do that than in a new country, with a newly liberated (but still independent) woman beside him, looking out over the marvellous lake, knowing every second that he was in an utterly new world; and there finally remaking the old one.

SONS AND LOVERS

I Coming Out Myself

'I *loathe* Paul Morel': thus, on 22 July, just before starting its last revision, Lawrence had contemplated his novel and his hero. He had been writing a letter about life with Frieda in Icking:

Here, in this tiny savage little place, F. and I have got awfully wild. I loathe the idea of England, and its enervation and misty miserable modernness. I *don't* want to go back to town and civilisation. I want to rough it and scramble through, free, free. I don't want to be tied down. And I can live on a tiny bit. I shan't let F leave me, if I can help it. I feel I've got a mate and I'll fight tooth and claw to keep her. She says I'm reverting, but I'm not – I'm only coming out wholesome and myself. Say I'm right, and I ought to be always common. I *loathe* Paul Morel. (i. 427)

He is making the old division between the sensitive, artistic person – the 'Paul Morel' he still was – and the sensual, common man he also insisted he was. But the letter also shows him admonishing himself about a proper attitude to his past and to his past sympathies: Paul Morel – with his sensitivity, his artistic temperament, his incipient middle classness, his still-lingering similarity to Cyril Beardsall and Cecil Byrne – was growing loathsome. Lawrence gave himself a day 'in thought (?)', to contemplate the novel; and then, with Garnett's 'awfully nice and detailed' (i. 427) notes beside him – only a few jottings of which survive – he started it again.[1]

Only ten days later, he and Frieda would be making final preparations to leave Icking and travel over the Alps to Italy. He had not time to do very much to the novel. And yet, in Icking and before setting out on the journey south, Lawrence managed to rewrite the first seventy-six pages of his novel (chapters I and II, and a few pages of chapter III) into practically their final form. Because the pages of 'Paul Morel' which he rejected still survive, it is possible to see exactly in what direction he was now working.[2]

The structure of the first two chapters was very much the same in the old 'Paul Morel' and in what he was now writing: similar events in a similar order. He inserted thirty-eight new pages, and reused thirty-three old ones. However, the final version makes far more use of the character of William; his rushing home from school and going to the Wakes have no equivalent in

'Paul Morel': and there are indications, too, that William's 'love for his mother' is 'vexing his young growth' rather than simply revealing him '⟨very thoughtful for his mother⟩'.[3] That is in accordance with the way Lawrence was starting to use William in the final manuscript; the novel, from the very beginning, was on its way to deserving the title Lawrence first suggested in October 1912, *Sons and Lovers*, with William as well as Paul affected by his mother's love for him. (It is also something which has been minimised for the novel's readers during the last eighty years, because of extensive cuts made before publication by Edward Garnett in episodes concerning William in the first third of the novel: Garnett cut the sentence about William's growth being vexed, for example.)

The primary narrative episode in these first seventy-six pages, in which Walter Morel goes to Nottingham for a day of holiday and returns home to turn Mrs Morel out of the house, shows how 'Paul Morel' had itself grown and developed. Lawrence had first written this section of the novel in Croydon in November 1911 before falling ill, and (beneath later revisions) the old pages of 'Paul Morel' show what he had then written. A description of the trials and tribulations of Mrs Morel had culminated in a lengthy passage showing her waiting for her husband to come home: she sits working at her sewing, 'churning her bitterness. As she sewed the baby-clothes, she cast her thoughts backwards and forwards, like a shuttle across the years of her life, weaving her own philosophy from the yarn of her experience.' Such sentences had demonstrated the habit of extended and precious metaphor which Lawrence had employed so often in *The White Peacock* and in *The Trespasser*; another sentence, astonishingly, had originally compared Mrs Morel to 'a wild fish stifling in the warm room'.[4]

In the course of revision of this chapter, either immediately in 1911 or sometime early in 1912, Lawrence cut the 'wild fish' comparison completely and deleted 'the yarn of' in the other passage: the metaphor is made less precious, though it still dominates the sentence. In November 1911 he had continued the passage with the sentence quoted in chapter 5 about Mrs Morel being like an artist, 'uncaught by life, watching', leading on to a sequence of would-be impressive and rather empty statements about women in general: how '⟨They take a man almost as a flower takes a bee: and if he be a fly, a drone, a creeping insect, a mere despoiler, they reject him and starve him.⟩'[5] These were along the lines of things he had written into *The Trespasser* in January 1912. In November 1911, Lawrence had also described how Walter Morel 'had given his wife children, according to the doctrine of Schopenhauer. But he would not take from her, and help her to produce, the other finer products, blossoms of beautiful living, of which he might make wisdom like honey, and dreams like worship.' Lawrence refers to Schopenhauer's description of the operations of instinct in the production of life: 'nature aims at the preservation of the species, and consequently at as great an increase in it as possible'.[6] In trying to be modern and scientific, however, Lawrence had made it sound as if Morel made love to his wife because he took Schopenhauer seriously.

Between February and June 1912, Lawrence had revised the metaphorical excesses of this passage. He cut Morel's unlikely-sounding 'wisdom like honey and dreams like worship'; and then, at a later date – probably May–June – he had also deleted the whole passage after the sentence describing Mrs Morel as an artist. The Schopenhauerean philosophy of 'the genius of the species',[7] with its associated metaphors, was abandoned: and the passage, which had substantially interrupted the flow of the action, was cut back to a description of Mrs Morel in the kitchen waiting for her husband.

On the other hand, the deletions meant that Lawrence had also removed some interlinear insertions which had started to show Mrs Morel in the new light which the spring 1912 version had developed: for instance, 'Therefore she nourished the souls of her unborn children on her own dissatisfactions. Her passionate yearning entered into her infants, poisoning, as it were, their naïve young spirits.'[8] Jessie Chambers, if she had observed such deletions, would have concluded that Lawrence was again trying to justify his mother: Walter de la Mare, who read the novel at Heinemanns in June 1912 and commented that 'the real theme of the story is not arrived at till half way through' (i. 424 n. 1), would have found such deletions helping to obscure one potential theme. However, Mrs Morel was still sending 'her thoughts backwards and forwards, like a shuttle' in the version of the novel Lawrence sent to Heinemann in June; a good deal of such florid metaphorical writing remained.

On the other hand, there had also been some judicious development of the study of the Morels as partners. The passage in the 'Paul Morel' sent to Heinemann in June had culminated in Mr Morel's arrival home:

It is a question whether she was more intoxicated with suffering than her husband with drink. He came at about twenty past eleven. He was not drunk, but in that wound-up state of intoxication whose precious calm and equipoise is easily shaken, when a little readjustment is irritating to make, when real thwarting maddens. He was perfectly amiable and serene when he got to the garden gate. But the latch was hard to find, and then it was stiff, so he swore nastily. He was sufficiently drunk to be oblivious of everybody save himself.

There was a step up from the scullery to the kitchen. The kitchen door was open.

He entered the scullery, a kind of porch, quite decently, but he stumbled up the step into the living room, into his wife's presence. He was not used to the house. She started up, a wave of madness going over her like flame.

"A nice way to come in—!" she cried.

"They shouldna put the fool's step there!" he said, loudly.

"It's not the step—it's the drunken nuisance that falls over it," she vibrated.

"Who's a drunken nuisance?" he resented, bullying.[9]

In Icking, Lawrence rewrote the episode completely. The new version is far simpler. There are now no extended metaphors, no preliminary commentary upon Mrs Morel, no analysis of 'women'; and where previously Mrs Morel had sat and sewed, the focus of her work is now a large saucepan in which she is boiling herb beer. She is working at it at the crucial moment of her husband's arrival: 'Mrs Morel took a panchion, a great bowl of thick red earth, streamed a heap of white sugar into the bottom, and then, straining herself to the weight, was pouring in the liquor. Just then, Morel came in . . .' The passage is focusing upon a man coming in after a day's holiday, and a still working woman: the fact that his wife is visibly 'straining' and inwardly furious, while Morel this time is not only tipsy but ill, irritable and guilty, creates an explosive situation. He brushes against the table:

The boiling liquor pitched. Mrs Morel started back.

"Good gracious," she cried, "coming home in his drunkenness!"

"Comin' home in his what—?" he snarled, his hat over his eye.

Suddenly her blood rose in a jet.

"Say you're *not* drunk!" she flashed.[10]

The 'boiling liquor' (a marvellous analogy for the situation) is dangerous and easily spilled: it suggests both Mrs Morel's unrelenting work for the household and the violence just below the surface of the marriage. As Mrs Morel strains to hold the pan, we are also reminded that she is pregnant. On the other hand, Lawrence not only cut the slightly wordy but also convincing analysis of exactly how tipsy Mr Morel is – something which had revealed a common human situation – but in his Icking revision he also made him much more violent. Morel is no longer 'amiable and serene' as he nears the house; he not only fumbles with the gate but kicks it open and breaks the latch; he does not simply fall up a step which is new to him and swear.[11] At his worst – and mostly when provoked by his wife – Morel had been 'bullying' in 'Paul Morel'; but in the Icking revision he snarls, he does not only speak loudly; while his 'hat over his eye' makes him both villainous and slightly ridiculous.

Mrs Morel's reaction is explained, in both accounts, by her own lonely and depressed state; but 'Paul Morel', by comparing her 'intoxication' to Mr

Morel's, had brought out an odd similarity in their feelings: it had shown an inevitable quarrel betwen two unhappy and irritable people. The Icking revision now made Mrs Morel more self-righteously angry: she takes the chance of a confrontation, just as her husband is confronting her. And where 'Paul Morel' had described Mrs Morel having her husband's 'soul in charge' – 'Like a sheep dog, she tried to keep him from straying. She barked in front of him, she fought with him. In two words, she turned the point of ⟨one of⟩ his own petty meannesses back into himself. He could not endure moral suffering: it drove him mad' – Mrs Morel's attitude is now far less forgiving and much more dangerous: 'She fought to make him undertake his own responsibilties, to make him fulfil his own obligations. But he was too different from her. His nature was purely sensuous, and she strove to make him moral, religious. She tried to force him to face things. He could not endure it—it drove him out of his mind.'[12]

These revisions are characteristic of those made in Icking. Lawrence is tightening the drama and cutting down on the metaphors; but he is also creating a new and dangerous feeling of moral superiority in Mrs Morel, while simultaneously making Mr Morel more violent, irresponsible and selfish, and unable to cope with his wife because he is 'too different'. The situation now shows Mrs Morel and her husband opposing each other because their marriage makes it inevitable. But Mrs Morel is now also rather frightening in her rigidity and her intense anger; her helplessness is not so significant. She is less to be sympathised with than understood: Lawrence has got a clue as to why she behaves as she does towards her children and to her husband. Where, in November 1911, he had written quite uncritically and rather ingenuously how 'The pity was' that Mrs Morel was 'too much above' her husband, he now wrote: 'The pity was, she was too much his opposite.'[13] It was the dreadful marriage of opposites which Lawrence began to create in those ten days in Icking: the first of his sequence of such fictional marriages: the first fruits, perhaps, of his finding in Frieda his own necessary adversary. He was also starting to turn his parents' lives into something schematic and fictional: the substance of a novel, not of an autobiography.

However, the final manuscript was now in danger of splitting Mrs Morel into two – the loving, caring, deeply sympathetic mother on the one hand, the ruthless moral martinet on the other; the two sides are only just perceived as aspects of each other. She is now seen as dangerous, and as partly responsible for the quarrels, but her point of view also regularly dominates the narrative of the marriage. Mr Morel also tended to become incoherent; although he is schematically an 'opposite', a sensual man in an intolerable position, and although the novel's narrative no longer simply supports Mrs Morel in her superior attitude towards him, there is still a very great deal of one-sided commentary in the book. And Mr Morel is not only made more drunken, and more violent: he is treated less forgivingly in other ways too. In 'Paul Morel', for example, he had been especially nice to his children when going off for his day out: 'He gave the two children a half-penny each. That was their share of the holiday, for their mother had not a penny to spare. William and Annie thought him generous. They got more pennies from him than from their mother, who was rather stern in the matter.' In the Icking revision, that passage was cut and exactly the opposite point made: Morel 'scarcely spared the children an extra penny, or bought them a pound of apples. It all went in drink.'[14] As if to give him 'character', Mr Morel is made meaner, more violent, more drunken and more unpleasant. Although Lawrence could start to create the women of his novel differently, he could not yet see a way – other than a moral way – of recreating the men. He later reacted against the 'dodge' of 'putting a thick black line' round his characters 'to throw out the composition' (i. 522): the portrait of Mr Morel was probably just the kind of thing he had in mind. In Icking he also cut a lengthy and rather attractive episode in the previous 'Paul Morel' drafts, in which Mr Morel's friend Jerry comes to see him when he is off work following his brain fever contracted on the Wakes day. Jerry secretly supplies him with beer (and parsley afterwards to take away the smell). The episode had had the effect of confirming that Mr Morel was rather self-pitying but not especially outrageous. Lawrence introduced instead a completely new episode at the end of the second chapter, in which Mr Morel pretends to leave home but never gets his bundle further than the coal-house at the bottom of the garden: Mrs Morel's discovery of it shows her husband up as both a bully and a coward.[15] In his portrayal of Mr Morel, for all his new and schematising fictional distance, Lawrence was still not able to free his writing (or himself) of the kinds of judgement which his experience had continually encouraged him to make upon his own father: and he more sharply defined the character's weaknesses, even though he was beginning to be clear about what was frightening and dangerous in Mrs Morel. He also found himself, in this final version of the novel, maintaining the status of a narrator who frequently shares the attitude of moral superior-ity in Mrs Morel – something he had also begun to see as a dangerous kind of emotional compensation.

II Italy

After completing the first seventy-six pages in Icking at the end of July, Lawrence probably did very little more work on the novel before settling in

Riva and then in Villa, in September. By 7 September – only two days after arriving in Riva – he was reading bits of the novel to Frieda, 'glad to be settling down, to get at that novel. I am rather keen on it' (i. 448). By 11 September he was 'working like Hell' at it: 'F. hates me for it, because it divides my attention' (i. 451). On the 17th – still in Riva, the day before they moved to Villa – he was at the 'labour of love' of shaping the book 'into form' (i. 455).

It was significant that Lawrence's revisions in Icking to those first seventy-six pages had not made Mr Morel more sympathetic. After Frieda, Italy was the most important new experience Lawrence had in these years. His very first letters about Italy had described its beauty and the happiness with which it filled him; but his months besides the Lago di Garda made him aware of the possibilities of Italy for symbolising the unconscious and the sensual: in which he had always believed, and knew was part of his own nature, but had always lacked expression for and confidence in. In 1911, for example, he had written about himself and the Italians in an opera company he had been to see in Croydon: 'if you were here tonight we'd go to *Carmen*, and hear those delicious little Italians love and weep. I am just as emotional and impulsive as they, by nature. It's the damned climate and upbringing and so on that make me cold-headed as mathematics' (i. 247). Italy helped him find his own sensibility illuminated by the lives he was now seeing around him. Frieda remembered the importance of Garda: 'Italy was a happy revelation for him'.[16] It was from beside the Lago di Garda that he would tell his artist acquaintance Ernest Collings, in January 1913, in phrases which have become famous, that 'My great religion is a belief in the blood, the flesh, as being wiser than the intellect' (i. 503). Lawrence made a direct link between that belief and his experience of Italy: 'That is why I like to live in Italy. The people are so unconscious. They only feel and want: they don't know. We know too much. No, we only *think* we know such a lot ...' (i. 504). It is not a new language for Lawrence, although it is now for the first time consciously articulated; it actually coheres perfectly with what he had believed 'when I was about twenty' (ii. 470). So that, for example, the new language chimed exactly with the way he had written about Walter Morel at the end of 1911. 'I conceive', he told Collings in January 1913, 'a man's body as a kind of flame, like a candle flame forever upright and yet flowing' (i. 503). He had written in 'Paul Morel' in November 1911 how Gertrude Coppard is attracted by Walter Morel: 'the dusky, golden softness of his sensuous flame of life, that flowed from off his flesh like the flame from a candle, not baffled and gripped into incandescence by thought and spirit as her life was, seemed to her something wonderful, beyond her'.[17] But Italy would give Lawrence the confidence of such language and such insight, as well as a much deeper awareness and control of it; he could commit himself to phrases about Italian men such as 'I think they haven't many ideas, but they look well, and they have strong blood' (i. 460), while castigating Englishmen for being 'swathed in restraint and puritanism and anti-emotion, until they are walking mummies': 'The flesh has been starved, denied, and impoverished, till it *is* weary, stiff, moribund' (ii. 102). But he would resurrect it: 'The real way of living is to answer to one's wants' (i. 504), he wrote in January 1913: 'Nowadays it costs more courage to assert ones desire and need, than it does to renounce' (i. 486). And it was in Italy that Lawrence would first put into words his belief in the polarity between flesh and spirit, love and law, father and mother; but, significantly, only after writing *Sons and Lovers*.

For although Villa had re-immersed Lawrence in an ordinary working village at times reminiscent of Eastwood – while also being a thorough contrast (for one thing, Lawrence found himself 'ranking here as quite a swell' (i. 505)) – *Sons and Lovers*, after all its vicissitudes, was in essence a novel concerned with elements of the past. Such a novel could not be much concerned with the present or the future; nor could it do what Lawrence began to do either in 1913 in 'The Sisters', or early in the 1920s, rather wistfully – to wish he had given a greater 'justice to his father' in his novel.[18] The way in which Italy *failed* to influence the novel is striking. Of course, the landscape of Garda was hardly that of the English Midlands:

There are vineyards and olive woods and lemon gardens on the hill at the back. There is a lovely little square, where the Italians gossip and the fishermen pull up their boats, just near. Everything is too nice for words – not a bit touristy – quite simply Italian common village ... Everything outside is Italian and weird and tumble-down, and seems to belong to the past ... (i. 453, 458)

But a family at home also 'reminds me so of home when I was a boy. They are all so warm with life. The father reaches his thick brown hand to play with the baby – the mother looks quickly away, catching my eye' (i. 460):

you can go in a wine place – and there's the family at supper by the fireplace, and you drink at another table. The father is a shortish, thick set, strong man – these Italians are *so* muscular – and the wife is straight and I like her – he *clicks-clicks* to the bambino in her arms, across the table. And the white grandfather scolds a little girl, and the old grandmother sits by the fire. And I drink a ¼ litre of red wine for 15 centesimi – about 1¼d – and I love them all. (i. 453)

Villa was a village, too, where – just as in Eastwood – Lawrence came to 'know all about everything'.[19] In December 1912, he would use the inn he went to half a mile away in Bogliaco to help him recreate an English Midlands eighteenth-century inn in the first of the 'Burns Novel' fragments; in Villa itself, the equivalent to Friday night in the English Midlands was Sunday night, when 'all the men get blind drunk' (i. 508). And in January 1913, while living in Villa, Lawrence wrote his most extended work in the dialect of the English Midlands, his play *The Daughter-in-Law*: appropriately, 'neither a comedy nor a tragedy – just ordinary' (i. 500–1).

But the pattern of Lawrence's treatment of the Morel family (father hateful and ignored, mother and children grouped in opposition to him) had been established over two years of writing, and had only been complicated, not altered, in Icking in July. So, for example, he had already written the episode in which Morel goes into the Palmerston Arms for 'a jolly night' to escape from the moral superiority of his family.[20] Italy could reinforce Lawrence's sense of what a family might be like together, 'warm with life'. But his experience of Italy would have far more effect on his subsequent writing than it could on *Sons and Lovers*.

III Frieda and *Sons and Lovers*

It has not, however, been sufficiently recognised how much Frieda influenced Lawrence as he settled into writing the final *Sons and Lovers*. He had always had an instinct for opposition: if Annable in *The White Peacock* had been necessary because otherwise the novel was 'too much *me*', so Frieda's influence would also prevent his writing being 'too much *me*'. She remembered, about their earliest days, 'I gave myself over completely to the adventure of his spirit. That was everything. I had no axe of my own to grind'. But she did; she commented in her biography:

In his heart of hearts I think he always dreaded women, felt that they were in the end more powerful than men. Woman is so absolute and undeniable. Man moves, his spirit flies here and there, but you can't go beyond a woman. From her man is born and to her he returns for his ultimate need of body and soul.[21]

Although Lawrence later remarked that 'I daren't sit in the world without a woman behind me' (i. 503), we can imagine his reaction to Frieda in *that* mood: fascination, outrage and probably violent derision. Her remarks exemplify exactly what he had found he had to cope with in her, and wanted to cope with: her sense of female and sensual superiority, her infuriating 'lack of sense of danger' (i. 406), an opposition which was the more potent because she presented an idea of 'woman' which opposed him almost incidentally. His quarrels with Frieda, however exhausting, were becoming necessary; he was learning that he had to prevent this astonishing, utterly different and deeply loved person from lording it over him, just as he needed *her* to prevent him from dominating. He had chosen in Frieda a woman as self-willed and as 'absolute and undeniable' as his mother had been. It would be nonsense to suggest that he chose Frieda because she resembled his mother, or because he wanted mothering. She was older than he was, and she was a mother; but, sensual, spontaneous, impractical, she bore almost no other resemblance to Lydia Lawrence – except in the one, vital respect that she demanded Lawrence's love and attention while opposing him implacably when she thought him wrong. He both rejoiced in his love for her and in her power, and sought (and needed) to overcome its threat. The contrast with his other women is extreme; none of them was able to stand up to Lawrence, because in the long run none of them wished to. Alice Dax felt frightened of disagreeing with him, Louie felt obliged to put up with him, Helen Corke felt sure she was right and did not bother to oppose him. Even Jessie Chambers, determined and independent, thought he was 'a living manifestation of God'.[22] But Lawrence could hammer out his opposition to Frieda and nevertheless accept what she meant, too: the conflicting (and contrary) states of the human sexes were becoming his natural territory as a writer.

The spring 1912 'Paul Morel' had been the first of his works Frieda had read; she had advised on its revision and then argued it through with him in Riva: 'we fight like blazes over it' (i. 449). During the autumn, she 'lived and suffered' it and 'wrote bits of it when he would ask me: "What do you think my mother felt like then?" I had to go deeply into the character of Miriam and all the others'.[23] Lawrence remarked early in October 1912 how 'I've got a heap of warmth and blood and tissue into that fuliginous [i.e. sooty, dusky] novel of mine – F. says it's her – it would be' (i. 462). By November, she was feeling 'quite responsible for "Paul". I wrote little female bits and lived it over in my own heart' (i. 479). As well as giving advice about Mrs Morel and Miriam, it seems likely that she helped in particular with the portrayal of Clara – the woman who leaves her husband. Frieda occasionally commented on the text, too; where Lawrence had originally written in 'Paul Morel' that 'the trees were blossoming out into shadows, like blossom of dark shape', Frieda inserted an Arabella-like 'hoyty-toyty' over the last phrase. Lawrence altered it to 'coming into shape, all shadow'.[24]

Frieda had also announced proudly to Garnett, in September, that 'I think L. quite missed the point in "Paul Morel". He really loved his mother more than any body, even with his other women, real love, sort of Oedipus, his mother must have been adorable ...' (i. 449). She writes with the assurance of someone putting a thick-headed author straight, but this highly significant moment shows something of what she had gleaned from Otto Gross. Freud's theory of the Oedipus complex had been in print in German since 1899 in *Die Traumdeutung* (translated into English as *The Interpreta-*

tion of Dreams in 1913); but few people outside the circle of professional psychoanalysts would have known about it. But Gross knew it: Frieda must have heard about it from him and passed it on to Lawrence. Frieda's grasp may have been as fragile as her phrase 'sort of Oedipus' suggests, and – without any knowledge of psychoanalysis – Lawrence had as early as December 1910 been in lucid possession of the idea that his mother's love for him had damaged him: 'It has been rather terrible, and has made me, in some respects, abnormal' (i. 190), he had with great candour told Rachel Annand Taylor. 'Nobody can have the soul of me. My mother has had it, and nobody can have it again' (i. 190–1).[25] But Frieda's excitement about what she now thought of as the real heart of the novel was because, in Freud's theory, the child was not rendered abnormal but was naturally dominated by incestuous feelings for its mother and by a desire to murder its father. Freud described a pattern which – although Lawrence had known all its details before – he can never have heard articulated so clearly as a theory; it was doubtless some comfort and reassurance to find that he had been thinking along the same lines as a revolutionary European intellectual. It gave him both clarity and distance; he could now see that it was Paul's growing up *out* of these childish feelings which constituted his crucial development: his killing of Mrs Morel rather than Mr Morel, for example, acquired a very special importance.

But Frieda's other contribution to the novel was quite different. She was a mother who had, in May 1912, for the sake of the man she loved, abandoned home and respectability and children: exactly what Mrs Morel does not and would not do. And she was also – in the words of Otto Gross – 'die Bestätigung in meinem Leben, das blühende und fruchtbare *Ja* [the affirmation in my life, the flowering fruitful yes]': 'das . . . *Weib der Zukunft* [the . . . woman of the future]', the new, liberated and erotically committed woman. She had not grown stunted and warped in marriage, compensating herself by devotion to her children (and stunting them in turn). Nor had she devoted herself to a man. She had kept her freedom, and was now literally on the loose: Gross, Frick, Dowson, von Henning, Lawrence and Hobson were the proof of that. Frieda would later send Weekley some of Gross's letters to help explain why she had left him;[26] Weekley blamed Gross for putting 'these "ideas" into her head' (i. 429).

This, however, almost certainly means that Lawrence also read Gross's letters; they would have offered him a major insight into the politics and language of fin-de-siècle liberation and self-fulfilment; Nietzschean, Freudian, vitalist. They affirmed the idea of the saving sexual relationship outside the bonds of society: they stressed how a sexually liberated woman could escape the trammels of the ordinary and be an inspiration for intellectual and striving men; they showed a passionately thinking man struggling to come to terms with the new and to escape the past. In many ways, they offered Lawrence the themes for his next eight years of writing; and (above all) they offered a way of thinking about Frieda.

What Frieda confronted Lawrence with, as they fought 'like blazes' over the novel, was not Freud but the confident, liberated and possessive woman (and mother) who had to be both loved and resisted. Lawrence's relations with Lydia Lawrence had, in her lifetime, always been conducted with duty, sensitivity and love: but he had no reserve from her and responded to her whole-heartedly. Until she died, she could not really *be* resisted. Violence and anger were taboo – inextricably linked as they were with Lawrence's father. The worst that ever happened between Lawrence and Jessie Chambers had been hard words and looks of anger and alienation: similarly with Helen Corke, Louie Burrows and Alice Dax. Not only were Lawrence's relations with Frieda often violent and frequently vituperative: they were a daily battle and a long-term war against a dominant and domineering opponent: a war which Lawrence felt never must be lost (or won).

What is more, every time Frieda grieved over her abandoned children, she was not only showing Lawrence her inability to accept that she had decided for him and against them but was showing the very desire to sacrifice herself to them which Lawrence found increasingly intolerable. He wrote at length about it to her sister Else in December 1912, in response to yet another letter from Else arguing that Frieda should go back to her children. Else was herself a mother who – Lawrence thought – surely ought to understand:

If Frieda and the children could live happily together, I should say 'Go' – because the happiness of two out of three is sufficient. But if she would only be sacrificing her life, I would not let her go if I could keep her. Because if she brings to the children a sacrifice, that is a curse to them ... if Frieda gave up all to go and live with them, that would sap their strength because they would have to support her life as they grew up. They would not be free to live of themselves – they would first have to live *for her*, to pay back. The worst of sacrifice is that we have to pay back. (i. 486)

There speaks at last the author of *Sons and Lovers*, the creator of Miriam Leivers and Gertrude Morel and the son of Lydia Lawrence. Back in the winter of 1910, Lawrence had himself made a very extraordinary remark about the guidance his mother had given him. He had been comparing himself with Will Holbrook, whose mother had died when he was 12, and had remarked ' "I wonder how I'd have turned out with no hand guiding me into a groove these last eleven years. I wonder ...." He flushed, opened his lips, but closed them again without speaking.'[27] Eleven years earlier

Lawrence had been at Nottingham High School. Again, he had written in December 1910 how – after his mother – 'Nobody can come into my very self again, and breathe me like an atmosphere' (i. 191). Being guided into a groove, being breathed, was love: but as the years went by, Lawrence was resentful as well as loving. In the novel, ideas of controlling motherly love were now linked with an understanding of the dreadful danger of self-sacrifice, and the danger of a possessive mother's children having to pay for living '*for her*'.

We can, then, imagine Lawrence in Riva in September 1912 contemplating his novel, and realising how different its concerns had become from those of his actual situation: how far he had moved on from the position not only of the central character, Paul, but also from the kinds of interest in women and love with which the book was concerned. He was living with a woman and mother who had abandoned her old life and her children for the sake of her fulfilment; in his fiction were a mother and two other women who not only would not, but could not have done that. Miriam and Clara are also self-sacrificing, but hardly ever self-fulfilling; even when Clara gives Paul 'Passion', it exists within the old structures of self-sacrifice and dependency. Lawrence may well have been coming to think that, in real life, the Weekley children were actually rather lucky to be clear of their mother's loving and wilful personality, because mothers like Frieda were clearly selfish and dominating: and if self-sacrificing too, then a real danger to their children. In the fiction, the loving and caring and creative mother is also the manipulative, morally self-righteous and strength-sapping mother, exacting repayment from her children for her dedicated but thwarted life. Paul's other women, too, are presented as wanting to possess the man they love even more than they themselves want to be loved. Frieda Weekley, however possessive of Lawrence's genius, had refused to be any of those people. She did not belong to Lawrence's old world: and Lawrence himself had – so far as he could – left behind its patterns, frustrations and satisfactions when he went away with her.

In such terms, Lawrence had begun not only to understand, but to dramatise his novel. Until his next completed novel 'The Sisters' – which became *The Rainbow* and *Women in Love* – the revised *Sons and Lovers* was Frieda's most important contribution to his writing. Her very existence must have been a provocation to Lawrence not only to recreate Clara – the angry married woman who walks out on her husband (even if she finally goes back to him) – but to recreate Mrs Morel, the married woman who never walks out or back: and Miriam, the self-sacrificing and sullen woman who loses everything: and Mr Morel, who although threatening to leave a nagging wife, never has the courage to do so. In *The White Peacock*, when

Lawrence had shown a father walking out on his wife and family it had been to demonstrate the father's resultant shame, ignominious drunkenness and death. After *Sons and Lovers*, Lawrence would constantly return to the theme of men and women (but especially women) breaking away from their security and risking themselves in their bid for self-fulfilment. When he revised his play *The Widowing of Mrs. Holroyd* in the autumn of 1913, he would show – in a situation very similar to that of *Sons and Lovers* – a loving man tempting a woman to leave the trap of a terrible marriage. Mrs Holroyd cannot in the end respond to the love, though she is far more tempted by it than Mrs Morel would be. Ursula, in *The Rainbow*, breaks free from her past; and in *Women in Love* she finds the man she loves: she also abandons her family. In *The Lost Girl*, Alvina Houghton breaks with her past, and with the expectations of men and marriage her small Midlands mining town has brought her up to accept: she goes away with a thoroughly 'unsuitable' man because she loves him and has been erotically liberated. And, seven years after *Sons and Lovers*, Lawrence revisited the exact territory of the novel and presented, in *Aaron's Rod*, the married collier with a family who does walk out on them, and into his own life. Aaron finds no Frieda, and is baffled; yet he is a kind of belated backward glance at Walter Morel.

That, however, suggests how Lawrence would use his novels after *Sons and Lovers*: to push back the boundaries of the possible – in language, in realisation, in experience itself. Walter Morel is a man too rooted in place and community ever seriously to contemplate leaving it, and Gertrude Morel always puts her children first; but Lawrence subsequently wrote very little about such people. With his third consecutive tragic novel behind him, he embarked on the kind of writing which the tragic and realistic forms of his first three novels did not permit. He wrote novels in which men not only resisted women, and women resisted men, but in which the creativity of both could be fulfilled by new relationships. His novel 'The Sisters', only six months later, would be about 'the establishment of a new relation, or the re-adjustment of the old one, between men and women' (i. 546). *Sons and Lovers*, like *The Trespasser*, could only be 'itself' (i. 358): a final confrontation with the past.

IV Escaping the Past

He had started to rewrite it around 10 September 1912. The work went fast: he averaged around seven large pages a day, in spite of the fact that he had temporarily stopped using any of the old 'Paul Morel' pages. Chapters III–VI were entirely new: William's relationship with 'Gipsy' Western was now both a result of his thwarted emotional growth and a way of opposing his mother: and it agonises him. Lawrence also made extensive revisions to some of the new passages about William as he wrote them: he was focusing sharply upon this feature of the novel, upon the way it was about *sons*. At first, for example, he had written how Mrs Morel was frightened that her son

was not going to come off. He would not get clear through things. They would trammel him up, and he would find himself enmeshed in his circumstances, unable to get any further. And her heart yearned over him. But her inward soul needed fulfilment, relentlessly. So much she had to give to the world, to life, and this she must give through one medium or another. She hoped ⟨for⟩ 'that' William might be this medium. She hoped that he, almost like a lover, might take out of her soul what stuff she had to present to ⟨the⟩ life, and enact it. Some force, some vitality of her own individual soul lay as yet unused. She wanted to get it forth, to give it to the world, through the medium of her son. Mary first, and then Jesus.

He then rewrote it:

Was he going to 'come off'? A grain of anxiety mingled with her pride in him. And she had waited so long for him, she could not bear it if he failed. She did not know what she wanted him to do. Perhaps she only wanted ⟨to be⟩ him to be himself, to develop and bring to fruit all that she had put into him. In him, she wanted to see her life's fruition, that was all. And with all the strength of her soul she tried to keep him strong and balanced and moving straight forwards. But he was baffling, without clarity of purpose. Sometimes he lapsed and was purely like his father. It made her heart sink with dismay and apprehension.[28]

Having first written a panegyric to Mrs Morel and what she has to give 'to the world', Lawrence made the revision far more complex. Mrs Morel is no less dangerous in wanting to see 'her life's fruition', but William is no longer 'almost like a lover'; that insight will grow disturbingly in the reader's mind rather than be made explicit. And Mrs Morel is up against a son who is also his father's son. Whatever had appeared in the spring 'Paul Morel', not until the very end of chapter VIII, 'Strife in Love', did Lawrence now use any of his earlier draft, apart from a short section of pages describing William's death and Paul's subsequent illness. This meant that not only the William passages but the whole of the 'Lad-and-Girl Love' chapter too, describing the start of the relationship between Paul and Miriam, were newly written in Riva and Villa. The comments Jessie had made in March and April had probably been met (so far as Lawrence wanted to meet them) in the draft he had revised in Eastwood and Waldbröl and submitted to Heinemann in June. It may have been Garnett's commentary and was certainly Frieda's influence which now led to his rewriting the chapter completely. On 3 October, he told Garnett that he was doing his novel

447

'well, I'm sure. It's half done' (i. 458).[29] On 4 October, he was thinking of altering the title (i. 460), but did not say to what.

By 15 October, however, telling Garnett that he had done '3/5 of Paul Morel', he asked 'Can I call it *Sons and Lovers*?' (i. 462). This extremely important moment came when he was around page 300: the 'Strife in Love' chapter ends (with a sequence of pages reused from the spring 'Paul Morel') on p. 304. It was at the end of that chapter that, in 'Paul Morel', Lawrence had given his clearest sign yet of Paul's love for his mother being in some degree abnormal, in the scene of Morel's angry and brutal return to find his son kissing Mrs Morel. The writing of the scene had however predated Lawrence's first meeting with Frieda; and – with Lawrence actually reusing the old 'Paul Morel' pages – it appeared with only small revisions in *Sons and Lovers*. It demonstrates that from sources like *Hamlet* Lawrence had understood the incest motif in the relationship of Paul and his mother (appropriately named Gertrude) before he had even heard of Freud; but doubtless Frieda (and, at the back of her, Gross) could confirm its accuracy. The tiny revisions he now made show he realised even more clearly what the scene meant. Mr Morel, coming in, had originally 'sneeringly' said ' "Hatching mischief again?" ' Now, 'venomously', he says, ' "At your mischief again?" ': as if he angrily recognises something in Paul's behaviour which before he had only suspected. The title *Sons and Lovers* was a fitting sign that, around 15 October, Lawrence had completed that scene, and – although altering it very little – was now investing it, Paul and Mrs Morel with the new significance which his writing about William had initiated. That, however, was characteristic of Lawrence's revisions. He was not, after all, writing a new novel: he was discovering things the old novel could articulate. And it was at last breaking away from the compulsions inherent in his autobiographical material: it was becoming a more complete fiction.

When, later in October and in November, he came to write about the sexual relationshp of Paul and Miriam and their final break in chapter XI, Lawrence once again reworked a chapter he had heavily revised in Eastwood, Waldbröl and Icking, following Jessie's desperate criticisms of the novel in March.[30] What he now did was crucial. Yet again he rewrote half the chapter: but this time he presented a particularly angry Paul. For the first time, Paul feels strongly that Miriam's love for him has not been real. Pretending to love him, she

had deceived him. She had despised him when he thought she worshipped him. She had let him say wrong things, and had not contradicted him. She had let him fight alone. But it stuck in his throat, that she had despised him whilst he thought she worshipped him. She should have told him when she found fault with him. She had not played fair. He hated her. All these years, she had treated him as if he were a hero, and thought of him secretly as an infant, a foolish child. Then why had she left the foolish child to his folly. His heart was hard against her.[31]

Paul's sense of betrayal, and demand for emotional plain-speaking and straightforwardness, are matched by Lawrence's creation of a kind of impotent anger in Miriam that she is still bound by him by her love for him.

She sat full of bitterness. She had known—oh well she had known. All the time he was away from her, she had summed him up, seen his littleness, his meanness, and his folly. Even she had guarded her soul against him. She was not overthrown, nor prostrated, not even much hurt. She had known. Only why, as he sat there, had he still this strange dominance over her. His very movements fascinated her as if she were hypnotised by him. Yet he was despicable, false, inconsistent, and mean. Why this bondage for her? Why was it the movement of his arm stirred her as nothing else in the world could? Why was she fastened to him? Why even now, if he looked at her and commanded her, would she have to obey? She would obey him now, in his trifling commands. But once he was obeyed, then she had him in her power, she knew, to lead him where she would. She was sure of herself. Only, this new influence! [i.e. Clara] Ah, he was not a man, he was a baby that cries for the newest toy. And all the attachment of his soul would not keep him. Very well, he would have to go. But he would come back, when he had tired of his new sensation.[32]

These passages offer a radically new account of the Paul–Miriam relationship: and although Paul's petulance is clear, the analysis offers a savage account of Miriam's frustrated hatred and contempt for Paul, her desire for power over him, her knowledge that she will get that power if she obeys him, and the manipulations she will use to get it. For the first time, Lawrence is making Miriam a deeply disturbed and frustrated character: a real forerunner of Hermione in *Women in Love*. The analysis shows precisely what Frieda remembered Lawrence trying to do in Villa: 'understand his relationship with Jessie and why he did not want to marry Jessie': 'I had to listen to him by the hour as he tried to understand her and their relationship'.[33] His continued thinking about the real person helped create this desperately yet helplessly egotistical fictional character, whose frustrated anger and contempt are all she has left after Paul abandons her. The analysis shows Lawrence now developing a character according to his own fictional logic – not according to the patterns of real life. He was creating a pattern of manipulative and frustrated desire: and he was concluding that what Miriam wanted was possession and power, to make up for her deep unhappiness. It was part of Lawrence's new emotional range as a writer that he could create such a character; and a sign of his ruthlessness that he should do so upon a basis of his feelings about Jessie Chambers. It hurt her more than anything else he ever did; he sent her his spare set of proofs of the novel in March 1913. He knew what the effect would be, telling his sister Ada 'You will see,

449

when you have read those proofs, why I sent them to J[essie]' (i. 531). The effect was devastating. Jessie wrote to Helen Corke:

Yesterday morning came the proofs of *Sons and Lovers* which makes no pleasant reading for me. I really can't think why David should have wished me to read the proofs, since nothing now can be altered. He must be extraordinarily inconsiderate. I shouldn't care if it didn't make me so sick, all this turmoil of emotionalism . . . The Miriam part of the novel is a slander, a fearful treachery. David has selected every point which sets off Miriam at a disadvantage, and he has interpreted her every word and action, and thought in the light of Mrs. Morel's hatred of her. Well, there's no altering things now . . . If I am to live at all it will be necessary to put David out of my life: – to ignore him entirely in thought and speech, there is no other way . . . I am sick, sick to death of David and all that concerns him.[34]

She had been destroying his old letters to her, tearing out his dedications in books. Now she sent back the letter accompanying the proofs: 'quite an inoffensive letter, I think' (i. 545), Lawrence commented – 'still, if J. did it on purpose – all the better' (i. 531). He never heard from her again: he had opened up another gap between him and the past. The person and the writer he was becoming, with Frieda, seemed a world away from the man who had struggled for so many years with Jessie and who had still been struggling only a few months earlier.

Perhaps not surprisingly, Lawrence seems to have taken a break from the novel after creating that chapter. Before going back to it and writing the 'last hundred or so pages', which he knew would be difficult – 'those I funk' (i. 466) – he turned to something else altogether: a play, *The Fight For Barbara*, entirely drawn from the events of the spring, summer and autumn of 1912. It must have been a great relief from the analysis of emotions in the novel: it existed entirely in dialogue, not in suppressed feeling articulated by a narrator. The play escaped both the past and Lawrence's profound need to write his way out of it. It was also something which directly concerned Frieda, just when she might have been becoming dubious about her contribution to the novel's account of female power play. In *The Fight for Barbara*, the married woman Barbara Tressider has eloped to Italy with the working-class Jimmy Wesson: her family and husband try to get her back – the latter, according to Frieda, using Weekley's 'very words' (i. 467). But although Barbara in the play is entirely drawn from Frieda, Lawrence makes her childless.[35] As a result, the most poignant aspect of Lawrence's and Frieda's situation was not transferred to a play which in almost every other way drew on their everyday life. He was clearly steering clear of the subject which continued most to hurt both of them; but a childless heroine was certainly more agreeable, too, for a man taking a break from *Sons and Lovers*. The play was also explicitly written as 'A Comedy', and Lawrence would have known that though audiences for comedies in 1912 would accept a woman who leaves her husband for another man, they would not have accepted in a comedy one who – like Nora in *A Doll's House* – abandons her children too.

The play was a relief from the novel: it celebrated a woman who had indeed run from her husband, and who was now living in Italy; Barbara is a forerunner of the Ursula character Lawrence would invent the following year and write about for many years afterwards. The play annoyed but flattered Frieda, cheered Lawrence up and made him hope for stage success.[36] And he had only a fortnight's more work on his novel left to do, for those final 'hundred or so pages'.

Chapter XI, 'The Test on Miriam', ends on p. 421, and p. 420 marks the last appearance of any of the 'Paul Morel' pages in the book. It seems very likely that when Lawrence settled down to the novel again around 1 November, he started with chapter XII ('Passion') and wrote the last 110 pages in a single burst of seventeen days writing, without using any of the old manuscript. He wanted a clean sweep of writing to carry him forward into the difficult areas ahead. It seems likely that his relationship with Frieda would have changed the way he wanted to write about Paul's affair with Clara: and that would have led to corresponding changes in the way the affair ended. His experience of Ernest Weekley influenced how he now wrote about the abandoned husband, Baxter Dawes; he had been forced to imagine – and in a way to sympathise with – the abandoned partner, even though Weekley had also aroused his indignation. Above all, he knew that he was going to re-enact the death of Lydia Lawrence when he wrote about the death of Gertrude Morel.

V Death of the Mother

The day after Lawrence restarted the novel, 2 November, was All Souls' Day; he and Frieda went up to the cemetery next to the main church in Gargnano 'to be made bright' (i. 467): along the avenue of cypresses, they saw processing 'the chanting choristers,/The priests in gold and black, the villagers. . . .' All Souls' Day was a strange and memorable experience for Lawrence, and an extraordinarily appropriate day for him to contemplate the last part of the novel. His poem 'All Souls' shows him linking the day with the death of his mother in Eastwood, nearly two years earlier: 'The naked candles burn on every grave./On your grave, in England, the weeds grow.'[37] Weeds and candles: for all its haunting power over his imagination, he was determined that the old relationship would become like that unkept grave. The novel would be its resting-place; he would light memorial candles to celebrate its end. As he worked towards that point in his novel during November, Frieda's memoir tells us how 'he was ill and his grief made me ill too, and he said: "If my mother had lived I could never have loved you, she wouldn't have let me go." '[38] Late in life, he described rather fearfully how 'Our habits of emotion go so deep, we almost die before they break: and our habits of relationship have so many cancer-like threads, any one of which will start the whole old thing again' (v. 471). Those 'cancer-like threads' are a tribute to the power – a truly malignant power, he now felt it to be – exercised over him by the dead Lydia Lawrence. But there in Villa, during the autumn, Frieda found that she too 'lived and suffered that book' as she watched Lawrence recreating Lydia Lawrence's love and death: a friend remembered hearing her once exclaim 'How I suffered, Lorenzo, when you killed your mother'. She remembered his desperate closeness to his subject – how on the little steamer which sailed from Gargnano he pointed out another passenger: 'Look, that little woman is like my mother.'[39] His hand-writing, often precise and always neat, becomes a clumsy scrawl on the manuscript pages of *Sons and Lovers* describing Mrs Morel's dying and death. The scrawl ends with the sentence describing Paul immediately after her death – 'When he took his face up from his warm, dead mother he went straight downstairs, began blacking his boots.'[40] Lawrence must have broken off writing at that point; the next sentence resumes precise and neat.

And yet, however sympathetic Frieda was, the novel (and Lawrence's obsession with it) also annoyed her. 'Towards the end of "Sons and Lovers" I got fed up and turned against all this "house of Atreus" feeling, and I wrote a skit called: "Paul Morel, or His Mother's Darling." ' Lawrence read it and remarked, 'coldly', 'This kind of thing isn't called a skit.'[41] Frieda's skit, which does not survive, was part of her answer to *The Fight for Barbara*, a play in which she thought Lawrence had made himself heroic and unflinching and her undecided and uncommitted. 'I did *not* wobble so' (i. 476), she insisted. The 'real love, sort of Oedipus' which in September she had been so proud to diagnose as Paul Morel's problem was turning out more disturbing than she had anticipated. Now she made him comic, as the mother-beloved son in whom she had discovered, she wrote to David Garnett, 'abysses of elusive, destructive, spiritual tragedy' (i. 494). Lawrence scribbled 'balls!' against that remark in her letter.

One of the troubles with thinking about *Sons and Lovers* – or any novel – as autobiographical is the danger of assuming that, what the character experiences, the author has also precisely experienced: and vice versa: no more and no less. In fact, the author of *Sons and Lovers*, unlike Paul, was by no means 'Derelict', in the last chapter of his tragic existence: and however distressed Lawrence was by Mrs Morel's death, he knew that Lydia

Lawrence's was very far indeed behind him. The self who wrote about it might well be in tears: but the self who at last grasped Mrs Morel's self-sacrificing domination of her children, and her incapacity to realise her own life, was struggling far beyond the confinement of such feelings. Exactly such a struggle appears in a dangerously sentimental poem which Lawrence wrote to Lydia Lawrence beside the Lago di Garda just as he was finishing the novel, in the late autumn of 1912.

From the Italian Lakes

Who do you think stands watching
The snow-tops shining rosy
In heaven, now that the darkness
Takes all but the tallest posy?

Who is it sees the two-winged
Black boat down there
Asleep on the snowy shadow
Like a moth that cannot hear?

The olive-leaves, light as gad-flies
Have all gone dark with the night
And far away, on the other shore
Twinkles a little light.

Yea, my little lady
And this is Italy,
And this is me, my darling,
And this is me.

So, there's an oxen-wagon
Comes darkly into sight
A man with a lantern swinging
Beaming the night.

He'll think I'm a ghost, such a stranger
Under the olive trees.
He says not a word, but passes
Staring at what he sees.

What does he see, my darling
Beside the darkening lake,
In the mountains sloping shadow
Lingering for your sake?

All the things that are lovely
I wanted to give them to you
And already the rose has vanished,
The night is blue.

And never now, my darling
Can I gather the mountain-tips
From the twilight like a nose-gay,
To hold to your lips.

And never the two-winged vessels
That sleep along the lake
Can I catch there between my hands like a moth
For you to take.

We have lost them all, and the darkness
Alone is left, of all
The wonderful things I had for you.
—So the fall

Of the latch through the night rings final.
And on opposite sides of the door
We are each shut out from the other now
For ever more.[42]

The poem's nostalgia shows a deep, continuing, loving attachment, hardly interrupted by death; and it was in the grip of such feelings that Lawrence was writing *Sons and Lovers*. Yet by the winter of 1912 he also knew that he was able (in the image of the poem) to keep the latch down, the door closed and the ghost the other side of it. However memorably he was haunted, he also knew that the ghost's love had to be let go. It was Lawrence's job as a writer to articulate that and make it real: old emotions were ghosts, too, and had to be mastered.

So although he remained deeply involved in that past and that love, his own continued work on the novel, coupled with Frieda's astringent attitude, assisted him over the final hurdle of his early life. We can see him directly addressing the same problem in the poem sequence *Look! We Have Come Through!* It was at exactly this point, among the poems belonging to late Autumn 1912, that he would place 'Lady Wife', a vicious attack upon the superior woman, the queen, the mother: both Lydia Lawrence and Frieda Weekley could have felt themselves targeted.

> Rise up and go, I have no use for you
>   And your blithe, glad mien.
> No angels here, for me no goddesses,
>   Nor any Queen.

The mother is conceited enough to believe that she and her child are the most important things on earth: but, asks the poem, 'What are you by yourself, do you think, and what/The mere fruit of your womb?'[43] Aimed at Frieda, or aimed at Lydia Lawrence, the question was equally devastating.

The other kind of rejection of Lydia Lawrence was no less complete, if more complex and less rancorous. In the poem 'All Souls', Lawrence had contemplated her grave in Eastwood, and had insisted:

> I forget you, have forgotten you.
> I am busy only at my burning,
> I am busy only at my life.
> But my feet are on your grave, planted.
> And when I lift my face, it is a flame that goes up
> To the other world, where you are now.
> But I am not concerned with you.
>   I have forgotten you.[44]

That is an assertion which the author of *Sons and Lovers* may have felt he was entitled to make, as he committed himself to write once and for all about the death of Mrs Morel. And, in spite of evidence of his continuing love for his mother such as that observed by Frieda, or of that in 'From the Italian Lakes', it was also something which Lawrence was now trying to make his own by creating.

VI Shedding Sicknesses

It was in that spirit that Lawrence finished his novel around 17 November, and immediately wrote Garnett a letter defending it:

I wrote it again, pruning it and shaping it and filling it in. I tell you it has got form – *form*: haven't I made it patiently, out of sweat as well as blood. It follows this idea: a woman of character and refinement goes into the lower class, and has no satisfaction in her own life. She has had a passion for her husband, so the children are born of passion, and have heaps of vitality. But as her sons grow up she selects them as lovers – first the eldest, then the second. These sons are *urged* into life by their reciprocal love of their mother – urged on and on. But when they come to manhood, they can't love, because their mother is the strongest power in their lives, and holds them. – It's rather like Goethe and his mother and Frau von Stein and Christiana –. As soon as the young men come into contact with women, there's a split. William gives his sex to a fribble, and his mother holds his soul. But the split kills him, because he doesn't know where he is. The next son gets a woman who fights for his soul – fights his mother. The son loves the mother – all the sons hate and are jealous of the father. The battle goes on between the mother and the girl, with the son as object. The mother gradually proves stronger, because of the tie of blood. The son decides to leave his soul in his mother's hands, and, like his elder brother, go for passion. He gets passion. Then the split begins to tell again. But, almost unconsciously, the mother realises what is the matter, and begins to die. The son casts off his mistress, attends to his mother dying. He is left in the end naked of everything, with the drift towards death.

It is a great tragedy, and I tell you I've written a great book. It's the tragedy of thousands of young men in England – it may even be Bunny's tragedy. I think it was Ruskin's, and men like him. – Now tell me if I haven't worked out my theme, like life, but always my theme. Read my novel – it's a great novel. If *you* can't see the development – which is slow like growth – I can. (i. 476–7)

He knew he had to defend it to Garnett with a statement about its 'form': but he had at last been so gripped by its dominant idea that he distorted the novel he had actually just finished. By the middle of November Lawrence was concerned less with what the novel had said than with what he had finally learned from it. And according to *that* Lawrence, Mrs Morel (for example) 'realises what is the matter' with Paul, and starts to die. That is not true of the novel: but it is another kind of truth, which the creative artist recognised and knew might well be right – and which the son (and lover) was using to help batter his way out of an old problem.

Again, in that letter, Lawrence says that Paul 'is left in the end naked of everything, with the drift towards death'. Perhaps only twenty-four hours earlier he had written the novel's last paragraph, which suggests the opposite. But the letter bears witness to the truly dreadful limitation of Paul, more strongly than the actual last paragraph does. All Paul can do is survive and walk towards a town, glowing or not: and Lawrence had learned enough from his own experience in 1911 to know just how close Paul is to giving up completely. He also knew, perhaps for the first time, just how weakened Paul had been by his upbringing. The fact that he himself had not only walked towards the town, but had been lucky enough to find Frieda Weekley in it, and with her help had managed to overcome the great burden of the past – and was now alive and well and living in Italy – would only have sharpened his sense of the tragedy of Paul.

It is at such a time that one feels the force of remarks such as those Lawrence later made to his friend the barrister Gordon Campbell about being a writer:

it really means something – I *wish* I could express myself – this feeling that one is not only a little individual living a little individual life, but that one is in oneself the whole of mankind, and ones fate is the fate of the whole of mankind, and ones charge is the charge of the whole of mankind. Not *me* – the little, vain, personal D. H. Lawrence – but that unnameable me which is not vain nor personal, but strong, and glad, and ultimately sure, but so blind, so groping, so tongue-tied, so staggering. (ii. 302)

The little, vain, personal D. H. Lawrence was doubtless overwhelmed by grief for his mother and for himself, in the middle of November 1912. Biographers generally prefer that figure, because he is thoroughly human and either sympathetic or antipathetic. But it is crucial to realise the importance for Lawrence of the 'unnameable me', whose experiences he was writing about, and whom at a time like this he could liberate only *by* writing. Such a self was aware, for example, of the dreadful and deadly self-sacrificial power of the beloved mother, and of the potential for loving death in the limited and in many ways hopelessly trapped son: just as it understood the possessive and destructive power within the beloved woman like Frieda. That was what being an autobiographical writer meant, to Lawrence: not simply reproducing what had happened to him, or to those close to him, but seeing where experience would most naturally take him (and them); and then following those consequences through in fiction, in the most desperate efforts of recreation.

This could be terribly painful to those recreated. Jessie Chambers, for example, was overwhelmed by anguish at the portraits of Paul and Miriam which Lawrence drew. She knew that what he wrote was in some ways a betrayal. Yet Lawrence wanted to understand how it was that Jessie Chambers had been so supportive – and yet, he was now sure, so destructive. He invented the fiction so as to answer the question, doing so without thought (or fear) of the consequences. Writing and understanding were always more important to Lawrence than any kind of personal loyalty. There was a ruthlessness in this which was apparently the opposite (but was perhaps a necessary concomitant) of the kind of sympathy and inwardness with others which he and his writing also demonstrated.

Thus he could attempt not only what another famous letter about *Sons and Lovers* spoke of – shed his 'sicknesses in books' (ii. 90) – but also what that same sentence goes on to assert: 'repeats and presents again' his emotions 'to be master of them'. The man overwhelmed with grief and love could also see deeply into the whole disastrous pattern of love between mother and son, and between man and woman: and could possess that knowledge and explore that possibility, not just on his own behalf but on behalf of others too. It was Frieda who remarked in her biography of Lawrence, just after telling the story of the writing of *Sons and Lovers*, that 'His courage in facing the dark recesses of his own soul impressed me always, scared me sometimes.'[45] Lawrence could work through the possibilities and potentialities of Paul Morel's existence long after the equivalent possibilities had actually passed out of his own life. To be the son of an angry and self-sacrificing mother who remained tragically incapacitated; to be a son who never saw how dangerous his beloved mother was and who never recognised his father within himself – this was to write out the logic of his own life in a way which came perilously close to the truth, and yet was not true.

And so it is not a contradiction to say that, in the early winter of 1912, by the Lago di Garda, Lawrence was both happy in love and overwhelmed by grief – and also able to stand clear and create mothers, and lovers, and sons and children, in very sharp and sometimes terribly critical relief. And he could also see the fate of Paul, tragic and overwhelmed hero, as another terrifying possibility: not only very close to himself indeed, but the danger of 'thousands of young men in England'. He wanted to lay that ghost too; and, as usual, his way of doing so was to write about it.

VII   *The Daughter-in-Law*

His final effort to lay these particular ghosts came less than seven weeks after finishing the novel, and before he worked on its proofs. Theatre had retained its fascination for him: he and Frieda had seen *Man and Superman* together in Nottingham in March, a Passion-play in the neighbourhood of Beuerberg at the end of May and Ibsen's *Ghosts* in Munich sometime during the summer of 1912. They had probably gone to the theatre in Bad Tölz; in October Lawrence had written *The Fight for Barbara*; and late in November or early in December he and Frieda had been to see Verdi's *Rigoletto* in Saló, at the southern end of the Lago di Garda. In December the Compagnia Drammatica Italiana Adelia Di Giacomo Tadini – a touring troupe of actors Lawrence referred to as 'peasants' – came to the theatre in Gargnano, and on 28 December Lawrence saw their version of *Ghosts* (very different from that in Munich). He saw D'Annunzio's play *The Light under the Bushel* on 6 January, Silvio Zambaldi's comedy *The Wife of the Doctor* on the 9th and *Hamlet* – as *Amleto* – on the 16th (i. 505).[46] And by the middle of January 1913 he had also written his play *The Daughter-in-Law*.

In this drama – and drama was a liberating genre for him, as *A Collier's Friday Night* had showed back in 1909 – he allowed himself to create the most powerful and dangerous of all his mother-figures. The widowed Mrs Gascoyne keeps her sons, married and unmarried, wholly under her thumb; she is magnificently dismissive of their independence, and wants revenge on the woman who has married her son Luther. In this astonishing play, Lawrence not only finally gave full release to his hatred of the dominant mother – of Gertrude, whoever she might be – but at last showed in Minnie, the woman who has married Luther, a young woman potentially every bit as dominant as her mother-in-law. At one point in *Sons and Lovers* Paul Morel had asked his mother 'Did *you* want to be a man, mother?' – because Miriam has told him that 'Men have everything.' Mrs Morel replies: 'Sometimes I have—but it's silly—and no, I don't really want to be anything but myself, and never did.' But as 'herself' Mrs Morel gets, in most ways at least, what she wants. In the play, Mrs Gascoyne apparently gets everything she wants, too, by behaving with a superb disdain for husbands, sons and daughters-in-law; but in spite of her feeling that 'The World is made o' men for me, lass—there's only the men for me', she also finds herself stricken with contempt for men as a kind of revengeful children: 'Nay, a childt is a troublesome pleasure to a woman, but a man's a trouble pure an' simple.'[47] After three acts in which her dominance has been absolute and her egotism superbly comic, Lawrence reveals the tragedy of her life and of her relationships with men: she herself knows that 'when a woman builds her life on men, either husbands or sons, she builds on summat as sooner or later brings the house down crash on her head—yi, she does'. And she predicts the same fate for Minnie:

Mrs Gascoyne: It's true. An' tha can ha'e Luther. Tha'lt get him, an' tha can ha' him—
Minnie: Do you think I shall?
Mrs Gascoyne: I can see. Tha'lt get him—but tha'lt get sorrow wi' 'im, an' wi' th' sons tha has. See if tha doesna.[48]

It is a reaction Minnie as yet refuses to share; in spite of her quarrels with her husband Luther, she insists that she loves him: and in the fourth act he finds he loves her too. And yet the ending of the play is thoroughly ambivalent about their love, as Minnie bandages Luther's head (he has been hit by a stone thrown by blacklegs during a strike) and takes his boots off for him:

Minnie: Let me do them. (*He sits up again.*)
Luther: It's started bleedin'. I'll do 'em i' hae'f a minute.
Minnie: No—trust me—trust yourself to me. Let me have you now for my own. (*She begins to undo his boots.*)
Luther: Dost want me? (*She kisses his hands.*)
Minnie: Oh my love! (*She takes him in her arms.*)
(*He suddenly begins to cry.*)[49]

Minnie's love trembles on the very verge of possessiveness: and never have the links between mother-in-law and daughter-in-law been stronger than in those few seconds of the ending – even though the love between husband and wife, both scarred and damaged people, has never been so real a possibility either. Luther is the man struggling free from his mother and from possessive women: and though, like Frieda, Minnie hates the man who has been his mother's boy – she flares at her husband '*She* mollycoddled and marded you till you weren't a man—and now—I have to pay for it'[50] – without recognising that she herself is exactly the kind of woman who helps create such a man.

Lawrence's work on this play is yet another example of his restless creative intelligence: it completed what he had done in the novel, and it also brought the problems of the novel up to modern times, as it were, with the man damaged by mother-love having to make his marriage with an independent and strongly individual woman contemptuous of just such love – contemptuous as Miriam could never be. The play was also by far Lawrence's most intensive and extensive work in the Nottinghamshire dialect, as well as his last extended work in that form. It is as if the moment when he came fully into his inheritance, as a man uninhibitedly speaking the language of his father's world as well as his mother's, was also the moment he declared his actual freedom from both his parents; declared that he was now the writer who, freed from his past, could move freely through a life which he and Frieda were now making.

VIII   Together

Three months later, in April 1913, one particular image captures the man and writer. Lawrence and Frieda had gone to stay for a few days up at the farm of San Gaudenzio, overlooking the Lago di Garda. The place was lovely; and just as at the Haggs Farm, the self-conscious, detached individual was happy to be swallowed up, and the outgoing man liberated, by dancing, talk, music, games and a continual intense involvement with people: 'One need never be alone': 'the folk are nice: warm and generous': '*fearfully* nice' (i. 535–6). But he would go to write in a deserted lemon house on the cliff-edge above the lake, looking across to Monte Baldo: 'sit and write in the great loft of the lemon house, high up, far, far from the ground, the open front giving across the lake and the mountain snow opposite flush with twilight'.[51] Perched there, he was quintessentially the stranger he had continued to be, even in a place as sympathetic as the Haggs had once been.

It is one of the great and doubtless deliberate gaps in the account of the relationship between Gilbert and Johanna during the months described in *Mr Noon* that Gilbert – a musician – shares none of his work with Johanna, although they discuss other things. But that, too, corresponds to a truth about Lawrence's writing. In spite of Frieda's sometimes intense involvement in it, it continued to be in the last issue Lawrence's lonely creation. Like the words with which he had responded to his attackers at Beauvale school, writing for this profoundly solitary man was a way of going out to other people on his own terms, not on theirs. For all the liberating, sensual and humanising influence of Frieda, Lawrence remained in danger of being, like Gilbert Noon in the novel's recreation of Icking, 'a separate, un-mixing specimen ... cut off from one half of man's life. With a curious blank certainty he knew it, as he leaned on the balcony, high up, and watched the men at work.'[52]

Lawrence's discovery in Frieda of the woman with whom he could live and share his life could not change that; but a profound instinct for his own psychic health (and for his healthy existence as a writer) demanded that he make his relationship with her the centre of his life. He did so in a way and with an intensity which, to begin with, frightened her. As he put it in *Mr Noon*: 'The life with Johanna was his all-in-all: the work was secondary . . .'[53]

And yet just as Frieda wanted more than Lawrence, she was not enough for him either. As she recalled, 'When I said, like a woman does: "But why do you bother about other people? You have me, isn't that enough?" he replied: "Yes, it's a lot, but it isn't everything."' Lawrence had found that he could not simply be a man living his own life with his partner: he needed to go on speaking with a public voice. The 'solitary, private business' of his writing paradoxically demanded readers and the sharing of experience.[54] It was a fundamental need in Lawrence to go out to others and explain what he had learned about himself: to try and be the man among men whom he eventually came to feel his father had been. He wrote and dreamed about that need for the rest of his life.

Between May and December 1912, Frieda and his writing began to transform him. They became his means of living as fully and creatively with himself and with others as he could. There were times when he hated both: fought with them, abandoned them, excoriated and denounced them. His relationship was often violent, his writing tumultuous and experimental: both had continually to be reimagined and recreated. Yet he knew that, together, they could make his life.

Cue-titles
and
Abbreviations

CUE-TITLES AND ABBREVIATIONS

Note The cue-titles and abbreviations are used in the Appendices, in the Note on Sources and in the Notes (the abbreviations in **Section A** and **Section F** are also used in the text.) Place of publication is London unless otherwise specified, here and elsewhere.

A Letters of Lawrence*

(i.) James. T. Boulton, ed. *The Letters of D. H. Lawrence*. Volume I. Cambridge: Cambridge University Press, 1979.

(ii.) George J. Zytaruk and James T. Boulton, eds. *The Letters of D. H. Lawrence*. Volume II. Cambridge: Cambridge University Press, 1982.

(iii.) James T. Boulton and Andrew Robertson, eds. *The Letters of D. H. Lawrence*. Volume III. Cambridge: Cambridge Unversity Press, 1984.

(iv.) Warren Roberts, James T. Boulton and Elizabeth Mansfield, eds. *The Letters of D. H. Lawrence*. Volume IV. Cambridge: Cambridge University Press, 1987.

(v.) James T. Boulton and Lindeth Vasey, eds. *The Letters of D. H. Lawrence*. Volume V. Cambridge: Cambridge University Press, 1989.

* Unpublished letters are quoted when possible from the manuscript or typescript.

B Works of Lawrence

A *Apocalypse and the Writings on Revelation*. Ed. Mara Kalnins. Cambridge: Cambridge University Press, 1979.

E [+no.] Manuscript [+no.] listed in Warren Roberts. *A Bibliography of D. H. Lawrence*. 2nd edn. Cambridge: Cambridge University Press, 1982. Section E.

EmyE *England, My England and Other Stories*. Ed. Bruce Steele. Cambridge: Cambridge University Press, 1990.

Hardy *Study of Thomas Hardy and Other Essays*. Ed. Bruce Steele. Cambridge: Cambridge University Press, 1985.

LAH   *Love Among the Haystacks and Other Stories.* Ed. John Worthen. Cambridge: Cambridge University Press, 1987.

LG   *The Lost Girl.* Ed. John Worthen. Cambridge: Cambridge University Press, 1981.

MN   *Mr Noon.* Ed. Lindeth Vasey. Cambridge: Cambridge University Press, 1984.

P   *Phoenix. The Posthumous Papers of D. H. Lawrence.* Ed. Edward D. McDonald. New York: Viking Press, 1936.

P II   *Phoenix II. Uncollected, Unpublished and Other Prose Works by D. H. Lawrence.* Ed. Warren Roberts and Harry T. Moore. Heinemann, 1968.

PO   *The Prussian Officer and Other Stories.* Ed. John Worthen. Cambridge: Cambridge University Press, 1983.

Poems   *The Complete Poems of D. H. Lawrence.* Ed. Vivian de Sola Pinto and Warren Roberts. Revised edn. Harmondsworth: Penguin Books, 1977. [The widely available paperback edition published by Penguin – and by Viking in the USA – has been cited rather than the identical revised text, with slightly different pagination, published in two hardback volumes by Heinemann in 1972.]

R   *The Rainbow.* Ed. Mark Kinkead-Weekes. Cambridge: Cambridge University Press, 1989.

SL   *Sons and Lovers.* Duckworth, 1913. [Quotations have been taken from the 1913 edition when it accurately reproduces the final manuscript (E373e) or when it presents an authorial revision. E373e has been quoted when its reading is not reproduced by the 1913 edition.]

T   *The Trespasser.* Ed. Elizabeth Mansfield. Cambridge: Cambridge University Press, 1981.

WL   *Women in Love.* Ed. David Farmer, Lindeth Vasey and John Worthen. Cambridge: Cambridge University Press, 1987.

WP   *The White Peacock.* Ed. Andrew Robertson. Cambridge: Cambridge University Press, 1983.

C   Other Printed Works

Ada   Ada Lawrence and Stuart Gelder. *The Early Life of D. H. Lawrence.* Secker, 1932.

Delavenay   Emile Delavenay. *D. H. Lawrence: L'Homme et la Genèse de son Oeuvre. Les Années de Formation: 1885–1919.* 2 volumes. Paris: Libraire C. Klincksieck, 1969.

E.T. E.T. [Jessie Chambers Wood]. *D. H. Lawrence: A Personal Record.* Jonathan Cape, 1935; reprinted Cambridge: Cambridge University Press, 1980.

Frieda Frieda Lawrence. *"Not I, But the Wind ..."* Santa Fe: Rydal Press, 1934.

Memoirs *Frieda Lawrence: The Memoirs and Correspondence.* Ed. E. W. Tedlock. Heinemann, 1961.

Nehls Edward Nehls, ed. *D. H. Lawrence: A Composite Biography.* 3 volumes. Madison: University of Wisconsin Press, 1957–9.

Neville George Neville. *A Memoir of D. H. Lawrence.* Ed. Carl Baron. Cambridge: Cambridge University Press, 1981.

OED Sir James A. H. Murray and others, eds. *A New English Dictionary on Historical Principles.* 10 volumes. Oxford: Clarendon Press, 1884–1928.

Taylor J. Clement Phillips Taylor. 'Boys of the Beauvale Breed', *Eastwood and Kimberley Advertiser,* 30 December 1960–17 August 1962.

D Manuscript Sources

BL British Library

Boulton James T. Boulton

Clarke W. H. Clarke

King Joan King

Lazarus George Lazarus

LB Papers Memoirs of D. H. Lawrence written by Louie Burrows, in the possession of Nora Haselden

NCL Nottingham County Libraries

NCRO Nottingham County Record Office

Needham Margaret Needham

NYPL New York Public Library

Sagar Keith Sagar

Till J. R. Till

UCin University of Cincinnati

UN University of Nottingham Library, Department of Manuscripts

UT Harry Ransom Humanities Research Center, University of Texas at Austin

Weekley   Ian R. Weekley

E People

DHL   D. H. Lawrence

Frieda   Frieda von Richthofen (m. Ernest Weekley 1899, m. DHL 1914, m. Angelo Ravagli 1950)

HC   Helen Corke

JC   Jessie Chambers (m. John Wood 1915)

LB   Louie Burrows (m. Frederick Heath 1941)

F Textual Symbols

⟨ ⟩   Deletion

⌜ ⌝   Insertion

[ ]   Authorial insertion

⟨...⟩   Illegible deletion

[...]   Illegible word

TA   Textual apparatus

*   Footnote

^{1} [etc.] Endnote

b.   Born

m .   Married

d.   Died

tr.   Translated

Appendices

APPENDIX I

◆

D. H. LAWRENCE'S PROSE WORKS,

1906–1913

Additional Cue-titles

ER	*English Review*
Facsimile	*Sons and Lovers Facsimile.* Ed. Mark Schorer. Berkeley: University of California Press, 1977.
Haystacks	D. H. Lawrence, *Love Among the Haystacks and Other Pieces.* Ed. David Garnett. The Nonesuch Press, 1930.
Huxley	*The Letters of D. H. Lawrence.* Ed. Aldous Huxley. Heinemann, 1932.
NG	*Nottinghamshire Guardian*
R&MS	*Renaissance and Modern Studies*
SWG	*Saturday Westminster Gazette*

DATE		TITLE	SURVIVING MS OR TS	PRINTED TEXT NEAREST TO MS OR TS	NOTES
1904	15 Nov.	'Nature Study'	LaB220	—	Copy of Ilkeston Pupil-Teacher Centre essay
1906	by Easter–June 1907	'Laetitia' I	E430a [48 pp. fragment]	*WP* 329–47	First version of *WP*
1906	9 Aug.	Diary Entry	MS Clarke	Ada 55–8	
1906	?Autumn–Winter	'Laetitia' I plot fragment	E318	Chapter 5, p. 139	In College notebook
1907	22 Feb.	'There's no art …'	LaL1	—	College essay
1907	15 March	'Character Sketch of: Lady Macbeth'	LaL1	—	College essay
1907	5 May	'The Fairies of:– "Midsummer Night's Dream"'	LaL1	—	College essay

471

APPENDIX I

DATE		TITLE	SURVIVING MS OR TS	PRINTED TEXT NEAREST TO MS OR TS	NOTES
1907	1 June	'The Character of Theseus'	LaL1	—	College essay
1907	Autumn	'The Vicar's Garden'	E359.5a	—	First version of 'Shadow in the Rose Garden'
1907	by 20 Oct.	'The White Stocking'	E430.3	—	NG entry: early version of story
1907	by 31 Oct.	'A Page from the Annals of Griseleia'	E140b	—	First version of 'Fragment of Stained Glass'. Rough draft of next entry
1907	by 31 Oct.	'Ruby Glass'	E140a [6 pp. fragment]	—	NG entry: by 'Herbert Richards'
1907	20 Oct.–8 Nov.	'A Prelude'	—	LAH 5–15	NG entry & winner
1907	late May 1908	'Laetitia' II	E430a [10 pp. fragment]	WP 348–51	WP second version
			E430b & c [half-page fragments]	Roberts 251 [one only]	Torn half pages
1908	March	'Art and the Individual' [version 1]	E24.3b	Hardy 223–9	—
1908	August	'Art and the Individual' [version 2]	E24.3a	Hardy 135–42	—
1908	Autumn–Nov. 1909	'Nethermere' I	E430d	—	WP third version: pp. copied by Agnes Holt & Agnes Mason ?Oct. 1909
1909	Summer–Autumn	'Goose Fair'	E150.7a	—	Collaboration with LB

472

DATE		TITLE	SURVIVING MS OR TS	PRINTED TEXT NEAREST TO MS OR TS	NOTES
1909	by Nov.	*A Collier's Friday Night*	E74a	—	—
1909	by Dec.	'Odour of Chrysanthemums'	E284a [6 pp. fragment]	*PO* 203–5	First version
1909	?Dec.	'A Lesson on a Tortoise'	E196.5a	*LAH* 16–20	—
1909	?Dec.	'Lessford's Rabbits'	E196.4a	*LAH* 21–7	—
1910	Jan.	'A Modern Lover'	E240.7	*LAH* 28–48	—
1910	Jan.	'The White Stocking'	—	—	Revision; see (i. 152)
1910	?Jan.	'Matilda'	E392a	—	—
1910	?Jan.	'Delilah and Mr Bircumshaw'	E90.5a [11 pp. fragment]	*LAH* 193–7	First version; revised in June 1912
1910	?Jan.	'Goose Fair'	—	*ER* Feb. 1910	Proof revision
1910	21 Jan.–11 April	'Nethermere' II	E430d	*WP* 1–325+ TA	Revision & new Part III: HC copies pp.
1910	?Feb.–Aug.	'The Saga of Siegmund'	E407 a & b [182 pp. fragment & pp. revised in E407b]	*T* 319–23 [E407a, 170–82]	First version of *T*
1910	April	'A Blot'	E135.5a	—	First version of 'The Fly in the Ointment'
1910	July	'Odour of Chrysanthemums'	E284c [ink revision]	*R&MS* (1969) 12–48	
1910	Aug.–Sept.	*The White Peacock*	E430e	*WP* 1–325+ TA	Proof revision
1910	?October	'Paul Morel' I plot	E320.1	Chapter 10, pp. 278–9	In College notebook
1910	October	'Paul Morel' I	—	—	First version of *SL*: see (i. 184)

DATE		TITLE	SURVIVING MS OR TS	PRINTED TEXT NEAREST TO MS OR TS	NOTES
1910	by 17 Nov.	*The Widowing of Mrs. Holroyd*	—	—	First version: see (i. 188).
1910	by 18 Nov.	'Rachel Annand Taylor'	E330.5	*Hardy* 145–8	—
1910	Nov.–Dec.	*The Merry-Go-Round*	E237a	—	—
1911	13 Mar.–?July	'Paul Morel' II	E373d & E373e ['Paul Morel' MS & 15 pp. in final MS]	—	Second version of *SL*
1911	March	'A Fragment of Stained Glass'	E140c	—	Revision
1911	March–April	'Odour of Chrysanthe-mums'	E284c [pencil revision]	—	Revision
1911	April	'Odour of Chrysanthe-mums'	E284b	—	DHL's revision of fair copy by LB
1911	April	'The White Stocking'	—	—	Revision: see (i. 258)
1911	?April	'The Shadow in the Rose Garden'	—	—	Possible revision
1911	?April	'Intimacy'	E438a	—	First version of 'The Witch à la Mode'
1911	May	'Odour of Chrysanthe-mums'	—	*ER* June 1911	Proof revision
1911	June	'The Old Adam'	[32pp. MS now lost]	—	(i. 276): E286 is later MS
1911	15–16 July	'Two Marriages'	E87a [1 p. fragment]	—	First version of 'Daughters of the Vicar'
1911	July	'A Fragment of Stained Glass'	—	*ER* Sept. 1911	Proof revision
1911	August	'Second-Best'	E356.5	—	—
1911	?Sept.	'The Old Adam'	E286	*LAH* 71–86	—

DATE		TITLE	SURVIVING MS OR TS	PRINTED TEXT NEAREST TO MS OR TS	NOTES
1911	?Sept.	'Intimacy'	E438a [revision]	—	Revision for Edward Garnett
1911	October	'Two Marriages'	E87b	*PO* 209–46	—
1911	October	Review of *Contemporary German Poetry*	—	*ER* Nov. 1911 *Encounter* Aug. 1969	—
1911	?October	'Love Among the Haystacks'	E211a [pp. 10–14 & 59]	—	First version
1911	3 Nov.–April 1912	'Paul Morel' IIIa	E373d [pp. 1–7] E373a [fragment of 58 pp.] E373b [pp. 204–26] E373e [fragments of 149 pp.]	—	Third version of *SL*; E373d a false start
1911	6–late Dec.	Reviews of *The Oxford Book of German Verse* and *The Minnesingers*	—	*ER* Jan. 1912 *P II* 269–72	—
1911	c. 16–23 Dec.	'The Harassed Angel'	E329.4a	—	First version of 'The Shades of Spring'
1912	Jan.–c. 8 Feb.	*The Trespasser*	E407b	*T* 41–230+ TA	—
1912	February	'The Miner at Home'	—	*Nation* (London), 16 March 1912: *LAH* 123–7	
1912	14–17 March	'A Sick Collier'	[E361.3]	[*PO* 165–61+ TA]	First version: E361.3 & *PO* are 1913 revision

DATE		TITLE	SURVIVING MS OR TS	PRINTED TEXT NEAREST TO MS OR TS	NOTES
1912	14–17 March	'Her Turn'	—	[*LAH* 128–33]	First version: *LAH* is 1913 revision
1912	14–17 March	'Strike-Pay'	[E381]	[*LAH* 134–40]	First version: E381 and *LAH* are 1913 revision
1912	March	'The Soiled Rose'	E359.4a	*Forum* (New York), March 1913	Second version of 'The Shades of Spring'
1912	April	*The Trespasser*	—	*T* 41–230+ TA	Proof revision
1912	April	*The Married Man*	E229a	—	—
1912	9–11 May	'In Fortified Germany'	—	—	—
1912	9–11 May	'French Sons of Germany'	—	*SWG* 3 Aug. 1912 [*P* 71–5]	—
1912	9–11 May	'How a Spy is Arrested'	—	—	—
1912	15–17 May	'Hail in the Rhine-Land'	—	*SWG* 10 Aug. 1912 [*P* 75–81]	—
1912	May–June	'Paul Morel' IIIb	E373d & e	—	Revision of 'Paul Morel' IIIa
1912	June	'The Christening'	[E68.2]	—	E68.2 is 1913 revision
1912	June	'The Fly in the Ointment'	[E135.5]	—	E135.5 is 1913 revision
1912	June	'Delilah and Mr Bircumshaw'	—	—	Revision of 1910 story: *LAH* 141–51 is 1913 revision
1912	June–July	'Once—!'	—	—	First draft: ? the 5th 'travel sketch' (i. 431)

DATE		TITLE	SURVIVING MS OR TS	PRINTED TEXT NEAREST TO MS OR TS	NOTES
1912	18 July	['a Comedy']	—	—	See (i. 427)
1912	23 July–4 Aug.	*Sons and Lovers*	E373e [pp. 1–75]	*Facsimile*	Final version of 'Paul Morel' (start)
1912	*c.* 8 Aug.	'A Chapel Among the Mountains'	E66	*Haystacks* 57–70	—
1912	August	'A Hay-Hut Among the Mountains'	—	*Haystacks* 71–82	—
1912	Aug.–Sept.	'Once—!'	E296a	*LAH* 152–60	Revision of July sketch
1912	September	'Christs in the Tirol'	E81.5	*P* 82–6	—
1912	Sept.– 18 Nov.	*Sons and Lovers*	E373e [pp. 76–540]	*Facsimile*	Final version of 'Paul Morel' (conclusion)
1912	27–30 Oct.	*The Fight for Barbara*	E130	—	—
1912	17–23 Dec.	'Burns Novel' fragments	E59.3 [13 pp. fragments]	*LAH* 201–11	—
1912	Dec.–Jan. 1913	'Elsa Culverwell'	E209a	*LG* 343–58	—
1913	Jan.–March	'The Insurrection of Miss Houghton'	—	—	Lost: reached 200 pp.: see (i. 536)
1913	by 12 Jan.	*The Daughter-in-Law*	E84a	—	—
1913	by 20 Jan.	'Foreword' to *Sons and Lovers*	E373.1	Huxley 95–102	—
1913	Feb.–March	*Sons and Lovers*	E373f & g	—	Proof revision

APPENDIX II

◆

D. H. LAWRENCE'S POETRY,

1897–1913

Establishing a certain order of composition for DHL's early poems is an impossible task: but the sequence below represents an approximation to a chronological order. It is based upon three main considerations.

(a) The order in which DHL inserted his poems into his two surviving early notebooks (E317 and E320.1). This does not prove, of course, when he wrote the poems he inserted: but it frequently indicates the sequence of composition. Only two poems that DHL is known to have written before the summer of 1911 ('Lilies in the Fire' and 'Red Moon-Rise') do not appear in either of the notebooks: and as they both belonged to the period of his affair with Jessie Chambers, that may have had something to do with their non-appearance. But the otherwise complete compilation offered by the notebooks confirms their significance as DHL's repository for poems he had, at least for the moment, completed. Late in 1910, DHL briefly reused the first notebook after having abandoned it for approximately a year; this may have something to do with his residence in Eastwood while his mother was ill; he may even have left the second notebook in Croydon.

(b) The notebooks' near-completeness in recording DHL's poetic *oeuvre* up to the summer of 1911. This strongly suggests that poems which do not appear in the notebooks were probably finished subsequently. From around July 1911 for about six months, however, a sequence of composition or completion is almost impossible to establish.

(c) The order DHL himself established for the poems which appeared in his 1917 volume *Look! We Have Come Through!* Where there is no reason to disrupt that order, it has been followed in the table. Various details – such as place names or implicit dates – suggest occasional modification of DHL's own order. Poems not included in the sequence have been inserted where most appropriate.

The table does not record all the manuscripts or printings of DHL's early poems. It simply provides the reader with the means of locating the text of a poem nearest to the time at which it was composed. The primary manuscript collections included in the table are the two notebooks described above (E317 and E320.1: the poems have been numbered according to the sequence of their appearance): the poems in a manuscript clearly originating from Croydon (E320.3): three sets of poems sent to Edward Garnett after October 1911 and probably before mid-1913 (E319.2, E320.4 and E446.5). Many early poems exist in still further manuscript copies: they will all be collated in the variorum edition of DHL's poetry to be published by Cambridge University Press.

Additional cue-titles

Amores	*Amores*. 1916
ER	*English Review*
Look!	*Look! We Have Come Through!* 1917. [Number in sequence follows]
LP	*Love Poems*. 1913
N	*Nation* (London)
NS	*New Statesman*
Poetry	*Poetry* (Chicago)
R&MS	F. Warren Roberts. 'D. H. Lawrence, The Second "Poetic Me": Some New Material'. *Renaissance and Modern Studies*, xiv (1970), 5–25

DATE	TITLE	SURVIVING MS OR TS	PRINTED TEXT CLOSE TO MS OR TS	NOTES
c. Spring 1897	'We sit in a lovely meadow'	—	Nehls, i. 32	Written for Mabel Thurlby
⟨?Summer 1908: Start of Notebook I (E317)⟩				
c. 1905	1 Campions	E317 no. 5	Illustration 24	See *Poems* 849
c. 1905	2 Guelder Roses	E317 no. 6	*Poems* 853–4	—
c. 1905	[13 The Wild Common]	E317 no. 16	*Poems* 894–5	Start torn out of notebook
c. 1906–8	3 From a College Window	E317 no. 7	—	—
	4 Study	E317 no. 8	—	—
	5 The Last Hours of a Holiday	E317 no. 9	—	—
	6 The Fall of Day	E317 no. 10	*Poems* 854–5	—
	7 Evening of a Week-day	E317 no. 11	—	—
	8 Eastwood—Evening	E317 no. 12	—	—
	9 The Piano	E317 no. 13	*Poems* 943	—

DATE	TITLE	SURVIVING MS OR TS	PRINTED TEXT CLOSE TO MS OR TS	NOTES
	10 Lightning	E317 no. 14	[*LP* version *Poems* 915]	*N* 4 Nov. 1911
	11 Married in June	E317 no. 15	*Poems* 855	—
	[12] —	E317 no. 15a	—	Torn out of notebook
c. 1908	14 The Worm Turns	E317 no. 17	*Poems* 855–6	—
	15 On the Road	E317 no. 18	*Poems* 856–7	—
	16 The Death of the Baron	E317 no. 19	*Poems* 857–8	—
c. 1908	17 Song ['Love has crept']	E317 no. 20	—	See (i. 150)
	Song ['Flapper']	E320.4 no. 31 E134.2	— (i. 150–1)	— —
	18 Love Comes Late	E317 no. 21	*Poems* 859	—
	19 A Tarantella Tarantella	E317 no. 22 E320.4 no. 36	— —	— —
by Dec. 1908	20 Song ['Up in the high']	E317 no. 23	*Poems* 859–60	See (i. 150)
	[21] An [. . .]	E317 no. 24	—	Torn out of notebook
by Jan. 1909	22 Cherry Robbers	E67b E317 no. 25 Acc.697 (UN)	(i. 109) — —	— — 22 March 1910
	23 In a Boat	E317 no. 26 E320.4 no. 12	— —	*ER* Oct. 1910
	24 Dim Recollections	E317 no. 27	—	—
by Jan. 1909	Renaissance	E342b E317 no. 28	(i. 110–11) *Poems* 895–6	— —
	A Failure	E317 no. 29	*Poems* 860–1	—
by Jan. 1909	A Winter's Tale	E436b E317 no. 30	(i. 109–10) —	— —
	A Decision	E317 no. 31	*Poems* 861	—
	Dog-tired	E317 no. 32	—	—

DATE	TITLE	SURVIVING MS OR TS	PRINTED TEXT CLOSE TO MS OR TS	NOTES
	A Train at Night	E317 no. 33	*Poems* 861	—
	Violets for the Dead	E317 no. 34	*Poems* 912–3 [1913 version *Poems* 913–14]	N 4 Nov. 1911
15 Jan. 1909	Baby Songs: Ten Months Old	E389.6b E317 no. 35	(i. 108–9) *Poems* 862	— (i. 106)
by Jan. 1909	Trailing Clouds	E317 no. 36 E320.4 no. 18	*Poems* 916 —	—
	Triolet	E317 no. 37	—	—
	Coming Home from School Rondeau Redoublé	E317 no. 38	—	—
	Eve	E317 no. 39	*Poems* 862–3	—
?Feb. 1909	After School	E317 no. 40	*Poems* 863–4	—
?Feb. 1909	School	E317 no. 41	—	—
Feb. 1909	A Snowy Day at School	E317 no. 42	*Poems* 864–5	See (i. 113)
April 1909	Letters from Town. The Almond Tree	E317 no. 43	—	See (i. 125): ref. in E74a
?April 1909	Letter from Town. The City	E317 no. 44	—	—
	Letters f[rom town.] Unte[. . .]	E317 no. 45	—	Torn out of notebook
April–May 1909	Reading in the Evening	E317 no. 49	*Poems* 865–6	See (i. 126)
by June 1909	Discipline	E317 no. 46	—	E.T. 157: copied by JC in June 1909: *ER* Nov. 1909
by June 1909	A Still Afternoon in School	E317 no. 47	—	—

DATE	TITLE	SURVIVING MS OR TS	PRINTED TEXT CLOSE TO MS OR TS	NOTES
by June 1909	A Still Afternoon in School	E317 no. 48	—	E.T. 157: copied by JC in June 1909: ER Nov. 1909
		E320.4 no. 14–15	—	—
Summer 1909	Movements.			
	1. A Baby Running Barefoot	E317 no. 50	—	E.T. 157: copied by JC in June 1909: ER Nov. 1909
		E320.4 no. 16	—	—
Summer 1909	2. A Baby Asleep after Pain	E317 no. 51	—	E.T. 157: copied by JC in June 1909: ER Nov. 1909
	3. The Body Awake	E317 no. 52	—	—
	4. A Man at Play on the River	E317 no. 53	*Poems* 866–7	—
	5. A Review of the Scots Guards	E317 no. 54	—	—
	Restlessness	E317 no. 55	—	—
	A Bell	E317 no. 56 E320.4 no. 27	— —	—
	Lost	E317 no. 57	—	—
?Summer 1909	After the Theatre	E317 no. 58	—	—
	Brotherhood	E317 no. 59	—	—
?August 1909	The end of another Home-holiday	E317 no. 60	—	—
	Brotherhood	E317 no. 61 E320.4 no. 37	— —	— —
Autumn 1909	End of another Home-holiday	E317 no. 62	—	—
Autumn 1909	The Songless			

DATE	TITLE	SURVIVING MS OR TS	PRINTED TEXT CLOSE TO MS OR TS	NOTES
	1. Today. Tonight	E317 no. 63	*ER* text *Poems* 919–20	*ER* April 1910
	Tired	E320.4 no. 32	—	
Autumn 1909	2. Tomorrow Tired But Dissatisfied	E317 no. 64	*ER* Text *Poems* 920–1	*ER* April 1910
		E320.4 no. 33	—	
Autumn 1909	'When on the autumn roses'	E317 no. 65	—	—
	Amour	E317 no. 66	*Poems* 867	—
Autumn 1909	At the Window	E317 no. 67	—	*ER* April 1910
		E320.4 no. 19	—	
	Weeknight Service	E317 no. 68	—	—
		E320.4 no. 13	—	
Autumn 1909	Fooled	E317 no. 69	*ER* text *Poems* 731	*ER* April 1910
	Fooled!	E320.4 no. 9	—	
	Dream	E317 no. 70	—	—
Autumn 1909	Dream	E317 no. 71	—	*ER* April 1910

————⟨September–October 1909: Agnes Holt starts Notebook II (E320.1)⟩————

DATE	TITLE	SURVIVING MS OR TS	PRINTED TEXT CLOSE TO MS OR TS	NOTES
copied Sept.–Oct. 1909	Discipline	E320.1 no. 1	*ER* text *Poems* 929	*ER* Nov. 1909 Agnes Holt copy/DHL revised
		E95d	—	Source for Agnes Holt
copied Sept.–Oct. 1909	A Still Afternoon	E320.1 no. 2	*ER* text *Poems* 908	*ER* Nov. 1909 Agnes Holt copy
		E104c	—	Source for Agnes Holt
copied Sept.–Oct. 1909	Baby Movements.			
	1. Running Barefoot	E320.1 no. 3	*ER* text *Poems* 916	*ER* Nov. 1909 Agnes Holt copy
		E34.5c	—	Source for Agnes Holt
copied Sept.–Oct. 1909	2. "Trailing Clouds"	E320.1 no. 4	*ER* text *Poems* 916	*ER* Nov. 1909 Agnes Holt copy

DATE	TITLE	SURVIVING MS OR TS	PRINTED TEXT CLOSE TO MS OR TS	NOTES
		E33c	—	Source for Agnes Holt
copied Sept.–Oct. 1909	Restlessness	E320.1 no. 5	—	Agnes Holt/DHL copy

——————————————⟨DHL continues Notebook II⟩——————————————

DATE	TITLE	SURVIVING MS OR TS	PRINTED TEXT CLOSE TO MS OR TS	NOTES
	A Beloved	E320.1 no. 6	*R&MS* 6–7	—
	The Punisher	E320.1 no. 7	—	—
	An Epistle from Thelma	E320.1 no. 8	*R&MS* 8	—
	An Epistle from Arthur	E320.1 no. 9	*R&MS* 8	—
	Epilogue from Thelma	E320.1 no. 10	*R&MS* 9	—
	Sickness	E320.1 no. 11	—	—
November 1909	A Day in November	E320.1 no. 12	—	—
by Nov. 1909	A Life History In Harmonies and Discords			Ref. in E74a
	First Harmony	E320.1 no. 13	Appendix III	—
by Nov. 1909	Discord	E320.1 no. 14	Appendix III	—
by Nov. 1909	Second Harmony	E320.1 no. 15	Appendix III	—
by Nov. 1909	Discord	E320.1 no. 16	Appendix III	—
by Nov. 1909	Third Harmony	E320.1 no. 17	Appendix III	—
by Nov. 1909	Discord	E320.1 no. 18	Appendix III	—
by Nov. 1909	Fourth Harmony	E320.1 no. 19	Appendix III	—
by Nov. 1909	Baiser	E320.1 no. 20	Appendix III	Title inserted over end of previous poem
by Nov. 1909	Discord	E320.1 no. 21	Appendix III	—
by Nov. 1909	Last Harmony	E320.1 no. 22	Appendix III	—

DATE	TITLE	SURVIVING MS OR TS	PRINTED TEXT CLOSE TO MS OR TS	NOTES
	Kiss	E320.1 no. 23	—	Perhaps added later
		E320.6 no. 8	*Poems* 892	
	The Street-Lamps	E320.1 no. 24	—	—
		E320.4 no. 30	—	
	The Complaint of the Soul of a Worker	E320.1 no. 25	*R&MS* 9–10	—
	Monologue of a Mother	E320.1 no. 26	—	—
	School—I Morning. The Waste Lands	E320.1 no. 27	*R&MS* 10	—
	The Street	E320.1 no. 28	*R&MS* 10	—
	Scripture	E320.1 no. 29	*R&MS* 10	—
	Afternoon	E320.1 no. 30	—	—
February 1910	Malade	E320.1 no. 31	—	See (i. 155)
March–April 1910	Do not hold me, Siegmund	E320.1 no. 86	—	First draft of E320.1 no. 32
March–April 1910	A Love-Passage. A Rift in the Lute	E320.1 no. 32 E320.4 no. 6	— *Poems* 875–6	—
	[Spring in the City]	E320.1 no. 33	—	—
?May 1910	Infidelity Ah, Muriel	E320.1 no. 34 E320.4 no. 10	— —	*ER* Oct. 1910
?May 1910	Scent of Irises	E320.1 no. 35	—	Delavenay 703–4
?May 1910	Lilies in the Fire	—	[1913 version LP]	Delavenay 703–4
?May 1910	Red Moon-Rise	—	[1913 version LP]	—
?Summer 1910	Sigh No More Cuckoo and Wood-Dove	E320.1 no. 36 E320.4 no. 35	— —	*ER* Oct. 1910

DATE	TITLE	SURVIVING MS OR TS	PRINTED TEXT CLOSE TO MS OR TS	NOTES
	Late at Night along the Home Road	E320.1 no. 37	*R&MS* 11	—
?Autumn 1910	New Wine	E320.1 no. 38	—	—
	Liaison	E320.1 no. 39	—	—
	Ophelia	E320.1 no. 40	—	—
	Liaison	E320.1 no. 41	—	—
	Beneath the Yew Tree	E320.4 no. 21	—	
?Autumn 1910	Dolor of Autumn	E320.1 no. 42	—	—
	Unwitting	E320.1 no. 43	*R&MS* 11	—
	Nocturne	E320.1 no. 44	—	—
?Autumn 1910	Nocturne	E320.1 no. 45	*R&MS* 12	—
?Autumn 1910	The Appeal	E320.1 no. 46	—	—
?Autumn 1910	Reproach	E320.1 no. 47 E320.4 no. 22	*R&MS* 13	—
	Nils Lykke Dead	E320.1 no. 48	—	Accepted for *ER* by 6 April 1911 (i. 254)
		E320.4 no. 38	—	Sent to Garnett 23 Oct. 1911
		LaB6	—	—
?November 1910	Anxiety	E320.1 no. 54	—	Copied at later position
?November 1910	Patience	E320.1 no. 55	—	Copied at later position
⟨Restart of Notebook I⟩				
November 1910	The Crow	E317 no. 1	—	—
November 1910	Honeymoon	E317 no. 2	—	—
November 1910	Honeymoon	E317 no. 77	—	—
?November 1910	Brooding	E317 no. 74	—	—
December 1910	Sorrow	E317 no. 76	—	by 6 April 1911 DHL believed accepted (i. 254)

DATE	TITLE	SURVIVING MS OR TS	PRINTED TEXT CLOSE TO MS OR TS	NOTES
December 1910	Sorrow	E317 no. 3	—	—
December 1910	Grief	E317 no. 75	*Poems* 869	—
December 1910	Loss	E317 no. 73	*Poems* 868	—
December 1910	Bereavement	E317 no. 72	*Poems* 868	—
?December 1910	Last Words to Muriel	E317 no. 4	Illustrations 23 and 24	—

⟨LB translations and other poems⟩

DATE	TITLE	SURVIVING MS OR TS	PRINTED TEXT CLOSE TO MS OR TS	NOTES
6 Dec. 1910	Self Contempt	LaB77	(i. 196)	—
6 Dec. 1910	Near the Mark	LaB77	(i. 196)	—
December 1910	Love Message	LaB7	*Poems* 871	—
December 1910	The Witch I	LaB7	*Poems* 871–2	—
December 1910	Good Night	LaB9	*Poems* 872–3	—
December 1910	Sympathy	LaB9	*Poems* 873	—
December 1910	Train	LaB10–11	*Poems* 873	—
December 1910	At Midnight	LaB12	*Poems* 874	LB copy
December 1910	Beloved	LaB12	*Poems* 874	LB copy
December 1910	The Prophet in the Rose Garden	LaB12	*Poems* 874	LB copy
December 1910	Moth and Rust	LaB12	*Poems* 874	LB copy
December 1910	Irreverent Thoughts	LaB12	*Poems* 874–5	LB copy
December 1910	Two-fold	LaB13	*Poems* 875	LB copy
13 Dec. 1910	Elixir	LaB8	(i. 200)	—
13 Dec. 1910	The Witch II	LaB8	(i. 201)	—
15 Dec. 1910	The Wind, the Rascal	LaB80	(i. 203)	—
15 Dec. 1910	The Physician	LaB80	(i. 204)	—
15 Dec. 1910	Dusk-flower, look hither	LaB80	(i. 204)	—
?December 1910	Thief in the Night	—	[*New Poems* 1919]	—

⟨DHL restarts Notebook II⟩

DATE	TITLE	SURVIVING MS OR TS	PRINTED TEXT CLOSE TO MS OR TS	NOTES
after 9 Dec. 1910	Submergence	E320.1 no. 49	—	Inserted later

DATE	TITLE	SURVIVING MS OR TS	PRINTED TEXT CLOSE TO MS OR TS	NOTES
?December 1910	Reminder	E320.1 no. 50	—	—
?December 1910	A Wise Man Teasing	E320.1 no. 51 E320.4 no. 11	— —	See (i. 246)
early 1911	A Plaintive Confession	E320.1 no. 52 E320.4 no. 5	— *Poems* 877	—
early 1911	To Lettice, my Sister	E320.1 no. 53	*Poems* 940–1	—
early 1911	Winter	E320.1 no. 56	—	False start
early 1911	Winter	E320.1 no. 57	—	—
?early 1911	Another Ophelia	E320.1 no. 58 E320.4 no. 17 E38b	— *Poems* 935–6	— Sent to Garnett 23 Oct. 1911 On verso of E140a: copied when latter rewritten as E140c in March 1911 (i. 248)

─────────────〈L B copies into Notebook II〉─────────────

DATE	TITLE	SURVIVING MS OR TS	PRINTED TEXT CLOSE TO MS OR TS	NOTES
copied early 1911	To my Mother—Dead	E320.1 no. 59	—	L B copy
copied early 1911	The Dead Mother	E320.1 no. 60	—	L B copy
copied early 1911	My Love, My Mother	E320.1 no. 61	Chapter 15, pp. 411–12	L B copy with annotation by Frieda

─────────────〈DHL recommences Notebook II〉─────────────

DATE	TITLE	SURVIVING MS OR TS	PRINTED TEXT CLOSE TO MS OR TS	NOTES
?April 1911	Transformations.			Sent to Garnett 23 Oct. 1911
	1. Evening	E320.1 no. 62		
	2. Morning	E320.1 no. 63	*R&MS* 15	—
	3. Men in the Morning	E320.1 no. 64	—	—
	4. The Inanimate, that Changes Not in Shape	E320.1 no. 65	—	—

DATE	TITLE	SURVIVING MS OR TS	PRINTED TEXT CLOSE TO MS OR TS	NOTES
	5. The Changeful Animate	E320.1 no. 68	—	—
	6. Corot	E320.1 no. 69	*Poems* 917–18	—
	7. Raphael	E320.1 no. 70	[*LP* version *Poems* 918–19]	—
	'Ah, with his being bright'	E320.4 no. 1	*Poems* 876–7	Stanzas 5–9
	The Town	E320.1 no. 66	—	Inserted earlier
	The Earth	E320.1 no. 67	—	Inserted earlier
	Blue	E320.1 no. 71	—	—
	II. Red/Passion and Death	E320.1 no. 72 E320.4 no. 8	— *Poems* 888–9	— —
	Blue	E320.1 no. 73 E320.4 no. 28	— —	— —
?April 1911	Silence	E320.1 no. 74	—	—
?April 1911	The Inheritance	E320.1 no. 75	—	—
?April 1911	A Drama	E320.1 no. 76 E320.4 no. 7	— *Poems* 879–84	— —
?April 1911	Mating	E320.1 no. 77 E320.4 no. 24	— —	— —
	Meeting	E320.1 no. 78	—	E.T. 197 claims early 1912
	Return	E320.1 no. 79	—	—
	Separated	E320.1 no. 80 E320.4 no. 4	— *Poems* 885	— —
?late Spring 1911	Troth with the Dead	E320.1 no. 81	—	—
	A Love Song	E320.1 no. 82 LAB6 (Fragment) E320.4 no. 25	— *Poems* 871 —	— — —
c. 19 July 1911	Her Birthday	E320.1 no. 83	—	—
?Summer 1911	Your Hands	E320.1 no. 84	Chapter 11, pp. 309–11	—
		E320.4 no. 23	—	—

489

DATE	TITLE	SURVIVING MS OR TS	PRINTED TEXT CLOSE TO MS OR TS	NOTES
?Summer 1911	Drunk	E320.1 no. 85 E320.4 no. 20	— —	— —

⟨end of notebook II⟩

DATE	TITLE	SURVIVING MS OR TS	PRINTED TEXT CLOSE TO MS OR TS	NOTES
?mid-1911	Martyr à la Mode ('Croydon')	LaB6	*Poems* 869–70	Part sent LH in 1911: *Look!* 4
?after Aug. 1911	The Collier's Wife	—	—	*LP*
?after Aug. 1911	Whether or Not	—	[*LP* version *Poems* 921–8]	*LP*
?after Aug. 1911	The Drained Cup	—	—	*LP*
Autumn 1911	Snapdragon	E320.4 no. 26	*Poems* 937–40	LB says 191 *ER* June 191 *Amores*
?Autumn 1911	A Spiritual Woman	—	[*Amores* version *Poems* 934–5]	*Amores*
?1911	Kisses in the Train	[E213]	—	—
?1911	Wedding Morn	[E213]	—	*LP*
?1911	Aware	[E213]	—	*LP*
?1911	A Pang of Reminiscence	[E213]	—	*LP*
?1911	A White Blossom	[E213]	—	*LP*
?1911	The Best of School	—	—	*WG* 1 June 1912: *LP*
?1911	School on the Outskirts	—	—	*New Poems*
?1911	Death-Paean of a Mother	(UN)	—	—
?1911	Mystery	—	—	*Amores*
?1911	Lotus and Frost	—	—	*Amores*
?1911	Twofold	—	—	*New Poems*
?1911	In Trouble and Shame	—	—	*Amores*
?1911	Call into Death	—	—	*Amores*

DATE	TITLE	SURVIVING MS OR TS	PRINTED TEXT CLOSE TO MS OR TS	NOTES
?1911	Afterwards	—	—	*Amores*
?1911	Grief	—	—	*Amores*
?1911	Twilight	—	—	*Amores*
?1911	Love Storm	—	—	*New Poems*
1911–12	And Jude the Obscure and his Beloved	E320.4 no. 34	*Poems* 878–9	—
1911–12	Two Wives	E320.4 no. 39	—	—
1911–12	Moon New-Risen	E320.4 no. 2	*Poems* 888	—
?1911–12	Erotic	E320.4 no. 3	*Poems* 887–8	—
?1911–12	Moonrise	E320.4 no. 29	—	*Look!* 1
Jan. 1912	The Sea ('Bournemouth')	E320.4 no. 29	—	*Look!* 6
early 1912	Elegy ('Eastwood')	—	—	*Look!* 2
early 1912	Nonentity	—	—	*Look!* 3
early 1912	Don Juan	E320.6	—	*Look!* 5
?early 1912	Assuming the Burden	E320.4 no. 43	*Poems* 885–6	—
?early 1912	The Chief Mystery	E320.4 no. 40	*Poems* 886–7	—
?Spring 1912	Hymn to Priapus	—	—	*Look!* 7
April 1912	Pear-Blossom	E320.4 no. 42	*Poems* 890–1	—
April 1912	She Was a Good Little Wife	E320.4 no. 44	*Poems* 890	—
late April 1912	At the Cearne	E320.4 no. 41	*Poems* 891–2	—
late April 1912	'Other women have reared'	E320.4 no. 45	*Poems* 892–3	—
9–11 May 1912	Ballad of a Wilful Woman ('Trier')	[E320.6]	—	*Look!* 8
11 May 1912	Bei Hennef ('Hennef am Rhein')	[E213]	—	*LP*

DATE	TITLE	SURVIVING MS OR TS	PRINTED TEXT CLOSE TO MS OR TS	NOTES
26 May 1912	First Morning ('Beuerberg')	—	—	*Look!* 9
26–31 May 1912	She Looks Back ('Beuerberg')	—	—	*Look!* 11
6 June 1912	Frohnleichnam	—	—	*Look!* 13
June–Aug. 1912	On the Balcony ('Icking')	[E318]	—	*Look!* 12
	And oh ... might cease to be ('Wolfrats-hausen')	—	—	*Look!* 10
	In the Dark	—	—	*Look!* 14
	Mutilation ('Wolfrats-hausen')	—	—	*Look!* 15
	Humiliation	—	—	*Look!* 16
	A Young Wife	—	—	*Look!* 17
	Green ('Icking')	[E318]	[*Poetry* Jan. 1914]	*Look!* 18
	River Roses ('Kloster Schäftlarn')	[E318]	Frieda 45 [*Poetry* Jan. 1914: *Poems* 945]	*Look!* 19
	Gloire de Dijon ('Icking')	[E318]	Frieda 45–6 [*Poetry* Jan. 1914: *Poems* 945–6]	*Look!* 20
	Roses on the Breakfast Table	[E318]	Frieda 46 [*Poetry* Jan. 1914: *Poems* 946]	*Look!* 21
	I am like a Rose	—	—	*Look!* 22
	Rose of all the World	—	—	*Look!* 23
	All of Roses: IV	[E318]	Frieda 46 [*Poetry* Jan. 1914: *Poems* 946]	—

DATE	TITLE	SURVIVING MS OR TS	PRINTED TEXT CLOSE TO MS OR TS	NOTES
	Song of a Man who is loved	[E318]	Frieda 42	Frieda 41 says 'Isartal'
	A Youth Mowing	[E318]	[*Poetry* Jan. 1914: *Poems* 947]	*Look!* 24
	Quite Forsaken	—	—	*Look!* 25
	Forsaken and Forlorn	—	—	*Look!* 26
	Fireflies in the Corn	[E318]	[*Poetry* Jan. 1914: *Poems* 947–8]	*Look!* 27
7 Aug. 1912	Song of a Man who is not Loved ('Glashütte')	—	—	*Look!* 29
11–15 Aug. 1912	Sinners ('Mayrhofen')	—	—	*Look!* 30
11–25 Aug. 1912	Meeting Among the Mountains ('Tuxtal')	[E233.5]	Frieda 48–9	—
by 13 Aug. 1912	The Young Soldier with the Bloody Spurs	E446.5	(i. 434)	—
30–31 Aug. 1912	Misery ('Sterzing')	—	—	*Look!* 31
?October 1912	Sunday Afternoon in Italy ('Gargnano')	—	—	*Look!* 32
?October 1912	A Bad Beginning	—	—	*Look!* 34
?October 1912	Why does she weep?	—	—	*Look!* 35
2 Nov. 1912	Giorno dei Morti	—	*NS* 15 Nov. 1913	*Look!* 36
2 Nov. 1912	All Souls	—	—	*Look!* 37

DATE	TITLE	SURVIVING MS OR TS	PRINTED TEXT CLOSE TO MS OR TS	NOTES
?mid-Nov. 1912	From the Italian Lakes [Everlasting Flowers: 'Lago di Garda']	[E318]	Chapter 16, pp. 453–4	*New Poems*
?Winter 1912	Lady Wife	—	—	*Look!* 38
?December 1912	Winter Dawn	—	—	*Look!* 33
?December 1912	Both Sides of the Medal	—	—	*Look!* 39
?December 1912	Logger-heads	—	—	*Look!* 40
December 1912	December Night	—	—	*Look!* 41
31 Dec. 1912	New Year's Eve	—	—	*Look!* 42
Winter 1912–13	Birth Night	—	—	*Look!* 45
Winter 1912–13	Rabbit Snared in the Night	—	—	*Look!* 46
c. 1 Jan. 1913	New Year's Night	—	—	*Look!* 43
c. 14 Feb. 1913	Valentine's Night	—	—	*Look!* 44
?early 1913	Paradise Re-Entered [Purity]	—	—	*Look!* 47
?March 1913	Coming Awake	—	—	*New Poems*
early April 1913	Spring Morning ('San Gaudenzio')	—	—	*Look!* 48

'A LIFE HISTORY
IN HARMONIES AND DISCORDS'

Note The final readings of E320.1 have been given throughout.

FIRST HARMONY

Folded there deep hidden in the red inter-quivering flesh
The secret speck in a dim grey nebula drew flushing around it
    The glow of life ⟨...⟩ luminous blood.

Hastening always urgent to the new dark Cherubim
Came the scalding blood, gladly, to the service of the Dim One,   5
      and drowned it
    In a passionate scarlet flood.

The dim, imperious Grey-Star drew round itself like a glory
The sparkling threads of the blood, and hid in brightness, Itself:
    Then it loosed the residue back.

DISCORD

A sullen red moon held away the red tides from the clamouring Matter:
The tide relaxed, and ⟨...⟩ swept up and stunned the strange elf,
    And waited, threaded with black.

Till the trammelled Matter awoke and wildly netted the Life
And with the life some of the scalded death, and in the threads kindled
      agony and hate   5
And kept them all, and laid them down in their tissued beds,
Ruddy joy with death, and black anger with Love for mate.

SECOND HARMONY

    "Once in the dusky mirror
    There only could I find
    Eyes to balance my sorrow,
    Lips to my bitterness lined.

    Once in the misty mirror   5
    I laid my aching cheek
    And warmed my tear-dimmed mirror
    Till I felt that my shadow could speak—

Now open at my bosom
Two eyes that are blue like mine,   10
Eyes like the outer twilight
Where the suns last sufferings shine

Now clinging over my bosom
Two little crisping hands
Plant my heart like a garden,   15
Grow lilies in brackish sands."

DISCORD

At the breast like a dawn on the bosom of darkness, ruddily,
    Dawned the Dark-star, obscured in flesh:
A star that is almost extinguished, grown large and red
    Lapped in the mist's close mesh.

Between the wombed-One, Night, and Day that must thresh   5
    The grain, went tramping the panther of scorn,
Skulked the hyaena of spite, which snarled and fled
    Brushing ⟨...⟩ bristles the ⟨...⟩ born

Voices tangled in ⟨...⟩   have torn
    In tatters the flesh   10
And the hour which ⟨...⟩   the ⟨...⟩
    In ⟨...⟩ and ⟨...⟩   behests

Between the voices, blind ⟨...⟩ snatched out of the nest's
    Soft, clasp ⟨...⟩   in moments of anguish
Rose the thin ⟨...⟩ of my child ⟨...⟩ lips ⟨...⟩ like the ⟨...⟩ of   15
    Lisping ⟨...⟩   languish.

THIRD HARMONY

Round the house were lilacs and strawberries
    And foal-foots spangling the paths
And far away on the sand-hills, the dewberries
    Caught dust from the sea's long swaths.

Up the wolds the woods were walking   5
    And nuts fell out of their hair:
At the gates the nets hung, balking
    The starlit rush of the hare.

In the autumn fields the stubble
    Tinkled the music of gleaning: 10
Between a mother's knees, a trouble
    Lost all its little meaning.

496

Look in the hutch at the end of the garden
    A wise old black and white rabbit:
In the bend of the chimney, a horse chestnut will harden   15
    If you dare ⟨...⟩ up and grab it.

The young white terrier barked like laughter
    Outside the school at noon.
A terrible pirate stalked abaft a
    ⟨...⟩   20

Softly through ⟨...⟩   floor
    ⟨...⟩
⟨...⟩
    A violin ⟨...⟩

DISCORD

Outside the house an ash-tree hung its terrible whips
And at night the wind rose and the lash of the tree
Shrieked and slashed the wind, as a phantom ship's
Weird rigging in a storm shrieks hideously.

In the house the two same voices woke when the ash   5
    Was still, a swift thin lash
Whistling, and a thick lash sweeping with a booming dreadful sound
    And uproaring, till the thin voice was drowned
In a fearful ominous silence and the spell of blood
    Held the night fast bound.   10

One by one the frail thin voices
    Thronged themselves for fight.
Hoarser roared the heavy anger
    Hoarser after each hiss and bite
Frayed, and fraught with lessening danger   15
    Untwisted, unable to requite.

FOURTH HARMONY

Shadows upon the pavement lying real
    Like a shadow in ink on a gold-grey cartoon
From the strange dark eyes of a painter of Japan:
    —The shadow awakes, and dances with fear:
        —An eclipse comes over the moon—   5
The leaf lies over the shadow like a lap-wing tinted fan.

Birds with level wings droop down from the night
   —The plane-leaves are falling in the violet dusk
Noiselessly crossing the lamp's gold space
     As a dark fish sinks through the watery light   10
       —A narwhals ivory tusk!—
I have caught the leaf for luck in my hands white interlace.

Swinging like sails in a dim regatta at night
    In and out of the dark, the faces
Pass over my soul, and the nimble light   15
    Paints pale daubs for my soul's delight.
       The haunting love at it ⟨...⟩ paces—
Little friend for my heart's love ⟨...⟩ have ⟨...⟩ and the love far dight.

Hush, do you see my house mate calm like a shadow
    The warm lamp casts at the door of the dark: 20
A red flower falls to its dim reflection
    Hastening down a quivering ladder
      —A kiss, or a mist-blurred spark!—
The red ⟨...⟩ blots out its shade in an intimate joyous connection.

DISCORD

   One by one the fingers of love loosened the petals
     from off the rose
   Fingers like fallen chrysanthemum petals
     ⟨...⟩ fingers ⟨...⟩like ⟨...⟩ ose

   Whorl by whorl the petals spread their tender   5
     sweet ⟨...⟩ love
   Showed the ⟨...⟩ wine ⟨...⟩ and circled
     ⟨...⟩ of love

   Slowly the flower leaned ⟨...⟩ ly from the ⟨...⟩ of the
     beloved and ⟨...⟩   10
   Strangely and sadly the innermost colour and fragrance
     least ⟨...⟩ now ⟨...⟩

   Heavy and deadly the scent, fierce and dreadful to
     the eyes of those women ⟨...⟩ the flower
   Packed itself like a pl ⟨...⟩ that quenched   15
     ⟨...⟩ underneath a shower

   Of their tears but ⟨...⟩ drove them back away in a g ⟨...⟩:
     and she ⟨...⟩ with hastening fingers
   Knowing the fragrance and the flower they had ⟨...⟩
     Flowers ⟨...⟩ dreadfully lingers   20

[? Replacement for last two lines]

> Of tidings of death down the dark, soft ⟨...⟩
> ⟨...⟩ unwearied singers

LAST HARMONY

Watch each pair of stepping feet trace a strange design
  With broken curves and faltering lines
I trace a pattern, mine or thine
  Patiently, and over-line

Ah the blindly stepping kindly feet   5
  Watch them tracing their design
The curves waver and meet and interwine
  Twisting and Tangling mine and thine

With pain did I carefully overline
  What part of my graph was plainly plotted   10
Where the curves were knotted I must define
  Pains that were clotted over mine

I have come

APPENDIX IV

◆

D. H. LAWRENCE'S AUTOBIOGRAPHIES

DHL wrote a considerable number of autobiographical pieces during the period 1926–9:

'Getting On' (October–November 1926)

'Return to Bestwood' (October–November 1926)

'Mushrooms' (?late 1926)

'Which Class I belong To' (January 1927) (draft of 'Myself Revealed', later 'Autobiographical Sketch')

'A Dream of Life' ('Autobiographical Fragment') (October 1927)

'Foreword' to *Collected Poems* (May 1928)

'Notes' ('Autobiography') for the publisher Kra (*c.* July 1928)

'Red-Herring', 'Climbing Up', 'A Rise in the World', 'Up he Goes—', 'Have Done with It' and 'The Saddest Day' (in *Pansies*: late 1928)

'Enslaved by Civilisation' (November 1928)

'Nottingham and the Mining Countryside' (?summer 1929)

In the same period there are also oddities like Mellors's accounts of his early loves in *Lady Chatterley's Lover*.[1]

As I have shown elsewhere, these pieces are often unreliable.[2] What connects them is their analysis of the way DHL no longer felt England was a place where he could (in any sense) be at 'home'. The subject appears to have grown out of his last visit to the Midlands in 1926; the essays and poems, in particular, represent a man and writer taking stock of himself in his early forties, and asking himself what his country's recent history had really been, and why he felt so excluded from it.

His unvarying answer is to say that England has changed: that the old working class, of which he was part, is gone. To make that last point, DHL engages in an extraordinary series of rewritings of his early history, and in particular of the lives of his parents. In his essays 'Return to Bestwood', 'Getting On' and 'Which Class I belong To' he creates a more sympathetic portrait of his father than he had ever previously committed to print (his father had died in September 1924), while simultaneously representing his mother as a snob who was primarily responsible for the family quarrels. Arthur Lawrence now appears as a charming, very ordinary man, 'a collier who drank, who never went to church, who spoke broad dialect, and was altogether one of the common colliers'. But Lydia Lawrence is a woman obsessed by class, and with her sons 'getting on': 'Now I am forty, I realise that my mother deceived me. She stood for all that was lofty and noble and delicate and sensitive and pure, in my life. And all the time, she was worshipping success, because she hadn't got it.' She is presented as taking out her sense of impoverishment on her husband:

My mother fought with deadly hostility against my father, all her life. He was not hostile, till provoked, then he too was a devil. But my mother began it. She seemed to begrudge his very existence. She begrudged and hated her own love for him, she fought against his natural charm, vindictively. And by the time she died, at the age of fifty-five, she neither loved him nor hated him any more. She had got over her feeling for him, and was "free". So she died of cancer.[3]

It is, as that extract suggests ('So she died . . .'), an extremely unsympathetic portrait; but it is repeated with variations in the other essays of the series. 'Which Class I belong To', of January 1927, shows Lydia Lawrence belonging 'potentially to the middle-classes', while Arthur Lawrence is 'a collier, and only a collier'; the 'Autobiography' for Kra, written in July 1928, goes further by stating categorically that Lydia Lawrence was 'from the bourgeoisie' and deriding the way she encouraged her sons to 'rise in the world'.[4] The 1927 essay had at least explained how Arthur Lawrence 'could with great difficulty write a few words for a letter, and he could spell down the columns of the local newspaper'; in the Kra piece, however, Arthur Lawrence is 'a coal-miner, scarcely able to read or write'. By the time DHL came to write 'Nottingham and the Mining Countryside', his version of the truth has become even more absolute: 'men of my father's age could not really read'. But that is not a criticism; it is a guarantee of Arthur Lawrence's instinctual life. Education is seen as inherently destructive, it means being 'really tamed', as DHL put it in 'Enslaved by Civilisation'.[5] In 'Nottingham and the Mining Countryside' and 'Enslaved by Civilisation', Lydia Lawrence no longer even appears by name; she is simply one of the group of 'colliers' wives' or 'the women of my mother's generation', though Arthur Lawrence is still 'my father'. The colliers' wives are marked by their 'nagging materialism', and the collier very naturally 'fled out of the house as soon as he could', away from it, 'fled away from the women and rackapelted with his own gang'. The distinction between the woman with nagging, middle-class aspirations, and the wild or untamed collier is made absolute. We hear how the colliers have a real love for the beauty of flowers: 'I have known it often and often, in colliers'; the colliers' wives, however, like most women, only 'love flowers as possessions, and as trimmings'. In Sons and Lovers, we had heard a good deal about Mrs Morel and her love for her garden, and we also know about Lydia Lawrence's love for her garden. But both are now turned against the woman; it is the man who really loves the garden.[6] The support, love and encouragement for education which Lydia Lawrence gave to her children are now represented only as a nagging insistence on commercial success and 'getting on'. The real, and (in retrospect) primarily influential parent is the father, who represents the spirit of the untamed old England; the mother only represents the spirit of sordid commercialism.

DHL also makes the family home of his childhood 'an absolutely working-class home' in 'Which Class I belong To', and then goes further (in the Kra 'Autobiography') by suggesting that he, too, was a perfectly ordinary working-class child who 'went to elementary school & was just like anybody else of the miners' children'.[7] The Lawrence family and especially DHL himself could in no sense be called *ordinary*, in Eastwood. But DHL's late autobiographies all suggest that his own original (and continuing) loyalties were not to the middle-class aspirations of his mother, but to his father. He writes, for example, in his 'Autobiography' for Kra how his mother wanted her children to 'rise in the world, step by step', but that 'D.H. however recoiled away from the world, hated its ladder, & refused to rise. He had proper bourgeois aunts with "library" & "drawing-room" to their houses – but didn't like that either — preferred the powerful life in a miner's kitchen . . .'[8] *A Collier's Friday Night* suggests how little either its author or its protagonist Ernest preferred that 'powerful life in a miner's kitchen'; while nothing about the young DHL's career suggest that he 'refused to rise'. On the contrary, he was educated out of the working class; his profession of elementary schoolteacher may have been humble, but it was certainly on the middle-class ladder. And while he never embraced his teaching career joyfully, there was also no question that it was what he was going to do, from the age of 16 onwards. DHL would write very truthfully in 'Which Class I belong To' how 'I have, as far as circumstances go, left the working-class world',[9] but he does not add that this was a process which had actually been in progress since his very earliest childhood.

In these late autobiographical pieces, however, DHL declares his inborn sympathy with the working class, and his lifelong recoil away from the middle class. That separation is both part of the message of his late writing, and yet another reminder of that division in family and in consciousness which marked the early part of his life, and which remained as a kind of vivid ghost to the end of it. As the novel *Lady Chatterley's Lover* shows, the theme of 'tenderness', of warmth and instinctual contact between human beings, was what DHL wanted to write about in these years. For the purposes of that writing, and out of his own longing for what he had been denied, or had lost, or had never experienced, he constructed a myth about his own early life which he could most usefully employ in his attack on England and on the middle classes. The autobiographical pieces supported his definition of what had gone wrong in England in the last thirty or forty years; womanhood has been allowed to triumph, in its declaration of material loyalties; real manhood and human warmth has been denied, together with real sexuality; men are now 'tame'. And DHL asserted his loyalty not to the working class as such, because (as he said) he no longer belonged to it; but created a loyalty to what it could be made to symbolise.

The essays show how hard it was for DHL, by 1926, to declare what it was he belonged to, in terms of country or class; they demonstrate an odd and rather moving kind of desire to assert attachment and belonging, when he actually found it very hard either to feel it or to substantiate it. By the late 1920s he no longer really 'belonged' to 'his' England or to his English folk any more. When his sister Emily and niece Margaret visited him in 1928, it was (he found) 'really rather suffering', and provoked him to unusual outspokenness: 'How I hate the attitude of ordinary people to life. How I loathe ordinariness! How from my soul I abhor nice simple people, with their eternal price-list. It makes my blood boil.' His sense of being cut off from his own family only made him the more determined to reassert the almost mythical England to which he *did* belong, even if that country had, for the sake of the argument, to be constructed. Denis Donoghue once remarked that Yeats 'invented a country, calling it Ireland':[10] in these late essays, DHL invented a country and called it England. 'Is England still a Man's Country?' asks the title of an essay he published in 1929 – and asserted the kind of country for which he wanted to write. In 'Nottingham and the Mining Countryside' he described life in nineteenth-century Eastwood and in the coal industry: but he was really creating his myth about what he thought men in the twentieth century had lost:

> The pit did not mechanize men. On the contrary. Under the butty system, the miners worked underground as a sort of intimate community, they knew each other practically naked, and with curious close intimacy, and the darkness and the underground remoteness of the pit "stall," and the continual presence of danger, made the physical, instinctive, and intuitional contact between men very highly developed, a contact almost as close as touch, very real and very powerful.[11]

Such writing is in very great danger of an idealising nostalgia, in its version of life in the pre-mechanised pit (which is what DHL means by 'Under the butty system'): we feel something rather rare in DHL, the writer's need to distort his material so as to make it say what he wants. Very different is his genuinely imagined version of life in the Eastwood of 2927, in 'A Dream of Life', where the narrator wakes up after a thousand-year sleep to find Eastwood regenerated as a kind of Etruscan hilltop walled city; agricultural in an old-fashioned English way, but – for its everyday life – dependent upon DHL's knowledge of ancient Etruscans and contemporary Indians.[12] He has to *make* his version of the 'very highly developed' physical, instinctive and intuitional contact between people; and he also, very beautifully, reveals his narrator's slight but insistent anger with what he sees, feeling (as he does) dispossessed of what might have been his birthright.

This was the kind of writing DHL most wanted to do, in the last years of his life, and for which the essays served him as a kind of argumentative support. But he gave himself continual problems when he tried to demonstrate the possibility of such a life from the facts and circumstances of his own childhood in late nineteenth-century Eastwood. The distortions of the late essays demonstrate his desire to assert what did not emerge from the facts.

He also had the burden of his early autobiographical novel *Sons and Lovers* to overcome; one with its own distortions within it. He wanted to redress a balance, and he attacked the life he thought his mother had impelled him towards. He only attacked the mother herself occasionally; he attacked her most savagely, perhaps, by omitting her. These essays may best be seen as a final swing of the pendulum, in the to-and-fro of the conflict which had surrounded his early life; but the more they assert the simple unity and simple choices of that life, the more they reveal its divisions. It is of such division that we must always be conscious, within DHL's environment, within his family, within the man himself: and within the very structures of his writing.

Notes
and
Sources

THE USE OF SOURCES

In every case but those to one correspondent, DHL's letters survive in texts accurately established by the Cambridge edition. His letters to JC are the one possible exception to the rule of accuracy; their texts exist only in the versions she published in her 1935 memoir *D. H. Lawrence: A Personal Record*. While she was, in the words of her brother David, 'an intensely truthful woman', her texts were memorial reconstructions of letters she had been sent many years earlier, and which she had probably destroyed before her marriage in 1915: possibly as early as 1912.[1]

In one case we are able to compare her memory of a letter written in 1908 with a version which DHL himself wrote down in the spring 1912 draft of his novel 'Paul Morel' (later *Sons and Lovers*). Much of the letter – because Edward Garnett severely cut it in the 1913 published version of the novel – JC cannot have seen in print. This enables us to make some assessment of how well, in the early 1930s, she remembered DHL's letters. It is unfortunately only a rough assessment, because DHL's version of the letter is itself a memorial reconstruction. But JC read the manuscript of the novel which contained it and made a handwritten correction to explain what Miriam subsequently did with the letter; she did not, however, alter the text of the letter itself. This suggests that she accepted it as an accurate copy.

'Paul Morel' text	JC's text
(A) See, you are a nun. I have given you what I would give a holy nun—	Look, you are a nun, I give you what I would give a holy nun.
(B) When I talk to you, I do not look at you, often, for, can you understand, I do not talk to your eyes, though they are dark and fine, nor to your ears, hidden under a graceful toss of silky hair—but to you away inside, beyond. So I shall continue to do a whole life-time, if fate does not intervene.	When I look at you, what I see is not the kissable and embraceable part of you, although it is so fine to look at, with the silken toss of hair curling over your ears. What I see is the deep spirit within. That I love and can go on loving all my life.
(C) I might marry in the years to come. It would be a woman I could kiss and embrace, whom I could make the mother of my children ...	So you must let me marry a woman I can kiss and embrace and make the mother of my children.[2]

JC is most accurate when quoting phrases which she could have read again in the published *Sons and Lovers* – for example, the whole of quotation (A). The last part of extract (C) shows, however, how well she could also recall a passage which did not appear in the published novel. Extract (B) – again, not in the published novel – nevertheless indicates that what she prints is equally likely to be only a rough paraphrase of what DHL believed he had written and which she had accepted as accurate in 1912. We must never rely too heavily upon the actual words of the letters she quotes. Her honesty is well vouched for; and though she herself seldom expressed doubt of her accuracy, it is not her fault that she did not possess a photographic memory.

The same applies to the other main category of doubtful material: the written and tape-recorded memories of people who knew DHL. Most of these were not written down or recorded until many years later. The lengthy conversations recorded by May Chambers, for example, were probably not noted down for at least three years, and perhaps not for as long as twenty-five years after they occurred.[3] However attractive her reporting, and it frequently offers an unusually convincing version of DHL's conversation, we must – as with the letters published by JC – take the spirit rather than the word as the most reliable part of her contribution. The most generally reliable early memoirists appear to be May Chambers, Ada Lawrence and JC. The latter provided an incomparable guide to the life of the young DHL; yet her memoirs are also coloured throughout by her interpretation of DHL's attachment to his mother. LB's recollections are fragmentary and were probably not written down until 1931: a correction she made in 1962, however, in her copy of Moore's *Collected Letters*, to a date of a letter DHL himself misdated, does suggest a person with a remarkable memory.[4] George Neville's memoirs, though full and detailed, suffer from occasional lapses of memory and at times conflate events and periods. The earlier HC's reminiscence dates from, the more accurate it is likely to be: as she got older, she trusted her memory even where she was contradicting what she had said earlier.[5] Frieda's memory was never particularly good, but her published book about DHL – and her fragmentary memoirs – provide a good deal of material for DHL's life after March 1912. Her memoirs regularly fictionalised names but apparently little else. At the bottom of any table of relative accuracy, sadly, must appear the reminiscences of Ford Madox Hueffer, which do not baulk at inventing events, conversations and even visits which never happened but which, for one reason or another (usually good) Hueffer felt *should* have happened.[6]

The tape-recorded recollections of DHL collected for Nottingham Public Library by David Gerard vary enormously in quality and accuracy; most of the people he and his associates interviewed were very old. Outstanding among the interviewees, however, is Alice Hall Holditch, whose memory was good and whose knowledge is extensive. Easily the worst is DHL's nephew William Ernest Lawrence, whose anecdotes about his uncle are frequently unreliable, though he may well only be embroidering things already distorted by his father George Lawrence.

The surviving sources for DHL's early life are also frequently one-sided. The fact that DHL's letters to LB survive almost *in toto*, while not a single one of hers to him survives, means that our picture of their engagement is radically unbalanced. I have quoted wherever possible from her 1931 memoirs of DHL in an attempt to redress the balance. On the other hand, while JC's recollections of DHL were carefully worked over and revised, his about her exist mostly in the form of fictions.

In general, I have quoted extensively from letters and memoirs, and frequently drawn upon the more accurate tape-recorded recollections. The letters bear witness to events and beliefs of the moment, and the memoirs and tape-recordings at least allow DHL's contemporaries to speak for themselves in their own voices. As became clear from the memoirs assembled by Edward Nehls in *D. H. Lawrence: A Composite Biography*, the more one reads of a memoir, the easier it is to understand a person's standpoint and prejudices, and thus to gauge their reliability.

I have described above the use I have made of DHL's novels *Sons and Lovers* and *Mr Noon*.[7] The 'autobiographies' of the last part of DHL's life are discussed in Appendix IV.

NOTES

Chapter One: Antecedents

1 W. E. Hopkin, Unpublished Autobiography, quoted in Noel M. Kader, *William Edward Hopkin* [Eastwood, 1976], p. 11.
2 LB Papers 24; Nehls, i. 21; Kader, *William Edward Hopkin*, p. 11.
3 E373d, p. 80. The drafts of 'Paul Morel' will be referred to in the notes as follows:

'Paul Morel' I		?September–October 1910
'Paul Morel' II	(E373d & e)	March–July 1911
'Paul Morel' IIIa	(E373a, b & e)	Nov. 1911, Feb.–April 1912
'Paul Morel' IIIb	(E373a & e)	May–June 1912
Sons and Lovers	(E373e)	July–August, Sept.–Nov. 1912

4 A. R. and C. P. Griffin, 'A Social and Economic History of Eastwood and the Nottinghamshire Mining Country' in *A D. H. Lawrence Handbook*, ed. Keith Sagar (Manchester, 1982), p. 139; Frieda 306.
5 See DHL to S. S. Koteliansky, 27 April 1927: 'Gertie has been a horrible business – in a hospital in London these last two months – left lung removed, six ribs removed, glands in neck – too horrible – better die.' Tom Cooper was the only one of his family not to die of tuberculosis: he died of kidney disease at the age of 63, in August 1918. Dr Andrew Morland's book *Pulmonary Tuberculosis in General Practice* (1933) has been consulted for contemporary medical understanding of the disease: it is of particular interest because Morland himself advised DHL on treatment in January 1930.
6 Edward Gilbert, notes of conversations with Emily King (Sagar); Nehls, iii. 391.
7 William Lawrence appeared at the christenings of his children as 'Whitesmith', 'Forger' and 'Brass Founder' (St Martin's Parish Church, Birmingham, christening of Sarah and Elizabeth, 6 September 1813 and 30 March 1815: St John Aston in Deritend, County of Warwick, christening of John, 25 December 1815) (Birmingham City Record Office); (iii. 282): subsequent references to the Cambridge edition of DHL's letters will appear in the text, using the symbols listed in Section A above.
8 *SL* 9; Nehls, iii. 23 and 658 n. 33; (ii. 165); 'French Sons of Germany' Galley proof sheet 1 (Lazarus); information from George Hardy; E.T. 106.
9 See Harry T. Moore, *The Priest of Love* (1974), p. 8; Ada 37; cf. DHL to Harry and Caresse Crosby, 26 May 1928: 'I shall buy some snuff and put it in the

snuff-box and take it as my grandfather did: and offer worthy souls a pinch and a sneeze, with little finger lifted.'

10 Ada 37; George Lawrence, taped interview with David Gerard (NCL); Ada 37.

11 'Nottingham and the Mining Countryside', *P* 133.

12 Ibid.; Ada 37.

13 Ada 40, 38.

14 *SL* 2.

15 Ada 24.

16 'Enslaved by Civilisation', *P II* 580 and note; R. W. Storer, *Some Aspects of Brinsley Colliery and the Lawrence Connection* (Selston, 1985), pp. 11–12 (see pp. 44–52 for an account of work at the coal-face in Brinsley pit). A 13-year-old collier at Brinsley (who had worked 'nearly seven years in pits' by 1842) reported that he had had 4½ years of Sunday school education, and was able to read 'the Testament'; the same year, an 11-year-old – at work since he was 8 – reported 4 years of Sunday school, and could read 'in the Testament; can write a little' (pp. 10–11).

17 'Benjamin Franklin', *Studies in Classic American Literature* (New York, 1923), p. 20: calendars and almanacs (Parish and Co-op) also appear in *PO* 42:27 and 46:9–12, *The Daughter-in-Law* E84a, p. 55 and *Lady Chatterley's Lover* E186c, p. 530.

18 Arthur Coleman, *Eastwood through Bygone Ages* (Eastwood, n. d.), p. 110; E. T. 20.

19 Storer, *Some Aspects*, p. 38.

20 E373e, p. 11; if – like Mr Morel's dancing-class – it had been 'in the Miners Arms Club-room' in Eastwood for 'over five year' (E373e, p. 19), it would probably have existed before 1869: Ada Lawrence also knew about her father's 'graceful dancing' (Ada 23), but JC recalled DHL telling the Chambers family that not only had his father danced 'when he was a young man' but that 'He ran a dancing class at one time': DHL also recalled his father's remark that 'one ought to be able to dance on a three-penny bit' (E.T. 30); Edward Gilbert notes.

21 'Matilda', E392a, p. 22. The piece was probably written early in 1910: see chapter 10, pp. 276–8.

22 1881 definition in *OED*: the description of him as an 'engineer' in Ada's biography of her brother (Ada 13) and on his daughters' marriage certificates suggests his attempt to upgrade his status: he appeared as 'machine fitter', however, on his wife's death certificate in 1900; Edward Gilbert notes.

23 1881 Census. The children were William and Louisa, the latter (at 14) already 'lace mender'.

24 Roy Spencer, *D. H. Lawrence Country* (1979), pp. 67–8.

25 Ibid., p. 80.

26 Ibid., pp. 71–4: Emily King also recalled that Lydia 'had a school of her own' in Sheerness (Edward Gilbert notes); E392a, pp. 42–8; *SL* 8.

27 *SL* 259–60, emended from E373e, p. 365.

28 *EmyE* 209:5.

29 E373e, p. 7.

30 Ada 23–4, 23; Edward Gilbert notes.

31 *SL* 11; Neville 51.

32 Ada 23, 24–5.

33 E373e, p. 106; Ada 23.

34 Ada 23.

35 *SL* 12–13: the Electoral Registers for 1885–7 and 1907 (the latter not updated after John Lawrence's death in March 1901) both record him as a voter by right of his ownership of 'freehold houses' (BL); Emily King was also sure that 'Arthur deceived Lydia over money before marrying her' (Edward Gilbert notes).

36 Ada 22.

37 John Burnett, *Plenty and Want* (1966), p. 95; John Richard Staynes is described as 'formerly a Lace Manufacturer' on his wife Nellie's 1908 death certificate; Krenkow was 25.

38 Nehls, iii. 564.

39 *SL* 10.

40 Ada 22; Edward Gilbert notes; cf. Frieda to Koteliansky, 'Monday' [1932]: 'Ada is awfully decent – she has his and her mother's uncompromising honesty' (BL Add. Mss. 48975, fol. 28).

41 Cf. a deleted passage in final manuscript of *The White Peacock*, in which Mrs Beardsall describes her marriage. Her son Cyril narrates the passage; her daughter Lettie has asked her

"Do you think we ought to calculate, mother—about—about choosing a man, for instance?"

"I did not calculate," replied my mother, meaningful.

"No!" said Lettie thoughtfully.

"You have to choose," said my mother, "either a man to be a companion, a husband—or—the man whose children you want."

Lettie blushed vividly . . .   (*WP* 370–1)

42 E392a, p. 5; *SL* 7, 10, 7.

43 E392a, pp. 7, 4, 7.

44 Ibid., pp. 34–5.

45 Ibid., p. 38.

46 Ibid., pp. 38, 39.

47 *Eastwood and Kimberley Advertiser*, 8 October 1897, p. 2.

48 Ada 21–3, 21, 23.

49 *SL* 16; cf. 'The Miner at Home', 'A Sick Collier', 'Her Turn' and 'Strike-Pay', all written between February and March 1912, when DHL was also writing a new and much more realistic version of *Sons and Lovers*: see *PO* xxiii–xxiv and *LAH* xxxii–xxxiii.

50 Ada 21–2. DHL later told the Rev. Robert Reid that 'My mother held you very high' (i. 244).

51 *Co-operative News*, 21 January 1911, p. 80. See Victoria Middleton, 'Happy Birthday, Mrs Lawrence', *D. H. Lawrence, 1885–1930: A Celebration*, ed. Andrew Cooper (Nottingham, 1985), pp. 8–16.

52 *SL* 52; Virginia Woolf, 'Introductory Letter', *Life As We Have Known It*, ed. M. Llewellyn Davies (1931), pp. xxxv–xxxvi.

53 *Life As We Have Known It*, ed. Llewellyn Davies, p. 48; E373e, p. 83; Catherine Webb, *The Woman with the Basket* (1927), p. 109.

54 Margaret Llewellyn Davies, speaking in 1889, quoted in Webb, *The Woman with the Basket*, p. 32; *Life As We Have Known It*, ed. Llewellyn Davies, p. 49; Webb, *The Woman with the Basket*, p. 37; Middleton, 'Happy Birthday, Mrs Lawrence', pp. 8–16; the book was *Working Men Co-operators: What They Have Done and What They are Doing* by Arthur H. D. Acland and Benjamin Jones (1884): the ideal essay was to describe the social and industrial conditions that existed when Owen formulated his views, his theories and practice and their results, the Rochdale system of co-operation and the running of a co-operative store – pricing, profits, distribution, etc.: ten women submitted papers but Lydia Lawrence's was not singled out as one of the best four: none of the essays survives (see *Co-operative News*, 13 August 1897, pp. 903–4); Margaret Llewellyn Davies, 'Foreword' to Webb, *The Woman with the Basket*, p. 10.

55 John Shuttleworth, Ilkeston, 3 July 1983; Ada 24.

56 Ada 24; the proverbial phrase actually derives from a letter from Alexander Pope to John Gay, 6 October 1727.

57 Lydia Lawrence to Lettice Berry, 18 May 1910 (Clarke).

58 'Autobiographical Sketch', *P II* 592.

59 E74a p. [3]; Ford Madox Hueffer (see 'The Use of Sources') described *New Age* readers as 'from widely different classes ... I have known it read regularly by board-school teachers, shop assistants, servants, artisans, and members of the poor generally' ('Women and Men IV', *Little Review*, iv, May 1918, 59): DHL may well have been the board-school teacher Hueffer remembered; 'Autobiographical Sketch', *P II* 592; the novels are by George Meredith (1828–1909) and Mrs Henry Wood (1814–87) respectively: the former 'the first of the author's novels to attain anything approaching general popularity', the latter a novel 'of remarkable popularity' (John W. Cousin, *A Short Biographical Dictionary of English Literature*, 1910, pp. 267 and 413): *East Lynne*, together with twenty-three other books by Mrs Henry Wood, was in the Mechanics' Institute Library in Eastwood (*A Catalogue of Books Belonging to the Library of the Eastwood and Greasley Mechanics' and Artizans' Institute*, Eastwood, 1895, NCL).

60 E373e, p. 188; Annie S. Swan was the pseudonym under which Mrs Burnett Smith (1872–1943) wrote; she was author of over 150 novels, 8 of which (including *Carlowrie*, which was known in the Lawrence family) were in the Mechanics' Institute Library, along with *Wuthering Heights* and 25 novels by Scott; E.T. 102, 25; Ada 21: we should probably add the *Life of Gladstone* (1903) by John Morley (1838–1923) to the list of her reading; DHL referred once to his mother's admiration for Mr Gladstone (see 'Autobiographical Sketch', E31.3, p. 1), and a reference in *The White Peacock* suggests that Morley's

biography was its source (*WP* 76: 1–2): the book was lectured on at Eastwood Congregational Literary Society (i. 4).

61 *SL* 9. One of DHL's very rare references to his father's family came in the 1913 version of his essay 'The Theatre':

> They are peasants in origin, these actors: so the Signore says. They nearly made me weep. I had a cousin, a collier's wife, whom I loved. She had twins when she had already eight children, but she said "The more the merrier." Her boast was, "All my children are named after kings." She also had a brooch made of a four-shilling piece, so she used to say: "I've got money when there isn't a penny in my pocket."
>
> The actors were like Hannah's children: "they were all named after kings."
>
> ('Italian Studies: By the Lago di Garda: III.–THE THEATRE', *English Review*, xv, September 1913, 228)

The cousin DHL had in mind was Hannah Foster, daughter of his paternal aunt Emma: born in Brinsley in 1861, in 1882 Hannah married the coal-miner William Andrews: among their children were Matilda, Arthur, George William, Mabel, Albert Edward, Harold and the twins Charles Frederick and Ernest Walter: the family moved from Brinsley to Eastwood in the early 1890s, which perhaps accounts for the fact that DHL knew Hannah so well.

62 E392a, pp. 21, 34, 21.

63 *SL* 7–8.

64 Neville 38; Nehls, iii. 589.

65 DHL's own late autobiographical writings (discussed in Appendix IV) had set the pattern by making the distinction in e.g. 'Autobiographical Sketch' (first published February 1929): 'My father was a collier ... My mother was, I suppose, superior. She ... belonged to the lower bourgeoisie' (*P II* 592). Middleton Murry ignored DHL's qualification by stating in *Son of Woman* (1931) that DHL was 'the fourth child of a collier father and a bourgeoise mother' (p. 24); and Ada Lawrence's biography *The Early Life of D. H. Lawrence*, in one of the sections written by G. Stuart Gelder (with whom she collaborated), went further still by allowing it to be thought that *Sons and Lovers* told the literal truth about DHL's early life, and also by portraying Lydia Lawrence as 'of a different breed' from her husband: 'a school teacher' and the daughter of 'an engineer' (Ada 13). The fact that Ada did not correct this demonstrates how she, too, had inherited such a version of her mother and her mother's family.

66 See Storer, *Some Aspects*, p. 35.

67 E373e, p. 83.

68 Taylor, 27 January 1961, p. 5.

Chapter Two: Home at Eastwood

1 *C. N. Wright's Directory of Nottinghamshire* (1883), p. 406.

2 A. R. and C. P. Griffin, 'A Social and Economic History', p. 127; *SL* 2.

3 John Benson, *British Coalminers in the Nineteenth Century* (1980), p. 78: see too note 28 below.

4 Storer, *Some Aspects*, p. 38; Ada 16.

5 'Getting On', E144, pp. 1–3. Henry Saxton died in 1927, and DHL wrote about him to his sister Ada:

> I shall shed no tears in his memory, for I never liked him. I hated him as Sunday School superintendent, so common and loud-mouthed. I often wonder why my mother respected him so much, and in a way looked up to him. Perhaps because he had such a fat successful belly, and bullied the poor parsons like Mr Reid. Pax! He's left Camilla high and dry on the shelf forever, like the selfish mean brute he was. They need to run a chapel, such men do. (v. 631)

6 W. E. Hopkin, 'The Early Life of D. H. Lawrence', *Gazette* (Ilkeston), vol. iii no. 143 (Friday, 18 January 1935).

7 E373a, p. 3.

8 214 houses were built between 1868 and 1875 to make up the 'New Buildings', including 94 houses in Princes Street and 16 houses in Victoria Street.

9 'Nottingham and the Mining Countryside', P 134; the name 'the Bottoms' DHL uses in *Sons and Lovers* probably comes from Beggarlee Bottoms, two hundred yards along Engine Lane from the Breach. (I am indebted for this point to George Hardy.)

10 Ada 19.

11 E373a, p. 3.

12 A. R. and C. P. Griffin, 'A Social and Economic History', p. 160 n. 32; Ada 19.

13 Taylor, 8 June 1962, p. 5; E373e, p. 121. The deleted remark in the *Sons and Lovers* manuscript that the houses in Scargill Street had been built 'chiefly by colliers who had got on' (E373e, pp. 121–2) probably refers not to Walker Street, but to the Lawrences' next house in Lynn Croft; see below.

14 Neville 54: 'winders' are the angled steps which turn the corners in a staircase; E373d, p. 254.

15 Nehls, iii. 553.

16 Ibid., i. 30; *SL* 76.

17 Nehls, iii. 554. The family group (Clarke) was a large (56×43 cm.), hand-coloured and comprehensively touched-up enlargement of the well-known family photograph (see Illustration 1) of 1897, giving the impression of a handsomely framed (90×73 cm.) painting.

18 Nehls, iii. 604.

19 Ibid., iii. 554.

20 Ada 20. The Taylor family of Walker Street had 'a seven-piece suite in horse-hair' and a piano in their parlour (Taylor, 15 September 1961, p. 8 and June 1962, p. 5).

21 Ada 20–1.

22 Neville 55; 'Adolf', *EmyE* 206:14–15.

23 Taylor, 3 February 1961, p. 5; Joan King in conversation with the author, 14 April 1988.

24 Steve Bircumshaw, taped interview with David Gerard (NCL).

25 Taylor, 3 February 1961, p. 5 (DHL repeated the anecdote in 'Odour of Chrysanthemums', *PO* 183:25–6); E84a, p. 53.

26 E373e, pp. 27–8; E74a, p. [40]; Neville 49.

27 *Kangaroo*, E182a, p. 537 (UT): by 1922, however, DHL's capacity for unbiased reminiscence had lessened: the early short story 'Odour of Chrysanthemums' had shown Elizabeth Bates's husband (who is drinking heavily at the time) keeping 10/- for himself and giving her only 23/- (*PO* 183:25–30).

28 *SL* 18: after his wife's death in 1910, however, Arthur Lawrence felt himself under less obligation to hand over what he earned. His daughter Ada – now keeping house for him – complained early in 1911 that 'he earned 28/6, and of this kept 6/8' (i. 219).

29 *SL* 17; Ada 54; Taylor, 24 February 1961, p. 5.

30 '[Return to Bestwood]', *P II* 257; see E373d, p. 290, E373e, p. 150.

31 Ada 35; 'Italian Studies: By the Lago di Garda', *English Review*, xv, 230; Nehls, iii. 37: DHL's friend Dorothy Brett noted down in 1926 his conversation about his childhood, but there is evidence either of her faulty memory (or hearing), or of DHL exaggerating: she reports him saying that his father never earned more 'than twenty-five shillings a week'; *Life As We Have Known It*, ed. Llewellyn Davies, p. 63.

32 Nehls, i. 29; Mabel Thurlby Collishaw, taped interview with David Gerard (NCL).

33 *SL* 73; Taylor, 8 June 1962, p. 5; W. E. Lawrence, taped interview with David Gerard (NCL): it is possible that he was remembering DHL's elder brother Ernest, who certainly was a cyclist and who won competitions on his bicycle; Ada 49: the piano is also described at *WP* 6:28–34 and in 'The Piano', E317, no. 13.

34 Neville 57.

35 Clarke MS; *Eastwood and Kimberley Advertiser*, 23 October 1896, p. 7; Alice Hall Holditch, taped interview with F. C. Tighe (NCL); Benson, *British Coalminers*, p. 80; E373d, p. 182; Burnett, *Plenty and Want*, p. 93.

36 'Italian Studies: By the Lago di Garda', *English Review*, xv, 219; E74a, pp. [102–3, 116–17]; *SL* 210–11.

37 Neville 57–8.

38 Storer, *Some Aspects*, pp. 106–7: see (i. 132).

39 Nehls, iii. 392.

40 Neville 41; Taylor, 26 January 1962, p. 7; Ada 42; E.T. 54; E74a, p. [40].

41 E.T. 54–5: DHL referred to Minnie in 1911 (i. 231), and she appears regularly in the later parts of *Sons and Lovers* (*SL* 369, 375–6, 378–9, 380, 394–5); Neville 38; Ada 42.

42 See *LG* 1:11–26.

43 Storer, *Some Aspects*, p. 38; John Henry ('Jack') (b. 27 April), son of Walter: Luther John (b. 22 October), son of George: John (b. 16 December), son of James: Arthur Lawrence's first son (b. 26 September 1876) had been named George Arthur, a combination of the names of his father and of his maternal

grandfather, George Beardsall: his second son (b. 22 July 1878) was named William Ernest.

44 *Ilkeston Pioneer*, 4 March 1880, p. [2]; the name (mis-spelled 'Alvinah' on her birth certificate and 'Alvinab' in the Baptism register of Brinsley church) came from her great-aunt Alvina Newton, the link between the Lawrence family and the Beardsall family: Arthur Lawrence's aunt, she had married Lydia Beardsall's uncle John Newton. DHL borrowed the name for the heroine of *The Lost Girl*.

45 Accident of 21 November 1903, reported incorrectly as happening to 'Mr. Walter Lawrence, of Walker-street' (*Eastwood and Kimberley Advertiser*, 27 November 1903, p. 2): he was in hospital more than a month (see *Eastwood and Kimberley Advertiser*, 23 December 1904, p. 2: 'Mr. Lawrence was suffering from a fractured leg a year ago, and was an inmate of the [Nottingham] Infirmary on Christmas Day as will be the case this year'); Benson, *British Coalminers*, p. 43.

46 E373e, p. 102.

47 Alice Hall Holditch, interview; George Lawrence to William Whitehead, 13 December 1906 (George Hardy). (I am grateful to Margaret Alchat for much helpful information about this branch of the Lawrence family.)

48 Nehls, iii. 131; *Eastwood and Kimberley Advertiser*, 24 April 1896, p. 5. The most Arthur Lawrence is known to have done in the community is help organise 'Smoking Concerts' for the benefit of men (probably friends or former workmates) who were unemployed: two such were held in local pubs in 1899 and 1900 (*Eastwood and Kimberley Advertiser*, 19 May 1899, p. 2; 9 March 1900, p. 2). Lydia Lawrence's reaction to such fund-raising may be imagined.

49 Edward Gilbert notes; Alice Hall Holditch, interview; Nehls, iii. 593.

50 Storer, *Some Aspects*, pp. 38–9.

51 Their eldest child, John Henry, b. 27 April 1877, was christened on 27 May in Eastwood parish church. Although his parents' address is correctly given as 'South Normanton', the parents' names appear as 'John and Louisa', the names of his Lawrence grandparents. This may have been a simple mistake, or an indication that they were taking care of the child and ensuring that he was christened: or, just possibly, covering up the fact that he had been born so soon after his parents' marriage.

52 Neville 49.

53 *Ilkeston Advertiser*, 31 March 1900, p. 5; E373b, pp. 294, 311–13; in *A Collier's Friday Night*, Mr Lambert also pulls the table away from his daughter Nellie to get it 'nearer the fire': 'He drags up his arm chair and sits down at the table, full in front of the fire' (E74a, pp. [11–12]).

54 *Ilkeston Advertiser*, 31 March 1900, p. 5.

55 William A. R. Thompson, *Black's Medical Dictionary* (1971), p. 667.

56 E74a, p. [109].

57 Neville 59.

58 E74a, pp. [105–6] (italic for stage directions supplied).

59 Nehls, iii. 584; *SL* 23–5; e.g. *Eastwood and Kimberley Advertiser*, 18 June 1897,

with its report of a miner summoned for locking his wife out of the house 'on Friday night last' (p. 2).

60 E.T. 28; Ada 30–1; Nehls, i. 17; '[Return to Bestwood]', *P II* 258.

61 Nehls, iii. 571; *The Daughter-in-Law*, E84a, p. 31; *SL* 200, 28–9.

62 Nehls, iii. 580.

63 'Autobiography', *P II* 300–1, corrected from E31.3. In *The White Peacock*, Mrs Beardsall is much attached to Morley's *Life of Gladstone*: it is her 'breviary and missal' (*WP* 76:1). Cf. '⟨"If I might only grow up to be like Mr Gladstone!" was my mother's early wish.⟩' (E430d, p. 195). (For textual symbols, see Cue-titles Section F.)

64 LB Papers 8.

65 See chapter 5, pp. 134–5.

66 Dorothy Brett, *Lawrence and Brett: A Friendship* (1933), p. 141; E373d, pp. 104–6, 103, 140; Ada 29: R. M. Ballantyne (1825–94), *Coral Island* (1857), J. D. Wyss (1743–1818), *The Swiss Family Robinson* (Eng. tr., 1814). 'Little Folks' is probably not the novel (1871) by Louisa M. Alcott (1832–88) but the magazine of the same name; the Mechanics' Institute Library contained many volumes of it and also held *Coral Island* and *The Swiss Family Robinson*.

67 Nehls, iii. 23; E373d, pp. 101, 125.

68 Nehls, i. 17.

69 *SL* 69.

70 'Adolf', *EmyE* 201:3–5.

71 E373d, p. 97; E373e, p. 108.

72 Alice Hall Holditch, interview; Neville 50, 52.

73 Spencer, *D. H. Lawrence Country*, p. 19; Ada 26.

74 E.T. 37; 'That Women Know Best', E390, p. 3; Spencer, *D. H. Lawrence Country*, pp. 19–20.

75 Alice Hall Holditch, interview.

76 For how long is not known: he himself claimed from '1901 . . . until we moved into Lynn Croft', which would be four years (W. E. Lawrence, interview), but the time was almost certainly shorter than that. It is quite likely that he went around the time his brother Edward Arthur was born, on 30 April 1900: it is also possible that Lydia Lawrence took the child as part of her process of getting over the trauma of the death of her son Ernest (another W. E. Lawrence) in October 1901.

77 Neville 186; W. E. Lawrence, interview.

78 George Lawrence, interview.

79 Ada 26–7; Alice Hall Holditch, interview; document in Beauvale Infant School, Eastwood.

80 E390, p. 3; *SL* 54–5; George Lawrence, interview; E390, p. 3.

81 See *Young Bert: An Exhibition of the Early Years of D. H. Lawrence* (Nottingham, 1972), p. 61 and cf. *SL* 53; Ada 28; E373e, p. 84; *SL* 55; *Eastwood and Kimberley Advertiser*, 28 February 1896, p. 4.

82 Ada 28.

83 Ada 28; 'Emily's nickname was Pamela, or *Virtue Rewarded*' (iii. 328), a reference to Samuel Richardson's novel (1740); Ernest Lawrence to Emily Lawrence, 20 March 1901 (King); Ernest Lawrence to DHL, 7 October 1897 (Clarke). See p. 526, note 64 for one poem; the other is marked 'WEL in Miss W[right]'s book' – presumably an entry in the album belonging to Fanny Wright (see p. 525, note 46):

> Then let me strive with each besetting sin
> Recall my wandering fancies, and restrain
> The sore disquiet of a restless brain.
> And as the path of duty is made plain
> May grace be given, that I may walk therein,
> Not like the hireling, for his selfish gain
> But cheerful in the light around me thrown,
> Walking as one to pleasant service led,
> Doing Gods will as if it were my own,
> Yet trusting not in mine, but in his strength alone.   (King)

84 Ernest Lawrence to DHL, 7 October 1897.
85 Ernest Lawrence to DHL and Ada Lawrence, 1 November 1899 (Clarke). An insight into his serious qualities comes through an inscription in a Bible he presented to his sister Emily in March 1898: 'Trusting she may receive such instruction from its pages as will enable her to grow up a good, pure and noble woman' (King).
86 Ada 42; E390, pp. 2–3; *SL* 49.
87 *SL* 58; Ada 35, 22.
88 *SL* 67; E373e, p. 102; *SL* 58.
89 Nehls, iii. 578; Ada 23.
90 Nehls, ii. 126.
91 Ada 21; George Lawrence, interview; I am particularly grateful for discussions with W. H. Clarke, Margaret Needham and Joan King.
92 Ernest Lawrence to Arthur Lawrence, 26 February 1901 (Clarke); George Lawrence, interview: he refers to *Sons and Lovers*; Nehls, i. 14; iii. 568, 570.
93 Nehls, i. 31; iii. 567–8.
94 Ibid., iii. 570; Neville 60; E.T. 138; E373d, p. 98.
95 See Nehls, i. 31; Neville 55.
96 Taylor, 14 April 1961, p. 5; E373e, p. 22 (the first draft of the sentence described him as 'very gentle, infinitely patient'): see too Neville 48; W. E. Lawrence, interview; Edward Gilbert notes.
97 *Sea and Sardinia* (New York, 1921), p. 142; Ada 54; Neville 107.
98 Neville 63; Emily King too remembered the 'honey jars' her brother decorated ('Son and Lover', BBC Third Programme, 8 May 1955).
99 A similar physical reaction against Walter Morel is shown by Gertrude Morel in *Sons and Lovers*, chapter 1:

> There seemed so much gusto in the way he puffed and swilled as he

washed himself, so much alacrity with which he hurried to the mirror in the kitchen, and, bending because it was too low for him, scrupulously parted his wet black hair, that it irritated Mrs Morel.   (*SL* 18–19)

Morel's washing is 'swilling', his gusto irritating. He is offensively and boisterously cheerful (*SL* 6–7, 18–19), characterised by the yelling and bawling of his voice (45, 22, 35), the thrusting forward of his face and moustache (22, 35, 40). His walk is a hurry (19), a lurch (21), a run (25), hastening (42), slinking quickly (45): he is 'all for activity' (42). Gertrude Morel can only breathe freely when he is out of the room, though even then the smell of pit dirt remains behind him (33).

100 Nehls, iii. 567; Neville 59.
101 E373e, p. 451.
102 Delavenay, ii. 665.
103 Ibid., ii. 666.
104 'Autobiographical Sketch', *P II* 592.
105 E373d, p. 129; Neville 50.
106 E74a, p. [105]; *SL* 17.
107 Nehls, i. 89, 83; (i. 206).
108 Neville 195.
109 *Poems* 490.
110 Nehls, iii. 579.
111 Ibid., i. 25.
112 Nehls, iii. 70; 'Nottingham and the Mining Countryside', *P* 135.
113 DHL to unidentified recipient, 11 July 1915 (F. Meerwein).
114 *SL* 33–4, 67, 120, 193.
115 Lydia Beardsall's marriage to Arthur Lawrence in Sneinton's parish church in 1875 was not unusual for a Methodist: it was quite normal to marry in the parish church. None of her five sisters married in Wesleyan chapels, and four of the five married in parish churches.
116 'Hymns in a Man's Life', *P II* 600.
117 *A* 62:15, 20–1; 'Hymns in a Man's Life', *P II* 600.
118 E.T. 16.
119 Donald Davie argued in *A Gathered Church* (1978) that DHL came at the tail end of such a tradition, and that the tradition was so debased by the time it reached him as to be practically worthless (pp. 91–7): but Davie did not know the evidence of DHL's letters to Robert Reid and the contents of Reid's Eastwood sermons, which demonstrate that the tradition of strenuous intellectual discussion and argument was alive and vigorous in the Eastwood Congregational Chapel of 1907: see (i. 36–7, 39–41) and chapter 7, pp. 169–72.
120 Alice Hall Holditch, interview (her father was a Chapel Deacon, so the family would have been particularly aware of such a thing); Lydia Lawrence's copy of the *Eastwood Congregational Psalter*, compiled Charles W. Butler (Eastwood, 1876), still survives (Needham); Nehls, iii. 554.

121 See p. 516, note 5 for DHL on Saxton, and *LG* chap. 1 for DHL's recreation of Cullen as James Houghton; 'Hymns in a Man's Life', *P II* 600; E.T. 17; *A* 59:28–9.

122 *LG* 9:3–8.

123 Nehls, iii. 555.

124 E.T. 15–16; Nehls iii. 555; *Young Bert*, p. 13. It was practically a family tradition; Ernest Lawrence had won a book as '2nd Prize' for 'Regular Attendance' in February 1891, and Emily Lawrence won book prizes in February 1893 and 1894 for attendance at Beauvale Board School (King).

125 E.T. 53.

126 Ernest Lawrence to Emily Lawrence, 14 March 1901 (King). For a description of the 1901 festival in Eastwood, see Neville 198–9.

127 'Hymns in a Man's Life', *P II* 599 ['. . . Thou Saviour . . .']: John Keble (1792–1866), 'Sun of my soul' (1827); John Hampden Gurney (1802–62), 'Fair waved the golden corn' (1851).

128 *The Plumed Serpent* (ed. L. D. Clark, Cambridge, 1987, 195:14–25) drew on 'Shall you? Shall I?' (1887) by James McGranahan (1840–1907); the Rev. E. S. Ufford (1851–1929), 'Throw out the Lifeline' (c. 1882); Georgiana M. Taylor (1848–1915), 'Oh to be Nothing, Nothing' (1881) (see Nehls, iii. 259); Nehls iii. 216–17.

129 *A* 59:9–11, 24–7.

130 *A* 59:15–16: see too *LG* 366–7.

131 *PO* 246:20–6.

132 James T. Boulton, 'D. H. Lawrence's *Odour of Chrysanthemums*: An Early Version', *Renaissance and Modern Studies*, xiii (1969), 17–18.

133 Ibid., pp. 16–17.

134 E74a, p. [13].

135 '*Odour of Chrysanthemums*: An Early Version', p. 14.

136 *SL* 14–15.

137 E373e, pp. 22–3.

138 Ibid., p. 23.

139 Ibid. See Graham Holderness, *D. H. Lawrence: History, Ideology and Fiction* (Dublin, 1982), pp. 143–4.

140 Ada 33, 32. Arthur Templeman (b. 1885) was known, before DHL met him, as 'Fussy Templeman' – 'fussy because I was usually happy and smiling': he acquired his nickname 'Pussy' from DHL's mishearing of 'Fussy' (LaM86 p. 1 – UN), which strongly suggests that the young DHL's pronunciation of the 'u' in 'Fussy' was southern, like his mother's.

141 'Adolf', *EmyE* 202:30–2; 'Rex', *EmyE* 215:41–216:2. 'Paul Morel' II also recounts Paul's excursions with his rabbit 'Adolphus' in his pocket (E373d, pp. 150, 167–70).

142 Ada 33; E373d, p. 146.

143 'Rex', *EmyE* 211:4–5; E373d, p. 260.

144 'Rex', *EmyE* 214:25–6, 215:11, 209:15–16, 211:34–5, 7–10.

145 Ibid., 211:15–18; *John Thomas and Lady Jane* (1972), pp. 167, 168.

146 Cf. Parkin in *John Thomas and Lady Jane*:

Parkin was one of them—with a difference. He had been sent down pit as a lad. But he could not bear it. And he could not really mix in. Colliers, in truth, are a tribe, they have an elementary tribal instinct. Parkin, who inherited the instinct, had also a recoil from the underground tribal association. He *had* to get clear. He *had* to be alone. (p.151)

Chapter Three: Launching into Life

1 A number of children first went at ages between 3 and 4: Gertrude Cooper went at 3 years 7 months and her sister Ethel at 3 years 10 months; Frances Cooper, however, went at 4 years 4 months, as did DHL's sister Ada.
2 Greasley Schools Attendance Register (NCRO); Ada Clarke to Koteliansky, 5 March 1930 (BL, Add. Mss. 48975, fol. 59). DHL attended Beauvale school rather than Albert Street School because the Lawrences' house at 57, The Breach, was just inside Greasley Parish boundary (which went through their garden). The reasons given in the Register as to why children withdrew from the school varied from the laconic 'Died' via 'Too delicate', 'Ring worms' and 'Had a very serious illness' to 'Will not attend' and (referring to the parent of one girl) 'Will not send her'. No reason is given in the Register for DHL's withdrawal. The fact that he did not return to school in the intermediate period is confirmed by a document of 17 December 1890 which announces Ernest Lawrence's award of a prize from the trustees of Beauvale Board School, and records his family as '5': 'at work . . .1' [George] and 'at school . . . 2' [Ernest and Emily] (Beauvale Infant School). DHL was still at home with Ada.
3 'Enslaved by Civilisation', *P II* 580.
4 Nehls, i. 21; George Lawrence, interview; Taylor, 25 August 1961, p. 5; Mabel Thurlby Collishaw, interview; *Eastwood and Kimberley Advertiser*, 20 February 1897, p. 2: such pupils were awarded prizes: they included Frances Cooper and Arthur Templeman.
5 *SL* 49: in 'Paul Morel' II, the crying starts when Paul is a 'four-year-old' and continues until he is 'about six or seven' (E373d, p. 91); Ada 35–6.
6 E373e, p. 76; D. W. Winnicott, *The Child, the Family, and the Outside World* (1964), p. 66.
7 Nehls, i. 23.
8 Mabel Thurlby Collishaw, interview.
9 E373d, p. 132; Ada 36; Neville 38.
10 E373d, pp. 174, 178–9, 132.
11 Ada 36; E.T. 73; Neville 186 n. 14; Ada 36.
12 Nehls, i. 33, 23; Kader, *William Edward Hopkin*, p. 11.
13 Nehls, i. 29, 23, 25.
14 David Lindley, 'Eastwood Revisited', *Human World* (May 1973), p. 51; Nehls, iii. 553.
15 Taylor, 30 December 1960, p. 2; Taylor, 10 February 1961, p. 5.
16 Nehls, i. 72; George Lawrence, interview; Neville 97; E390, p. 1.
17 Ada 34, 30.

18 Nehls, i. 29; Steve Bircumshaw, interview; E. C. Carlin, taped interview with David Gerard (NCL).

19 Nehls, i. 25, 33; Beauvale School (Boys) Log Book, pp. 133 and 150 (Beauvale Infant School); Nehls, i. 33: he also won a certificate in the 'Recreative Drawing Competition', results announced on 10 October 1898 (Beauvale School (Boys) Log Book, p. 165); Beauvale School (Boys) Log Book, p. 154; Neville 39.

20 Neville 39; Beauvale School (Boys) Log Book, p. 90; Neville 39.

21 LaM86, p. 2 (UN). Clem Taylor had been another possible candidate, but his family also knew very little of what was involved: 'When the scholarship was first mooted my father applied for me to sit, only to be told that I was too young. I was more than a year older than Lawrence. When it was all over my father was told I was too old. It was then my father asked the schoolmaster [W. Whitehead] if he did not think he himself ought to have sat for it' (Taylor, 2 June 1961, p. 5).

22 Nehls, iii. 557–8.

23 Annie Morel in 'Paul Morel' II 'was put to dressmaking. She worked very earnestly, so that at sixteen she brought in ten shillings per week' (E373d, p. 211).

24 LaM86, p. 4; Taylor, 20 January 1961, p. 5; Taylor, 13 April 1962, p. 5.

25 SL 99–100, corrected from E373e, p. 148.

26 The Widowing of Mrs. Holroyd (New York, 1914), p. viii: Edwin Björkman's introduction contains biographical information supplied to the play's publisher, Mitchell Kennerley, by DHL himself in August 1913 (see ii. 26 and n. 13), which at times probably reproduces DHL's actual wording; Nehls, iii. 558.

27 Neville 40; E.T. 73.

28 Letter from E. J. Woodford to Michael Sharpe, 4 November 1957, p. 2, in the possession of J. T. Boulton; notes made by E. J. Woodford, c. 1955, in the possession of J. R. Till; George Lawrence lived in Sycamore Road, just off the Woodborough Road in Nottingham.

29 Letter from Woodford to Sharpe, pp. 1 and 3.

30 Ibid., p. 3.

31 Nottingham High School Register; Neville 67; E.T. 23. The Meakin family eldest daughter ('Kitty') had what the Eastwood and Kimberley Advertiser called a 'Fashionable Marriage' (10 September 1897, p. 2).

32 E.T. 19; Ernest Lawrence to DHL, 7 October 1897: a 'sleever' was a tall glass of beer and presumably also slang for a 'silker' – a silk top hat – though this sense is otherwise unrecorded.

33 Ada 28.

34 'Autobiography', P II 300, corrected from E31.3.

35 'Enslaved by Civilisation', P II 580–1; Taylor, 20 January 1961, p. 5. 'Ripping' meant making the roofs of the underground roads a height convenient for men and ponies, during 'road-laying'.

36 E. J. Woodford notes.

37 Frieda 54–5.

38 Birthday Book (King).

39 Elizabeth Marsden (1852–1913) had at least one niece (Ethel, 1885–1912) who stayed with her, and attended Wirksworth Grammar School. The house of 'Mrs Forbes' described in *The Rainbow* is modelled on Miss Marsden's (*R* 85:28–30). Tommy Marsden continued as an acquaintance of DHL's sister Ada and her husband after DHL went abroad in 1912; he struck their son W. H. Clarke as 'a rather ineffectual if not pathetic character' (W. H. Clarke to the author, 16 April 1987).

40 Clarke: there were three terms in the school year.

41 Nottingham High School Calendars.

42 Ibid.; Neville 40.

43 *Eastwood and Kimberley Advertiser*, 30 March 1900, p. 3.

44 *Eastwood and Kimberley Advertiser*, 23 and 30 March 1900, p. 3; *Nottinghamshire Guardian*, 24 and 31 March, pp. 3 and 8.

45 She died on 16 May 1900: George Beardsall had died on 27 June 1899. See DHL's reminiscence of his 'old grandmother', 'who was never anything but worse and fading fast, for forty years, till she was dying, at 75 [actually 71], when she protested she felt a bit better, and a bit better: and so she passed out' (to Earl Brewster, 8 November 1927).

46 E373e, p. 94: see too *SL* 61, 66, 70; the Cullen family's governess (see G. Hardy and N. Harris, *A D. H. Lawrence Album*, Ashbourne 1985, p. 69) was a 'very highly educated woman, and she spared no pains in helping Bert in his education – many times in after life he expressed his gratitude for what she had done' (Nehls, i. 71). She had been an assistant teacher at Eastwood's National School in the early 1890s (National School Log Book, p. 382): according to Joan King, she also gave music lessons to Emily Lawrence. DHL included her in the draft outline for 'Paul Morel' I, and recreated her as 'Miss May' in 'Paul Morel' II: she also appears as 'Miss Frost' in *The Lost Girl*: see *LG* 6:34 and n. When she died in October 1904, 'Mrs Lawrence' was listed as one of the 'chief mourners', and there was a floral tribute from 'Mr & Mrs Lawrence & family' (*Eastwood and Kimberley Advertiser*, 14 October 1904, p. 2): a funeral announcement card survives in the King family, and Emily Lawrence's Birthday Book noted under 9 October: 'Dear Miss Wright left us and entered her eternal home' (King). DHL also received coaching in Latin from the Rev. Robert Reid in 1906–7 (i. 31, 34): see chapter 7, p. 186.

47 E373e, pp. 115, 117, 145; *SL* 89.

48 E373e, p. 115. Paul in 'Paul Morel' II is 'always second or third from the top of the class; rarely first, rarely fourth, rarely remarked by his teacher' (E373d, p. 141).

49 E373e, p. 122.

50 *SL* 77.

51 Nehls, i. 29.

52 *R* 16:37, 18:5, 24–6, 28–9.

53 *R* 17:18, 18:13–15.

54 *R* 18:40–19:1; *SL* 89.

55 *R* 245:26–7, 30–2, 250:30–3, 251:9, 16.

56 *R* 388:26–7, 31–389:3.

57 There is just one moment in 'Paul Morel' II when Paul directly expresses the loneliness of being different and envies other boys their chance of going down pit: 'I should have known folk there' (E373d, p. 185); *R* 389:1–2.

58 *SL* 90.

59 *Nottingham Daily Guardian*, 5 July 1901, p. 1.

60 *SL* 97; E373d, p. 190.

61 E.T. 25; E373d, p. 205; Moore, *The Priest of Love*, p. 40.

62 E. J. Woodford notes; *SL* 102–9.

63 E373e, p. 161; Nehls, iii. 393, 573.

64 On the back of the photograph of 'Gipsy' he gave to his family appears the note 'Taken by me' (King). The poem 'To LLWD' appears in what is probably Lydia Lawrence's handwriting on a slip of paper now inserted in the King family Bible:

> Forgive me if the evil years
> Have left on me their sign.
> Wash out Oh soul ⟨most⟩ ⌜so⌝ beautiful
> These many stains of mine
> In tears of love divine

65 Ernest Lawrence to Emily Lawrence, 14 and 20 March 1901 (King); Neville 91–2, 197–9; the face can become badly swollen, often closing the eyes. Further symptoms are chills and a very high fever, with severe intense intermittent headaches plus nausea and vomiting as the body tries to fight off septicaemia (blood-poisoning). The basic danger is septicaemia; complications can include pneumonia, nephritis and rheumatic fever. Oral penicillin is now successful against this once dangerous disease, which could be particularly serious if the victim were also suffering from tuberculosis. Ernest Lawrence's lungs almost certainly contained the tuberculosis bacillus endemic in his community, and this may have been why the disease moved so fast and so tragically.

66 Ada 29.

67 Nehls, iii. 574.

68 *Eastwood and Kimberley Advertiser*, 18 October 1901, p. 2.

69 Nehls, iii. 574.

70 E.T. 31; King. The words cut on Ernest Lawrence's tombstone in Eastwood cemetery, though conventional, also suggest a subdued protest: 'He asked life of Thee, and Thou gavest it him, Even length of days, for ever and ever' (Psalm xxi. 4): in 'Him With His Tail in His Mouth' in 1925, DHL noted 'man's difficulty is, that he can't have life for the asking', added the quotation from Psalms and commented: '— There's a pretty motto for the tomb!' (*Reflections on the Death of a Porcupine and Other Essays*, ed. Michael Herbert, Cambridge, 1988, 310:38–40).

71 Nehls, iii. 574; Clarke.

72 Neville 91.

73 *SL* 137; E373e, p. 358.

74 *SL* 140; Nehls, iii. 574. The oddly precise date 'December 23' given in *Sons and Lovers* (*SL* 40) for the onset of Paul's illness (a Monday in 1901) may also mark the start of DHL's own.

75 Neville 89.

76 Taylor, 13 April 1962, 5; Neville 67; Ada 51.

77 Neville 37–8, 88–9.

78 F. Lyons, *The Hills of Annesley* (1973), p. 236.

79 Neville 90.

80 Ibid. 89.

81 Nehls, iii. 574.

82 Nehls, iii. 575. It has been claimed that DHL's illness 'made him sterile'; the claim rests on an assumption that DHL's pneumonia was followed by 'a serious illness, rather like mumps' – for which there is no evidence – and upon Barbie Weekley's belief that, because her mother Frieda Weekley had no children by DHL after they started their relationship in 1912, his illness at 16 had rendered him incapable of having children (Jeffrey Meyers, *D. H. Lawrence: A Biography* (New York, 1990, p. 93). Although Frieda had had three children by Ernest Weekley, and none by DHL, nor did she have any children by any of her other lovers between 1904 and 1912 (Dowson, Gross, Frick, von Henning, Hobson): and it seems that, after finding her period late (in mid-May 1912), and fearing she was pregnant, she insisted on DHL's using a contraceptive. See his protest against the idea (i. 402–3). DHL did not believe that he was incapable of having children: 'I want you to have children to me', he wrote in that same letter. The case for his sterility is unproven.

83 *SL* 90.

84 *EmyE* 39:37.

85 Ellen Staynes's boarding-house was in South Parade, Skegness (*Kelly's Directory of Lincolnshire*, 1905).

Chapter Four: Widening Circles

1 Nehls, iii. 740 n. 4; E.T. 16; in March 1887, Edmund Chambers described himself as 'Grocer (master)' when he registered JC's birth.

2 E.T. 16.

3 David Chambers, 'Memories of D. H. Lawrence', *Renaissance and Modern Studies*, xvi (1972), 6–7.

4 Ibid., p. 10; Nehls, iii. 561.

5 DHL to David Chambers, 14 November 1928.

6 Nehls, iii. 563.

7 Nehls, iii. 586, 572, 578; Emily King, BBC 'Son and Lover'; *SL* 46; *Memoirs* 131; Neville 187.

8 Chambers, 'Memories', p. 10; Nehls, iii. 578; Chambers, 'Memories', p. 10.

9 DHL to David Chambers, 14 November 1928; E.T. 35–6.

10 Nehls, iii. 611.

11 Chambers, 'Memories', p. 11; E.T. 28.

12 Chambers, 'Memories', p. 10.

13 E.T. 28; Nehls, iii. 589. See too Nehls, iii. 607 and E.T. 80–1.

14 JC to HC, 1 June 1933, 'The Collected Letters', p. 58; just as he kept recreating the place, so the idea of the family continued to haunt him: in the middle 1920s, in *The Boy in the Bush*, occurs young Jack Grant's extraordinary panegyric about a family: 'Ah the family! the family! Jack still loved it. It seemed to fill the whole of life for him. He did not want to be alone, save at moments . . . He didn't want his own children. He wanted this family: always this family' (*The Boy in the Bush*, ed. Paul Eggert, Cambridge University Press, 1990, 71:28–36).

15 JC to Koteliansky, 21 January 1937, 'The Collected Letters', p. 143; E.T. 134; Chambers, 'Memories', p. 11.

16 JC to HC, 1 June 1933, 'The Collected Letters', p. 58.

17 E.T. 28.

18 Nehls, iii. 592, 591.

19 'Autobiography', *P II* 301.

20 E.T. 18, 24, 63.

21 Nehls, iii. 593.

22 Ada 41; Sarah Walker, 'Memories of Eastwood', ed. Carol Herring, *Staple* (Winter, 1983), p. 49.

23 Delavenay, i. 310; see p. 519, note 66; *P* 94; Ada 41 (the magazines cost 3d a month); Ada 24; 'Nathaniel Hawthorne and the "Scarlet Letter"', *Studies in Classic American Literature*, p. 125; E373e, p. 188; *SL* 131.

24 Emily won Charles Kingsley's *Madam How and Lady Why* as a Sunday school prize in 1896, 'for having passed successfully the Scholar Scripture Examination' (King: see the *Eastwood and Kimberley Advertiser*, 5 June 1896, p. 5): her copy of *The Motherless Bairns and Who Sheltered Them*, published by the Religious Tract Society (*Young Bert*, p. 13), also sounds like a Sunday school prize; Neville 199.

25 E.T. 92.

26 E374a, pp. [2], [1] (italic for stage directions supplied).

27 Nehls, iii. 600; Chambers, 'Memories', p. 7.

28 Neville 40; Asher Tropp, *The School Teachers* (1957), p. 170.

29 Albert Street School (Boys) Log Book, pp. 301–2 (NCRO).

30 Clarke.

31 Nehls, iii. 596.

32 Ibid., iii. 587.

33 Ibid., iii. 587–8. Clem Taylor also records seeing DHL there 'about 1904' (Taylor, 17 February 1961, p. 7).

34 *The Widowing of Mrs. Holroyd*, p. viii; Nehls, iii. 583.

35 Albert Street School (Boys) Log Book, pp. 303, 307.

36 Keith Evans, *The Development and Structure of the English School System* (1975), p. 117.

37 See report in the *Ilkeston Advertiser*, 31 March 1900, p. 5.

38 Albert Street School (Boys) Log Book, pp. 318–19.

39 Nehls, i. 43; Mrs S. Cotterell, taped interview with David Gerard (NCL); E.T. 74.

40 Nehls, i. 43-4.

41 Mrs Cotterell's interview offers another account of the journey to Ilkeston by a contemporary. For Gilbert Noon, see Lindeth Vasey and John Worthen, 'Mr Noon/*Mr Noon*', *D. H. Lawrence Review*, xx (1988), 186-9. The report on Gilbert Noon in the College Register runs:

> Has a strong and pleasant voice, well managed; a manner energetic & forcible as a rule, with some hastiness of temper which needs control; a good flow of language but a tendency to talk too much rather than to make the boys contribute a large share and with a good deal of colloquialism used in the ordinary speech of class-management[;] considerable intelligence & natural power of teaching but without much real enthusiasm for the work[.]
>
> Mr Noon has great possibilities; but a[t] present there is a certain slackness of moral fibre which makes it doubtful whether he will really succeed and become a good teacher in the higher sense of the words.
> (University College, Nottingham, Day Training College Students' Register 1906-8, UN)

The last paragraph's hint at moral failings could perhaps be a clue to DHL's presentation of his character Gilbert Noon in *Mr Noon*. The College report on DHL printed above (chapter 7, p. 187) was written by the same teacher, probably Professor Amos Henderson. Gilbert Noon's College marks were CBBB+ in Teaching, Reading, Drawing and Music respectively: see below, pp. 539-40, note 52. Richard Pogmore and George Neville both inscribed their names in Emily Lawrence's Birthday Book before November 1904 (King). Alice Hall Holditch's interview mentions Pogmore, as does the rather unreliable interview with E. C. Carlin, which suggests that Pogmore 'got a bit sweet on Bert's sister'; see too Nehls, i. 54-5.

42 Minutes of Nottinghamshire Education Committee, 1 July 1904, p. 300 (NCRO).

43 Minutes of the Educational Committee, Ilkeston Council (1903-4), 1 December 1903; *Schoolmaster*, 4 March 1905, p. 470.

44 Nehls, iii. 584. In 1920, he would wonder why 'we are so frightened of that toothless old lion of *want*?' ('Education of the People', *Reflections on the Death of a Porcupine*, ed. Herbert, 91:2-3).

45 *Ilkeston Pioneer*, 5 April 1905, p. 5; Emily King, BBC 'Son and Lover'; *Schoolmaster*, 4 March 1905, p. 470; *The Widowing of Mrs. Holroyd*, p. viii.

46 Albert Street School (Boys) Log Book, p. 327, p. 328.

47 Neville 41.

48 *The Widowing of Mrs. Holroyd*, p. ix.

49 'Autobiographical Sketch', *P II* 593; Albert Street School (Boys) Log Book, 27-9 March 1906, p. 335; testimonial, written 18 July 1908 (UN).

50 Albert Street School (Boys) Log Book, p. 339.

51 Neville 41; Joan King to the author, 14 April 1988; Ada 72; E373e, pp. 86–7, E74a, p. [40]; Ada 72.

52 Neville 186; she married Sam King (1880–1965) on 5 November 1904.

53 Nehls, iii. 590; LB Papers 21; Helen Corke, *D. H. Lawrence: The Croydon Years* (Austin, Texas, 1965), pp. 20–1; in 1915 JC married a Nottinghamshire schoolmaster, John R. Wood, but never had the children she would have liked. She remained working as a teacher until her husband came back from the war in 1919. Under the name 'E.T.', she published her book *D. H. Lawrence: A Personal Record* in 1935; she suffered a severe stroke in April 1939, and never fully recovered; she died on 3 April 1944.

54 E.T. 15.

55 Chambers, 'Memories', p. 14.

56 Nehls, iii. 537.

57 E.T. 25; Chambers, 'Memories', p. 13; E.T. 46.

58 E.T. 28–9.

59 E.T. 92, 93.

60 E.T. 94, 96.

61 *R* 11:7–13, 12:21, 341:39–40.

62 E.T. 99, 97–8, 63, 101, 99, 101. Numerous editions of Blake's poems were printed in the nineteenth century: the 16°, 1868 printing of Richard H. Shepherd's edition is typical.

63 *Schoolmaster*, 4 March 1905, p. 470; Nehls, i. 127; ibid., i. 116.

64 E.T. 95.

65 E.T. 101–2.

66 E.T. 102, 172, 145.

67 Underwood School Log Book, 23 January 1903; Infants' Section Log Book, 16 October 1903 (NCRO); Chambers, 'Memories', p. 14.

68 Nehls, iii. 537.

69 Chambers, 'Memories', p. 14.

70 *Young Bert*, p. 31.

71 Neville 68; Mrs Bryce [Polly Goddard], taped interview with David Gerard (NCL). DHL recalled in 1926 his particular association of the Coopers with 'Lynn Croft, when I was going to college' (v. 582); the flute-playing of Thomas Cooper contributed to the character of Aaron Sisson in DHL's novel *Aaron's Rod*: the fact that the real-life Aaron Sisson (d. 1916) was a witness to the marriage of Cooper's daughter Mabel in June 1909 (when DHL was also present, perhaps as best man: Taylor, 15 September 1961, p. 5) shows the links between the Coopers, Sissons and Lawrences.

72 *SL* 77; *Eastwood and Kimberley Advertiser*, 8 August 1913, p. 2. The family had known the Limbs from at least March 1901, when a letter from Ernest Lawrence to his sister Emily remarked 'You must thank Emmie Limb from me for helping you, and tell her that when I come over I will take her photo, all by myself' (King). The photograph does not survive.

73 Steve Bircumshaw, 'The following is a list of the Pagans' (NCL); Nehls, iii. 606.

74 See (i. 85, 95): the only other early correspondent to get kisses is his cousin Alvina Lawrence (card of 31 October 1903, UN).

75 Nehls, iii. 569–70.

76 *R* 388:33–4.

Chapter Five: Writing and Painting

1 E.T. 57.

2 *SL* 52; see Middleton, 'Happy Birthday, Mrs Lawrence', pp. 8–16; see above, chapter 1, pp. 21–2.

3 Clarke. The MS is unsigned, but is in a hand identical with that of Lydia Lawrence's letters, while deletions and corrections indicate that it is not a copy of a poem by another person. DHL himself was also extremely conscious of hands: see Black, *D. H. Lawrence: The Early Fiction*, pp. 275–6. During his final illness in 1930, he declared that Maria Huxley – who helped nurse him – had 'his mother's hands' (Nehls, iii. 436).

4 See p. 520, note 83 and p. 526, note 64.

5 Nehls, iii. 560.

6 E.T. 57.

7 'Getting On', E144, p. 5; *SL* 175.

8 For Burns, see *LAH* xxxvii and n. 60. The fact that in the second draft of *Lady Chatterley's Lover* DHL gave Parkin a father who was – like Wells's – a part-time professional cricketer shows that he was probably aware of Wells's background: see *John Thomas and Lady Jane*, p. 198, and Anthony West, *H. G. Wells: Aspects of a Life* (1984), p. 175.

9 *Poems* 849.

10 In 1926, DHL commented on 'that Hopkinish impudence' and described Hopkin's daughter Enid as 'impudent, a real Hopkin' (v. 548).

11 E.T. 58.

12 E.T. 75; E144, p. 5. He also found that 'she twigged . . . and she read the things when I wasn't there': it is possible that George Neville read them at the same time (Neville 188).

13 See *Young Bert*, pp. 32, 59; a painting of flowers by JC survives in private hands; Moore, *The Priest of Love*, p. 28.

14 'Making Pictures', *P II* 603–4; e.g. the jug of Nasturtiums he painted in oil on glass (Needham) for his aunt Ada in October 1908 (i. 78 and n. 1), and the still-life of the Ginger Jar and Oranges (King) which had been the exam subject for his art class at Davidson Road on 14 December and which he finished the following day (i. 201 and n. 4): see *Paintings of D. H. Lawrence*, ed. M. Levy (1964), Monochrome Plate 1, and *Young Bert*, p. 50.

15 'Making Pictures', *P II* 604.

16 Nehls, iii. 597.

17 The album of Ethel Harris (UN) – a fellow teacher at Underwood school with JC – is dated 11 April 1903; Emily Lawrence's album (Needham) has a first drawing dated 1904; the album of Grace Hardwick (1887–1957) (UN) – a

fellow student of DHL at Nottingham University College – was started in 1904, but DHL's contribution was probably made several years after that. Her album also contains contributions from J. Barrie Robinson (1886–1945) and Lois Mee, student contemporaries of DHL (see i. 357 and 142).

18 *Young Bert*, p. 59; (i. 78 and n. 1, 263); (i. 88 n. 4); *D. H. Lawrence – A Life in Literature*. ed. Alan Cameron (Nottingham, 1985), p. 34; (i. 196–7, 242–3); (i. 282 and n. 2); (i. 242–3); LaT69 (UN); (i. 488).

19 Carl Baron, 'D. H. Lawrence's Early Paintings', *Young Bert*, p. 36.

20 DHL to Giuseppe Orioli, 7 August 1929.

21 'Enslaved by Civilisation', *P II* 581. HC and Blanche Jennings both called him David, as did the Brewster family in the 1920s; JC used 'David' when writing to HC and 'Bert' when writing to LB ('The Collected Letters', pp. 5–6); UN. Arthur Templeman also recalled: 'He never used the name David. His papers were always headed by – "Herbert Lawrence". In the early days he was called Bertie, a name he cared little for. Later the boys called him Bert, while the girls held to the name Bertie' (LaM86, p. 1, UN).

22 The first exception is his appearance as 'your ever estimable   Uncle Bert' to his nephew Jack Clarke in December 1925 (v. 360).

23 Ernest Lawrence to Arthur Lawrence, 26 February 1901. Cf. DHL to Enid Hopkin Hilton, 31 August 1928, when his sister Emily and niece Margaret were visiting: 'I am not really "our Bert." Come to that, I never was.' His play *The Daughter-in-Law* shows how possessive the local 'our' can be, in Mrs Gascoyne's references to 'our Luther' and 'our Joe' (E84, p. 50).

24 E.T. 69.

25 Neville 195; Alice Hall Holditch, interview.

26 E.T. 91, 28.

27 Ada 57–8, corrected from MS (Clarke): although the diary reads as though the launching took place at Theddlethorpe, the lifeboat 'Heywood' (presented in 1883) was at Mablethorpe.

28 E.T. 117.

29 E.T. 103.

30 Ibid.

31 E74a, pp. [56–8] (italic stage directions supplied).

32 E.T. 116.

33 E.T. 117, 116.

34 E.T. 104.

35 The identification of the surviving early fragment with the writing which ended in June 1907 is made by Andrew Robertson (*WP* xviii and n. 5), but he does not connect the fragment with the surviving plot. The latter is written, in pencil, on the front fly-leaf of DHL's Nottingham University College Notebook E320.1, and at some stage was heavily erased. An alternative plot (reaching roman numeral XVI, XVII or XVIII) which once existed on the two following leaves was torn out of the notebook: two surviving stumps of leaves show traces of roman numerals along their left-hand edges. A poem was inserted in ink over the

surviving pencil plot after the latter had been erased. As DHL used the notebook for the insertion of poems from November 1909 onwards (see p. 551, note
25) the plot was probably erased at some time after that.

The outline of the last two numbered chapters (XIX and XX) in the plot
corresponds closely to that of the surviving fragment of the novel (part of
chapter XVII and chapter XVIII) printed in *WP* 329–47. The plot was just
possibly preliminary work for 'Laetitia' II (written between late 1907 and May
1908). However, as it starts with chapter XIV, and its position on the notebook
fly-leaf shows that nothing can have preceded it, it is much more likely to be a
draft outline, composed sometime after October 1906 (when DHL acquired
the notebook), of the proposed ending of 'Laetitia' I. It would therefore
represent DHL's plan for finishing his work in progress. It is possible that the
plot on the following (and missing) leaves contained the outline which he
actually followed.

36 *WP* 331:8–12.

37 *WP* 341:15, 24; *LAH* 14:22–3; *WP* 341:32; 342:7–9.

38 *WP* 347:16–19.

39 'Autobiography', *P II* 300.

40 E144, p. 5.

41 *WL* 19: 15–37.

42 Nehls, i. 72; E.T. 117; the surviving manuscript fragment shows that this
happened in the penultimate chapter, XVII.

43 Lydia Lawrence to Ada Krenkow, 8 February 1910 (Clarke); to Lettice Berry,
11 July 1910 (Clarke).

44 LB Papers 40.

45 'Autobiography', *P II* 300–1, corrected from E31.3; Nehls, i. 72.

46 Nehls, iii. 618.

47 E.g.

His intrinsic beauty was evident now ⟨. . .⟩. ⌜She had not been mistaken in
him as ⟨she had⟩ often & often ⌜⌜she had⌝⌝ bitterly confessed to herself she
was. The beauty of his youth, of his eighteen years, of the time when life
had settled on him, as, in adolescence, it settles on youth, bringing a
mission to fulfil and equipment therfor, this beauty shone almost unstained
again. It was this adolescent 'he', the young man looking round to see
which way, that Elizabeth had loved.⌝ He had come from the discipleship
of youth, through the Pentecost of adolescence, pledged to keep with
honor his own individuality, ⟨. . .⟩ to be steadily and unquenchably himself, electing his own masters & serving them till the wages were won.
(E284c, pp. [31–3])

48 'Autobiographical Sketch' *P II* 592; 'Autobiography', *P II* 301.

49 Neville 188.

50 'Introduction' to Edward McDonald, *A Bibliography of D. H. Lawrence*
(Philadelphia, 1925), p. 10 (*P* 232). Ernest Hooley (1859–1947), born in Sneinton, Nottingham, accumulated a fortune by stock-exchange speculation before

going bankrupt in 1898: after further dealings he was sentenced in 1922 to three years penal servitude for fraud: he and his *Confessions* both came out in 1925.

51 E373a, p. 32.
52 *SL* 6, 40.
53 E.g. E373e, pp. 267, 269; 'The Right Thing to Do', E359.4a, p. 2; (i. 214).
54 Nehls, iii. 568; E74a, p. [100].
55 George Lawrence, Blanche Bircumshaw and Mrs Bryce, taped interviews with David Gerard (NCL).
56 *Villette* (1853), chapter xxiii ('Vashti'). There is no direct evidence that DHL knew the novel, but Charlotte Brontë's *Jane Eyre* and *Shirley* were two of his 'favourite English books' (i. 88) and he knew Mrs Gaskell's *Life of Charlotte Brontë* (i. 105).
57 See *WP* 5:34–6: Cyril is a painter at 46:9–10, 127:3–4 and 239:15–19; *WP* 91:4–5; 267:8.
58 E.T. 117; LB Papers 28.
59 John Worthen, 'Introduction' to *The White Peacock*, ed. Alan Newton (Harmondsworth, 1982), p. 27.
60 In the words of DHL's 1915 essay 'The Crown', such a person is 'looking for ever at himself', 'within the envelope', incapable of getting outside himself and incapable of love (*Reflections on the Death of a Porcupine*, ed. Herbert, 281:15, 24).
61 *SL* 364.
62 *LAH* 179:22–33.
63 E320.3, p. 40 (see chapter 15, p. 412); *LAH* 78:15, 27.
64 *LAH* 46:12–14; 47:34, 38; 48:8–9, 16–17.
65 E.T. 117.

Chapter Six: Spirit Love

1 E373b, p. 213; E373c, p. 2; E373b, p. 224.
2 See Helen Baron, 'Jessie Chambers' plea for justice to "Miriam"', *Archiv*, cxxxvii (1985), 63–84.
3 Alice Hall Holditch, interview.
4 Information from Joan King, September 1989; Alice Hall Holditch, interview; *SL* 163.
5 Nehls, i. 32–3; Neville 72–4; in *Sons and Lovers* both Miriam and Paul are bewildered and disgusted by the idea that 'the mare was in foal' (*SL* 163); Neville 81–3.
6 Neville 75. DHL's continuing ignorance of cricket is shown by his description of a game in *The Boy in the Bush* (chapter viii), where he makes a number of mistakes.
7 See, e.g. *Fantasia of the Unconscious* (1923), when the parent advises his child about sex and tells it to 'leave yourself alone':
   don't you go creeping off and doing things on the sly. It won't do you any good—I know what you'll do, because we've all been through it. I know

the thing will keep coming on you at night. But ... remember that I want you to leave yourself alone. I know what it is, I tell you. I've been through it all myself. You've got to go through these years, before you find a woman you want to marry, and whom you can marry. I went through them myself, and got myself worked up a good deal more than was good for me. (p. 101)

See too 'Pornography and Obscenity':

Sex must go somewhere, especially in young people. So, in our glorious civilization, it goes in masturbation ... In the young, a certain amount of masturbation is inevitable, but not therefore natural. I think, there is no boy or girl who masturbates without feeling a sense of shame, anger, and futility ... The only positive effect of masturbation is that it seems to release a certain mental energy, in some people. ... The outstanding feature of such consciousness is that there is no real object, there is only subject ... The author never escapes from himself, he pads along within the vicious circle of himself. (P 178–80)

8 E.T. 125–6.
9 E.T. 127. The power of the moon for representing alluring but unresponsive, even hostile, female sexuality is also expressed in chapter xix ('Moony') of *Women in Love* (*WL* 245:19–248:33).
10 Delavenay, ii. 699; cf. *SL* 178–9; E.T. 128.
11 E.T. 128.
12 Nehls, i. 49.
13 *LAH* 179:30; E373b, p. 213.
14 *MN* 225:16–17.
15 *WP* 221:22–223:3.
16 *WL* 502:37; Delavenay, ii. 666: see chapter 7, p. 174, for further commentary on this passage, which occurs in *Essays of Schopenhauer*, tr. Mrs Rudolf Dircks (n.d.), p. 179.
17 *WL* 502:2–3.
18 E.T. 116; 'Autobiographical Sketch', *P II* 593; E373b, p. 220.
19 Nehls, iii. 589, 603.
20 Sarah Elizabeth Walker (b. 1896), memories of Eastwood and DHL given to Carol Herring, 1981: I am grateful to the latter for supplying me with materials omitted from the selections in *Staple* (Winter 1983), pp. 46–53 and (Summer 1984), pp. 34–9; Nehls, iii. 603.
21 E373e, p. 298.
22 *SL* 212.
23 Lydia Lawrence to Lettice Berry, 11 July 1910.
24 E373e, p. 300.
25 See E.T. 47 and (i. 243); Olive Hopkin, taped interview with David Gerard (NCL); see E74a, pp. [46–7], where Nellie deliberately leaves so as not to meet Maggie and p. [86], where she rejoices to hear of Maggie's discomfiture; *WP* 373 (note on 97:21).
26 Nehls, iii. 588.

27 E.T. 66.

28 E.T. 69.

29 E.T. 66.

30 Ibid. The wording JC wrote down in March 1912 in her commentary upon 'Paul Morel' IIIa was: 'And I've tried to find out, and I don't think I love you as a man ought to love his wife' (E373c, 'Easter Monday').

31 E.T. 133.

32 E.T. 136–7, 67; E373b, p. 204.

33 E.T. 67–8.

34 E373b, p. 225; E.T. 125.

35 E.T. 67.

36 E373e, p. 226; E373e, p. 287.

37 *SL* 195; E373e, pp. 277–8; E373e, p. 277.

38 Such passages were among those which JC particularly objected to in her later comments on the novel: see Helen Baron, 'Jessie Chambers' plea for justice to "Miriam"', pp. 75–84.

39 E373e, pp. 350–2.

40 Delavenay, ii. 701.

41 E373c, p. 10: see Helen Baron, 'Jessie Chambers' plea for justice to "Miriam"', pp. 70, 73–5.

Chapter Seven: College

1 E.T. 76.

2 E.T. 81.

3 *LG* 20:30–21:5.

4 Cf. the weekly programme of Chapel goers in the Yorkshire village of Castleford in the 1890s (Benson, *British Coalminers*, p. 170):

Monday	Christian Endeavour
Tuesday	Chapel Class Meeting
Wednesday	Mother's Night
Thursday	Band of Hope
Friday	Men's Friday Night Bible Class
Saturday	Socials

5 E.T. 53; Nehls, i. 55.

6 Neville 37, 183–5 n. 1; Alice Hall Holditch, interview.

7 Nehls, i. 152.

8 John Beer, 'Ford's Impression of the Lawrences' (*The Times Literary Supplement*, 5 May 1972, p. 520). See too Duncan McGuffie, 'Lawrence and Nonconformity', *D. H. Lawrence 1885–1930: A Celebration*, ed. Cooper, pp. 31–8. The *Hibbert Journal* (which started in 1902) was a quarterly review of religion, theology and philosophy, written by clergymen, scientists and philosophers, and costing 2/6 a number: see below, p. 558, note 30 and p. 560, note 38.

9 E.T. 83; *Eastwood and Kimberley Advertiser*, 13 December, p. 2, 20 December,

p. 2; 3 January 1908, p. 3. A card was distributed advertising the series: W. E. Hopkin (as 'Anglo Saxon') commented: 'I feel proud we have a teacher bold enough to face the whole situation, and I know it will receive able handling' (ibid., 6 December 1907, p. 2).

10 E.T. 85.

11 E.T. 48–9; 'Nature Study', LaB 220 (UN).

12 Nehls, iii. 593; HC, *In Our Infancy: An Autobiography; Part I: 1882–1912* (Cambridge, 1975), p. 143; Nehls, iii. 593.

13 Edward Fitzgerald (1809–83), *The Rubáiyát of Omar Khayyám*, 4th edn (1899), pp. 43 and 51.

14 E.T. 84.

15 E.T. 84; see Gordon Haight, *George Eliot* (1968), pp. 39–44.

16 Nehls, i. 74, iii. 593.

17 See Christa Jansohn, 'Zu Schopenhauers Einfluss auf D. H. Lawrence', *arcadia*, xxi (1986), 263–75: Mrs Dircks not only in general reproduced extracts from Schopenhauer, rather than the full essays her titles suggest, but her translations were in many respects faulty: she also censored some of Schopenhauer's most outspoken remarks: 'Sätze wie *ein altes, d.h. nicht mehr menstruirtes Weib erregt unsern Abscheu* werden erst gar nicht übersetzt und das Wort *Leidenschaft* wird ebenso wie das Wort *Geschlechtsliebe* meist nur mit *love* wiedergegeben ...' [Sentences like *an old, i.e. no longer menstruating woman arouses our abhorrence* are simply not translated and the word *passion* as well as *sexual love* is generally reproduced just as *love* ...]' (ibid., p. 269); E.T. 111.

18 *Essays of Schopenhauer*, p. 173; E.T. 111–12.

19 E.T. 112; see *The Literary Notebooks of Thomas Hardy*, ed. Lennart A. Björk (1985), ii. 28–31, entries 1782–1800 (13 May 1891).

20 E.T. 86.

21 See E.T. 84–5; JC assumed that 'the thought of his mother held him back' but it did not: see (i. 36–7, 39–41).

22 Nehls, iii. 600.

23 R. P. Blatchford, *God and My Neighbour* (1903), p. 10.

24 Chambers, 'Memories', p. 15.

25 Ibid.; Edward Gilbert notes. For DHL's opinion of the vicar of Greasley, the Rev. Rodolph, Baron von Hube, see the character of Baron Rudolf von Ruge in *The Merry-Go-Round*, 'The Death of the Baron' (*Poems* 857–8), *PO* 258 (note on 88:2) and *R* 183: see too Moore, *The Priest of Love*, pp. 71–2.

26 'Autobiography', *P II* 300–1.

27 *R* 404:6–7; E.T. 88.

28 Nehls, iii. 610.

29 Nehls, i. 50. The original last paragraph of chapter VIII of *The White Peacock*, with its recreation of the friendship of DHL and Alan Chambers in the summer and early autumn of 1908, ended: '⟨it was then I repeated to him Swinburne's lyrics, and Meredith's, till he learned them from me; it was then, and at such times, I showed him how to read Ibsen, and Synge's fine dramas. So long as I chose for him he read, and grew; but when I no longer gave him my choice, he

ceased to grow〉' (E430d, p. 553). Those months apparently marked the high point of DHL's friendship with Alan Chambers. DHL gave him a present of six books (now unlocated), perhaps on the occasion of his marriage (which DHL could not have attended: he was in Hampstead that day) at Basford Registry Office on 15 October 1910 to DHL's cousin Alvina Reeve. The books were all from the 'British Library of Continental Fiction' (one was Rudolf Golm's *The Old Adam and the New Eve*: see *LAH* 247, note on 161:1). DHL inscribed one 'Alan A. Chambers "memor / Actae non alio rege puertiae / Mutataesque simul togae" / D. H. Lawrence' ['recalling boyhood passed under the self-same king and their togas changed together'] (Horace, *Odes*, I. 36: see note 48 below). Changing to the man's togas at the same time means 'reached manhood together'. DHL was still in touch with Alan Chambers early in 1911, when he entered into his address book the name 'Alan' and his address (Berkeley).

30 Edward Gilbert notes; Alice Hall Holditch, interview; see *Ilkeston Advertiser*, 24 September 1900, p. 8; Ernest Lawrence commented on the change in a letter to Emily Lawrence, 20 March 1901 (King).

31 Nehls, i. 74, 72; *Hardy* 223:2–4, xli.

32 E.T. 112; in his paper, 'Art and the Individual', his reference to Darwin was taken from Tolstoy's essay *What is Art?* (*Hardy* 139:16–18, 225:29 and p. 273, note on 139:18). May Chambers, however, recalled DHL bringing 'Darwin's *Origin of Species*, and Huxley and Haeckel' to the Haggs (Nehls, iii. 609).

33 William James, *Pragmatism* (1907), p. 16; E. Haeckel, *The Riddle of the Universe*, tr. J. McCabe (1902): the 6d edition, published by the Rationalist Press in 1902 and many times reprinted, is likely to have been DHL's source.

34 Haeckel, *The Riddle of the Universe*, p. 102; William James, *A Pluralistic Universe* (1909), p. 316; E.T. 112.

35 E.T. 113; *OED* definition from James; William James, 'Postscript', *The Varieties of Religious Experience* (1902), p. 525; 'William James and Pluralism' by Joseph H. Wickstead, *English Review*, iii (September 1909), 357–681. DHL found James's books sympathetic (E.T. 113) and took over some of his arguments and attitudes: e.g. in 'Pragmatism and Religion' in *Pragmatism*, James described man's desire for

> a universe where we can just give up, fall on our father's neck, and be absorbed into the absolute life as a drop of water melts into the river or the sea.
>
> The peace and rest, the security desiderated at such moments is security against the bewildering accidents of so much finite experience. Nirvana means safety from this everlasting round of adventures of which the world of sense consists ... to men of this complexion, religious monism comes with its consoling words: 'All is needed and essential – even you with your sick soul and heart. All are one with God, and with God all is well. The everlasting arms are beneath ...' (pp. 292–3)

DHL's own lighthearted expression of ridicule for Buddhism in April 1908 (i. 46) and his arguments against (and attraction to) 'the everlasting arms' in July 1908 (i. 62) indicate his indebtedness to James.

36 E.T. 76.

37 *R* 414:17–19, 20; 442:11–12; 443:37–8.

38 According to JC, DHL probably read Spencer around 1906–7 (E.T. 113): DHL mentioned him in October 1907 as important (i. 36), and referred to him again in April 1908 as an appropriate subject for an Eastwood discussion group ('Art and the Individual', *Hardy*, 229:9): see too note 43.

39 *R* 405:26, 27–30.

40 *R* 406:1–2, 10–12, 18–19; 406:7; 405:39.

41 *R* 408:20–21, 16: cf. a deleted passage in *The White Peacock*: Cyril Beardsall recalls a University professor who could 'see no reason why Life should be considered as anything fundamentally different from the other physical forces, a thing whose secret is only temporarily hid, as electricity was' (E430d, p. 152); *R* 408:31–3, 36–9.

42 *R* 409:3–6.

43 *SL* 153; E373e, pp. 230, 286; Spencer's evolutionary theory of ethics strongly influenced the *Manual of Ethics*, by John S. Mackenzie, which Paul offers to send Miriam (E373e, p. 352), and Paul cites Spencer to his mother as a representative modern intellectual (*SL* 213).

44 E.T. 79; 'Madame' was probably Edith Mary Becket, lecturer in the Department of Education.

45 Nehls, ii. 126–7; William Harold King, taped interview with David Gerard (NCL): Bart Kennedy (1861–1930), popular author.

46 LaL1 (UN).

47 Tropp, *The School Teachers*, p. 168.

48 LaL2 (UN). In *A Collier's Friday Night*, Ernest Lambert asks his mother for money to buy 'two books of Horace Quintus Horatius Flaccius [sic], dear old chap' (E74a, p. [24]). DHL quoted from the *Odes*, Book III, in 1908 and 1911 (i. 47, 224: *WP* 211:35–8), and regularly from Book I (i. 56, ii. 36, 46, 352, iii. 65: *WP* 85:38–40, 216:23–4). See too note 29 above.

49 E.T. 75; two references from October 1908, after the course at Nottingham was over, indicate that 'maternal advice' (i. 85) ensured that he was still considering studying for a degree: 'I am making a vain attempt to study' (i. 84) and 'I ought to continue to study for a degree, but I do not want to study' (i. 85). This would have been an external degree of the University of London; he never followed up the idea, however.

50 *WP* 111:38–9, 113:19–21.

51 E.T. 77–8, 76; Frieda recollected that her husband Ernest Weekley had his attention caught by DHL as a student, and on seeing his reaction to a reference which Weekley made to Rossetti's 'The Blessed Damozel', remarked 'I am sure he is a poet I could see it in his face' (i. 51 n. 1); 'Autobiography', *P II* 300; see chapter 5, p. 139 and pp. 532–3, note 35.

52 BABB in Teaching, Reading, Drawing and Music respectively (University College Students' Register). DHL did not, however, do as well as a number of the female students; his friend Lois Mee, for example – see pp. 531–2, note 17 and (i. 142 and n. 6) – got AAAA. For LB's report and marks see p. 553, note 6: for

Gilbert Noon's see p. 529, note 41; University College Students' Register 1906–8.

53 Ibid.

54 LB Papers 34: full stops and inverted commas supplied.

55 *List of Training College Students who completed their period of training on 31st July 1908* (HMSO, 1909), p. 41; Delavenay, ii. 690.

56 *Nottinghamshire Guardian*, 10 August 1907, p. 1.

57 JC to Professor W. Lutoslawski, 23 June 1935, 'The Collected Letters', p. 113.

58 In DHL's English syllabus printed in Delavenay, ii. 659, the earliest work studied is Spenser's *Faerie Queene*, but one of his college notebooks contains three pages of notes on Langland and Chaucer (LaL1, UN).

59 E.T. 155.

60 E.T. 155, 156.

61 *WP* 348:9–30.

62 E.T. 117.

63 See JC to Professor W. Lutoslawski, 23 June 1935, 'The Collected Letters', p. 114: 'Lettie was supposed to be his sister Ada, but it is much more the feminine side of Lawrence himself.'

64 E317, no. 17. 'Saprophyte' means any vegetable organism which lives on decayed organic matter. DHL numbered the poem '14': it was one of the twenty-four poems he copied into the notebook when he first began using it to collect his poems, probably in the summer of 1908.

65 E317, no. 8, ll. 21, 23–4, 7–12. DHL numbered the poem '4'.

66 E317, no. 7, ll. 11–12, 13–18. DHL numbered the poem '3'.

67 *R* 399:28–34, 400:3–5.

68 *R* 403:15–17; 403:34–404:2.

Chapter Eight: Success

1 E.T. 88, 89. DHL's difficulties were compounded by the fact that the increase of training college student places 'meant that a much larger number of newly trained teachers were thrown upon the market at one time. As early as 1907 it was found that a certain number of ex-students were finding it impossible to obtain employment as trained certificated teachers on leaving college' (Tropp, *The School Teachers*, p. 188).

2 E.T. 89.

3 HC, *In Our Infancy*, pp. 133, 151–2; Nehls, i. 85.

4 E.T. 149–50.

5 In March 1908 the Jones family had been living at 13 Blackhorse Lane (Hilda Mary Jones Birth Certificate); E.T. 152.

6 Neville 51.

7 Nehls, i. 83, 89.

8 HC, *In Our Infancy*, p. 153.

9 'A Snowy Day at School', E317, no. 42, ll. 15–16, 19–20, 21–30, 34–6.

10 HC, *In Our Infancy*, p. 160.

11 Nehls, i. 93, 98, 90, 141; Aldous Huxley, 'Introduction', *The Letters of D. H. Lawrence*, ed. Aldous Huxley (1932), p. xxxi; Nehls, i. 89.

12 Charles Leeming, taped interview with David Gerard (NCL).

13 Nehls, i. 85, 90.

14 Ibid., i. 90.

15 Ibid., i. 86.

16 Ibid., i. 87–8.

17 Frieda to Amy Lowell, 5 April 1918, *The Letters of D. H. Lawrence & Amy Lowell, 1914–1925*, ed. E. Claire Healey and Keith Cushman (Santa Barbara, 1985), p. 132; Nehls, i. 86–7.

18 Nehls, i. 90, 85–7; LaT 70 (UN).

19 Nehls, i. 90: LaT 70.

20 E240.7, p. [17]: he first wrote 'Nietsche', then changed it to 'Nietzche'; E407a, p. 56 [verso]: the reference has not been identified; *T* 66:16–17. Writing the word in 'Paul Morel' IIIa in the spring of 1912, he started 'Niets ...', then adjusted the spelling in mid-word to 'Nietzsche' (E373b, p. 208).

21 Patrick Bridgwater, *Nietzsche in Anglosaxony* (Leicester, 1972), pp. 12–13, 56–8, 104–5; David S. Thatcher, *Nietzsche in England 1890–1914* (Toronto, 1970), pp. 139–73, 175–217; see e.g. the *New Age* of 4 January 1908, advertising Orage's two books (produced by its own books department): 'No Socialist can afford to leave unconsidered the ideas of Friedrich Nietzsche, the greatest teacher of the aristocratic philosophy' (p. 200). Orage reviewed a reissue of *Thus Spake Zarathustra* on 20 June 1908 (p. 153), and reviews of and articles on Nietzsche were common (e.g. 12 September 1908, p. 392; 19 September 1908, pp. 408–9; 26 September 1908, pp. 428–9). DHL heard about the magazine from either Alice Dax or Sallie Hopkin sometime in 1908; the 'Jacob Tonson' column, which JC recalled in particular, started in March that year (see E.T. 120, where the year is misdated). There is direct evidence that DHL knew the issue of 8 August 1908 (*Hardy* 271 note on 135:6).

22 See *WL* 150:26 and Explanatory note.

23 'The Georgian Renaissance', *Rhythm* (March 1913), xvii–xviii; Colin Milton, *Lawrence and Nietzsche* (Aberdeen, 1987), p. 2.

24 'The Despisers of the Body', 'Reading and Writing', *Thus Spake Zarathustra*, First Part, tr. Thomas Common (Edinburgh, 1906), pp. 28–9, 33. The earlier edition of Common's translation (London, n.d. [*c.* 1901]) runs as follows:

> And thy little intelligence, my brother, which thou callest 'spirit', is but an instrument of thy body, a little instrument and plaything of thy big intelligence.
> Behind thy thoughts and feelings, my brother, there stands a powerful governor, an unknown sage, called self – which resides in thy body, which is thy body.
> There is more intelligence in thy body than in thy best wisdom ...
> Of all that is written, I only love that which a person writes with his blood. Write with blood, and thou wilt find that blood is thought. (p. [4])

25 E.T. 120.

26 *LAH* 33:16–25.

27 HC, *In Our Infancy*, pp. 157–8; Nehls, i. 89.

28 HC, *In Our Infancy*, pp. 160–1, 166, 167.

29 E.T. 119; Nehls, i. 91.

30 This contradicts the spirit, if not the letter, of his own later account of his career, when he observed:

> I never starved in a garret, nor waited in anguish for the post to bring me an answer from editor or publisher, nor did I struggle in sweat and blood to bring forth mighty works, nor did I ever wake up and find myself famous.
>
> I was a poor boy. I *ought* to have wrestled in the fell clutch of circumstances, and undergone the bludgeonings of chance before I became a writer ... But I didn't. It all happened by itself and without any groans from me.   ('Autobiographical Sketch', *P II* 592)

31 Ford Madox Hueffer to Arnold Bennett, 10 March 1909 (UT); see too (i. 11–13). For details of the financing of the *English Review*, see Arthur Mizener, *The Saddest Story* (1971), pp. 157–64. Hueffer changed his surname to Ford in June 1919.

32 E.T. 156.

33 E.T. 156–7.

34 E.T. 157–8.

35 E.T. 159.

36 'Autobiographical Sketch', *P II* 593.

37 Ford Madox Ford, *Return to Yesterday* (1931), p. 399.

38 Nehls, i. 108–9.

39 Ibid., i. 116; see *LAH* xxv–xxvi.

40 *Poems* 852.

41 E.T. 164–5; see too *WP* 282:6–34.

42 E.T. 166–7.

43 E.T. 167–8; Delavenay, ii. 702.

44 HC, *Neutral Ground* (1933), p. 284 ['duvet']; the book is a fictionalised account of the events of HC's life up to 1912; *Hardy* 146:20–1.

45 Keith Sagar, 'Lawrence and the Wilkinsons', *Review of English Literature*, iv (October 1962), 73; E.T. 168.

46 E.T. 171–2; Nehls, i. 127; E.T. 174.

47 HC, *The Croydon Years*, p. 49; 'Autobiographical Sketch', *P II* 593–4; the final manuscript, as it now stands, contains the handwriting of DHL himself and four other people. His friends Agnes Holt and Agnes Mason had saved him the expense of a typist by making clean handwritten copies of the manuscript's most heavily revised pages, and HC also copied out five pages early in 1910. A final copyist (who worked only in Part III, in March–April 1910) remains unidentified.

Andrew Robertson has suggested that the work of copying was done between

Hueffer reading the manuscript and the manuscript being sent to Heinemann (*WP* xxvi–xxvii). However, there seems to have been no time for such work in December; the manuscript was in Hueffer's hands between 1 November and mid-December and – via Violet Hunt – went straight to Heinemann, almost certainly before Christmas 1909, where it stayed until 20 January 1910. Some of HC's corrections (which she started to make in February 1910) appear on pages written out by Agnes Holt and Agnes Mason; and although Agnes Holt had copied into DHL's poetry notebook those of his poems published in the November 1909 *English Review*, their relationship cooled during the winter: JC believed that 'after my visit in November [27th–28th] 1909 he told her that he really belonged to me' (Delavenay, ii. 675). This suggests that Agnes Holt was less likely to have copied for DHL in the period January–February 1910 and that she did her stint earlier. As Agnes Mason's copying directly followed on from hers (she had written out pp. 1–76, Agnes Mason went on with pp. 77–82), their work probably represents DHL's attempt to get the manuscript into a presentable form for Hueffer during October 1909. HC's pages were, however, certainly written in the spring of 1910, when she was active in helping DHL with the novel (four of her five pages appear in the Part III of the novel, which DHL rewrote after getting the manuscript back from Heinemann in January). She appears to have helped correct Parts I and II in February and March, and Part III in March-April. (I am grateful for the help of Tony Atkins in establishing these points.)

48 Lazarus: in DHL's hand, marked 'Copy'.

49 William de Morgan (1839–1917), artist and potter, who published his first novel *Joseph Vance* (1906) at the age of 57, became extremely successful; his novels *Alice-for-Short* (1907), *Somehow Good* (1908) and *It Never Can Happen Again* (1909) made him and his publisher Heinemann 'a steady flow of money':

> when some friend asked him what was the nature of his contract with Heinemann he responded contentedly, 'I never really worry about contracts. When I want some money, I just write to Heinemann for £1,000 and he sends me a cheque, and when that is gone, I write for another. It's much simpler!' (A. M. W. Stirling, *William de Morgan and his Wife*, New York, 1922, pp. 313–14)

Hueffer's comparison with *The White Peacock* was therefore very much to Lawrence's advantage, though the great length and extraordinarily prolix detail of de Morgan's novels (*It Never Can Happen Again* had just been published in two volumes in November 1909) also indicated one of Hueffer's criticisms of DHL's novel.

50 E. V. Lucas, *Reading, Writing and Remembering* (New York, 1932), p. 290; E.T. 179.

51 HC, *The Croydon Years*, pp. 6, 50; *WP* xxvi; E.T. 180–1.

52 Corrected from MS.

53 *WP* 83:40–84:5; 13:24–5.

54 *WP* 324:5–8.

55 *WP* 324:32–3.

56 'Introduction' to McDonald, *A Bibliography of D. H. Lawrence*, p. 9 (P 232); Nehls, ii. 414.

57 *WP* 302:37–9, 304:8–10.

58 *LAH* 35:1–3.

59 JC and May Chambers both described an encounter with a gamekeeper in High Park Wood in which Alan Chambers and DHL had their names taken (E.T. 117–18 puts the episode in 1903: Nehls, iii. 594–5 puts it two or three years later); May Chambers also described taking DHL to the keeper's hut in High Park Wood in 1901 (Nehls, iii. 562). LB also recalled a meeting between DHL and a gamekeeper: see chapter 7, p. 188.

60 See *WP* 147:3 and n.

61 Black, *D. H. Lawrence: The Early Fiction*, p. 47; H. M. Daleski, 'Lawrence and George Eliot: The Genesis of *The White Peacock*', *D. H. Lawrence and Tradition*, ed. Jeffrey Meyers (Amherst, 1985), pp. 51–68.

Chapter Nine: Strife

1 Joseph Conrad to Norman Douglas, 25 December 1909 (UT).

2 Nehls, i. 127, 128.

3 See Kim A. Herzinger, *D. H. Lawrence in His Time: 1908–1915* (1982), p. 185; Nehls, i. 130, 131.

4 Nehls, i. 137; *Hardy* xlii–xliii. The meeting at the Rhyses' house is also recreated in *WP* 282–4.

5 Grace Lovat Fraser [née Crawford], *In the Days of my Youth* (1970), p. 133.

6 Ibid., pp. 134–5.

7 Ibid., p. 144: David Garnett also recalled the ear-ring, 'which was considered very scandalous by certain ladies' (*The Golden Echo*, 1953, p. 130); information from Mrs Nesta Macdonald, July 1986.

8 *Hardy*, 145:19–20, 24–6; 'sublimating' here retains the older meaning of 'refining into something nobler, higher and less real', and has no connection with the exactly contemporary psychoanalytic meaning adopted by the English translators of Freud (the word first appearing in this sense in 1910).

9 Hardy 146:29–36.

10 Nehls, i. 121.

11 Ibid.

12 E135.5a, p. 2 (original readings in all quotations): *LAH* 50:14–15.

13 Ibid., p. 4.

14 Ibid., pp. 5, 6.

15 Ibid., p. 7.

16 Ibid.

17 Ibid., p. 8.

18 HC, *In Our Infancy*, p. 135.

19 *LAH* 23:14–23, 25–6, 27–8.

20 *LAH* 24:4, 25:13–14; 26:35–40.

21 *LAH* 24:2; 25:32–4.
22 *LAH* 16:27–8, 30–1.
23 *LAH* 17:24, 29–31; 18:4–5.
24 *LAH* 18:7, 13–17.
25 *LAH* 18:40, 19:1, 13–14, 21–2.
26 *LAH* 19:36–20:1; 17:4.
27 *LAH* 20:27–36, 24.
28 E.T. 165.
29 '*Odour of Chrysanthemums*: An early version', p. 44.
30 E284c, p. [33] (original reading).
31 E317, no. 48, ll. 49–51.
32 Although DHL stated that he wrote it 'when I was twenty-one, almost before I'd done anything' (E74a, p. [1]), JC was correct in asserting that it was written in 1909: 'He certainly wrote it that autumn' (Delavenay, ii. 694). The references to the death of Swinburne (and to Meredith, in manuscript), in April and May 1909, to the baby born to his sister Emily (Margaret, b. 9 February 1909), and to his poem sequence 'A Life History' written late in the year (see chapter 10, pp. 276–8) confirm her dating (E74a, pp. [31, 47, 58]).
33 E74a, p. [1].
34 E74a, p. [24].
35 E74a, p. [25].
36 E74a, p. [40].
37 *Memoirs* 131.
38 E74a, p. [124] (italic for stage directions supplied).
39 E74a, p. [133–4] (italic for stage directions supplied).
40 Nehls, iii. 610–11.
41 See *LAH* xxvi and *PO* xlii–xliv.
42 *LAH* 31:6–13.
43 *LAH* 32:9–10, 12–13.
44 E359.4a, p. 8 (original reading).
45 Ibid., p. 9 (original reading).
46 See chapter 4, pp. 104–5. Although JC reported that there were 'no uproarious charades' at the Haggs at Christmas 1908 (E.T. 152), DHL was not only present on several occasions (E.T. 151, 152, 156) but saw a good deal of Alan Chambers (i. 104). He also made JC jealous by flirting with LB (i. 103, 105). He was there again around 19–26 August 1909, when he told the Chambers family about the desertion of Sir James Barrie by his wife Mary for Gilbert Cannan (Nehls, iii. 582), and he was still visiting the Haggs at Christmas 1909 (Delavenay, ii. 702), though his visits were obviously fewer than during the years 1901–8.
47 E.T. 164.
48 *WP* 226:10–11; E.T. 168.
49 See pp. 542–3, note 47.
50 E317, no. 55, ll. 30–1.
51 E.T. 165.

52 Delavenay, ii. 656.

53 E.T. 141, 140; Delavenay, ii. 702.

54 Delavenay, ii. 701; DHL told George Neville about a visit to the house of LB and her family which may well have happened in the spring of 1910: after DHL had got his coat dirty, LB took it outside to brush it, and accidentally tipped out the contents of its pockets, depositing 'about a half dozen rubber protectors, just in their transparent flimsy slips' on the lawn (Neville 85–6). See too (i. 286) and its reference to 'the two little articles Jones gave me months back, and which were my articles of temptation'.

55 Delavenay, ii. 705.

56 Neville 86.

57 Delavenay, ii. 704.

58 Delavenay, ii. 702; in 'Paul Morel' IIIb, when Paul finally breaks off from Miriam, she remarks that it has been 'three months' (E373d, p. 415, page renumbered from 371) since their sexual relationship started: DHL broke off from JC on 1 August 1910; Delavenay, ii. 703.

59 Edward Gilbert, notes of conversations with Willie Hopkin (Sagar); E373e, p. 496.

60 Delavenay, ii. 703: 'gives much of his time to his mother; they only have walks and conversations . . . fine weather; they are happy.'

61 E320.1, no. 35, ll. 15–18; E213a, ll. 24–5.

62 E213a, ll. 30–3, 39–42.

63 Delavenay, ii. 704; Lydia Lawrence to Lettice Berry, 11 July 1910.

64 E.T. 181.

65 HC, *Neutral Ground*, p. 274; HC to the author, July 1968; *T* 6.

66 *T* 299, 301.

67 *LAH* 64:35–6; HC, *In Our Infancy*, pp. 157–8.

68 *T* 8, 318.

69 See *T* 325–7 and Explanatory notes; *T* 12.

70 It has been argued that the appearance of the name could be accounted for by his familiarity with HC's story since the autumn of 1909, and their using that name for Macartney in their discussions: 'DHL could easily have had "Siegmund" on his mind before he began "The Saga"' (*T* 9 n. 31).

But for it to be so readily on his pen, as well as on his mind, DHL had probably already started writing about Siegmund in the other novel. He had written at least one poem about Siegmund, 'A Love-Passage': it appears in his second college notebook (E320.1, no. 32) immediately after a poem which can be dated (in its conception) to late February 1910. That would make 'A Love-Passage' coincide with DHL's use of the name 'Siegmund' in *The White Peacock*, and helps confirm the possibility that 'The Saga' was begun well before Easter 1910. 'A Love-Passage' is a savagely ironical title; the poem is spoken by the 'Helena' figure, and shows her turning the (unnamed) Siegmund into the lover she wants ('Oh what were you, what were you but the stuff of my soul!'). DHL's other two poems on the subject of Siegmund, 'Red' and 'A Love Song', both however date from 1911: the first belongs to a sequence of 'colour' poems and has little to do with the novel. To believe that DHL did not start writing 'The Saga' before April 1910 is to put too great a weight upon HC's statement that he began it 'during the fortnight succeeding the Easter Holidays', and upon JC's assertion that he started it in May (E.T. 181). Since he had by his own account written 'about half' of it by 27 April (i. 159), and was working on *The White Peacock* until 11 April, it is inconceivable that he wrote perhaps 200 pages of 'The Saga' between then and the 27th. It was the book of his which JC knew least about, and HC's own accounts of its starting date are inconsistent (*T* 8 n. 26).

71 E.T. 181.

72 E407b, p. 285.

73 Ibid., p. 283 (original reading).

74 HC, *In Our Infancy*, p. 181.

75 *T* 225:36–227:25. DHL originally used the name Ernest Lambert throughout the last chapter of 'The Saga' for the character he had (in chapter I) called Cecil Byrne; Lambert, the central figure in the November 1909 *Collier's Friday Night*, perhaps represented a tougher self-image than Cecil Byrne (C.B. like Cyril Beardsall), and may suggest a new astringency in the way Helena/Sieglinde is to be treated.

76 Olive Schreiner ['Ralph Irons'], *The Story of an African Farm* (1883), Part II, chapter II ('Waldo's Stranger') and chapter IX ('Lyndall's Stranger'): see too Delavenay, ii. 685 and HC, *In Our Infancy*, p. 184; HC, *Neutral Ground*, p. 284.

77 *T* 112:21–5.

78 DHL wrote in 1920 how his writings were 'somewhere . . . the crumpled wings of my soul. They get me free before I get myself free' (iii. 522).

79 Nehls, i. 121.

80 E320.1, no. 36, ll. 13–15; at some stage DHL added another line ('For better is bereaving than deceiving') between ll. 13 and 14.

81 Delavenay, ii. 704; E.T. 182.

82 E359.4a, p. 22 (original reading): in April 1916, he would describe a woman's feeling for a man which sounds very similar to JC's for him: 'Like a priestess she kept his records and his oracles, he was like a God who would be nothing if his worship were neglected.' When Birkin offends Hermione in the discarded 'Prologue' to *Women in Love* by behaving as a 'common, vulgar man who turned her to scorn' instead of as the 'pure, incandescent spirit burning intense with the presence of God' (*WL* 492:8–10, 26–7, 28–9), Hermione's soul is

convulsed with cynicism. She despised her God and her angel. Yet she could not do without him. She believed in herself as a priestess, and that was all. Though there was no god to serve, still she was a priestess. Yet having no altar to kindle, no sacrifice to burn, she would be barren and useless. So she adhered to her god in him, which she claimed almost violently, whilst her soul turned in bitter cynicism from the prostitute man in him. She did not believe in him, she only believed in that which she

could gather from him, as one gathers silk from the corrupt worm. She was
the maker of gods.   (*WL* 494:8–17)
DHL had come to that final understanding only slowly and painfully.

83 HC, *The Croydon Years*, p. 21; see too *In Our Infancy*, p. 188.
84 E.T. 182; JC to Professor W. Lutoslawski, 23 July 1935, 'The Collected
    Letters', p. 117.
85 E.T. 182, 221.
86 E.T. 182; 'felt herself going mad': Delavenay, ii. 704.
87 E.T. 182.
88 J. M. Barrie, *Tommy and Grizel* (1900), pp. 179, 193, 194, 279.
89 *LG* 70:33–4.
90 See too pp. 559–60, note 14.
91 In his 1914 revision of 'The Shades of Spring', when the narrator makes his
final attempt to work out what has gone wrong between himself and Hilda,
DHL came to his first deeper understanding of the 'Miriam' experience. Syson,
after breaking with Hilda, sees a kingfisher, and is 'extraordinarily moved. He
climbed the bank to the gorse bushes, whose sparks of blossom had not yet
gathered into a flame. Lying on the dry brown turf, he discovered sprigs of tiny
purple milkwort and pink spots of lousewort. What a wonderful world it
was—marvellous, for ever new.' And yet, however conscious the narrator is of
that 'wonderful world', he finds he cannot escape himself and what his own
tortured vision brings. The passage continues:

> He felt as if it were underground, like the fields of monotone hell, notwith-
> standing. Inside his breast was a pain like a wound. He remembered the
> poem of William Morris, where in the Chapel of Lyonesse a knight lay
> wounded, with the truncheon of a spear deep in his breast, lying always as
> dead, yet did not die, while day after day the coloured sunlight dipped
> from the painted window across the chancel, and passed away.

Such a feeling gives Syson a clue to his years of relationship with Hilda: 'He
knew now it never had been true, that which was between him and her, not for a
moment. The truth had stood apart all the time' (*PO* 110:24–36). It 'never had
been true' because the 'uncorporeal' relationship had left out so much of the
person he was. The peculiar intensity of the relationship had meant that he
lived for sensations, not for realities; his vividest life lay within his own consciousness, not outside it in experience of what was 'other' to him. Such self-
consciousness could never really acknowledge another person. And that was a
terrifying fate: to lie 'always as dead' yet with the self unable to die, because
always aware.

    Between the years 1910 and 1916, this was one of the most important
understandings which DHL came to of himself and his contemporaries. In
1915 his poem 'New Heaven and Earth' explored the experience of being
trapped within such a consciousness:

> I was so weary of the world,
> I was so sick of it,
> everything was tainted with myself,

NOTES TO P. 267

skies, trees, flowers, birds, water,
people, houses, streets, vehicles, machines,
nations, armies, war, peace-talking,
work, recreation, governing, anarchy,
it was all tainted with myself, I knew it all to start with
because it was all myself.

When I gathered flowers, I knew it was myself plucking my own flowering.
When I went in a train, I knew it was myself travelling by my own invention.
When I heard the cannon of the war, I listened with my own ears to my own
      destruction.
When I saw the torn dead, I knew it was my own torn dead body.
It was all me, I had done it all in my own flesh.

                         (*Poems* 256–7: ll. 13–26)

DHL had never previously managed to write about the experience of self-consciousness so clearly as in this poem. But he had become one of the great writers about the experience of self-consciousness; of being not only aware of the self, but being trapped within the awareness and unable to escape oneself. In 1920 he used the character Albert Witham in *The Lost Girl* first to refer to the fate of Tommy in *Tommy and Grizel* (see note 88 above) and then to portray a bland disregard of the handicap of self-consciousness: 'I wonder why self-consciousness should hinder a man in his action? Why does it cause misgiving? —I think I'm self-conscious, but I don't think I have so many misgivings. I don't see that they're necessary' (*LG* 70:39–71:2). DHL then made the process of the child's growing up into self-consciousness one of the centres of his book *Fantasia of the Unconscious* in 1921; but he had already carried the process of understanding one stage further when writing the 'Prologue' to *Women in Love* in the spring of 1916: he had actually then managed to understand, in fictional form, the pattern of the 'Miriam' relationship. Birkin's love for Hermione is

a love based entirely on ecstasy and on pain, and ultimate death. He *knew*
he did not love her with any living, creative love. He did not even desire
her; he had no passion for her, there was no hot impulse of growth
between them, only this terrible reducing activity of phosphorescent consciousness, the consciousness ever liberated more and more into the void,
at the expense of the flesh, which was burnt down like dead grey ash. (*WL*
496:38–497:5)

It had taken DHL years to discover a language which marked his understanding of self-consciousness or 'phosphorescent consciousness', though HC and 'The Saga' in 1910 had given him his first insight into it.

Chapter Ten: The Bitter River

1 *SL* 303; Lydia Lawrence to Ada Krenkow, 8 February 1910. Harry Mitchie [sic] (M.B. C.M. Aberd., Surgeon) lived at 27 Regent Street, Nottingham.

2 Lydia Lawrence to Lettice Berry, 11 July 1910; to Ada Krenkow, 8 February 1910.

3 Storer, *Some Aspects*, pp. 106–7: in 1911 he was apparently working as a dayman in other butties' coal-getting teams, only working three-quarters of a shift or odd shifts at 5/- or 5/6 a shift (p. 107) and earning 28/6 a week at the best time of the year (i. 219). We can, however, favourably compare his earnings – at the age of 65 in 1911, after being a collier for more than fifty years – with those of the elderly collier in *The Daughter-in-Law*, who having 'worked fifty years for th' cumpany, an' isn't but sixty-two now' is declared not 'equal to stall working', works on maintenance of the underground roadways and earns only 'a guinea a week' (E84a, p. 5).

4 Neville 10, 152.

5 Ernest Wilson, taped interview with David Gerard (NCL).

6 Ellen Staynes died on 22 April 1908 of 'Chronic Glandular Nephritis' at 26 Stretton Road, South Leicester: (i. 46 n. 2) is incorrect in implying that the ailing person was Ada Krenkow. Ellen Staynes had been separated from her husband for many years (information from Joan King, April 1988): Ada Krenkow's husband Fritz registered her death.

7 Ada Lawrence stated it was Lynn Croft when she sent George Neville a copy of the photograph (Neville 66). Richard Aldington thought it showed Lydia Lawrence with *The White Peacock* in her hand, shortly before her death (*Portrait of a Genius, but . . .*', London 1951, p. 86), but failed to consider why a dying woman should have been exposed in her garden during December.

8 HC, *The Croydon Years*, p. 51.

9 LB Papers 40; E.T. 188.

10 See *WP* xxx–xxxiii; (i. 184) is emended from MS; see (i. 161 n. 4): Lydia Lawrence described the details of the contract in her letter to Lettice Berry of 11 July 1910.

11 Gillespie would certify Lydia Lawrence's death: he had also treated Lawrence's friend Mabel Limb and certified her death in 1909; New Eastwood Schools Log Book, 11 November 1910, p. 165 (NCRO).

12 Nehls, iii. 619.

13 *SL* 395.

14 Neville 66; Nehls, i. 140 (corrected from BBC 'Son and Lover'). On 8 April 1923 Frieda, writing to Adele Seltzer about cancer, remarked that DHL 'has a *horror* of it' (UT).

15 Nehls, iii. 619.

16 *SL* 394–7; Lina D. Waterfield, *Castle in Italy* (1961), p. 139; *SL* 396. DHL's brother George claimed to have heard DHL asking Gillespie for 'something to end it' and Gillespie replying 'You know I can't' (George Lawrence, interview); but George's claim in the interview to have gone to see his mother 'every day, cycle after eight o'clock every night, go over to see her' is certainly unreliable (Margaret Needham recalls her mother Emily King's anger that George went so rarely), and his recollection of Gillespie may well be untrustworthy too.

17 *WP* 23:5, 370, 7:14–15, 28, 30, 101:14, 7:30–8:8: see E.T. 149, Nehls, iii. 554.
   Lydia Lawrence was b. 19 July 1851. See too p. 513, note 41.

18 *WP* 33:9–13.

19 Maggie Pearson (a version of JC) is looking at some of Ernest Lambert's
   poems, and Ernest comments to her: 'That one "A Life History"'s' best . . . It is.
   It means more. Look how full of significance it is, when you think of it. The
   profs. would make a great long essay out of the idea. Then the rhythm is finer;
   it's more complicated.' (E74a, p. [58])

20 'Twenty Years Ago' was first printed in *New Poems* (1918), 'Discord in Childhood' in *Amores* (1916).

21 *Poems* 850.

22 E74a, p. [2].

23 Roberts E392a, following E. W. Tedlock's *The Frieda Lawrence Collection of
   D. H. Lawrence Manuscripts: A Descriptive Bibliography* (Albuquerque, 1948), pp.
   37–9, is described as 'An unfinished story' (*A Bibliography of D. H. Lawrence*,
   Cambridge 1982, p. 530). (I am grateful to Dr Helen Baron for helping me
   identify this fragment.)

24 *SL* 8: E392a, pp. 41–8.

25 The plot is written, in ink, on side 8 of Lawrence's Nottingham University
   College Notebook E320.1, opposite Botany notes; the plot fragment for the
   end of 'Laetitia I' (see pp. 532–3, note 35) appears earlier in the same notebook.
   The 'Paul Morel' I plot was, however, probably written after Lawrence began
   to use the notebook for inserting poems, around the start of November 1909.
   Its appearance 'right-way-up' on a previously totally blank page, when nearly all
   the poems in the notebook are written starting from the back of the book
   (therefore 'wrong-way-up'), shows that the plot was inserted well before the last
   poem was inserted (in the summer of 1911). A date for the plot's insertion
   between late 1909 and early 1911 is thus probable from internal evidence, and
   September–October 1910 most likely from external evidence.

26 E320.1.

27 See (i. 52); JC recalled DHL's sister Emily asking him 'When are you coming
   to see me, our William?' (E.T. 64).

28 *The White Peacock* (E430d) was 802 pages long; 'The Saga of Siegmund' (E407a
   & b) was 503 pages long.

29 Keith Sagar, *D. H. Lawrence: Life into Art* (1985), p. 53.

30 E237a, pp. 10–11.

31 Ibid., pp. 41–2.

32 *Hardy* xlii and 141:40.

33 *WP* 29:9, 13, 16, 26, 28–9. The passage was freshly copied by Agnes Holt,
   almost certainly in October 1909; it is not possible to say when it was first
   drafted. Her making of a fair copy suggests a heavily revised and therefore not
   particularly recent original draft.

34 *WP* 29:11–12, 36, 33–5.

35 Ada's copy (Clarke) is reproduced in colour on the dust jacket of this volume;

Agnes Holt's copy (UN) was reproduced in colour on the cover of the Penguin Books *The White Peacock*, ed. Alan Newton (Harmondsworth, 1982); LB's copy (in private hands) is reproduced (reversed) in black-and-white in Sotheby's Catalogue for 6 December 1984, item. 218. The colour reproduction of Greiffenhagen's original painting which DHL most probably used in 1910–11 appeared in the issue for the latter half of May of *100 Popular Pictures*, ed. M. H. Spielmann, issued fortnightly in 1910, size 14.15 × 27.66 cm.; DHL's copies for Ada and Agnes Holt are both approximately 14.1 × 27.6 cm. A modern colour reproduction of the original appears on the cover of *D. H. Lawrence & the Visual Arts*, the catalogue of the 1985 exhibition at the Castle Museum, Nottingham.

George Neville claimed to have influenced DHL's copies by posing for him when he had problems painting the half-naked man (Neville 77–81). But Lydia Lawrence is still alive in Neville's account, which puts the making of the copies nearer 1908 than 1910–11; and he also assumes that DHL needed to see a real back to make his copy. The man's back does not appear in the painting; while DHL's habit of inch-by-inch copying did not require a model (he actually preferred not to work from life). DHL's copies, after the original sketch made in Eastwood in December 1910 as his mother was dying, were all made in 1911, when he was hardly ever in Eastwood. For these reasons I have ignored Neville's account of DHL and the painting. Neville probably helped DHL with life-studies and posed for him; but it seems unlikely that he assisted with *An Idyll*. See however the arguments of Dr Carl Baron for a directly contrary opinion (Neville 172–80).

36 Nehls, iii. 620; Ada 25; E.T. 184. The poems were 'To My Mother—Dead' (later called 'The End'), 'The Dead Mother' (later 'The Bride'), and 'My Love, My Mother' (later 'The Virgin Mother'): the identical poems which LB later copied into his notebook for him (E320.1, nos. 59–61).

Chapter Eleven: The Sick Year

1 LB Papers 22.
2 Ibid. 23.
3 Ibid. 21.
4 Ibid. 15. Her visit on Wednesday 26 December 1906 was expected – see (i. 33); hence the dating of this episode to the previous year.
5 Neville 81–2; E.T. 139–40, 142. JC's comment 'although he had apparently satisfied himself as to the nature of his feeling, he took no action of any kind, but remained as suspended as before' is misleading; the poem belongs not to 1907 (as she believed) but to 1911, the year of DHL's engagement to LB. LB annotated it in her copy of *Look! We Have Come Through!*: 'Written during our engagement because I challenged his ability to write such love poems as Richard Middleton's' (Neales of Nottingham Sales Catalogue, 24 October 1985). The date is confirmed by the poem's non-appearance in either of DHL's poetry notebooks (which he stopped using in the summer of 1911).

6 Her college marks were CBBA (Teaching, Reading, Drawing, Music); see pp. 539–40, note 52. Her report runs:

> Miss Burrows is a teacher with plenty of intelligence & a good manner but no system. She is most successful in teaching Literature, History, Geography & Drawing – but often digresses & fails to impress important points. She has a good fund of general information – Descriptions are graphic – very good flow of language – but she talks too much, & at times makes large statements and uses colloquial expressions. Questions intelligent but often indefinite – too 'wordy' –
>
> Discipline not a strong point – want of system shows itself particularly here. Manner genial but not sufficiently dignified in class. Great interest shown in children's games. (University College Students' Register)

She obtained a distinction in her Education examination in 1908.

7 LaB243 (UN).

8 E320.1, no. 50, ll. 12, 21, 26–33; autumn 1910 was the period when, according to JC, HC became DHL's mistress: JC linked the poem with her (Delavenay, ii. 705). There is, however, no other evidence to support JC's belief about the poem's origins, or to subvert HC's continued testimony against her being DHL's mistress. See chapter 11, pp. 307–8.

9 *R* 234:21–3.

10 DHL set the final exchange between Paul Morel and Miriam in *Sons and Lovers* at a time when 'the floods were out' (*SL* 416): and in the novel, too, 'the silent water and the darkness' drive the two of them together.

11 On 6 January 1910, her neighbour in Ratcliffe-on-the-Wreake mentioned that two ladies, 'hearing that I had a Suffragist neighbour asked your name' (LaB193, UN).

12 HC, *The Croydon Years*, p. 22.

13 LB Papers 9.

14 *PO* 234:21–2, 36–7.

15 LaB6 (UN): *Poems* 871.

16 LaB6 (UN): *Poems* 869; *SL* 141.

17 LB Papers 14.

18 The black vases were probably the 'two, squat, dark pieces of majolica' described in 'Paul Morel' II (E373d, p. 287).

19 Frieda, 'Introduction' to *Look! We Have Come Through!* (Ark Press, Brushford, Dulverton 1971), p. 11; *WL* 104:6.

20 E.T. 189; Hilda Shaw to LB, 'Tuesday' [*c.* February 1911], LaB195 (UN).

21 James T. Boulton, General Editor of the Cambridge Edition of Lawrence's *Letters*, advises that this letter should be assigned the date of 29 May 1911, not 29 April 1911, DHL having made the same mistake in the month which he began to make on 26 May (i. 271 and n. 4).

22 See Helen Baron, '*Sons and Lovers*: The Surviving Manuscripts from Three Drafts Dated by Paper Analysis', *Studies in Bibliography*, xxxviii (1985), 303.

23 E373d, pp. 210, 211.

24 Ibid., pp. 171–2, 292, 321.

25 E373d, p. 327; Helen Baron, '*Sons and Lovers*', pp. 302–3.

26 E373d, p. 288.

27 Ibid., p. 165.

28 Letters nos. 306 and 312, to Edward Garnett, 10 and 25 September 1911, are both on mourning paper. DHL was, however, probably also using the paper because it was of good quality, and he was writing to a new and potentially important correspondent. His previous last surviving letter on mourning paper (no. 243) dates from March 1911.

29 E.T. 201; Frieda 74.

30 LB Papers 17.

31 'Scarcely believes in my love for you'.

32 E320.1, no. 51, ll. 17–24 (original reading); see too (i. 246).

33 *Poems* 851.

34 *SL* 412, 422.

35 E373e, p. 534; *SL* 413; E320.1, no. 81, ll. 34–5.

36 *LG* 45:4.

37 *LG* 47:34–9.

38 E320.1, no. 81, ll. 21–2, 25–8 (original readings).

39 *LAH* 71:26–7.

40 E320.1, no. 85, ll. 3–12.

41 *SL* 413; Edward Thomas, 'Out in the Dark', *Collected Poems*, ed. R. George Thomas (Oxford, 1978), p. 375.

42 'I'll bring you nothing but sorrows'.

43 Nehls, i. 142, 143.

44 Delavenay, ii. 705: 'H. C. became his mistress' (see note 8 above).

45 In the version of these relationships DHL gave to Mellors in *Lady Chatterley's Lover*, Mellors's anger with 'Lesbian women' – 'When I get with a Lesbian woman, whether she knows she's one or not, I see red' (E186c, p. 469) – relates to his experiences with a recreation of HC: a 'soft, white-skinned, soft sort of woman, older than me' who 'played the fiddle'. Mellors notes that 'if you forced her to the sex itself, she just ground her teeth and sent out hate. I forced her to it: and she could simply numb me with hate because of it. So I was balked again' (E186c, p. 462).

46 E320.1, no. 85, ll. 66–7.

47 LB Papers 17; *Poems* 127.

48 'Your Hands', E320.1, no. 84. Ll. 23–4 originally ran 'Gluttonous bird that stirs on my thigh and eats on the / Warmth and thickness . . .' But DHL did not finish l. 24, and must immediately have revised to the reading printed. L. 34 originally ran 'For her; she crushes with them her bosom, her heart,' but DHL made the rhyme word in l. 36 'sleep', so must immediately have revised the line.

49 Delavenay, ii. 705.

50 E438a, pp. 17–18.

51 E438a, pp. 23–4.

52 LB Papers 7.

53 E438a, p. 28; HC, *In Our Infancy*, p. 207: see too (i. 240); E438a, p. 35.

54 E438a, pp. 35, 36.

55 *Poems* 878.

56 LB Papers 14.

57 Especially given her own mother's reaction; according to David Chambers, Ann Chambers 'used to shudder when the subject of sex was mentioned' (Nehls, iii. 536).

58 E438a, pp. 23–4; 'Your Hands', E320.1, no. 84, ll. 42–3.

59 'I long for you, mouth and throat, to kiss you' [neither DHL nor LB probably knew that 'gorge' also meant 'breasts']; 'Alas, how far you are from me, how far your body from mine'; 'A kiss on the mouth'.

60 LB Papers 14, 25.

61 Ibid. 19.

62 Delavenay, ii. 705; E.T. 165.

63 See too (i. 104).

64 *PO* 280.

65 Neville 103; Delavenay, ii. 706.

66 The quotation is given the date 'post 13 March 1911' in *Letters*, i., because of the reference to a Croydon visit by LB ('here for the week-end'): LB was in Croydon 11–12 March 1911. In E.T. 154, however (the source of the quotation), LB's visit to Croydon is dated 'Soon afterwards' a visit DHL made to JC at the Haggs Farm, which the Chambers family left in the summer of 1910. LB's weekend visit to Croydon is therefore more likely to have been the one she paid on Saturday 10 July 1909 (i. 130).

67 LB Papers 19. The evidence for his relationship with Marie Jones is, however, very slight. DHL's short story 'The Old Adam', written in the summer of 1911, describes 'Edward Severn', a lodger in a recreation of DHL's Croydon lodgings, who finds himself overwhelmed by a violent sexual awareness of his rather older landlady 'Mrs Thomas' (*LAH* 77:8–78:28). DHL said an emotional goodbye to an unidentified London woman he called 'Jane' on 9 February 1912 (i. 364). The most striking evidence, however, is that in May 1913 DHL sent one of his five precious author's copies of *Sons and Lovers* to Marie Jones (the other copies went to his two sisters, his brother and his close friend Arthur McLeod). To do this nearly eighteen months after last seeing her suggests the repayment of some debt of loyalty or feeling: it may not be a coincidence that Paul Morel has an affair with an older, married, woman who returns to her husband.

68 In the late nineteenth century the word 'tart' was regularly used to mean 'prostitute': see the 1887 and 1894 citations in *OED*; Neville 86; *PO* 67:36–9, *R* 20:3–5, 21:37–22:4; address book at the Bancroft Library, University of California at Berkeley. There is only one other woman recorded solely by her first name in it: the flirtatious and titillating Gussie Cooper – see (i. 286) – of Purley. It is possible that 'the sequel – which startled *me*' (i. 366) to seeing LB off by train at Nottingham's Midland station, after finally breaking with her on 13 February 1912, involved an encounter with such a woman. DHL's address book entry for 'Pauline' immediately follows the address of the Brinton sisters – whom he had met in Bournemouth by 12 January 1912 (i. 350) – and was

almost certainly made before he went away in May. There may be some connection with the 'red-haired Pauline' at Haywoods: see chapter 3, p. 279. On 13 February DHL was clearly in a demonic mood and he made it sound like a sexual adventure: 'I will tell you personally some time. It shall not be committed to paper' (i. 366). Cf. Lawrence's writing in the 1916 'Prologue' to *Women in Love* about Birkin's attraction to both spiritual women and to prostitutes (*WL* 498:40–501:5). The startling 'sequel' may, however, have been an encounter with Alice Dax: see chapter 13, p. 367.

69 'Elegy', *Poems* 193–4.
70 LaT69 (UN).
71 Nehls, i. 83–4; Garnett's loan of 7 guineas in December must have helped (i. 337 and n. 1).
72 Ada Lawrence to LB, 'Tuesday' [28 November 1911] (LaB203; UN): see too Ada Lawrence to Edward Garnett, 26 November 1911 (NYPL); Ada Lawrence to LB, 'Tuesday 10. p.m.' [28 November 1911] (LaB204, UN).
73 Ada Lawrence to Edward Garnett, 17 December 1911 (NYPL).
74 Ada Lawrence to LB, 'Wednesday' [20 December 1911] (LaB205, UN).
75 *Poems* 851; the phrase comes from DHL's 1926 short novel *The Virgin and the Gipsy*, in which the strikingly named Major Eastwood refers to the gypsy of the title as one who 'Nearly died of pneumonia. I thought he *was* dead. He's a resurrected man to me. I'm a resurrected man myself, as far as that goes . . .' (E420a, p. 115).
76 E373e, p. 540: MS damaged and text partly supplied from *SL* 422; *SL* 423.

Chapter Twelve: Breaking Off

1 Ada Lawrence to LB, 'Wednesday' [20 December 1911]. We can compare DHL's feelings for the Villa Mirenda in Italy after he had been ill there in July 1927; see DHL to Baroness Anna von Richthofen, [20 October 1927]; Delavenay, ii. 656.
2 HC, 'D. H. Lawrence as I Saw Him', *Renaissance and Modern Studies*, iv (1960), 13.
3 'Getting On', E144, p. 5.
4 E.T. 184–5; JC to HC, 11 September 1911, 'The Collected Letters', p. 15; JC to Émile Delavenay, 1 February 1935, 'The Collected Letters', p. 97. The poem was 'Sonnet d'Automne'.
5 E.T. 122–3: the book, which survived in JC's possession, is inscribed 'Christmas 1911'. 'Coteshael' was the name of the Burrows' house in Quorn.
6 E320.1, no. 78, ll. 5–6. JC saw the poem (then probably with its later title 'After Many Days') in the spring of 1912, and assumed it was written then (E.T. 197); E.T. 190.
7 He sent LB 'this mass . . . a quarter of the book', probably pp. 1–166, on 29 May 1911 (i. 263: letter redated: see p. 553, note 21). She saw at least some

more of it, as there are eleven later corrections in her hand. DHL may have given her some more manuscript pages at Whitsun, 3–11 June 1911; but 'her alterations are minor one-word corrections of inconsistencies in names or dates, and small slips' (Helen Baron, 'Sons and Lovers', p. 302). Although 'Paul Morel' II continued to at least p. 353, LB's writing does not appear in it after p. 188.

8 E373d, p. 238.

9 E.T. 190.

10 E.T. 190–1. JC also says that DHL was 'telling the story of his mother's married life'; but Mr Morel dies fifty pages before the end of E373d (something JC never mentions). JC's memory of 'Paul Morel' II appears to have been particularly faint.

11 E.T. 192.

12 E.T. 193. A section of what she wrote has been identified by Dr Helen Baron as E373c, 'Again, the first time . . .': this is all which can now be identified as JC's response to 'Paul Morel' II. All the other 'Miriam Papers' at UT are commentaries on DHL's February–April 1912 revision, 'Paul Morel' IIIa. See Helen Baron, 'Jessie Chambers' Plea for Justice to "Miriam"', pp. 70, 73–5.

13 Helen Baron, 'Sons and Lovers', pp. 308–9.

14 PO 118:8–9; the character Jimmy Wesson is also DHL's recreation of himself in his play The Fight for Barbara, written in October 1912; PO 116:18–19.

15 E365.5, p. 14.

16 E373e, p. 25 (original reading).

17 E.T. 194; DHL admitted in March 1912 that he had completely forgotten the earlier story (i. 372–3 and n. 5).

18 E359.4a, p. 10. Not until his 1914 revision of the story for The Prussian Officer collection did DHL add 'It was the old, delicious sublimation, the thinning, almost the vaporising of himself, as if his spirit were to be liberated' (PO 103:40–104:2).

19 E359.4a, pp. 21–2 (original reading).

20 HC, The Croydon Years, p. 9; In Our Infancy, p. 184; see (i. 230).

21 Helena and Siegmund's landlady on the Isle of Wight ('Mrs Curtis' in T 66) is 'Mrs Brinton' in E407b, pp. 65, 68, 71; DHL knew Margaret and Irene Brinton by 12 January (i. 350) and saw them in April (see Illustration 45); T 32.

22 A couple of years later, he would probably have discarded it, as he did discard whole drafts of novels he thought unsuccessful; in 1921 he abandoned Mr Noon when it was more than 400 manuscript pages long (see MN xxxii–xxxiii).

23 T 323 (corrected from E407a).

24 T 33.

25 Ibid.

26 LB Papers 29–30.

27 See (i. 361 n. 2).

28 Copy (once belonging to LB) of The Collected Letters of D. H. Lawrence, ed. Harry T. Moore (1962), i. 100. (I am grateful to William Baker for transcribing for me, while the book was in his possession, LB's comments.)

29 E.T. 184. Alan Chambers, whose 'sceptical materialism' had made him 'one of the few men friends' DHL had 'at this time', was also 'fond of quoting' the phrase (Nehls, i. 50).

30 A note in LB's typing explains what she experienced:

It was arranged that I should see him at the station on his return from Nottingham on the Sunday [11 June 1911] as his train passed through Loughboro'.

It was a crowded train. He rose and stood in the doorway, Holding at his breast a current copy of the Criterio. I vaguely wondered how he had obtained it on a Sunday. But I was puzzled most by his strange manner aloof and supercilious, and his rather silly clipped speech. I thought He is sorry to be disturbed in his reading, and felt terribly hurt at the slight, or again perhaps I thought it is to impress the trippers in the compartment with him. I was left tearful and very puzzled as the train steamed away.

That holiday was I think the beginning or resumption of his affair with professor Weekleys wife T [sic] tho I have no proof whatever. My intuition was very strong.   L.B.   (LaB243, UN)

The incomplete title suggests that LB wondered whether the *Criterion* was the right magazine. It was not: the *Criterion* did not commence publication until 1922. She may have meant the *Hibbert Journal*, which was linked with both Alice Dax and Helen Corke (see i. 359 and n. 3). Her 'intuition' perhaps relates to the start of DHL's affair with Alice Dax: it certainly did not relate to Frieda.

31 LB Papers 29–30.

32 Nehls, iii. 449; *Lawrence in Love*, ed. James T. Boulton (1968), p. xxviii.

33 *MN* 291:8, 10–12; Nehls, iii. 449.

Chapter Thirteen: Spring

1 See Richard Ellmann, *James Joyce*, rev. edn (Oxford, 1983), pp. 179–94 and Noel Stock, *The Life of Ezra Pound* (Harmondsworth, 1974), pp. 62–6, 138–53.

2 Lydia Lawrence to Ada Krenkow, 8 February 1910.

3 Nehls, i. 116.

4 Neville 154–5.

5 DHL was responsible for renaming his niece: 'She's too big to be called "Baby", and "Margaret" is such a mouthful. I'm going to call her Peggy' (Margaret Needham to the author, 13 April 1988): Arthur Lawrence moved to lodgings in Bishop Street, Eastwood (later to 11 Princes St and finally to Bailey Grove) when the family gave up the Queen's Square house in the summer of 1912: the Kings went to Glasgow, and Ada moved in first with the Limb family and then with her cousins John and Nellie Watson in Percy Street: see Ada Lawrence to LB, 10 June 1912 (LaB207, UN); E.T. 198.

6 When Ada got married in 1913 the choir of the Congregational chapel presented her with a set of cutlery (*Eastwood and Kimberley Advertiser*, 8 August 1913, p. 2); Sarah Walker, 'Memories of Eastwood', p. 51.

7 'The Miner at Home' (*Nation*, x (16 March 1912), 981–2): 'Her Turn' (*West-

minster Gazette, 6 September 1913, p. 2); 'Strike-Pay' (heavily cut, *Westminster Gazette*, 13 September 1913, p. 2); 'A Sick Collier' (*New Statesman*, i (13 September 1913), 722–4). See *LAH* xxxii–xxxiv, 123–42 and *PO* xlviii, 165–71.

8 E373e, p. 537.

9 Delavenay, ii. 706.

10 E.T. 196, 197.

11 E.T. 197, 201; JC to HC, 1 June 1933, 'The Collected Letters', p. 58.

12 E.T. 203; E373e, pp. 227–30, 351.

13 DHL's copy of Alphonse Daudet's novel (1872), ed. Otto Siepmann (Macmillan, 1900), signed 'DHL' and 'Lawrence', survived in the possession of LB (information from William Baker); for Spencer, see p. 539, note 43; *SL* 213, 224; E373e, p. 279 (original reading); *SL* 192.

14 *SL* 316. Late in 1927, DHL rewrote, for the third time, his novel *Lady Chatterley's Lover*; and introduced into it an account of Mellors's love affairs before meeting his wife. The first of these is described with a particularly ironic kind of hindsight, and is, of course, primarily an explanation of how and why Mellors should be as he is; but it is also a fictional version of what had happened between DHL and JC between 1901 and 1912.

> "I'll tell you," he said. "The first girl I had, I began with when I was sixteen. She was a schoolmaster's daughter over at Ollerton—pretty, beautiful really. I was a ⟨poetic⟩ 'supposed-to-be clever' sort of young swain from Sheffield Grammar School, with a bit of French and German, very much up aloft. She was the romantic sort that hated commonness. She egged me on to poetry and reading: in a way, she made a man of me. I read and I thought like a house on fire, for her. And I was a clerk in Butterley Offices, thin, white-faced fellow fuming with all the things I read. And about *everything* I talked to her: but everything. We talked ourselves into Persepolis and Timbuctoo. We were the most literary-cultured couple in ten counties. I held forth with rapture to her, positively with rapture. I simply went up in smoke. And she adored me.—The serpent in the grass was sex. She somehow didn't have any—at least, not where it's supposed to be. I got thinner and crazier. Then I said we'd got to be lovers. I talked her into it, as usual. So she let me. I was excited, and she never wanted it. She just didn't want it. She adored me, ⟨but⟩ she loved me to talk to her and kiss her: in that way, she had a passion for me. But the other, she just didn't want. And there are lots of women like her. And it was just the other that I *did* want. So there we split. I was cruel and left her."

(E186c, pp. 461[a]–2)

The passage is cruel to the youthful aspirations of both JC and DHL. Its version of their discussions, reading and writing suggests the absurdity of such proceedings: the things most exciting for DHL in his relationship with JC are either subjected to merciless parody or simply omitted. JC found the novel 'interesting mainly because it casts a beam of light upon his tortured spirit' (to Professor W. Lutoslawski, 23 July 1935, 'The Collected Letters', p. 118).

The fictional account also demonstrates how touchy DHL had become, by

1927, about any suggestion that as a young man he had been highly educated academically, or was thoroughly well-read. Aldous Huxley remarked that 'Lawrence had a large store of knowledge, he didn't like to say so, but *he did*. He was very well read . . .' (Sybille Bedford, *Aldous Huxley: A Biography*, i. (1973), 192); and Richard Aldington reported the same: 'he read omnivorously, though he pretended not to' (Nehls, iii. 456). In the late 1920s DHL was constructing a new version of his own early life in which his loyalties and instincts had always remained thoroughly working-class. Making Mellors – a very different kind of person from himself – participate, fictively, in some of his own formative experiences inevitably meant subjecting those experiences to irony.

15 *SL* 195, 143; *WP* 4:15, 32–37, etc.
16 Helen Baron, 'Jessie Chambers' Plea for Justice to "Miriam"', p. 81.
17 E373b, p. 214, p. 215; the survival of the original pp. 204–26 of 'Paul Morel' IIIa, with JC's handwritten comments (E373b, UT), is probably due to DHL's preserving them for later reference.
18 E.T. 204.
19 Delavenay, ii. 673.
20 (i. 531 n. 1); E.T. 203.
21 E.T. 202, 203.
22 E.T. 216.
23 E.T. 200.
24 E.T. 201.
25 E.T. 201, 203.
26 JC to HC, 18 December 1910, 'The Collected Letters', p. 11.
27 Nehls, iii. 537; E373b, p. 225.
28 E.T. 143.
29 HC, *The Croydon Years*, p. 44.
30 E.T. 201–2; JC to Professor W. Lutoslawski, 23 June 1935, 'The Collected Letters', p. 114; *Memoirs* 196.
31 E.T. 213.
32 Delavenay, ii. 707.
33 E.T. 216.
34 *Memoirs* 246, corrected in this and subsequent quotations from MS (UT).
35 Enid Hilton, Memoir of Alice Dax (Hil. 2/12, UN), p. 4; *Memoirs* 246–7; Alice Hall Holditch, interview.
36 Enid Hilton memoir, p. 2.
37 Nehls, i. 135; letter from E. C. Dax to J. T. Boulton, 5 August 1975; Enid Hilton memoir, p. 4.
38 A. J. Balfour, 'Creative Evolution and Philosophic Doubt', *Hibbert Journal*, x (October 1911), 1–23; Emile Delavenay, *D. H. Lawrence and Edward Carpenter* (1971), pp. 22, 247; see *Hardy* xli; letter from Mrs L. Butcher to J. T. Boulton, 28 May 1975.
39 Nehls, i. 135.
40 Ibid., i. 135–6; Enid Hilton memoir, p. 2; Alice Hall Holditch, interview.
41 Alice Hall Holditch, interview; Nehls, i. 136.

42 *D. H. Lawrence – A Life in Literature*, p. 34.
43 E373e, p. 337.
44 Enid Hilton memoir, p. 2; Alice Hall Holditch, interview.
45 Notes by Lewis Richmond (NCRO).
46 Moore, *The Priest of Love*, p. 112; *Memoirs* 140–1.
47 JC to Emile Delavenay, 24 November 1933, 'The Collected Letters', p. 67.
48 Delavenay, ii. 703. Martin Green argues that the opera's 'erotic gospel' would have affected them (*The von Richthofen Sisters*, New York, 1974, p. 187), but DHL described the opera in November 1910 as 'emotionally insufficient' (*Hardy* 147:5).
49 JC to 'Sieglinde' [HC], 15 October 1910, 'The Collected Letters', p. 8.
50 Delavenay, ii. 671; JC to Emile Delavenay, 24 November 1933, 'The Collected Letters', p. 67.
51 See pp. 555–6, note 68.
52 *Memoirs* 247; Enid Hilton memoir, p. 5.
53 The undated card, sent in an envelope (now missing), has been given the date of 'c. 26 August 1909' in the Cambridge Edition of DHL's *Letters* because its Laocoon illustration is identical with that on a card sent to Arthur McLeod that day (i. 137). But as the card to Alice Dax mentions a visit to Lincoln – where DHL went in August 1911, shortly after visiting Shirebrook – it is more likely to date from 1911.
54 Enid Hilton memoir, pp. 4–5.
55 *Memoirs* 246.
56 Copy (once belonging to LB) of *The Collected Letters of D. H. Lawrence*, i. 100 (information from William Baker); *SL* 331–2; see pp. 555–6, note 68. DHL also went to the theatre with Frieda in March 1912: see chapter 14, p. 381.
57 See pp. 562–3, note 5; *Memoirs* 245, 247; Enid Hilton memoir, p. 6.
58 *Memoirs* 245.
59 Ibid. 246; Enid Hilton memoir, p. 6.
60 JC to HC, 13 November 1911, 'The Collected Letters', p. 18; *Memoirs* 246, 247.
61 E.T. 216; Delavenay, ii. 708. The name of Frieda's first husband, Ernest Weekley, was avoided in publications about DHL for many years: it appears nowhere in Huxley's *Letters of D. H. Lawrence* (1932), nor in Frieda's own biography *"Not I, But the Wind ..."* and probably first appeared in Richard Aldington's biography *Portrait of a Genius, but ...* in 1951. JC's friendship with Nora Lavrin, the wife of a colleague of Weekley, would have ruled out any mention of the name in JC's own book. On only two occasions (in a quotation from a letter from DHL) does the name 'Frieda' (E.T. 219) appear in JC's book; she left the impression that his new 'attachment' was unimportant. Writing about Paul Morel's relationship with Clara Dawes in *Sons and Lovers*, too, she noted that 'The events described had no foundation in fact' (E.T. 202): she deliberately avoided the part Frieda played in the final creation of the character of Clara. In 1938, in spite of never having seen or corresponded with Frieda, she commented: 'I am not, and never have been, jealous of Frieda. From the

very first I said "She does not take the man I wanted, because she is incapable of realising him . . ."' (JC to S. S. Koteliansky, 20 December 1938, 'The Collected Letters', p. 176). Frieda felt much the same: after reading JC's published comments on DHL in April 1930 in the *Star* (Nehls, iii. 467–70), she drafted a letter to JC from Vence (*c.* May 1930): '*Don't* read his things, they were not written for you & your sort!' (King).

62 Enid Hilton memoir, p. 6; *Memoirs* 245.
63 JC to HC, 'Thursday' [May 1913], 'The Collected Letters', p. 36.

Chapter Fourteen: Frieda Weekley

1 Frieda 18.
2 George Lawrence, interview.
3 See Keith Sagar, 'Lawrence and Frieda: The Alternative Story', *D. H. Lawrence Review*, ix (Spring 1976), 117–25, and Steve Bircumshaw, interview. Evidence in favour of their meeting in March 1912 can be found at (i. 394), (ii. 72), Frieda 24 and *Twilight in Italy* (1916), p. 154; see note 5 below.
4 E.T. 196.
5 Delavenay, ii. 707. Frieda once referred to the period she and DHL knew each other before going away as 'six weeks' (Frieda 24), and DHL also once mentioned 'six weeks' (*Twilight in Italy*, p. 154). The date of Sunday 17 March, six weeks and five days before 3 May, is proposed by the Cambridge Edition of DHL's *Letters* for the date of the meeting: we know DHL was in Nottingham that day (i. 374 and n. 4). And the meeting seems to have been on a Sunday.

However, DHL also referred, on 9 May 1912, to 'eight weeks of acquaintance' with Frieda (i. 394): and this reference is closer in time to the events it describes than any other. It would make Sunday 10 March as likely as 17 March (10 March to 9 May seeming very like 'eight weeks'); and Sunday 3 March would also perhaps become a possibility – except that we know DHL planned and expected to be in Shirebrook that weekend, not in Nottingham.

By the week 18–23 March 1912 DHL knew Frieda well enough to go to the theatre with her (see note 36 below); by 27 March he had told May Chambers about her and had considered a visit with her to the Chambers's cottage at Moorgreen (i. 377). That all seems a little sudden, if he had indeed met her only on the 17th: he had also been away in Staffordshire, visiting George Neville, for three of those ten days. The timetable of events given by JC in letters to Emile Delavenay supports a date early in March rather than later (Delavenay, ii. 706–7); while Alice Dax, in 1935, claimed that DHL told her about Frieda 'the day after the event' (*Memoirs* 245). This would be impossible to reconcile with the date of 17 March, but it seems likely that DHL told her about Frieda personally. After his visit to the Daxes at the start of March, he does not seem to have gone to Shirebrook again before going away on 3 May, though he might, of course, have met Alice Dax somewhere else: he had met her in Nottingham, for example, on 14 February (i. 365–6).

But there is also the question of DHL's visit to the Weekleys being – JC remembered (Delavenay, ii. 707) – at first put off. It is hard to see why DHL would do this, unless he had been very annoyed indeed at manipulation by the Krenkows: he was going to Germany and needed all the help he could get. However, a visit to someone important, planned in advance, would be such a reason: and a visit to the Daxes, planned to start on Saturday 2 March (see i. 369), would be a natural reason for a postponement. A letter DHL addressed from Shirebrook on Monday 4 March (i. 370–1) confirms that he was indeed there by that day; a reference in it to another letter having 'come on to me here' shows that his mail had been forwarded to him from Eastwood, either on the Saturday or the Sunday.

There is, however, also the matter of Frieda's own recollection of the circumstances of the meeting. She thought it had been in April (which cannot be true); but she always remembered the windows being open, because of the fine weather, and her children playing in the garden. Of all the possible Sundays in March, Sunday 3 March stands out for its particularly brilliant weather: the 'temperature has been almost exactly that usually experienced during the opening days of April . . . a typical April day' (*Nottingham Guardian*, 4 March 1912, p. 12). The especially fine weather would account for Frieda later assuming that the meeting had been in April and not in March. In contrast, Sunday 17 March was marked by 'general rainfall' (*Nottingham Guardian*, 18 March 1912, p. 12), and was not especially warm: while Sunday 10 March was overcast.

It seems at least possible, therefore, that DHL at first told Weekley he could not come on Sunday 3 March, because of his planned visit to Shirebrook: then changed his mind and postponed his visit to the Daxes for thirty-six hours, going to the Weekleys for lunch on that brilliant Sunday: to the Chambers family for tea and on to Shirebrook that same evening or the following day – thus indeed telling Alice Dax literally 'the day after the event' about meeting Frieda. On 6 March, while still at Shirebrook, DHL wrote to Garnett that 'I'm not going to tell you any stories, because at breakfast you are a sort of Father Anthony, and I am afraid of you' (i. 372). He clearly had some story to tell. In recollection, however, both he and Frieda remembered 'six weeks' rather than nine as the period they had known each other before going away: the 'six weeks' may relate to the occasion of their first sleeping together, rather than to their first meeting (though see chapter 14, pp. 382–3).

6 'Seltsame Geschichte des Mr. Ernest Weekley', '*Freiburger Zeitung*', 29 August 1899: an imitation newspaper produced at the University of Freiburg printing press on the occasion of the Weekley/von Richthofen wedding (Weekley). Its poems, imitation advertisements and pretended news items all testify to the affection Weekley commanded in Freiburg.

7 See Robert Lucas, *Frieda Lawrence* (1973), pp. 16–17; Frieda to Else Jaffe, n.d. [1898] ['Carissima! Nimm einen . . .'] (UT); *Memoirs* 69.

8 *Memoirs* 70–1, 423, corrected from MS (UT). These woodland meetings characterised the early relationship of Ernest Weekley and Frieda, as is shown by a poem in the '*Freiburger Zeitung*':

'Geheimnis'
Am Eichberg in Littenweiler
Grosse Gesellschaft war,
Man streifte durch die Wälder,
Es schloss sich Paar an Paar.

Und als zurück man kehrte,
Kam *ein* Paar nicht mit an,
Es war ein deutsches Mädchen
Und ein englischer Mann.

Es währte eine Stunde,
Da trafen sie endlich ein,
Man fragte sie neugierig,
Wo sie gewesen sei'n.

"Wir suchten Farrenkräuter",
Errötend das Mädchen sprach,
Aber den leeren Händen
Jedwedes Grün gebrach.

"Und was habt Ihr gefunden?"
Das Mädchen sagte nichts,
Geheimnis bargen die Züge
Des lieblichen Gesichts.

['The Secret'. A large company of people was at the Eichberg in Littenweiler; people roamed through the woods in pairs. And as they returned, *one* pair failed to arrive: it was a German girl and an English man. An hour went by, at last they arrived; people asked them curiously where they had been. "Looking for ferns", the girl said, blushing, but her empty hands lacked all trace of green. "And what have you found?" The girl said nothing, the features of her lovely face kept the secret.]

9 *Memoirs* 69.
10 His mistress was named Selma: see Frieda to Else Jaffe, n.d. [September 1913] ['Liebe Else! schon kommt . . .'] (UT) for his problems in paying her. In *The Fight for Barbara* DHL gave the father of his recreation of Frieda a mistress named Selma and an illegitimate son (E130a, pp. 4–5); in *Mr Noon*, DHL used the name 'Elena' and again referred to an illegitimate son (*MN* 180:39–40).
11 *Memoirs* 390.
12 Birth Certificate, Bürgermeisteramt Metz (Weekley).
13 Weekley's younger brother the Rev. Bruce ('Ted') Weekley (1868–1940) conducted the religious service in the English Church at Turnseestraße 59, Freiburg; the official marriage certificate records Weekley as 'Ernst Weekley' and Frieda as 'Emma Maria Frieda Johanna Freiin von Richthofen' (Somerset House, Divorce Register).
14 *Memoirs* 397; Frieda to Otto Gross, n.d. [*c.* 1907) ['wo Du bist . . .'] (UT); Frieda to Frieda Gross, n.d. [*c.* 1907] ['Es ist nichts . . .'] (UT).

15 Frieda to Otto Gross ['wo Du bist . . .']; *Memoirs* 73, 74; D. Garnett, *Great Friends*, p. 78.

16 D. Garnett, *Great Friends*, p. 78; *Memoirs* 69–70.

17 Frieda to Otto Gross, n.d. [*c.* 1907] ['glüht in wahrer . . .'] (UT).

18 Montague Weekley, taped interview with David Gerard (NCL); Nehls, iii. 58.

19 *Memoirs* 355, 97.

20 *MN* 123:33–5, 38–40; Else Jaffe to Montague Weekley, 11 August 1966 (La We18, UN).

21 Otto Gross to Frieda, n.d. [*c.* 1907] ['Ich habe Dir . . .'] (UT): for Otto Gross see Martin Green, *The von Richthofen Sisters*, pp. 32–73; *Memoirs* 69.

22 *Memoirs* 76.

23 *Memoirs* 167; Schiller, *Select Ballads*, ed. Frieda Weekley (n.d. [1902]); *Bechstein's Märchen*, ed. F. Weekley (n.d. [1906]); W. B. Yeats, *Das Land der Sehnsucht* (Englisches Theater in deutscher Übertragung, Heft. 1), tr. Frieda Weekley and Ernst Leopold Stahl (Düsseldorf, 1911) [tr. of *The Land of Heart's Desire*]. (I am grateful to Dr S. J. Hills of Cambridge University Library for bringing the last to my attention.) See too *The Times Literary Supplement*, 6 September 1985, p. 975.

24 Frieda 22.

25 *Memoirs* 75, corrected from MS.

26 Ibid. 92; Otto Gross to Frieda, n.d. [*c.* 1907] ['ich sehe jetzt . . .'] (UT). (I am indebted in particular to Dr John Turner's transcription and – with Cornelia Rumpf-Worthen – translation of the Frieda/Otto Gross correspondence.)

27 Otto Gross to Frieda, n.d. [*c.* 1907] ['Du meine wunderbare . . .'] (UT); *Memoirs* 91; see Martin Green, *Mountain of Truth* (Hanover, 1986), pp. 38–9.

28 See *Memoirs* 82 and Lucas, *Frieda Lawrence*, p. 33, drawing on information from Frieda's daughter Barbara. William Enfield Dowson (1864–1934), the eldest of the ten children of the Nottingham solicitor Benjamin Dowson, was a partner in the firm of Farmer and Dowson, Machine Holders. Until *c.* 1907 he lived at Walton House, 10 Mapperley Road, Nottingham, only a short distance from the Weekley house in Vickers Street. He was one of the earliest motor-car owners in Nottingham, and also owned and ran pleasure boats on the Trent. DHL's story 'The Overtone' (*St. Mawr and Other Stories*, ed. Brian Finney, Cambridge, 1983, pp. 5–17), dated to 1924 by Finney, was written February–March 1913 (information from Mark Kinkead-Weekes). It recreates both the young Frieda (in Elsa Laskell) and Will Dowson (in Will Renshaw), who 'drove to all kinds of unexpected places, in his motor car, bathed where he liked, said what he liked, did what he liked' (10:9–11); the story ends with his proposing 'Come a drive with me tomorrow, Miss Laskell' (17:14). The drive into Sherwood forest taken by Birkin and Ursula in *Women in Love*, chapter XXXIII, also draws on Frieda's memories of Dowson.

29 Montague Weekley, interview; Angelo Ravagli to Montague Weekley, 1 September 1956 (Weekley); Frieda to Frieda Gross, n.d. [*c.* 1907] ['Es ist nichts . . .'] (UT).

30 Otto Gross to Frieda, n.d. [*c.* 1907] ['ich danke Dir . . .'] (UT).

31 *Memoirs* 84; Ernest Weekley to Montague and Vera Weekley, 13 October 1930 (Weekley).

32 Barbara Barr, taped interview with David Gerard (NCL); Frieda 22; *Look! We Have Come Through!* (Ark Press), p. 10.

33 Delavenay, ii. 707; E.T. 199–200.

34 *R* 41:3; Frieda 22.

35 Frieda 21.

36 Ibid. 22–3; JC to Emile Delavenay, 24 November 1933, 'The Collected Letters', p. 67: Bernard Shaw's *Man and Superman* (1903) was performed by B. Iden Payne's company at the Theatre Royal, Nottingham; Nehls, i. 162–3.

37 Frieda 23, 307–8.

38 Barbara Barr, interview.

39 Frieda 307.

40 Notes by Lewis Richmond; *MN* 123–31; Frieda 21, 23.

41 'She Was a Good Little Wife' and 'Pear-Blossom' (E320.4 nos. 44 and 42). It is just possible that the poems relate to Alice Dax, but the pear-blossom season (April–May) rules out February–March 1912, and April–May 1911 is unlikely.

42 Frieda 23; Enid Hilton memoir, p. 6; Montague Weekley, interview.

43 'At the Cearne' (E320.4 no. 41).

44 Phyllis Cahill's memoir of a conversation with Frieda (UT); Frieda 23. Late in life Frieda concluded the process of forgetting her actual caution, and described instead a commitment of the kind she felt she ought to have demonstrated: she remarked in 1954 that 'Lawrence before we went made me tell my husband I would leave him. I didn't seem to have any choice' (*Look! We Have Come Through!*, Ark Press, p. 10). Phyllis Cahill's memoir also recalls Frieda saying that – confronted by an ultimatum from DHL that she leave Weekley – 'I went to the nursery and kissed my children good-bye & stepped into a new life' (UT).

45 E229a, p. 68.

46 Ibid., pp. 68–9.

47 *R* 29:24.

48 *T* 112:12–16. Nietzsche's *Der Fall Wagner* (a translation of which was in Croydon public library) offers a striking parallel to this diagnosis of unhealthy love:

> ... die Gefahr der Künstler, der Genies – und das sind ja die 'ewigen Juden' – liegt im Weibe: die *anbetenden* Weiber sind ihr Verderb ... In vielen Fällen der weiblichen Liebe, und vielleicht gerade in den berühmtesten, ist Liebe nur ein feinerer *Parasitismus*, ein Sich-Einnisten in eine fremde Seele, mitunter selbst in ein fremdes Fleisch ... [... the danger of artists, of geniuses – for these are the 'Wandering Jews' – lies in woman: *adoring* women are their ruin ... In many cases of feminine love (perhaps precisely in the most celebrated cases), love is only a more refined *parasitism*, a nestling in a strange soul, sometimes even in a strange body ...] (*Der Fall Wagner*, Nietzsche Werke, ed. G. Colli and M. Montinari (Berlin 1969), vi (3), 12:7–9, 13–17; *The Case of Wagner*, tr. T. Common, 1896, p. 12).

49 Frieda 22.

50 HC, *In Our Infancy*, pp. 162, 150.

51 *Memoirs* 246; cf. the comment by JC's husband, John R. Wood, after her death: 'she was such a delightful pal' ('Foreword' by P. Beaumont Wadsworth to D. H. Lawrence, *A Prelude*, Thames Ditton, 1949, p. 25).

52 Frieda 53.

53 *Memoirs* 79; Frieda 56–7.

54 Frieda 56; Frieda to Richard Aldington, n.d. [1950], *Frieda Lawrence and Her Circle*, ed. Harry T. Moore and Dale B. Montague (1981), p. 98.

55 Frieda 22; *Memoirs* 90, 92.

56 *Memoirs* 92.

57 Ibid. 425.

58 Barbara Barr, interview; Montague Weekley, interview.

59 *LAH* 176:19–20, 21–3; 177:18–21.

60 *LAH* 177:9–11. See too *MN* 139:23–4, 140:1–2 for a version of what Frieda gave Udo von Henning in May 1912.

61 *Memoirs* 92.

62 Frieda 57; *Memoirs* 43–4; Robert Nichols, quoted by Sybille Bedford, *Aldous Huxley*, i. 226.

63 See Bedford, *Aldous Huxley*, i. 179, 228; information from Barbara Barr.

Chapter Fifteen: Abroad

1 See (i. 389 n. 1); a first-class ticket cost £2-19-10: a return ticket, valid sixty days, would have cost only £3-14-0, and Frieda might have taken one for her summer visits to Germany but *MN* 202:23–24 suggests that she may have planned to return in August. Weekley would not have expected his wife to buy her own tickets.

2 Frieda 25; *WL* 387:27, 389:29.

3 *MN* 146:37.

4 *MN* 143:14; Nehls, i. 165.

5 Frieda 25; *MN* 150:22–3; see chapter 15, pp. 400–1.

6 *MN* 150: 29–31.

7 Green, *Mountain of Truth*, p. 39; *Memoirs* 178; Ernest Weekley to Anna von Richthofen, 26 September 1912 (UT).

8 *MN* 154:34–5; Frieda 25; Nehls, i. 165.

9 Nehls, iii. 162.

10 *MN* 179:15; 178:39–40.

11 *MN* 179:2–3.

12 The accounts of these events in DHL's surviving letters and in *Mr Noon* do not tally. In the novel, a cable comes to 'Detsch' (Metz): 'Believe you have gone with Berry. Wire *ganz richtig* or *nicht wahr*' (*MN* 144:32) – and in spite of Gilbert's demands that she reply '*ganz richtig*', Johanna cables '*Nicht Berry— Schreibe—Not Berry, am writing*' (*MN* 150:37). A letter DHL wrote on 21 May describes, however, how Weekley wrote a letter saying 'if it is true, wire to me

"Ganz recent" ... I saw the letter – we were sitting under the lilacs in the garden at Trier ... I took F. straight to the post-office and she wired "ganz recent". Came back a wire "kein moeglichkeit" – (no possibility – i.e. all is over)' (i. 409). However, since there were 'wires and letters, something awful' (i. 409), it is possible that both accounts are true: i.e. that Weekley first wired (to Metz) about the person Frieda had gone with, to which she replied ambiguously: and that Weekley then wrote a letter demanding the truth, which Frieda took to DHL in Trier on Friday 10th May, and to which DHL ensured that Frieda replied truthfully by telegram. The account given above assumes that both accounts are true. It is possible, however, that the version in *Mr Noon* misremembers 'Ganz recent' as 'ganz richtig'.

13 'How a Spy is Arrested', E170.2a, pp. 3–4 (Lazarus).

14 Frieda 26; *MN* 169:35; *MN* 169:9–13, 23–31.

15 *MN* 160:14–35; the letter was given that date in the account of the divorce decree nisi proceedings of October 1913 (see i. 392 and n. 1).

16 'How a Spy is Arrested', pp. 10–11; *MN* 171:35–6.

17 *MN* 171:28; Frieda 26.

18 The envelope containing the four essays bears a note: 'That in MS has been refused by Spender' – John Alfred Spender (1862–1942), editor of the *Saturday Westminster Gazette* – 'as being too violently anti-German' (Lazarus).

19 Information from Marianne von Eckardt (I am grateful to her for allowing me to make many copies of family photographs, and for sharing with me her memories of her mother and father Else and Edgar Jaffe); see *Memoirs* 61–2, 275–6.

20 'French Sons of Germany', Galley proofs sheet 1 (Lazarus).

21 Ibid.; 'In Fortified Germany', Galley proofs sheet 1 (Lazarus).

22 'In Fortified Germany', Galley proofs sheet 2.

23 *MN* 178:6–9, 179:28–33. See too E130a, pp. 16–21.

24 *Memoirs* 92; *MN* 181:21–2; *Memoirs* 92; *MN* 181:24–5.

25 In *Mr Noon* she gives him 70 Marks – 'seventy shillings' (*MN* 172:23–4).

26 *MN* 107:39.

27 E373e, pp. 411–12; *Memoirs* 141.

28 *Memoirs* 180, 181, 179: the month cited in *Memoirs* – 'April' – is an error for the 'May' of MS (UT).

29 Ibid. 179, 180.

30 Frieda Lawrence, *Memoirs and Correspondence* (New York, 1962), p. 166.

31 *Memoirs* 179, 181.

32 *Memoirs and Correspondence* (New York), p. 167 (Lily Kipping).

33 For Udo von Henning see (i. 404, 406, ii. 221) and *MN* 139:13–141:35; *MN* 188:16–18.

34 He was working on the start and finish of chapter II (E373e, pp. 45–9a and 68–9), on the quarrel between Morel and his wife when he throws the drawer at her (E373e, p. 64), and on the 'Test on Miriam' chapter (E373e, pp. 397–9, 402–6 and 414–17). All these are on German paper: see Helen Baron, '*Sons and Lovers*', pp. 327–8.

35 'Hail in the Rhine-Land', Galley proofs sheet 2 (Lazarus), *P* 79. See too Dieter Mehl, *Notes & Queries*, xxxi (March 1984), 78–81.

36 Frieda to Richard Aldington, 2 January 1949 (*Frieda Lawrence and Her Circle*, ed. Moore and Montague, p. 91).

37 *Memoirs* 95; *MN* 134:40; *Poems* 204; *MN* 131:7, 9–10; cf. the relationship between Paul Morel as a boy and his mother: 'there was between them that love and intimacy which makes the mere walking down the street together a glorious adventure, an experience. They were as happy as the day together, and neither knew it' (E373d, p. 192). A later reflection of this occurs in the 1916 MS of *Women in Love*, when Birkin and Ursula are together at the Saracen's Head in Southwell: 'And he knew it was the first time in his life he had ever been happy, as flowers are happy, as the heedless things of the earth are happy. He had known ecstasy and delight before, but now, for the first time, he knew the grace of happiness' (E441c, pp. 26–7, UT).

38 Frieda to Richard Aldington, 2 January 1949 (*Frieda Lawrence and Her Circle*, ed. Moore and Montague, p. 91); *MN* 135:1–10.

39 Frieda 54; *MN* 228:28; Frieda 53; Frieda to S. S. Koteliansky, 'Sunday' [3 July 1932] (BL Add. Mss. 48975, fol. 21); Otto Gross to Frieda Weekley, n.d. [*c.* 1907] ['ich danke Dir . . .'] (UT).

40 *MN* 135:6–8.

41 Frieda 20.

42 Information from Marianne von Eckardt.

43 *MN* 199:20; 199:23–31; 200:39–201:5. As late as 1929 Lawrence wrote how 'Die Frieda und ich haben unseres Zusammenleben in Beuerberg im Isartal angefangen – in Mai, 1912 – und wie schön es war! [Frieda and I started our life together in Beuerberg in the Isartal – in May, 1912 – and how lovely it was!]' (DHL to Max Mohr, 22 August 1929).

44 *MN* 185:35.

45 *MN* 134:23, 27; Frieda 60.

46 Constance Garnett to Edward Garnett, 'Saturday' [5 July 1913] (Eton College).

47 Ibid.

48 *MN* 213:32–214:23.

49 E320.1 no. 67; Frieda's comments are indicated by italics: she also underlined ll. 10–12.

50 See *MN* 229:4–230:25. Frieda also 'ran away from L. for two days' late in June 1913 (ii. 23): they were quarrelling very badly at the time (Constance Garnett to Edward Garnett, 'Saturday' [5 July 1913]), probably over Weekley and the children.

51 Josef (1850–1924) and Walburga (1859–1928) Leitner: their fictional surname 'Breitgau' suggests the region of Germany ('Breisgau') in which Freiburg (where Frieda had met and married Weekley) lies; *MN* 206:18–21.

52 *MN* 207:5–12.

53 *MN* 225:15–19.

54 *MN* 252:6–8.

55 *MN* 202:20–5.

56 *MN* 204:31–2.

57 Recording of Else Jaffe made by Dirk and Lois Hoffmann (*c.* 1964) (UT).

58 *Memoirs* 97–8; Frieda 58.

59 'She Looks Back', *Poems* 208; in 'Education of the People' in 1922 DHL would write polemically how 'babies should invariably be taken away from their modern mothers . . . There should be a league for the prevention of maternal love, as there is a society for the prevention of cruelty to animals' (*Reflections on the Death of a Porcupine*, ed. Herbert, 121:21–2, 24–5).

60 *MN* 229:4–5; 'Mutilation', *Poems* 212, ll. 8–12.

61 'Meeting Among the Mountains', Frieda 71, ll. 41–2, 40, 43–4; Ernest Weekley to Anna von Richthofen, 26 September 1912.

62 Delavenay, ii. 690.

63 Cf. DHL to Blair Hughes-Stanton, 26 May 1928: 'Perhaps if I'd have had children, I'd have been a comfortable body with all my novels circulating like steam among all the safe people, and everybody pleased.'

64 See *PO* xlix; *LAH* xxvii, xxxiv.

65 See Helen Baron, '*Sons and Lovers*', pp. 319–20.

66 Nehls, i. 173–4.

67 He claimed that Frieda proposed making love with him at the Cearne in the summer of 1913 (*Great Friends*, 1979, p. 81).

68 *LAH* 153:19–20; 153:22–3, 26–7.

69 *LAH* 160:5–14, 17–27.

70 In addition to the four sketches written in Metz, Trier and Waldbröl in May (in one of which the character Anita appears), 'Once—!', 'A Chapel Among the Mountains' and 'A Hay-Hut Among the Mountains' (all containing Anita and drafted no later than August 1912) and 'Christs in the Tirol' (probably drafted in September 1912) would have made up the book. But, instead, the last sketch – rewritten as 'The Crucifix Across the Mountains' – became the first item in DHL's 1916 book about Italy, *Twilight in Italy*, and the German book was abandoned.

71 *MN* 237:11–17.

72 *Look! We Have Come Through!* (Ark Press), p. 13.

73 'A Chapel among the Mountains', *P II* 29.

74 The Baedeker guide to *SüdBayern, Tirol, Salzburg* (Leipzig, Verlag von Karl Baedeker, 1912) would have told DHL and Frieda about a path 'Vom *Gerblbauern*, ¼ St. hinter Winkel, MW. [markierter Weg] l. [links] durch Wald hinan zur (2 St.) *Hochalpe (1428 m), mit prächtiger Aussicht; Abstieg zur (1½ St.) Stuben-A. an der Achentaler Straße (S. 78)' (p. 72). The time this would have taken – 3½ hours – corresponds exactly to the time DHL mentioned in his essay 'A Chapel Among the Mountains': 'They had told us there was a footpath over the mountain, three and a half hours to Glashütte' (*P II* 29). The folding map in Baedeker opposite p. 69 showed exactly that path from Winkel to Hochalpe (though not its continuation down to the Achentaler Straße); this path still exists on the modern map, and – just as Baedeker says – it comes out at Stubenalm (i.e. Stuben-A) on the Achentaler Straße, not at Glashütte. The

place Baedeker mentions as its starting point – Gerblbauern – is not on the modern map, but corresponds to the modern Hohenwiesen, just along the road from Winkel and with a path direct to Hochalm. But the Baedeker map also showed another path going due e. from Winkel before curving s., and apparently going direct over the hills, to come out where DHL hoped to, at Glashütte, a little further n. along the Achentaler Straße than Stubenalm. This is almost certainly the path DHL and Frieda were on, taken either because the map showed it (and it avoided the peak of Hochalm), or because they mistook it for the marked path to Hochalm. In fact, the path going e. from Winkel simply peters out after the waterfall at Klaffenbach. However, the map in Baedeker – confirmed by the modern map – also shows the existing path (now road) to Röhrlmoos, well to the n. and e.; this was the path which DHL and Frieda actually managed to cross over to after the first path disappeared.

Baedeker also provided details of the walks to follow round Mayrhofen, and included reliable estimates of the time it would take on foot to get to destinations such as Ginzling from Mayrhofen, the Dominicus-Hütte from Ginzling, the Pfitscherjoch from the Dominicus-Hütte, Sterzing from the Pfitscherjoch, etc.: this was vital information to travellers such as DHL and Frieda. DHL had known Baedeker's guides since at least 1911 (i. 322); it is almost certain that he carried one in 1912. He certainly did to Sardinia in 1921: '"Where is the Albergo d'Italia?" I was relying on Baedeker' (*Sea and Sardinia*, p. 170).

75 *MN* 244:36–245:1.
76 'A Chapel Among the Mountains', *P II* 29. DHL's two postcards written from this part of the journey, nos. 479 and 480, postmarked Kufstein (where he went over the border to post them), both apparently derive from Glashütte: one is of 'Glashü[tte . . .] Café Hubertus', the other of 'Glashütte – Stuben'. DHL, drafting his essays ('A Chapel among the Mountains', *P II* 29) certainly thought he had come out at Glashütte (his essay 'A Hay-Hut Among the Mountains' says they 'came out in the level valley at Glashütte' – *P II* 43), but in spite of the apparent evidence of the postcards, it is most unlikely that they did. From the Röhrlmoos Alm (meadow), where they spent the night, it is impossible to come down to the road anywhere else than on the e. side of the Schliffbach, the lower part of which is in a gorge or gulley, and uncrossable without extreme effort: the path comes out about 2 km. e. of Glashütte. DHL and Frieda may have stopped at the foot of the path in a 'village of about four houses' (*MN* 246:20–1); there are still two houses at the place where the path beside the Schliffbach comes out on to the main road, one of the houses being old. They may, however, have ignored the houses (or house), turned right (i.e. west) at the bottom of the path, and walked 8–9 minutes along the road to the Café Hubertus; the essay 'A Hay-Hut among the Mountains', written very soon after the event, describes them coming out 'in the level valley . . . We pushed on to a little Gasthaus, that was really the home of a forester' (*P II* 43). They stayed for coffee and their beds for the morning in that house, which DHL's postcards more graphically describe as 'the cottage of a hunter' and 'a hunter's cottage' (i.

432). The Café is not, however, in a 'village of about four houses' but is a single house, set by itself. It is therefore possible that they went along the road for a further 9–10 minutes, as far as Glashütte, where (according to Baedeker) there was an inn with some other houses. Yet in that case it is extremely odd that they did not stop at the Café Hubertus, beside the road and nearer: they were tired and hungry, and it was pouring with rain. It seems likely that the name Glashütte was still in DHL's mind as the place he and Frieda had been aiming for (see note 74) – it may well have been the place he asked directions to, at the top of the path – and he assumed that, when they finally came out on the road and found houses, that they had reached it. The fictional account in *Mr Noon* was written, however, long after the event; not only is its account of 'a village of four houses' suspect, but DHL describes how Gilbert and Johanna actually meet the forester, whereas in the essay the forester is away for a couple of days. It seems most likely that DHL and Frieda came down the e. side of the Schliffbach, turned right and walked along to the Café Hubertus, stayed there for a few hours, and that DHL bought and wrote his postcards there. They would have seen Glashütte itself that afternoon, as they drove past it in the post-omnibus on the way to the Achensee.

77 DHL's postcard to Edward Garnett (no. 481) from Mayrhofen saying 'We got here last night', and postmarked '11. VIII. 12', is given the date of Sunday 11 August 1912 in *Letters*, i. 433. It was, however, almost certainly written on Saturday 10th and franked on Sunday 11th. In it, DHL announced that there were 'no letters postlagernds' for him in Mayrhofen – i.e. letters awaiting collection in the post office: he would not have been able to check this on Saturday night or on the Sunday; while if DHL and Frieda spent the Friday night on the road somewhere between Jenbach and Mayrhofen, it would be the only night on the entire journey for which we could not account either from DHL's letters or from *Mr Noon*. DHL and Frieda almost certainly could not have covered the 30 km. to Mayrhofen from Jenbach on foot, during Friday, after travelling from Kufstein in the morning; but if they had taken the little railway for some of the way, the journey would have been quite possible in one day. On Monday 5 August, their railway journey from south of Wolfratshausen (probably from Bolzwang to Bichl) had saved them 15–20 km. walking on the roads (Bolzwang to Bichl by train being 20.2 km.): they had walked at least 9 km. (Icking to Bolzwang) before taking the train, and they walked a further 15 km. (Bichl to Bad Tölz) after it.

78 'Christs in the Tirol', *P* 83–4; see 'Sinners' ('Mayrhofen') and 'Meeting Among the Mountains' ('Tuxtal') in *Look! We Have Come Through!*: the Tuxertal runs w. and s. from Mayrhofen. Garnett remembered that in Mayrhofen DHL was 'just finishing *Sons and Lovers*, he was writing some stories and a lot of poems' (*The Golden Echo*, 1953, p. 245).

79 Copy in Eastwood Public Library; Gilbert's sudden awareness of the 'Aphrodite' in the forty-year-old Patty Goddard in *Mr Noon* – 'the flame that ran from his heels to his head' when he looks at her – suggests that DHL may at some stage have been aware of similar feelings towards the 45-year-old Sallie

Hopkin (*MN* 39:2–3). His poem 'Spirits Summoned West', written shortly after Sallie Hopkin's death in October 1922, describes how

> England seems full of graves to me,
> Full of graves . . .
> Women who were gentle
> And who loved me
> And whom I loved
> And told to die . . .
> Women of the older generation, who knew
> The full doom of loving and not being able to take back.

(Poems 410, ll. 1–2, 7–10, 15–16)

80 David Garnett, 'Frieda and Lawrence', *D. H. Lawrence: Novelist, Poet, Prophet*, ed. Stephen Spender (1973), p. 39.
81 *MN* 277:20.
82 'Christs in the Tirol', *P* 85 and *MN* 268:3–7.
83 David Garnett, *Great Friends*, p. 81; 'Christs in the Tirol', *P* 84.
84 *MN* 272:33.
85 *MN* 279:30–4.
86 Frieda 72; *MN* 287:11–13.
87 Frieda 72.
88 Ernest Weekley to Anna von Richthofen, 26 September 1912.
89 *Memoirs* 99.

<h3 align="center">Chapter Sixteen: Sons and Lovers</h3>

1 See Helen Baron, '*Sons and Lovers*', pp. 319–20.
2 Ibid., pp. 322–3. The so-called 'Sons and Lovers Fragments' (E373a) are in fact fifty-eight pages from the start of 'Paul Morel' IIIb, the draft superseded by the final manuscript E373e. DHL's method of revision, both in Icking and in Italy, was to write either completely new manuscript pages (e.g. pp. 1–8 and 26–34 in chapter I and pp. 41a–60 and 70–3 of chapter II in the final manuscript E373e), or – slightly less often – to reuse, revise and incorporate the rather smaller pages of his previous draft (e.g. pp. 9–25 and 35–41 in chapter I and pp. 61–9 in chapter II). Sometimes he revised the old pages heavily as he incorporated them, sometimes only lightly. He probably left behind with Else Jaffe those pages of the beginning of 'Paul Morel' IIIb which he had rewritten and not reused. However, after he went to Italy with the new first seventy-six pages, and the rest of the old manuscript of 'Paul Morel' IIIb to work from, and began rewriting, he did not keep the unused old pages. The only survivals of the third draft of 'Paul Morel' after p. 85 (apart from a section with JC's comments on them from 'Paul Morel' IIIa, which he had probably replaced as early as April), are a further sixty pages scattered through the book which were also revised and incorporated into the final manuscript of *Sons and Lovers*. And from p. 422 (the start of chapter XIII, 'Passion') to the end of the novel at p. 540, the pages were all written in Villa. Since this last part of the book has no equivalent section in

573

the 1911 'Paul Morel' II manuscript either, there is no way of knowing how DHL had handled such matters as Paul's affair with Clara, his relation with Baxter Dawes, the later relation with Miriam and the death of Mrs Morel in previous drafts – if, indeed, all these things had been in 'Paul Morel' IIIb. They may well have been: but it is probable that, since DHL chose not to use any of the old pages, they were very differently handled. When he turned 'The Saga' into *The Trespasser* in January–February 1912, he used more and more of the old pages as he went on (see chapter 12, p. 332): the opposite is true of *Sons and Lovers*.

3 E373e, p. 31, E373a, p. 30.
4 E373a, pp. 32, 33 (original readings).
5 Ibid., p. 32; see chapter 5, p. 145.
6 E373a, p. 32 (original reading); DHL had also ended the extended passage, before Morel arrives home, with a further comment on Mrs Morel: 'She was too much of a woman, too much of the stuff of life, to despair for herself. She was still first producing life, and religion of life for her children' (E373a, p. 33, original reading): quotations taken from the translation of Schopenhauer we know DHL possessed: *Essays of Schopenhauer*, tr. Mrs R. Dircks (Walter Scott Ltd., n.d. [1897]), p. 182 (see Nehls, i. 66–70, 548 n. 95). The original German sentence runs: 'Dies ist eine Folge des Zwecks der Natur, welche auf Erhaltung und daher auf möglichst starke Vermehrung der Gattung gerichtet ist'. For Schopenhauer and DHL, see chapter 7, p. 174.
7 *Essays of Schopenhauer*, p. 191.
8 E373a, pp. 32–3.
9 Ibid., pp. 34–5.
10 E373e, pp. 32, 33.
11 Ibid., p. 33.
12 Ibid., p. 21 (original and revised readings).
13 E373e, p. 25; *SL* 16.
14 E373a, p. 28; E373e, p. 27.
15 E373a, pp. 69–78; E373e, pp. 72–3.
16 Frieda to Richard Aldington, 2 January 1949 (*Frieda Lawrence and Her Circle*, ed. Moore and Montague, p. 90).
17 E373e, p. 13.
18 Nehls, ii. 126; Frieda remembered DHL saying 'Did I write this? I would be much fairer to my father now, now I know how devastating was my mother's love' (Frieda to Vivian de Sola Pinto, 30 January 1953, *D. H. Lawrence After Thirty Years 1930–1960*, ed. V. de S. Pinto, Nottingham, 1960, p. 19).
19 'Italian Studies: By the Lago di Garda: III.—THE THEATRE', *English Review*, xv (September 1913), 233.
20 E373e, pp. 69–70.
21 E.T. 117; *Memoirs* 131; Frieda 74–5.
22 Nehls, iii. 471.
23 Frieda 74.
24 She would later tell Mabel Luhan that she 'actually wrote pages into it' (Mabel

Dodge Luhan, *Lorenzo in Taos*, New York 1934, p. 50); but this is not borne out by the surviving final manuscript E373e; her handwriting appears only twice (pp. 126, 334). The 'little female bits' she felt responsible for were passages influenced by her arguments and insistencies. As well as 'hoyty-toyty' (p. 334) – see Thomas Hardy, *Jude the Obscure* (1893), I. v., p. 41 – she also altered the idiomatic 'There were never such preparations' to the more standard 'There had never been such preparations' (p. 126). (I am grateful to Dr Helen Baron for pointing out these two passages to me.)

25 DHL used the idea again in the last paragraph of the 'Foreword' to *Sons and Lovers* he wrote in January 1913 (E373.1, p. 7).

26 Otto Gross to Frieda, n.d. [*c.* 1907] ['ich sehe jetzt . . .'] and ['ich danke Dir . . .'] (UT); Ernest Weekley to Anna von Richthofen, 26 September 1912.

27 Nehls, iii. 618.

28 E373e, p. 93.

29 It is not known how long the manuscript of 'Paul Morel' IIIb had been, so it is hard to judge how far DHL had got into the final draft. But it is clear from a letter he wrote at the end of October that he expected to end up with a manuscript of around 500 pages (i. 466). By 3 October, 'half done', he had thus perhaps started the 'Strife in Love' chapter, which begins on E373e, p. 256.

30 Out of the chapter's twenty-eight pages, fourteen originated in Villa and fourteen survived from the 'Paul Morel' IIIb revision in Waldbröl. What he had written February–March was thus entirely rewritten, suggesting how seriously he had taken JC's criticisms. Out of the descriptions of Miriam in 'Paul Morel' IIIa as written between February and April 1912, only the six page 'letter to Miriam' in chapter IX – almost an historical document – survived into the final manuscript. This contradicts JC's assertion that, when she saw the novel in proof in March 1913, 'I found both story and mood alike unchanged' (E.T. 220).

31 E373e, p. 418: the page was added in Villa and inserted between two pages originating in Eastwood in the spring of 1912.

32 E373e, pp. 418–19.

33 Frieda to Vivian de Sola Pinto, 30 January 1953 (*D. H. Lawrence After Thirty Years 1930–1960*, p. 19); Frieda to T. S. Mercer, 30 May 1951 (Lazarus).

34 JC to HC, [16 March 1913], 'The Collected Letters', pp. 26–8.

35 DHL at first made Barbara leave her husband-to-be before the wedding-day (E130a, p. 5, original reading) but changed his mind. (I am grateful to Dr Hans Schwarze for pointing this out to me.)

36 DHL sent the play to Edward Garnett, but Garnett did not think much of it (i. 475): he also probably wanted DHL to work on the novel for Duckworth.

37 'Giorno dei Morti', *Poems* 232, ll. 1, 3–4; 'All Souls', *Poems* 233, ll. 8–9.

38 Frieda 74.

39 Frieda 74; Brigit Patmore, 'A Memoir of Frieda Lawrence', *A D. H. Lawrence Miscellany*, ed. Harry T. Moore (1961), p. 137; Frieda 74.

40 E373e, p. 522.

41 Frieda 74.

42 Text from E320.2 (manuscript compiled in 1916: the title 'Too Late' deleted): first published in *New Poems* as 'Everlasting Flowers: For a Dead Mother'. DHL himself inserted it in his 1928 *Collected Poems* as the first of the '*Lago di Garda*' poems (pp. 54–5). It is impossible to date the initial writing of the poem exactly, but DHL first mentioned seeing snow on Monte Baldo on 19 November 1912 (i. 478). He wrote to Garnett the same day about finishing *Sons and Lovers*: it is therefore probable that the poem was written simultaneously with the ending of the novel. The poem's light 'on the other shore' is mentioned in a letter of 2 December (i. 483).

43 *Poems* 234–5, ll. 17–20, 35–6.

44 *Poems* 233, ll. 17–24.

45 Frieda 74.

46 'Italian Studies: By the Lago di Garda: III.— THE THEATRE', *English Review*, xv, 221, 224–5, 227: the opera – directed by Ernesto Sebastiani – was reviewed in *La Provincia di Brescia* (3 December 1912, p. 2). The actor-director DHL recreated as Enrico Persevalli in 'The Theatre' was Enrico Marconi, while the actress he called Adelaida was actually the leading actress after whom the company was named, Adelia Di Giacomo Tadini. (I am grateful to Dr Paul Eggert for supplying me with this information.) *Moglie del Dottore*, by Zambaldi (1870–1932), had first been performed in Milan in 1908.

47 E373e, p. 221–2; E84a, p. 60.

48 E84a, p. 61.

49 Ibid., p. 63.

50 Ibid., p. 41.

51 'San Gaudenzio', *Twilight in Italy*, pp. 151, 173.

52 *MN* 228:6, 18–20.

53 *MN* 227:30.

54 *Memoirs* 133; *MN* 227:31.

Appendix IV

1 See pp. 559–60, note 14.

2 John Worthen, 'Lawrence's Autobiographies', *The Spirit of D. H. Lawrence*, ed. G. Salgado and G. K. Das (1988), pp. 1–15.

3 'Getting On', E144, pp. 1, 2–3, 4.

4 'Which Class I belong To', E428, p. 2; 'Autobiography', *P II* 300, 301.

5 E428, p. 2; 'Autobiography', *P II* 300; 'Nottingham and the Mining Country-side', *P* 135: 'Autobiographical Sketch', *P II* 581.

6 'Nottingham and the Mining Countryside', *P* 136–7, 'Autobiographical Sketch', *P II* 580–1; e.g. the description of Mrs Morel's garden as 'an endless joy to her' (*SL* 165): even at the Breach house, where 'a bit of space made a drying ground for the wash, its line-post between the house and the ash pit' Lydia Lawrence made a garden: 'A tiny spot like a tablecloth was protected by a few bits of board for palings, and here bloomed a handful of flowers' (Nehls, iii. 555).

7 E428, p. 3; 'Autobiography', *P II* 300.

8 'Autobiography', *P II* 301.

9 E428, p. 5.

10 DHL to Aldous Huxley, 'Sunday, after Tea' [2 September 1928]; Denis Donaghue, *W. B. Yeats* (1971), p. 14.

11 'Nottingham and the Mining Countryside', *P* 135–6.

12 '[Autobiographical Fragment]', *P* 817–36. The title 'A Dream of Life' is Keith Sagar's suggestion.

The Use of Sources

1 Chambers, 'Memories', p. 17. JC gave her precious copy of Browning's poems – which she and DHL had read together 'many times' (Nehls, iii. 453) – to her sister May: it is inscribed 'Muriel M. Holbrook, Moorgreen, 1912'. This suggests that JC started parting with her memorabilia of DHL soon after May 1912.

2 E373e, pp. 350–1; E.T. 139.

3 It is possible that DHL's reference on 13 July 1912 to her 'notes' – 'Your notes were *good* – rather fascinating – do go on, I should love the rest' (i. 425) – refers to an early version of the memoirs; this would make them far closer in time than those of JC to the events they describe.

4 A number of LB's papers refer to the visit Emily King and her daughter Margaret paid DHL and Frieda in Switzerland in 1929. Emily, with her daughters Margaret and Joan, went to see LB at Quorn in 1931, and it seems likely that LB then heard about the visit. There are also documents among the papers which can be dated to 1931: hence the suggested dating. Moore dated the letter from DHL to Garnett '12 February 1912': LB re-dated it '13 February 1912': see p. 557, note 28.

5 Neville 183 n. 1, 187 n. 20, 189 nn. 29 and 30, 191 n. 7, 200 n. 8: see too p. 552, note 35. For HC, see *T* 3 and n. 3, 8 nn. 23 and 26.

6 See Beer, 'Ford's Impression of the Lawrences', p. 520, and Ford Madox Ford, *Return to Yesterday*: 'Where it has seemed expedient to me I have altered episodes that I have witnessed but I have been careful never to distort the character of an episode. The accuracies I deal in are the accuracies of my impressions' (p. viii).

7 See asterisked footnotes in chapter 1 p. 10 and chapter 14 p. 382.

ACKNOWLEDGEMENTS

I am grateful for the permission of the Literary Executor of the Estate of Frieda Lawrence Ravagli, Gerald Pollinger, and Laurence Pollinger Limited, as well as of Lawrence's publishers, Messrs William Heinemann Ltd. and Cambridge University Press in Britain and Viking Press and Cambridge University Press in the USA, to quote from D. H. Lawrence's and Frieda Lawrence Ravagli's published and unpublished work.

My fellow biographers Mark Kinkead-Weekes and David Ellis have been incomparably helpful at all stages of the writing of this book. My only way of thanking them, Joan Kinkead-Weekes and Geneviève Ellis for many years' care of me and of my writing will be to read the second and third volumes of this biography with the same eye for detail, and a grasp of the larger movement of thought, which my collaborators have unstintingly awarded me and mine.

Michael Black, Susan Gagg, John Turner, Lindeth Vasey and F. M. Worthen read the (quite different) first draft of this book. Their comments resulted in major changes of shaping and understanding. Cornelia Rumpf-Worthen read the second draft: without her, the subsequent versions would not have been written. Sam Dawson read the penultimate version with a fine eye for infelicities and solecisms; John Turner's comments on the final draft were most helpful. I am very grateful to all these readers. James T. Boulton assisted me by opening his Lawrence files to me and by helping me at every stage on a project which he himself might well have undertaken; Gerald Pollinger, Margaret Pepper and the D. H. Lawrence Estate have been helpful in every possible way; Lindeth Vasey has edited the book with the passion for detail and the wide knowledge of Lawrence which makes all of her work so remarkable. Errors remaining must be attributed to the irredeemable old Adam of the author.

Other people have helped me in ways that need special acknowledgement. Without George Lazarus's collection of manuscripts – and George's generosity over two decades – it would not have been possible to write this book. W. H. Clarke gave me most generous access to his pictures, manuscripts and papers. Joan King and Margaret Needham have over the years offered me hospitality and numerous insights into the Lawrence family: I am very grateful to them both. Nora Haselden discovered, and then gave me permission to draw upon, her sister Louie Burrows's writings about Lawrence; she also untiringly answered my questions. Ian Weekley answered my numerous questions about his father and grandfather. Helen Baron has helped me enormously in discussions about Lawrence going back for many years, and in placing the research done by her and Carl Baron on *Sons and Lovers* at my disposal. Marianne von Eckardt, George Hardy, Joan King, Margaret Needham, Margaret Ridgway, Keith Sagar, Harald Szeemann and Ian Weekley were all of the greatest help in gathering photographs: Roger Davies produced beautiful prints for me from often unpromising originals. The La Trobe University English Review *Meridian*, vii (October 1988), 99–115 and the *Swansea Review*, no. 6 (July 1989), 23–44 both printed an early draft of chapter 14. A sabbatical year and leave of absence from the University College of Swansea allowed me much necessary time to work on the book. I am very grateful to all these people and institutions.

A number of books by other people have been indispensable. Roy Spencer's book *D. H. Lawrence Country* did more to change our understanding of the Lawrence family than any other work; it has been an invaluable aid. I must also thank Roy Spencer for assisting me with two difficult points. Ronald Storer's book *Some Aspects of Brinsley Colliery and the Lawrence Connection* contains a great deal of information about the coal-mining industry, Brinsley and the Lawrence family. But above all I am indebted to the late Edward Nehls's monumental compilation, *D. H. Lawrence: A Composite Biography*, which remains in many ways the most important biography of D. H. Lawrence.

I am also very grateful to the following for their courtesy in making manuscripts, photographs, official records, recordings and essential printed books available to me:

Archiv Museo Casa Anatta, Ascona

Michael Bennett and the staff of Eastwood Library

Ford Madox Ford letter © 1991 by Janice Biala

Eton College Library

Bob and Eileen Forster

Richard Garnett

Kevin Grace and the Archives and Rare Books Department, University of Cincinnati Libraries

Cathy Henderson and the staff of the Harry Ransom Humanities Research Center, University of Texas

Dorothy Johnston and the staff of the Manuscripts Department of Nottingham University Library

Judy Kingscott and the staff of the Local Studies Department of Nottingham City Library

F. Meerwein

Keith Sagar

Connie Winsor and Beauvale Infants School

D. T. Witcombe and Nottingham High School

I should also like to thank the following for their particular contributions:

Barbara Andrews, Valerio Arosio, Tony Atkins, William Baker, Moina and Tom Brown, Janet Byrne, Brian Cainen, Alan Cameron, †Beatrice Campbell, Christopher Collard, †Helen Corke, †Waldo Dowson, Paul Eggert, Andrea Fletcher, Lou Gollin, Alan Griffin, John Harries, Alex Hatz, Paul Heapy, Carol Herring, Stephen Hill, Rosemary Howard, Mary Jaffe, Christa Jahnson, Frederick Jeffrey, Ruth Jenkins, Mara Kalnins, Ruma Kinkead-Weekes, Alois Kranebitter, Pamela Lewis, Nesta Macdonald, Margaret Masson, Dieter Mehl, Hildegund Mehl, Victoria Middleton, Howard Mills, Colin Milton, Phyl Nunn, Eddie Owens, David and Marion Parry, Helen Perkins, Reginald H. Phelps, Hermann Ritter von Poschinger, John Poynter, Peter Preston, Neil Reeve, Joyce and Gordon Richards, Oswald and Maria von Richthofen, Patrick von Richthofen, Warren Roberts, Erhard Rumpf, †Helmut Rumpf, Waltraud Rumpf, Hans Schwarze, Michael Squires, Christopher Terry, J. R. Till, Gabriella Wasiniak, Rita Williams, D. G. Worthen, Peter Worthen.

Over the years, people on the roads of Nottinghamshire, France, Germany and Italy have pointed me in the right direction on numerous occasions: I rarely knew their names. I am also grateful to the generations of students in my Lawrence seminar at Swansea who have found themselves engaging in the arguments of this book.

2 March 1990   J.W.

INDEX

Note

Individuals named in the text as the sources of quotations from letters or memoirs have not been indexed. Fictional characters are indexed under the works in which they appear. 'L' stands for Lawrence; 'App.' refers to entries in Appendix I and Appendix II.

Burrows, Louisa (*cont.*)
rules of engagement, 295, 296–7, 306–7, 326, 385, 386, 406, 416; DHL gives copy of *An Idyll*, 133–4, 285–6; sends wreath for Lydia L, 287; copies poems into DHL's notebook, 411; proud of *WP*, 296; DHL selects what he sends her and tells her, 300, 314–15; and his writing, 296–7, 300, 303–4, 556–7; visits DHL in London, 301, 555; DHL warns against himself, 300–1; moves back to Quorn, 302; fears DHL's other women, 303; critical of DHL, 306, 314; problems of engagement, 306–9; cannot express anger, 442, 444; continues to excite DHL, 313–14; suspicious of DHL, 366, 558; DHL on verge of breaking engagement, 315–16; summer holiday, 319; not allowed to see or write to DHL during his illness, 322–3; goes to Croydon for Christmas, 322, 323–4, 326; JC gets book LB wants, 326; to Red Hill with DHL, 324, 334; future with DHL uncertain, 325; DHL apparently offers to marry, 334–5; DHL deceives with HC and Alice Dax, 339, 367; DHL writes ending the engagement, 336–7, 355; protests and writes, 337–8; meets DHL in Nottingham, 338–9, 367; parting, 338; compared with JC and Alice Dax, 339, 368, 370; blames DHL's illness, 339; believes Frieda 'seducer' of DHL, 340, 558; feelings about DHL and herself, 340; never renounces her love for DHL, 340–1; youth and career recreated in *R*, 340–1; DHL calls 'good to me', 341; DHL does not write about life solutions of women like her, 370; goes to see DHL's grave, 341; hears about DHL from Emily King, 577; reliability as memoirist, 508–9; marries at age 53, 341, 386; in 1962 comments on DHL's letter to Edward Garnett, 338
Butler, Charles W., compiler, *Eastwood Congregational Psalter*, 521
Butty system described, 11; Arthur L as butty, 11, 12, 33, 40; DHL comments on, 503
Byron, George Gordon, DHL teaches 'The Assyrian Came Down', 208

Cambridge, Trinity College, Ernest Weekley attends, 372
Campbell, Gordon, DHL writes to, 456
Canaan, 67; DHL thinks of LB as, 294
Canada, see *White Peacock, The*
Cannan, Gilbert, and Mary Barrie, 545
Carlin, George, picture framer, George L apprenticed to, 44, 53
Carlyle, Thomas, DHL and JC read, 122, 288; *Sartor Resartus, The French Revolution, Lectures on Heroes, Past and Present* important to DHL, 122; and modern world, 169; in 'A Modern Lover', 212
Carmen, DHL sees in Croydon, 439
Carpenter, Edward, works lent to JC and DHL, 360
Case of Wagner, The, see Nietzsche, Friedrich
Cassell's *Dictionaries*, 111
Caunt, Ben, boxer and 'Champion of England', 8
Century, see Garnett, Edward
Chambers family, 358; neighbours of Ls in Greenhills Road, 35, 103; move to Haggs Farm, 104; animals, 105; children shy of DHL at first, 104; learn to love him, 106–8; strong-willed family, 106–10; disagreements, 106, 219, 264; resentment of L family, 108–9; poverty, 109; children become schoolteachers and coal-miners, 109; books and literature, 109–10; reaction to DHL going to London, 246–8; move to farm at Arno Vale, 263, 267, 268, 380
Alan, born, 104; eldest son, 106; aloof, 107; particular friend of DHL, 119; DHL attracted to, 50, 157; sees dangers of DHL writing, 144; chapel, 170; and the 'Pagans', 170; materialism, 178, 558; 'bosom friend' of DHL, 191, 201, 537–8; 545; after 1908 DHL sees less of, 178; marries DHL's cousin Alvina Reeve, 270, 348, 538; living in Nottingham, 348, 538; defines 'superfluous' sense, 369; meets gamekeeper with DHL, 544
Ann, née Oats, daughter of Nottingham joiner, marries Edmund Chambers, 103; meets Lydia L at chapel, 103–4; self-sacrificing, 106; and DHL, 108, 166; adores Barrie, 109; and religion, 173; self-centred, 356; and sex, 555

Chambers, Jessie (*cont.*)
369, 561–2; compared with Alice Dax, 368–70; DHL's revision of 'Paul Morel' III takes her criticisms seriously, 353, 447, 448; DHL creates new fictional account of Paul–Miriam relationship in *SL*, 448–9, 457; DHL sends proofs of *SL*, 449–50; puts DHL out of her life, 450; destroys letters, gives away books, tears out dedications, 450, 577; sends back DHL's letter from Villa, 450; DHL does not write about life solutions of women like her, 370; marries John Wood in 1915, 386, 530; teaches until 1919, 530; no children, 530; on *Lady Chatterley's Lover*, 559; as memoirist, 356, 358, 507–8; stroke in 1939, 530; dies in 1944, 530; *for* 'Emily' *see* 'Laetitia', 'Nethermere', *White Peacock, The*; *for* 'Hilda' *see* 'Harassed Angel, The', 'Shades of Spring, The'; *for* 'Miriam' *see Sons and Lovers*; *for* 'Muriel' *see* 'Modern Lover, A', 'Blot, A', 'Fly in the Ointment, The', 'Last Words to Muriel'
WRITING
Annotations on 'Paul Morel' III, 152 and n, 353, 356
E.T., *D. H. Lawrence: A Personal Record*, 138, 215, 263–4, 354–8, 368–9, 507–8
Novel, 266
Chambers, Jonathan ('Pawny'), Eastwood pawnbroker and owner of off-licence in Breach, 103; and wife, chapel goers, 103
Chambers, May, born, 104; shows DHL around Haggs, 105, 119; aloof from DHL, 107; pupil-teacher, 114, 116; independent-minded, 123; and the 'Pagans', 170; marries Will Holbrook, 107; living in Moorgreen, 271; DHL tells about Frieda, 562; DHL and Frieda visit, 381, 383; DHL writes poems about house, 383; JC visits and meets DHL for last time, 357–8; writes 'notes', 577; reliability as memoirist, 508
Chapels and Churches in Eastwood
Baptist, 34
Congregational, 29; Henry Saxton deacon of, 31; Lydia L attends, 64; DHL and, 64–8, 125, 163, 169–72, 173; L family and, 64–5, 84, 96, 104; architect designed, 65; 'Butty's Lump', 65; intellectual and

cultural tradition, 65, 104, 170; social life, 66, 169–70; Chambers family and, 103; JC sees DHL, 119; Literary Society, 170, 171, 360, 515; chapel as focus of discussion, 170–1: *see also* Reid, Rev. Robert *and* Loosemoore family
Parish Church (Church of England), 64, 65, 518; DHL christened, 64, 135
Primitive Methodist, 64–5; split with Wesleyans, 65; links with Labour party, 65; chapel designed by F.W. Stubbs, 65
Wesleyan, 29; Tory rather than Liberal, 64
Chatterbox, The, read by L children, 110
Chatterton, Thomas, 170
Chaucer, Geoffrey, DHL studies at college, 190, 540
Chekhov, Anton, DHL reads, 346
Chesterton, G. K., in *New Age*, 24; DHL sends writing to, wife returns, 190
Child's Own, read by L children, 110
'Chorus from *Atalanta*', *see* Swinburne, Algernon Charles
Christian Endeavour, 536; DHL attends, 68, 169; DHL mimics attenders, 62
Christiana, *see* Vulpius, Christiane
Clare, John, DHL probably ignorant of, 130
Clarke, William Edwin ('Eddie'), engaged to Ada L, 243–4; at theatre with Ada, 268; Christmas 1911 in Croydon with Ada, LB and DHL, 324, 332
Clarkson, J. J., student on day-training course at Nottingham, 188
Class
Middle class, and the Beardsall family, 26; and Lydia L, 501–2, 515; literature a middle-class phenomenon, 130–1; DHL and Blanche Jennings, 191–2, 232; and Grace Crawford, 232–3; DHL's problems with, 236–7, 247; in *WP*, 274; in 'Paul Morel' I, 280; DHL attacks, 501–2; schoolteaching as middle-class profession, 502
Working class, and the L family, 20, 41, 48–9, 50, 501–2; and the Beardsall family, 20, 26; DHL's myth of, 75, 500–3; rural working-class life, 109, 247; working-class writers, 130–1, 531; DHL's problems with, 236–7; working-class life in *A Collier's Friday Night*, 274; missing in *WP* and 'Paul Morel' I, 279; intelligent working-class and lower-middle-class women reversing traditional roles, 385; careers as

teachers, 385–6; DHL's class important to Frieda, 388; *see also* Gamekeepers

Clay, J. S., dancing classes in Eastwood, 55

Clifford, George, *see* Lawrence, James

Coal-mining

Brinsley pit, 7, 9; deepened and extended, 10; children working, 10, 512; James L killed, 6–7; George and Walter L work, 7; Arthur L signs on, 31; works, 10–12, 30; hostile to his superiors, 37; coal seam variable, 37–8; walks through countryside on way, 103; still there at age of 66, 349

Eastwood region, 11–12, 29–30; conditions, 11–12, 21, 512; development of industry in region, 29–30; growth in coal sales, 29; prosperity of miners compared with farm workers, 30; financial problems of mining families, 36–8; industry and unspoiled country, 103; 1893–4 lock-out, 22, 39; injuries at work, 43; 1910 Eastwood pit strike, 267, 271; 1912 national pit strike, 348, 350; *see also* Butty system

High Park pit, 10; Clem Taylor working, 81

Moorgreen pit, 10, 51; smuts from, 33

Underwood pit, 10

Watnall pit, 10

Collected Letters of D. H. Lawrence, The, see Moore, Harry T.

Collins, T., student on day-training course at Nottingham, 188

Collins, Wilkie, melodrama tradition, 140; DHL links title of *WP* with, 224

Collishaw, Mabel, *see* Thurlby, Mabel

Cologne, *see* Waldbröl, 372

Conrad, Joseph, DHL reads, 210, 346; 'Some Reminiscences' in *English Review*, 214; on Ford Madox Hueffer, 230

Contemporary Belgian Poetry, DHL gives to JC, 326

Co-operative Society (Co-op), newspaper 22; support for miners' wives, 22; L family number, store, 38; share and quarterly dividend, 38; estimates of cost of groceries, 39n

Cooper family, next-door neighbours of the Ls in Lynn Croft, 125, 153, 530

Ethel, at school, 523; dies, 6, 124

Florence Cooper Wilson, 124; dies, 6

Frances ('Frankie'), at school, 124, 523; attracted to DHL, 124; DHL sends 'love', 125; sees dangers of DHL writing, 144; chapel, 170; and the 'Pagans', 170; DHL visits, 124; dies, 6

Gertrude ('Gertie', 'Grit'), at school, 523; protects DHL at school, 78; DHL sends 'love', 125; sees dangers of DHL writing, 144; and the 'Pagans', 170; makes home with Ada L, 124; DHL on her illness, 271, 511; dies, 6; recreated as Gertie Coomber in *A Collier's Friday Night*, 124, 244

Mabel Hannah Cooper Marson, and the 'Pagans', 170; DHL attends wedding, 124, 530; dies, 6

Thirza, dies, 6

Tom, owns L house, 6, 41; flute-playing, 530; dies, 511

Cooper, Gussie (of Purley), 555

Cooper, James Fenimore, DHL reads, 110; JC and DHL read, 121; and Annabel in *WP*, 228

Coral Island, see Ballantyne, R.M.

Corke, Helen, upbringing, 386; character and appearance, 212–13, 254–5; sexuality, 212–13, 257, 308, 386; teacher at Philip Smith's old school, 212; tragic relationship with Herbert Macartney ('Siegmund'), 212–13, 254, 386; called 'Sieglinde' by Macartney, 254; relationship with Agnes Mason, 213, 254; DHL's early relationship with, 213, 254–5; writes about experience with Macartney, 254–5; calls DHL 'David', 192, 532; and Nietzsche, 212; and Wagner, 254–5; shares DHL's intellectual pursuits, 346, 558; helps DHL with 'Nethermere', 222–3, 254, 542–3; DHL attracted to, 166, 251, 252; assists with 'The Saga', 253–62; praises it, 331; DHL's increasing involvement with her, 258–9; plays JC's role, 258–9; encourages DHL's writing, 261; DHL's 'maîtresse', 290, 307, 309, 553; Lydia L tells LB about, 142; DHL's problems with, 291, 444; DHL wants to sleep with her, 302–3, 307–8, 309; her rejections, 308, 385, 442; poems provoked by, 303; criticises DHL for his engagement, 312; relationship with JC, 213, 327, 330, 357; reliability as memoirist, 508; novel *Neutral Ground,*

Corke, Helen (*cont.*)
220; play 'The Way of Silence', 254; 'The Freshwater Diary', 254–5
Cornwall, 245; DHL thinks of applying for job with LB, 341; goes with Frieda, 341
Cosford, Samuel, *see* Lawrence, James
Cossall, Burrows family home until 1908, 288
'Coteshael', Burrows family house, 326, 556
'Cotter's Saturday Night, The', *see* Burns, Robert
Coulson family, Miss Coulson, letter to Lydia L, 97; Mr and Mrs Coulson, wreath for Ernest L, 98
Court, Ernest, admirer of LB, 302
Crawford, Grace, 231–3; middle-class, 231; parents, 233; too fond of DHL, 233; DHL's poetic writing to, 232, 261
Crich Stand, seen from Walker Street, 34, 41
Crichton, Kyle, DHL tells about *WP*, 225
Cricket, 534
Crime and Punishment, see Dostoevsky, F. M.
Criterion, 558
Cromford canal, 29
Cronin, A. J., Alice Dax recommends, 360
Croydon, 142; DHL interviewed for job, 201; DHL in, 75n, 194; situation, 202; growing town, 202–3, 204; poverty of, 204
  Colworth Road, 12 and 16, John and Marie Jones's residences, 166, 203, 325
  Crown Inn, 203, 320
  Davidson Road, *see* Schools, Davidson Road School
  Dering Place, *see* Schools, Dering Place School
  Education Committee, reduce DHL's salary, 348
  Empire Music Hall, 238
  English Association branch, 202, 233
  George Street, 202
  Gordon Home for Waifs and Strays, Morland Road, 204, 238–9
  Grand Theatre, 202; *Tristan und Isolde*, 255; *Carmen*, 439
  Greyhound Inn, 203
  Public Library, Nietzsche holdings, 210, 212
  Theatre Royal, 202
  Whitgift Grammar School, 202
Crystal Palace, 204, 206
Cuer, Elizabeth, *see* Lawrence, Elizabeth

Cullen, Florence ('Flossie'), daughter of George Henry Cullen, family friend, 171; in 'Paul Morel' I, 124–5, 278–80; and DHL, 280; death of governess Fanny Wright and mother Lucy in 1904, 280; *see also* Wright, Fanny
Cullen, George Henry, grocer, 66, 280; Sunday school teacher, 66; superintendent in 'Paul Morel' I, 278; DHL recreates him and family in 'Paul Morel' II, 'The Insurrection of Miss Houghton' and *LG*, 280
Cullen, Lucy, *see* Cullen, Flossie
Cummin, Maria, 110

D.H.L., significance of initials, 134–6, 246
D. H. Lawrence: A Composite Biography, see Nehls, Edward
Daily News, DHL sends article to, 321
D'Annunzio, Gabriele, DHL and Frieda see *The Light under the Bushel*, 458
Dale Abbey, DHL and friends to, 170
Daleski, H. M., on *WP*, 228
Daly, Dominic, defends Walter L in court, 47n
Dame aux Camélias, La, DHL sees Sarah Bernhardt in, 147
Dare-Devil Dorothy, musical, 202
Darwin, Charles, 171, 174, 175, 179, 346; *Origin of Species*, 179, 538; in the *International Library*, 111n; in 'A Modern Lover', 212; *see also* Science
Daudet, Alphonse, *Tartarin de Tarascon*, 351, 559
Daudet, Leon, DHL gives JC copy of *Le partage de l'enfant*, 326
Davie, Donald, *A Gathered Church*, belief in a debased Congregational tradition, 521
Dawn of Day, The, see Nietzsche, Friedrich
Dax, Alice Mary, née Mills
  1878–1910 born, 358–9; impoverished childhood, 359, 386; Liverpool Central School, 359; hatred of father and men, 359; character, 360–1, 362, 364; unconventionality, 360–1, 364; appearance, 359, 360; intelligence, 360–1, 369; writes poems and plays, 360; suffragist, 360–1, 362, 369; agnostic, 361; 'advanced', 360, 362–3; post-office job, 360; transferred to Isle of Man, 360; marries Harry Dax, 359, 367, 386; to East-

Emerson, Ralph Waldo, DHL and JC read, 122

'Emmeline', *see* Pankhurst, Emmeline

English Review, 229, 321, 348; contents of first number, 214; reaction of Chambers family to, 214; serialises H. G. Wells's *Tono-Bungay*, 214; Alice Dax reads, 360; review of William James's *A Pluralistic Universe*, 180; JC sends DHL's poems to, 214–15; left-wing bias, 216; publishes DHL's poems, 216, 268, 321; publishes 'Goose Fair', 142, 268, 289; cannot serialise 'Nethermere', 221–2; loses money, 214, 542; delays publication of 'Odour of Chrysanthemums', 262; publishes and pays for it, 306, 309; *see also* Harrison, Austin *and* Hueffer, Ford Madox

Erewash river, Eastwood on, 29

Etruscans, DHL's knowledge of, 503

Euripides, Gilbert Murray's translations of, 224; DHL reads *Bacchae*, 224

Evolution, *see* Science

Eyte, Miss, teacher of Arthur L, 10

Far From the Madding Crowd, *see* Hardy, Thomas

Farmworkers pay, 29

Felley, Arthur L's story about, 53; DHL at millrace, 155

Feltrinelli, Signora, friend of Frieda, 432; *see also* Villa

'Fisher of Men, A', *see* Galsworthy, John

Fitzgerald, Edward, *see* Rubáiyát of Omar Khayyám

Flamborough, Yorkshire, L family holiday, 23n; DHL and JC, 155

Flaubert, Gustave, 171; Lydia L reads *Sentimental Education*, 24, 268; *Madame Bovary* in 'A Modern Lover', 212; Alice Dax and Emma Bovary, 368; Hueffer's ideal of art, 234, 260

Folkestone, Birkin and Ursula sail from in *WL*, 393

Ford, Ford Madox, *see* Hueffer, Ford Madox

Forster, E. M., DHL lends work to HC, 258

Foster, George, marries Emma L, 9

Foster, Hannah, daughter of George and Emma Foster, marries William Andrews, 515; children named, 515

France, DHL's desire to go to, 62, 308; fictional characters go to, 308

France, Anatole, DHL brings books to the Haggs, 110

Franco-Prussian war, *see* Richthofen, Friedrich von

Frankenstein, Dr, *see* Rainbow, The

Freiburg (in Breisgau), Ernest Weekley Lektor at University, 372–3, 563, 569; Professor A. Schröers and wife, 373; Frieda and Weekley marry, 375, 564; *see also* Eichberg, Haus

French, Lawrence family connections, *see* Lawrence family, of Eastwood; *and* Languages, Foreign

French Revolution, The, *see* Carlyle, Thomas

Freshwater, *see* Isle of Wight

'Freshwater Diary, The', *see* Corke, Helen

Freud, Dr Siegmund, 544; *Die Traumdeutung (The Interpretation of Dreams)*, 400, 442; Oedipus complex, theory of, 442–3; and Otto Gross, 442–3; ideas reach DHL via Gross and Frieda, 443, 444; DHL understands incest motif in *SL* without Freud, 448

Frick, Ernst, German painter, lives with Frieda Gross, 379; affair with Frieda Weekley, 379, 389, 443; Ernest Weekley hears about, 395

Gaddesby, LB headmistress, 302

Galsworthy, John, 'A Fisher of Men' in *English Review*, 214; William Dowson lends work to Frieda, 388

Gamekeepers, DHL confronts, 188; from the working-class, déclassé, 227–8; Alan Chambers and DHL have their names taken by, 544

Garda, Lake (Lago di), 334, 368, 423, 425, 431, 432, 439, 453, 458, 460; Saló, 458

Gargnano, Hotel al Cervo and Maria Samuelli, 431; cemetery and church, 451; steamer, 452

Garnett, Constance, and the quarrels of DHL and Frieda, 409–10

Garnett, David ('Bunny'), son of Constance and Edward Garnett, visits DHL and Frieda, 420; admires Frieda, typecasts DHL, 421; with DHL, Frieda and Harold Hobson in Mayrhofen, 427, 428; and walks over Pfitscherjoch, 428; out-

Holt, Agnes (*cont.*)
285–6, 306; recreated as Agnes D'Arcy in *WP*, 249
Hooley, Ernest, 144, 533–4
Hopkin, Sarah Annie ('Sallie'), wife of Willie Hopkin, sympathetic to DHL, 178, 427, 572–3; shares DHL's intellectual pursuits, 346, 541; unconventional, 364; DHL asks her about LB, 427; recreated as Patty Goddard in *MN*, 572–3; *see also* 'Spirits Summoned West'
Hopkin, William Edward ('Willie'), shopkeeper, 5, 31; intellectual, 5, 361; sees DHL in pram, 5; attitude to Women's Co-operative Guild, 22; talks dialect with DHL, 63; sympathises with DHL at school, 78; as writer, 131; on Lydia L and *WP*, 141, 143; socialist and agnostic, 178, 538; intellectual and political interests shared with DHL, 178, 346; Eastwood Debating Society at his house, 178; scared of Alice Dax, 361; tells story of her and DHL, 364; on Frieda and DHL, 382–3; DHL calls impudent, 531; praises Rev. Robert Reid, 537
Horace, 243; *Odes*, Book I, 186, 538, 539, Book III, 539
Houses, L family, *see* Eastwood
Hube, Rev. Rodolph, Baron von, 537
Hudson, W. H., 'Stonehenge' in *English Review*, 214
Hueffer, Ford Madox, editor, *English Review*, 142, 214–17; loses money, 142, 542; removed as editor, 142; argument with Arnold Bennett, 214; JC sends DHL's poems, 214–15; takes up DHL, 215–17; prints poems in *English Review*, 216–17; asks to see, reads 'Nethermere', 216–17, 249, 543; approves of 'Odour of Chrysanthemums', 216, 229; impressed by DHL's background, 216–17; by his reading, 121–2; DHL and JC go to see, 218, 220–1; writes crucial introductory letter, 221–2; introduces DHL as genius, 230; irritated by DHL, 234; imaginative account of chapel in Eastwood, 171; reacts against 'The Saga' as inartistic, 143, 234, 260, 331–2, 334; as 'erotic', 143, 234, 334; and the 'high things of culture', 346; unreliability as memoirist, 508, 577; change of name to

Ford, 542
Humphreys, Ernest Arthur, colleague in Croydon, 206; annoyed by *T*, 334
Hunger, Max, 39n
Hunt, Violet, Ford Madox Hueffer's companion, 218, 220–1; impressed by DHL's knowledge of literature, 121; DHL visits, 220–1; with JC, 221; on DHL, 230; DHL describes, 231
Huxley, Aldous, on Frieda, 390; on DHL's reading, 560; editor, *The Letters of D.H. Lawrence*, 561
Huxley, Maria, 531
Huxley, T. H., 179, 538; in the *International Library*, 111n; *Man's Place in Nature*, 179; in 'A Modern Lover', 212
Hymns, DHL's knowledge of, 67

Ibsen, Henrik, 346; DHL brings work to the Haggs, 110; in the *International Library*, 111n; in 'A Modern Lover', 212; in revised passage of *WP*, 537; DHL links title of *WP* with, 224; Alice Dax reads, 360; *The Fight for Barbara* and the ending of *A Doll's House*, 450; DHL and Frieda see *Ghosts* in Munich and Gargnano, 458
Icking, 419, 421, 423, 428, 433, 436, 437, 461; 'tiny savage little place', 433; DHL and Frieda live in Alfred Weber's flat, 413–25; Frieda missing children, 414–16; DHL and Frieda leave, 425
Idyll, An, see Greiffenhagen, Maurice
Igea, Villa, *see* Villa
Ilkeston, Walter L family, 45–7, 88; Pupil-Teacher Centre, 115–17, 122, 125, 172, 288; Gladstone Street Schools, 115; Education Committee, 116; DHL and LB, 290
Indians, 503
Ineson, Rev. George, visits Lydia L, 98
International Library of Famous Literature, The, ed. Dr Richard Garnett, Ernest buys, 111; JC borrows a volume, 111; in stage direction for *A Collier's Friday Night*, 111; not for serious study, 111n, 121
Interpretation of Dreams, The, see Freud, Siegmund
Inwood, Alfred John, *see* Beardsall, Emma
Irschenhausen, Edgar Jaffe builds house, 413; DHL and Frieda borrow it, 413

Lawrence, D.H. (*cont.*)

problems at school, 205, 206–9; teaching methods, 208–9; reading extends, 210–12; and Nietzsche, 210–12; making friends, 212–13; sends JC writing, 214; ironical about Alice Dax, 361; JC sends poems to *English Review*, 215; Ford Madox Hueffer asks to see him, 215–16; meets Hueffer, 215–17; as working-class writer, 216–18; Hueffer's support, 220–2; 'Nethermere' accepted by Heinemann, 222–4; disillusionment with literary life, 230–2, 261; problems with the 'artistic', 232–5; problems in Croydon and London, 235–40; writes plays, 242–6; warmth and detachment, 247–8; wishes to sleep with, breaks with Agnes Holt, 248–9; wants JC to sleep with him, 219, 249–50; reaction against her devotion, 220, 281

1909–1910 start of sexual relationship with JC, 248–51, 293; attracted to other women, 248, 251–2; weekend in London with JC, 251; HC and 'The Saga', 253–62; polarised between HC and JC, 257–9, 383; relationship with HC during writing of 'The Saga', 257–9, 262; Whitsuntide 1910 with JC, 252–3, 262–3; critical of and worried about 'The Saga', 260–1; JC's idealisation and possessiveness, 263, 457; breaks off with JC in August, 263–6; compares himself to Barrie's Tommy, 264–5; at home in August, 267–8; to Blackpool with George Neville, 269; Lydia's illness, 269–73; visits from Croydon, 269; sends proofs of *WP*, 269; and Flossie Cullen, 280; HC 'sa maîtresse', 307, 309; sends books to JC, 326; off school during mother's illness, 270–1; describes parents' marriage, 281–2; engagement to LB, 288, 317–19, 508–9; with Ada, ends mother's life, 272–3; tells JC of his engagement, gives her poems, 287; in charge of funeral, 287

1910–1911 attraction of LB, 288–94, 316–18; would like to marry at once, 295; reservations, 294–6, 427; problems over money, 295–7, 306–9; desire to be a full-time writer, 296, 317, 328; work on 'Paul Morel', 297–300; still in mourning, 299; selective in what he sends and tells LB,

300, 303–4; LB and his writing, 300, 303–4; contrast with JC, 304, 314, 315; misses JC, 320, 326; warns LB against himself, 300–1, 315–16; LB visits, 301–2; urges HC to sleep with him, 302, 307–8; problems of engagement, 306–9; gives up HC, 308–9; criticism of LB, 309–11; fiction about engagement, 311–13; no time for short-story volume, 320; sexual frustration with LB, 313–14, 366, 401; signs of break with LB, 315, 319, 320; starts affair with Alice Dax, 319, 366, 558; desperate, 320; cannot publish, 320–1; tries journalism, 321; sees JC at theatre with HC, gives her 'Paul Morel' II, 327; restarts novel, 328; needs to write it, 328; collapse, 304, 320, 322–4; double pneumonia, 322–3; LB kept away, 322–3; slow recovery, 323–4; first beard, 323; parallel to 1901 illness, 324; freed by illness, 324; writing, 326; sees JC again, 330; Christmas in Croydon, 324

1912 January–May needs a novel to publish, 331; Edward Garnett helpful, 331–2; with LB in Red Hill, 324, 334; apparently offers to marry LB, 334–5; convalesces in Bournemouth, 335; plans to go to Germany, 335; letters to LB casual, 335; writes *T*, 332–4, 336; considers problem of hopeless marriage, 336; decides to break off with LB, 336; to Cearne, 336; asks HC to sleep with him, 336, 356; writes to LB breaking engagement, 336–7; LB protests, meets her in Nottingham, 337–9; writes to Garnett, 338; writes to LB, 339; uses LB's life and career in *R*, 340–1; what achieved by spring 1912, 345–7; financial problems, 348; cannot repay Garnett, 348; precipitated into being full-time writer, 348; living at home again, 349; shocks Ada, 349; writes mining sketches, 349–50; sees JC again, 350–8; offers to marry JC, 350; suggests running away with her, 350; shows her 'Paul Morel' III, 350–4, 357; affair with Alice Dax, 355–6, 366–8; idea of work in Germany, 372, 380, 384; visit to Weekley house postponed, 372, 563; date of visit, 562–3; goes, meets Frieda, 371, 380, 456, 562–3; sees JC same day, 380–1; sees Alice Dax same or next day,

poems in French, 62

professional writer, as, 131–2, 331, 334, 341, 348

real lives recreated in fiction, 225, 339, 449–50, 452–3, 456–7

role-playing as artist, 144–51, 157, 232

tragedy, interest in, 224–5, 260, 329, 446, 452, 456

writing and the writer, 144, 145–51, 232, 347, 452–3, 457, 460–1

WORKS

Aaron's Rod, experience of man who leaves Midlands, 246; Aaron walks out on family, 446; backward glance at Walter Morel 446; real-life Aaron Sisson, 530

'All Souls', 451, 455; App. 493

Amores, 412

'And Jude the Obscure and his Beloved', 312–13; App. 491

'Art and the Individual', given as paper heard by Willie Hopkin and Alice Dax, 178, 360; socialist, 178, 234; reference to Darwin, 179; completed, 190; fuller version, 191; App. 472

'At the Cearne', 383; App. 491

'Autumn', college essay (not extant), 185

'Ballad of a Wilful Woman', 421; App. 491

'Bei Hennef', 403; App. 491

'Blot, A', see 'Fly in the Ointment, The'

Boy in the Bush, The, Jack Grant and the Ellis family, 528

'Burns Novel' fragments, use of landscape near Haggs Farm, 105; recreation of inn in Bogliaco, 440–1; App. 477

'Campions', 131, 131n; App. 479

'Chapel in the Mountains, A', 426, 570; Anita, 426; part of projected book of German sketches, 423, 570; App. 477

'Character of Theseus, The', criticised, 185; App. 472

'Character Sketch of: Lady Macbeth', criticised, 186; App. 471

'Christening, The', 69n; revised, 419; App. 476

'Christs in the Tirol', crucifix in Klamm gorge, 427; Christus im Elend in Wieden, 429; part of projected book of German sketches, 423, 570; rewritten as 'The Crucifix Across the Mountains', 570; App. 477

'Climbing Up', 500

Collier's Friday Night, A, 242–6, 274, 458; written, 217, 218, 242, 545; and James L, 24, 43; contrast with 'Odour of Chrysanthemums', 71; and L family kitchen, 111, 502; and JC, 138, 218, 243; DHL's poems in, 138; drawn from life of mining community, 217, 244–5; and Burns's 'The Cotter's Saturday Night', 242; stage directions in, 245; and HC, 254; parallel with 'A Life History in Harmonies and Discords', 275, 551; like *The Merry-Go-Round*, 282; *characters*, Eddie (Clarke), 243; Gertie Coomber, 124, 244; Ernest Lambert, 24, 138, 161, 195, 243–5, 502, 547; Mr Lambert, 47–8, 62, 71, 243, 518; Mrs Lambert, 24, 37, 118, 243–5; Ada L recreated as Nellie Lambert, 161, 243–4, 518; Maggie Pearson, 138, 161, 243; App. 473

Daughter-in-Law, The, 458–60, 550; 'ordinary', 441; written in Villa, 441, 458; Midlands dialect in, 441, 460; possessive love, 265, 458–60; and Lydia L, 266; and Gertrude Morel, 458–9; completes *SL*, 460; *characters*, Mrs Gascoyne, 458–9; Joe, 37; Luther, 458, 459; Minnie, 458, 459–60; App. 477

'Daughters of the Vicar'

'Two Marriages', 320; no children in, 69n; Alfred attracted to Louisa, 291; Alfred awaiting his mother's death, 293; and 'Paul Morel' III, 300; Alfred's marriage, 300–1; the Lindleys, Mary Lindley, 301; and 'fulfilment', 301; Louisa, 312; approval of mother, 318–19; DHL sends to Garnett, 320–1; App. 474, 475

'Daughters of the Vicar', portraits of John and Louisa L, 24; early version, 69–70, 69n, 291, 293, 300–1, 312, 318–19, 320–1; Louisa Lindley, 69, 70; Alfred Durant, 69, 70, 320; fiction without artist-hero, 150; App. 474

David, use of Bible in, 67; especially personal, 261

'Delilah and Mr Bircumshaw', revised, 419; App. 473, 476

'Discipline', JC sends to Hueffer, 215; App. 481

'Discord in Childhood', originally part of 'A Life History in Harmonies and Discords', 274, 275; App. 484

Lawrence, D.H. (*cont.*)
  Sterzing, 429; J demands meal on train, 430; J has to keep Burberry on, 430; G and Patty Goddard, 572–3
  Divergences from real life, episodes amalgamated and heightened, 382n; G unaffected by attachment to a mother, 382n; J has few problems with leaving her children, 382n, 414; G musician, not writer, 418–19; G does not share his work with J, 460–1; fictional version of Glashütte, 572
'Modern Lover, A', use of landscape near Haggs Farm, 105; Cyril Mersham as autobiographical hero, 148, 149–50, 184, 212, 246–7; hero leaves Midlands and returns, 246; Muriel, 149–50, 212, 266, 329; Tom Vickers, 156, 329; reference to Nietzsche, 210, 212; family, 246–7; seen by JC, 304; difference from 'The Harassed Angel', 330; App. 473
'Mushrooms', [vii], 500
'Mutilation' 416, 570; App. 492
'My Love, My Mother', Frieda's annotations, 411–12; 'The Virgin Mother' in *Amores*, 412; App. 488
'Nethermere' I–II, see *White Peacock, The*
'New Eve and Old Adam', Richard Moest, 148; as autobiographical hero, 389; Paula Moest's fascination with the artist, 388–9; Moest as Paula's 'mission', 389; Paula as recreation of Frieda, 389
'New Heaven and Earth', and self-consciousness, 548–9
'Notes' ('Autobiography'), for Kra, 500, 501, 502
'Nottingham and the Mining Countryside', 500, 501, 503
'Odour of Chrysanthemums', 216, 217, 218; role of Louisa L in, 24; and death of James L, 24; Lydia L, 25, 37; dialect speech in, 70; compared with *A Collier's Friday Night*, 71; Lydia L knows, 142, 143; problematic 1910–11 revisions to, 143, 241–2, 244, 301, 533; fiction without artist-hero, 150; compared with *SL*, 150; Ford Madox Hueffer impressed by, 216–17, 241; drawn from life of mining community, 217, 233, 241; ending, 241; compared with *The Widowing of Mrs. Holroyd*, 242; Austin Harrison

delays publication, 262; parallel with 'A Life History in Harmonies and Discords', 275; compared with version of marriage in 'Paul Morel' II, 299, 300; heavily revised, 300; published, 306, 420; earns £10, 306; *characters*, Elizabeth Bates, 69–71, 241; John Bates, 70; Mr Bates, 241; children, 69, 241; narrator, 241; App. 473, 474
'Old Adam, The', written, 320; and marriage, 300; interferes with writing of 'Paul Morel' II, 300; 'green fire' in, 305; and violence, 317; Edward Severn as autobiographical hero, 62, 148; Severn educated in France, 308; Severn's relationship with Mrs Thomas, 148, 555; App. 474
'Once–!', 148, 421–3; begun in Icking, finished in Italy, 421, 423; perhaps continued in Mayrhofen, 427; heroine Anita partly recreation of Johanna von Schreibershofen, 421–2; part of projected book of German sketches, 423, 570; App. 476, 477
'Overtone, The', recreations of Frieda and William Dowson, 565
'Paul Morel' I–III, see *Sons and Lovers*
'Pear-Blossom', 566; App. 491
Plumed Serpent, The, Sankey hymn in, 67
'Pornography and Obscenity', masturbation, 535
'Prelude, A', use of landscape near Haggs Farm, 105; version of Chambers family, 189; Giordani song used in 'Laetitia' I, 140; entered by JC, wins *Nottinghamshire Guardian* Competition, 189–90; App. 472
Prussian Officer and Other Stories, The, suggestion for improvement to dialect in, 63–4
'Prussian Officer, The' ['Honour and Arms'], and violence, 317
'Rachel Annand Taylor', 233–4; App. 474
Rainbow, The, written 1914–15, 89, 181; grows out of 'The Sisters', 445; especially personal, 261; education in, 89, 92–4; DHL covers ground not studied in *SL*, 93; Tom Brangwen at Derby Grammar School, 92–3; Brangwen women and JC, 121; Tom Brangwen and the prostitute, 320; Tom Brangwen seeing Lydia Lensky, 385; Tom Brang-

wen courting, 381; Will Brangwen after death of Tom, 290–1; Ursula Brangwen goes to Nottingham Grammar School, 93–4; algebra and French, 93; separation from village, 93–4, 126; Ursula and JC, 121, 123; Ursula and DHL as teachers, 207, 386; Ursula at college and DHL, 177, 195, 197; botany, 182; Ursula's progress away from scientific materialism, 181–4; Ursula undergoes many of DHL's formative experiences, 181, 197; last relationship with Skrebensky, 181–2; Ursula breaks with past, 446; 'Shame', 93; 'The Man's World', 123, 386; Dr Frankstone as Dr Frankenstein, 182

'Red', provoked by HC, 303, 546; App. 489

'Red-Herring', 62–3, 500

'Reminder', and LB, 290; and HC, 290, 553; App. 488

'Restlessness', 249; App. 482

'Return', provoked by HC, 303; App. 489

'Return to Bestwood', 500

'Rex', 73–4

'Rise in the World, A', 500

'Ruby-Glass', see 'Fragment of Stained Glass, A'

'Saddest Day, The', 500

'Saga of Siegmund, The', see Trespasser, The

'Scent of Irises', 252; App. 485

Sea and Sardinia, 571

'Second-Best', written, 320, 328–9; ending, 329; use of landscape near Haggs Farm, 105, 328–9; Frances, 329; Jimmy Barrass, 329; Tom Smedley, 329; App. 474

'Shades of Spring, The', use of landscape near Haggs Farm, 105; John Adderley Syson as autobiographical hero, 148, 548; hero leaves Midlands and returns, 246; and the 'Miriam' figure, 265, 266, 548; 1914 revisions, 548, 557; App. 475, 476

'Shadow in the Rose Garden, The', rewritten version of 'The Vicar's Garden', 300; App. 474

'She Looks Back', 570; designated 'Beuerberg', 415; App. 492

'She Was a Good Little Wife', 566; App. 491

'Sick Collier, A', 69n, 513; fiction without artist-hero, 150; App. 475

'Sinners', 572

'Sisters, The', novel after SL, 445, 446;

becomes R and WL, 445; Barbara in The Fight for Barbara forerunner of Ursula character, 451

'Snapdragon', 289; dated by LB, 552; App. 490

'Snowy Day in School, A', 205, 235, 238; App. 481

Sons and Lovers, use of in biography, 10n, 509
'Paul Morel' I, 511; plot, 124, 125, 126, 278–9, 551; started, 218, 261, 273, 281; Paul called William, 124, 279, 281; and the mining community, 241–2; and 'A Life History in Harmonies and Discords', 275; and 'Matilda', 278–9; absence of Mrs Morel, 279, 280; character Flossie and JC, 124–5; and LB, 280; in progress, 281; abandoned, 281; App. 473; characters, Aunt Ada, 124–5, 278–9; Cullen, 278; Flossie, 124–5, 278–9, 280; Fred, 279; Gertie, 124–5, 279; Mrs Limb, 124–5, 278; Mabel, 124–5, 278–9; mother, 278; Walter Morel, 278–9; Newcombe 278–9; sister, 278; Miss Wright, 124–5, 278–9, 280, 525; features, Mr Bates' School, 279, 281; Breach house, 278; Engine Lane, 278; Haywoods, 124–5, 279
'Paul Morel' II, 511; started, 282, 297; ten pages to be produced regularly, 297, 298, 299, 300; writing, 278, 297; LB does not see later part, 327, 556–7; children in, 69; Mrs Morel rips pages out of Tristram Shandy, 143; working-class marriage in, 282, 285–6; saintly Mrs Morel, 300; Paul Morel a painter, 298–9, 351; part of MS survives into SL, 298; defuses real-life conflicts, 299, 327, 328; and 'Odour of Chrysanthemums' versions of marriage, 299, 300; no death of Mrs Morel, 299, 304; Miriam's life unlike JC's, 351; and Alice Dax, 366; unreality, 299–300, 327–8; abandoned, 297, 299, 321; DHL gives MS to JC, 327; JC thinks sentimental, 327; JC's faint recollection, 557; DHL decides to rewrite, 328; asks JC for recollections, 328; App. 474; characters, Miss May, 298, 525; Miriam, 265, 266, 298, 351, 353; Arthur Morel, 297, 299; Gertrude Morel, 143, 278, 297, 298, 299, 304; Paul Morel, 73, 77, 90, 297, 298–9, 351, 353, 523, 525, 526; Walter Morel, 24, 45–6, 297–8, 299; William Morel, 299; Frances Radford, 'Clara' figure, 298,

of 'Paul Morel' II survives into *SL*, 298;
contrast between 'Paul Morel' II and *SL*,
299; *see also* 'Paul Morel' I–III
Characters
Barker, 49
Chambers, Alice, 91
Dawes, Baxter, 366, 451
Dawes, Clara, 149, 252, 291, 361, 365,
  370, 442, 445, 449, 451, 455–6, 561
Field, John, 277
Jordan, Thomas, 90
Leivers, Miriam, 60, 365, 370, 422, 444,
  445, 447, 448–50, 455, 457, 458–9,
  460, 534, 553
Morel, Annie, 89
Morel, Arthur, 52, 90
Morel, Gertrude, 21, 24, 25, 27, 37, 38,
  49, 60, 64, 69, 71–2, 76, 89, 94, 99,
  127–8, 267, 271, 275, 278, 354–5,
  435–8, 441, 442, 444, 445, 446, 447,
  448, 450, 451–3, 455–6, 458–9, 501,
  520–1, 576
Morel, Paul, 25, 39, 43, 46, 52, 56–7, 64,
  76, 77, 82, 89–90, 94, 95, 99, 130, 132,
  148, 149, 159–60, 181, 183, 275, 291,
  293, 304, 306, 324, 329, 361, 365, 422,
  441, 433, 445, 447, 448–9, 451, 455–6,
  457, 458–9, 527, 534, 553, 561
Morel, Walter, 12, 16, 21, 24, 25, 26–7,
  37, 45–6, 49, 52, 58–9, 60, 61, 62, 69,
  71–2, 99, 110, 333, 435–9, 441, 445,
  446, 447, 448, 455, 520–1
Morel, William, 27, 54–5, 64, 71–2, 89,
  99, 118, 299, 446–7, 448, 455
Western, Lily ('Gipsy'), 24, 64, 446
Chapters VII 'Lad-and-Girl Love', 447;
  VIII 'Strife in Love', 447, 448, 575; XI
  'The Test on Miriam', 353, 448–9,
  451, 575; XII 'Passion', 445, 451; XV
  'Derelict', 452
*Significant fictional correspondences to real
life*
LB and Clara Dawes, 282
JC and Miriam Leivers, 152–3, 160,
  164–5, 212, 265, 350, 352–4, 357,
  448–9
Alice Dax and Clara Dawes, 361, 363,
  365–7
Arthur L and Walter Morel, 12, 16, 21,
  26–7, 49, 99, 110, 438
DHL and Paul Morel, 25, 39, 43, 52,

56–7, 58, 76, 82, 89–92, 94, 95, 99,
  101, 130, 132, 148, 149, 152–3,
  159–60, 164–5, 195, 252, 272–3, 350,
  456
Lydia L and Gertrude Morel, 14, 15, 16,
  18, 21, 25, 27, 37, 40, 49, 56, 76, 98,
  99, 127–8, 145, 266, 267, 271, 354–5,
  438, 444, 451
Frieda and Clara Dawes, 442, 445, 561
Significant fictional alterations of real life
Lydia L's religion omitted from Mrs
  Morel, 18; Arthur L's family hardly
  appear, 25–6; Walter Morel's con-
  sistently bad stalls at pit not true of
  Arthur L, 37; Mrs Morel's attraction
  to Mr Morel not true of Lydia L, 60;
  Mrs Morel 'uncaught by life', 145;
  Paul more independent than DHL,
  52; Paul hardly ever speaks dialect, 63;
  Paul shares none of DHL's connections with chapel, 64, 195; Paul has no
  problems at school, 89–92; Jordan's
  work-girls loving and sensitive, 100–1;
  Paul does not go to college, 181, 195;
  Paul makes no progress towards scientific materialism, 181, 195; Paul ordinary, 317–18, 352–3; Paul's love for
  mother makes him unable to love
  Miriam, 355; Paul and Miriam's relationship always sexual, 165, 352–4;
  Mrs Morel jealous of Miriam as a
  rival, 160–1; Miriam makes no struggles for career or independence, 352
'Spirits Summoned West', written after
  death of Sallie Hopkin, 573
'Still Afternoon in School, A', quoted
  242; App. 481, 483
'Strike-Pay', 69n, 513; fiction without artist-hero, 150; App. 476
'Study', submitted to *Gong*, 189; quoted,
  196; App. 479
'Teasing', *see* 'To my Usurper Love'
'Tickets Please', 101n
'To my Usurper Love', first title of 'Teasing'; poem for LB, 303; App. 488
Trespasser, The
  'Saga of Siegmund, The', HC's experience behind, 254–6, 257–9; DHL
  writing, 253–4, 255–62, 277, 278, 383,
  546–7; finished, 256, 259, 268, 277,
  278; JC knows little about, 256–7,